INSPIRE / PLAN / DISCOVER / EXPERIENCE

CALIFORNIA

CALIFORNIA

CONTENTS

Victorian houses in San Francisco

DISCOVER 6

EXPERIENCE 52

NEED TO KNOW 520

DISCOVER

Downtown San Francisco at sunset

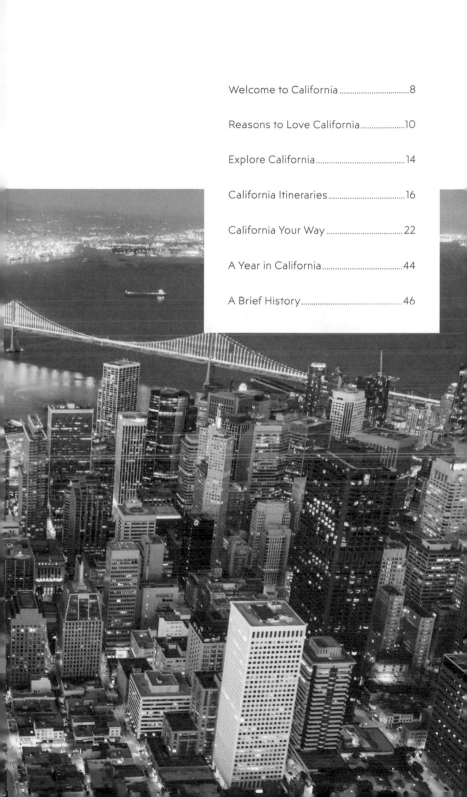

WELCOME TO
CALIFORNIA

Surf beaches and soaring snowcapped peaks. Tranquil deserts and dense redwood forests. Fine wines, gourmet food trucks, and spicy Mexican cuisine. California sates the senses with a blend of cultures and landscapes. Whatever your dream trip to California entails, this DK Eyewitness travel guide is the perfect companion.

1 Mount Whitney, part of the Sierra Nevada range.

2 Browsing fresh produce in a California market.

3 Cable car on a steep hill in San Francisco.

4 A beach in San Diego, a prime area for surfing.

The Golden State encompasses a mind-bending array of landscapes, inhabited by a population passionate about the great outdoors. Whether they're surfing along the coasts of San Diego or hiking through the High Sierras, Californians embrace their natural surroundings. Here, you can climb one of the highest peaks in the US, Mount Whitney, or wander through Death Valley, the lowest expanse of dry land in the country. Beautiful beaches range from enviable resorts in the south to driftwood-strewn strands in the north. Inland are the ancient towering trees of Redwood National Park and the mythical Mojave Desert landscapes, pin-pricked with giant cacti.

When it comes to urban pleasures, few places in the world can match Los Angeles for variety: icons grace the sidewalks of Hollywood Boulevard, world-class art flanks the walls of the Getty Center, and Venice Beach remains as freewheeling as ever. San Francisco isn't just about old cable cars and iconic Golden Gate Bridge, it is California at its most creative. Here, LGBTQ+ community bookshops welcome regulars, farm-to-table restaurants entice with innovative organic dishes, and Silicon Valley bursts with visionary high-tech industries.

From Mount Shasta to San Diego, and everything in between, we break California down into easily navigable chapters with detailed itineraries, expert local knowledge, and colorful, comprehensive maps. Whether you're here for a flying visit or a long road trip, this DK Eyewitness guide will ensure that you see the very best that California has to offer.

REASONS TO LOVE
CALIFORNIA

Abundant natural beauty, picturesque cities, glamorous movie stars, sun-kissed beaches, and trend-setting cuisine – there are so many reasons why visitors fall in love with the Golden State. Here are some of our favorites.

1 HOLLYWOOD

From silent movies to big blockbusters, Hollywood has been at the epicenter of the global film industry. See the names of your favorite stars on the Walk of Fame *(p97)*.

SURFING 2

Surfing has been part of California life since the early 1900s. Surf the gnarly breaks of Malibu *(p73)* or Huntington Beach *(p222)*, or dip into the California Surf Museum *(p245)*.

3 THE MOJAVE DESERT

The ghostly outlines of long-abandoned mining shacks, 1950s gas stations, twisted Joshua trees, and the salt pans of Death Valley: you won't forget the stunning landscapes of the Mojave *(p260)*.

CULINARY DELIGHTS 4

California's food scene enjoys a mix of cultural influences and an abundance of superb fresh produce. From food trucks to lauded gourmet restaurants, this is foodie heaven.

WINE COUNTRY 5

Whether you're after crisp Sauvignon Blanc or fruity Zinfandel, it's all here, with tastings in Spanish missions or French-style chateaus, wrapped in vast fields of vines.

SCENIC JOURNEYS 6

California was made for road trips, but don't forget the train: Amtrak's *Coast Starlight* glides past snowy peaks, lush redwood forests, and misty stretches of Pacific Ocean shoreline.

SKIING IN THE SIERRAS *7*

Come winter, the High Sierras are enveloped in snow under deep-blue skies. Snowboard the trails around Lake Tahoe *(p490)* or tackle the runs on Mammoth Mountain *(p494)*.

PALM SPRINGS MODERNISM *8*

From the iconic A-Frame houses by Charles Dubois to Richard Neutra's skeletal steel frames, some of the world's best Modernist architecture is found in Palm Springs *(p250)*.

9 REDWOODS

Towering coastal redwoods are the tallest trees in the world and can be over 1,000 years old. Walk among these awe-inspiring giants in California's plentiful forests.

10 SAN FRANCISCO

Watch the fog roll in under the Golden Gate Bridge, ride rattling cable cars, visit Chinatown markets, and savor tortillas in The Mission – welcome to the "cool, gray city of love."

STUNNING COASTLINE 11

Untouched surf beaches, towering cliffs, dense redwood forests, rustic seaside towns, and a host of wildlife, from otters to elephant seals: California's coastline has it all.

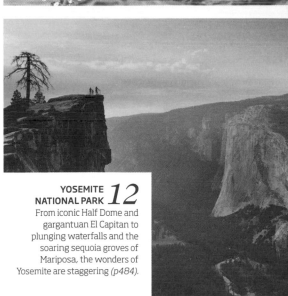

YOSEMITE NATIONAL PARK 12

From iconic Half Dome and gargantuan El Capitan to plunging waterfalls and the soaring sequoia groves of Mariposa, the wonders of Yosemite are staggering (p484).

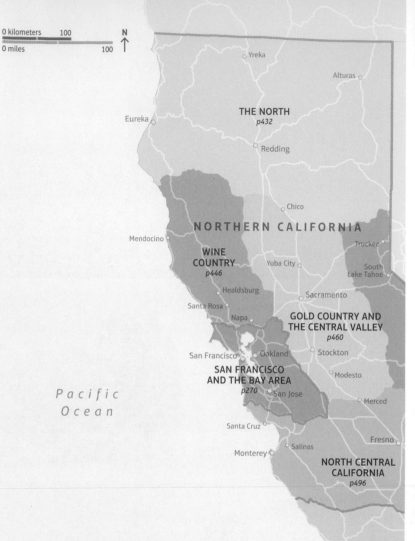

0 kilometers 100

0 miles 100

N ↑

Yreka

Alturas

THE NORTH
p432

Eureka

Redding

Chico

NORTHERN CALIFORNIA

Mendocino

Truckee

WINE COUNTRY
p446

Yuba City

South Lake Tahoe

Healdsburg

Sacramento

Santa Rosa

Napa

GOLD COUNTRY AND THE CENTRAL VALLEY
p460

San Francisco   Oakland

Stockton

SAN FRANCISCO AND THE BAY AREA
p270   San Jose

Modesto

Pacific Ocean

Merced

Santa Cruz

Fresno

Monterey   Salinas

NORTH CENTRAL CALIFORNIA
p496

San Luis Obispo

EXPLORE
CALIFORNIA

Santa Barbara

This guide divides California into four main sections: Los Angeles *(p54)*; Southern California *(p170)*; San Francisco and the Bay Area *(p270)*; and Northern California *(p420)*. These have been split into 12 color-coded sightseeing areas, as shown on the map here.

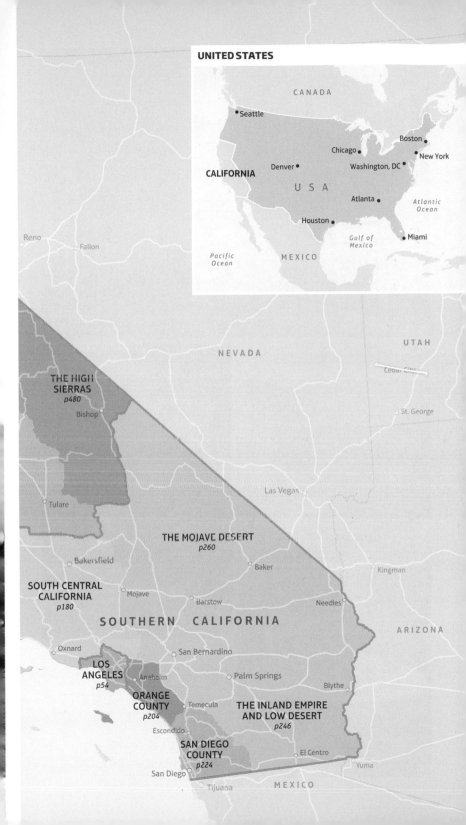

UNITED STATES

CANADA

●Seattle

Boston ●
Chicago ●   ● New York
Denver ●   Washington, DC ●

CALIFORNIA

U S A

Atlanta ●   *Atlantic
Ocean*

Houston ●

*Pacific
Ocean*   MEXICO   *Gulf of
Mexico*   ● Miami

Reno   Fallon

NEVADA   UTAH

Cedar City

**THE HIGH
SIERRAS**
p480
Bishop

St. George

Las Vegas

Tulare

THE MOJAVE DESERT
p260

Kingman

Bakersfield   Baker

**SOUTH CENTRAL
CALIFORNIA**
p180   Mojave   Barstow   Needles

ARIZONA

S O U T H E R N   C A L I F O R N I A

Oxnard   San Bernardino

**LOS
ANGELES**   Anaheim   Palm Springs
p54   Blythe

**ORANGE
COUNTY**   Temecula   **THE INLAND EMPIRE
AND LOW DESERT**
p204   *p246*

Escondido

**SAN DIEGO
COUNTY**   El Centro
p224
San Diego   Yuma

Tijuana   MEXICO

←

1 Lively Muscle Beach, Venice, Los Angeles.

2 *Coast Starlight* train arriving in Santa Barbara.

3 Breakfast at the Ferry Building, San Francisco.

4 The historic Ahwahnee hotel, Yosemite National Park.

California bursts at the seams with magnificent natural scenery, unique cultural sights, and fabulous cuisine. Taking in dynamic cities and spectacular landscapes, these itineraries will help you make the most of your visit to the state.

2 WEEKS
A Tour of California

Day 1

Begin your tour in downtown Los Angeles, exploring historic El Pueblo (p116), the original Spanish settlement from which the city sprung, and Little Tokyo (p122) before admiring the art at The Broad (p114). After lunch at the museum's restaurant, take the LA Metro to Hollywood/Vine and stroll Hollywood Boulevard (p96). Dine at Musso & Frank Grill (p97) before turning in for the night at the Sunset Tower Hotel (p98).

Day 2

Ride the LA Metro to Santa Monica (p68) and hit the legendary Santa Monica Pier. Stroll along the boardwalk to Venice Beach (p70), taking in the kooky action and Muscle Beach before munching a burger at Hinano Café (p71). In the afternoon take a taxi to the Getty Center (p80) to soak up its phenomenal art. End the day on the Sunset Strip (p98), with dinner at Rainbow Bar & Grill (p99), followed by a live show.

Day 3

At LA's Union station hop onto the Coast Starlight train (www.amtrak.com) for two and a half hours along the hilly Pacific shoreline to Santa Barbara (p184). Explore this beautiful city, beginning with its Spanish past at El Presidio. Build your own salad for lunch at Savoy (p187) before admiring the Spanish Revival architecture on State Street. On the bayfront, take in the seafaring history at Santa Barbara Maritime Museum (p186), then grab a seafood dinner at Santa Barbara Shellfish Company (p187). Stay the night at Hotel Californian (www.hotelcalifornian.com).

Day 4

Head north on the Coast Starlight train for the 11-hour journey to San Francisco – the railway hugs the Pacific past miles of untrammeled sands. Disembark at Emeryville and take the free bus transfer to downtown San Francisco (p282). Dine at Tadich Grill, the oldest continually run restaurant in California (p299). Hotel G (www.hotelgsanfrancisco.com) is a great centrally located place to stay.

Day 5

After breakfast in the Ferry Building (p290), wander down Market Street, then past the Transamerica Pyramid into Chinatown (p307). Be sure to stop at the Golden Gate Fortune Cookie Factory (p316) before tramping up the slopes to catch a cable car at Powell and Jackson. Disembark at Fisherman's Wharf, where you can sample fresh crab near PIER 39. It's a pleasant hike from here along the bay to the Golden Gate Bridge (p384) via the Maritime National Historical Park. For dinner head back to the Cow Hollow area for a splurge at Atelier Crenn (www.ateliercrenn.com).

Day 6

Rent a car and drive 200 miles (322 km) west to Yosemite, with a stop for lunch at the small town of Oakdale. Spend the afternoon exploring the plunging cascades, snowy peaks, and gargantuan granite monoliths of Yosemite National Park (p484). Be sure to hike up to Lower Yosemite Falls, and along the trail to Mirror Lake. End the day with dinner and an overnight stay at the 1920s Ahwahnee hotel.

→

Day 7

Start at dawn to see the sunrise at Tunnel View (p484). Then take the short hike to Bridalveil Falls before driving to Mariposa Grove where you can stroll among sequoia giants. After lunch at Wawona, traverse Yosemite National Park on scenic Tioga Road (Hwy-120; closed Nov–May) to Lee Vining on the shore of Mono Lake (p492). End the day with a walk by the lake to view its ghostly tufa formations. Check into El Mono Motel (www.elmonomotel.com) and grab a bite at Nicely's diner (US 395 4th St).

Day 8

Drive 172 miles (277 km) from Lee Vining to Panamint Springs along Owens Valley (p494), making a short detour to Devils Postpile National Monument (p492) to see its bizarre basalt columns. Stop for a light lunch at Erick Schat's Bakkery (www. schatsbakery.com) in Bishop. You can learn about 19th-century pioneer life at the Eastern California Museum (p494) in tiny Independence. End your day with dinner and a stay at Panamint Springs Resort (p265), on the edge of Death Valley.

Day 9

Spend the day exploring Death Valley National Park (p264). From Panamint Springs drive around the Mesquite Flat Sand Dunes before heading north for a guided tour of whimsical Scotty's Castle (p266) and a hike around the rim of ancient Ubehebe Crater. You can have lunch at Furnace Creek, just a little south of here. In the late afternoon head out to overlooks at Dante's View and Zabriskie Point – the latter perfect for sunset. Dine and stay at the Inn at Death Valley (p265).

Day 10

Rise early for a 270-mile (435-km) drive through the Mojave Desert to Joshua Tree National Park (p252). Leave Furnace Creek on the Badwater Road and take in the multicolored formations at Artist's Palette and the US's lowest point at Badwater Basin (p264). Driving deep into Mojave National Preserve, continue south to Amboy, where Roy's Motel & Café on Route 66 displays its futuristic Googie architecture sign (p268). Cut south to Twentynine Palms; check into quirky 29 Palms Inn (www.29palmsinn.com).

① Tufa formations surrounding Mono Lake.

② Erick Schat's Bakkery, Bishop.

③ Driving through Death Valley National Park.

④ Joshua Tree National Park.

⑤ Spanish Village Art Center, Balboa Park, San Diego.

⑥ Tacos at South Beach Bar & Grille, San Diego.

Day 11

Today will be a leisurely drive through Joshua Tree National Park. Enter the park at Joshua Tree town, where the main road winds around the huge rocks at Hidden Valley and Skull Rock, before running south to Cottonwood Spring – a good spot for a picnic lunch. It's a swift drive along I-10 from the park's southern entrance to Palm Springs (p250). Stay at the Movie Colony Hotel (www.moviecolonyhotel.com).

Day 12

Begin your day in Palm Springs by viewing the European and Native American art at Palm Springs Art Museum (p251), followed by lunch at Pinocchio in the Desert (www.pinocchiops.com). In the afternoon, roam the Indian Canyons (p251) – verdant palm-filled valleys amid arid hills. Dine at elegant Spencer's (www.spencersrestaurant.com) before sampling the city's lively nightlife.

Day 13

Head into the San Jacinto Mountains today, stopping at Idyllwild to browse the stores and sip coffee at the Red Kettle (p256). From here snake through the San Bernardino National Forest, then drive toward the Pacific, making a detour to the Mission San Antonio De Pala (p240). For lunch, continue 7 miles (11 km) to Nessy Burgers (www.nessyburgers.com). From here it's a short drive down Hwy 76 to beautiful Mission San Luis Rey (p240) and then to Oceanside (p245), where the California Surf Museum makes a fitting introduction to the coast. Enjoy a soul food dinner at Miss Kim's by That Boy Good (www.thatboygoodbbq.com) before taking the I-5 down to San Diego, where you can stay at the Horton Grand Hotel (p231).

Day 14

Spend the last day of your tour exploring sunny San Diego, beginning with the colonial buildings and shops in Old Town San Diego State Historic Park (p232). After lunch at Old Town Mexican Café (p233), visit Balboa Park (p234), home to museums and the Spanish Village Art Center. Dine at South Beach Bar & Grille (www.southbeach ob.com) while watching the sunset.

7 DAYS

Along the California Coast

Day 1

Start your journey along the Pacific coast by hopping onto the Coast Starlight train *(www.amtrak.com)* at Union Station in Los Angeles. It's a relaxing two-and-a-half-hour ride to Santa Barbara, with expansive views of crashing surf and rolling hills. Spend the afternoon exploring the Spanish heritage of downtown Santa Barbara *(p184)*, including the Presidio and Santa Barbara Mission, before turning in at Hotel Indigo Santa Barbara *(www.ihg.com)*.

Day 2

After picking up a rental car, drive inland to Solvang *(p196)*, with its Danish architecture and bakeries. Spend the rest of this morning exploring the wine country around Santa Ynez *(p202)*, stopping for lunch at Los Olivos Wine Merchant Café *(www.winemerchantcafe.com)*. Continue to Pismo Beach *(p195)*, allowing time to stroll the famous sand dunes before arriving in the historic city of San Luis Obispo *(p194)*. For dinner, sample the local tri-tip steak at Firestone Grill *(www.firestonegrill.com)* and then hunker down for the night at Garden Street Inn *(www.gardenstreetinn.com)*.

Day 3

Start early for the one-hour drive north to San Simeon and a guided tour of Hearst Castle *(p188)*, the lavish mountaintop palace built by media tycoon William Randolph Hearst. After an early lunch in San Simeon, view the honking elephant seals at nearby Piedras Blancas *(p193)* before driving up the rugged, forest-smothered Big Sur coast *(p510)*, arriving in Carmel-by-the-Sea *(p506)* by the evening. Reserve well in advance for dinner at Mission Ranch Restaurant *(www.mission ranchcarmel.com)*, owned by local movie star Clint Eastwood. It offers sensational ocean and mountain views (especially at sunset) and classic American food; you can also stay overnight here.

Day 4

Visit restored Carmel Mission *(p508)* to get an impression of 18th-century Spanish mission life, then continue to Monterey *(p502)*. Focus on the Monterey Bay Aquarium and waterfront Cannery Row *(p506)*, originally made famous by John Steinbeck's novels. The old warehouses have been transformed into shops and

1 Santa Barbara Mission.
2 The Big Sur coastline.
3 Cannery Row, Monterey.
4 Trolley bus, San Francisco.
5 The iconic Drive-Thru Tree, Leggett Valley.

restaurants. Have a leisurely lunch at Lalla Oceanside Grill *(lallaoceansidegrill. com)* before driving north, via surfer haven Half Moon Bay, along the thrilling coastal route to San Francisco. Check into YOTEL San Francisco in the heart of SOMA *(p293)*.

Day 5

Spend the day exploring San Francisco. Either pick a day from the San Francisco itinerary *(p278)* or follow the 49-Mile Scenic Drive *(www.sftravel.com/article/49-mile-scenic-drive)* for an all-encompassing tour of the area.

Day 6

Drive across the Golden Gate Bridge *(p384)* to stroll the waterfront in upscale Sausalito *(p410)*, then traverse the Marin Headlands via Muir Woods on the twisting Panoramic Highway. Continue north along the shore of Tomales Bay to arrive in Bodega Bay *(p458)* in time for a seafood lunch with a view at Tides Wharf & Restaurant *(www. innatthetides.com)*. After lunch soak up the scenic vistas on the 97-mile (156-km)

winding coast road (Hwy 1) to the quaint cliff-top village of Mendocino *(p456)*, with its New England-style architecture. End the day with cocktails and locally sourced cuisine at elegant MacCallum House Inn overlooking the Pacific Ocean, where you can also stay overnight *(www.maccallum house.com)*

Day 7

Get an early start for the drive north via Fort Bragg to the Leggett Valley *(p457)*, famed for its Drive-Thru Tree – a huge redwood big enough to drive a car through. You will be awestruck by the tallest trees in the world as you pass through the Avenue of the Giants *(p442)*, 45 miles (72 km) farther on. Continue to Eureka *(p442)*, for a lunch of oysters and fried fish at the Café Waterfront *(www. cafewaterfronteureka.com)* in a beautifully preserved Queen Anne building. In the afternoon visit the incredibly ornate Carson Mansion, then wind through the leafy giants of Redwood National Park *(p436)* to end your coastal adventure in Crescent City, staying at the Ocean View Inn *(www.oceanviewinncrescentcity.com)*.

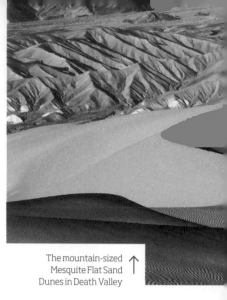

CALIFORNIA'S SUPER BLOOM

The low desert of the Inland Empire *(p246)* and Anza-Borrego Desert State Park *(p256)* sometimes experiences the spectacular phenomenon known as a "super bloom." If a few years of drought are followed by a heavy rainy season and a burst of hot weather, the desert erupts with wildflowers. The super bloom in 2018 could be seen from space.

The mountain-sized Mesquite Flat Sand Dunes in Death Valley ↑

CALIFORNIA FOR
AWE-INSPIRING
LANDSCAPES

Hike vast expanses of cactus-studded desert, climb snowcapped mountains, gaze in awe at dizzying redwood giants, and kayak emerald lakes – the dramatically varied landscapes and mesmerizing natural wonders of California will stay with you forever.

Fabulous Forests

The leafy giants of California soar above the forest like wooden skyscrapers, with trunks wider than buses. Redwood National Park *(p436)* and Sequoia and Kings Canyon National Parks *(p488)* are the best places to spy super-sized sequoias, while bristlecone pines, some of the world's oldest trees, grow in the White Mountains *(p494)*. The Muir Woods National Monument *(p410)* is also full of old-growth redwoods.

←

Giant sequoia trees rising above a hiking trail in Redwood National Park

Just Deserts

Home to some of the driest climates in North America, the deserts of California are surprisingly accessible. Experience the sun-blasted rocks, salt pans, and furnace-like temperatures of Death Valley *(p264)*, or wander slopes sprinkled with giant cacti in Joshua Tree National Park *(p252)*. Drive through the Mojave *(p260)* to abandoned gold mines, ghost towns, and ancient craters.

Did You Know?

California has more active volcanoes than any other US state.

Mountain Highs

Craggy ice-covered peaks, ancient slumbering volcanoes, and sharp pine-smothered ridges: California's mountains offer real adventure. Tackle granite monoliths like iconic Half Dome in Yosemite *(p484)* or the conical summit of Mount Shasta *(p445)*. In the High Sierras, scale the heights of Mount Whitney *(p494)* for a view to end all views, high above the clouds.

← View from Glacier Point, overlooking Half Dome, in Yosemite National Park

Dazzling Lakes

With over 3,000 lakes of all sizes, California offers a rich array of water-based activities. Kayaking on Lake Tahoe *(p490)*, fringed by snowy peaks and idyllic spruce forest, is hard to beat for scenic beauty. Spot myriad birdlife on low-lying Salton Sea *(p257)*, or ghostly columns of limestone in Mono Lake *(p492)*. For paddleboarding and canoeing, make for Big Bear Lake.

↑ Kayaker paddling across renowned beauty spot Lake Tahoe at sunset

Celebrate the Written Word

See authors reading from their work, discover upcoming writers, and browse for new books at California's literary festivals. Long Beach, Pasadena, San Francisco, and even Hesperia, in the Mojave Desert, host popular annual events, but the mother of them all is the LA Times Festival of Books. Held over a weekend in April at the University of Southern California campus *(p144)*, this spring bookfest attracts 150,000 literati from across the globe. Admission to the festival and the main stage events is free for all.

→

Festival-goer browsing books on a stall at the LA Times Festival of Books

CALIFORNIA FOR
BOOKWORMS

The Golden State beckons bibliophiles from far and wide, with opportunities aplenty to browse independent bookshops, attend literary fairs or festivals, and discover the scenes that inspired some of America's most celebrated authors.

THE BEATS

The San Francisco-based Beats were led by the writers Allen Ginsberg (1926–97), Jack Kerouac (1922–69), and William Burroughs (1914–97). The "Beatnik" era began in December 1955, when Ginsberg gave a public reading of his poem "Howl" at San Francisco's Six Gallery (it was later published by the San Lawrence Ferlinghetti, founder of City Lights bookstore). Two years later, Kerouac's novel *On the Road* spread the Beats' bohemian ethic nationwide. Kerouac also wrote *Desolation Angels, Big Sur,* and *The Dharma Bums,* all set in California.

If You're Going to San Francisco...

Numerous novels are set in what poet George Sterling called the "cool, gray city of love." Stroll Russian Hill's atmospheric narrow lanes for a taste of Armistead Maupin's *Tales of the City* or trawl the teahouses of Chinatown *(p306)* for characters straight from the pages of novels by Amy Tan, Lisa See, and Maxine Hong Kingston.

→

Russian Hill, the San Francisco neighborhood featured in *Tales of the City*

Once Upon a Time in Los Angeles

Countless literary favorites have called LA home, and it's easy to trace the places that inspired them. Unleash your inner Charles Bukowski at the poet's beloved hangout, the Frolic Room (p105), or sip martinis at Musso & Frank Grill (p97) where Nathanael West penned *The Day of the Locust*. Raymond Chandler's iconic hardboiled detective Philip Marlowe trawled the streets of Downtown, while James Ellroy's bestselling neo-noir crime novels explore the seedier side of Tinseltown.

SHOP

Book Soup
This indie store is a Sunset Strip icon, home to towering bookcases, knowledgeable staff, and author events.

🅰G3 🏠8818 Sunset Blvd, West Hollywood 🌐booksoup.com

The Last Bookstore
A gargantuan book mecca in downtown Los Angeles selling used and new books, as well as records.

🅰O4 🏠453 S Spring St, Los Angeles 🌐lastbookstorela.com

← Literary hangout Musso & Frank Grill

Jack London's cottage in the Jack London State Historic Park ↑

Leading Lights
Get under the skin of literary titans by exploring the places they lived and worked in. Visit Salinas (p517), the home of John Steinbeck; retrace *Call of the Wild* author Jack London's steps in Oakland (p404) and at the Jack London State Historic Park (p459); wander the streets of Monterey (p502), location of Robert Louis Stevenson's brief sojourn in California; or seek out Joan Didion's childhood haunts in Sacramento (p464).

Discover Native American Art

The State Indian Museum *(p467)* in Sacramento gives an overview of Indigenous art and culture but to fully grasp California's legacy of Native American art visit the Autry Museum of the American West *(p135)* or see the folk arts at the Antelope Valley Indian Museum *(www. avim.parks.ca.gov)*.

← California Hall in the Antelope Valley Indian Museum

CALIFORNIA FOR
ART LOVERS

From the Carmel art colony to David Hockney's iconic swimming pools, California has been both a magnet and a breeding ground for artists. View Old Masters and great works at art museums, take a street mural tour, or soak up the latest trends at indie gallery events.

BAY AREA FIGURATIVE MOVEMENT

Considered the first globally significant West Coast art school, the Bay Area Figurative Movement was a post-World War II rejection of Abstract Expressionism. Born in Oakland's California School of Fine Art in the 1940s to 1960s, the movement portrayed subjects realistically while still embracing the spirit of abstraction, as exemplified in the work of Elmer Bischoff, Richard Diebenkorn, and David Park.

Street Art

California has a long tradition of street art, concentrated in urban locations. See the exuberant murals of San Francisco's Mission District on a guided tour from Precita Eyes Muralists *(p370)*, or take a self-guided stroll around Fresno's vibrant Mural District *(p516)*. Los Angeles's Melrose Avenue *(p107)* has been a magnet for street artists since the 1980s.

→ *Jazz Mural* by artist Bill Weber, at the corner of Broadway and Columbus

Contemporary art on display at the Volakis Gallery in Napa ↑

Cutting-Edge Art Galleries

While the big-name museums contain world-famous works, California's indie gallery scene showcases exciting new talent. Wander the Arts District in downtown Los Angeles for artists' lofts, specialist art museums, and small galleries showcasing innovative art (p152). Discover the strong local art scenes in Palm Springs (p250) and Napa (p450), or explore the many galleries in artist retreat Carmel-by-the-Sea (p506) and La Jolla (p238), San Diego's arty neighborhood.

💬 INSIDER TIP
Oakland Art Walks

On the first Friday of every month, the free Oakland Art Murmur Art Walk (www.oakland artmurmur.org) sees 50 galleries extend their opening hours from 6pm to 9pm.

Stellar Museums

Almost every Californian city has an exceptional art museum. In LA you can peruse Gauguins and David Hockneys at the Getty Center (p80), see Andy Warhol's Single Elvis at The Broad (p114), and admire the English collection at the Huntington (p140). French Impressionist fans should make for San Francisco's Legion of Honor (p382), while for Renaissance masters, San Diego's Timken Museum of Art (p234) is hard to top.

↑ Frans Hals's Portrait of a Man at the Timken Museum of Art and (inset) the Legion of Honor

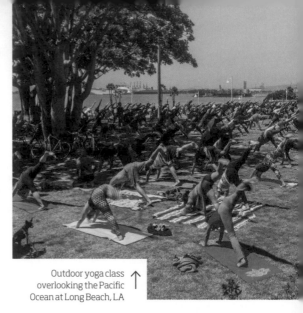

Yoga with a Difference

You'll find yoga classes all over the state, but LA is an especially good place to try beach yoga. In Santa Monica, Beach Yoga Socal holds classes directly on the beach *(www.beachyogasocal.com)* and at Long Beach, Yogalution Movement has daily free Yoga on the Bluff overlooking the Pacific Ocean *(www.yogalutionmovement.com)*. You can even do yoga on stand-up paddleboards at Marina del Rey *(www.yogaqua.com)*. For yoga classes with a difference hit Trap Yoga Bae in San Francisco, with trap beats and live DJs pulling in a diverse crowd *(www.itsyogabae.com)*.

Outdoor yoga class overlooking the Pacific Ocean at Long Beach, LA ↑

CALIFORNIA FOR
HEALTHY LIVING

With its novelty diets, hot yoga, and Gwyneth Paltrow's LA-headquartered Goop, California does health and wellness better than anywhere else. Visitors can sample local produce, attend yoga and meditation schools, or choose from numerous activities to get the heart pumping.

Wacky Workouts

Beach volleyball, southern California's most popular workout, is the perfect way to burn calories, but the state offers plenty of more unusual ways to exercise. Try underwater hockey for free with the San Francisco Sea Lions *(www.sfuwh.org)*, bike polo in LA *(www.facebook.com/labikepolo)*, or hilarious (and surprisingly exhausting) trampoline dodgeball in San Francisco *(www.houseoffair.com)*. Disc golf is all the rage in San Francisco's Golden Gate Park, where enthusiasts can throw a small disc around an 18-hole course free of charge *(www.sfdiscgolf.org)*.

←

Playing disc golf in Golden Gate Park, San Francisco

Food, Glorious Food

Natural, organic, or vegan – California doesn't mess around when it comes to healthy food. Farm-to-table cuisine leads the way in San Francisco, where many restaurants build their menus around ingredients sourced from local ranchers and farmers. Those with a plant-based diet never need to look far for a good meal – the only difficulty is narrowing the options down. Don't know where to start? Sample the much-celebrated meatless "bleeding" Impossible Burger, the brainchild of Redwood City's Impossible Foods (*www.impossiblefoods.com*). Don't miss Monty's dairy-free vanilla milkshakes, too.

← Vegetarian Impossible Burgers, created by Redwood City-based Impossible Foods

💬 **INSIDER TIP**
Spa by App

Book made-to-order massage and other spa treatments via apps. The one from Squeeze in LA's Studio City (*www.squeezemassage.com*) is a firm favorite.

New Age Nirvanas

If you are in search of yoga and meditation retreats, California has plenty to offer. The Self-Realization Fellowship Encinitas Retreat, founded by renowned Indian guru Paramahansa Yogananda *(p244)*, offers spiritual renewal programs (*www.yogananda.org*). Ojai's Krishnamurti Visitor Center *(p198)* hosts lectures based on the teachings of the Indian philosopher and in Big Sur, the Esalen Institute has yoga workshops and hot springs *(p513)*.

→ Esalen's hot springs, part of the Esalen Institute, a retreat in Big Sur focusing on humanistic alternative education

The Spanish Connection

California is peppered with 18th-century Spanish missions, many beautifully restored, such as the Mission San Diego de Alcalá *(p238)*. To travel back to the early days of European settlement, wander the streets of Old Monterey *(p502)* and Los Angeles's El Pueblo *(p116)*. For more recent Mission Revival styles, visit Santa Barbara *(p184)*, largely rebuilt after the 1925 earthquake.

Rooftops of Santa Barbara, a city largely built in Mission Revival style

CALIFORNIA FOR
ARCHITECTURE

Elegant Spanish missions, adobe ranches, grand Victorian mansions – despite its relatively short recorded history, California has built up a startling array of architectural treasures. Its dynamic cities continue to develop, with skyscrapers and bold designs offering something new on every corner.

Contemporary California

The Golden State is a hub for contemporary architecture thanks to local "Starchitects" such as Frank Gehry, as well as the architecture schools of the Southern California Institute of Architecture, University of California LA, and University of Southern California. Visit Frank Gehry's Walt Disney Concert Hall *(p120)*, Diller Scofidio + Renfro's honeycomb-like Broad *(p114)*, and Renzo Piano's glass-paneled Academy Museum of Motion Pictures *(p107)* in LA. Also check out Norman Foster's "spaceship" Apple Park in Cupertino, headquarters of Apple Inc.

Did You Know?

Frank Gehry originally wanted the Walt Disney Concert Hall to be built in stone, not metal.

Futuristic metal exterior of the Walt Disney Concert Hall in LA ↑

California's Tall Giants

With buildings ranging from the Art Deco towers of the 1930s to 21st-century skyscrapers, California's cities have provided an inviting stage for architecture's leading players since the early 20th century. Modern highlights include San Francisco's Transamerica Pyramid (p293) and the gleaming Salesforce Tower (p298), designed by César Pelli. Soaring landmarks in LA include the Wilshire Grand Center, the tallest building in the state, and the US Bank Tower (p124).

← The striking Transamerica Pyramid in downtown San Francisco

DESERT MODERNISM

Reaching its pinnacle in the 1950s, this aesthetic was pioneered by architects such as Richard Neutra, John Lautner, and Robert Wexler. Sleek, minimalist homes and public buildings were built throughout the desert. Palm Springs (p250) is home to the world's largest collection of this Modernist style.

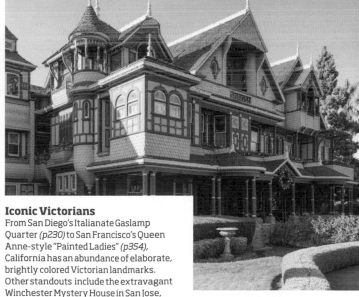

Iconic Victorians

From San Diego's Italianate Gaslamp Quarter (p230) to San Francisco's Queen Anne-style "Painted Ladies" (p354), California has an abundance of elaborate, brightly colored Victorian landmarks. Other standouts include the extravagant Winchester Mystery House in San Jose, decorated with Tiffany stained glass (p408), and Carson Mansion in Eureka (p442), California's ultimate Victorian folly.

↑ The Queen Anne-style Winchester Mystery House in San Jose

Life's a Beach

Balmy temperatures year-round (almost), fresh sea breezes, the scent of sunscreen, and the cries of volleyballers – Southern California's beach culture is an assault on the senses. LA's iconic boardwalk between Santa Monica (p68) and Venice (p70), heaving with in-line skaters, buskers, Muscle-Beach enthusiasts, and joggers, is not to be missed. In the south, the beaches of San Diego (p228) are the main draw, while to the north, the old fishing ports of Morro Bay (p195) and Monterey (p502) offer a great escape.

Waves crashing against a palm-fringed beach in San Diego

CALIFORNIA
ON THE COAST

With wild, fog-bound beaches in the north and sun-kissed sands in the south, California encompasses over 1,000 miles (1,600 km) of Pacific Ocean coastline. It's little wonder that, whether for a refreshing early morning surf or a whale-watching tour, the seaside is a favorite for locals and visitors.

Sensational Seafood

With so much coastline, it's no surprise California is home to some of North America's freshest seafood. This is the home of the California sushi roll (likely invented in LA) and the adopted home of the fish taco. Sample *cioppino* (fish stew) in San Francisco, or dine on salmon in northern California. If you're serious about your fish, pop by the many local shacks in Morro Bay, or the famed Dory Fleet Seafood Market (www.dory fleet.com) in Newport Beach.

Did You Know?

Cioppino was created by Italian immigrants who lived in San Francisco in the late 19th century.

↑ Entrance to the famous Dory Fleet Seafood Market in Newport Beach

Kayakers exploring the ↑
crystal-clear waters of
Santa Cruz Island

Island Hopping

California's Channel Islands *(p199)* are pristine natural reserves off the state's south coast, an untrammeled paradise ideal for leisurely exploring. Glimpse the brown pelican colony and explore the nature trails on Anacapa Island; swim, dive, snorkel, and kayak off Santa Cruz Island; or seek out Chumash archaeological sites on Santa Rosa Island. Hardier visitors can make for fog-bound San Miguel Island, full of elephant seals and sea lions.

💬 INSIDER TIP
Whale-Watching Hotspots

Each year an estimated 20,000 gray whales make the epic journey between the Bering Sea and Baja California – and back again – via the coast of California. In the north, the best place to spot them from land is Mendocino *(p456)*. The San Francisco Bay Area, Santa Cruz, and Monterey are also great for whale watching.

Magnificent Marine Life

Whales can be spotted all along the coast of California – gray whales, humpbacks, blue whales, and orcas all make the coastal trip between Alaska and Mexico north and south each year. Sightings of seals and sea lions are also common, including the raucous elephant seal colony south of Big Sur *(p510)*. It's even possible to kayak with basking sea otters near Monterey *(p502)*, a rare treat.

↑ A humpback whale and her calf surfacing in Monterey Bay and *(inset)* a sea otter

INSIDER TIP
Foodie Tours

Foodie walking tours have exploded in California. In LA, try Sidewalk Food Tours *(www. sidewalkfoodtours.com)* or sample bites from various restaurants on a Bite San Diego tour *(www.bitesandiego.com).*

Markets

Join the locals at food markets, a favorite weekend pastime for many Californians, who take pride in the state's quality produce, from olive oil to just-picked strawberries. Thursday evenings see downtown San Luis Obispo morph into a giant street market, while on Tuesday afternoons it's Santa Barbara's turn.

→

Vendor selling strawberries and spring onions at Santa Barbara Farmers' Market

CALIFORNIA FOR
FOODIES

From Googie diners to some of the world's top restaurants, California's vibrant food scene should be a key part of any visit to the Golden State. All the ingredients are here: a heady mix of cultural influences and flavors, from Mexican to Chinese, and an abundance of high-quality local produce.

New California Menus

New California cuisine got its start in Berkeley in the early 1970s, when Alice Waters began preparing French dishes at her restaurant Chez Panisse *(www.chezpanisse. com)* using fresh local produce. Los Angeles's Wolfgang Puck of Spago fame *(p87)* helped further popularize the trend. For a particularly special Michelin-starred New California cuisine experience, dine at Thomas Keller's French Laundry in Napa Valley's Yountville *(p451),* widely considered the finest restaurant in the US.

←

Beautifully presented dish at Wolfgang Puck's Spago in Beverly Hills, LA

GOOGIE DINERS

These 1950s futuristic roadside restaurants with upswept roofs and plenty of neon were intended to herald the Space Age. Great examples include Mel's Drive-in on LA's Sunset Boulevard *(www.melsdrive-in.com),* Pann's in LA *(www.panns.com),* and Burbank Bob's Big Boy *(www.bobs.net).*

Cal-Mex Cravings

California invented its own take on Mexican cuisine called Cal-Mex, a style that is less saucy than Tex-Mex and incorporates plenty of fresh vegetables and seafood. Try a super burrito in San Francisco's Mission District, where it was first concocted. Fish tacos originated in Baja California but swiftly migrated north – you can find some of the best at hole-in-the-wall taco joints like El Metate in San Francisco *(2406 Bryant St).*

←

Cal-Mex fish-and-shrimp tacos, a California classic

California Food Icons

California has spawned some iconic chains, including In-N-Out Burger and King Taco. You'll find distinctive local dishes on your travels, too. The rustic mountain town of Julian *(p242)* knocks out sumptuous apple pies, French dip sandwiches are a specialty of LA, and Tri-Tip steak was made famous in Santa Maria. And don't forget avocado toast – the hipster favorite was popularized in San Francisco.

→

Customers dining inside Los Angeles's bustling In-N-Out burger joint

▷ Surf's Up

Surf culture went mainstream in Malibu, Huntington Beach, and Oceanside in the late 1950s. From San Diego to the cooler waters of Half Moon Bay, California offers waves for every type of surfer. Spectators can check out the pros at the US Open of Surfing at Huntington Beach every summer *(p222)*.

Did You Know?

An ancient Polynesian sport, surfing was introduced to California by Hawaiian princes in the 1920s.

CALIFORNIA FOR
OUTDOOR ADVENTURES

With its vast tracts of mountains, deserts, beaches, and rivers, the landscapes of California are made for outdoor adventures. Tramp along hiking trails deep into the High Sierras, surf the waves off beautiful strands, or soar down ski runs under sunny blue skies.

▽ Scale New Heights

Rock climbing is big in California, with several outfits offering tours or programs for beginners. Cliffhanger Guides *(www.cliffhangerguides.com)*, for example, offers adventures in Joshua Tree National Park. Fearless adventurers can tackle the awe-inspiring Half Dome *(p484)* in Yosemite for vertiginous views over the valley below.

▷ By the Boots
California is a hiker's paradise. State and national parks have well-marked trails, from easy day hikes to wilderness routes. Long-distance paths include the 211-mile (340-km) John Muir Trail, which cuts through dense pine forest and snowy plateaus from Yosemite's high country *(p484)* to Mount Whitney *(p494)*.

◁ Hit the Slopes
There's superb skiing to be had in the High Sierras of California. Several world-class ski resorts can be found at Lake Tahoe *(p490)* and there are over 150 runs at Mammoth Mountain *(p494)*. Beginners can hone their skills at Big Bear Lake *(p259)*, while snowboarders hit the slopes of Mount Shasta Ski Park *(p445)*.

▷ Whitewater Thrills
California offers all manner of whitewater action, from lazy rivers to insane torrents. Sample everything from Class II to Class V rapids in the Kern River *(p199)*; ride the rapids of the beautiful Tuolumne River (the "T"); or glide along the family-friendly American River (South Fork). For an untrammeled wilderness experience, take a trip down the Lower Klamath and Smith rivers near the Oregon border.

◁ On Two Wheels
Many Californian state parks allow mountain bikes on their hiking trails, while High Sierra resorts such as Mammoth Lakes adapt their ski slopes for mountain bikes in the summer. The spectacular trail at High Camp in Squaw Valley, Lake Tahoe, involves a 2,000-ft (610-m) ascent via an aerial tram, followed by a downhill ride to Shirley Lake. For a more relaxed bike ride, tackle the Jedediah Smith Memorial Trail, which winds from Folsom to Old Sacramento *(p464)*, paralleling the American River.

Fruit of the Vine

California is by far the largest wine-producing state in the US. Chardonnay, Sauvignon Blanc, Cabernet Sauvignon, Merlot, and Zinfandel are the dominant grapes, produced on the slopes of the Central Valley and Coastal Ranges. Sample some of the best on tours of the Napa *(p450)* or Sonoma *(p452)* valleys, or in the Paso Robles *(p192)* wine region.

CALIFORNIA
BY THE GLASS

Sun-kissed vineyards, lush hopfields, bountiful orchards, and icy mountain water: California has all the ingredients for quality beverages. Craft beer, a refreshing frozen margarita, a glass of Napa Zinfandel, or just a healthy fresh-fruit smoothie – the choice is endless.

Cocktail Culture

Several cocktails are thought to have originated in the Golden State – the Appletini, White Russian, Tequila Sunrise, and the (non-alcoholic) Shirley Temple among them. Sample local favorite the margarita (tequila, orange liqueur, and lime juice) at beach bars throughout the state; head to an old-school tiki bar for a Mai Tai (rum and Curaçao liqueur); or sip a classic martini (gin and vermouth) at venerable Musso & Frank Grill in LA *(p97)*.

$\rightarrow$

Cocktails on the bar at Nepenthe restaurant, overlooking Big Sur

JUICE BARS

Californians tend to be very health-conscious, and fresh fruit and vegetable juices and smoothies are popular everywhere. Juice bars are almost as ubiquitous as fast-food joints. Here, patrons can get fresh produce – from strawberries to kale – pressed or squeezed to order. Nutritious seeds or spirulina are often added to smoothies.

← Wine tasting in Napa Valley and (inset) sign pointing to wineries in Sonoma Valley

The Craft Beer Scene

Craft beer, often created in small breweries with no-frills taprooms attached, is booming in California. Fruity (and potent) IPAs are most common, but local brewmasters cook up all sorts of flavors and hues, from peach-infused, hazy and golden ales to malty stouts and porters. Pop into your nearest brewery – San Diego has over 150 – and ask to taste a few, or opt for a "flight," usually a sample set of five small pours.

→ Tasting room of the Ballast Point Brewing Company in San Diego

Just for Laughs

Tiffany Haddish groomed her comedy chops in LA and the city remains a major hub for live shows; you might see Jay Leno testing material at the Comedy & Magic Club *(www.comedyandmagicclub.info)*, or other big names at Second City Studio Theater *(p109)*. In San Francisco, try Cobb's Comedy Club *(www.cobbscomedy.com)* or Punch Line *(www.punchlinecomedyclub.com)*.

←

Audience watching a stand-up performance in Cobb's Comedy Club

CALIFORNIA FOR
ENTERTAINMENT

From the Beach Boys to Billie Eilish, Californian artists have created a diverse live music scene – to say nothing of the Californian contribution to live theater, comedy, the movies, and sports. Plug into the latest sounds at a gig, have some laughs at a comedy club, or catch a classic flick at a drive-in.

TOP 4 LIVE MUSIC VENUES

Casbah
W casbahmusic.com
Intimate rock venue in San Diego since 1989.

Santa Barbara Bowl
W sbbowl.com
Spectacular outdoor amphitheater hosting a variety of acts from April to October.

Great American Music Hall
W gamh.com
Historic jazz and rock venue in San Francisco.

The Troubadour
W troubadour.com
Legendary LA club that helped launch Elton John and James Taylor.

The Sporting Life

Watching baseball at San Francisco's Oracle Park *(p301)* and LA's Dodger Stadium *(p153)* is a summer tradition. Baseball not your thing? Top NFL games are held at Levi's Stadium in Santa Clara and SoFi stadium in LA County, and NBA games at the Chase Center in San Francisco and LA's Staples Center *(p121)*.

→

A baseball game at Dodger Stadium in Los Angeles

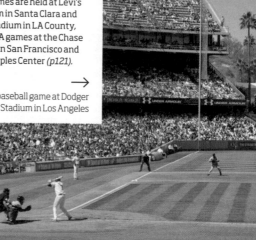

California Live

California's cities provide a wealth of live music. LA teems with iconic locations, from Whisky a Go-Go on the Sunset Strip *(p99)* to Santa Monica jazz and blues favorite Harvelle's *(www.santamonica.harvelles.com)*. For classical music, the Walt Disney Concert Hall *(p120)* is hard to top. Tap into the San Francisco music scene at the Fillmore *(www.thefillmore.com)* or unleash your inner cowboy at Bakersfield's Buck Owens' Crystal Palace *(www.buckowens.com)*. For the mother of all music festivals, head to Coachella, held in Indio every April *(p255)*.

↑ Green Day performing at Whisky a Go Go in West Hollywood

On the Stage

It may be the home of the movies, but theater is also big in California. The San Francisco Bay Area's Golden Gate Theatre *(www.broadwaysf.com)* stages touring Broadway shows, Cal Shakes offers open-air performances, while The Marsh *(www.themarsh.org)* hosts indie productions. Check out top talent at LA's Geffen Playhouse *(p85)*. In summer, pay homage to the Bard at the Lake Tahoe Shakespeare Festival *(www.laketahoeshakespeare.com)*.

←

A Cal Shakes performance of Bertolt Brecht's *The Good Person of Szechwan*

Nights at the Movies

Watch movies with a difference: travel back in time at a 1950s-style drive-in *(www.electricduskdrivein.com)*, or, if you visit LA in summer, catch a Cinespia screening in the Hollywood Forever Cemetery *(p104)*. For an authentic old-school movie experience, complete with a live organ, attend a show at San Francisco's Castro Theatre *(p367)*.

→ Picnicking during a Cinespia screening in Los Angeles

Small-Town Vistas ▷

Plenty of movies have been set in California's small towns. Ventura *(p197)* features in the 2000-made drama *Erin Brockovich (right)* about the environmental activist. If you're a fan of *The Goonies* (1985), visit Goat Rock Beach in the small town of Jenner in Bodega Bay , Sonoma County, where the final scene was shot.

◁ Around the Golden State

Movie backdrops can be found wherever you turn. Grab a bite in the Mojave Desert at the Bagdad Café, Newberry Springs *(p269)*, the location of the eponymous 1988 film. Visit state capital Sacramento *(p464)* for scenes from Greta Gerwig's 2017 *Lady Bird (left)*.

CALIFORNIA
ON SCREEN

Parts of California can feel surprisingly familiar, even for first-time visitors. The state has served as a backdrop for thousands of movies and TV shows. From biographical dramas such as *Milk* to cult classics like *Top Gun*, you'll be sure to come across the locations of some of your favorites.

◁ San Franciscan Scenery

San Francisco has long been a movie set. Wander around Castro to spy locations in *Milk* (2008) about the first openly gay elected official in California *(p281)*. Head to Alcatraz to re-imagine scenes from *Escape from Alcatraz* (1979), the famous film set on the island *(p328)*. Stand under the Golden Gate Bridge *(p385)* to capture the iconic shot in Hitchcock's *Vertigo* (1958).

◁ Hooray for Hollywood

It's not surprising that a popular subject on screen is Tinseltown itself. Head to the top of Mount Hollywood in Griffith Park *(p134)* for the location of the famous dance scene in *La La Land (left)*. Also in Griffith Park, the Greek Theatre is the setting for a big stage scene in the 2018 remake of *A Star is Born*.

◁ City of Angels?

LA isn't just glitz and glamour. Iconic films have captured the corruption that dogged the city in the early 1900s. Head to Echo Park *(p153)* or Catalina Island *(p218)* to see locations in Roman Polanski's *Chinatown* (1974). The dark side of the city is also shown in 1973's noir thriller *The Long Goodbye (left)*. Here the Italian campanile-style High Tower in Hollywood Heights appears as Philip Marlowe's apartment.

TOP 3 MOVIE SET TOURS

San Francisco
This bus tour led by friendly actors will show you your favorite movie locations *(www.sanfran ciscomovietours.com)*.

Warner Bros.
See movie sets from some of the most iconic films ever made on this studio tour in LA *(p149)* .

Sony Pictures
Another iconic LA studio offers behind-the-scenes walking tours *(www.sonypictures studios.tours.com)*.

△ San Diego in the Movies

With glorious beaches, plentiful sunshine, and atmospheric bars and restaurants, San Diego often stars on the silver screen. Chill out on Coronado's beach *(p242)*, the site of scenes in *Some Like it Hot* (1958). Walk in the footsteps of Tom Cruise in *Top Gun* at the tiny Kansas City Barbecue sports bar *(www.kcbqq.net)* on the edge of the Gaslamp Quarter *(p230)*, which still looks just the same as did in the 1986 movie. The New Point Loma Lighthouse near Cabrillo National Monument *(above; p239)*, from where there are fabulous ocean views, is another *Top Gun* landmark.

A YEAR IN
CALIFORNIA

JANUARY

△ **Rose Parade & Rose Bowl Game** *(Jan 1)*. Pasadena's parade of flower-covered floats is followed by the Rose Bowl, one of the major games in college football.

Napa Truffle Festival *(late Jan)*. Enjoy black truffle orchard tours, gourmet lunches, and wild mushroom forays at this Napa Valley event.

FEBRUARY

Chinese New Year Celebration *(late Jan or early to mid-Feb)*. Parades and performances across San Francisco make up the nation's largest Chinese New Year festival.

△ **Riverside County Fair and National Date Festival** *(mid- to end Feb)*. Carnival rides, date dishes, and live music concerts in Indio.

MAY

△ **Cinco de Mayo** *(May 5)*. Big block parties in Los Angeles and San Francisco celebrate Mexico's victory over the French in 1862.

Redwood Coast Music Festival *(early May)*. Dance along to live performances of jazz, swing, blues, soul, country, rockabilly, and more in Eureka.

Bay to Breakers *(late May)*. This 7.5-mile (12-km) race in San Francisco attracts tens of thousands.

JUNE

△ **Pride Week** *(various dates in Jun)*. America's biggest, most hedonistic celebrations of LGBTQ+ culture take place in San Francisco and Los Angeles.

Tuolumne Lumber Jubilee *(late Jun)*. This popular event celebrates the history of California's lumber industry with three days of carnival, arm wrestling, axe throwing, food, and live music.

SEPTEMBER

△ **Monterey Jazz Festival** *(third weekend in Sep)*. Epic jazz concert featuring around 500 artists performing on nine stages.

Los Angeles County Fair *(whole month)*. This vast county fair in Pomona includes horse races, an operational farm, an outdoor miniature railroad, and live entertainment.

OCTOBER

△ **Black Cowboy Parade** *(early Oct)*. This Oakland festival and parade commemorates the role of African Americans in settling the American West.

Sonoma County Harvest Fair *(early Oct)*. A popular agricultural fair held in Santa Rosa.

Grand National Rodeo *(mid-Oct)*. Held in Daly City, the largest two-day rodeo in the US features rodeo performances and a livestock exposition.

MARCH

△ **Los Angeles Marathon** (*early Mar*). More than 25,000 runners participate in this 26-mile (42-km) race, which has been held in the heart of Los Angeles since 1986.

St. Patrick's Day Parade (*mid-Mar*). San Francisco's bars fill with green-clad patrons, who gather to watch one of America's oldest parades down Market Street.

APRIL

△ **Coachella Music & Arts Festival** (*mid-Apr*). This huge music and arts festival is held in Indio on two consecutive three-day weekends. It features live performances from the biggest global names in rock, R&B, hip-hop, dance, and pop.

San Francisco International Film Festival (*mid-Apr*). Enjoy screenings every day for two weeks in theaters across the city.

Northern California Cherry Blossom Festival (*mid- to late Apr*). Japantown in San Francisco hosts a celebration of Japanese arts, crafts, food, and performers, with a colorful parade.

JULY

California State Fair (*mid-Jul*). Expect to see everything from star-studded entertainment to cooking demos at this show in Sacramento.

Comic-Con International: San Diego (*mid- to late Jul*). An epic four-day celebration of pop culture, with exhibitions, screenings, forums, and thousands of fans dressed up.

△ **International Surf Festival** (*late Jul/Aug*). Watch bodyboarding and surfing events at Torrance, Redondo Beach, Hermosa Beach, and Manhattan Beach in Los Angeles.

AUGUST

Old Spanish Days (*early Aug*). A celebration of Spanish and Mexican heritage in Santa Barbara.

△ **Outside Lands** (*mid-Aug*). This huge eco-friendly festival is held in Golden Gate Park, San Francisco.

Bigfoot Daze (*last Sat of Aug*). Watch Willow Creek's parades and logging contests in homage to California's legendary Sasquatch.

NOVEMBER

Dia de los Muertos (*Nov 2*). This Mexican celebration of the dead is marked by processions in Los Angeles's El Pueblo and San Francisco's Mission District.

△ **Doo Dah Parade** (*late Nov*). This fun costumed parody parade in Pasadena features irreverent satire.

DECEMBER

Hollywood Christmas Parade (*first Sun after Thanksgiving*). Hollywood and Sunset boulevards are crowded with this celebrity-heavy extravaganza, held since 1931.

△ **Newport Beach Christmas Boat Parade** (*mid-Dec*). Almost a hundred glittering vessels light up the Newport waterfront over five nights.

New Year's Eve (*Dec 31*). Enjoy spectacular fireworks over the harbor in San Francisco.

A BRIEF
HISTORY

Settled by diverse cultures over millennia, California has a rich and varied history. The 1848 Gold Rush, the birth of Hollywood in the early 1900s, and the flourishing of the LGBTQ+ community in the 1960s are just some pivotal moments that have shaped California into the state it is today.

Early California

Little is known about today's California before European contact, though its Indigenous population may have been as high as 300,000. Major early civilizations included the tool-making La Jolla and Pauma peoples, both dating from 6050 BC. By the 16th century, numerous peoples inhabited the area, such as the Chumash in the south, the Paiute in the Great Basin area, and the Hupa in the northwest. These peoples lived peacefully in hundreds of small autonomous communities connected by trade. They spoke different languages and practiced different religions.

1 Map of California from 1652.

2 Kumeyaay pictographs in Anza-Borrego Desert State Park.

3 Spanish celebrating Mass at Monterey, 1876.

4 Prospectors washing for gold, 1849.

Timeline of events

c 6050 BC
Indigenous peoples first settle the area.

1542
The first European to reach California today was Spanish Juan Cabrillo, at San Diego Bay.

1769
Gaspar de Portolá lands at San Francisco Bay. California's first mission is founded at San Diego.

1775
Monterey becomes capital of Spanish California.

1777
Foundation of Mission Dolores - the precursor of San Francisco - by Juan Bautista de Anza expedition members.

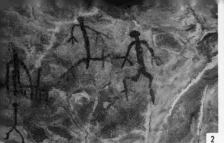

Spanish Settlement

Although the Spanish first landed in California in 1542, they did not colonize the area until the 18th century. Spanish rule was enforced through a trio of institutions – the mission (church), the presidio (fort), and the pueblo (town). Of these, the mission was the most influential. Beginning at San Diego in 1769, Franciscan friars founded 21 missions along El Camino Real as far as Sonoma. After Mexico achieved independence from Spain in 1821, California officially came under Mexican rule.

America and the Rush for Riches

Following the Mexican–American War (1846–48) California became part of the US in 1848, the same year that newspaperman Sam Brannan brandished nuggets that had been found in the Sacramento Valley, shouting "Gold! Gold!" The hordes of prospectors who thereafter stampeded into California changed the area forever. By 1850 San Francisco's population shot from 812 to 25,000, while Sacramento, closer to the mines, became the capital after California became a state In 1850. By the late 1800s, the US government had forced the Indigenous peoples to live only on small pieces of land called reservations.

1821
Mexican War of Independence ends Spanish rule of California.

1835
English sailor William Richardson settles Yerba Buena, later renamed San Francisco.

1846
US troops led by John Frémont claim California from Mexico.

1848
California is annexed by the US. The discovery of gold at Sutter's Mill.

1850
California becomes the 31st state in the Union.

IRECTING A SCENE IN "DOUGLAS FA
HOLLYWOOD, CALI

1

2

The Boom Years

The late 19th century was a time of massive expansion in California, thanks to train connections with the East, completed in 1869. California oranges could be exported easily to New York markets; taking the return trip were European immigrants hoping for a better life on the West Coast. In the north, Eureka and Mendocino were founded in 1850 and 1852 respectively, soon becoming "timber capitals," as well as hubs for fishing, shipping, and boating. In the 1860s San Francisco enjoyed an even bigger boom as a result of the Comstock Lode silver mines in Nevada, owned mainly by Californians, who displayed their wealth by building grand mansions on Nob Hill – by 1900 the city's population exceeded 300,000. In 1906 a massive earthquake devastated San Francisco, but the city recovered impressively fast.

The Rise of Hollywood

In 1887, Kansas prohibitionist Harvey Henderson Wilcox wanted to call his farm and the LA suburb surrounding it "Figwood," after his chief crop. His wife chose instead a name of a town in Ohio she had overheard on a train: "Hollywood." The nascent

NATIVE CALIFORNIA

California's Indigenous population suffered maltreatment and slavery under Spanish and American rule. The introduction of new diseases reduced the population to about 16,000 by 1900. The survivors were restricted to reservations, where their descendants still live: the Cahuilla (Palm Springs), the Hupa (northwest coast), and the Paiute-Shoshone (Owens Valley).

Timeline of events

1861–65
US Civil War - California is largely unaffected.

1869
Transcontinental railroad is completed.

1882
US Congress limits Chinese immigration.

1890
Yosemite wins national park status.

1906
San Francisco is struck by the worst ever US earthquake, at about 8.3 on the Richter scale.

NKS IN ROBIN HOOD "
NIA

US film industry began moving here from the East Coast in 1911, attracted by the state's temperate climate, in which directors could shoot outdoors year-round, and by the relatively cheap land, on which large indoor studios could be built at low cost. Silent film stars such as Mary Pickford and Charlie Chaplin were succeeded by icons of a more glamorous Hollywood, such as Mae West and Errol Flynn in the 1920s and 1930s.

The Depression and World War II

California's idealized image had a magnetic effect during the Great Depression of the 1930s, when thousands of people from all over the US headed West. From the Midwest's Dust Bowl, entire families, who came to be known as Okies, packed up everything they owned and set off for the farms of the Central Valley, an epic journey captured by John Steinbeck's bestselling novel The Grapes of Wrath.

World War II brought heavy industry to California, and shipyards and airplane factories sprang up. After the war, most of these industries stayed on, and today several California companies still make up the roll call of suppliers to the US military and space programs.

① Workers laying a logging railroad track at Mendocino, c 1890s.

② Directing on a Hollywood film set, 1922.

③ A migrant camp, 1935.

④ Shipbuilding yard in Los Angeles, 1943.

Did You Know?

The first actor to cement her footprints at Hollywood's Chinese Theatre was Norma Talmadge in 1927.

1917
The US enters World War I.

1932
LA hosts its first Olympic Games.

1941
Japanese attack on Pearl Harbor – US enters World War II.

1911
The Law of the Range, shot by William and David Horsley, is the first film made in Hollywood.

1929
The Wall Street Crash precipitates the Great Depression.

1945
End of World War II. International delegates meet at San Francisco to found the United Nations.

Post-War California and Civil Rights

Movies and the new medium of television made the state the symbol of America's postwar resurgence through the 1950s. The anti-conformist "Beat Generation" in San Francisco kicked off an era of experimental art, recreational drugs, and sexual freedom that peaked with the 1967 Summer of Love.

This liberal atmosphere enabled progressive ideas to flourish, with UC Berkeley's role in America's Free Speech Movement, the foundation of the Black Panther Party in Oakland, and the occupation of Alcatraz by Indians of All Tribes all part of a growing campaign for greater civil rights. In particular San Francisco became a key center of activism for gay rights. In 1992, however, the beating of Black motorist Rodney King by LAPD officers, and the subsequent acquittal of those officers, sparked fierce rioting. Racism in law enforcement remains a contentious issue.

Urban Regeneration and the Tech Boom

The 1970s ushered in an era of major expansion of key cities. Certain areas – particularly working-class, non-white neighborhoods – were torn down in favor of new

1 The Summer of Love in Haight-Ashbury, San Francisco, 1967.

2 Los Angeles Riots, April 1992.

3 Kamala Harris, the 49th Vice President of the United States.

Did You Know?

California is the most populous state in the US today.

Timeline of events

1955
Disneyland opens in Anaheim.

1966
The Black Panther Party, a Black Power political organization, is founded in Oakland.

1991
AIDS becomes San Francisco's number one killer of men.

1992
LA Riots following the beating of Rodney King.

1976
Apple is founded by Steve Jobs and Steve Wozniak.

1978
San Francisco mayor George Moscone and his deputy Harvey Milk are assassinated.

3

developments, and the cost of living dramatically increased, with wealth inequality mushrooming in the 1980s. The devastating 1989 Loma Pieta earthquake near Sant Cruz did not dampen Californians' energy, and renewal in San Francisco and the Bay Area and beyond continued apace. At the same time, high-tech industries began to transform the Silicon Valley between San Jose and San Francisco, ushering in the dot.com boom.

California Today

California is a forward-thinking state, confronting the challenges of the 21st century with the continued development of new technologies and investment in clean energy and a low-carbon economy to combat climate change and the ongoing threat of devastating wildfires and drought. Since the early 1990s the state has been a Democratic stronghold, with a reputaton for progressive politics: Gavin Newsom, the former mayor of San Francisco, was elected governor in 2018 and in 2021 Oakland-born Kamala Harris became Vice President of the United States.

However, housing prices, which have continued to rocket, and escalating homelessness in a state with the world's fifth-largest economy, remain highly pressing issues.

THE RISE OF SILICON VALLEY

The birthplace of Silicon Valley is attributed to the garage in Palo Alto where students William Hewlett and David Packard made their first products in 1938. In 1976, Apple ushered in the era of personal computers. Internet innovation began with Yahoo! in 1994, followed by Google in 1998, Facebook in 2004, and YouTube in 2005, all founded and head-quartered in California.

1998
Google founded by Larry Page and Sergey Brin while they were students.

2003
Electric car maker Tesla founded in San Carlos by Martin Eberhard and Marc Tarpenning.

2004
Facebook founded by Mark Zuckerberg.

2013
Same-sex marriage is legalized in California, two years ahead of nationwide legalization.

2018
The deadliest wildfire season ever recorded in California.

2021
Kamala Harris becomes Vice President of the United States.

EXPERIENCE

Santa Monica Boulevard, Los Angeles

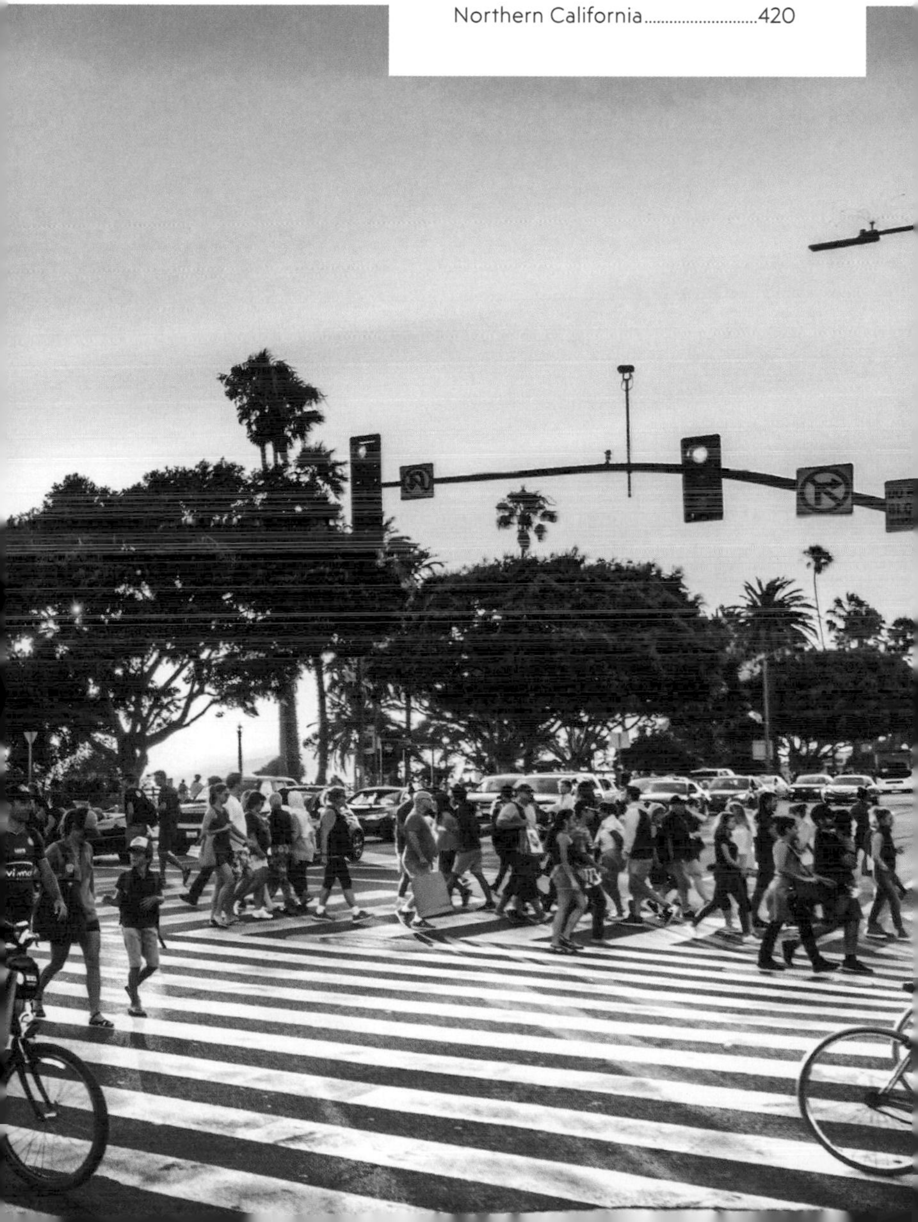

LOS
ANGELES

Sunseekers at Santa Monica Beach

EXPLORE
LOS ANGELES

This guide divides Los Angeles into six sightseeing areas, as shown on the map below. Find out more about each area on the following pages.

TOPANGA

Topanga State Park

Santa Monica Mountains

SANTA MONICA BAY
p64

MALIBU

Santa Monica Bay

CALIFORNIA

Pacific Ocean

LOS ANGELES

0 kilometers 10

0 miles 10

N

SAN FERNANDO

SUN VALLEY

Verdugo Mountains

ALTADENA

BURBANK

VAN NUYS

Griffith Park

GLENDALE

PASADENA

SAN GABRIEL

HOLLYWOOD AND WEST HOLLYWOOD
p92

BEVERLY HILLS, BEL AIR, AND WESTWOOD
p76

DOWNTOWN
p110

MONTEREY PARK

SANTA MONICA

CULVER CITY

AROUND DOWNTOWN
p126

VENICE

MARINA DEL REY

SOUTHGATE

DOWNEY

INGLEWOOD

WATTS

HAWTHORNE

PARAMOUNT

COMPTON

BELLFLOWER

REDONDO BEACH

CARSON

TORRANCE

SIGNAL HILL

LONG BEACH, SAN PEDRO, AND PALOS VERDES
p154

PALOS VERDES

LONG BEACH

NAPLES

SAN PEDRO

San Pedro Bay

GETTING TO KNOW
LOS ANGELES

The City of Angels is the sun-blessed, traffic-jammed, surf- and celebrity-mad entertainment capital of the US and the country's second-most populous city (after New York). Enclosed by mountains, LA's sprawling mass of vibrant, multicultural neighborhoods back onto golden beaches of the Pacific Ocean.

SANTA MONICA BAY

PAGE 64

With its warm sun, cool sea breezes, long sandy beaches, and excellent surf, Santa Monica Bay epitomizes the best of seaside California. The beach and pier at Santa Monica itself are major attractions, but this neighborhood is also justly celebrated for its restaurants, outdoor shopping areas, and active arts scene. Immediately south, Venice is the eccentric, kooky version of LA, home to skaters, bronzed bodybuilders, streetballers, buskers, and street artists. To the northwest, Malibu is a surfing hotspot and home to many Hollywood stars.

Best for
Beaches, surfing, and shopping

Home to
Santa Monica

Experience
LA beach culture by strolling along the boardwalk from Santa Monica to Venice Beach

PAGE 76

BEVERLY HILLS, BEL AIR, AND WESTWOOD

Synonymous with wealth and luxury, Beverly Hills, together with adjacent Bel Air, has been the entertainment industry's favorite residential address since the 1920s. Today Rodeo Drive and the Golden Triangle are crammed with posh restaurants, boutiques, and coffee bars. South of ritzy Bel Air, Westwood Village caters to UCLA students, whose campus features several enticing museums. High above it all, the Getty Center is one of the world's great caches of art.

Best for
High-end shopping, celebrity sightings, and restaurants

Home to
The Getty Center, UCLA, and Westwood Village

Experience
A guided tour of the stars' homes in Beverly Hills

PAGE 92

HOLLYWOOD AND WEST HOLLYWOOD

Hollywood remains forever associated with the Golden Age of movies. Hollywood Boulevard is lined with historic theaters, the Walk of Fame, and movie-themed attractions. Teeming with nightclubs, bars, and comedy clubs, West Hollywood is LA's party zone and is also home to a large LGBTQ+ community. Trendy Melrose Avenue features vintage and unique boutiques, while the section of Wilshire Boulevard known as Miracle Mile has some of LA's finest museums.

Best for
Museums, nightlife, and classic movie history and memorabilia

Home to
Historic Hollywood Boulevard, Sunset Strip, Los Angeles County Museum of Art

Experience
A live comedy show at the Groundlings

→

PAGE 110

DOWNTOWN

Downtown Los Angeles is home to the city's oldest district, El Pueblo de Los Angeles, a reminder of its Spanish origins. To the north of El Pueblo, Chinatown brims with shops and restaurants, while to the south, Little Tokyo is the heart of the largest Japanese American community in North America. Full of skyscrapers, the city's financial center lies along Flower and Figueroa streets. The Broad museum and the Arts District are full of cutting-edge art and the vast LA Live complex houses LA's premier sports and entertainment venues.

Best for
Art, Chinese and Japanese food, striking skyscrapers, and LA's oldest historic structures

Home to
The Broad, El Pueblo de Los Angeles

Experience
Watching the Los Angeles Lakers play at their home venue, the Staples Center

PAGE 126

AROUND DOWNTOWN

Emanating from LA's central core is a vast sprawl of neighborhoods and districts. Key draws include the upscale city of Pasadena, the art displays in the Huntington Library, and hilly Griffith Park, with its precious open spaces and the Griffith Observatory. Nearby, Universal Studios offers tours of its backlots as well as theme park rides, and is one of several studios based in Burbank, which has replaced Hollywood as the headquarters of the film and TV industries. South of Downtown, Exposition Park is a hub for wide-ranging museums and the University of Southern California.

Best for
Hollywood studios and theme parks, Korean food, and hilly wilderness

Home to
Universal Studios Hollywood, Griffith Park, Pasadena, Exposition Park and University of Southern California

Experience
Driving along Mulholland Drive with spectacular views of LA

PAGE 154

LONG BEACH, SAN PEDRO, AND PALOS VERDES

LA's southern coastal districts offer plenty of variety. Mansions dot the rolling hills of the affluent Palos Verdes Peninsula, a magnificent stretch of clifftop coastline. To the southeast, working-class San Pedro is home to the Port of Los Angeles and maritime-themed museums. Long Beach city is aptly named for its 5.5-mile (9-km) expanse of white sand, and is best known as the resting place of the *Queen Mary* ocean liner.

Best for
Beaches, museums, and maritime history

Home to
Queen Mary, *Battleship USS Iowa Museum*

Experience
Hiking the rugged Palo Verdes coastline

1

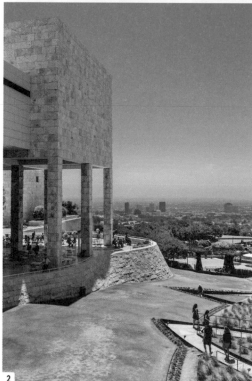

2

3

4

1 Angels Flight, a vintage rail car in downtown LA.

2 The Getty Center.

3 The Comedy Store on Sunset Strip.

4 The Academy Museum of Motion Pictures.

5 DAYS
in Los Angeles

Day 1

Start your LA odyssey at El Pueblo de Los Angeles (p116), the site of the original 1818 Spanish settlement. Then stroll south into lively Little Tokyo (p122), and explore the Japanese American National Museum. After lunch at Daikokuya (p122), wander through the Financial District and ride the historic Angels Flight funicular (p118) before taking in the eye-popping art at The Broad (p114). Visit the Grammy Museum (p120), open until 8pm Friday and Saturday, or take in a show or basketball game at the Staples Center (p120), then head up to Spire Bar (www.spire73.com), an open-air perch atop LA's tallest edifice.

Day 2

Begin the day at the Getty Center (p80), loaded with masterpieces. Then take a taxi to Santa Monica's Third Street Promenade (p68), peruse the shops, and grab a seafood lunch at STRFSH (www.strfsh.com). Walk down to iconic Santa Monica Pier and stroll along the boardwalk to Venice Beach (p70), past skaters, bodybuilders, and buskers. Have a drink and burger at Hinano Café (p71) before heading back to Santa Monica and catching some live blues at Harvelle's (www.santamonica.harvelles.com).

Day 3

Get up early for a bracing hike up to Griffith Observatory (p134), also reachable by bus. Check out the exhibits and admire the view of the Hollywood Sign – this is one of the best spots to see it. On the path back down, have lunch at The Trails (2333 Fern Dell Dr), and continue to Hollywood Boulevard (p96). Follow the famous stars on the Hollywood Walk of Fame and the celebrity handprints at TCL Chinese Theatre. Make sure you have a drink at the legendary Musso & Frank Grill (p97) before heading to the Sunset Strip for a live show at the Comedy Store (p99).

Day 4

Take a trip back to LA's prehistoric past at La Brea Tar Pits and Museum (p109) before wandering over to the Los Angeles County Museum of Art (p100) where you can also grab lunch at on-site Ray's and Stark Bar. The 2021 Renzo Piano-designed Academy Museum of Motion Pictures (p107) stands next door. In the afternoon, catch a bus along Wilshire Boulevard to Beverly Hills and wander Rodeo Drive, peeking at swanky boutiques. In the evening take a bus or taxi to Westwood to stroll the UCLA campus (p84) and catch a show at the Geffen Playhouse (p85).

Day 5

Ride the LA Metro to Pasadena (p136) and explore the streets of Old Pasadena, full of cafés, galleries, and theaters, then soak up the paintings at the Norton Simon Museum (p138). After lunch at the museum café, walk up Orange Grove Boulevard to visit either the Pasadena Museum of History (p137) or Gamble House (p136), an Arts and Crafts-style mansion. In the evening head to the Pasadena Pavilion for the Performing Arts (85 E Holly St) for some live music.

SANTA MONICA BAY

Santa Monica Bay was inhabited by the Tongva and Chumash peoples for thousands of years before the arrival of explorer Juan Cabrillo, who sailed here on behalf of the Spanish Empire in 1542. The Spanish started to colonize the region in the late 18th century and most of the bayfront was parceled out to ranchers, beginning with Rancho San Pedro (1784) and Rancho Topanga Malibu Sequit (1804). The area was then absorbed by the US in 1848, but development remained low-key until the opening of a railway between downtown LA and Santa Monica in 1875. In the late 19th century, the beaches and piers of Santa Monica Bay developed rapidly as tourist attractions, while Venice was laid out as a replica of the Italian city to form a resort town in the marshlands of Ballona Creek in 1905 by developer Abbot Kinney. The network of canals and waterfront homes didn't catch on and by the 1950s Venice was known as the "Slum by the Sea," a low-rent suburb that attracted the Beats literary counterculture movement and rock bands like The Doors in the 1960s. Beginning with Santa Monica in the 1990s, much of the coast has since been gentrified, creating the affluent beach communities that exist today.

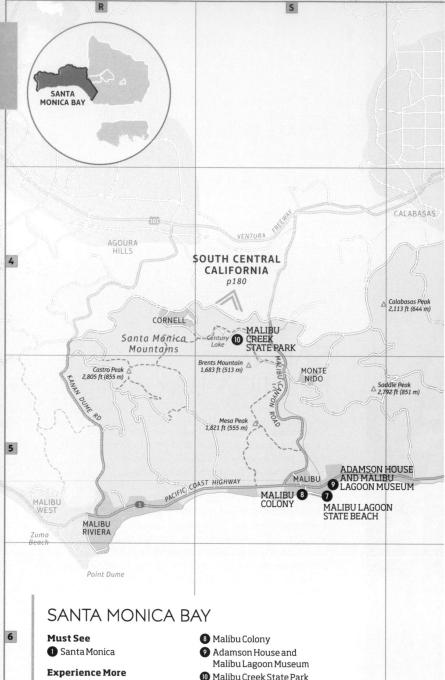

4

SOUTH CENTRAL
CALIFORNIA
p180

CALABASAS

△ Calabasas Peak
2,113 ft (644 m)

AGOURA
HILLS

CORNELL

*Santa Monica
Mountains*

Century
Lake

MALIBU
CREEK
STATE PARK

10

Castro Peak
2,805 ft (855 m) △

Brents Mountain
1,683 ft (513 m) △

MONTE
NIDO

△ Saddle Peak
2,792 ft (851 m)

KANAN DUME RD

Mesa Peak
1,821 ft (555 m)

5

MALIBU
WEST

PACIFIC COAST HIGHWAY

MALIBU

ADAMSON HOUSE
AND MALIBU
LAGOON MUSEUM

MALIBU
COLONY **8** **9**

7

MALIBU LAGOON
STATE BEACH

*Zuma
Beach*

MALIBU
RIVIERA

1

Point Dume

6

SANTA MONICA BAY

Must See

1 Santa Monica

Experience More

2 Venice
3 Museum of Flying
4 Topanga State Park
5 Will Rogers State Historic Park
6 Getty Villa
7 Malibu Lagoon State Beach

8 Malibu Colony
9 Adamson House and
Malibu Lagoon Museum
10 Malibu Creek State Park

Drink

① High Rooftop Lounge
② Hinano Café
③ Venice Ale House

7

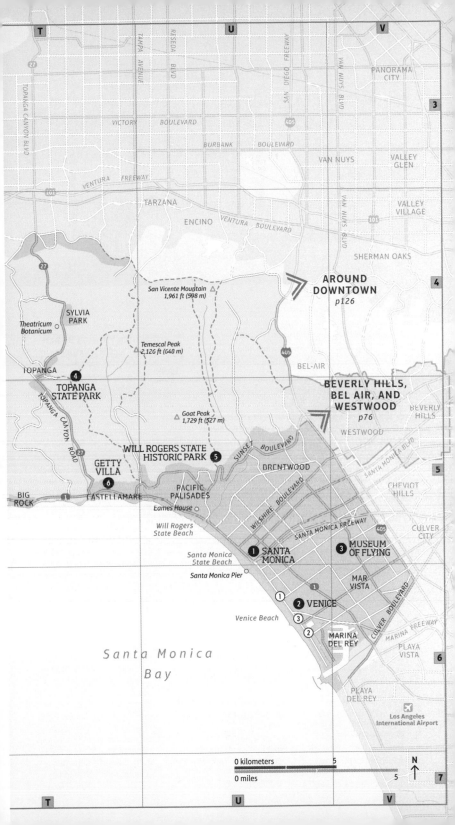

Paddling on the beach at sunset beside Santa Monica Pier ↑

SANTA MONICA

◎ U5 ✈ LAX, 8 miles (13 km) SE of Santa Monica ⊟ 4th St & Colorado Blvd ℹ 1400 Ocean Av; santamonica.com

A fresh sea breeze, mild climate, and pedestrianized streets make this one of the best places in LA to go for a stroll. In the early days, it lived a dual life as a sleepy coastal town and a gambling outpost until movie stars started moving in during the 1920s and 30s, creating the so-called "Gold Coast." The beach and pier are still major attractions, and the city's arts scene is flourishing.

Santa Monica Pier

◎ Colorado Av & Ocean Av
ⓦ santamonicapier.org

This popular 1909 landmark is the West Coast's oldest amusement pier, with bumper cars, an arcade, popcorn, and cotton candy. At the western end, Pacific Park has an 11-story Ferris wheel. Nearby, you can hone your circus skills at the Trapeze School and ride on the 1922 Looff Carousel, which has 44 handcrafted horses. Beneath the pier, the Heal the Bay Aquarium displays over 100 species of local marine life.

Palisades Park

◎ Ocean Av between Colorado Av & Adelaide Dr
◷ 6am–11pm daily

Stretching 1.5 miles (2.5 km) along a bluff overlooking the ocean, this narrow, manicured park is one of the best spots to take a walk, go for a jog, or watch the sun go down. The landscaping is beautiful, with semitropical trees towering overhead. At the northern end, the aptly named Inspiration Point has great views of the bay, stretching from Malibu to Palos Verdes.

Santa Monica Beach

Dozens of movies and TV shows have been filmed on this world-famous beach. The International Chess Park and original Muscle Beach adjoin the pier. The beach has plenty of volleyball courts and invites long walks or bicycle rides. The North Beach Playground and Annenberg Community Beach House pool are great for kids.

Third Street Promenade

One of the liveliest places in LA, Third Street's pedestrian blocks are lined with shops, coffee houses, restaurants, bookstores, and cinemas. The mood is especially festive at night. Nearby, on Arizona Avenue, the farmers' market on Saturdays and Wednesdays is one of the best in the city.

The other major shopping area is Main Street, which runs south toward Venice (p70) and abounds with shops, restaurants, and art galleries. A fine example of Mission Revival architecture is at the northwest corner of Main Street and Pier Avenue. Nearby is the "Binoculars Building," fronted by the huge binocular sculpture by artists Claes Oldenburg and Coosje van Bruggen.

⑤ Bergamot Station

🅰 2525 Michigan Av
🕐 10am-6pm Tue-Fri,
11am-5:30pm Sat
🌐 bergamotstation.com

Bergamot Station stands on the site of an abandoned Red Line trolley station. Over 25 galleries and a small museum showcase the latest works in contemporary and radical art, including painting, sculpture, photography, and glass, plus collectibles and African art.

⑥ California Heritage Museum

🅰 2612 Main St 🕐 11am-4pm Wed-Sun 🌐 california heritagemuseum.org

This fabulous Queen Anne-style building was built in 1894 by architect Sumner P. Hunt as the home of Roy Jones, son of the founder of Santa Monica. On the first floor, the rooms depict the lifestyle of various periods in Southern California history: a Victorian dining room, an Arts and Crafts living room, and a 1930s kitchen. Upstairs, there are revolving exhibitions on topics such as surfing, the Hollywood Western, handmade quilts, and Rancho Monterey furniture.

⑦ Santa Monica History Museum

🅰 1350 7th St 🕐 Noon-8pm Tue & Thu; 10am-5pm Wed, Fri, & Sat 🌐 santamonica history.org

Cartoonist Elzie C. Segar based his famous cartoon character Popeye on real-life Santa Monica fisherman Olaf Olsen. A permanent exhibit of Popeye history is among the fascinating displays at this museum. Its six galleries are chock-full of exhibits highlighting everything from the early Native Americans and the

RAYMOND CHANDLER

Novelist Raymond Chandler (1888–1959) – author of *Farewell, My Lovely*, *The Big Sleep*, and *The Long Goodbye* – set several of his works in Santa Monica. There was some truth in his seedy portrayal of the city; corruption and vice in the 1920s and 1930s are well documented, and illegal gambling ships were sometimes anchored offshore in Santa Monica Bay.

founding of the city to the amusement pier and modern skate culture. Interactive exhibits include a touch-screen map.

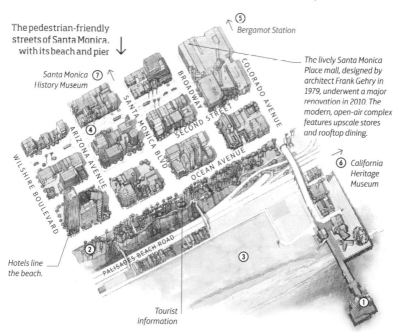

The pedestrian-friendly streets of Santa Monica, with its beach and pier ↓

⑤ Bergamot Station

Santa Monica ⑦ ↖ History Museum

The lively Santa Monica Place mall, designed by architect Frank Gehry in 1979, underwent a major renovation in 2010. The modern, open-air complex features upscale stores and rooftop dining.

BROADWAY
COLORADO AVENUE
SANTA MONICA BLVD
SECOND STREET
ARIZONA AVENUE
OCEAN AVENUE
WILSHIRE BOULEVARD

④

⑥ California Heritage Museum

 Hotels line the beach.

②

PALISADES BEACH ROAD

③

Tourist information

①

↑ A tree decorated with glass ornaments along a canal in Venice

The area's creative scene is best evidenced by the famous Venice Art Walls. Featuring street art, murals, and graffiti, the vibrant walls line Venice Beach boardwalk and Abbot Kinney Boulevard, which has colorful shops, galleries, and Botticelli's *Venus* on roller skates.

3

Museum of Flying

📍V5 🏠3100 Airport Av
🕙10am–5pm Fri–Sun
🌐museumofflying.org

The Museum of Flying places heavy emphasis on the history of the Santa Monica Airport, where it is located, as well as the prominent role that the Douglas Aircraft Company played in the early development of commercial and military aviation.

The museum exhibits an impressive collection of aircraft, artifacts, aviation art, and memorabilia, plus educational offerings with hands-on, interactive exhibits. Nearly two dozen aircraft chronicle the history of flight, from a Wright Flyer replica to aircraft from the jet age.

EXPERIENCE MORE

2

Venice

📍U6 🌐visitveniceca.com

Since its inception, Venice has attracted a colorful crowd, from the rowdy partygoers that frequented its dance hall and bathhouse in the 1910s to the 1950s beatniks. Today this freewheeling neighborhood remains the epicenter of Southern California bohemia.

The community was founded in 1905 by tobacco magnate Abbot Kinney as a US version of Venice, Italy and remained an independent town until 1926 when it merged with LA. Kinney built a system of canals and imported gondolas and gondoliers to punt along the waterways. Unfortunately, Kinney's design failed to account for the tides, which led to sewage problems in the area. Most of the original 7 miles (11 km) of canals have since been filled in; a small quadrant remains on Dell Avenue, where boats and ducks grace the waterways.

Today's top draw is Venice Pier and the surrounding beach and boardwalk, most notably for people-watching. On weekends, scantily clad men and women whiz along the boardwalk on bicycles and skates, while a zany array of street performers captivates the crowds. Muscle Beach, where Arnold Schwarzenegger used to work out, still attracts bodybuilders.

Did You Know?

The Venice sign across Windward Street is a replica of the original, installed in 1905 by Abbot Kinney.

4

Topanga State Park

📍T4–5 🏠20825 Entrada Rd, Topanga 🕗8am–sunset daily 🌐parks.ca.gov

The area that is now Topanga State Park was inhabited by the Tongva/Gabrielino and Chumash peoples 5,000 years ago. The marked entrance to the huge park lies just north of Topanga village, off Hwy 27 on Entrada Road. Most of the land falls within the LA city boundary, making it the largest city park in the US. As such, it vastly improves the region's air quality and provides ample space for hiking and riding.

As you ascend the Santa Monica Mountains, canyons,

CALIFORNIA'S HOUSING CRISIS

Due to rising poverty, a lack of affordable housing, and other complex issues, California's cities have been undergoing a homelessness crisis for some years. Large numbers of people are living in tents or in the open in cities large and small. In LA there are homeless people on the streets throughout the city, including near Venice Beach and in much of Downtown.

cliffs, and meadows give way to vistas of the ocean and the San Fernando Valley. Four trails begin from the park's headquarters at Trippet Ranch: a 1-mile (1.6-km) self-guided nature trail; the Dead Horse Trail; Musch Ranch Trail (which leads to a camp site); and East Topanga Fire Road, which connects with Eagle Junction. The 2.5-mile (4-km) Eagle Rock/Eagle Spring Trail from Eagle Junction is one of the most popular.

Bicycles are allowed on the park's dirt fire roads, and horses on most of the trails.

Nestled in a hillside off SR27 in Topanga Canyon is the Theatricum Botanicum, which hosts summer performances.

5

Will Rogers State Historic Park

U5 **1501 Will Rogers State Park Rd, Pacific Palisades** **8am–sunset daily** **Jan 1, Thanksgiving, Dec 25** **parks.ca.gov**

Will Rogers (1879–1935) started life as a cowboy and went on to become a movie star, radio commentator, and newspaper columnist. Called the "Cowboy Philosopher," he was famous for his homespun humor and shrewd comments on current events, usually made while performing rope tricks. His show business career lasted from 1905 until his death. When his widow, Betty, died in 1944, she deeded the house and the surrounding land to the state, stipulating that nothing in the house be changed and that polo matches be held here on weekends (Rogers was an avid polo player).

Hiking trails lead up from the ranch. The lawn just east of the house is an ideal setting for a picnic. Tours of the house include the living room where Rogers used to practice his roping skills.

DRINK

High Rooftop Lounge

Enjoy panoramic sunset views over the ocean while sipping a seasonal cocktail.

U6 **Hotel Erwin, 1697 Pacific Av** **hotelerwin.com**

Hinano Café

Formerly Jim Morrison's favorite hangout, Hinano is a fun pier-top bar with a jukebox and pool tables. It serves free popcorn.

U6 **15 Washington Blvd** **hinanocafe venice.com**

Venice Ale House

This boardwalk bar draws a huge crowd to sample its selection of local craft beers.

U6 **2 Rose Av** **veniccalchousc.com**

Mountain bikers on a dirt road near Eagle Rock, Topanga State Park

Getty Villa

⑥

📍 T5 🏠 17985 Pacific Coast Hwy 🕐 10am–5pm Wed–Mon 🚫 Jan 1, Independence Day, Thanksgiving, Dec 25 holidays 🌐 getty.edu

The Getty Villa is the home of the Getty Center's *(p80)* antiquities collection. Getty's vision – of a museum where antiquities could be displayed in a place where such art might originally have been seen – came to fruition in 2006. The museum displays around 1,200 works of ancient art from Greece, Rome, and Etruria, dating from 6,500 BC to AD 400.

The villa is based on the Villa dei Papiri, the country estate

↑ The Outer Peristyle garden at the Getty Villa and *(inset)* kids on a guided tour

of a Roman consul. The Outer Peristyle garden is spectacular, with its large pool lined by bronze statuary replicas and plants favored by the ancient Romans.

Getty's original home on this property, and the site of the first Getty Museum, holds a research library, seminar room, classroom, reading room, conservation labs, and offices for scholars and staff. The outdoor amphitheater presents Greek drama and dance performances, and there is an upscale café. Admission to the villa is free, but tickets are timed.

---

⑦

Malibu Lagoon State Beach

📍 S5 🕐 8am–sunset daily 🌐 parks.ca.gov

The Chumash people built Humaliwo, their largest village, on the shores of this lagoon. By the 16th century,

about 1,000 people had their home here, making it one of the most populated Native American villages north of what is now Mexico.

The estuary supports a wide range of marine life and is an important feeding ground for up to 200 species of migratory and native birds. To the east of the lagoon, Surfrider County Beach is devoted to surfers. Malibu is one of the finest surfing spots in southern California.

---

⑧

Malibu Colony

📍 S5 ℹ️ 23554 Malibu Colony Rd

In 1928, to raise money for an ongoing battle to keep Malibu in the family, May Rindge sold

---

HIDDEN GEM
Eames House

Set atop an oceanside cliff in Pacific Palisades, a few miles east of Getty Villa, this 1949 building is a perfect exemplar of mid-century Modernist architecture in LA *(www. eamesfoundation.org)*.

> **A varied landscape of forests, volcanic rocky outcrops, and meadows in Malibu Creek State Park creates the illusion of a vast wilderness, far away from civilization.**

this section of shoreline to movie stars such as Bing Crosby, Gary Cooper, and Barbara Stanwyck. Today the colony is a private, gated compound, still favored by people working within the entertainment industry. Public access to the beach is difficult, but stars can often be spotted in the Malibu Colony Plaza, located near the entrance.

 9

Adamson House and Malibu Lagoon Museum

📍 S5 🏠 23200 Pacific Coast Hwy ⏰ For tours only: 11am-3pm Fri & Sat; Grounds: 8am-6pm daily 🚫 Jan 1, Jul 4, Thanksgiving, Dec 25 🌐 adamsonhouse.org

Adamson House was built in 1930 for husband and wife Merritt and Rhoda Adamson. Rhoda was the daughter of Frederick and May Rindge, the last owners of the Rancho Malibu Spanish land grant. Until 1928, the family owned 24 miles (39 km) of Malibu coastline. Situated on the beach, the idyllic house, designed by Stiles Clements, and its 6 acres (2.5 ha) of land and gardens overlook Malibu Pier and Malibu Lagoon. The Spanish Revival-style building is covered with vivid tiles from the Malibu Potteries – a ceramics firm that was started by May Rindge and owned by the family. Hundreds of these individually designed tiles are featured throughout the house and grounds. The floors, walls, doorways, and fountains are all intricately decorated. The house's original 1920s furnishings are also on display.

Located in the converted garage of Adamson House is the Malibu Lagoon Museum, which is devoted to the history of Malibu. Artifacts, documents, and photographs tell the story not only of the Rindge family but also of the early Chumash population and José Tapia, who in 1802 became Malibu's first Spanish landowner.

 10

Malibu Creek State Park

📍 S4 ⏰ Dawn-dusk daily 🌐 parks.ca.gov

This 10,000-acre (4,000-ha) park was inhabited for centuries by the Chumash people until the mid-1800s. A varied landscape of forests, volcanic rocky outcrops, and meadows creates the illusion of a vast wilderness, far away from civilization.

Some 2,000 acres (800 ha) of the park were once owned by 20th Century Fox, which made it a favorite location for movie-making. *M*A*S*H* (1970), *Butch Cassidy and the Sundance Kid* (1969), and *Planet of the Apes* (1968) were all filmed here. The state bought the land back from the film company in 1974.

The information center is close to the parking lot and has exhibits on the area's history, flora, and fauna. The stunning Gorge Trail starts from the center of the park and leads to a rock pool, which was used as a pseudo-tropical location to film the movies *South Pacific* (1958) and *Tarzan* (1959).

Off Crags Road, the marshy Century Lake harbors catfish, bass, bluefish, red-winged blackbirds, coots, and mallards. In spring the meadows are a riot of colorful wildflowers. Groves of live and valley oaks, redwood, and dogwood trees are scattered throughout the park, which was badly damaged by a fire in 2018.

Within the park there are 20 trails for hiking, cycling, or horseback riding; a nature center; and many picnic areas.

MALIBU SURF

In the 1920s, surfing pioneers began catching rides "where the waves…crash against the shore like … rocket bombs"– as Frederick Kohner wrote in *Gidget*, the 1957 novel about a surfing teenager that launched Malibu to fame. Surfrider Beach is considered the cradle and epicenter of LA's surfing culture; its waves are packed with surfers in the early morning and late afternoon, while tourists gather to soak in the beach-party atmosphere.

A DRIVING TOUR
NORTH LOS ANGELES COASTLINE

Length 30 miles (50 km) **Stopping-off points** There is a restaurant and a coffee kiosk at Getty Villa. Malibu, Santa Monica, and Venice have many beachside restaurants and cafés.

The coastline north of Los Angeles is lined with tempting strips of sand and cultural attractions, including the renowned city beaches at Santa Monica and Venice. As you drive along the Pacific Coast Highway, the urban sprawl soon morphs into exclusive beachside communities such as Pacific

Palisades and Malibu, hemmed in by arid hills. The waters off Malibu Pier, Leo Carrillo, and Topanga are surfing hotspots, while inland, the rugged Santa Monica Mountains and Malibu Creek State Park are largely unspoiled, with plenty of hiking trails leading to panoramic views of the ocean.

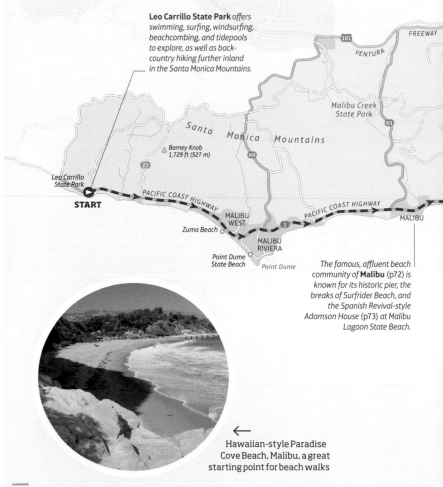

Leo Carrillo State Park *offers swimming, surfing, windsurfing, beachcombing, and tidepools to explore, as well as back-country hiking further inland in the Santa Monica Mountains.*

FREEWAY

101

VENTURA

Malibu Creek State Park

N1

Santa Monica Mountains

N9

△ Barney Knob
1,729 ft (527 m)

23

Leo Carrillo
State Park

START

PACIFIC COAST HIGHWAY

PACIFIC COAST HIGHWAY

MALIBU

MALIBU WEST

1

Zuma Beach

MALIBU RIVIERA

Point Dume
State Beach   Point Dume

The famous, affluent beach community of **Malibu** *(p72) is known for its historic pier, the breaks of Surfrider Beach, and the Spanish Revival-style Adamson House (p73) at Malibu Lagoon State Beach.*

←
Hawaiian-style Paradise Cove Beach, Malibu, a great starting point for beach walks

↑ Pacific Wheel, the world's first solar-powered Ferris wheel, Santa Monica Pier

Locator Map
For more detail see p66

SANTA MONICA BAY
North Los Angeles Coastline

Perched high above the shoreline, the **Getty Villa** *(p72) holds a precious cache of Etruscan, Greek, and Roman antiquities.*

Located just off the Coast Hwy, **Eames House** *(p72) is a landmark of mid-20th-century modern architecture. Reserve guided tours in advance.*

Santa Monica Pier *(p68) is crammed with attractions, including Pacific Park's iconic Ferris wheel, a carousel, and an aquarium.*

Topanga Beach *is divided in two by the mouth of Topanga Creek. It is popular with kite- and windsurfers.*

Named after the Hollywood actor, **Will Rogers State Beach** *(p70) is a sandy spot good for bodysurfing and beach volleyball.*

Venice Beach *(p70) offers a mix of beach shacks, golden sands, street performers, skaters, and bodybuilders working out at Muscle Beach.*

WOODLAND HILLS
TARZANA
CALABASAS
ENCINO

Calabasas Peak 2,113 ft (644 m)
Temescal Peak 2,126 ft (648 m)

TOPANGA
Topanga State Park

Saddle Peak 2,792 ft (851 m)

Getty Villa
BRENTWOOD
Topanga Beach
Will Rogers State Beach
Eames House
SANTA MONICA
Santa Monica Pier
MAR VISTA
Venice Beach
VENICE
MARINA DEL REY
FINISH

0 kilometers 5
0 miles 5

N ↑

75

Palm tree-lined Rodeo Drive

BEVERLY HILLS, BEL AIR, AND WESTWOOD

Beverly Hills is actually a city in its own right, independent of Los Angeles. It was originally settled by Spanish ranchers and the land was subdivided and developed from the 1880s. In 1912, the iconic Beverly Hills Hotel opened and visitors drawn to the area by the hotel started to purchase land, including movie stars such as Douglas Fairbanks and Mary Pickford, who moved here in 1919 – since then Beverly Hills has been the entertainment industry's favorite residential address. Rodeo Drive's current incarnation as a luxury shopping strip dates back to 1961, when Giorgio Beverly Hills, a former luxury boutique, was opened by Swiss-born Fred Hayman, later dubbed "the father of Rodeo Drive."

Similarly wealthy is adjacent Bel Air (which unlike Beverly Hills is administered as part of LA). The area was founded by oil tycoon Alphonzo Bell in 1923 – he also built the luxury Bel Air Country Club two years later, which remains an exclusive golf and tennis club today.

Westwood, a collection of low-slung Spanish Revival buildings that went up in the 1920s around Broxton Avenue, is one of LA's more pedestrian-friendly neighborhoods. The University of California, Los Angeles (UCLA) campus moved here from East Hollywood in 1929, and today Westwood is an affluent, youthful area, as well as a hub for the Persian community in Los Angeles.

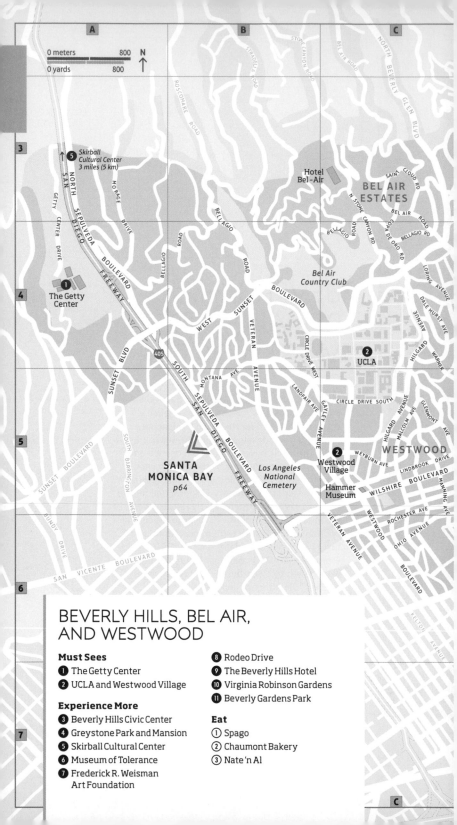

0 meters   800
0 yards   800

N

3

🅢 Skirball
Cultural Center
3 miles (5 km)

Hotel
Bel-Air

**BEL AIR
ESTATES**

GETTY CENTER DRIVE

MORAGE DRIVE

NORTH SEPULVEDA BOULEVARD

ROSCOMARE ROAD

STONE CANYON ROAD

BEL AIR ROAD

NORTH BEVERLY GLEN BLVD

SAINT CLOUD RD

N STONE CANYON RD

BEL AIR RD

COPA DE ORO RD

BELLAGIO RD

LORING AVENUE

4

🅘 The Getty
Center

SAN DIEGO FREEWAY

BELLAGIO ROAD

BELLAGIO ROAD

SUNSET   BOULEVARD

Bel Air
Country Club

BELLAGIO ROAD

DALE HURST AVE

HILGARD AVENUE

WARNER AVE

AVENUE

405

SUNSET BLVD

SOUTH SAN DIEGO BOULEVARD

WEST   SUNSET

VETERAN AVENUE

CIRCLE DRIVE WEST

🅱 UCLA

MONTANA AVE

CIRCLE DRIVE SOUTH

HILGARD AVENUE

MALCOLM AVE

GLENMONT AVE

5

SANTA
MONICA BAY
p64

Los Angeles
National
Cemetery

LANDFAIR AVE

GAYLEY AVENUE

🅱 Westwood
Village

WEYBURN AVE

WESTWOOD

Hammer
Museum

WILSHIRE BOULEVARD

LINDBROOK DRIVE

MANNING AVE

SUNSET BOULEVARD

SOUTH BARRINGTON AVENUE

VETERAN AVENUE

WESTWOOD BOULEVARD

ROCHESTER AVE

OHIO AVENUE

BUNDY DRIVE

SAN VICENTE BOULEVARD

6

KELTON AVENUE

7

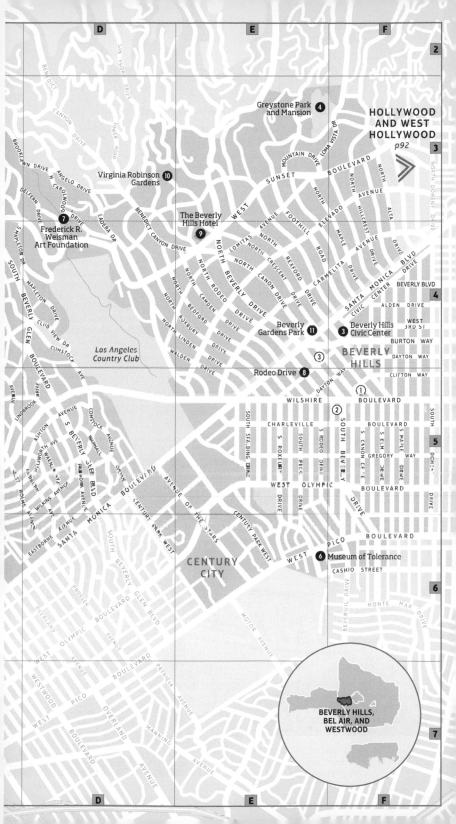

THE GETTY CENTER

A4 **1200 Getty Center Dr** **10am–5pm Tue–Sun** **getty.edu**

A spectacular art collection, stunning architecture, and gorgeous gardens combine with a hilltop location to create one of LA's finest cultural destinations. Designed by architect Richard Meier, the Getty Center opened in 1997; it houses an array of exquisite European art, from illuminated manuscripts to contemporary photography.

J. Paul Getty made his fortune in the oil business and became an ardent collector of art. He was a bold collector, who enjoyed the pursuit of an object almost more than the possession of it. He wanted his remarkable collection, which focuses on European art from the Renaissance to Post-Impressionism, to be open to the public without charge.

Situated amid the wild beauty of the Santa Monica Mountains, the Getty Center houses not only the museum but also the Getty's research, conservation, and grant programs (the Getty Foundation). Hundreds of pre-20th-century paintings, drawings, sculptures, and decorative arts and 19th- to 21st-century photographs are displayed on rotation. Greek, Etruscan, and Roman antiquities are exhibited at the Getty Villa in Malibu (p72).

GUIDE TO THE GETTY CENTER

A tram brings visitors from the parking area to the complex. The museum has a tall, airy foyer that opens onto a central courtyard, from which radiate five pavilions. The Conceptualist artist Robert Irwin created a garden to the west of the museum. Opposite the tram station there is a café and restaurant. Another café and a bookstore are located in the museum.

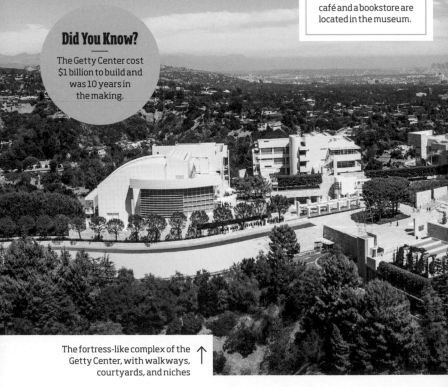

Did You Know?

The Getty Center cost $1 billion to build and was 10 years in the making.

↑ The fortress-like complex of the Getty Center, with walkways, courtyards, and niches

1 *Irises* (1889) was painted by Vincent van Gogh while he was in the asylum at St-Rémy.

2 Paul Cézanne experiments with shape, color, and light in *Still Life with Apples* (1893).

3 This bust of Maria Capranica (c. 1640) is attributed to Italian sculptor Alessandro Algardi.

Exploring the Getty Museum

The North Pavilion houses Medieval and Renaissance sculpture, decorative arts, and paintings up to 1600, as well as illuminated manuscripts from the Byzantine, Ottoman, Romanesque, Renaissance, and Gothic periods, spanning the 6th to the 16th centuries. Exhibits in the East Pavilion showcase Baroque 17th-century Dutch, Flemish, French, and Spanish paintings, and sculpture and Italian decorative arts from 1700 to 1800. The South Pavilion displays 18th-century paintings and a large collection of European decorative arts, including lavishly furnished paneled rooms. The West Pavilion has sculpture and Italian decorative arts dating from 1700 to 1900, as well as Neo-Classical, Romantic, and Symbolist decorative arts. It also houses the Center for Photographs. A fifth pavilion hosts temporary exhibitions. The grounds are dotted with modern sculptures.

→
Cabinet on Stand (1675-80) attributed to the French master craftsman André-Charles Boulle

A fountain at the Getty Center, which incorporates modern design and open spaces ↑

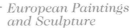

Must See

Gallery Guide

INSIDER TIP
GettyGuide

Hear curators and artists talk about the collections and exhibitions in the Getty Center by picking up a GettyGuide. This free mobile device, with audio tours and music, enables you to take your own self-guided tour. The guides are in multiple languages and can be collected from the desk in the main entrance hall.

European Paintings and Sculpture

▷ The museum has a superb collection of European paintings, dating from the 13th century to the late 19th century. These range from Italian, Flemish, and Dutch works from the Renaissance and Baroque periods to key Impressionist and Post-Impressionist pieces. European sculptures in the Getty span the 16th century to the end of the 19th century, encompassing High Renaissance, Mannerist, Baroque, and Neo-Classical styles.

Drawings

◁ The purchase in 1981 of Rembrandt's red chalk study of *Nude Woman with a Snake* (c.1637) marked the beginning of the museum's drawings collection. Today the collection contains more than 400 works in a wide range of media, spanning the 15th to the late 19th century. Highlights of the collection include Leonardo da Vinci's *Studies for the Christ Child with a Lamb* (c.1503-6) in pen and ink, Peter Paul Rubens' *Korean Man,* one of several portrait drawings, and *Self-Portrait* (c.1857-8) by Edgar Degas, executed in oil on paper and showing the young artist on the threshold of his extraordinary career.

Decorative and Applied Arts

Decorative arts were Getty's first love as a collector, after he rented a New York penthouse furnished with 18th-century French and English antiques. Originally, his collection focused on furnishings from the reign of Louis XIV to the Napoleonic era (1643-1815), encompassing the Regency, Rococo, and Empire periods. The age of Louis XIV saw the development of French furniture reach great artistic heights. The premier craftsman during that time was André-Charles Boulle (1642-1732), who was noted for his complex veneers and marquetry. Several of his pieces are housed in the museum. Other highlights include glass and earthenware from Italy and Spain and metalwork from France, Germany, and Italy, dating from 1650 to 1900.

Photographs

▷ The museum launched its photographic department in 1984 with the purchase of several major private collections. The holdings focus on European and American photography up to the 1950s. Exceptionally rich in works from the early 1840s, the collection features many of the pioneers of photography. The museum has one portrait of photographer Louis-Jacques-Mande Daguerre, taken in 1848 by Charles R. Meade. *Oak Tree in Winter* (1841) is a lovely example of the work by Englishman William Henry Fox Talbot, the first photographer to make prints from negatives. Other early practitioners on display include Hyppolyte Bayard (1801-87), portraitist Julia Margaret Cameron (1815-79), war photographer Roger Fenton (1819-69), and Gustave Le Gray (1820-82). Among the early 20th-century artists are Edward Weston (1886-1958), creator of beautiful still lifes, and Walker Evans (1903-75), a pivotal influence in American documentary photography.

UCLA AND WESTWOOD VILLAGE

 C4 20, 21, 22 🚇 UCLA Campus: www.ucla.edu; Westwood Village: 2990 S Sepulveda Blvd, www.thewestwoodvillage.com

A large university with a first-rate reputation, the University of California, Los Angeles (UCLA) has a wide range of academic departments and professional schools, including the respected UCLA Hospital. The original campus, set in beautiful landscaped grounds, was designed in 1925 to resemble the Romanesque towns of southern Europe. As the university expanded, more modern architecture was favored.

① Royce Quadrangle

🏛 Dickson Plaza ⏱ Daily

The four buildings surrounding a grassy space that make up the Royce Quadrangle are the oldest on UCLA's Westwood campus. Built of red brick in the Italian Romanesque style, Royce, Kinsey, and Haines halls, and Powell Library far surpass the other buildings at UCLA in beauty. The best of them all is Royce Hall, which is based on the basilica of San Ambrogio in Milan, Italy. Across the quad, Powell Library's grand rotunda was modeled on the basilica of San Sepolcro in Bologna, Italy.

② Hammer Museum

🏛 10899 Wilshire Blvd ⏱ 11am–8pm Tue–Fri, 11am–5pm Sat & Sun 🚫 Jan 1, Jul 4, Thanksgiving, Dec 25 🌐 hammer.ucla.edu

The museum presents selections from the collection of businessman Armand Hammer (1899–1990). Works are principally by Impressionist or Post-Impressionist artists such as Mary Cassatt (1845–1926), Camille Pissarro (1830–1903), Claude Monet (1840–1926), John Singer Sargent (1856–1925), and Vincent van Gogh (1853–90). Contemporary paintings, sculptures, and lithographs are also shown on a rotating basis.

③ Franklin D. Murphy Sculpture Garden

🏛 245 Charles E. Young Dr E ⏱ Daily

This is the largest sculpture garden on the West Coast, with more than 70 20th-century

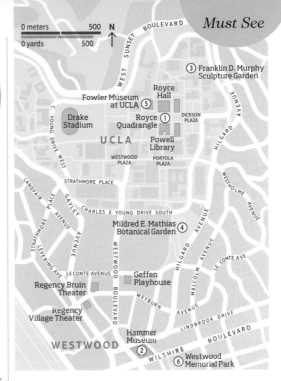

sculptures. The highlights include Henry Moore's *Two-Piece Reclining Figure, No. 3* (1961) and Jacques Lipchitz's *Baigneuse* (*Bather*, 1923–5).

---

④

Mildred E. Mathias Botanical Garden

🏛 707 Tiverton Av ⏰ 8am-4pm Tue-Fri, 9am-4pm Sat & Sun 🚫 Federal hols 🌐 botgard.ucla.edu

Named after an acclaimed American botanist, this serene garden is tucked away in a small shady canyon and contains more than 3,000 rare and native species. The gardens are divided into 13 thematic sections, and feature both subtropical and tropical plants. The spectacular trees include some outstanding Australian eucalyptus and large dawn redwoods.

↑ A fountain gushing outside Royce Hall on the pristine UCLA campus

⑤ 🏛

Fowler Museum at UCLA

📞 310-825-4361 ⏰ Noon-8pm Wed, noon-5pm Thu-Sun 🚫 Federal hols 🌐 fowler.ucla.edu

This university museum is committed to enriching the community's understanding of the diverse cultures, peoples, and religions of the world. Its exhibitions focus on the prehistoric, historic, and contemporary societies of Africa, Asia, the Americas, and Oceania.

---

⑥

Westwood Memorial Park

🏛 1218 Glendon Av 📞 310-474-1579 ⏰ 8am-5pm daily

This small cemetery is located behind the iPic theaters. The tranquil grounds are now the final resting place for celebrities such as Dean Martin,

Peter Lorre, Buddy Rich, Natalie Wood, and Marilyn Monroe. For years after her death, Monroe's second husband, Joe DiMaggio, had six red roses placed on her tomb every week.

THEATERS AND HISTORIC CINEMAS OF WESTWOOD

Westwood Village is an epicenter for historic theaters. Visitors are often treated to parades of movie stars arriving for premieres at the landmark Regency Village Theater. Opposite, the Art Deco Regency Bruin Theater is a Los Angeles Historic-Cultural Monument. The Geffen Playhouse is one of the original 12 structures built in Westwood Village; since 1995 it has hosted contemporary and classic plays.

EXPERIENCE MORE

Beverly Hills Civic Center

♀F4 **🏛455 N Rexford Dr**
🕐7:30am-5:30pm Mon-Thu, 8am-5pm Fri
🔒Federal hols **🌐laconservancy.org/locations/beverly-hills-civic-center**

The Spanish Renaissance City Hall, with its majestic tower capped by a tiled cupola, was designed in 1932 by local firm Koerner and Gage. Over the years, this striking building has become a symbol of the elegant, European-inspired city of Beverly Hills.

In 1990, architect Charles Moore linked the building to a new Civic Center by a series of diagonal landscaped and pedestrianized courtyards. On the upper levels, balconies and arcaded corridors continue the Spanish Renaissance theme. The harmonious modern addition houses a beautiful public library as well as the local fire and police stations.

Billboards are banned in the area, and a height restriction of three stories or 45 ft (14 m) is imposed on any new buildings, leaving City Hall to dominate the skyline.

 INSIDER TIP
The Manor by Theatre 40

This play is staged with actors in period costume in Greystone Mansion every February. It is a fictionalized re-enactment of the tragic events that took place here *(www.theatre40.org)*.

Greystone Park and Mansion

♀E3 **🏛905 Loma Vista Dr**
📞(310) 285-6830 **🕐Park: daily, call ahead for details; Mansion: only for special events**

In 1928 oil millionaire Edward L. Doheny built this 55-room mock-Tudor manor house for his son. Just three weeks after moving in with his family, Doheny's son was found dead in his bedroom with a male secretary, an apparent murder-suicide.

Now owned by the city of Beverly Hills, Greystone has been used in films, such as the 2007 film *There Will Be Blood*, and the house's staircase is one of the most famous sets in Hollywood. The house is closed to the public except for events such as the Music in the Mansion chamber music program that takes place on Sundays from January to June. Visitors are allowed to walk or picnic in the terraced gardens, which offer views across the city.

Skirball Cultural Center

♀A3 **🏛2701 N Sepulveda Blvd**
🕐Noon-5pm Tue-Fri, 10am-5pm Sat & Sun
🌐skirball.org

This modern complex celebrates 4,000 years of Jewish heritage and interprets the American Jewish experience, emphasizing the

↑ The Beverly Hills Civic Center, overlooked by the Spanish Renaissance City Hall

↑ Sculpture in the courtyard of the Museum of Tolerance

parallel influence of all other immigrants on American society and its institutions. Engaging temporary exhibitions have included the art of Roy Lichtenstein, the fashion of Rudi Gernreich, and the history of the American Jewish deli. Live concerts and special screenings are offered throughout the year. The Noah's Ark, made from recycled materials, is a fun and interactive play area for children.

6

Museum of Tolerance

E6 9786 W Pico Blvd 10am-5pm Sun-Fri Jan 1, Thanksgiving, Dec 25, and all major Jewish holidays museumof tolerance.com

This fascinating museum examines discrimination and prejudice around the world in both historical and contemporary contexts, with a particularly strong focus on the Holocaust.

In the Tolerancenter, visitors are challenged to confront racism and bigotry through interactive exhibits. Meanwhile, a 16-screen video wall depicts the 1960s civil rights struggle in America.

At the beginning of the Holocaust section, each visitor is given a photograph of a child whose life was in some way altered by that period. Throughout the tour, the child's history is updated and, at the end, his or her fate is revealed. In a re-creation of the Wannsee Conference, the Third Reich leaders decide on the Final Solution of the Jewish Question. Videotaped interviews with concentration camp survivors shown in the Hall of Testimony tell of their harrowing experiences. The Anne exhibit displays Anne Frank's original letters and memorabilia from the camps, as well as featuring a dramatization of her life in the secret annex. A separate fee is charged for this exhibit.

Visitors must call ahead for reservations, as tickets are issued for allocated slots and specific exhibitions. Some of the exhibits, including the Holocaust portion, are not recommended for children under the age of 12.

7

Frederick R. Weisman Art Foundation

D4 265 N Carolwood Dr 10:30am-1:30pm Mon-Fri weisman foundation.org

The son of Russian immigrants, the late Frederick R. Weisman started his first business at the age of 17, achieving entrepreneurial success and wealth by the time he reached his 30s. His real passion, though, was philanthropy and art, and he soon gained an international reputation as one of the top collectors of modern and contemporary art in the world.

This museum in a 1920s Mediterranean-style estate and an adjoining contemporary annex sensitively showcases Weisman's collection of 400 extraordinary works of art that periodically rotate. Visitors can explore the history of 20th-century art through the works of more than 150 artists, including Cezanne, Picasso, Kandinsky, Miro, and Magritte. There is also a large section displaying Pop Art by the likes of Warhol, Lichtenstein, Oldenburg, and Rosenquist. A beautifully landscaped garden contains fine sculptures, including works by Colombian figurative artist Fernando Botero. Visiting the estate is by docent-led tour only, which lasts about 90 minutes.

EAT

Spago

Wolfgang Puck's flagship restaurant guarantees unforgettable fine-dining. Reserve well in advance.

F5 176 N Canon Dr Lunch Sun & Mon wolfgangpuck. com/dining/spago-2

$$$

Chaumont Bakery

This French bakery and café serves divine savory croissants, pastries, and sandwiches.

F5 143 S Beverly Dr chaumont bakery.com

$$$

Nate 'n Al

Opened in 1945, this classic deli clings to tradition. Menu highlights include its trademark corned beef Reuben sandwich.

E4 414 N Beverly Dr natenals.com

$$$

8

Rodeo Drive

E5

With its Italian boutiques, the best of French fashion, and world-class jewelers, Rodeo Drive is unrivaled as a venue for shopping and celebrity spotting.

Its broad, tree-lined sidewalks are inset with Walk of Style bronze plaques, modeled on Hollywood's Walk of Fame, honoring the big names in fashion. The walk's focal point is *Torso*, a 14-ft (4-m) solid aluminum sculpture at the junction with Dayton Way. To its east side, and built in 1990, is Two Rodeo, one of the world's most exclusive retail centers. It resembles a film set of a European street, complete with a public square and Victorian-style street lamps. Chic shops such as Versace and Jimmy Choo line Via Rodeo, the cobbled lane that bisects the center and meanders south to the Spanish Steps, which descend to Wilshire Boulevard.

> Rodeo Drive's broad, tree-lined sidewalks are inset with Walk of Style bronze plaques, modeled on Hollywood's Walk of Fame, honoring the big names in fashion.

Among Rodeo Drive's luxury retailers are such fashion luminaries as Louis Vuitton (No. 295), for the finest in luggage and accessories; Gucci (No. 347), the Italian boutique known for its leather goods and colorful scarves; Valentino (No. 324), the elegant Italian fashion house; and House of Bijan (No. 420), the world's most expensive menswear store.

Fans of Sprinkles cupcakes – or anyone craving a 24/7 snack or the novelty of purchasing a cupcake from a banking machine – can visit **Sprinkles'** "ATM" dispenser attached to its 24-hour flagship bakery, a couple of blocks from Rodeo Drive. It's a favorite with celebrities.

Sprinkles
9635 S Santa Monica Blvd
sprinkles.com

9

The Beverly Hills Hotel

E4 9641 Sunset Blvd
Daily dorchester collection.com

Dubbed "the Pink Palace," this extravagant Mission Revival-style hotel was built in 1912, before the city even existed. The iconic hotel has been a playground for Hollywood royalty for over a century; numerous movie deals have been made in the lavish Polo Lounge Restaurant, while the

←
Elegant Rodeo Drive, lined with the stores of world-famous fashion designers

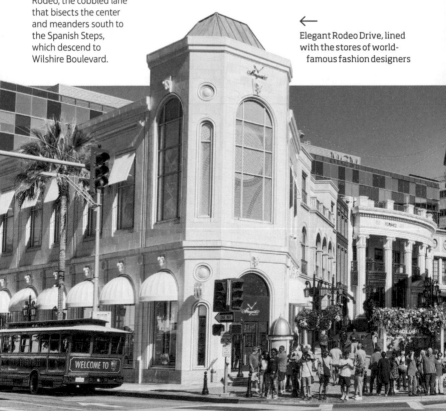

hotel's secluded bungalows, set in 12 acres (5 ha) of landscaped gardens, are the perfect hideaway for stars seeking solitude.

In 2019 the hotel's current owner, the Sultan of Brunei, imposed Sharia law in his country, which led to a celebrity and LA City Council boycott of the hotel.

Virginia Robinson Gardens

📍 D3 🏠 1008 Elden Way
🕐 9am–4pm Mon–Fri, with advance reservations only
🌐 robinsongardens.org

In 1908, department-store heir Harry Robinson and his wife, Virginia, bought a plot of land in Beverly Hills. Three years later, the Robinsons had not only completed the city's first ever house here, they had also planted 6 acres (2.5 ha) of lush landscaped gardens set among many terraces, ponds, and fountains.

Virginia Robinson became known as the "First Lady of Beverly Hills," legendary for her card games and lavish parties, which were often attended by celebrities.

Bequeathed to LA County, the gardens were opened to the public in 1982. One of the most impressive sights is the palm forest, where you can see the largest king palms outside Australia.

The organized tour includes part of the house, which still has its original furnishings. Be sure to make a reservation in advance since walk-up visits are not allowed.

↑ People taking pictures of the iconic Beverly Hills Sign at leafy Beverly Gardens Park

Beverly Gardens Park

📍 E4 🏠 Santa Monica Blvd, between Doheny Dr & Wilshire Blvd

Spanning 23 blocks, this large tree-shaded park stretches nearly 2 miles (3 km) along Santa Monica and Wilshire boulevards. Studded with sculptures, its three central blocks were laid out in 1911 with a lily pond and the iconic Beverly Hills Sign, which was re-created in a modern style in 2009. Narrower sections – including palm, rose, and cactus gardens – were added in the late 1920s.

At its southern end, the Electric Fountain is topped by a kneeling Tongva tribe member and sits in a basin that shows scenes from California history in bas-relief.

In May and October, the park hosts the prestigious Beverly Hills Art Show.

💬 INSIDER TIP
Celebrity Home Tours

Starline Tours offers a two-hour tour of upscale hillside neighborhoods, giving you a real sense of the lifestyles of the rich and famous *(www. starlinetours.com)*.

A SHORT WALK
THE GOLDEN TRIANGLE

Distance 1.5 miles (2.5 km) **Time** 30 minutes
Nearest bus 20, 720, 786

The area bordered by Santa Monica Boulevard, Wilshire Boulevard, and North Crescent Drive, known as the "Golden Triangle," is the shopping district of Beverly Hills. The shops, restaurants, and art galleries lining the streets are some of the most luxurious in the world. Cutting through the middle is Rodeo Drive, where many international designer boutiques are to be found. On Wilshire Boulevard, the cream of American department stores offer a heady mix of style and opulence. This walk will also lead you past the beautifully manicured Beverly Gardens Park, a great place for a stroll past various sculptures, cactus and rose gardens, and the elegant Civic Center with its landmark City Hall.

The golden Electric Fountain shimmering in Beverly Gardens Park

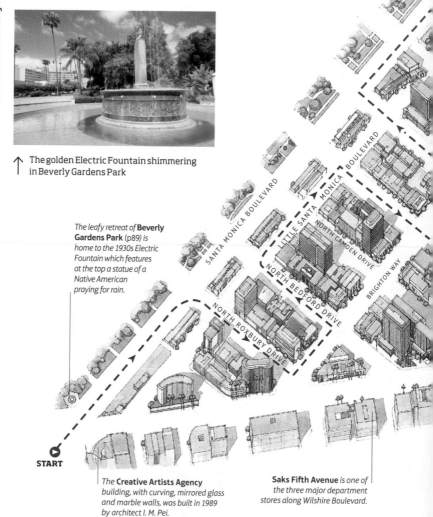

The leafy retreat of **Beverly Gardens Park** (p89) is home to the 1930s Electric Fountain which features at the top a statue of a Native American praying for rain.

SANTA MONICA BOULEVARD

SANTA MONICA BOULEVARD

LITTLE SANTA MONICA BOULEVARD

NORTH CAMDEN DRIVE

NORTH BEDFORD DRIVE

BRIGHTON WAY

NORTH ROXBURY DRIVE

START

The **Creative Artists Agency** building, with curving, mirrored glass and marble walls, was built in 1989 by architect I. M. Pei.

Saks Fifth Avenue is one of the three major department stores along Wilshire Boulevard.

↑ Colorful shops lining the high-end hub of Two Rodeo

FINISH

The **Beverly Hills Civic Center** (p86) *features the restored 1932 Spanish Renaissance City Hall.*

NORTH CRESCENT DRIVE

NORTH CANON DRIVE

DAYTON WAY

NORTH BEVERLY DRIVE

Did You Know?

The store where Julia Roberts' character in *Pretty Woman* gets rebuffed was on Rodeo Drive.

When built in 1990, the **Two Rodeo** *center included the first new street in Beverly Hills since the city established Independence from LA in 1914.*

NORTH RODEO DRIVE

WILSHIRE BOULEVARD

The MGM Building *was built in the 1920s by film producer Louis B. Mayer. The Art Deco structure was the headquarters of the Metro-Goldwyn-Mayer film studios.*

Rodeo Drive (p88) *is among the most famous shopping areas in the world. Look out for the Rodeo Drive Walk of Style (plaques commemorating important people in fashion).*

Anderton Court Shops *was designed by architect Frank Lloyd Wright in 1953.*

The iconic **Beverly Wilshire** *first opened in 1928 in a stunning Beaux-Arts building. The hotel restaurant has a patio overlooking Rodeo Drive.*

| 0 meters | 100 |
| 0 yards | 100 |

N ↑

Exterior of the Petersen Automotive Museum

HOLLYWOOD AND WEST HOLLYWOOD

In 1887, Harvey H. Wilcox and his wife, Daeida (the "Mother of Hollywood"), started selling lots on land they had purchased eight miles (13 km) west of downtown Los Angeles – they called it Hollywood. The community was initially conceived as fiercely Christian, free of saloons and gambling – alcohol, pool halls, and even bowling alleys were formally banned in 1904. Encouraged by subsequent developer H.J. Whitley (the "Father of Hollywood") and attracted by cheap labor, low taxes, compliant government, and guaranteed sunshine, the first Hollywood film studio opened here in 1911 – two years later Cecil B. DeMille began filming *The Squaw Man* and Charlie Chaplin arrived in LA. The Hollywood movie industry blossomed from the 1920s on, generating wealth and glamour. A few decades later, however, and most of the major studios began migrating to Burbank in southeast Los Angeles county, pushing Hollywood into a period of decline during the 1970s and 80s. Things picked up again in the 1990s, with the area becoming a major tourist draw and a hub for Los Angeles nightlife. West Hollywood became an independent city in 1984, known for its lively nightlife and commercial districts. To the south of West Hollywood, Wilshire Boulevard between La Brea and Fairfax avenues, too, has seen something of a renaissance: once a thriving retail district and so-called "Miracle Mile", Wilshire Boulevard declined during the 1980s, only to see the arrival of museums and offices a decade later. This stretch of Wilshire Boulevard is now known as "Museum Row."

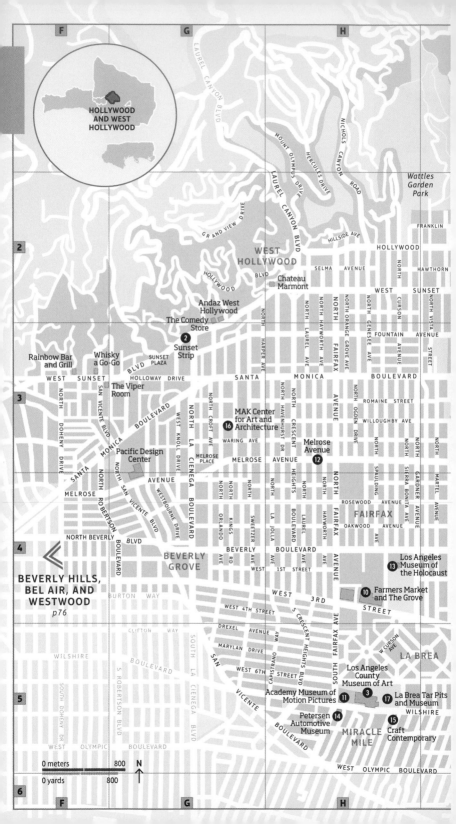

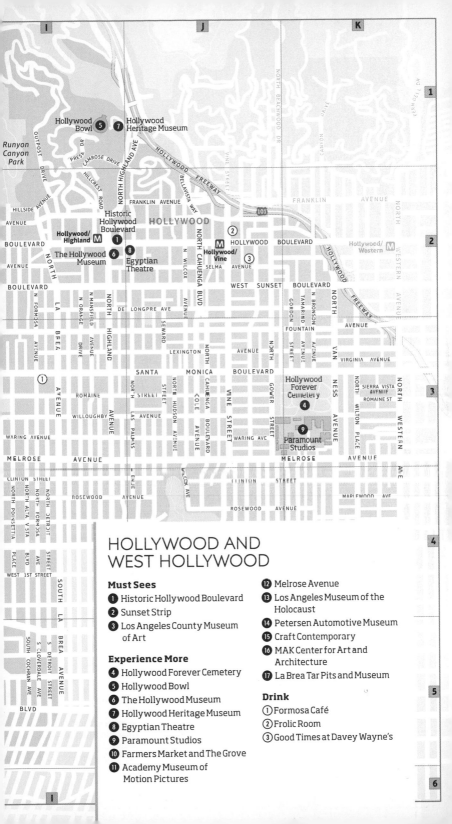

HOLLYWOOD AND WEST HOLLYWOOD

Must Sees

1. Historic Hollywood Boulevard
2. Sunset Strip
3. Los Angeles County Museum of Art

Experience More

4. Hollywood Forever Cemetery
5. Hollywood Bowl
6. The Hollywood Museum
7. Hollywood Heritage Museum
8. Egyptian Theatre
9. Paramount Studios
10. Farmers Market and The Grove
11. Academy Museum of Motion Pictures
12. Melrose Avenue
13. Los Angeles Museum of the Holocaust
14. Petersen Automotive Museum
15. Craft Contemporary
16. MAK Center for Art and Architecture
17. La Brea Tar Pits and Museum

Drink

1. Formosa Café
2. Frolic Room
3. Good Times at Davey Wayne's

HISTORIC HOLLYWOOD BOULEVARD

📍 I2

Hollywood Boulevard is one of the most famous streets in the world, and its name is still redolent with glamour. Explore the Golden Age of film with a visit to the autograph patio at the TCL Chinese Theatre and stroll down the Walk of Fame to spot the marble stars of icons such as Marilyn Monroe and James Dean.

The Hollywood Roosevelt Hotel

🏛 7000 Hollywood Blvd
🌐 thehollywood
roosevelt.com

The unassuming exterior of this landmark hotel, built in 1926, belies its stunning Spanish Renaissance lobby and its glamorous history as a haunt for movie stars. Visitors can be thrilled at The Magic Show, enjoy a treatment in the Massage Garden, and savor a meal at the Tropicana Pool & Café overlooking the famous pool with its million-dollar David Hockney mural.

El Capitan Theatre

🏛 6838 Hollywood Blvd
🌐 elcapitantheatre.com

Built in 1926 as a legitimate theater, El Capitan was later converted to a movie house. It was the venue for many premieres, such as Orson Welles' *Citizen Kane* (1941). The theater was renamed the Hollywood Paramount in 1942 but it was bought by Disney in 1991, who restored its original name and its Art Deco interior. Today the theater hosts screenings and opening nights of Walt Disney films.

Madame Tussauds™

🏛 6933 Hollywood Blvd
🕐 11am–6pm daily
🌐 madametussauds.com

This three-story structure features wax figures of cultural icons and Hollywood stars, including former president Barack Obama, Taylor Swift, Tom Hanks, Lady Gaga, Clarke Gable, and Marilyn Monroe, plus action figures such as

---

 INSIDER TIP
Jimmy Kimmel

The hugely popular late-night talk show *Jimmy Kimmel Live!* films at 5pm in the El Capitan Entertainment Center, next to the El Capitan Theatre. Tickets are essential, but it's easy to request them online (*www.1iota.com/show/ 1/jimmy-kimmel-live*).

←

Dusk settling over Hollywood Boulevard beneath the hills

the Marvel superheroes. Over 80 figures are displayed in 11 themed areas, including "The Red Carpet."

TCL Chinese Theatre

🏠 6925 Hollywood Blvd
🕐 Daily 🌐 tclchinese theatres.com

One of the most famous sights in Hollywood has not changed much since it opened in 1927. The ornate exterior is a medley of Chinese temples, pagodas, lions, and dragons, reflecting the keen sense of showmanship of creator Sid Grauman.

Grauman also thought up one of the longest-running publicity stunts in Hollywood history: inviting movie stars to impress their handprints, footprints, and autographs in the cement courtyard. Anyone can visit the courtyard, but only filmgoers and those on guided tours can see the extravagant interior.

Hollywood and Highland

🏠 6801 Hollywood Blvd
🕐 10am–10pm Mon–Sat, 10am–7pm Sun 🌐 holly woodandhighland.com

This shopping and entertainment complex features restaurants, clubs, shops, a hotel, and a cinema. Visitors can also see a play or concert and take a tour of the Dolby Theatre, the home of the Academy Awards® shows.

Walk of Fame

ℹ️ 7018 Hollywood Blvd; www.walkoffame.com

Since 1960, celebrities from the worlds of film, radio, TV, theater, and music have been immortalized with a marble star on the Walk of Fame, set on Hollywood Boulevard and Vine Street. Each star has to be sponsored and approved by the Chamber of Commerce and requires a $40,000 fee. Among the 2,600-plus stars are Charlie Chaplin (No. 6751) and Alfred Hitchcock (No. 6506).

EAT

Pink's Hot Dogs

This tiny stand draws celebrities for cheap hot dogs lathered in chilies and other goodies.

🏠 709 N LaBrea Av
🌐 pinkshollywood.com

$⑤$$⑤$

Alfred

Hip West Hollywood java shop with tasty breakfast burritos, pastries, and drinks.

🏠 8428 Melrose Place
🌐 alfred.la

$⑤$$⑤$

Mel's Drive-in

The world's most famous 24/7 drive-in chain, perfect for nighthawks hungry for a burger.

🏠 1660 North Highland Av
🌐 melsdrive-in.com

$$$⑤

The Musso & Frank Grill

Hollywood's oldest restaurant serves up great steaks and chops.

🏠 6667 Hollywood Blvd
🌐 mussoandfrank.com

$$$⑤

SHOP

Larry Edmunds Book Shop

A renowned landmark, this unique one-stop shop has enough movie-related books, photos, and posters to make your head spin.

🏠 6644 Hollywood Blvd
🌐 larryedmunds.com

2 🍴 🏛

SUNSET STRIP

📍 **G3** 🏠 **Sunset Blvd between Crescent Heights Blvd and Doheny Dr**

Wedged between Hollywood and Beverly Hills, this 1.7-mile (2.7-km) strip of the Sunset Boulevard is crammed with cool nightclubs, hip rock venues, and fashionable boutiques. A haven of hedonism since Prohibition days, it still lives up to its pleasure-seeking reputation.

Sunset has been associated with the movies since the 1920s, but it wasn't until Prohibition ended in 1933 that it began to flourish. During Hollywood's Glamour Age in the 1930s to 1950s, the stars trysted at the Chateau Marmont, partied at Trocadero, and talked shop at Schwab's Pharmacy. Today's hotspots rub shoulders with these historical landmarks. From glamorous bars to legendary comedy clubs, there's entertainment here to suit everyone.

← The grand Chateau Marmont, in the style of a French castle

STAY

Sunset Tower Hotel
In Hollywood's heyday this Art Deco high-rise was an apartment complex and home to Jean Harlow, Clark Gable, and other luminaries. Today it is a classy hotel with a great bar and restaurant.

🏠 **8358 Sunset Blvd**
Ⓦ **sunsettower hotel.com**

💲💲💲

Sunset Strip, a nightlife hotspot, with restaurants, bars, music venues, and nightclubs ↑

LA'S HAND-PAINTED BILLBOARDS

Mammoth stretch-vinyl advertisements crowd every available space along Sunset Strip. Los Angeles has a special relationship with the art of the ad, having once been at the heart of the hand-painted billboard industry. Some of Hollywood's finest artists painted huge adverts. During the 1960s the billboards were dominated by the music industry, with advertising space along Sunset Strip even being written into some rock stars' contracts. Nowadays they mostly advertise luxury brands and new TV shows.

The Comedy Store

▷ Opened in 1972, this world-famous spot for stand-up comedy, at No. 8433, puts on quality comedy acts and is a mecca for stand-up fans.

Sunset Plaza

This two-block stretch is lined with European-style restaurants and designer shops teeming with fashionable crowds. It's prime territory for star-spotting.

Andaz West Hollywood

▽ Formerly known as the "Riot Hyatt," the Andaz West Hollywood (No. 8401) is part of rock history. It was party central for British bands in the 1960s and 1970s, and Led Zeppelin even cruised down the halls on motorcycles.

Whisky a Go-Go

A Strip fixture since 1963, the Whisky (No. 8901) gave the world go-go dancing and The Doors, its house band in 1966. Other stars, such as Jimi Hendrix and Janis Joplin, also played here.

The Viper Room

At No. 8852, the Viper Room is a popular live music club co-founded and once owned by the actor Johnny Depp. Few remember its earlier incarnation as the Melody Room, a favorite with Bugsy Siegel and his mobster pals.

Chateau Marmont

This hotel at No. 8221 was modeled on a Loire Valley château. When it opened in 1929, it attracted actors such as Errol Flynn and Greta Garbo. Other regulars included Humphrey Bogart, Howard Hughes, and Mick Jagger.

Rainbow Bar & Grill

▷ Formerly the Villa Nova restaurant, where Vincente Minnelli proposed to Judy Garland, this rock 'n' roll bar (No. 9015) fills with rockers every night.

③ 🗝 🎨 🍴 🖼 🛍

LOS ANGELES COUNTY MUSEUM OF ART

📍H5 📍5905 Wilshire Blvd 🕐11am–5pm Mon, Tue & Thu, 11am–8pm Fri, 10am–7pm Sat & Sun 🚫Thanksgiving, Dec 25 🌐lacma.org

The largest art museum west of Chicago, LACMA has one of the finest collections of art in the US. Its vast holdings feature work from Europe, the Americas, Asia, and the Middle East.

Founded in 1910, LACMA moved to its current premises in 1965. A trip to this modern powerhouse offers visitors a comprehensive survey of the history of art throughout the world – more than 140,000 objects can be found here, dating from prehistoric to contemporary periods. Museum highlights include pre-Columbian finds, American and Latin American art, and the largest Islamic art collection in the western United States. An extensive decorative arts collection also features, with pieces dating from medieval times to the present exhibited alongside paintings and sculpture from the same period. There is a lively program of concerts, lectures, and film screenings, too. Due to ongoing construction work, art from LACMA's permanent collection is currently on display in the Resnick Pavilion and the Broad Contemporary Art Museum at LACMA.

Urban Light, an installation by the late Chris Burden, illuminating LACMA's campus ↑

1. A section of LACMA's bright terrace is dotted with tropical plants.

2. The facade of the Broad Contemporary Art Museum at LACMA, designed by Renzo Piano.

3. Paintings and sculptures from a wide range of periods are on display in LACMA.

EAT

C+M (Coffee + Milk)
Stop by this stylish café for strong espresso drinks as well as fruit shakes and irresistible sweet and savory pastries.

⌂ 5905 Wilshire Blvd
ⓦ patinagroup.com/cm-lacma

$\$$$$\$$$$\$$

Ray's and Stark Bar
Grab a seat on the outdoor patio of this upscale restaurant which offers a globally inspired feast and seasonal fare.

⌂ 5905 Wilshire Blvd
ⓦ patinagroup.com/rays-and-stark-bar

$\$$$$\$$$$\$$

Exploring LACMA

As part of a continuing expansion project, LACMA's four main buildings are closed and will be replaced by a new structure, the David Geffen Galleries, which will house the permanent collection, in 2024. During the construction phase, art from the permanent collection and temporary exhibitions can still be seen on rotating display in the Resnick Pavilion and the Broad Contemporary Art Museum buildings. The Broad, designed by Renzo Piano, was added to the complex in 2008 to house the private collection of contemporary art donated by its billionaire founder and art connoisseur Eli Broad. The vast, light-filled Resnick Pavilion, also designed by Renzo Piano, opened in 2010 to display multiple rotating exhibitions.

 INSIDER TIP
Take a Tour

There are short guided tours of key exhibits held around lunchtime every Saturday and Sunday. Check the museum website for further details. Private tours of the collection and tours for visitors with specific requirements are also available – call or email ahead for more information.

↑ *John the Baptist* by Jeff Koons, currently on display at the Broad

Examining the ↑ contemporary art from LACMA's vast collection

Must See

Top Collections

THE MIRACLE MILE

LACMA sits on a historic stretch of Wilshire Boulevard called the "Miracle Mile." Created in 1921 by developer A. W. Ross, it was the city's first shopping district outside of Downtown and the first designed with easy access for wheelchair users. The idea was a success, as many department stores moved in, but it also marked the start of LA's decentralization. By the 1960s, a new innovation, the shopping mall, spelled the end of the "miracle." The area still attracts crowds today for its galleries and Art Deco buildings.

American Art

The collection of paintings traces the history of American art from the 1700s to the 1940s. Highlights include John Singleton Copley's *Portrait of a Lady* (1771), Mary Cassatt's *Mother About to Wash her Sleepy Child* (1880), George Bellows' *Cliff Dwellers* (1913), and Childe Hassam's *Avenue of the Allies* (1918).

European Painting, Sculpture, and Decorative Arts

▶ The collection of European art spans the 12th to early 20th centuries. One of the collection's strengths is its 17th-century Dutch and Flemish canvases; Rembrandt's *The Raising of Lazarus* (c.1630) and Anthony van Dyck's *Andromeda Chained to the Rock* (1637-8) are among the highlights. The sculpture collection features more than 40 works by Auguste Rodin (1840-1917). Among the finest decorative arts pieces is a Venetian enameled and gilded blue glass ewer, dating from about 1500.

Modern and Contemporary Art

The Broad contemporary art museum, on the LACMA campus, houses some 200 pieces from Eli Broad's collection, plus LACMA's growing assemblage of modern holdings and visiting collections. Its span covers painting, sculpture, and installations from 1945 to the present day.

Photography, Prints, and Drawings

The museum's outstanding photography holdings range from early 19th-century daguerreotypes and albumen prints to abstract mixed-media images. LACMA's holdings of prints and drawings includes the Robert Gore Rifkind Collection of German Expressionist works.

Ancient and Islamic Art

◀ The Ancient Art collection includes carved stone panels from a 9th-century BC Assyrian palace; a rare Egyptian bronze from the 25th Dynasty; ceramic vessels and statues from Central America; and delicate Iranian figures, dating from 3,000 BC. The Islamic Art collection's Iranian and Turkish holdings are particularly strong.

Asian Art

With more than 5,000 works dating from the 3rd century BC, the museum has one of the most comprehensive collections outside Asia. It is especially strong in Indian arts, from splendid sculpture to intricate watercolors on cloth and paper, and manuscripts from Southeast Asia. The highlight of the Far Eastern Art holdings is the Shin'enkan Collection which features 200 screens and scroll paintings from the Edo period (1615-1868).

Costumes and Textiles

▶ The collection represents more than 300 of the world's cultures. The oldest pieces are embroidered Peruvian burial shrouds from 100 BC and a 5th-century AD Egyptian Coptic tunic. One of the most important pieces is the 16th-century Iranian "Ardebil" carpet.

↑ A mausoleum on an island in a small lake at the Hollywood Forever Cemetery

EXPERIENCE MORE

Hollywood Forever Cemetery

📍 K3 🏛 6000 Santa Monica Blvd ⏰ 8:30am–5pm daily 🚫 Federal hols 🌐 hollywoodforever.com

The map of this cemetery (available at the front office) reads like a history of film, with figures from Hollywood's heyday buried here, all within sight of the Hollywood Sign.

Some of the most notable residents include actor Tyrone Power, who has a white memorial overlooking a pond on the eastern side. Next to him, the mausoleum of Marion Davies, an actress perhaps better known as the mistress of media tycoon

---

> 💬 INSIDER TIP
> ## Cinespia
>
> From May to October, Hollywood Forever Cemetery's Fairbanks Lawn is the atmospheric location for classic movies under the stars. Book early, and bring blankets and snacks (*www.cinespia.org*).

William Randolph Hearst, bears her family name of Douras. Douglas Fairbanks Sr.'s grave has a reflecting pool and monument, reputed to have been paid for by his ex-wife, the silent film star Mary Pickford. Inside the gloomy Cathedral Mausoleum is the tomb of Rudolph Valentino, still the cemetery's biggest attraction. Every year, on August 23, a "Lady in Black" pays her respects to the actor on the anniversary of his death. Look out, too, for the graves of director and producer Cecil B. DeMille, singer and actor Nelson Eddy, and superstar Judy Garland.

A tour of the cemetery (usually 10am on Saturday) is recommended.

Hollywood Bowl

📍 I1 🏛 2301 N Highland Av ⏰ Late Jun–late Sep; Box office: noon–6pm Tue–Sat; Hollywood Bowl Museum: Times vary, check website 🌐 hollywoodbowl.com

Situated in a natural amphitheater, once revered by the

Cahuenga Pass Gabrielino people, the Hollywood Bowl is now considered sacred by Angelenos. Since 1922 it has been the summer home of the LA Philharmonic.

Thousands of locals gather on warm evenings to picnic – often in high style – under the stars and listen to the orchestra. Jazz, country, folk, and pop concerts are also performed here, while popular events include the Fourth of July concert with fireworks, the Easter Sunrise Service, and a Tchaikovsky Spectacular with cannons, fireworks, and a military band.

The iconic shell-shaped stage was originally designed in 1929 by Lloyd Wright, son of architect Frank Lloyd Wright, and the Bowl and its privately-owned front-row boxes seat 18,000 people.

The Hollywood Bowl Museum explores the rich history of the venue through a permanent display of old programs and posters, plus rotating exhibitions of memorabilia of the artists who have come here to perform, from violinist Jascha Heifetz to The Beatles.

The Hollywood Museum

📍 I2 🏛 1660 N Highland Av ⏰ 10am–5pm Wed–Sun 🌐 thehollywoodmuseum.com

This museum is housed in a restored 1930s Art Deco building, which was once make-up artist Max Factor's studios. Three floors display fabulous costumes worn in films by stars such as Marilyn Monroe, Judy Garland, Elizabeth Taylor, Humphrey Bogart, and Jodie Foster. The collectibles exhibition displays Sylvester Stallone's boxing gloves and WC Field's top hat among other oddities. The basement contains Hannibal Lecter's entire prison cell.

7

Hollywood Heritage Museum

I1 **2100 N Highland Av** **Noon-4pm Sat & Sun** **hollywoodheritage.org**

In 1913, Cecil B. DeMille and the Jesse L. Lasky Feature Play Company rented this barn, then located on Vine Street, just north of Sunset Boulevard. That year DeMille used the building to make *The Squaw Man*, the first feature-length movie that was produced in Hollywood. In 1935 the company was renamed Paramount Pictures.

The barn was moved to its present site, in the parking lot of the Hollywood Bowl (*p104*), in 1983. Thirteen years later a fire prompted a major renovation, and the barn was turned into a museum, displaying props, costumes, photographs, and other memorabilia from the early days of filmmaking.

8

Egyptian Theatre

J2 **6712 Hollywood Blvd** **american cinematheque.com**

The oldest of Hollywood Boulevard's themed 1920s movie palaces, the Egyptian Theatre was the birthplace of the glitzy Hollywood premiere. Today it is the home of the American Cinematheque, a non profit organization that arranges screenings, retrospectives, and live panel discussions with Hollywood actors and directors. Past high-profile guests have included the likes of Martin Scorsese, Julianne Moore, and Clint Eastwood.

DRINK

Formosa Café
The red booths at this legendary haunt are perfect for schmoozing with craft Martinis.

I3 **7156 Santa Monica Blvd** **theformosacafe.com**

Frolic Room
Dim lighting, strong drinks, and an eclectic clientele can be found at this classic dive bar.

J2 **6245 Hollywood Blvd** **(323) 462-5890**

Good Times at Davey Wayne's
A retro bar famed for alchohol-infused snow cones and tiki drinks.

J2 **1611 N El Centro Av** **goodtimesat daveywaynes.com**

↑ An exhibition room full of historic photographs in the Hollywood Museum

↑ The famous wrought-iron gates at the entrance to Paramount Studios

Paramount Studios

Q K3 **A** 5555 Melrose Av; Visitors' Center and Ticket Window: 860 N Gower St **O** For tours: 9am-6pm Mon-Fri (reservations only; last tour starts at 3:30pm) **Q** Jan 1, Easter Sun, Thanksgiving, Dec 25 **W** paramountstudiotour.com

The last major studio still located in Hollywood, Paramount was also the first in operation. Cecil B. DeMille, Jesse Lasky, and Samuel Goldwyn joined forces with Adolph Zukor in 1914 to form what became known as the directors' studio. The roster of stars was equally impressive: Gloria Swanson, Rudolph Valentino, Mae West, Marlene Dietrich, Gary Cooper, and Bing Crosby all signed with Paramount.

Aspiring actors still hug the wrought-iron gates at Bronson Avenue and Marathon Street. Seeking luck, they quote Norma Desmond's final line in *Sunset Boulevard*: "I'm ready for my close-up, Mr. DeMille."

Classics such as *The Ten Commandments*, *The War of the Worlds*, *The Greatest Show on Earth*, and *The Godfather Parts I, II*, and *III* were all made in Paramount's backlot and sound stages. There are three available tour options: the Studio Tour, VIP Studio Tour, and Paramount After Dark Tour. These tours give visitors a behind-the-scenes view of the past and present legacy of the Paramount Studios.

Farmers Market and The Grove

Q H4 **A** 6333 W 3rd St **O** 9am-9pm Mon-Fri, 9am-8pm Sat, 10am-7pm Sun **Q** Jan 1, Easter Sun, Memorial Day, Jul 4, Labor Day, Thanksgiving, Dec 25 **W** farmersmarketla.com

In 1934, during the Great Depression (p49), a group of farmers began selling their produce directly to the public in a field then at the edge of town. Since then, Farmers Market has become a favorite meeting place for Angelenos and tourists. There are stalls

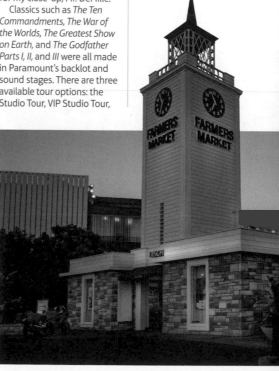

TOP 3 LGBTQ+ HOTSPOTS

Fubar
A 7994 Santa Monica Blvd **W** fubarla.com
Raunchy, dark bar serving strong drinks.

The Abbey
A 692 N Robertson Blvd **W** theabbeyweho.com
Hugely popular gay bar with a dance floor.

Micky's
A 8857 Santa Monica Blvd **W** mickys.com
Wild late-night club.

selling fresh flowers, meats, cheeses, fruit, vegetables, breads, and gourmet foods. There are also more than 100 shops selling everything: antiques, T-shirts, garden supplies, and more. Among the numerous cafés and restaurants are Bob's Donuts; Magee's Kitchen for roast or corned beef, turkey, and ham platters; and The Gumbo Pot, with sweet *beignets* (dough fritters) and classic Cajun food. Next to the market complex is The Grove, a deluxe retail complex containing shops, restaurants, and a cinema.

Academy Museum of Motion Pictures

🔲 H5 🏛 6067 Wilshire Blvd
🕐 Hours vary, check website
🌐 academymuseum.org

This museum, opened in 2021, is dedicated to the history, art, and business of movie-making. It draws on the Academy of Motion Picture Arts & Sciences' unparalleled collection of 12 million photographs and 61,000 posters, plus costumes, props, technology, and other film-related objects. Among the most iconic objects in the collection are Bela Lugosi's cape from *Dracula*, and the *Aries 1B* spaceship model from *2001: A Space Odyssey*. Italian architect Renzo Piano redesigned the 1939 May

Company Building to house two floors of permanent exhibits. His design includes a stunning glass dome, The Sphere, atop the new, 1,000-seat, state-of-the-art David Geffen Theater.

Melrose Avenue

🔲 H3 🌐 melroseavenue-shop.com

Stretching between Silver Lake and Santa Monica Boulevard, Melrose Avenue rose to fame in the 1980s as LA's hub of underground culture. It has since mellowed, but the street is still full of vintage shops and quirky venues. At Melrose Avenue's western end is LA's Design District, anchored by the architecturally stunning Pacific Design Center – a triptych of blue, green, and red buildings by César Pelli. Nearby, Hamilton-Selway Fine Art boasts an impressive collection of Andy Warhol prints and paintings.

Walking east, Melrose Place is lined with designer boutiques, plus Alfred Coffee (No. 8428), a major draw for those looking for their next caffeine fix. This stylish stretch hosts a who's who

of high-end tenants, from Irene Neuwirth (No. 8458) for designer jewelry to The Row (No. 8440), celebrity twins Mary-Kate and Ashley Olsen's haven of California fashion.

Hints of Melrose Avenue's punk past live on at Vivienne Westwood (No. 8320) and the Melrose Trading Post Sunday flea market (No. 7850). Melrose Place hosts a farmers' market on Sundays.

Los Angeles Museum of the Holocaust

🔲 H4 🏛 100 The Grove Dr
🕐 10am–2pm Mon & Fri, 10am–5pm Sun, Thu & Sat
🌐 lamoth.org

Founded by Holocaust survivors in 1961, the Los Angeles Museum of the Holocaust (LAMOTH) moved to its current site in 2010. Its eight galleries house the West Coast's largest archive of Holocaust-era artifacts, photos, and videos dedicated to commemorating the six million Jews murdered by Nazis in World War II. The 70-screen Tree of Testimony displays nearly 51,000 survivor testimonies. Tours are offered on weekends; Sunday tours include a Holocaust survivor talk. In front of the museum, six imposing black-granite columns comprise the Holocaust Monument.

←

The Farmers Market and kiosks lining the way to The Grove

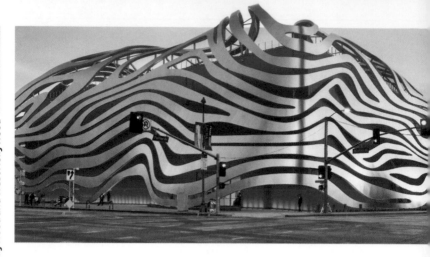

The futuristic exterior of the Petersen Automotive Museum; *(inset)* a close-up of the building's steel-ribbon structure

Petersen Automotive Museum

📍H5 🏛6060 Wilshire Blvd
🕐10am-5pm Tue-Sun
🚫Jan 1, Thanksgiving, Dec 25 🌐petersen.org

The evolution of Los Angeles from sleepy outpost to sweeping megalopolis is directly linked to the rise of the motor industry. Housed in a building wrapped in steel "ribbons," this museum illustrates that development, showcasing the history of the automobile and its central place in American culture.

On the first floor there are detailed displays featuring cars such as the 1911 American Underslung "Stuck in the Mud" and Earl Cooper's 1915 "White Squadron" Stutz Racer. A 1922 Ford Model-T is shown in a scene from a Laurel and Hardy film, and a trio of beautiful vintage cars appear in a 1920s street setting. Other displays include a 1920s garage; a 1930s car showroom, whose opulence defied the Great Depression; and a 1950s

drive-in restaurant. A billboard from the 1930s illustrates how advertising was used to boost the popularity of the car.

Upstairs, five galleries showcase everything from hot rods and motorcycles to vintage classics and cars of the stars. Among the vehicles that fall into the last category are Rita Hayworth's 1953 Cadillac and Clark Gable's 1941 Cadillac Coupe.

Craft Contemporary

📍H5 🏛5814 Wilshire Blvd
🕐11am-5pm Wed-Sun
🚫Jan 1, Thanksgiving, Dec 25 🌐cafam.org

The brainchild of folk art collector Edith Wyle, this museum was originally launched in 1965 as a small gallery space. Today the collection includes more than 3,000 folk art and craft objects from around the world, ranging from 19th-century American quilts to contemporary

furniture, to African masks. Mexican artworks on display here include papier-mâché pieces made by Mexico City's Linares family.

Special exhibitions on subjects such as toys, glassware, and textiles are held throughout the year. In addition, the museum organizes regular art talks, workshops on crafting techniques such as mask making and clay throwing, and other events for a range of different age groups, plus tours on Wednesdays.

MAK Center for Art and Architecture

📍G3 🏛835 N Kings Rd
🕐11am-6pm Wed-Sun
🌐makcenter.org

The MAK Center – the California branch of the Museum of Applied Arts (MAK) in Vienna, Austria – is a multidisciplinary exhibition center and laboratory for the development of ideas in art and architecture.

> **The La Brea Tar Pits contain the largest collection of fossils from the Pleistocene epoch ever found in one place - a whopping 3.5 million specimens to date.**

La Brea Tar Pits and Museum

📍H5 🏠5801 Wilshire Blvd 🕐9:30am–5pm daily 🚫Jan 1, Jul 4, Thanksgiving, Dec 25 🌐tarpits.org

The ancient tar pits at Hancock Park have been forming for some 50,000 years. During this time, gooey asphalt has been rising to the earth's surface from an underground oil field. An entire menagerie of Ice Age creatures, including mastodons, giant ground sloths, and saber-toothed tigers, became trapped, died, and preserved in the tar. A highlight of the site is the model of a trapped mammoth in Lake Pit, a legacy of late 19th-century mining operations turned to bubbling pools of asphalt.

The pits contain the largest collection of fossils from the Pleistocene epoch ever found in one place – a whopping 3.5 million specimens to date. In summer, you can watch scientists excavating bones from Pit 91 and then analysing their discoveries in a glass-walled laboratory in the adjoining Page Museum. Its galleries exhibit fossils, as well as life-sized replicas of sloths, mammoths, and mastodons, so visitors can marvel at the scale of today's species' ancient relatives. In the Observation Pit, you can learn to identify creatures whose bones are encased in asphalt.

TOP 4 **COMEDY CLUBS**

Improv
🏠8162 Melrose Av
🌐improv.com/hollywood
Many comedians, from Richard Pryor to Ellen DeGeneres, got their start here.

Comedy Store
🏠8433 Sunset Blvd
🌐thecomedystore.com
Comedian Marc Maron was once a doorman at this mecca of improv.

Groundlings
🏠7307 Melrose Av
🌐groundlings.com
Melissa McCarthy and Kristen Wiig took their first steps in comedy at this club.

Second City Studio Theater
🏠6560 Hollywood Blvd
🌐secondcity.com
Tina Fey and Stephen Colbert are alumni of this cozy comedy house.

Spread across three strikingly Modernist buildings designed by visionary Austrian American architect Rudolph M. Schindler, the MAK Center has its headquarters at the landmark Schindler House, his former home and studio in West Hollywood. Built in 1922, this airy property became known as a hub of social, intellectual, and political activity in the 1920s and 1930s. The other two locations – the 1939 Mackey Apartments, located in Mid-City, and the dramatic 1936 L-shaped Fitzpatrick-Leland House, set in the Hollywood Hills – are used by artists, architects, and students in residence. All three buildings are must-see sights for anyone with an interest in Modernist design.

The center features a year-round roster of lectures, panel discussions, fundraisers, and musical performances, and is open for architecture tours; visits are free on Friday afternoons and on Schindler's birthday, September 10.

↑ Models at La Brea Tar Pits depicting how animals became trapped in the tar

DOWNTOWN

Spanish-speaking settlers arrived in today's Downtown area in 1781. They named their settlement Los Angeles after the Spanish phrase for "Our Lady Queen of the Angels." After flooding, the town was moved to the present site of El Pueblo de Los Angeles in 1818. Even after being absorbed by the US after the Mexican–American War (1846–48), LA remained a small town with a population of less than 5,000. The arrival of the transcontinental railroad in 1876 gave the city a massive boost, with thousands arriving from the eastern states to live in what was billed as a Mediterranean-style paradise. Between 1870 and 1900 LA's population exploded to over 100,000 and by 1920 it was over half a million. In the 1920s, Broadway became the nightlife, shopping, and entertainment district of the city, while LA's Civic Center was developed between the 1930s and 1950s. In the 1960s, Bunker Hill's Victorian buildings were replaced with a forest of glass and steel skyscrapers that form LA's Financial District today. After a long period of decline, Downtown entered a renaissance with the opening of the Staples Center in 1999 and the revitalization of the Arts District in the 21st century.

DOWNTOWN

Must Sees
1. The Broad
2. El Pueblo de Los Angeles

Experience More
3. Angels Flight
4. Los Angeles Central Library
5. Grand Central Market
6. Broadway Historic Theater District
7. LA Live
8. Museum of Contemporary Art
9. Walt Disney Concert Hall
10. Geffen Contemporary at MOCA
11. Chinatown
12. Little Tokyo
13. Japanese American National Museum
14. Cathedral of Our Lady of the Angels
15. Fashion Institute of Design and Merchandising Museum
16. Los Angeles City Hall

Eat
1. Original Pantry Café
2. Philippe the Original
3. Daikokuya
4. Mitsuru Café
5. Sushi Gen
6. Fugetsu-Do Bakery Shop
7. Sugarfish

Drink
8. Traxx Bar
9. Upstairs at the Ace Hotel

Stay
10. Hotel Figueroa

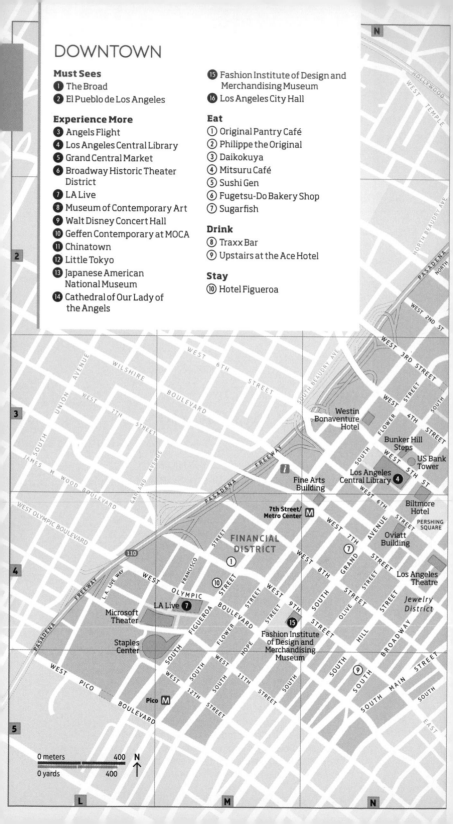

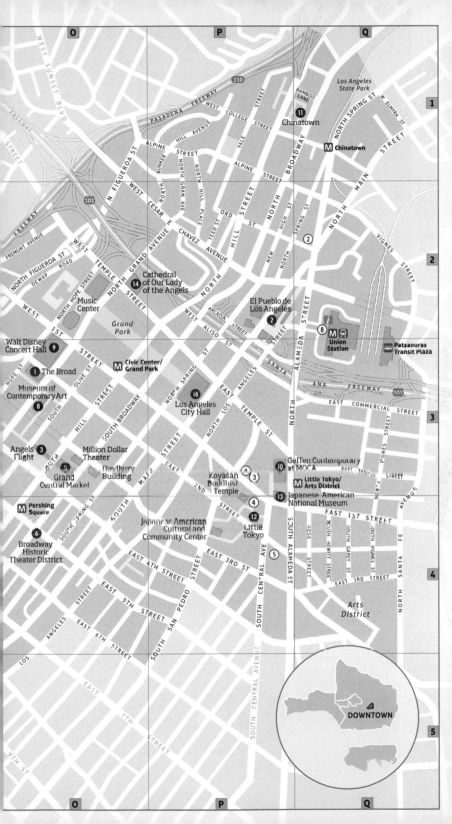

1 🏛 🍴 🛍

THE BROAD

📍 03 🏠 221 S Grand Av 🕐 11am–5pm Tue & Wed, 11am–8pm Thu & Fri, 10am–8pm Sat, 10am–6pm Sun 🚫 Thanksgiving, Dec 25 🌐 thebroad.org

Housed in a stunning, cutting-edge building, the Broad contains one of the world's leading collections of art from the 1950s to the present day. Among the works on display are paintings by Jean-Michel Basquiat, images by Barbara Kruger, cutouts by Kara Walker, and a range of art by Andy Warhol.

The museum features 2,000 postwar and contemporary artworks by more than 200 artists – both established and emerging – from the collection of philanthropists Eli and Edythe Broad, who gifted the museum to Los Angeles in 2015 with the aim of making contemporary art accessible to all. Works are displayed over two floors of gallery space. The building is also home to the

←

Visitors examining the contemporary art on display in the museum

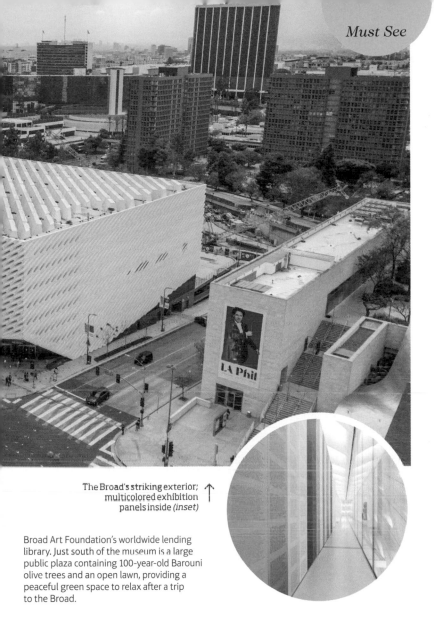

The Broad's striking exterior;
multicolored exhibition
panels inside *(inset)* ↑

Broad Art Foundation's worldwide lending
library. Just south of the museum is a large
public plaza containing 100-year-old Barouni
olive trees and an open lawn, providing a
peaceful green space to relax after a trip
to the Broad.

ARCHITECTURE OF THE MUSEUM

Designed by architectural firm Diller Scofidio +
Renfro in collaboration with Gensler, the Broad
building has been dubbed "the veil and vault,"
describing its two functions: exhibition space and
collection storage. The vault storage space contains
artworks not on display; it has windows through
which the public can peer into it. The vault is
enveloped by the "veil," a honeycomb-like
structure spanning the gallery, which provides
natural filtered daylight.

↑ Bandstand in the Plaza of El Pueblo de Los Angeles, the oldest part of LA

EL PUEBLO DE LOS ANGELES

📍 P2 🏠 Avila Adobe, 10 Olvera St; www.elpueblo.lacity.org

Located close to the site where 44 settlers from Mexico established El Pueblo de Los Angeles in 1781, this State Historic Monument is LA's oldest neighborhood. A century later, Chinese and Italian immigrants settled here, and El Pueblo reflects these different heritages.

Our Lady Queen of the Angels Church

🏠 535 N Main St

Worshippers have gathered in LA's oldest church since 1822. Highlights are the painted ceiling, the altar framed in gold leaf, and *The Annunciation*, a 1981 mosaic by Isabel Piczek.

Avila Adobe

🏠 10 Olvera St
🕐 9am-4pm daily

LA's oldest surviving house, built by mayor Don Francisco Avila in 1818, went through several incarnations as a military headquarters and boarding house. Today it is furnished as it would have been in the 1840s and contains a visitor center.

La Plaza de Cultura y Artes

🏠 501 N Main St 🕐 Noon-5pm Wed-Mon 🌐 lapca.org

This museum and cultural center, known also as LA Plaza, displays art and artifacts that celebrate the history and cultural influence of Mexicans, Mexican Americans and all Latin Americans in LA. It offers a wide-ranging program of music, dance, cooking, art, and other workshops and events.

Chinese American Museum

🏠 425 N Los Angeles St
🕐 10am-3pm Tue-Sun
🌐 camla.org

The Chinese first settled in this area in the late

THE MOTHER OF OLVERA STREET

Christine Sterling (1881-1963), an LA socialite-turned-civic activist, was dismayed by the seediness of El Pueblo de Los Angeles. In 1926 Sterling launched a campaign to save it, backed by *LA Times* publisher Harry Chandler and others. In April 1930, Olvera Street was reincarnated as a busy Mexican market. The Avila Adobe contains an exhibit on her triumph.

19th century. This museum, housed in the 1890s Garnier Building – the oldest surviving structure in historic Chinatown – traces the community's history and narrates the experiences and contributions of Chinese Americans in the US through changing exhibitions, lectures, workshops, and events.

⑤ Italian American Museum of Los Angeles

🏠 644 North Main St
🕐 10am–3pm Tue–Sun
🌐 iamla.org

Constructed in 1908, the Italian Hall served as a meeting place for the Italian community. The Italian American Museum of Los Angeles (IAMLA) opened in the hall in 2016 and presents the history and culture of

Did You Know?

In 2015, the American Planning Association named Olvera Street one of the "Great Places of America."

Italian Americans and Southern California's Italian roots through exhibits and a varied program of events.

⑥ América Tropical Interpretive Center

🏠 125 Paseo de la Plaza
🕐 10am–3pm Tue–Sun (Nov–Mar: 10am–noon)
🌐 theamericatropical.org

Dedicated to the legacy of Mexican social realist artist David Alfaro Siqueiros (1896–

1974), this center aims to preserve his 1932 controversial mural, *América Tropical*, a political statement about the exploitation of Mexican workers, and an emblematic part of the Mexican muralism movement.

⑦ Old Plaza Firehouse

🏠 501 N Los Angeles St
🕐 10am–3pm daily

This two-story brick building, completed in 1884, is the oldest purpose-built fire station in LA. With an all-volunteer crew and horse-drawn equipment, it was operational until 1897. Today it is a museum displaying firefighting apparatus from the late 19th and early 20th centuries.

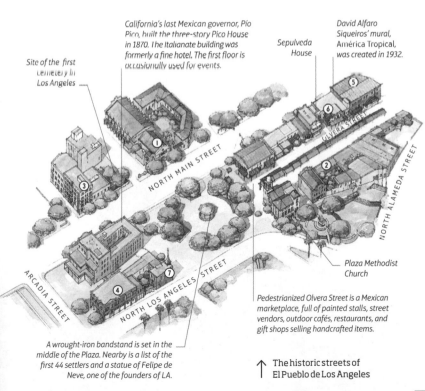

California's last Mexican governor, Pío Pico, built the three-story Pico House in 1870. The Italianate building was formerly a fine hotel. The first floor is occasionally used for events.

Sepulveda House

David Alfaro Siqueiros' mural, América Tropical, was created in 1932.

Site of the first cemetery in Los Angeles

Plaza Methodist Church

Pedestrianized Olvera Street is a Mexican marketplace, full of painted stalls, street vendors, outdoor cafés, restaurants, and gift shops selling handcrafted items.

A wrought-iron bandstand is set in the middle of the Plaza. Nearby is a list of the first 44 settlers and a statue of Felipe de Neve, one of the founders of LA.

↑ The historic streets of El Pueblo de Los Angeles

EXPERIENCE MORE

3

Angels Flight

📍 O3 🏛 Between Grand,
Hill, 3rd & 4th sts
🕐 6:45am–10pm daily
🌐 angelsflight.org

Billed as the "shortest railroad
in the world," Angels Flight
transported riders the 315 ft
(96 m) between Hill Street
and Bunker Hill for almost
70 years. Built in 1901, the
funicular quickly became
a familiar and much-loved
method of travel. However,
by 1969, Bunker Hill had
sadly degenerated and was
considered an eyesore. The
city dismantled Angels Flight,
but promised to reinstall the
funicular once the area had
been redeveloped. It reopened
in 1996 but was closed for
almost a decade after an
accident. In early 2017, the city
agreed to restore and run the
funicular for the next 30 years.
This charming landmark makes
an appearance in several
blockbuster movies, from
The Muppets to *La La Land*.

4

Los Angeles Central Library

📍 N3 🏛 630 W 5th St
🕐 10am–8pm Mon–Thu,
10am–5:30pm Fri & Sat,
1–5pm Sun 🚫 Federal hols
🌐 lapl.org

Built in 1926, this civic treasure
was struck by an arson attack
in 1986. It was closed for seven
years while a $213.9 million
renovation program was
carried out. Sympathetic to
the original architecture, the
improvements have doubled
the library's capacity to more
than 2.1 million books.

The building's original design
combines Beaux-Arts grandeur
with Byzantine, Egyptian, and
Roman architectural elements,
inscriptions, and sculpture on
the theme of "the Light of
Learning." The murals in the
rotunda, painted by celebrated
American muralist Dean
Cornwell (1892–1960), depict
the history of California and
are well worth seeing.

The attention given to
detail in the Tom Bradley
wing is impressive. One
example is the three atrium
chandeliers, created by

INSIDER TIP
Walking Tours

The nonprofit LA
Conservancy *(www.
laconservancy.org)*,
devoted to preserving
the unique architecture
of LA, gives excellent
walking tours of
Downtown every
Saturday morning.
Themes include the
old-time glamour of
Art Deco, the history
of Downtown and its
architecture, and the
iconic Union Station.

Therman Statom as
whimsical representations of
the natural, ethereal, and
technological worlds.

The Central Library's garden
is situated by the Flower Street
entrance. Weary sightseers
will appreciate its fountains,
sculptures, shaded benches,
and restaurant.

The library's varied program
of events includes prose
and poetry readings,
lectures, concerts,
exhibitions,
and plays.

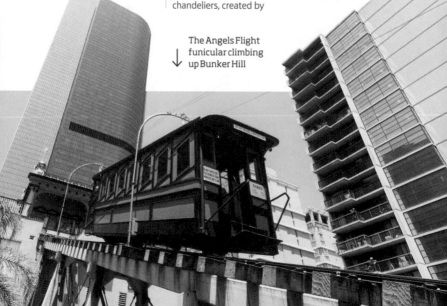

← The Angels Flight
funicular climbing
up Bunker Hill

↑ Stalls heaped with a variety of fresh produce at the Grand Central Market

5

Grand Central Market

📍 OJ 📍 OJ17 S Broadway
🕐 8am–9pm daily 🚫 Jan 1, Thanksgiving, Dec 25
🌐 grandcentralsquare.com

Angelenos have been coming to this vibrant indoor bazaar since 1917. Today more than 40 stallholders operate inside the marketplace. Neatly arranged mounds of bargain-priced fresh fruits and vegetables line the many produce stands, and friendly stallholders frequently offer free samples of fruit.

Among the many cafés and food stands in the market is China Café, which has been serving its popular chow mein since the 1930s, and Roast-to-Go, established in the 1950s and serving Mexican street food and roast meats. More Mexican stalls, such as Ana Maria, sell tacos and burritos, which are filled with all kinds of meat and seafood. Visitors can enjoy watching a rickety assembly-line machine turn *masa* (corn flour dough) into tortillas and then partake of the free samples offered on the counter.

6

Broadway Historic Theater District

📍 O4

Once LA's shopping and entertainment nucleus, this neon-drenched National Historic District stretching from 3rd to 9th streets is today a hub of revitalization. Its 12 movie theaters, built between 1910 and 1931, comprise the world's highest concentration of cinemas. The most ornate is the opulent French Baroque Los Angeles Theatre (No. 615). Inspired by the Hall of Mirrors in the palace of Versailles, near Paris, the theater opened on January 30, 1931, with the premiere of Charlie Chaplin's masterpiece *City Lights*. The 1918 Million Dollar Theater (No. 307) has a striking, heavily ornate fade, while on the opposite side, the restored Bradbury Building (No. 304) features an awe-inspiring light-filled Victorian court, with a lacework of wrought-iron railings, oak paneling, glazed brick walls, two open-cage elevators, and a glass roof.

EAT

Original Pantry Café

Marilyn Monroe and Martin Luther King, Jr. are among the luminaries who've dined at this historic 24-hour café. The pancakes, Southern fried chicken, burgers, and peach cobbler are perfect comfort food.

📍 M4 📍 877 S Figueroa St 🌐 pantry cafe. restaurant

⑤⑤⑤

Philippe the Original

The French Dip sandwich is the specialty of the house. Here it's accompanied with heaps of optional tangy coleslaw, potato salad, and pickled eggs.

📍 Q2 📍 1001 N Alameda St 🌐 philippes.com

⑤⑤⑤

DRINK

Traxx Bar

Inside the gorgeous Union Station, this stylish bar serves beer, wine, and craft cocktails.

📍 Q2 📍 800 N Alameda 🌐 traxxunion.com

Upstairs at the Ace Hotel

Enjoy drinks with a view of Downtown from the rooftop bar of this old Broadway building.

📍 N5 📍 921 S Broadway 🌐 acehotel.com/ upstairs

LA Live

M4 **lalive.com**

Once overlooked as a residential and shopping district, downtown LA now has an abundance of trendy apartments, theaters, hotels, restaurants, and clubs surrounding the Los Angeles Convention Center and the Staples Center. All were part of the ambitious LA Live sports and entertainment district development project that was completed in 2010.

Also here is the Grammy Museum *(www.grammy museum.org)*, where you can record and perform a song and explore the history of the music industry.

Museum of Contemporary Art

03 **250 S Grand Av**
11am-6pm Mon, Wed & Fri, 11am-5pm Sat & Sun
Jan 1, Jul 4, Thanksgiving, Dec 25 **moca.org**

The building of the Museum of Contemporary Art (MOCA), an intriguing combination of

---

BASKETBALL AT THE STAPLES CENTER

In the fast-paced, high-scoring National Basketball Association (NBA) pantheon, the city's pre-eminent team, the LA Lakers, has the biggest fan base and holds the NBA record with a 33-game winning streak. Such illustrious players as Magic Johnson, Kareem Abdul-Jabbar, and the late Kobe Bryant have helped the team win the NBA Championship 16 times. The LA Clippers also play in the NBA; however, they have never won a championship, conference, or division. The city's women's team, The Sparks, has qualified for the Women's National Basketball Association playoffs more than any other team in the league. All three teams play in the state-of-the-art Staples Center *(www.staplescenter.com)* located adjacent to LA Live.

---

pyramids, cylinders, and cubes designed by Japanese architect Arata Isozaki, is as interesting as its collection.

Founded in 1979, MOCA has a respected selection of post-1940 work from artists such as Piet Mondrian, Jackson Pollock, Louise Nevelson, and Julian Schnabel. Added weight is given by the Panza Collection of 80 works of Pop Art and Abstract Expressionism by American artists such as Robert Rauschenberg, Mark Rothko, and Claes Oldenburg.

In 1995, MOCA acquired the 2,100-print Freidus Collection of photographs, which traces the history of documentary photography in the country from the 1940s to the 1980s. The collection includes works

by the likes of Diane Arbus and Robert Frank. Advance, timed-entry tickets are required for visiting MOCA.

Walt Disney Concert Hall

03 **111 S Grand Av**
musiccenter.org

Part of The Music Center – a complex made up of four performing arts venues – the Walt Disney Concert Hall was designed by architect Frank Gehry and completed in 2003. This striking 2,265-seat venue, with outstanding acoustics, is the home of the Los Angeles Philharmonic and Los Angeles

---

STAY

Hotel Figueroa
This boutique hotel began life in 1926 as a hostel for lone women travelers. Rooms here have a contemporary Spanish charm and there's also a bar and pool on site.

M4 **939 S Figueroa St** **hotel figueroa.com**

$$$

Master Chorale. A self-guided audio tour narrated by actor John Lithgow offers insights into the architecture of the hall.

Built in 1964, the oldest and largest theater in the Music Center complex is the Dorothy Chandler Pavilion, which is the venue for the Los Angeles Opera. The Ahmanson Theatre stages musicals and Broadway productions, while the intimate Mark Taper Forum, the smallest of the theaters, presents innovative plays.

↑ A store-lined street decorated with red paper lanterns in Chinatown

Geffen Contemporary at MOCA

📍P3 🏛152 N Central Av ⏰11am–6pm Mon, Wed & Fri, 11am–5pm Sat & Sun 🚫Jan 1, Jul 4, Thanksgiving, Dec 25 🌐moca.org

In 1983, this old police garage was used as a temporary exhibition space for MOCA (p120). Frank Gehry's bold renovations of the building in the 1980s were so successful that the gallery in the warehouse became a permanent fixture. Exhibitions often include highlights from MOCA's large permanent collection as well as more esoteric shows.

🍴 💬 🛍

Chinatown

📍Q1 ℹ727 N Broadway, Suite 208; www.china townla.com

The Chinese first came to California during the Gold Rush to work in the mines and build the railroads. Confronted by prejudice, they developed tightknit communities. LA's first Chinatown was established in 1870 on the present-day site of Union Station, and relocated about 900 yds (820 m) north in 1938. Today it is the home of more than 21,000 people who live and work in the area.

The ornate East Gate on North Broadway leads into Gin Ling Way and the New Chinatown Central Plaza, a pedestrian precinct lined with brightly painted buildings with pagoda-style roofs. Here shops sell everything from exquisite jade jewelry to inexpensive trinkets.

In the surrounding streets, tantalizing restaurants offer all manner of Chinese food, from dim sum (steamed or grilled dumplings), to spicy Szechuan dishes.

The Chinese New Year Parade and festivities (p44) include dragon and lion dancers accompanied by drums, floats, and firecrackers.

The sleek Walt Disney Concert Hall, designed ↓ by Frank Gehry

EAT

Daikokuya

This hole-in-the-wall is renowned for its excellent ramen.

📍P3 🏠327 E 1st St
🌐daikoku-ten.com

💲💲💲

Mitsuru Café

A one-stop destination for traditional Japanese finger foods such as *imagawayaki* (hot griddle cakes stuffed with red-bean paste).

📍P4 🏠117 Japanese Village Plaza Mall
🕐Mon 🌐mitsuru. top-cafes.com

💲💲💲

Sushi Gen

Patrons wait in line to savor the sashimi special or the *omakase* (chef's own choice) selection at this huge restaurant.

📍P4 🏠422 E 2nd St
🕐Sun & Mon
🌐sushigen-dtla.com

💲💲💲

Fugetsu-Do Bakery Shop

This long-standing family-owned "sweet shop" is all about *mochi* – small, round, sticky rice cake confections.

📍P3 🏠315 E 1st St
🌐fugetsu-do.com

💲💲💲

Sugarfish

Everything is served *omakase* at this sushi restaurant.

📍N4 🏠W 7th St
🌐sugarfishsushi.com

💲💲💲

12 Little Tokyo

📍P4 🚇244 S San Pedro St; www.visitlittletokyo.com

Lying between 1st, 3rd, Los Angeles, and Alameda streets is the bustling area of Little Tokyo. One of the largest Japantowns in the US, it is dotted with Japanese markets, shops, restaurants, and temples, giving a taste of American Japanese culture.

The first Japanese settled here in 1884. Today the heart of the area is the Japanese American Cultural and Community Center at No. 244 South San Pedro Street, from which cultural activities and festivals, such as Nisei Week, which celebrates Japanese American history, are organized. The fan-shaped Japan America Theater often hosts performers from Japan, such as the Grand Kabuki.

The Japanese Village Plaza at No. 335 East 2nd Street resembles a rural Japanese village, with blue roof tiles, exposed wood frames, and paths landscaped with pools and rocks. A traditional fire watchtower marks the plaza's 1st Street entrance. Stores include Nijiya Market and the Mikawaya Candy Store. Off San Pedro Street, Onizuka Street offers more upscale shops.

13 Japanese American National Museum

📍P4 🏠100 N Central Av
🕐11am–5pm Tue–Sun
🕐Jan 1, Thanksgiving, Dec 25 🌐janm.org

This somber museum, housed in a handsome contemporary structure in the Little Tokyo district, chronicles the story of Japanese Americans, from the first migrants in 1882 to present-day culture. The sprawling main exhibition, "Common Ground: The Heart of Community," provides a thorough historical survey, with a worthwhile focus on the forced incarceration of 120,000 Japanese Americans during World War II. It includes a reconstruction of a barracks from the Heart Mountain internment camp in northern Wyoming. Videos preserve oral histories, while temporary exhibitions, plus a resource center, provide further understanding and appreciation of the contributions made by Japanese Americans.

Facing the entrance, the Go For Broke National Education Center (355 E 1st St) offers exhibitions and events drawing on the achievements of World War II American veterans of Japanese ancestry.

↑ Film costumes at the Fashion Institute of Design and Merchandising Museum

HIDDEN GEM
Koyasan Temple

In Little Tokyo, at the end of an unmarked alley off East 1st Street, stands this charming temple, adorned with lanterns, Buddhist statues, and effigies of other deities *(www.koyasanbetsuin.org)*.

Cathedral of Our Lady of the Angels

📍 O2 🏛 555 W Temple St
🕐 Early morning-6pm daily
🌐 olacathedral.org

LA's Catholic cathedral is a massive Cubist complex designed by Spanish architect José Rafael Moneo. It includes monumental bronze doors, thin alabaster windows, a 6,109-pipe organ, a Carrara marble altar, and the gilt 17th-century Retablo Ezcaray altarpiece from Spain. Actor Gregory Peck is buried in the crypt, as are the bones of Saint Vibiana, a 3rd-century Roman virgin martyr (and LA's patron saint) whose remains were discovered in ancient catacombs in 1853.

Fashion Institute of Design and Merchandising Museum

📍 M4 🏛 919 S Grand Av
🕐 10am-5pm Tue-Sat
🌐 fidmmuseum.org

The Fashion Institute of Design and Merchandising Museum pays homage to the fashion, entertainment, interior design, and graphics industries. Ranging from the late 18th century to the present day, there are some 12,000 pieces in the collection, from ready-to-wear garments to couture, film and theater costumes, fabrics, and accessories.

↑ The iconic tower of Los Angeles City Hall, with an observation deck for expansive city views

World-renowned designers such as Christian Dior, Issey Miyake, and Yves Saint Laurent are all represented here. Many of the garments on display were worn by famous stars such as Marlene Dietrich, Fred Astaire, and Carole Lombard.

Los Angeles City Hall

📍 P3 🏛 200 N Spring St
📞 (213) 485-2121 🕐 8am-5pm Mon-Fri 🚫 Federal hols

Until 1957, this 28-story structure was the tallest in Downtown – all others were limited to 12 floors. Today City Hall is dwarfed by surrounding skyscrapers, but its distinctive tower is still one of Los Angeles's most familiar landmarks. Among its many film and television roles, it has been the location for the *Daily Planet*, Clark Kent's place of work in the 1950s television series *Adventures of Superman*.

Inside, the rotunda has a beautiful inlaid-tile dome and excellent acoustics. The dome is decorated with eight figures representing the City Hall's major concerns: education, health, law, art, government, service, protection, and trust. An observation area in the tower, which has been lovingly restored after damage by the 1994 Northridge earthquake, offers panoramic views across the city. Call (213) 978-1995 to book the 45-minute tour.

Many of the garments on display were worn by famous stars such as Marlene Dietrich, Fred Astaire, and Carole Lombard.

A SHORT WALK
BUSINESS DISTRICT

Distance 1.5 miles (2.5 km) **Time** 30 minutes
Nearest metro 7th Street/Metro Center

The 20th century saw LA expand west toward the ocean, temporarily relegating Downtown to a minor role in the city. Today a revitalized business district has developed around Flower Street, and the sidewalks are once more filled with tourists and Angelenos alike. California's banking industry has its headquarters here, housed in striking skyscrapers such as the Wells Fargo Center. Walking eastward, you'll see that the jewelry, toy, food, and garment wholesale industries are flourishing. A commitment to the arts has also been successful. The Museum of Contemporary Art (MOCA), the Walt Disney Concert Hall, and the Los Angeles Central Library have sparked a thriving cultural environment that has drawn people back to the city's center.

The **US Bank Tower** *is a 73-story office block designed by I. M. Pei. At 1,017 ft (310 m) it is the tallest building in LA.*

The **Westin Bonaventure Hotel** *has external elevators with views of the business district.*

The beautiful Beaux-Arts **Los Angeles Central Library** (p118) *is decorated with carvings and inscriptions based on the theme "the Light of Learning."*

SOUTH FLOWER STREET

START

Fine Arts Building

7th Street/ Metro Center station

SOUTH HOPE STREET

WEST 6TH STREET

WEST 7TH STREET

The **James Oviatt Building** *(1925) is a marvelous example of Art Deco styling.*

The **Millennium Biltmore** *was one of LA's most luxurious hotels when it opened in 1923.*

← The eye-catching pyramid of Los Angeles Central Library

The **Wells Fargo Center**, the LA branch of this California company, has a sculpture court, with works by artists such as Jean Dubuffet.

The sandstone building of the **Museum of Contemporary Art** (p120) was praised when it opened in 1986. The collection gives an overview of post-1940 art.

Angels Flight (p118) is a funicular that runs from South Hill Street to Bunker Hill.

Locator Map
For more detail see p112

FINISH

Bright lights hover above stores in the busy Grand Central Market ↑

The atrium of the unassuming **Bradbury Building** is one of the finest of its kind in the US.

Grand Central Market (p119) is an indoor market at the heart of the movie theater district.

SOUTH GRAND AVENUE

SOUTH OLIVE STREET

SOUTH HILL STREET

WEST 4TH STREET

WEST 5TH STREET

SOUTH BROADWAY

M

Pershing Square Metro station

Pershing Square was designated the city's first public park in 1866. The now-concreted square is still a popular meeting place and has been landscaped with trees, benches, and statuary.

| 0 meters | | 200 | N |
| 0 yards | | 200 | ↑ |

125

AROUND DOWNTOWN

Northeast of LA, the San Gabriel Valley gets its name from the Mission San Gabriel Arcángel, which was established here by Franciscan priest Junípero Serra in 1771. The local Tongva people were subsequently almost wiped out by disease, brought to the area by the arrival of European colonizers, and some 6,000 are buried at the mission. Pasadena is the largest city in the valley. It was established in 1874 by a group of wealthy Midwesterners, who set up a health and wellness community – called the Indiana Colony – here as a result of the area's mild climate. In 1886, this resort became known as Pasadena and was incorporated as a city. Today Pasadena and the San Gabriel Valley, have become popular bedroom communities for commuters working in LA.

South LA is better known by its previous moniker South Central. LA City Council voted to change the name in 2003 in the hope of disassociating the area with long-term gang violence (notoriously between the Bloods and Crips). In 1965, a long record of police brutality by the LAPD against the local African American community led to the Watts Riots, which lasted six days and left 32 dead. Riots occurred again in 1992, after LAPD officers were acquitted of beating local man Rodney King. In the 2000s, the crime rate declined significantly, leading to gentrification in some areas. The 2028 Los Angeles Olympics is expected to further boost South LA's fortunes.

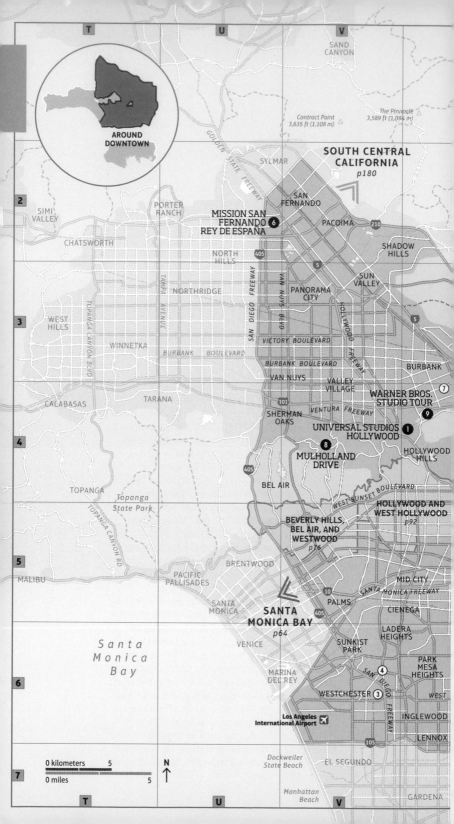

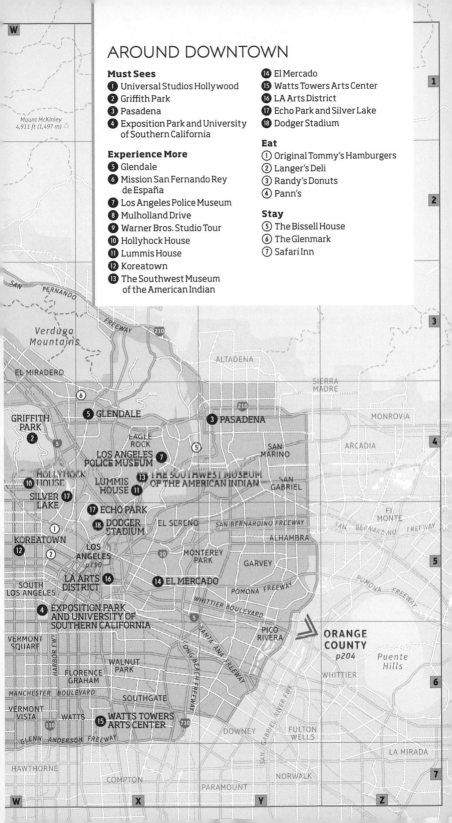

AROUND DOWNTOWN

Must Sees

1. Universal Studios Hollywood
2. Griffith Park
3. Pasadena
4. Exposition Park and University of Southern California

Experience More

5. Glendale
6. Mission San Fernando Rey de España
7. Los Angeles Police Museum
8. Mulholland Drive
9. Warner Bros. Studio Tour
10. Hollyhock House
11. Lummis House
12. Koreatown
13. The Southwest Museum of the American Indian
14. El Mercado
15. Watts Towers Arts Center
16. LA Arts District
17. Echo Park and Silver Lake
18. Dodger Stadium

Eat

1. Original Tommy's Hamburgers
2. Langer's Deli
3. Randy's Donuts
4. Pann's

Stay

5. The Bissell House
6. The Glenmark
7. Safari Inn

The Universal Studios globe fountain in front of the main gate and *(inset)* the tour tram

UNIVERSAL STUDIOS HOLLYWOOD

◉W4 📍100 Universal City Plaza, Universal City 🕐Jun-Aug: 9am-8pm daily; Sep-May: 10am-6pm daily; times can vary 🌐universalstudioshollywood.com

Spread over 415 acres (169 ha), Universal Studios Hollywood is the world's largest working movie and television studio and theme park. The attractions, from family favorites such as Shrek and Jurassic Park® to the latest virtual-reality thrill ride, create a fantastical world of magic and Hollywood glamor.

The movie and television studio sprang from the imagination of Carl Laemmle, who in 1915 bought a former chicken ranch on the site, moved his film studio here from Hollywood, and started making silent films. He charged visitors 25 cents to see the films being made, and guests could also purchase fresh eggs. With the advent of the "talkies" in 1927, the sets needed quiet and the visits stopped. The theme park began taking shape in 1964 when Universal Studios Hollywood was launched as a behind-the-scenes tram ride.

Today Universal Studios is divided into upper and lower sections. As soon as visitors walk through the gate, they stroll through the Streets of the World, which are actual working sets depicting anything from 1950s America to a quaint European village. The Studio Tour is the only way of seeing Universal's major television and movie stages and sets. The lower level is where the major thrill rides can be found.

> 💬 INSIDER TIP
> **Beat the Crowds**
>
> The Universal Express ticket provides single access to all attractions, and includes priority seating. With the VIP Experience ticket you can explore areas not open to the public. Download the Universal Studios Hollywood app for maps, show times, and free Wi-Fi.

STUDIO TOUR

The original Universal Studios attraction, this classic Studio Tour gives visitors an up-close and personal view of the past, present, and future of movie-making in Hollywood. Guests are ferried about in trolley buses fitted with state-of-the-art, high-definition monitors and digital playback systems. Comedian Jimmy Fallon, the star of *Late Night with Jimmy Fallon*, is the video host of the tour and augments the live Studio Tour narration by introducing hundreds of clips from hit films and TV shows. Visitors see King Kong, Jaws, and plenty of dinosaurs, and survive a collapsing bridge, flash flood, earthquake, and avalanche. The tour passes the Bates Motel from *Psycho* (1960), the startlingly realistic Boeing 747 crash from *War of the Worlds* (2005), and Wisteria Lane from *Desperate Housewives*. The 35 different soundstages,

↑ King Kong: 360-3-D, featuring a re-created version of Skull Island

various movie and TV sets, props, cameras, lights, and action give guests a glimpse into filmland's realities and illusions, while special installations of "The Mummy," "Earthquake – The Big One," "King Kong," and "Jaws Lake" let visitors experience the drama of each working set. The Studio Tour is really what a visit to Universal Studios is all about, and it's included in the general admission ticket.

UNIVERSAL CITYWALK

In 1993, American architect Jon Jerde designed a festive assortment of facades for the shops and restaurants on CityWalk's promenade. Today, with its numerous attractions, including bars, restaurants, shops, nightclubs, and theaters, Universal's CityWalk is hailed as the entertainment mecca of Southern California. Tapping into guests' whimsy is a giant neon-lit baseball player who swings his bat above a sports store and an icecream store fronted by an upside-down pink convertible that has crashed through a Hollywood Freeway sign. The seven-story IMAX® 3-D theater shows the latest blockbusters, and the i-FLY Indoor Skydiving experience is an adrenaline-pumping alternative to the plethora of retail shops, name-brand outlets, and glitzy restaurants. CityWalk is nothing short of a spectacular venture into Californian fantasy and entertainment.

← Bright lights and city sights at Universal Studios Hollywood's CityWalk Mall

RIDES AND SPECIAL EFFECTS

Thrill rides are what theme parks do best, and Universal offers some of the most spectacular rides, all coupled with incredible special effects. Revenge of the Mummy™ – The Ride is a firm favorite with visitors of all ages thanks to a mix of high-speed roller coaster and space-age robotics, while many of the other attractions simulate the sense of movement by using flight-simulation technology and 3-D effects. In WaterWorld® the audience needs to be prepared for a soaking. Guests can also see King Kong on the world's largest and most intense soundstage and may get the rare chance to get a sneak peek at one of dozens of the films currently in production. Each attraction here is a thrill ride in itself, where the excitement of movies literally comes alive.

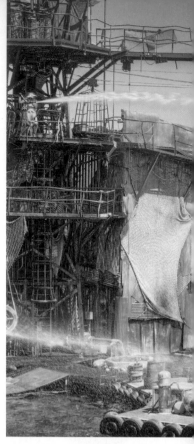

Dinosaur seen in Jurassic World - The Ride

Dazzling pyrotechnics, battle scenes, and extraordinary stunts, all part of the Waterworld® show ↑

Revenge of the Mummy™ – The Ride

California's fastest indoor roller coaster uses some of the most advanced animatronics and space-age robotics ever engineered to create an exciting, scream-worthy ride. Light levels change from daylight to total darkness. Watch out for the skeleton warriors!

Top Rides

Transformers™: The Ride-3D

▲ This ride is based on the popular movie franchise that spun out of the success of transforming robot toys. It uses 3-D effects and flight-simulation technology to provide an immersive, excitingly realistic experience. The adventure puts you in a war zone, fighting alongside the Transformers™ to save the human race from the Decepticons.

The Simpsons Ride™

▲ Homer, Marge, Bart, Lisa, and Maggie Simpson - stars of TV's longest running cartoon series - ride along with visitors on a hysterical adventure in this mega-attraction. On the way guests experience a side of Springfield previously unexplored, as they enjoy the ride's interpretation of the thrill rides, dark rides, and "live" shows that make up a fantasy amusement park dreamed up by the show's cantankerous Krusty the Clown.

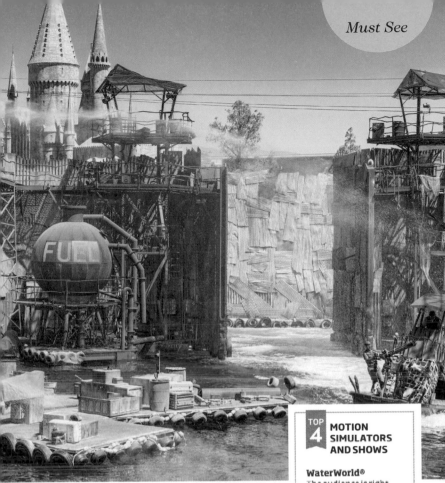

The Wizarding World of Harry Potter™

▽ Thrilling rides include 4K-HD imagery projected at twice the usual frame rate for a supremely realistic feeling. The highlight is Flight of the Hippogriff, where young wizards soar over Hogwarts.

Jurassic World – The Ride

△ An upgrade to the previous ride, this is part expedition and part thrilling water ride based on the film franchise. Visitors are hurled into a steamy prehistoric wilderness, where huge dinosaurs swoop to within inches of riders' faces.

TOP 4 MOTION SIMULATORS AND SHOWS

WaterWorld®
The audience is right in the middle of this thrilling, high-tech show based on the 1995 film.

Despicable Me Minion Mayhem
This simulator ride uses 3-D HD animation to transport you into the Despicable Me world.

Shrek 4-D™
Picking up where the original DreamWorks movie left off, this show features "Ogre Vision" animation.

Special Effects Stage
Learn the secrets behind the special effects in today's blockbusters at this live show.

2 🖼️ 🍴 💻 🛍️

GRIFFITH PARK

📍 W4 🚌 96 🕐 5am-10:30pm daily ℹ️ 4730 Crystal Springs Dr; www.laparks.org/griffithpark

The country's largest urban park, Griffith Park is a vast wilderness of rugged hills, forested valleys, and green meadows in the center of LA. People come here to escape from the city crowds, visit the sights, picnic, hike, or go horseback riding.

① 🖼️

Griffith Observatory

🏠 2800 Observatory Rd
🕐 Noon-10pm Tue-Fri,
10am-10pm Sat & Sun
🌐 griffithobservatory.org

Located on the south-facing slope of Mount Hollywood, Griffith Observatory offers stunning views of the LA basin. The Art Deco observatory is divided into three main areas: the Hall of Science, the planetarium, and the telescopes.
The planetarium has the world's most advanced projector, and visitors can journey through space and time, as stars, moons, and planets are projected onto the ceiling. In the Main Rotunda of the Hall of Science, the Foucault Pendulum demonstrates the earth's rotation. Characters from Classical mythology are depicted on the domed ceiling. On the roof, the Zeiss Telescope is open to the public on clear nights.

② 🛍️

Travel Town Museum

🏠 5200 W Zoo Dr 🕐 10am-5pm Thu-Tue 🚫 Dec 25
🌐 traveltown.org

The spirit of the rails comes alive at this outdoor collection of vintage trains and cars. Children and adults can climb aboard the exhibits or ride on a miniature railway.

③ 🖼️

Greek Theatre

🏠 2700 N Vermont Ave
🕐 For performances only
🌐 lagreektheatre.com

Styled after an ancient Greek amphitheater, this open-air music venue has outstanding acoustics. On summer nights, over 6,000 people can sit under the stars and enjoy performances by major popular and classical musicians. Evenings can be chilly, so bring a sweater.

④ 🖼️ 💻 🛍️

Los Angeles Zoo

🏠 5333 Zoo Dr 🕐 10am-5pm daily 🚫 Dec 25 🌐 lazoo.org

This hilly compound has more than 1,200 mammals, reptiles, and birds living in simulations of their natural habitats.
Many newborn creatures can be seen in the Animal Nursery, including some from the zoo's breeding program for rare and endangered species. The Koala House is dimly lit to encourage the nocturnal creatures to be more active. Adventure Island focuses on Southwestern animals and habitats. Visitors can also enjoy the Pachyderm Exhibit,

HOLLYWOOD SIGN

The Hollywood Sign is an internationally recognized symbol of the movie business. Set high up in the Hollywood Hills, it is visible for miles from many parts of LA. Erected in 1923, it originally advertised the Hollywoodland housing development. The "land" was removed in 1949. Three trails (from easy to difficult: Mt Hollywood, Brush Canyon, and Cahuenga Peak) lead up to the sign, with views out over the downtown LA sprawl (www.hollywoodsign.org).

↑ Griffith Observatory overlooking the downtown
Los Angeles skyline

the Rainforest of the Americas, and the Insect Interpretation Center. Be prepared to walk long distances, or use the Safari Shuttle bus.

Autry Museum of the American West

📍 4700 Western Heritage Way (opposite the zoo)
🕐 10am–4pm Tue–Sun
🚫 Thanksgiving, Dec 25
🌐 theautry.org

The Autry Museum explores the many cultures that have shaped the American West. Artworks by such artists as Albert Bierstadt and Frederic Remington depict a somewhat romanticized view of life in the region. Tools, firearms,

INSIDER TIP
Renting Bikes at Spokes 'N Stuff

For zippy tours around Griffith Park, stop at Spokes 'N Stuff on Crystal Springs Drive, where you can rent out anything from kids' mountain bikes to a four-seater surrey *(www. spokes-n-stuff.com).*

tribal clothing, and religious figurines are some of the artifacts that show Native American traditions and the diversity of the people who have lived here. Founded by the film star Gene Autry, "The Singing Cowboy," the museum also houses a collection of Hollywood Western movie and television memorabilia. The museum's ethnobotanical garden offers a glimpse of the local vegetation and geology with a wetlands cove, pond, waterfall, and basalt columns.

LA Live Steamers Railroad Museum

📍 5202 Zoo Dr 🕐 11am–3pm Sun (Walt's Barn: 3rd Sun of month) 🌐 lalsrm.org

Founded in 1956 by a group of train enthusiasts, LALSRM educates visitors in railroad history and takes them out on its model trains. The museum is also home to Walt's Barn, where Walt Disney had a workshop for his own home railroad.

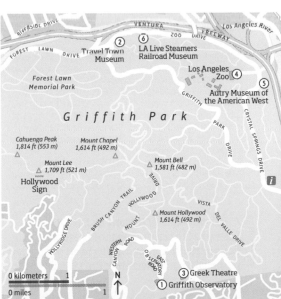

↑ Palm trees lining the streets of Pasadena, overlooked by the mountains

3

PASADENA

📍 Y4 🚌 79 from downtown LA ℹ️ 300 E Green St; www.visitpasadena.com

With the completion of the Santa Fe Railroad in 1887, Pasadena evolved from an orange-growing cooperative to a winter resort for wealthy East Coast visitors. The real estate boom graced the nascent city with splendid Victorian, Spanish Revival, and Art Deco buildings.

①

Old Pasadena

🌐 oldpasadena.org

A National Register Historic District, Old Pasadena is a model of historic preservation and revitalization, having been recouped from neglect since the 1960s. Its 22 blocks are abuzz with hip stores, top-class restaurants, and restored movie theaters, many tucked neatly into charming European-style piazzas and alleys. The Pasadena Heritage organization offers walking tours.

②

Rose Bowl

📍 1001 Rose Bowl Dr
🌐 rosebowlstadium.com

This large stadium was built in 1922 for the annual Rose Bowl football game, which matches college teams from the West Coast and the Midwest. This is the home of UCLA's football team, the Bruins. Numerous Super Bowl games have also been played here as well as the World Cup Championships in 1994 and the 1984 Summer Olympics soccer competitions.

> **A National Register Historic District, Old Pasadena is a model of historic preservation and revitalization, having been recouped from neglect since the 1960s.**

> ### THE TOURNAMENT OF ROSES PARADE
>
> In 1890 the Pasadena Valley Hunt Club held the first Tournament of Roses to celebrate the region's balmy winters. Little did they know their horse-drawn carriages would be the start of this world-famous New Year's day extravaganza, with marching bands and gigantic floats covered in flowers and seeds.

③

Gamble House

📍 4 Westmoreland Pl
🕐 10:30am-1pm Tue, 11:40am-3pm Thu-Sat, noon-3pm Sun 🚫 Federal hols 🌐 gamblehouse.org

A masterpiece of the era, this wooden house epitomizes the Arts and Crafts movement, which stressed simplicity of design and superior craftsmanship. The dwelling was built in 1908 for David Gamble, of the Procter and Gamble Company.

Gamble House was tailor-made for LA's climate, with its terraces, open porches, and broad overhanging eaves.

Pacific-Asia Museum

📍 46 N Los Robles Av
🕐 11am–5pm Wed–Sun
(to 8pm Thu) 🌐 pacificasia
museum.usc.edu

Built in 1924 to a traditional northern Chinese design, the Pacific-Asia Museum houses a collection of Far Eastern art founded by collector Grace Nicholson. The museum's enchanting courtyard garden is one of only a few authentic Chinese gardens in the country.

Pasadena Museum of History

📍 470 W Walnut St
🕐 Noon–5pm Wed–Sun
🌐 pasadenahistory.org

Occupying the former estate of Hungarian physician and entomologist Dr. Adalbert Fenyes, this museum is the key archival repository of the city's heritage. The History Center exhibits early life in Southern California. Hour-long docent-led tours of the palatial 1905 Beaux Arts Fenyes mansion, with its sumptuous furnishings

and art collection, provide a peek into erstwhile life on Pasadena's South Orange Grove Boulevard, previously known as "Millionaire's Row." After Fenyes' granddaughter married a Finnish consul, the mansion served as the Finnish consulate. A cabin, in the style of a 19th-century farmhouse in the gardens, today houses the Finnish Folk Art Museum.

Mount Wilson Observatory

📍 Mt Wilson Rd 🕐 10am–4pm daily 🌐 mtwilson.edu

Mount Wilson Observatory opened in 1904 atop the San Gabriel Mountains, and for several decades the world's biggest telescopes and top astronomers – including Edwin Hubble – trailblazed discoveries here that revolutionized our understanding of the universe. The observatory is open for free self-guided tours daily; docent-led tours are held for a small fee twice-daily on weekends, and it hosts concerts, lectures, and special events throughout the year.

Must See

EAT

Fair Oaks Pharmacy & Soda Fountain
Retro decor and old-fashioned favorites, such as patty melts and hot fudge sundaes.

📍 1526 Mission St
🌐 fairoakspharmacy.net

💲💲💲

La Grande Orange Café
Regional takes on American classics in the 1935 Del Mar station.

📍 260 S Raymond Av
🌐 lgostation cafe.com

💲💲💲

Urth Caffé
Organic coffee and tea, healthy soups, and decadent desserts.

📍 594 E Colorado Blvd
🌐 urthcaffe.com

💲💲💲

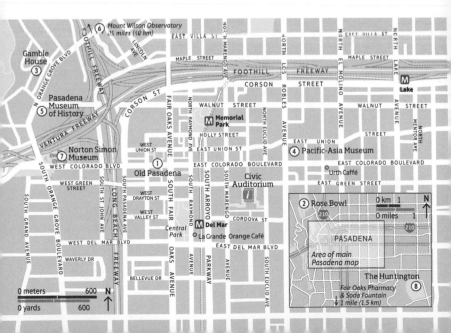

⑦ 🖉 🎨 🖥 🛍

NORTON SIMON MUSEUM

🏠 411 W Colorado Blvd 🚍 180, 181 🕐 Noon–5pm Thu–Mon
🗓 Jan 1, Thanksgiving, Dec 25 🌐 nortonsimon.org

One of the most remarkable private art collections in the world, the Norton Simon Museum is packed to the rafters with invaluable Raphaels, Rembrandts, Van Goghs, and Picassos.

Norton Simon (1907–93) was a successful businessman who combined running his multinational corporation with forming an internationally acclaimed collection of works of art. From the 1950s onward, he amassed masterpieces spanning more than 2,000 years of Western and Asian art, and, having taken over the Pasadena Art Museum in 1974, his collection continued to expand through the 1980s. Within the European holdings, the Old Masters and Impressionist paintings are especially strong; Renaissance, Post-Impressionism, German Expressionism, and the modern period are also well represented. Sculptures from India and Southeast Asia are among the finest outside the region and offer an insight into the complex roles art and religion play in these cultures.

GALLERY GUIDE

European paintings, prints, sculpture, and tapestries, dating from the Renaissance to the 20th century, are on the first floor. The lower galleries showcase an impressive collection of Indian and Southeast Asian works. Visitors can also enjoy the outdoor space, which takes the form of a huge sculpture garden with a natural pond.

A selection of the museum's distinguished collection of European oil paintings ↑

1 The sculpture garden has a large natural pond.

2 This ceremonial mask of Bhairaval is from Nepal.

3 These ancient sculptures depict Hindu deities.

Must See

TOP 5 ARTWORKS AT NORTON SIMON

Woman with a Book (1932)
Marie-Thérèse Walter featured in a number of Picasso's paintings.

Still Life with Lemons, Oranges and a Rose (1633)
Francisco de Zurbarán excelled at contemplative still lifes.

Self-Portrait (c. 1636-8)
Rembrandt painted nearly 100 self-portraits during his lifetime.

Buddha (8 AD)
This bronze was made in Kashmir, India and inlaid with silver and copper.

Saints Paula and Frediano (c. 1483)
One of a pair of panels by Filippino Lippi.

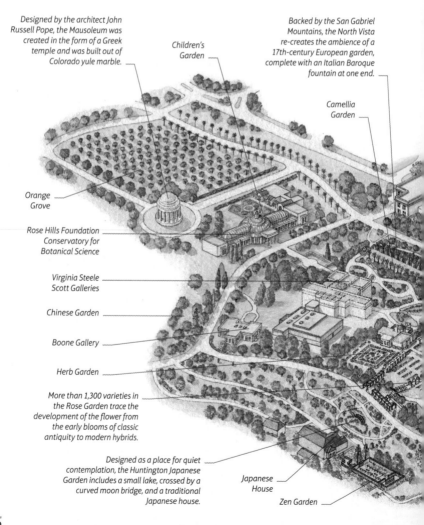

⑧ 🛶 Ⓜ 🖥 🛍

THE HUNTINGTON

📍 1151 Oxford Rd 🕐 10am–5pm Wed–Mon (advance reservations recommended, required on weekends) 🚫 Federal hols 🌐 huntington.org

Visitors and scholars alike are united in their love of the Huntington institution, comprising stunning research libraries, an outstanding art collection, and botanical gardens with plants from around the world.

The original Beaux-Arts mansion here was built between 1909 and 1911 for Henry Huntington (1850–1927), who made his fortune building a network of interurban trams (Red Cars) in Los Angeles. In 1913 he married his uncle's widow, Arabella, and together they amassed one of the most significant book, art, and botanical collections in the world. In 1919 Henry and Arabella put their home and gardens into a trust, creating a nonprofit research institution, with modern educational and cultural facilities added later.

Designed by the architect John Russell Pope, the Mausoleum was created in the form of a Greek temple and was built out of Colorado yule marble.

Children's Garden

Backed by the San Gabriel Mountains, the North Vista re-creates the ambience of a 17th-century European garden, complete with an Italian Baroque fountain at one end.

Camellia Garden

Orange Grove

Rose Hills Foundation Conservatory for Botanical Science

Virginia Steele Scott Galleries

Chinese Garden

Boone Gallery

Herb Garden

More than 1,300 varieties in the Rose Garden trace the development of the flower from the early blooms of classic antiquity to modern hybrids.

Designed as a place for quiet contemplation, the Huntington Japanese Garden includes a small lake, crossed by a curved moon bridge, and a traditional Japanese house.

Japanese House

Zen Garden

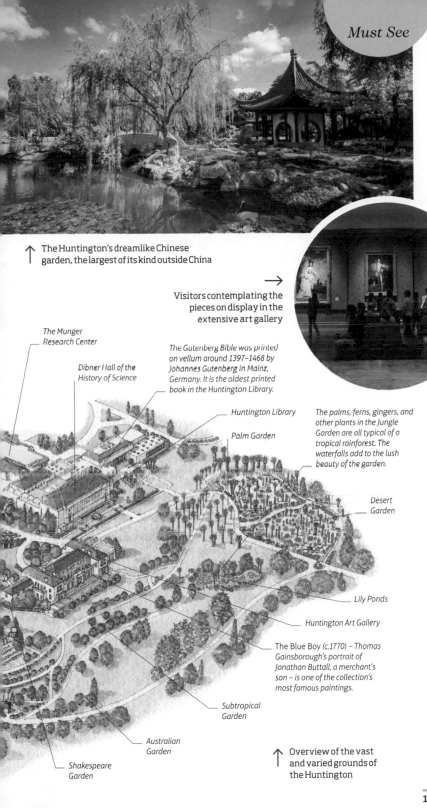

↑ The Huntington's dreamlike Chinese garden, the largest of its kind outside China

→ Visitors contemplating the pieces on display in the extensive art gallery

The Munger Research Center

Dibner Hall of the History of Science

The Gutenberg Bible was printed on vellum around 1397–1468 by Johannes Gutenberg in Mainz, Germany. It is the oldest printed book in the Huntington Library.

Huntington Library

Palm Garden

The palms, ferns, gingers, and other plants in the Jungle Garden are all typical of a tropical rainforest. The waterfalls add to the lush beauty of the garden.

Desert Garden

Lily Ponds

Huntington Art Gallery

The Blue Boy (c.1770) – Thomas Gainsborough's portrait of Jonathan Buttall, a merchant's son – is one of the collection's most famous paintings.

Subtropical Garden

Australian Garden

Shakespeare Garden

↑ Overview of the vast and varied grounds of the Huntington

EXPLORING THE HUNTINGTON

Huntington Library

Built in 1920, the library specializes in British and American history and literature. It attracts nearly 2,000 scholars every year. The public can view key items and exhibits in the Library Exhibition Hall.

Among the 440,000 rare books and 8 million manuscripts are such treasures as Benjamin Franklin's autobiography and the beautiful 15th-century Ellesmere manuscript of Chaucer's *Canterbury Tales* (c. 1410). The collection also includes a Gutenberg Bible (c. 1397–1468) – one of only 12 surviving copies printed on vellum in the world.

> **The idea behind the Dibner Hall exhibit is to appreciate the beauty of science and how certain historical breakthroughs have changed the world.**

There are first editions and manuscripts by noted authors, including Mark Twain, Charles Dickens, and Lord Tennyson, and some early editions of Shakespeare's plays. Personal correspondence written by George Washington, Benjamin Franklin, and Abraham Lincoln are also part of the collection.

Dibner Hall of the History of Science

The idea behind the Dibner Hall exhibit is to appreciate the beauty of science and how certain historical breakthroughs have changed the world. The Burndy Library, formerly housed at MIT, plus the Huntingdon's own history of science collection, are elegantly combined here in four galleries to present the findings of world-renowned scientists all the way from Ptolemy to Einstein. Visitors will be able to make use of a reading room to study translations and modern editions of work in the collection.

Virginia Steele Scott Galleries of American Art

Two major expansions in 2014 and 2016 added several thousand square feet of extra gallery space to the old Virginia Steele Scott Gallery, combining it with the former Lois and Robert F. Erburu Gallery. The space is one of the largest presentations in Southern California of American art from the early days of Spanish settlement through to the mid-20th century. Some of the most well-known works in the collection are *The Meeting of Lear and Cordelia* (1784), by Benjamin West (1738–1820); *Chimborazo* (1864), by Frederic Edwin

→

Sculpture of the goddess Diana in the Virginia Steele Scott Galleries

↑ Paintings and period
furnishings in the
Huntington Art Gallery

Church (1826–1900); and
Breakfast in Bed (1897), by
Mary Cassatt (1844–1926).
The gallery also features the
marble sculpture *Zenobia
in Chains* (1859), by Harriet
Hosmer (1830–1908), which
was discovered in a private
collection after years of being
presumed lost or destroyed.
Other notable artists include
Edward Hopper (1882–1967);
and there is a group of seminal photographs by Edward
Henry Weston (1886–1958).

Huntington Art Gallery

The Huntington's mansion
houses the majority of the
art collection – some 1,200
European pieces from the 15th
century and beyond, including
British and French art from the
18th and early 19th centuries.
The most famous works are
those held in the Thornton
Portrait Gallery, which provide
an unrivaled opportunity to
study British art. On display
are Thomas Gainsborough's
The Blue Boy (c. 1770) and
Thomas Lawrence's *Pinkie*
(1794), as well as paintings by
Constable, Romney, Reynolds,
Van Dyck, and Turner.

The Large Library Room
contains some outstanding
18th-century furnishings,
which include two Savonnerie
carpets made for Louis XIV,
and five Beauvais tapestries.

On the second floor of
this palatial home, formerly
occupied by the Huntingtons
themselves, are Renaissance
paintings and bronzes and
more choice pieces of French
and British art.

Boone Gallery

The Boone Gallery is home
to temporary exhibitions of
American and English art, rare
books and manuscripts, and
items from the Huntington's
permanent collection.

Built in 1911 as a garage
for Mr Huntington's fleet of
automobiles, the Neo-Classical
building later fell into disrepair.
Its restoration in 2000, funded
by philanthropists MaryLou
and George Boone, provides
some 4,000 sq ft (370 sq m) of
additional exhibition space.

Botanical Gardens

In 1904, Henry Huntington
hired landscape gardener
William Hertrich to develop
the grounds, which now
contain 15 principal gardens.

The vast Desert Garden
has more than 4,000 drought-
tolerant species from around
the world. In the Rose Garden,
a walkway traces the history of
the species, with more than

1,300 varieties. The oldest
of these are found in the
Shakespeare Garden.

One of the most popular
areas is the Japanese Garden,
with a moon bridge, a Zen
Garden, and Japanese plants.

HUNTINGTON'S BIG RED CARS

Henry E. Huntington
made his vast fortune
by marrying real-estate
speculation with public
transportation. The
largest landowner in
Southern California, he
established the Pacific
Electric Railway in 1901,
primarily to get people
out to the far-flung new
suburbs he was develop-
ing. Soon Huntington's
fleet of interurban red
trolleys – dubbed the
"Big Red Cars" – became
the world's largest
electric-transit system,
linking communities
all across Southern
California. By the time
he sold most of his hold-
ings to the Southern
Pacific Railroad in 1910,
the population of LA
had tripled to around
310,000. The last trolley
made its voyage in 1961.

↑ An array of cactuses and succulents
occupying the Desert Garden

The Doheny Memorial Library in the center of the University of Southern California campus ↑

 ④ ⑭

EXPOSITION PARK AND UNIVERSITY OF SOUTHERN CALIFORNIA

📍 W5 🚌 DASH Shuttle F from Business District, 81 🌐 usc.edu

A cultural landmark, Exposition Park includes three museums surrounding a rose garden with more than 19,000 rose bushes. Across the street, the large campus of the University of Southern California (USC) is attended by about 28,000 students. Founded in 1880, it is the oldest and largest private university in the western United States.

↑ A *Tyrannosaurus rex* in the Natural History Museum of Los Angeles County

 ①

Natural History Museum of Los Angeles County

🏠 900 Exposition Blvd, Exposition Park
🕐 9:30am–5pm daily
📅 Jan 1, Jul 4, Thanksgiving, Dec 25 🌐 nhm.org

This museum is one of the most significant natural and cultural history museums in the US. With around 35 million specimens and artifacts covering around 4.5 billion years of history, the collection highlights Southern California's natural and cultural treasures.

 (3)

Doheny Memorial Library

📍 **3550 Trousdale Pkwy, USC** 📞 **(213) 740-2924**

A majestic building with Italian Romanesque, Egyptian, and Moorish design influences, USC's main reference library was built in 1932 in memory of Edward L Doheny, Jr., a trustee of the university. There is a monumental marble staircase at the entrance, and ornate stone throughout.

(4)

Mudd Memorial Hall

📍 **3709 Trousdale Pkwy, USC**

USC's philosophy department's hall is mainly pre-Renaissance Tuscan in style. Statues of great philosophers adorn the exterior, with the Cynic Diogenes over the entrance. With more than 60,000 volumes, the Hoose Library of Philosophy is considered to be one of the best in the US.

EAT

Chichen Itza

USC students and Angelenos flock to this Mexican restaurant serving fast-casual Yucatan dishes.

📍 **3655 S Grand Av**
🌐 **chichenitza restaurant.com**

💲💲💲

Jacks N Joe

An all-day breakfast menu reigns supreme at this Hawaiian-themed restaurant. Creative flapjacks (pancakes) entice with names like Pudgie Elvis, Fight On, and Totally LA. The restaurant also serves delicious French toast.

📍 **2498 S Figueroa St**
🌐 **jacksnjoe.com**

💲💲💲

Did You Know?

The bell tower of Mudd Memorial Hall featured in the 1939 film *The Hunchback of Notre Dame*.

The museum includes the Age of Mammals exhibit and the Dinosaur Hall, while in the Nature Lab you can learn about LA's wild plants and animals through live animal habitats. The Nature Gardens explore Californian and other plants from around the world and include the seasonal Butterfly Pavilion (Sep/Oct) and Spider Pavilion (Oct/Nov).

(2)

Frank Sinatra Hall and Hugh Hefner Hall

📍 **900 West 34th St, USC**
🕐 **10am–4pm Mon–Fri**
🌐 **cinema.usc.edu**

Located in the Eileen Norris Theatre complex, part of the USC School of Cinematic Arts, the Frank Sinatra Hall showcases unique memorabilia from the legendary singer and actor's career. Also here is the Hugh Hefner Hall, featuring rotating displays of classic Hollywood memorabilia.

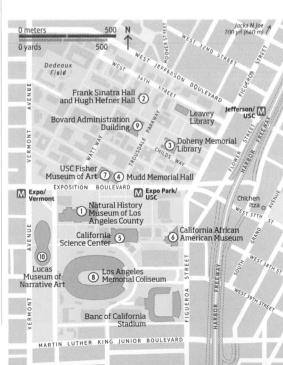

⑤ Ⓜ
California Science Center

🏛 700 Exposition Park Dr ⏰ 10am–5pm daily 🚫 Jan 1, Thanksgiving, Dec 25 🌐 californiascience center.org.

This dynamic museum and learning center aims to make science accessible to people of all ages. The World of Life exhibit in the Kinsev Hall of Health explores how living things function, with Body Works, a 50-ft- (15-m-) long transparent human figure with illuminated organs. The Creative World area shows how people create what they need, following an idea from

↑ Sculptures and paintings on display in the California African American Museum

inception to production. Ecosystems exploreseight different environments, while the IMAX® Theater has a seven-story-high screen presenting nature-related movies.

Winged craft, from a Wright Brothers' glider to a *Gemini 11* space capsule, can be seen in the Air & Space section. The space shuttle *Endeavour* is on display in the Samuel Oschin Pavilion. Note that the museum requires advance timed-entry reservations.

The space shuttle *Endeavour* and *(inset)* the forecourt of the California
↓ Science Center

⑥
California African American Museum

🏛 600 State Dr, Exposition Park ⏰ 10am–5pm Tue-Sat, 11am–5pm Sun 🚫 Jan 1, Thanksgiving, Dec 25 🌐 caamuseum.org

Through more than 4,000 objects from the 1800s to the present day, this museum explores the history, art, and culture of African Americans, with a particular focus on the western United States. The permanent art collection includes works by Martin Pierré, Betye Saar, Noah Purifoy, and the 19th-century landscape painter Robert

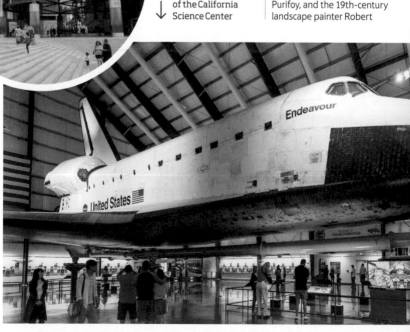

Duncanson. The rest of the collection features sculptures, photographs, films, and historical documents. Frequent temporary exhibitions and regular events are held in the sculpture court.

USC Fisher Museum of Art

⌂ 823 S Exposition Blvd, USC ⏰ Noon–5pm Tue–Fri, noon–4pm Sat ⛔ Federal hols & summer ⊞ fisher.usc.edu

Named after the gallery's benefactor, Mrs. Walter Harrison Fisher, the collection here includes 19th-century French and American landscapes and works by Peter Paul Rubens.

> **Through more than 4,000 objects, the California African American Museum explores the history, art, and culture of African Americans.**

USC TROJANS

The University of Southern California ranks as a powerhouse of collegiate sports; it has won more men's National Collegiate Athletic Association championships (84 in total) than any other college in the US, as well as spawning the most male and female Olympians. National champions in football (11 times), water polo (9 times), and women's basketball (3 times), the USC Trojans - the name given to all the athletics teams - have been at the top of their game for decades, including four consecutive tennis victories between 2009 and 2012 *(usctrojans.com)*.

Los Angeles Memorial Coliseum

⌂ 3911 S Figueroa St, Exposition Park ⏰ For events ⊞ lacoliseum.com

Opened in 1923 as a memorial to veterans of World War I, this is the only facility in the world to have hosted two Olymplads, two Super Bowls, and a World Series. Home court for the USC football team, the Los Angeles Memorial Coliseum has also hosted numerous rock concerts, Nelson Mandela's triumphant return to the US in 1990, Pope John Paul II's Mass in 1987, and John F. Kennedy's 1960 acceptance speech as the Democratic party's candidate for president. It also benefits from a sound system and videoboards.

> 💬 INSIDER TIP
> **Coliseum Tours**
>
> The Los Angeles Memorial Coliseum offers guided and self-guided tours, where you can learn about the venue's history and gain access to the Court of Honor, locker rooms, and views of the field.

⑨ Bovard Administration Building

⌂ 3551 Trousdale Parkway, USC

One of the most iconic of USC's buildings, this Italian Romanesque structure was named after USC's fourth president, George Bovard. The former bell tower has sculpted figures of John Wesley, Abraham Lincoln, Theodore Roosevelt, Cicero, and Plato. Tommy Trojan, a statue of a Trojan warrior by the main entrance, was sculpted in 1930 by Roger Nobel Burnham.

Lucas Museum of Narrative Art

⌂ Bill Robertson Lane, Exposition Park ⏰ Times vary, check website ⊞ lucasmuseum.org

Founded by filmmaker George Lucas, this museum, set to open in late 2021, celebrates the power of visual storytelling through illustrations, paintings, comic art, photography, digital art, and film.

EXPERIENCE MORE

⑤ Glendale

❾X4 **ℹ️613 E Broadway; www.glendaleca.gov**

A somewhat amorphous city in the eastern San Fernando Valley, Glendale is straddled by the lush Verdugo Mountains and scythed by picturesque canyons. It has a meticulously preserved downtown that features 11 buildings on the respected National Register of Historic Places.

The offbeat Museum of Neon Art (216 S Brand Blvd; www.neonmona.org) offers a glowing tribute to the world of contemporary and vintage neon signs. It also runs the fascinating Neon Cruise, a tour of LA landmarks by double-decker bus. For another cool retro experience, watch a classic movie under the stars at the Electric Dusk Drive-In (236 N Central Av), one of only three remaining such venues in Los Angeles. It has monthly screenings.

Glendale's unmissable site, however, is Forest Lawn (1712 S Glendale Av), a vast, leafy cemetery studded by European-style churches.

A "who's who" of LA's finest is interred here, from Walt Disney to Humphrey Bogart. Its world-class art museum displays stunning statuary and paintings that include the Old Masters. Don't miss the massive stained-glass recreation of *The Last Supper* in the Great Mausoleum, and Polish artist Jan Styka's 195-ft- (60-m-) long painting *The Crucifixion* in the Hall of the Crucifixion-Resurrection.

⑥

Mission San Fernando Rey de España

❾U2 **🏠15151 San Fernando Mission Blvd, Mission Hills** **🕐9am–4:30pm daily** **❌Thanksgiving, Dec 25**

One of 21 Franciscan missions located in California, San Fernando Rey de España was founded in 1797 and named after King Ferdinand III of Spain. The present church is an exact copy of the original, which was destroyed in the 1971 earthquake. The *convento* (living quarters) features a 21-arch portico, plus residential rooms, a chapel, kitchen, winery, and storehouse. It is the largest mission building still standing in California.

⑦ Los Angeles Police Museum

❾X4 **🏠6045 York Blvd** **🕐10am–4pm Mon–Fri, 9am–3pm third Sat of each month** **🌐laphs.org**

Located in Highland Park's 1925 police station, this quirky museum covers all aspects of the city's world-famous police force, the LAPD. Handcuffs, firearms, and uniforms are all on display, along with former patrol cars, some with bullet

← Interior and *(inset)* entrance of the reconstructed church of Mission San Fernando Rey de España

↑ Sweeping view of the bright lights of night-time Los Angeles from Mulholland Drive

holes and shot-out windows. You can have your mugshot taken, sit in a holding cell, or take the controls of a grounded LAPD helicopter.

Mulholland Drive

 V4 ⬚ Off Hwys 1 & 27, from Hollywood Fwy to Leo Carrillo State Beach 🛈 Malibu Chamber of Commerce, 23805 Stuart Ranch Rd, Ste 100; (310) 456-9025

Mulholland Drive, one of the most famous roads in Los Angeles, is a 20-mile (32-km) stretch of road that forms part of the Muholland Highway from northern Hollywood to the Malibu coast (p74). As it winds along the ridge of the Santa Monica mountains, the route has spectacular panoramic views across the city, San Fernando Valley, and some of LA's most exclusive

neighborhoods. Its spirit was captured in David Hockney's eponymous painting, which hangs in LACMA (p100).

The road was named after the famous civil engineer William Mulholland. Although better known for his work on the LA Aqueduct, he oversaw the completion of Mulholland Drive in 1924.

Warner Bros. Studio Tour

V4 ⬚ 3400 Warner Blvd, Burbank ⏰ 9am–3:30pm Thu–Mon 🚫 Thanksgiving, Dec 25 🖥 wbstudio tour.com

Hop aboard a tram for a guided tour of this stalwart studio, founded in 1923 at the base of the Hollywood Hills. You'll zip through 110 acres (44.5 ha) of sprawling film lots, and maybe spot some of your favorite stars as you witness scores of movie and TV settings, from *Casablanca* to the set of *Friends*.

The Studio Tour takes you behind the scenes, including the props department and the two-floor interactive archive of fascinating movie memorabilia, which displays such items as Superman's kryptonite. Take the six-hour Deluxe Tour for a VIP insider's look into the actual movie-making process.

> **HIDDEN GEM**
> ### Six Flags Magic Mountain
> Some 25 miles (40 km) north of Mulholland Drive, this theme park has more roller coasters, games, and attractions than any other in the world (*www.sixflags.com/magicmountain*).

EAT

Original Tommy's Hamburgers
This beloved shack on the busy Beverly and Rampart intersection has outside counter seating only.

W5 ⬚ 2575 Beverly Blvd 🖥 original tommys.com

$⑤⑤

Langer's Deli
A kosher-style deli renowned for its hand-carved pastrami rye-bread sandwich. Sandwich #19 is accompanied by a bowl of matzo-ball soup.

W5 ⬚ 704 S Alvarado St 🖥 langersdeli.com

$⑤⑤

Randy's Donuts
There's no missing this 1950s landmark movie location with a giant donut on its roof. There's always a line at both drive-through and walk-up windows for its huge and fluffy donuts.

V6 ⬚ 805 W Manchester Blvd, Inglewood 🖥 randysdonuts.com

$⑤⑤

Pann's
An iconic 1950s coffee shop, Pann's boasts a throwback menu that includes buttermilk biscuit breakfasts, liver and onions, tapioca pudding, and malts.

V6 ⬚ 6710 La Tijera Blvd 🚫 Dinner 🖥 panns.com

$⑤⑤

→

Frank Lloyd Wright's Hollyhock House, reminiscent of an ancient Mayan temple

Hollyhock House

📍 W4 🏛 4800 Hollywood Blvd ⏰ Park: 6am-10pm daily; House: for tours 11am-4pm Thu-Sun 🌐 barnsdall.org/hollyhock-house

Hollyhock House was the first house to be built in LA by American architect Frank Lloyd Wright. An excellent example of Wright's fascination for pre-Columbian styles, the hilltop residence was inspired by Mayan temples and is built around a courtyard.

It was completed in 1921 for oil heiress Aline Barnsdall, who asked that her favorite flower, the hollyhock, be used as a decorative motif throughout the building. A band of stylized hollyhocks, fashioned in concrete, adorns the exterior of the house. The flowers also feature as ornamentation inside, such as on the dining room chairs and other Wright-

Did You Know?

Hollyhock House was the only house in LA that Frank Lloyd Wright built in the Prairie style.

designed furnishings. The large Barnsdall Park, once the grounds of the estate, is now a public art park with galleries.

Lummis House

📍 X4 🏛 200 E Av 43 ⏰ 10am-3pm Sat & Sun 🌐 laparks.org/historic/lummis-home-and-gardens

This house was the home of Charles Fletcher Lummis (1859–1928), who built it between 1898 and 1910 out of concrete and rocks from the local riverbed. The design elements – Native American, Mission Revival, and Arts and Crafts – reveal the main influences on Lummis's life.

Lummis was a writer, historian, photographer, and activist. He played a central role in the city's cultural life, editing the *Los Angeles Times*. As co-founder of the California Landmark Club, he campaigned successfully for the preservation of the state's missions. His vast collection of Native American artifacts was the basis of the holdings at the Southwest Museum of the American Indian. Some Native American objects are displayed in the house.

The garden grows drought-tolerant and native Southern Californian plant species.

Koreatown

📍 W5

A generation ago, "K-Town," located west of downtown LA and south of Hollywood, was a low-rent flashpoint for the April 1992 LA riots, when much of the district went up in flames. Today this 3-sq-mile (8-sq-km) community is one of LA's hippest and most diverse areas, thriving on its Korean-Latin American culture. With densely packed K-pop stores, shopping malls, restaurants, and nightclubs, it also has quieter palm-lined streets.

The **Koreatown Galleria Supermarket** teems with groceries and fresh produce. For a profile on the Korean community's cultural heritage, visit the **Korean American National Museum**. To the southwest, at Olympic Boulevard and Wilton Place, is the exquisite Thal Mah Sah Buddhist Temple. Farther west, in neighboring Brookside, the **Korean Cultural Center** houses a museum and also hosts screenings and exhibitions.

Koreatown Galleria Supermarket
🏛 3250 W Olympic Blvd ⏰ 10am-8pm Mon-Sat, 11am-7pm Sun 🌐 korea towngalleria.com

Korean American National Museum

⌂ 3727 W 6th St No.519
🕐 10am-6pm Mon-Fri
🌐 kanmuseum.org

Korean Cultural Center

⌂ 5505 Wilshire Blvd
🕐 9am-5pm Mon-Fri
🌐 kccla.org

13

The Southwest Museum of the American Indian

📍 X4 ⌂ 234 Museum Dr
🕐 10am-4pm Sat
🌐 theautry.org

A part of the Autry Museum of the American West *(p135)*, this museum is one of the oldest in Los Angeles and is officially named the Historic Southwest Museum Mount Washington Campus. It was founded by Charles Fletcher Lummis, a writer, ethnographer, and prolific historian of the southwestern United States. In 1884, Lummis walked from Ohio to California in a pair of knickerbockers and street shoes to take a job as a reporter for the *Los Angeles Times*, and sent reports to the newspaper chronicling his trip. During his journey, he gained a deep appreciation for both the natural beauty and cultural diversity of the Southwest, where he remained for the rest of his life. In 1903, Lummis set out to create "a great, characteristic Southern California museum," which opened in 1914 with halls of conchology and Asian and European art, displays of Southwestern and California archaeological materials, and two libraries.

In the 1920s the museum narrowed its focus to anthropology and the cultural history and prehistory of the Indigenous peoples of the Americas, work it continues to this day.

14

El Mercado

📍 X5 ⌂ 3425 E 1st St
📞 (323) 268-3451
🕐 9am-8pm daily

East Los Angeles is the heart of the Mexican American community, and this marketplace is a favorite with the locals. It has three floors that bustle with taco vendors, *mariachis* (Mexican street musicians), and families out for a meal. Unlike Olvera Street *(p116)*, found to the north of LA, El Mercado was not intended as a tourist spot. Its best attractions include authentic Mexican food and regional music. On the main floor, stands offer everything from chilies to snack food. A *tortillaria* sells fresh, hot tortillas; bakeries display traditional Mexican breads and pastries; and delis offer meats you may never have seen before. To hear the *mariachis*, go to the mezzanine level, where the cafeteria-style restaurants are located.

In the Whittier district to the southeast, the Latin American Walk of Fame honors historic Latin American figures, from labor activist César Chávez to baseball pitcher Fernando Valenzuela, with circular sun plaques in the sidewalks of Whittier Blvd.

← Colorful vase on display at the Southwest Museum of the American Indian

---

15

Watts Towers Arts Center

X6 **1727 E 107th St, Watts** **For restoration until further notice** **wattstowers.org**

Watts Towers is a masterpiece of folk art that embodies the perseverance and vision of Simon Rodia, an artist and tile-worker born in Campania, Italy and settled in LA in 1895. It is the world's largest single construction created by one individual. Between 1921 and 1954, Rodia sculpted steel rods and pipes into a huge skeletal framework. At its highest point, the structure reaches 100 ft (30 m). Rodia adorned the towers' cement facades with seashells, tiles, china, and glass. He never gave a reason for building the towers and, upon finishing, he deeded the land to a neighbor and left Los Angeles.

Despite several attempts to have Watts Towers razed, it is now a State Historic Site. It stands as a symbol of hope in this area that, in 1965, was the site of the worst riots in LA.

Adjacent to the monument is the Watts Towers Arts Center. This complex displays temporary exhibitions of work by African American artists in the community and hosts workshops for artists of all ages.

South LA, which includes the Watts area, was once known for high poverty and crime rates. Today it is a relatively safe neighborhood, although visitors are advised to take the same common-sense precautions that they would take anywhere.

While the entire site undergoes restoration until further notice, free guided tours operate outside the fence (Thu to Sun).

← The iconic Watts Towers, built in the mid-1900s by an Italian folk artist

↑ A kaleidoscopic mural decorating a building in the LA Arts District

INSIDER TIP
Flower Market

In the hours before sunrise the city's florists flock to this two-block-long area to buy wholesale flowers and plants. The huge range offered includes California varieties, but also plants from Colombia, New Zealand, France, and Holland. Arrive early – supplies tend to sell out quickly.

16

LA Arts District

X5 **East of Downtown**

The flourishing Arts District, located roughly east of Little Tokyo and west of the LA River, has become one of the hippest destinations on the West Coast. Former factories and abandoned warehouses have been converted into stylish galleries, artists' studios, and trendy boutiques. Showcasing urban art, many of the warehouses are painted with vibrant murals, making this a colorful district to walk around. The area is also dotted with specialty coffee roasters and some of the most fashionable restaurants and bars in the city. The neighborhood has emerged as a popular home for local artists and film and TV professionals.

Among the venues worth visiting is the A+D Architecture & Design Museum *(900 E 4th St)*, which organizes eclectic cross-disciplinary exhibitions. Just around the corner, the Hauser & Wirth gallery *(901 E 3rd St)* offers a dynamic events program ranging from artist-led conversations to film screenings – all within a former flour mill. About a mile south, the Institute of Contemporary Art *(1717 E 7th St)* has galleries open for free viewings, as does ArtMovement's Project Space *(2049 S Santa Fe Av)*, known for its pop-up exhibitions.

Echo Park and Silver Lake

W4 & X5

Located north of Downtown, these two diverse, low-key Eastside neighborhoods and hipster enclaves are loaded with cool cafés, bars and restaurants, and quirky sites to discover.

Echo Park is famously home to Dodger Stadium. Its downtown side includes Echo Park Lake, which offers swan pedal boats for rent, and Baxter Stairs, a zigzagging 231-step stairway to Elysian Park, where trails and the birdlife-rich Chavez Ravine Arboretum afford fabulous views over Los Angeles.

In Silver Lake, you can stroll the path around the rehabilitated Silver Lake Reservoir, then check out the Neutra VDL Studio and Residences *(2300 Silver Lake Blvd)*: the

→

A statue on the banks of tranquil, palm-lined Echo Park Lake

iconic Modernist home of famed architect Richard Neutra and justifiably a National Historic Landmark.

Dodger Stadium

X5 **1000 Vin Scully Av (at Stadium Way)**
Tickets: (323) 224-1471
For games and special events only **mlb.com/dodgers**

This baseball stadium has a huge capacity, seating 56,000 spectators. Built in 1962 for the Brooklyn team, which had moved to LA in 1958, the stadium has a cantilevered design that guarantees every seat an unobstructed view of the action on the field.

From the stadium there are equally impressive panoramic views of the city. To the south is downtown LA and to the north and east are the San Gabriel Mountains. The stadium underwent a multimillion-dollar renovation in 2008, resulting in a sleek, contemporary, and luxurious sports venue.

LONG BEACH, SAN PEDRO, AND PALOS VERDES

Originally Tongva land, the Los Angeles coastline and Palos Verdes Peninsula was divided up into ranches by Spanish settlers in the 1780s. This farmland was further subdivided and developed in the 1880s. In 1897, one of these ranches – Rancho Los Cerritos – was incorporated as the city of Long Beach and soon abandoned cattle and sheep for oil and manufacturing. The Port of Long Beach was established in 1911 and today forms America's largest container hub along with the adjacent Port of Los Angeles, which opened in San Pedro in 1907.

San Pedro emerged as a small fishing community and harbor in the 19th century, and was connected to downtown Los Angeles by rail in 1868. The construction of the port brought a huge influx of foreign labor and the city is proudly multicultural, with the largest Italian American community in Southern California, and sizeable Croatian and Norwegian diasporas.

The hilly tracts on the Palos Verdes Peninsula were some of the last areas to be developed. Palos Verdes Estates – the city situated on the peninsula – was master-planned by celebrated American architect Frederick Law Olmsted Jr. in the 1920s. Today the peninsula is sprinkled with relatively affluent communities.

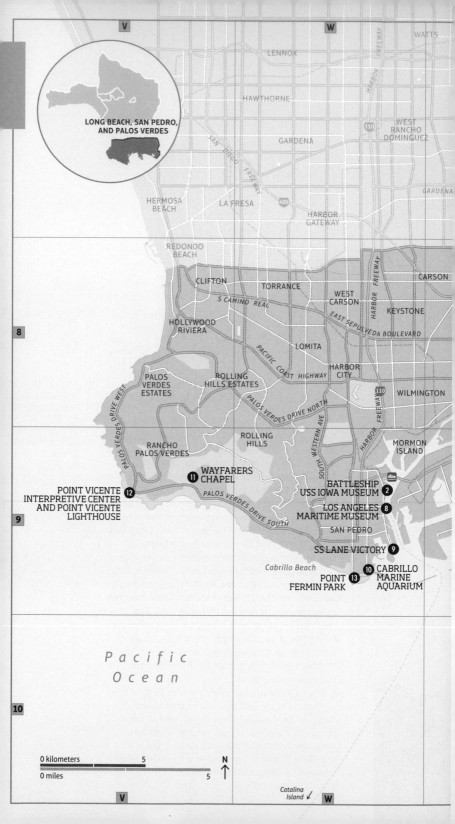

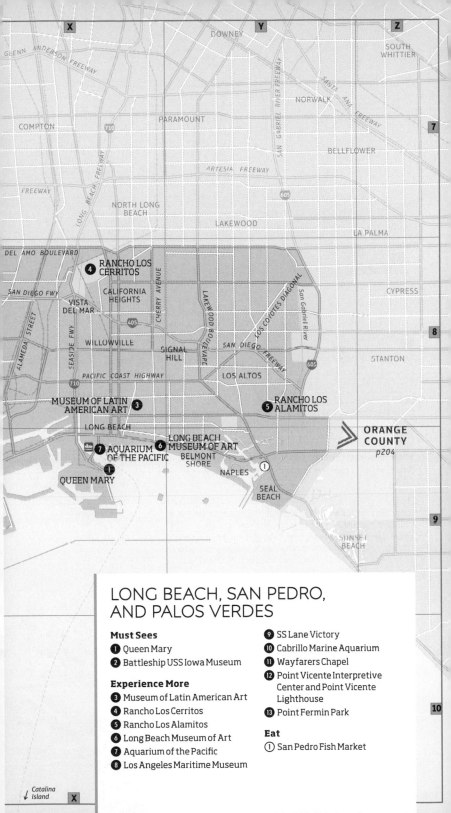

LONG BEACH, SAN PEDRO, AND PALOS VERDES

Must Sees
1. Queen Mary
2. Battleship USS Iowa Museum

Experience More
3. Museum of Latin American Art
4. Rancho Los Cerritos
5. Rancho Los Alamitos
6. Long Beach Museum of Art
7. Aquarium of the Pacific
8. Los Angeles Maritime Museum
9. SS Lane Victory
10. Cabrillo Marine Aquarium
11. Wayfarers Chapel
12. Point Vicente Interpretive Center and Point Vicente Lighthouse
13. Point Fermin Park

Eat
1. San Pedro Fish Market

ORANGE COUNTY p204

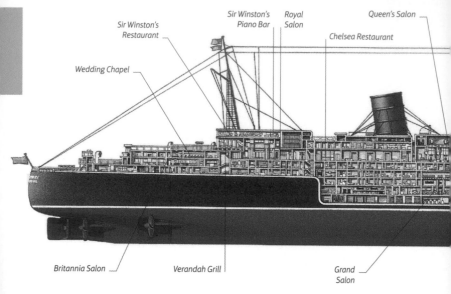

Sir Winston's Piano Bar

Royal Salon

Queen's Salon

Sir Winston's Restaurant

Chelsea Restaurant

Wedding Chapel

Britannia Salon

Verandah Grill

Grand Salon

QUEEN MARY

📍 X9 🏨 Pier J, 1126 Queens Hwy, Long Beach
🔧 For renovation, check website 🌐 queenmary.com

Named after the wife of British King George V, this enormous liner – now a floating museum, hotel, and entertainment center – set new standards in ocean travel with its maiden voyage of May 27, 1936.

The jewel in the crown of the Cunard White Star Line, the *Queen Mary* sailed regularly from Southampton, England to New York City. On its five-day trips, the liner carried an average of 3,000 passengers and crew. There were two swimming pools, two chapels, a synagogue, a gym, a ballroom, and playrooms for children. Anyone who was anyone sailed on the *Queen Mary*, from royalty to Hollywood stars.

From 1939 to 1946, it was converted into a troopship called the *Grey Ghost*, carrying more than 800,000 soldiers during its wartime career. At the end of the war, it transported more than 22,000 war brides and children to the US during "Operation Diaper."

In 1967, the liner was bought by the City of Long Beach and permanently docked for use as a hotel and tourist attraction. Today visitors can view the original engine room, examples of the different travel accommodations, and an exhibition on the war years. Many of the original Art Deco features, created by more than 30 artists, still decorate the interior. The Grand Salon and Observation Lounge are fine examples of period styling.

1,001

The number of transatlantic crossings made by the *Queen Mary* between 1936 and 1967.

→

The *Queen Mary* permanently moored in Long Beach at the mouth of the Los Angeles River

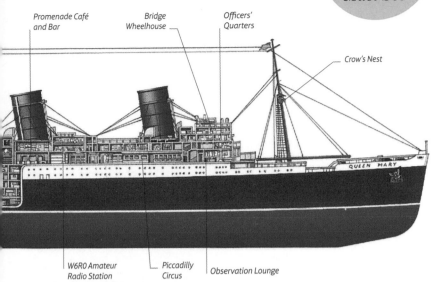

Promenade Café and Bar

Bridge Wheelhouse

Officers' Quarters

Crow's Nest

QUEEN MARY

W6RO Amateur Radio Station

Piccadilly Circus

Observation Lounge

↑ Illustration of the *Queen Mary* ocean liner, Long Beach's most famous landmark

← Original controls on display inside the *Queen Mary*'s engine room

INSIDER TIP
Tours and Events

The excellent Glory Days Historical Tour takes place daily, lasting about one hour, and whisks visitors around some of the most historic rooms on the ship. Murder mystery dinner shows, Sunday brunches, and other events also take place regularly (book via the website).

BATTLESHIP USS IOWA MUSEUM

⊞ W9 **⌂ 250 S Harbor Blvd, San Pedro** **⊙ 10am–5pm daily**
⊘ Thanksgiving, Dec 25 **🖥 pacificbattleship.com**

Launched on August 27, 1942, this massive WWII-era battleship was one of the last of its kind commissioned by the US Navy. USS *Iowa* saw action in the Atlantic and Pacific oceans, and later in the Korean War, and today thrills visitors at its berth on the LA Waterfront.

Weighing 55,450 tons and covered in armor plating more than 12 inches (30 cm) thick, the 887-ft- (270-m-) long USS *Iowa* was the world's second-largest battleship after the *Yamato* when it was constructed. Capable of 33 knots (38 mph/ 61 km/h), she served for more than 50 years. Decommissioned in 1994, the ship now serves as a floating museum, with interactive exhibits, including a kid-friendly scavenger hunt. The self-guided tour takes in the bridge, gun turrets, and missile decks, or you can take a tour with a US Navy veteran to gain an in-depth understanding of life at sea.

> **💬 INSIDER TIP**
> **Heli-Fun**
>
> Look out for the Piasecki HUP-2 Retriever Helicopter on the ship's flight deck. Battleship Flight – A Naval Aviation Experience lets you "fly" a twin-rotor HUP helicopter in a virtual reality flight simulator. If that doesn't take your fancy, you can also choose from five other VR in-flight experiences.

[1] The USS *Iowa* is armed with nine guns, each 66 ft (20 m) long.

[2] Veterans show visitors around the ship, explaining its history.

[3] The ship is docked alongside other vessels.

BATTLESHIP OF PRESIDENTS

One of the *Iowa*'s most important missions was to ferry President Franklin D. Roosevelt to Algeria en route to meet with Winston Churchill and Josef Stalin at the Tehran Conference in 1943. A guided 45-minute President's Tour reveals fascinating insights from this top-secret voyage. Various modifications had to be made to the *Iowa* in secret at Norfolk Navy Yard in Portsmouth, Virginia before the voyage. Being a wheelchair user due to polio, Roosevelt couldn't use the shower in the Captain's Cabin, so a bathtub - the only one aboard a US Navy vessel - was installed, as well as an elevator shaft between decks.

↑ The hulking USS *Iowa*, now an important museum of military history

EXPERIENCE MORE

3

Museum of Latin American Art

🚩 X8 🏠 628 Alamitos Av, Long Beach ⏰ 11am–5pm Wed–Sun (to 9pm Thu) 🌐 molaa.org

Dedicated to modern and contemporary Latin American art and culture, the Museum of Latin American Art (MOLAA) is located in a sun-drenched building designed by Mexican architect Manuel Rosen in the city's East Village Arts District. MOLAA's building is integrated with a 1920s roller-skating rink, hence its high vaulted ceiling and beautiful wooden floor. The permanent collection has more than 1,600 exhibits. At its core is the Long Gallery, which displays one work by an artist from every Latin American country. Temporary exhibitions and special events take place regularly.

> MOLAA's building is integrated with a 1920s roller-skating rink, hence its high vaulted ceiling and beautiful wooden floor.

4

Rancho Los Cerritos

🚩 X8 🏠 4600 Virginia Rd ⏰ 1–5pm Wed–Fri & Sun, 10am–5pm Sat 🚫 Jan 1, Easter Sun, Thanksgiving, Dec 25 🌐 rancholos cerritos.org

Rancho Los Cerritos was once part of a 470-sq-mile (1,200-sq-km) land grant, given between 1784 and 1790 to Spanish soldier Manuel Nieto. Mission San Gabriel reclaimed nearly half of the property in 1790, and the rest was left to Nieto's children on his death in 1804. In 1844 John Temple bought the ranch, built the two-story adobe house, and later sold it to the firm Flint, Bixby & Co. The ranch was gradually sold off, but in 1955 the City of Long Beach bought the house and its remaining land. Today it is a museum,

focusing on those who lived here from 1840 to 1940. The Monterey-style house *(p30)* is furnished to reflect the interiors typical of the late 1870s. Guided tours take place on Saturdays and Sundays.

---

 ⑤

Rancho Los Alamitos

📍Y8 🏠6400 Bixby Hill Rd 🕐1–5pm Wed–Sun ⊘Jan 1, Easter Sun, Thanksgiving, Dec 25 🌐rancholosalamitos.com

On a mesa inhabited since AD 500, the site of Rancho Los Alamitos formed part of the Manuel Nieto land grant in 1790. The house was built in the early 19th century and changed hands frequently until it was bought by the Bixby family firm in 1881. In 1968 the ranch was given to the City of Long Beach, and today the house, furnished as it was in the 1920s and 1930s, forms a museum of the area's history. The grounds are an example of a pioneer garden.

 ↑ Whale sculpture hanging from the ceiling in the Aquarium of the Pacific

⑥

Long Beach Museum of Art

📍X9 🏠2300 E Ocean Blvd, Long Beach 🕐11am–5pm Thu–Sun 🌐lbma.org

Set atop a bluff overlooking the Pacific Ocean and the port, the Long Beach Museum of Art (LBMA) occupies a 1911 Craftsman-style house and a modern two-story pavilion. It exhibits American decorative arts and early 20th-century European works, as well as contemporary Californian art drawn from its collection of more than 3,200 pieces. Highlights include abstract works by Vasily Kandinsky, sculptures by Peter Voulkos, furniture by Charles and Ray Eames, and a wide range of Staffordshire ceramics dating from the 17th to the 19th centuries. The Sculpture Garden shows works by Californian artists.

Claire's at the Museum Restaurant has an outdoor dining area surrounding a water sculpture by Claire Falkenstein, with magnificent ocean views.

Located at 356 E 3rd St, LBMA Downtown is an off-shoot of the museum and showcases dynamic works by local Long Beach artists.

⑦

Aquarium of the Pacific

📍X9 🏠100 Aquarium Way, Long Beach 🕐9am–6pm daily ⊘Long Beach's Grand Prix weekend (Apr), Dec 25 🌐aquariumofpacific.org

One of the largest aquariums in the US guides visitors on a journey through the Pacific's three major regions: Southern California, the Tropical Pacific, and the Northern Pacific.

> **LONG BEACH OPERA**
>
> Founded in 1979, the Long Beach Opera company *(www.long beachopera.org)* has hosted countless great singers, such as Jerome Hines, Ruth Ann Swenson, James Morris, and Jerry Hadley. It's known for its wide-ranging repertoire, from established classics to lesser-known works, and radical artistic innovations character-ized by visual drama. The company performs at various venues across the Long Beach area, including the Aquarium of the Pacific.

 ↓ The colorful building housing the Museum of Latin American Art

8

Los Angeles Maritime Museum

📍 W9 🏛 Berth 84, 6th St, San Pedro 🕐 10am–5pm Tue–Sun 🚫 Easter Sun, Thanksgiving, Dec 25 🌐 lamaritimemuseum.org

Housed in a restored ferry terminal building, the Los Angeles Maritime Museum contains an array of nautical paintings and memorabilia, including a wooden figure-head of British Queen Victoria. Highlights of the exhibition include its extensive model ship collection. Also on display is the bow and bridge of US Navy cruiser USS *Los Angeles*, and there are ever-changing temporary exhibitions. Early 20th-century fishing boats from Monterey (*p502*) can be seen in the dock.

9

SS Lane Victory

📍 W9 🏛 Berth 49, 3011 Miner St, San Pedro 🕐 Noon–6pm Wed, 9am–5pm Sat–Sun 🌐 lanevictory.org

Built in San Pedro by the California Shipbuilding Corporation and launched on May 31, 1945, this Victory Class merchant ship served in World War II and the Korean and Vietnam wars, and as a national merchant carrier. After years of deterioration, the vessel was restored and is now a National Historic Landmark and museum. Visitors can explore the entire ship, from the bridge to the engine room, learning how merchant marines of the World War II era lived and worked. Videos bring the ship's engaging history to life.

→

The glass and wood frame of Wayfarers Chapel

Did You Know?

California has some of the most diverse marine life in the world.

10

Cabrillo Marine Aquarium

📍 W9 🏛 3720 Stephen White Dr, San Pedro 🕐 Noon–5pm Wed–Sun 🚫 Thanksgiving, Dec 25 🌐 cabrillomarineaquarium.org

Designed by architect Frank Gehry and surrounded by a geometric chain-link fence, the Cabrillo Marine Aquarium contains a large collection of Southern California marine life, including sharks, moray eels, and rays. The exhibition space is divided into three environments – rocky shores, beaches and mudflats, and open ocean.

An outdoor rock pool tank contains sea cucumbers, sea anemones, urchins, and starfish. Another exhibit shows how human activities have altered Los Angeles Harbor, and a tidal tank allows visitors to see what happens below a wave. All in all, this small aquarium contains an impressive 14,150 gallons (64,400 liters) of circulating seawater.

The Point Vicente headland and its lighthouse ↑

11

Wayfarers Chapel

📍 V9 🏛 5755 Palos Verdes Dr S, Rancho Palos Verdes 🕐 9am–5pm daily 🌐 wayfarerschapel.org

This glass and redwood-framed chapel sits on a hilltop above the ocean. From the street below, all that can be seen is a thin stone and concrete tower rising from the greenery. The chapel was designed in 1949 by architect Lloyd Wright (son of Frank Lloyd Wright) as a natural place of worship, surrounded by trees. Today its charm makes it a popular venue for weddings.

Point Vicente Interpretive Center and Point Vicente Lighthouse

9 V9 **A** Palos Verdes Dr W, Rancho Palos Verdes **C** (310) 544-5375 **O** 10am–5pm daily **Q** Jan 1, Thanksgiving, Dec 24 & 25

No other location along the Southern California coastline has such expansive views as the Point Vicente headland. It is topped by the 67-ft- (20-m-) tall Point Vicente Lighthouse, built in 1926 with a 2-million candlepower Paris-made Fresnel lens dating from 1886 (but removed in 2019). Now automated, the lighthouse still projects a beam 20 miles (32 km) out to sea. Tours are offered once a month.

A path winds north to the Point Vicente Interpretive Center, which has exhibits on the natural and cultural history of the Palos Verdes Peninsula. Emphasis is placed on the Pacific gray whale as the headland is an ideal spot to watch their winter migration from Alaskan waters to the lagoons of Baja California.

Point Fermin Park

9 W9 **A** 807 Paseo del Mar, San Pedro **O** 6:30am–10pm daily **W** laparks.org; pointferminlighthouse.org

This tranquil oceanfront park at the southernmost tip of Los Angeles surrounds the charming Point Fermin Lighthouse, which dates from 1874. A National Historic Landmark, the clapboard lighthouse hasn't been in use since 1941. In 2003, it opened to the public for guided tours – see the lighthouse website for opening hours and tour times.

To the rear, Angels Gate Park's sloping lawns are popular for kite-flying, thanks to consistent winds. However, the main draw here is the Korean Friendship Bell, a massive bronze bell, among the largest in the world, and a blue-tiled traditional pavilion. Both monuments were donated by the Republic of Korea to celebrate the bicentennial of the US in 1976.

The park occupies the site of Fort MacArthur, which once protected Los Angeles Harbor (1914–74). The **Fort MacArthur Museum**, in the galleries of the Battery Osgood-Farley historic site, illustrates the history of LA's coastal defences.

There are spectacular views of Catalina Island from Point Fermin Park, and in winter it is possible to spot migrating gray whales offshore.

Fort MacArthur Museum

 A 3601 S Gaffey St, San Pedro **O** Noon–5pm Tue, Thu, Sat & Sun **Q** Federal hols **W** ftmac.org

---

💬 INSIDER TIP
Whales Ahoy!

Between December and April, spot gray whales as they migrate between Alaska and Baja California to breed. May to November is the best time for seeing magnificent blue whales. Companies such as Harbor Breeze Cruises (www.2seewhales.com) offer trips to see whales and other marine wildlife from Long Beach and nearby harbors.

A SHORT WALK
LONG BEACH

Distance 1.5 miles (2.5 km) **Time** 30 minutes
Nearest metro 1st Street

With palm trees and the ocean as a backdrop, downtown Long Beach is a mixture of carefully restored buildings and modern glass high-rises. At its heart, Pine Avenue still retains the early midwestern charm that gave the city its nickname of "Iowa by the Sea." The lively atmosphere attracts locals, who come to relax, enjoy a cup of espresso, and sample some of the best food in the area. Nearby, Long Beach Convention and Entertainment Center is home to the Terrace Theater, with its respected music and dance programs. As you walk along the ocean, the shops and restaurants in Shoreline Village offer views of the ocean liner the *Queen Mary*.

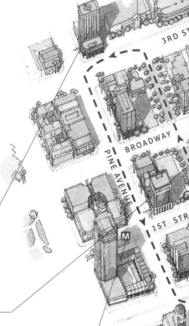

Long Beach Municipal Auditorium Mural *is a 1938 mural of a day at the beach.*

When erected in 1922, the terracotta **Farmers and Merchants Bank Tower** *was Long Beach's first skyscraper. Its hall is a fine example of period styling.*

The Promenade *is the site of Long Beach's farmers' market. Every Friday the street is filled with stands selling fruit, vegetables, and crafts.*

Transit Mall Metro station

The 1929 **Ocean Center Building** *was a key feature of the Pike Amusement Park (or simply The Pike).*

The center of downtown Long Beach, **Pine Avenue** *is lined with stores, cafés, and restaurants. Some of these businesses are housed in historic buildings, such as the 1903 Masonic Temple at No. 230.*

←
The wide boardwalk of Pine Avenue pier, in downtown Long Beach

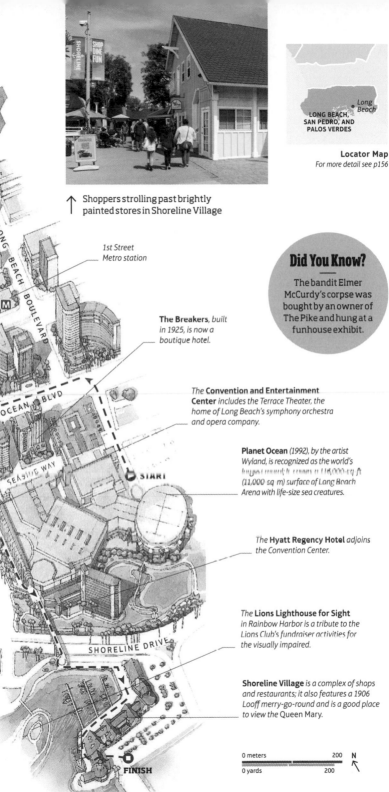

↑ Shoppers strolling past brightly
painted stores in Shoreline Village

Locator Map
For more detail see p156

1st Street
Metro station

Did You Know?

The bandit Elmer
McCurdy's corpse was
bought by an owner of
The Pike and hung at a
funhouse exhibit.

The Breakers, *built
in 1925, is now a
boutique hotel.*

The **Convention and Entertainment
Center** *includes the Terrace Theater, the
home of Long Beach's symphony orchestra
and opera company.*

Planet Ocean *(1992), by the artist
Wyland, is recognized as the world's
largest mural. It covers a 116,000-sq ft
(11,000 sq m) surface of Long Beach
Arena with life-size sea creatures.*

The **Hyatt Regency Hotel** *adjoins
the Convention Center.*

The **Lions Lighthouse for Sight**
*in Rainbow Harbor is a tribute to the
Lions Club's fundraiser activities for
the visually impaired.*

Shoreline Village *is a complex of shops
and restaurants; it also features a 1906
Looff merry-go-round and is a good place
to view the Queen Mary.*

START

FINISH

0 meters 200
0 yards 200

N

A DRIVING TOUR
SOUTH LOS ANGELES COASTLINE

Length 32 miles (52 km) **Stopping-off points** Manhattan Beach, Redondo Beach, and Long Beach have many beachside restaurants and cafés.

The South Los Angeles coastline encompasses popular city beaches and wilder sections of coast, as well as a roster of cultural attractions. The route begins near Manhattan Beach; the shallow waters and wide stretches of sand here are ideal for families. As you drive south you'll hit the rocky bluffs and coves of the Palos Verdes Peninsula, littered with light-houses and state parks. Beyond lie the museums and aquariums of rejuvenated San Pedro and Long Beach, separated by the sprawling dockyards of LA port.

Backed by the coastal cycle path, upscale **Manhattan Beach** *is known for good swimming, surfing, and beach volleyball. The free Roundhouse Aquarium sits at the end of the pier.*

START PLAYA DEL REY WESTCHESTER

Los Angeles International Airport

Dockweiler State Beach

Manhattan Beach

MANHATTAN BEACH

NORTH REDONDO

HERMOSA BEACH

The 1,000-ft- (300-m-) long **Hermosa Beach Pier**, *dating from 1913, offers fabulous views of the coast and ocean.*

Hermosa Beach Pier

Redondo Beach Pier

REDONDO BEACH

Horseshoe-shaped **Redondo Beach Pier** *features numerous restaurants, shops, and entertainment venues. It is adjacent to the International Boardwalk, Redondo Marina, and family-friendly swimming of Seaside Lagoon.*

Torrance County Beach

ROLLING HILLS

The **Wayfarers Chapel** *(p164) is known as "The Glass Church" because of its geometric, light-filled design by architect Lloyd Wright (son of Frank Lloyd Wright).*

RANCHO PALOS VERDES

Wayfarers Chapel

Point Vicente Interpretive Center

Perched on the Palos Verdes Peninsula some 130 ft (40 m) above the rocky shoreline, **Point Vicente Interpretive Center** *(p165) contains informative exhibits on the area's natural and cultural history.*

↑ Redondo Beach Pier, lined with a variety of places to eat, shop, and be entertained

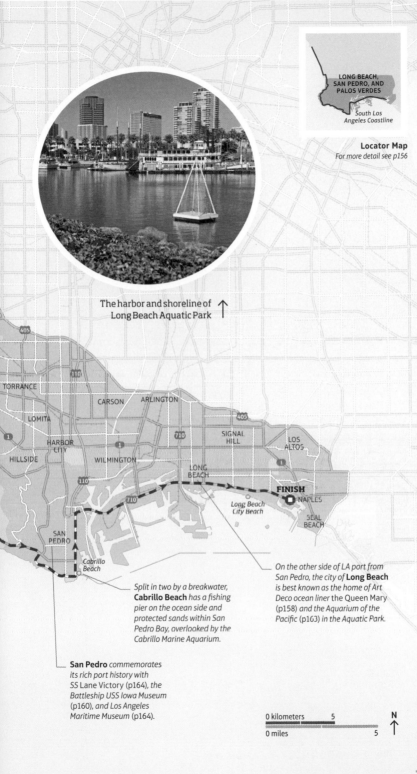

The harbor and shoreline of ↑
Long Beach Aquatic Park

On the other side of LA port from
San Pedro, the city of **Long Beach**
is best known as the home of Art
Deco ocean liner the Queen Mary
(p158) and the Aquarium of the
Pacific (p163) in the Aquatic Park.

Split in two by a breakwater,
Cabrillo Beach has a fishing
pier on the ocean side and
protected sands within San
Pedro Bay, overlooked by the
Cabrillo Marine Aquarium.

San Pedro commemorates
its rich port history with
SS Lane Victory (p164), the
Battleship USS Iowa Museum
(p160), and Los Angeles
Maritime Museum (p164).

0 kilometers   5

0 miles   5

N
↑

SOUTHERN CALIFORNIA

Paragliders floating over Black's Beach, La Jolla, San Diego

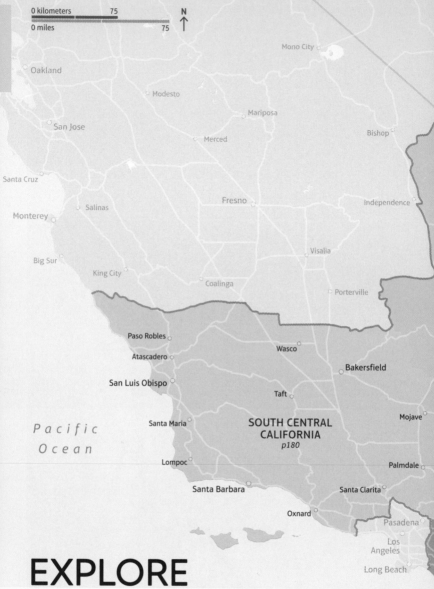

EXPLORE
SOUTHERN
CALIFORNIA

This guide divides Southern California into five color-coded sightseeing areas, as shown on this map. Find out more about each area on the following pages.

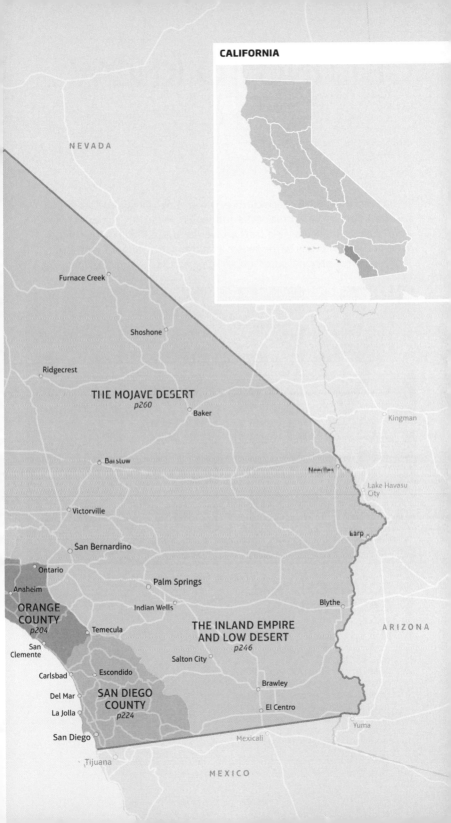

GETTING TO KNOW SOUTHERN CALIFORNIA

Surf towns, a laid-back beach culture, snowcapped peaks, and scorching deserts: Southern California packs enormous variety into a relatively small area. From the museums and craft breweries of San Diego to the theme parks of Orange County to the twisted cacti and salt pans of Death Valley and Joshua Tree national parks, each region has its own unique flavor.

SOUTH CENTRAL CALIFORNIA

PAGE 180

A region of small, affluent towns, South Central California encompasses a beautiful coastline and the heavily farmed southern end of the San Joaquin Valley. Its Spanish heritage is highly visible, especially in Santa Barbara, with its red-tile Mission Revival-style architecture. To the north, Santa Ynez is an up-and-coming wine-growing area, while at San Simeon the opulent Hearst Castle®, built by millionaire William Randolph Hearst, is a historical landmark. Inland, Bakersfield has its own country music scene, and the Kern River offers exhilarating white-water rafting.

Best for
Beaches, seafood, Mission Revival architecture, and live country music

Home to
Santa Barbara, Hearst Castle®

Experience
A wine tour of the Santa Ynez Valley

ORANGE COUNTY

The subject of countless movies, documentaries, and reality TV shows, much of Orange County today serves as suburbs to LA, its population of three million enjoying perennial sunshine and a high standard of living. Though the primary attraction is Disneyland® Resort, the coastline is lined with wide, sandy beaches and a succession of legendary surfing haunts, marinas, and artists' enclaves. Inland, open spaces can be found in the chaparral-covered Santa Ana Mountains.

Best for
Beaches, theme parks, and art museums

Home to
Disneyland® Resort, Knott's Berry Farm and Soak City, Mission San Juan Capistrano, Catalina Island

Experience
Surfing off Huntington Beach Pier

→

PAGE 224

SAN DIEGO COUNTY

With its affluent beach communities, serious surfers, and seemingly perfect, year-round weather, San Diego County is the California of popular imagination. Its appeal goes far beyond major showstoppers like Mission Beach and San Diego Zoo Safari Park to the historic Old Town and Gaslamp quarters and a clutch of fine museums in Balboa Park. North of the city, the rugged Pacific Coast is lined with arty seaside towns such as Encinitas, while inland, historic mining settlements such as Julian lie within the tranquil mountains of the Peninsular Ranges.

Best for
Surfing, Italian food, Spanish settler history and architecture, and craft beer

Home to
San Diego, Balboa Park

Experience
A tour of the local microbreweries

PAGE 246

THE INLAND EMPIRE AND LOW DESERT

The landscape here is one of the most varied in California – the terrain can change from pine forest to searing desert in just a few miles. At the heart of the region is Palm Springs, with luxurious resorts, art museums, and verdant golf courses. To the east lies Joshua Tree National Park, a land of giant yuccas, hot, dry days, and immense outcrops of rock. Farther south is the salty Salton Sea lake and arid Anza-Borrego Desert State Park.

Best for
Modernist architecture, Palm Springs' LGBTQ+ culture, shopping, and desert national parks

Home to
Palm Springs, Joshua Tree National Park

Experience
A night camping in the desert in Joshua Tree National Park

PAGE 260

THE MOJAVE DESERT

The mythical landscapes of the Mojave Desert present an arid, otherworldly terrain of brilliantly colored, bizarrely eroded rocks, mountains, and sand dunes. For a few weeks each year, when yellow and orange wildflowers appear amid the arid hills, it becomes hauntingly beautiful. Broiling Death Valley National Park is the region's main attraction, along with wonderfully preserved sections of Route 66. The rest of the desert is peppered with ghost towns, abandoned mining shacks, and giant US military bases.

Best for
Classic Americana, desert landscapes, cinder cones and giant dunes, ghost towns

Home to
Death Valley National Park

Experience
Driving the original Route 66

1 The desert town of Palm Springs, Coachella Valley.

2 Sunset view at Zabriskie Point, Death Valley.

3 The iconic Alien Fresh Jerky store in Baker.

4 Pool at the Inn at Death Valley, Furnace Creek.

4 DAYS
in the Desert

Day 1

The resort town of Palm Springs (p250) is the perfect place to start your tour of the California deserts. First, visit the Palm Springs Art Museum, with its world-class contemporary works. Lunch on a burger at hotspot Kaiser Grille (www.kaisergrille.com). In the afternoon head 20 miles (30 km) southeast of town to learn about desert ecosystems as you wander the trails of The Living Desert Zoo and Botanical Garden (p255). End the day sampling the bars and clubs of downtown Palm Springs before retiring to the Three Fifty Hotel (www.thethreefiftyhotel.com).

Day 2

Set off early into the High Desert via Yucca Valley (p255) and Pioneertown, which was built in 1947 as a Western movie film set. Then drive north into Joshua Tree National Park (p252) and stop for a hike past bristling Joshua trees and eerie rock formations. A little north of here is Twentynine Palms, with the charming Kitchen in the Desert (kitchen inthedesert.com), a perfect spot for lunch. After lunch, continue north to Amboy (p268) and stop for photos of the iconic Googie architecture of Roy's Motel & Café on Route 66. Then spend the rest of the afternoon traversing the arid Mojave National Preserve, admiring or climbing the Kelso Dunes (p268) and the ancient lava flows of Cinder Cone National Natural Landmark (p269). Grab a snack from the kooky Alien Fresh Jerky store (www.alien freshjerky.com) in the tiny

town of Baker, before driving north and ending the day with a refreshingly therapeutic bathe at Tecopa Hot Springs Resort (www.tecopa hotsprings.org).

Day 3

Heading north through the Mojave Desert, enter Death Valley National Park (p264) at Shoshone. Begin exploring the major sites south to north, being sure to include Badwater Basin – the lowest point in North America (p264) – the baking salt pans of Devil's Golf Course (p264), multi-hued Artist's Palette (p267), and the Furnace Creek Visitor Center (p264), where you can have lunch at the Western-themed Last Kind Words Saloon & Steakhouse (www.oasisatdeathvalley.com). In the afternoon drive out to Dante's View overlook, timing the ride back to Furnace Creek to catch sunset at Zabriskie Point. Stay overnight at the Inn at Death Valley at the mouth of Furnace Creek (p265).

Day 4

Start the day by exploring the remains of the Harmony Borax Works at the Borax Museum (p265) before driving north for a guided tour of Scotty's Castle (p266), a beautiful 1920s ranch. Then walk the rim of Uhebebe Crater (p266), an ancient volcanic cone, before returning to Furnace Creek and exiting the Death Valley National park at Panamint Springs. From here you can drive south towards LA via the ghost town of Randsburg and rejoin Route 66 at Barstow (p268).

SOUTH CENTRAL CALIFORNIA

Present-day Santa Barbara and the Channel Islands were inhabited by the Chumash and their ancestors for some 13,000 years. After the arrival of the Spanish in the 18th century, the Chumash population declined. The area's Spanish heritage is highly visible, no more so than in Santa Barbara, which was founded as a military garrison or "presidio" in 1782. The legendary structure that came to be known as "Queen of the Missions" was built four years later. Santa Barbara became a seaside resort from the late 1870s, but was devastated by a major earthquake in 1925. In the aftermath, virtually the entire city was rebuilt to look like a Spanish town. The city's red-tiled, Mission Revival-style architecture has been imitated throughout the state ever since.

In the early part of the 20th century much of the Central Coast became a popular vacation destination, drawing thousands of people each summer to seaside towns such as Pismo and Avila Beach. At San Simeon, millionaire William Randolph Hearst built his own personal playground, Hearst Castle®, between 1919 and 1947.

Inland, Bakersfield has its roots in a farm and stagecoach rest stop built by the eponymous Colonel Thomas Baker in 1863. Oil was discovered in the region in 1899 and today Kern County, of which Bakersfield is the county seat, produces 10 percent of all US output. The agricultural sector also remains strong, with Bakersfield acting as the hub of a vast network of orange, pistachio, and almond groves.

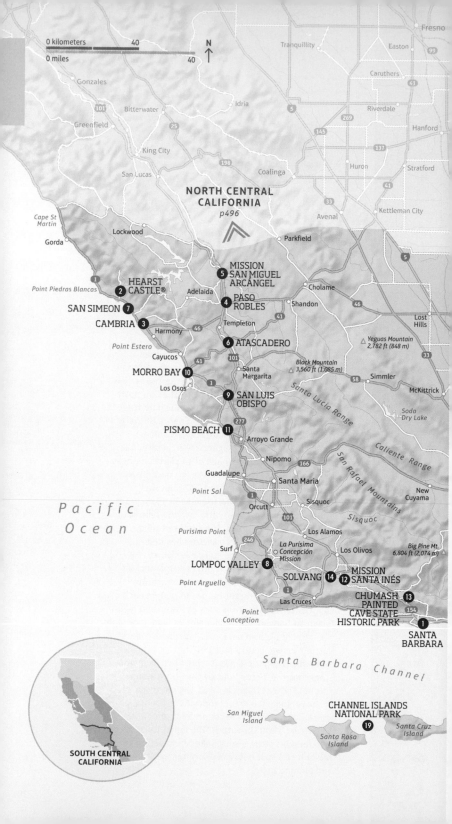

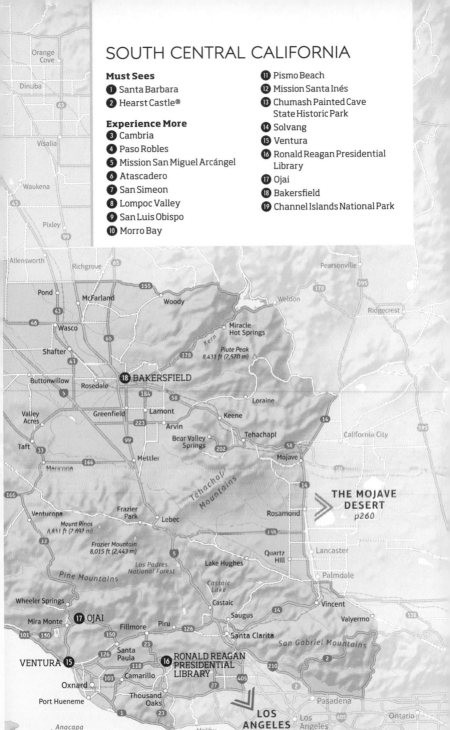

SOUTH CENTRAL CALIFORNIA

Must Sees
1. Santa Barbara
2. Hearst Castle®

Experience More
3. Cambria
4. Paso Robles
5. Mission San Miguel Arcángel
6. Atascadero
7. San Simeon
8. Lompoc Valley
9. San Luis Obispo
10. Morro Bay
11. Pismo Beach
12. Mission Santa Inés
13. Chumash Painted Cave State Historic Park
14. Solvang
15. Ventura
16. Ronald Reagan Presidential Library
17. Ojai
18. Bakersfield
19. Channel Islands National Park

↑ Mediterranean-style architecture lining the Santa Barbara coastline

❶

SANTA BARBARA

🅐D6 ✈Santa Barbara Airport, 8 miles (13 km) N of Santa Barbara 🚌34 W Carrillo 🚊Stearns Wharf 🛈1 Garden St; www.santabarbaraca.com

Santa Barbara is a Southern Californian rarity: a city with one main architectural style. Following a devastating earthquake in 1925, the center was rebuilt according to strict rules that dictated Mediterranean-style architecture. The original city was founded as a Spanish garrison in 1782. During the 19th century Santa Barbara was a quiet pueblo; a handful of adobes from that era have survived. Today Santa Barbara is a favorite resort with sand beaches, fine cafés and restaurants, boutiques, and art galleries.

①

Santa Barbara Museum of Art

🅐1130 State St 🕙11am–5pm Tue-Sun (to 8pm Thu) 🚫Federal hols 🌐sbma.net

This outstanding art collection includes Asian art, antiquities, American art, contemporary regional art, prints, drawings, and photography.

②

County Courthouse

🅐1100 Anacapa St 🕙8am–5pm Mon-Fri, 10am–4:30pm Sat & Sun

The 1929 Spanish Revival-style courthouse is still in use. It is decorated with Tunisian tiles and wrought-iron metal-work. Murals by Californian illustrator Dan Sayre

Groesbeck in the Mural Room depict California history. There are panoramic views from the clock tower. Free guided tours take place daily.

③

El Presidio de Santa Bárbara State Historic Park

🅐123 E Canon Perdido St 🕙10:30am–4:30pm daily 🌐parks.ca.gov

When the crown of Spain populated Alta California to protect it from encroaching Russian and British interests along the coast, it did so in three ways: the establishment of missions, pueblos, and presidios. Santa Barbara's strategic location between San Diego and Monterey was an ideal site for a presidio, the last of four to be built in California beginning in 1782. It served as a military head-quarters and regional center of government well into the 19th century.

Neglect and natural disasters eventually brought down the adobe brick pueblo, but two buildings have survived and remain relatively well preserved. The Cañedo Adobe, former residence of a non-commissioned officer during the Mexican period, now serves as the park's headquarters where you can pick up information about the park. Dating from 1788, El Cuartel Adobe is the oldest remaining building in Santa Barbara and the second oldest in the state of California. It now holds historical exhibits. Other rooms re-create the sparsely furnished commander's quarters and an unsophisticated *cocina* (kitchen).

④ Casa de la Guerra

🏠 15 E De La Guerra St
🕐 Noon-4pm Tue-Sun
🌐 sbthp.org

Built in the 1820s by José de la Guerra, the fifth Presidio commander, this historic, whitewashed adobe is now a restored house museum. In the early days of Santa Barbara the house would have served an important role in community events. Twelve rooms, situated around a courtyard, are furnished with antiques of the era and hold rotating exhibits dedicated to early California history and Hispanic heritage. Still serving as a traditional civic gathering place, the front of the casa is where Santa Barbara holds community events and festivals.

⑤ Santa Barbara Historical Museum

🏠 136 E De La Guerra St
🕐 Noon-5pm Wed, Fri & Sat, noon-7pm Thu 🕐 Federal hols 🌐 sbhistorical.org

The Santa Barbara Historical Museum's collections encompass local history and are housed in two adobe buildings. The collections include paintings, furniture, saddles, decorative arts, and costumes spanning some 500 years of history, from the days of the Chumash, to Mexican and Spanish rule and the American era. Among the many artifacts is a statue of the 4th-century martyr St. Barbara.

⑥ The Waterfront

📍 132A Harbor Way; www.santabarbaraca.gov

Scattered palm trees along a promenade, boat masts bobbing in the harbor, the Santa Ynez Mountains to one side and the vast Pacific Ocean on the other: Santa Barbara's Waterfront is the quintessential California postcard scene. Boat tours, kayaking, surfing, lounging on the beach, or riding a bike are just a few choices on the activity menu. Take a short walk out to the end of Stearns Wharf, thought to be the oldest wooden pier in California, dating back to 1872. Sometimes you can spot sea lions down below.

URBAN WINE TRAIL

Grape vines thrive in Santa Barbara, where mineral-rich soil and a mild climate help the grapes reach perfection. Over 30 of the city's wineries have tasting rooms in the center of town, where you can sample world-class Pinot Noir and Chardonnay varieties. Most are located in the hip Funk Zone, right between Highway 101 and the Amtrak station, and up in the historic Presidio neighborhood. A shuttle runs along State Street between the two areas *(www.urbanwinetrailsb.com)*.

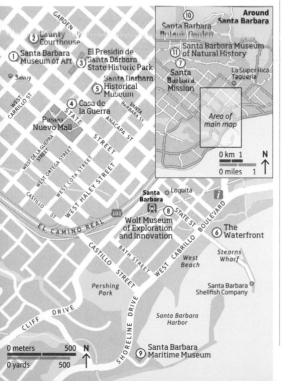

7

Santa Barbara Mission

📍 2201 Laguna St ⏰ 9:30am–5pm daily (last tour 4:15pm) 🌐 santabarbaramission.org

Labeled the "Queen of the Missions," Santa Barbara is the most visited mission in the state. Founded in 1786 on the feast day of St. Barbara, and in use ever since, it was the tenth mission built by the Spanish (p47). The third adobe church on the site was destroyed by an earthquake in 1812, and the present structure was completed in 1820. Its twin towers and mix of Roman, Moorish, and Spanish styles served as the main inspiration for what came to be known as Mission Style. The mission was again hit by an earthquake in 1925, and the entire front was rebuilt in 1953.

8

Wolf Museum of Exploration and Innovation

📍 125 State St ⏰ 10am–5pm daily; advance reservations recommended 🌐 moxi.org

Kids and adults can engage with science through play in this activity-filled museum. It's three stories of fun where you can build and launch a rocket, design and race a car, and step inside a giant guitar. The museum provides all the tools to discover the laws of light, aerodynamics, or kinetics. At Sky Garden, the open-air top floor, science themes cover wind, sound, and water. You can experiment with the concept of fluid dynamics at Whitewater, an interactive water feature, or peer through five different scopes in the Lookout Tower.

9

Santa Barbara Maritime Museum

📍 113 Harbor Way, Ste 190 ⏰ 10am–5pm Sun-Tue & Thu-Fri, 9am–3pm Sat 🌐 sbmm.org

Perfectly located at the Santa Barbara Waterfront, everything about the maritime history of the central coast is presented through compelling and interactive exhibits. Visitors can learn how the early Chumash people built their canoes, the environmental impact of oil extraction, and even the history of surfing. Sit in the sport-fishing simulator, pick the fish you want to land, and when the rod starts jerking, reel in your fish. Little ones will enjoy peering through a working US Navy periscope or watching films on the deep sea.

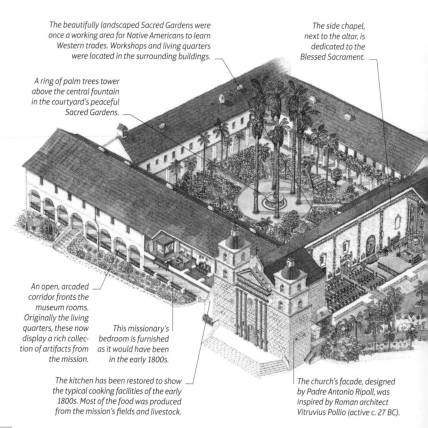

The beautifully landscaped Sacred Gardens were once a working area for Native Americans to learn Western trades. Workshops and living quarters were located in the surrounding buildings.

The side chapel, next to the altar, is dedicated to the Blessed Sacrament.

A ring of palm trees tower above the central fountain in the courtyard's peaceful Sacred Gardens.

An open, arcaded corridor fronts the museum rooms. Originally the living quarters, these now display a rich collection of artifacts from the mission.

This missionary's bedroom is furnished as it would have been in the early 1800s.

The kitchen has been restored to show the typical cooking facilities of the early 1800s. Most of the food was produced from the mission's fields and livestock.

The church's facade, designed by Padre Antonio Ripoll, was inspired by Roman architect Vitruvius Pollio (active c. 27 BC).

Conservation center at the Santa Barbara Botanic Garden in Mission Canyon

EAT

La Super Rica Taqueria
Authentic Mexican taqueria where the tortillas are freshly made and the meat slow cooked.

🏠 622 N Milpas
📞 (805) 963-4940

Santa Barbara Shellfish Company
A homey shack at the end of Stearns Wharf. Indulge in crab sandwiches, lobster tacos, or clam linguine while gazing at the Pacific.

🏠 230 Stearns Wharf
🌐 shellfishco.com

Savoy
A local favorite, with an astonishing variety of ingredients on offer to build your own salad or order from a set menu. Breakfast is one of the best in town.

🏠 24 W Figueroa St 🕐 Sun
🌐 savoycafe.weebly.com

Loquita
Spanish-influenced tapas, paella, and wood-fired meats and seafood served with flair in a romantic atmosphere.

🏠 202 State St
🌐 loquitasb.com

$$$

---

⑩ 🚴 Ⓜ 🖥 🛍

Santa Barbara Botanic Garden

🏠 1212 Mission Canyon Rd
🕐 9am–5pm daily
🌐 sbbg.org

More a nature walk than a traditional garden, the Botanic Garden specializes in the Indigenous plants of California.

The width of the nave was determined by the height of the trees used as cross-beams.

The cemetery garden contains the graves of some 4,000 Native Americans as well as friars.

↑ The Santa Barbara Mission quadrangle and Classical-style church

Over a thousand species can be seen on trails leading through the desert, chaparral, and arroyo environments that are so typical of California. Of note is a small grove of coast redwood trees, unusual this far south. Spring is the best time to view floral displays. Research into biodiversity and conservation of rare plants is the mission of the garden, and admission fees support that work. Visitors are encouraged to learn how plants contribute to healthy ecosystems, and docent-led tours are offered on weekends and Mondays.

---

⑪ 🚴 🛍

Santa Barbara Museum of Natural History

🏠 2559 Puesta Del Sol
🕐 10am–5pm daily
🌐 sbnature.org

Housed in a series of Spanish-style buildings and courtyards, the Santa Barbara Museum of Natural History is devoted to the paleontology, native wildlife, and marine life of the region. Displays showcase plenty of stuffed creatures and skeletons – you can't miss the blue whale. In the Mineral and Gem Gallery, brilliant samples will teach you the difference between minerals and gemstones. An adjacent planetarium features live shows as well as a monthly star party. The museum also holds the largest collection of Chumash artifacts in the world.

② 🚲 🛌 🍴 🖥 🛍

HEARST CASTLE®

Ⓐ C5 🏠 750 Hearst Castle Rd 🚌 To San Simeon 🕐 9am–4pm daily
🗓 Jan 1, Thanksgiving, Dec 25 🌐 hearstcastle.org

Hearst Castle® perches on a hill above the village of San Simeon. The private playground and museum of media tycoon William Randolph Hearst is today one of California's top tourist attractions.

Hearst Castle® epitomizes the extravagance and glamour of the West Coast in the 1930s and 1940s, home to lavish guest houses, gardens, pools, and even a winery. The guest houses – Casa del Mar, Casa del Sol, and Casa del Monte – are superb buildings, but the highlight is the twin-towered Casa Grande or "Big House," which lives up to its name and then some. Designed by the Paris-trained architect Julia Morgan and built in stages from 1922 to 1947, its 115 exquisitely decorated and furnished rooms house a treasure trove of valuable art.

WILLIAM RANDOLPH HEARST

The son of a multi-millionaire, W. R. Hearst (1863–1951) was an ebullient personality who made his own fortune in magazine and newspaper publishing. He married Millicent Willson, an entertainer from New York, in 1903. On his mother's death in 1919, Hearst inherited the San Simeon property and began to build the castle and grounds. On moving in, he installed his companion, actress Marion Davies. The couple entertained royalty at San Simeon over the next 20 years. Hearst died from heart complications in 1951.

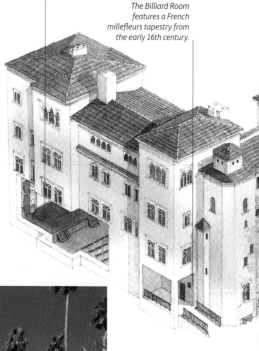

The walls of Hearst's private theater and cinema are lined with damask. Lamps held by gilded caryatids (female figures from Classical architecture) light the 50 seats.

The Billiard Room features a French millefleurs tapestry from the early 16th century.

← Mediterranean Revival facade with ancient architectural fragments

Timeline

1865
George Hearst buys a large plot of land near San Simeon.

1919
△ W. R. Hearst inherits family fortune. Plans a house on "Camp Hill."

1922
Work begins on the twin-towered main house, Casa Grande.

1921
Casa del Mar guest house completed.

1924
▽ Casa del Sol guest house completed.

1951
Hearst dies in Beverly Hills.

1958
Hearst Castle® is opened to the public.

Casa Grande – the "Big House" of the vast Hearst estate ↓

When in San Simeon, Hearst ran his empire from the Gothic Study, where he kept his valuable book collection behind grilles.

Tapestries, choir stalls, and colorful banners cover the walls of the massive dining hall or refectory.

The two Celestial Suite bedrooms are located high up in the north and south towers. They are linked by a spacious sitting room.

Main entrance

An enormous 16th-century French fireplace dominates the Assembly Room. Italian choir stalls line the walls, which are hung with Flemish tapestries.

EXPLORING HEARST CASTLE®

Casa Grande: the "Big House"

Casa Grande is built from steel-reinforced concrete in order to withstand California's earthquakes. Despite the concrete, the building was designed to look like a masonry cathedral in the Mediterranean Revival style.

Houseguests stayed in one of dozens of luxurious bedrooms, surrounded by works from the magnate's eclectic art collection. Hearst himself lived in the third-floor Gothic Suite. His extraordinary bedroom was decorated with a 14th-century Spanish ceiling and a renowned

Did You Know?

Casa Grande has a total of 38 bedrooms, 30 fireplaces, and 42 bathrooms.

Madonna and Child painting from the School of Duccio di Buoninsegna (c. 1255–1318). A sitting room with ocean views linked it to the bedroom of his companion, the actress and philanthropist Marion Davies.

Across the hall, the Gothic Study housed Hearst's most prized books and manuscripts. It was from this room that he directed his media empire.

The Assembly Room, on the first floor, was designed around a massive 16th-century French fireplace. The high-ceilinged Refectory, next door, features a Renaissance dining table, misericord seats, and a flagstone floor in the Italian style. Guests at the castle were required to attend their late evening meals here.

The Billiard Room, with its Spanish Gothic ceiling, show-cases an early 16th-century tapestry of a stag hunt. Adjoining this room is Hearst's private movie theater. Here, up to 50 guests would watch films. The screen could be removed, revealing a small stage,

INSIDER TIP
Tours

Visitors to Hearst Castle® must take one of half a dozen guided tours, all of which start from the Visitors' Center. The Grand Rooms Tour is recommended for first-time visitors. During spring and fall, evening tours of the estate feature "guests" in 1930s costume.

where famous actors and actresses would sometimes put on plays.

The exquisite indoor Roman Pool, entirely decorated with mosaics of hammered gold and Venetian glass, is further furnished with eight marble statues and was a favorite haunt among his guests.

The house was continually being developed in accordance with Hearst's ever-evolving ideas, much to the consternation of architect Julia Morgan. Her relationship with Hearst was based on mutual respect but was often tempestuous. After spending long hours together finalizing a plan,

↑ Marble statues and gold mosaics surround the Roman Pool

> **Hearst transformed the rocky California hillside into a veritable Garden of Eden, hauling huge fan palms and cypresses up the dirt road.**

↑ Roman-style features ringing the Neptune Pool, the showpiece of the castle

Hearst would sometimes telegraph Morgan with last-minute changes. One supporting wall was moved at great cost to make room for a bowling alley that was never built.

The Grounds and Neptune Pool

Hearst transformed the rocky California hillside into a veritable Garden of Eden, hauling huge fan palms and cypresses up the dirt road at great expense, and planting thousands of flowers each year.

Massive loads of topsoil were brought up to create flowerbeds for the vast gardens. Several greenhouses supplied colorful plants throughout the year. To hide the water reservoirs on a distant hill, 6,000 Monterey pines were planted in holes blasted out of the rock. Many varieties of fruit trees were planted, providing an abundance of fresh fruit.

Ancient and modern statues were collected to adorn the terraces. Among the finest are four statues of Sekhmet, the Egyptian goddess of war. The oldest works date from 1560–1200 BC.

The pièce de résistance is the 104-ft- (32-m-) long Neptune Pool. Made in white marble, it is flanked by colonnades and features Roman architectural elements and a temple facade. The latter is made from ancient columns and decorated with authentic friezes. The statues around the pool were carved in the 1930s by Charles-George Cassou, a Parisian sculptor.

A great lover of the outdoors, Hearst had a 1-mile- (1.6-km-) long pergola so that he could ride in all weather. Two tennis courts were also built on the roof of the indoor Roman Pool.

Hearst even went as far as to build a private zoo on "Camp Hill." The remains of the enclosures, where animals such as lions, bears, elephants, pumas, and leopards were once kept, can still be seen. Giraffes, ostriches, zebras, and even a baby elephant were free to wander the grounds.

The Guest Houses

Until the mid-1920s, when Casa Grande became ready for occupancy, Hearst lived in the 15-room Casa del Mar, the largest of the three guest houses. He enjoyed his years in the smaller house, but on viewing the completed Casa Grande he admitted, "If I had known it would be so big, I would have made the little buildings bigger." The "little buildings," however, are really mansions in their own right.

Casa del Sol is built on three levels. It has fabulous views of the Californian sunset, and in one of the broad lower terraces you will find a tall fountain topped with a cast bronze copy of Donatello's *David*. The smallest of the guest houses, Casa del Monte, faces toward the hills and has nine rooms.

JULIA MORGAN

Julia Morgan, the architect of Hearst Castle®, was one of the first women to graduate in engineering from Berkeley, and was also the first to receive a certificate in architecture from the Ecole Nationale et Spéciale des Beaux-Arts in Paris. This multitalented artist designed almost every aspect of the castle, and rigorously supervised the project's many contractors.

EXPERIENCE MORE

③

Cambria

🅐C5 🚌 ℹ️ 767 Main St;
www.cambriachamber.org

Cambria, situated between rugged seashore and pine-clad hills, began as a mercury mining settlement in 1866. Today it is a popular location for artists and craftspeople, its Main Street lined with art galleries and specialty shops.

To the north of the town, the Leffingwell Landing offers excellent views of the surf. At low tide it is also possible to climb down to the rock pools at the bottom of the cliffs.

---

④

Paso Robles

🅐C5 🚌 ℹ️ 1225 Park St;
www.pasorobleschamber.com

Paso Robles, or "Pass of the Oaks," was once part of the El Paso de Robles ranch. In 1857, a sulfurous hot spring was transformed into a health resort. With the arrival of the Southern Pacific railroad in

Did You Know?

A few miles east of Paso Robles, the James Dean Monument sits close to where the actor lost his life.

1886, the town fast developed. Today Paso Robles is ringed with horse ranches, vineyards, wineries, and almond orchards. The hot springs have now been capped but the town still has much to offer. On Vine Street are restored buildings from the 1890s, and in a historic former car dealership nearby, **Studios on the Park** features art exhibitions and tours of the open studios of local artists.

Studios on the Park

◈ 🏠1130 Pine St 🕐Noon-4pm Sun-Thu, noon-9pm Fri-Sat 🅦studiosonthepark.org

⑤ 🛍️

Mission San Miguel Arcángel

🅐C5 🏠775 Mission St, San Miguel 🕐10am-4:30pm daily 🅦missionsanmiguel.org

This mission, the 16th in the Californian chain, was founded in 1797 by Father Fermín de Lasuén, the successor to Father Junípero Serra (p225). Nine years later the original church was

→ The bell tower of Mission San Miguel Arcángel

↑ Wandering among the rock pools at Cambria's Leffingwell Landing

destroyed by fire and the present building, which was used as a parish church, was completed In 1819. A team of Te'po'ta'ahl peoples, working under the guidance of artist Esteban Munras, painted the frescoes that can still be seen today.

In addition to growing grain and raising cattle, the padres produced their own sacramental wine, and today the surrounding hills shelter more than 30 wineries.

The mission was damaged in the San Salinas earthquake of 2003; it reopened in 2009, but retrofitting continues.

The six rooms in the mission's museum are furnished as they would have been in the early 1800s. There is also a gift shop and a pleasant courtyard.

 6

Atascadero

C5 San Luis Obispo Dial-A-Ride (805 466-7433) 6904 El Camino Real; www.atascadero chamber.org

Atascadero, which means "muddy place" in Spanish, was founded in 1913 by the publisher Edward G. Lewis,

who bought the 36-sq-mile (93-sq-km) ranch to build his ideal town. His headquarters were in an impressive Italian Renaissance-style building, constructed in 1914 for almost half a million dollars and now home to the City Hall. The building used to house the Atascadero Historical Society Museum, which contained photographs taken by Lewis's official photographer as well as artifacts. However, the building was damaged by a major earthquake in late 2003, reopening ten years later. Portions of the collection are on display at the Colony House until the building is restored.

Lewis went bankrupt before Atascadero was finished. The town continued to grow steadily from the 1950s as more people were attracted by its rural atmosphere. It became an official city in 1979.

Today's visitors frequent the city's antique shops, stylish boutiques, and weekly farmers' market.

During the week-long Colony Days celebration in October, the city remembers its early history with a parade and other festivities.

 7

San Simeon

C5 250 San Simeon Av; www. visitsansimeonca.com

San Simeon started life as a whaling station. Its fortunes changed when publishing

---

INSIDER TIP
See a Seal

Up to 25,000 great northern seals hang out at the Piedras Blancas Elephant Seal Rookery in San Simeon. The best time to see them is from December to March, when males fight and pups are born (www. elephantseal.org).

EAT

tycoon William Randolph Hearst built a new wharf In the bay for unloading the precious materials destined for his nearby castle, which now dominates the town from a wooded hilltop.

Gentle waves make William Randolph Hearst Memorial Beach an ideal spot to splash in the ocean or rent a kayak, while the **Coastal Discovery Center** has interactive displays on the area's spectacular natural and cultural history.

Coastal Discovery Center
William Randolph Hearst Memorial Beach 11am-5pm Fri-Sun monterey bay.noaa.gov

8 Lompoc Valley

🅐C6 🔁 Santa Barbara
🚃Lompoc 🛈111 S I St,
Lompoc; www.lompoc.com

Lompoc Valley is one of the world's major producers of flower seed. The hills and flower fields surrounding the valley are a blaze of color between late spring and mid-summer. Among the varieties grown are marigolds, sweet peas, and asters. A map of the fields in the area is distributed by the town of Lompoc's Chamber of Commerce. The Civic Center Plaza, between Ocean Avenue and C Street, has a display garden in which all the flowers are identified.

La Purísima Concepción Mission, 3 miles (5 km) north-east of the town, was the 11th mission to be founded in California. It was declared a State Historic Park during the 1930s. The early 19th-century buildings have been reconstructed, and the complex and grounds provide real insights into missionary life. Visitors are able to view the priests' living quarters, furnished with original pieces. The simple church is decorated with colorful stencilwork. In the adjacent workshops, cloth, candles, leather goods, and furniture were at one time produced for the mission.

La Purísima's gardens have been faithfully restored. The varieties of fruit, vegetables, and medicinal herbs that are grown here were all common in the 19th century.

La Purísima Concepción Mission

 🅐2295 Purísima Rd, Lompoc ⏰10am–4pm Tue–Sun (Jul & Aug: also 11am–3pm Mon) 🚫Jan 1, Thanksgiving, Dec 25
🌐 lapurisimamission.org

EAT

The Cracked Crab
The specialty at this informal seafood restaurant is shellfish served in a bucket. It also offers fish, meat, and vegetable dishes.

🅐C6 🅐751 Price St, Pismo Beach
🌐crackedcrab.com

💲💲💲

Hofbrau
Famous for its fine, hand-carved roast-beef sandwiches, this long-standing eatery also has burgers, seafood, and salads on the menu.

🅐C5 🅐901 Embarcadero, Morro Bay
🌐hofbraumorrobay.com

💲💲💲

9 San Luis Obispo

🅐C5 🔁 San Luis Obispo
🚃🚌 🛈895 Monterey St; www.visitslo.com

This small city, in a valley in the Santa Lucia Mountains, developed around the **Mission San Luis Obispo de Tolosa**. The mission was founded on September 1, 1772, by Father Junípero Serra. Fifth in the chain of 21 missions built by the Franciscan Order, and one of the wealthiest, it is still in use as a parish church.

Beside the church, the mission's museum displays Chumash artifacts, such as baskets, vessels, and jewelry; the padre's bed; and the mission's original altar. In front of the church is Mission Plaza, a landscaped public square bisected by a tree-lined creek. During the 1860s, bullfights and bear-baiting took place in the park; today these activities are thankfully over. Just off the plaza, on Broad Street, the San Luis Obispo Museum of Art displays works by contemporary Californian artists. Nearby, at 800 Palm Street, is the Ah Louis Store. Founded in 1874 by a Chinese railroad laborer, it grew to be the center of a then-thriving Chinatown. It is now a gift shop, but is only open at irregular hours.

On the outskirts of town, rocky Bishop Peak is laced with hiking trails for varying abilities, rising to a 1,550-ft (475-m) summit. The paths offer outstanding views.

Mission San Luis Obispo de Tolosa

🅐751 Palm St 📞(805) 781-8220 ⏰9am–4pm daily (Mar-Oct: to 5pm) 🚫Federal hols
🌐missionsanluisobispo.org

The stately Mission San Luis Obispo de Tolosa facade ↓

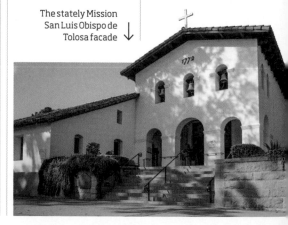

Morro Bay's harbor, with Morro Rock in the background →

 10

Morro Bay

🅰 C5 🚌 ℹ️ 695 Harbor St; www.morrobay.org

This seaside port was founded in 1870 to ship produce from the area's cattle-ranching and dairy-farming businesses. Today tourism has become the town's main industry, and the waterfront Embarcadero is lined with galleries, shops, an aquarium, and seafood restaurants. Whale-watching trips, bay cruises, and a commercial fishing fleet also operate from here. A redwood stairway descends from a stone pelican at clifftop level down to the Embarcadero. The view from Black Hill Lookout is worth the easy hike from the parking lot to the mountain's summit.

The bay's principal feature is Morro Rock, a dome-shaped 576-ft- (175-m-) high volcanic peak. Named "El Moro" by

---

GREAT VIEW
Morro Rock

One of the best views of Morro Rock and the surrounding coastline is from the top of Cerro Alto, a 2,624-ft (800-m) volcanic cone 9 miles (14 km) east of Morro Bay. It can be reached via Highway 41.

GUADALUPE-NIPOMO DUNES NATIONAL WILDLIFE REFUGE

About 15 miles (24 km) south of Pismo Beach, this protected area covers one of the largest coastal dune systems in California. The refuge protects endangered species such as Morro butterflies, brown pelicans, California least terns, and Western snowy plovers. The Dunes Center (www.dunescenter.org) provides information about the dunes and has an exhibit on the 1923 silent movie *The Ten Commandments*, by Cecil B. DeMille, which was shot in the dunes near Guadalupe.

Juan Rodríguez Cabrillo (João Rodrigues Cabrilho) in 1542, who thought it resembled a Moor's turban, it was connected to the mainland by a causeway in 1933. Today Morro Rock is a wildlife preserve housing nests of peregrine falcons and gull species, while Coleman Park, at the rock's base, is a highly popular fishing spot.

Across town, Morro Bay State Park offers both water sports and birdwatching activities.

 11

Pismo Beach

🅰 C6 🚆 San Luis Obispo 🚍 San Luis Obispo 🚌 ℹ️ 581 Dolliver St; www. experiencepismobeach.com

Pismo Beach is famous for the Pismo clam. At the turn of the 20th century up to 40,000 clams were harvested per day; now, a fishing license is

required and there are strict size and quantity restrictions. A clam festival is held in the fall. Pismo State Beach offers campsites, boating, fishing, and picnic facilities. The sand is firmly compacted, so cars can go onto the beach via ramps at Grand Avenue in Grover Beach and Pier Avenue in Oceano. Sand dunes shelter birdlife, wildflowers, and other seashore plants, along with the occasional foxes, rabbits, and coyotes. Shell mounds in the dunes, especially near Arroyo Grande Creek, mark sites where the Chumash people once lived. Valuable information on Chumash culture is available at the Oceano Dunes Visitor Center.

During the 1930s and 1940s the dunes were the center of a cult of artists and nudists, who saw them as a place of spiritual enlightenment and freedom. Pismo Beach Pier, which was renovated in 2018, was also built at this time.

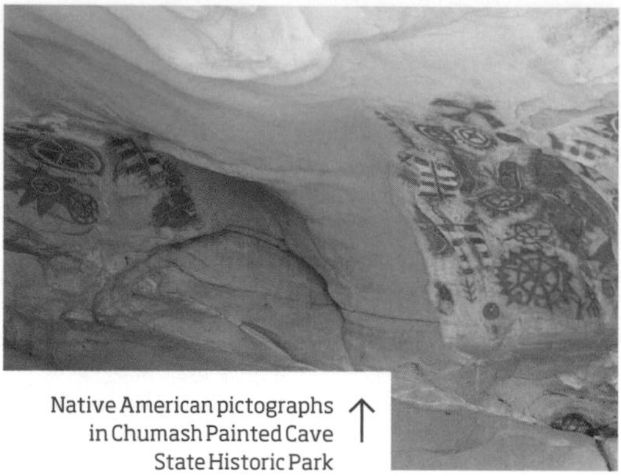

Native American pictographs in Chumash Painted Cave State Historic Park

12 Mission Santa Inés

D6 1760 Mission Dr, Solvang 9am-5pm daily Easter, Thanksgiving, Dec 25 missionsantaines.org

Founded within the territory of the Chumash people in 1804, Santa Inés was the 19th in the chain of California missions. After secularization in 1834, it fell into disrepair and most of the Native Americans left. Restoration work began after World War II, including the campanile (financed by W. R. Hearst, *p188*). The mission has a small museum, with period furnishings, the vestments worn by early priests, and Native American murals.

13 Chumash Painted Cave State Historic Park

D6 Painted Cave Rd From Santa Barbara parks.ca.gov

In the Santa Ynez Mountains, 8 miles (13 km) northwest of Santa Barbara, are a number of remote and scattered caves with Chumash drawings. The most famous example is a 20- by 40-ft (6- by 12-m) cave just off Hwy 154. Inside is an egg-shaped cavity covered in elaborate ocher drawings.

Some drawings resemble lizards, snakes, and scorpions, executed in red, black, or white paint. Tribes are known to have traded pigments with each other. Many experts believe the drawings are symbolic of the Chumash religion or cosmology. Getting the bus to the park is recommended since parking is limited to two vehicles.

14 Solvang

D6 1639 Copenhagen Dr; www.solvangusa.com

In 1911 a group of three Danish educators bought 14 sq miles (36 sq km) of land on which to build a Danish colony and school. The original schoolhouse, a two-story frame structure on Alisal Road, is now the Bit o' Denmark Restaurant. Located above a bookstore, the small **Hans Christian Andersen Museum** pays tribute to the life of the Danish fairy-tale author, while the **Elverhøj Museum of History and Art**, in a building styled after an 18th-century Danish farmhouse, displays original furnishings and folk art.

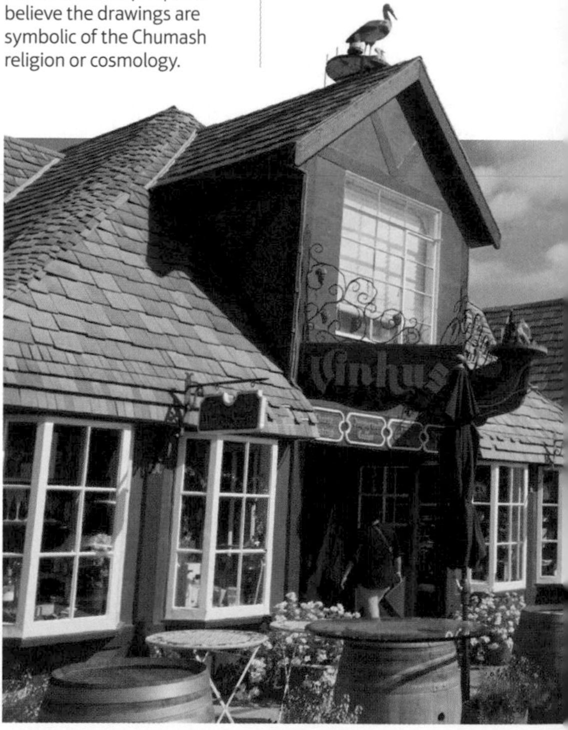

A quaint street in Solvang, a former Danish settlement

MONARCH BUTTERFLIES

Each year, around October, millions of monarch butterflies migrate from the western US and Canada to winter in Southern and Central California and Mexico. In season you can see them around Montaña de Oro State Park *(p200)*, Pismo Beach *(p195)*, and Ventura. After the mating season in January and February, the butterflies attempt the journey back to their summer habitat.

On a walk through the town, visitors can see windmills, roofs with wooden storks, and gas streetlights. Restaurants serve *aebleskiver* (a type of Danish pancake), during the town's Danish Days festival in September.

Hans Christian Andersen Museum

🏠 1680 Mission Dr
🕐 10am–6pm daily
🌐 bookloftsolvang.com/hca-museum

Elverhoj Museum of History and Art

🏠 1624 Elverhoy Way 🕐 11am–5pm Fri–Mon
🌐 elverhoj.org

15

Ventura

🅰 D6 🚌 🛈 101 S California St, Suite C; www.visit venturaca.com

All that remains of the 1872 **San Buenaventura Mission** is a church with a courtyard garden and tiled fountain. A museum details the buildings of the original complex.

The tiny, mid-19th-century **Ortega Adobe** reveals the harsh living conditions many experienced at that time. In contrast, the Monterey-style **Olivas Adobe** is a two-story ranch hacienda, furnished in period style, with rose and herb gardens.

Fishing charters and whale-watching cruises, as well as boats to the Channel Islands National Park, depart from Ventura Harbor.

San Buenaventura Mission

🏠 211 E Main St 🕐 10am–5pm daily 🚫 Jan 1, Easter, Thanksgiving, Dec 25 🌐 san buenaventuramission.org

Ortega Adobe

🏠 215 W Main St 📞 (805) 658-4726 🕐 Daily 🚫 Jan 1, Easter Sun, Labor Day, Thanksgiving, Dec 25

Olivas Adobe

🏠 4200 Olivas Park Dr
🕐 Sat & Sun; Grounds: daily
🚫 Jan 1, Easter, Thanksgiving, Dec 25 🌐 olivasadobe.org

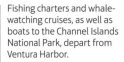

DRINK

Clean Slate Wine Bar

Fifty limited-edition wines from independent producers are served by the glass.

🅰 D6 🏠 448 Atterdag Rd, Solvang
📞 (805)302-1787

___

Arrowsmith's Wine Bar

Owners Anna and Tim Arrowsmith serve a wide choice of European wines, including their own label.

🅰 D6 🏠 1539C Mission Dr, Solvang
🌐 arrowsmithwine.com

___

Poseidon Brewing Company

This nautical-themed microbrewery pours high-quality craft beers.

🅰 D6 🏠 5777 Olivas Park Dr, Unit Q, Ventura
🌐 poseidonbrewing co.com

↑ Shopping for certified produce at Ojai's Sunday farmers' market

Ronald Reagan Presidential Library

🅐 D6 🅐 40 Presidential Dr, Simi Valley 🕙 10am–5pm daily 🚫 Jan 1, Thanksgiving, Dec 25 🌐 reaganfoundation.org

Housed in a Mission Revival-style structure, this library documents the life of President Reagan and his wife, Nancy. Reagan's papers are all archived here, and temporary exhibitions display gifts, costumes, and other objects related to his eight-year tenure in the White House; a highlight is a large piece of the Berlin Wall. There is also an exact full-size replica of the Oval Office, as well as bronze statues of Ronald and Nancy at the library's entrance. In the Air Force One Pavilion, visitors can board the aircraft which was used by six presidents from 1973 to 2001.

⓱ Ojai

🅐 D6 🚌 ℹ 109 N Blanche St; www.ojaivisitors.com

Founded in 1874, Ojai takes its name from the Chumash word for "moon," a reference to the crescent-shaped valley where the town sits. Many local residents feel a deep spiritual connection with the environment, which has given rise to meditation centers and alternative healing retreats.

Trendy shops line Ojai's arcaded, Spanish-style main street. On Sunday mornings, a farmers' market is held nearby.

The area is blessed with a Mediterranean climate, and olive trees thrive in the Ojai Valley, with some groves dating

← Statues of Ronald and Nancy Reagan at the Ronald Reagan Presidential Library

back to the mid-1800s. At **Ojai Olive Oil Company** visitors can learn about the process of making extra virgin olive oil.

Located inside an early 20th-century Catholic church, the **Ojai Valley Museum** aims to preserve the area's culture and history, with two rooms full of paintings, photographs, Chumash artifacts, and more.

Fitting with Ojai's spiritual side, the **Krishnamurti Visitor Center and Library** is dedicated to the teachings of the Indian philosopher Jiddu Krishnamurti. At Pine Cottage, where he once lived, visitors can study, meditate, and explore the grounds.

Ojai Olive Oil Company
🅐 1811 Ladera Rd 🕙 10am–4pm daily 🌐 ojaioliveoil.com

Ojai Valley Museum
🅐 130 W Ojai Av
🕙 10am–4pm Tue–Sat
🌐 ojaivalleymuseum.org

Krishnamurti Visitor Center and Library

 1098 McAndrew Rd
⏱ Noon–4pm Tue-Fri, 10am–5pm Sat & Sun, 11am–4pm hols 🌐 kfa.org

---

18

Bakersfield

🅰 D5 🚌 ℹ 515 Truxton Av; www.visitbakers field.com

Bakersfield was named after Colonel Thomas Baker, a settler who planted a field of alfalfa here in 1863. Its modern history began with the discovery of oil in the following decades.

Enjoying the view from Anacapa Island, Channel Islands National Park ↓

At the **Kern County Museum**, 50 historic structures and exhibits illustrate the history and culture of the area, while the **Bakersfield Museum of Art** has a collection of modern and contemporary works.

Bakersfield also features some architectural curiosities, like the landmark town sign that straddles across four lanes at Sillect Avenue and the shoe-shaped building at 931 Chester Avenue, which houses the Big Shoe Repair shop. The latter typifies Programmatic architecture, where the structure mimics the building's purpose.

The **California Living Museum** houses animals that have been injured and cannot be returned to the wild. There are more than 200 California species here, and residents include a bald eagle, condor, bears, and bighorn sheep.

Kern County Museum
⊘ 3801 Chester Av
⏱ 9am–4pm Wed-Sun
📅 Jan 1, Thanksgiving, Dec 24, 25, 31 🌐 kerncounty museum.org

Bakersfield Museum of Art
⊘ 1930 R St ⏱ 10am–4pm Tue-Sat 🌐 bmoa.org

California Living Museum
⊘ 10500 Alfred Harrell Hwy ⏱ 9am–4pm daily 🌐 calmzoo.org

19

Channel Islands National Park

🅰 D6 🚌 Ventura 🚢 Island Packers (805 642-1393)
ℹ 1901 Spinnaker Dr, Ventura; www.nps.gov/chis

The volcanic islands of Santa Barbara, Anacapa, San Miguel, Santa Cruz, and Santa Rosa make up this National Park. Access to the islands is strictly monitored, and permits are issued at the Visitors' Center at Ventura Harbor. Camping is allowed, but be sure to make reservations at least two weeks in advance. You must also bring your own food and water supplies, since none are available on the islands.

The best time to visit is between February and April, when you may spot whales, dolphins, and brown pelicans. Wildlife on the islands includes cormorants, sea lions, elephant seals, and gulls.

Guided walks conducted by park rangers offer insights into this remarkable coastal ecosystem. Visitors must stay on the designated trails.

The rock pools on all of the islands are rich in marine life, and the kelp forests surrounding them provide shelter for more than 1,000 plant and animal species. The islands' many sea caves make sea-kayaking a unique and exciting experience. The snorkeling and scuba diving in this area are superb.

A DRIVING TOUR
CALIFORNIA'S SOUTH CENTRAL COASTLINE

Length 170 miles (275 km) **Stopping-off points** Morro Bay is known for its seafood shacks; Pismo Beach and Santa Barbara have many seaside restaurants and cafés.

California's South Central coast offers accessible, broad, sandy beaches and some of the best surfing in the state. Most of this route follows coastal Hwy 1, from laid-back Morro Bay to hip Ventura, via the stately city of Santa Barbara. Opportunities for swimming, sunbathing, and surfing abound, and there are great seafood stop-offs almost everywhere. Plus, it's easy to tap into the region's history at Spanish missions.

Morro Rock is one of California's most distinctive landmarks. Used as a navigation point by the first Spanish explorers, it is best seen at sunrise or sunset.

START
William R. Hearst Memorial State Beach
San Simeon
Cambria
Harmony
Cayucos
Morro Rock
Morro Bay
Atascadero
Santa Margarita
San Luis Obispo
Montaña de Oro State Park
Avila Beach
Pismo Beach
Arroyo Grande
Guadalupe
Purisima Point
Surf
Point Arguello

*Rugged cliffs, wild sandy beaches, and canyons characterize **Montaña de Oro State Park**. Hiking trails include a path up the 1,347-ft- (411-m) Valencia Peak.*

*The tranquil seaside town of **Avila Beach** has a wooden fishing pier constructed in 1908 (partially closed for renovation) and a sandy beach, popular in the summer for surfing and swimming.*

*Known primarily for its clams and clam chowder-serving cafés, **Pismo Beach** (p195) is a small town with a long beach, giant sand dunes, and a wooden pier.*

↑ Hiking in the hills of Montaña de Oro State Park

Did You Know?

Clams must be at least 4.5 inches (11 cm) to be harvested legally from Pismo Beach.

SOUTH CENTRAL CALIFORNIA

California's South Central Coastline

Locator Map
For more detail see p182

El Capitan State Beach, backed ↑
by rolling green hills

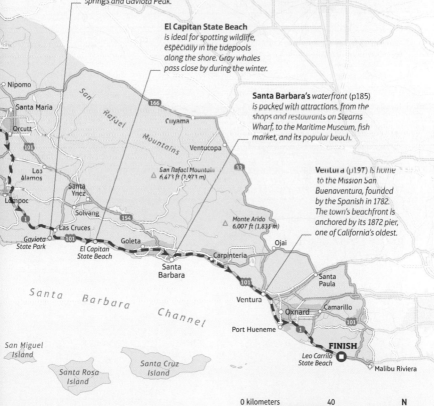

Gaviota State Park *includes a narrow beach with a fishing pier beneath the cliffs, as well as an inland section of trails leading to hot springs and Gaviota Peak.*

El Capitan State Beach *is ideal for spotting wildlife, especially in the tidepools along the shore. Gray whales pass close by during the winter.*

Santa Barbara's *waterfront (p185) is packed with attractions, from the shops and restaurants on Stearns Wharf, to the Maritime Museum, fish market, and its popular beach.*

Ventura (p197) *is home to the Mission San Buenaventura, founded by the Spanish in 1782. The town's beachfront is anchored by its 1872 pier, one of California's oldest.*

Nipomo

Santa Maria

Orcutt

Los Alamos

Lompoc

San Rafael Mountains

Cuyama

Ventucopa

San Rafael Mountain
△ *6,473 ft (1,973 m)*

Monte Arido
△ *6,007 ft (1,831 m)*

Santa Ynez

Solvang

Las Cruces

Gaviota State Park

El Capitan State Beach

Goleta

Carpinteria

Ojai

Santa Paula

Santa Barbara

Ventura

Oxnard

Camarillo

Port Hueneme

FINISH

Leo Carrilo State Beach

Malibu Riviera

Santa Barbara Channel

San Miguel Island

Santa Rosa Island

Santa Cruz Island

0 kilometers	40
0 miles	40

N ↑

A DRIVING TOUR
THE SANTA YNEZ VALLEY WINERIES

SOUTH CENTRAL CALIFORNIA

The Santa Ynez Valley Wineries

Locator Map
For more detail see p182

Length 30 miles (48 km) **Stopping-off points**
The Los Olivos Wine Merchant Café is great for lunch or dinner. Most wineries have picnic areas, where you can enjoy a local wine with your meal.

Santa Ynez Valley is one of the youngest and most distinctive wine regions in the state and enjoys a longer growing season than Northern California. The area experiences coastal fog, shifts in altitude, and sea breezes, all of which produce micro-climates. These unique conditions, coupled with varied soils, produce a selection of classic grape varieties. So, bring a designated driver and unwind in the valley's beautiful surroundings.

Did You Know?

The winds here can be so strong that they cause trees to twist and turn, creating unique shapes.

Pinot Noirs, Syrahs, and Rieslings are produced at **Fess Parker Winery**, *the eponymous former actor's winery. Tastings are available in an attractive building.*

Firestone Vineyard, the region's largest producer, presents distinctive Cabernet Sauvignons, Chardonnays, and Merlots in a large tasting room adjoining the winery.

The specialty at **Andrew Murray Vineyards** *is Rhone Varietal and Syrahs, which can be enjoyed in a tasting room adjoining the cellar.*

Los Olivos, a picture-perfect country town, is home to the award-winning Los Olivos Wine Merchant Café, which serves fresh produce grown on their organic farm.

Established in 1975, **Brander Vineyard** *offers award-winning Sauvignon Blancs and other wines in a French-style building overlooking the vineyards.*

Santa Ynez *town is full of 19th-century-style buildings. Just outside town, Sunstone Vineyard and Winery farms its vineyards in an organic, bio-sustainable way.*

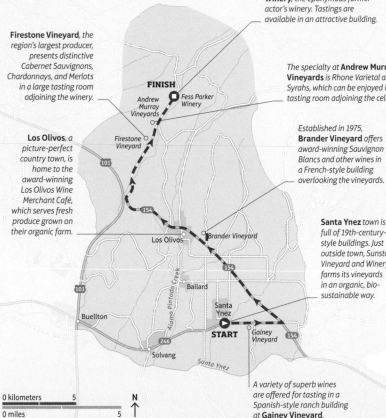

FINISH
Andrew Murray Vineyards
Fess Parker Winery
Firestone Vineyard
101
154
Los Olivos
Brander Vineyard
154
Ballard
Alamo Pintado Creek
101
Santa Ynez
Buellton
246
START
Gainey Vineyard
154
Solvang
Santa Ynez

0 kilometers 5
0 miles 5
N

A variety of superb wines are offered for tasting in a Spanish-style ranch building at **Gainey Vineyard**.

↑ Road leading through lush vineyards in Santa Ynez valley

ORANGE COUNTY

This area was once inhabited by the Tongva, Acjachemen, and Payomkowishum but, when the Spanish established Mission San Juan Capistrano in 1776, their culture was suppressed by mass conversions to Christianity and forced labor. European diseases decimated their population. Like much of Southern California, the land was carved up into giant ranches, which in turn were sold off into lots in the late 19th century. Anaheim was founded in 1857 as a grape and winemaking community by German Americans, and Orange County was formally created in 1889.

A century ago, much of Orange County still lived up to its name – it was dominated by extensive orange groves until the mid-1950s. Everything changed in 1955 when Disneyland opened in Anaheim, and now oranges have given way to urban sprawl. Today's Orange County is almost two worlds. The older cities in the center and northern areas have traditional downtowns with diverse architecture and populations, while south Orange County features homogeneous, upscale developments. Despite declaring bankruptcy in 1994 after an investment scandal, the county remains one of the wealthiest in the US. However, the high cost of living here has led many people to move farther out to the neighboring suburbs and commute to the county for work.

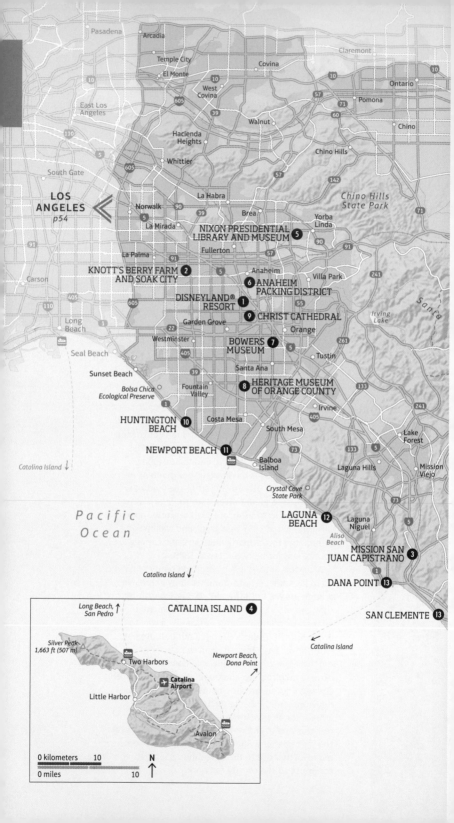

Pasadena

Arcadia

Temple City

El Monte

West Covina

Covina

Claremont

Ontario

East Los Angeles

Hacienda Heights

Walnut

Pomona

Chino

South Gate

Whittier

Chino Hills

LOS ANGELES *p54*

Norwalk

La Mirada

La Habra

Brea

Yorba Linda

Chino Hills State Park

Carson

La Palma

KNOTT'S BERRY FARM AND SOAK CITY ②

Fullerton

Anaheim

Villa Park

NIXON PRESIDENTIAL LIBRARY AND MUSEUM ⑤

Long Beach

DISNEYLAND® RESORT ①

ANAHEIM PACKING DISTRICT ⑥

CHRIST CATHEDRAL ⑨

Irving Lake

Seal Beach

Garden Grove

Orange

Santa

Sunset Beach

Westminster

BOWERS MUSEUM ⑦

Tustin

Bolsa Chica Ecological Preserve

Fountain Valley

Santa Ana

HERITAGE MUSEUM OF ORANGE COUNTY ⑧

Irvine

HUNTINGTON BEACH ⑩

Costa Mesa

South Mesa

Lake Forest

NEWPORT BEACH ⑪

Balboa Island

Laguna Hills

Mission Viejo

Catalina Island ↓

Crystal Cove State Park

Pacific Ocean

LAGUNA BEACH ⑫

Laguna Niguel

Aliso Beach

MISSION SAN JUAN CAPISTRANO ③

Catalina Island ↓

DANA POINT ⑬

SAN CLEMENTE ⑬

Catalina Island ↙

Long Beach, San Pedro ↑

CATALINA ISLAND ④

Silver Peak 1,663 ft (507 m)

Two Harbors

Newport Beach, Dona Point ↗

Little Harbor

Catalina Airport

Avalon

0 kilometers   10

0 miles   10

N ↑

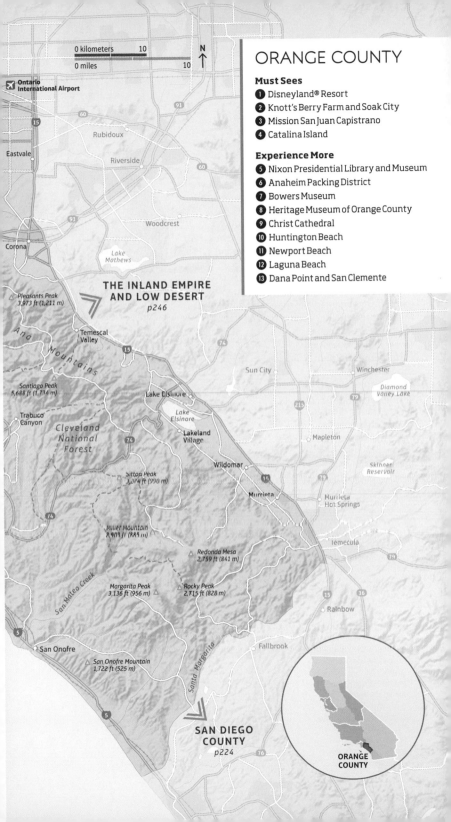

ORANGE COUNTY

Must Sees

① Disneyland® Resort
② Knott's Berry Farm and Soak City
③ Mission San Juan Capistrano
④ Catalina Island

Experience More

⑤ Nixon Presidential Library and Museum
⑥ Anaheim Packing District
⑦ Bowers Museum
⑧ Heritage Museum of Orange County
⑨ Christ Cathedral
⑩ Huntington Beach
⑪ Newport Beach
⑫ Laguna Beach
⑬ Dana Point and San Clemente

1 ⟨icons⟩

DISNEYLAND®
RESORT

A B7 **⌂** Disneyland Dr, Anaheim **✈** From LAX
🚌 435 **🕐** Jun-Aug: 8am-midnight daily; Sep-May:
9am-8pm daily **🌐** disneyland.com

Disney's "Magic Kingdom" in Anaheim is one of the top tourist attractions in California. Encompassing the original Disneyland® Park, the adjacent Disney California Adventure™ Park, and Downtown Disney®, the resort has become the model for theme parks around the globe and is as American as apple pie. Disneyland® Park and Disney California Adventure™ Park are divided into "lands," each offering themed experiences that celebrate the California dream. Visitors to "The Happiest Place on Earth" find fantasy, thrill rides, glittering shows, and shopping in a brightly orchestrated land of long lines, fireworks, and Mickey Mouse. It takes at least three days to make the most of a visit. The nightly fireworks show in Disneyland® Park is well worth losing a little sleep for.

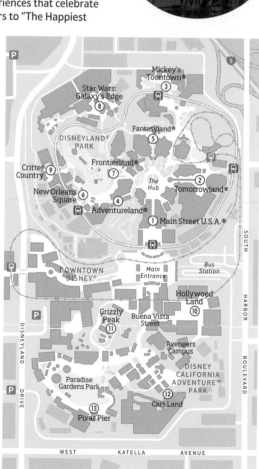

INSIDER TIP
Tickets

Disneyland Park® and Disney California Adventure™ Park have separate admission. You can visit both in one day with a Park Hopper ticket, while multiday tickets and Annual Passports give unlimited access. A FastPass+ provides assigned times for rides so you can avoid long lines. You can buy tickets at any Disney Store or online. The Disney MaxPass app lets you book attractions on your phone.

Map labels:

P
5
Mickey's Toontown® 3
Star Wars: Galaxy's Edge 8
Fantasyland® 5
DISNEYLAND PARK
Critter Country 9
Frontierland® 7
The Hub
Tomorrowland® 2
New Orleans Square 6
4
Adventureland®
Main Street U.S.A.® 1

DOWNTOWN DISNEY®
Main Entrance
Bus Station
SOUTH
HARBOR
Hollywood Land 10
Grizzly Peak 11
Buena Vista Street
Avengers Campus
DISNEY CALIFORNIA ADVENTURE™ PARK
BOULEVARD
DISNEYLAND DRIVE
Paradise Gardens Park
Cars Land 12
Pixar Pier 13

WEST   KATELLA   AVENUE

↑ Mickey, Goofy, and Minnie
welcoming visitors and
(inset) nightly fireworks

DISNEYLAND® PARK

① MAIN STREET U.S.A.®

This spotlessly clean, colorful street lined with early 20th-century buildings welcomes visitors to Disneyland®. The

Town Square, near City Hall, is a good place to view the daily parade and meet many of the famous Disney characters. If you are lucky, you can find ample opportunities here for photographs and videos. City Hall offers maps and other information about the park, while the Main Street Cinema screens early Disney silent films. Main Street itself has a large selection of attractions, shops, and places to eat.

← Bustling Main Street U.S.A.®, lined with shops and attractions

② TOMORROWLAND®

Visions of the future inspire the attractions here, which change regularly to keep ahead of technology and still retain a sense of fantasy. One of the first attractions in 1955 was Autopia, which takes guests into a parallel universe from a car's point of view, winding through Tomorrowland®, as well as Fantasyland®.

Buzz Lightyear Astro Blasters is an interactive experience in which guests pilot their own Space Cruisers. A hands-down Disneyland® favorite, Space Mountain® provides a high-speed roller-coaster ride. The ride has meteoric flashes, celestial showers, and space-age music (not suitable for very young children).

③ MICKEY'S TOONTOWN®

This is where visitors are most likely to find Mickey, Goofy, and other well-known Disney characters having their pictures taken with guests. The most popular places are Mickey's house and Minnie's cottage. Most of the attractions are geared toward kids from age three up. The bustling interactive downtown area offers gentle excitement for this younger set. Roger Rabbit's Car Toon Spin is Toontown®'s largest and most popular attraction, providing a madcap taxi drive through a surreal cartoon world. Gadget's Go Coaster is a gentle roller coaster for kids.

↑ Mickey Mouse Fountain standing in front of Mickey's Toontown®

↑ Elephant spraying passengers on the Jungle Cruise in Adventureland®

④ ADVENTURELAND®

The jungle atmosphere in Adventureland® offers dark, humid waterways lined with tropical plants. The Enchanted Tiki Room showcases mechanical singing birds in a musical romp through the tropics.

Inspired by the film trilogy, the Indiana Jones™ Adventure takes passengers on a jeep-style drive through the Temple of the Forbidden Eye. Theatrical props, a realistic soundtrack, sensational images, and the physical sensation of a roller coaster make this one of the most thrilling rides in Disneyland®. Jungle Cruise is a safari-style boat ride that glides along steamy waters through a jungle forest full of rampant apes and threatening hippos. It is narrated by an on-board captain, who tells his captive audience terrible puns and amusing jokes. Tarzan™'s Treehouse is a climb-up, climb-through experience with a play area at the base of the tree.

⑥ NEW ORLEANS SQUARE

This town square is modeled on the New Orleans French Quarter, as it was in its heyday in the 19th century. The Haunted Mansion® attraction promises realistic holographic figures of 999 "ghosts and ghouls" in a spooky world of mischievous spirits and grave-diggers. The Pirates of the Caribbean® ride provides a floating tour through a yo-ho-ho world of ruffians and wenches empowered with the gifts of song and dance by Audio-Animatronics.

⑤ FANTASYLAND®

Dominated by the pink and gold towers of Sleeping Beauty Castle and a replica of the Matterhorn, Fantasyland® is a shrine to children's dreams and adult nostalgia. Nursery heroes such as Peter Pan, Dumbo, and Snow White provide the themes for gentle fairy-tale rides in vehicles that range from flying galleons and canal boats to the Mad Hatter's giant spinning teacups. There are almost twice as many attractions here as in most of the other lands. "It's a Small World"® ferries passengers in boats past hundreds of singing-and-dancing dolls, all in national costumes from around the world. The two Matterhorn Bobsleds rollercoasters, on the other hand, are more for thrill-seekers. Bobsleds climb up to Matterhorn Mountain's summit, then drop into a steep, high-speed descent past glacier caves and waterfalls. At the end of the trip, riders in the front seats are splashed as the sleds careen into a pond.

Star Wars: Galaxy's Edge and *(inset)* Splash Mountain® ↑

⑦ FRONTIERLAND®

This area is inspired by the adventurous days of the Wild West. Skirt-lifting songs and dances take place on the Golden Horseshoe stage featuring Billy Hill and the Hillbillies. Every evening on weekends the spectacular Fantasmic! show, with fireworks, sound effects, and live performers, lights up the skies above Frontierland®.

The Mark Twain Riverboat offers visitors a 15-minute cruise on a paddle-wheel boat. While it crosses the Rivers of America, look out for the plastic moose and deer. Take time to visit the scary Pirate's Lair on Tom Sawyer Island.

Thrill-seekers love the Big Thunder Mountain Railroad roller-coaster ride. Open ore trucks set off from the 1880s mining town of Big Thunder without a driver. The runaway train then speeds through the cavernous interior of Big Thunder Mountain, narrowly escaping boulders and waterfalls. For an even wilder experience, secure a car at the rear.

WALT DISNEY'S VISION

Walt Disney (1901–66) was a pioneer in animation. Watching his own children at play in an ordinary amusement park, he was inspired to build a place filled with attractions that would capture the imagination of kids and adults alike. When the Magic Kingdom opened in 1955, and 28,000 people stormed in, tears reportedly streamed down Disney's cheeks.

⑧ STAR WARS: GALAXY'S EDGE

In a galaxy far, far away, visitors enter the total-immersion experience of the planet Batuu. Its stellar attraction, *Star Wars*: Rise of the Resistance, consists of several different ride systems featuring more than 300 animated objects and lasting about 18 minutes. On Millennium Falcon: Smugglers Run, passengers take on the role of pilot, engineer, or gunner on Han Solo's famous ship and embark on a secret mission. In the village of Black Spire Outpost, guests can build a light saber, chat in Batuuese with Chewbacca, or have a drink at Oga's Cantina. For an enhanced experience throughout the galaxy, be sure to download the Disney Play app.

⑨ CRITTER COUNTRY

Based on the rugged American Northwest, Critter Country is home to Splash Mountain®, a winding, watery log flume and one of the most popular attractions in Disneyland®. Brer Rabbit and Brer Fox are among the furry, singing characters who inhabit the mountain. On Davy Crockett's Explorer Canoes, groups take to the water and row down-river frontier-style. Guides provide lessons and ensure safety. The world's most beloved bear and his friends go on a charming hunt for honey in the Many Adventures of Winnie the Pooh.

→

Dancing roasters in Cars Land, and *(inset)* the Guardians of the Galaxy ride in Hollywood Land

DISNEY CALIFORNIA ADVENTURE™ PARK

⑩ HOLLYWOOD LAND

Movie soundstages and backlot scenery evoke the atmosphere of the Golden Age of Hollywood. Backstage demonstrations reveal some of the magic that goes into movie making, but for a real thrill, head over to the Guardians of the Galaxy—Mission: Breakout! Step into a lift that climbs a 13-story tower and suddenly propels up and down while intense visual effects assault the senses.

⑪ GRIZZLY PEAK

Grizzly Peak is dedicated to the natural beauty of the California wilderness. The idea here is a Californian National Park as experienced in the 1950s. Its focal point is Grizzly Peak, a 110-ft- (34-m-) high mountain in the shape of a grizzly bear, the iconic symbol on the state flag. At Grizzly River Run visitors are guaranteed to get wet as they run the rapids on a rubber raft. Another popular ride, Soarin' Around the World takes visitors beyond California on a simulated hang-glider ride that portrays the earth's landscapes on a huge screen.

↑ A water wheel on the white-water Grizzly River Run ride

EAT

Plaza Inn
Home-cooked buffets in a Victorian setting.

 Main St U.S.A., Disneyland® Park

⑤⑤⑤

Corn Dog Castle
The go-to place for hand-dipped corn dogs.

Disney California Adventure™ Park

⑤⑤⑤

Pacific Wharf Cafe
Soups and chilis served in "bread bowls."

 Disney California Adventure™ Park

⑤⑤⑤

Catal Restaurant
Classic Catalan Mediterranean-style fine dining.

 Downtown Disney®

⑤⑤⑤

⑫ CARS LAND

Guests step into the imaginary 1950s town of Radiator Springs, located somewhere along Route 66 and nestled at the foot of the 125-ft- (38-m-) tall Cadillac mountain range. Disney Imagineers actually took a road trip along the real Route 66 to make sure they got the details right. The premier attraction is Radiator Springs Racers, where a six-person, smiling convertible races through the desert.

⑬ PIXAR PIER

Pixar Pier is a waterside area of the park that seeks to re-create a Victorian-era version of the famed amusement parks that once dotted the boardwalks of California's coast, but with everything themed to Disney's Pixar movies. Drop, loop, twist, and turn on the white-knuckle Incredicoaster, or ride the gentler Jessie's Critter Carousel. Toy Story Midway Mania! is a popular interactive ride, where guests shoot projectiles at moving objects while passing through a virtual midway of carnival game booths.

↑ 360-degree thrills and spills on the Incredicoaster at Pixar Pier

DOWNTOWN DISNEY®

Located between the entrances to Disneyland® Park and Disney's California Adventure™ Park, Downtown Disney® is a lively walking street filled with restaurants, shops, and entertainment venues. The fact that this area has no admission fee makes it one of the more popular – but crowded – spaces. A 12-screen theater, ESPN Zone™, and a LEGO Imagination Center® are the top attractions. The snack shops and restaurants, plus a vast range of specialty and more general shops and a travel center, create a total Disney experience.

← Carthay Circle Restaurant in Downtown Disney®

2

KNOTT'S BERRY FARM AND SOAK CITY

🅰 B7   📍 8039 Beach Blvd, Buena Park   🕐 Times vary, check website
🌐 knotts.com

Located in Buena Park, 6 miles (10 km) from Disneyland® Resort, Knott's Berry Farm evolved from a boysenberry farm in the 1920s to a 21st-century entertainment complex. Today it offers more than 165 different rides and attractions, including dozens of live-action stages, shows, thrill rides, shopping, dining, and a full-service resort hotel. Next door, Soak City is a large water adventure park.

① Camp Snoopy

Inspired by the majestic High Sierra, Camp Snoopy's 6-acre (2.4-ha) wonderland is an interactive participatory kids' paradise. There are over 30 attractions and pint-sized rides, hosted by the beloved *Peanuts* characters Snoopy, Lucy, and Charlie Brown. Children under 12 delight in the Timberline Twister roller coaster, the Red Baron's airplanes, and an old-fashioned Ferris wheel, where parents can also enjoy wonderful views. The Charlie Brown's Kite Flyer features two-passenger swings that rise 18 ft (5.5 m) in the air. Woodstock's Airmail is a child-sized version of Supreme Scream®, simulating a rocket launch. Kids of all ages can come aboard Lucy's Tugboat, take a spin on the Sierra Sidewinder roller coaster, or watch a show at the Camp Snoopy Theatre.

② Fiesta Village

Celebrating California's Spanish legacy, Fiesta Village offers a superb collection of Mexican-themed adventures and high-energy thrills. Sol Spin takes riders six stories into the air in all directions. A ride on the world's oldest Dentzel Carousel is a nostalgic treat for all ages. Two large roller coasters, the family-pleasing Jaguar! and, for the more adventurous fun-seeker, Montezooma's Revenge, provide exciting thrill rides.

③ Indian Trails Stage

The music, dance, and folklore of Native Americans are celebrated through these dance presentations that relay the culture and history of tribes such as the Navajo, Cherokee, and Chumash.

④ Old West Ghost Town

This 1880s Goldrush town has authentic 19th-century buildings. An 1880 steam

Did You Know?

Knott's Berry Farm became a theme park in the 1940s - over a decade before Disneyland® opened.

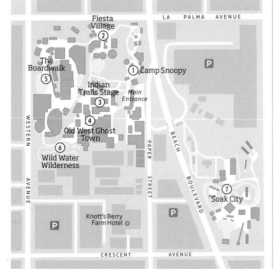

↑ Timber Mountain Log Ride
in Old West Ghost Town,
Knott's Berry Farm

train, the Ghost Town & Calico Railroad, circles the park, and an original Butterfield Stagecoach takes passengers on a trip into the past.

The Gold Trails Hotel and Mercantile, a restored Kansas schoolhouse, and the Western Trails Museum are chock-full of Wild West memorabilia. Visitors can join a line-dance at Calico Square or float through a real 1880s sawmill before plunging down a water-fall on the Timber Mountain Log Ride.

At the heart of Ghost Town, the GhostRider wooden roller coaster towers over the park while the Silver Bullet steel coaster suspends riders beneath the track and climbs to a height of 146 ft (45 m). Round off your visit with the Wild West Stunt Show and a drink and live entertainment in the Calico Saloon.

The Boardwalk

A continuous beach party is the theme here, where everything centers around Southern California's seaside culture. Beachside concessions and the most radical thrill rides rule: Supreme Scream® simulates a rocket launch and

the Coast Rider and Xcelerator are also not for the nervous, while HangTime, a gravity-defying dive coaster, provides the steepest vertical drop in California. Afterwards, visitors can relax by taking in a big-stage show featuring the *Peanuts* characters at the Charles M. Schulz Theatre.

Wild Water Wilderness

Experience the magic of the river wilderness with a raging white-water river excursion. With soaring geysers, a giant waterfall, and indigenous wildlife, Calico River Rapids will fulfill your wildest dreams. The circular raft ride, which seats six passengers, passes through rushing waters and currents, making twists and turns along the way.

Soak City

Adjacent to Knott's Berry Farm's main park, and separately gated, Soak City is Southern California's largest water adventure park, with 23 awesome water rides, themed on California's surfing

culture. It serves up 13 water logged acres (5.3 ha), replete with tube and body slides, extreme water slides, surfing pipelines, a six-lane super slide, the relaxing Sunset River, where you can float while drifting one-third of a mile along a river-like pool, and Tidal Wave Bay, a special pool with gentle to moderate wave action. Gremmie Lagoon is a wet playground with hands-on fun for younger kids.

There are changing rooms and lockers for personal belongings and a couple of pizza and burger restaurants.

STAY

Knott's Berry Farm Hotel

The 320-room hotel offers a Snoopy-themed wing, pools, a fitness center, and children's activity area.

🏠 7675 Crescent Ave, Buena Park Ⓦknotts. com/stay

③ ⟨⟩ Ⓜ 🛍

MISSION SAN JUAN CAPISTRANO

🅰 E7 🏠 26801 Ortega Hwy, San Juan Capistrano
🕘 9am–4pm Wed–Sun 🚫 Thanksgiving, Dec 25 🌐 missionsjc.com

Father Junípero Serra founded Mission San Juan Capistrano, known as the "Jewel of the Missions," in November 1776. Today it is one of the state's most important historical and cultural centers.

San Juan Capistrano was one of the first missions to be set up along the coast, and its chapel is the only surviving building in California in which Father Junípero Serra *(p225)* preached. One of the largest and most prosperous in the whole chain of 21 missions established between 1769 and 1833, the mission was crowned by the Great Stone Church, completed in 1806. Six years later this was destroyed by an earthquake, leaving a ruined shell amid a rambling complex of adobe and brick buildings. Walking among its preserved features, ornamental gardens, and historical exhibits, it's not hard to imagine the mission in its former days.

The kitchens have corner ovens and displays of utensils.

This kicha (domed hut), built from reeds, is a re-creation of the traditional dwellings of Native American villages at the time of the mission.

The padres of Mission San Juan Capistrano lived in sparsely furnished rooms and slept on hard plank beds. Visitors enjoyed more comfortable accommodations.

The original four sacred bells from the Great Stone Church now hang in the wall of this small garden. The larger pair date from 1796.

1,361

The number of people living in the mission at its peak in 1812.

A statue of the founder, Father Junípero Serra, and a Native American boy stands in a corner of the gardens.

↑ Flourishing plant life around the fountain in the mission's courtyard

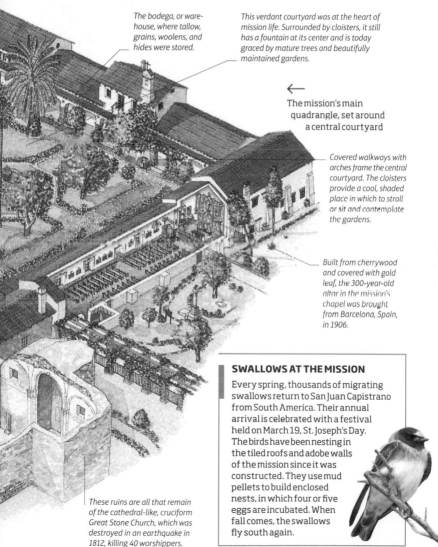

The bodega, or warehouse, where tallow, grains, woolens, and hides were stored.

This verdant courtyard was at the heart of mission life. Surrounded by cloisters, it still has a fountain at its center and is today graced by mature trees and beautifully maintained gardens.

← The mission's main quadrangle, set around a central courtyard

Covered walkways with arches frame the central courtyard. The cloisters provide a cool, shaded place in which to stroll or sit and contemplate the gardens.

Built from cherrywood and covered with gold leaf, the 300-year-old altar in the mission's chapel was brought from Barcelona, Spain, in 1906.

These ruins are all that remain of the cathedral-like, cruciform Great Stone Church, which was destroyed in an earthquake in 1812, killing 40 worshippers.

SWALLOWS AT THE MISSION

Every spring, thousands of migrating swallows return to San Juan Capistrano from South America. Their annual arrival is celebrated with a festival held on March 19, St. Joseph's Day. The birds have been nesting in the tiled roofs and adobe walls of the mission since it was constructed. They use mud pellets to build enclosed nests, in which four or five eggs are incubated. When fall comes, the swallows fly south again.

Pleasure boats lined up in beautiful Avalon Bay on Catalina Island

4

CATALINA ISLAND

E7 From San Pedro, John Wayne Airport, & Long Beach From San Pedro, Long Beach, Dana Point, & Newport Beach Green Pleasure Pier, Avalon; Isthmus Pier, Two Harbors; visitcatalinaisland.com

Just 22 miles (50 km) from the mainland, Catalina Island is the most accessible of California's Channel Islands. Much of the island's mountainous landscape remains unspoiled, and it has long been a favorite weekend and vacation destination.

①

Little Harbor

From Two Harbors or Avalon

This out-of-the-way spot on the island's west shore has a sheltered cove with a beach and a scenic harbor. There are also several hiking trails along the bay and a good campsite.

②

Avalon

Surrounding scenic Avalon Bay, the town of Avalon is home to about 4,000 people. Locals get around in golf carts, which you can rent from Golf Cart Rentals, 625 Crescent Avenue. Known locally as Front Street, Crescent Avenue is also where you will find many of the best restaurants and shops, while Pleasure Pier is the hub for Catalina's boat tours. Tour Plaza is where you pick up the Safari Bus connecting Avalon to Two Harbors.

③

Catalina Island Museum

217 Metropole Ave, Avalon 8am-5pm daily catalinamuseum.org

This museum has exhibits showing how Catalina Island has historically been used for ranching, mining, tourism, and as a film location. Artifacts include pottery and tiles dating to the 1920s–30s. Photographs show island life from the late 19th century to

CATALINA WILDLIFE

Over the centuries, Catalina has become a sanctuary for plants and animals that do not inhabit the mainland. Unusual animal subspecies have evolved, such as the Catalina Island fox *(right)*. Many animals have been introduced to the island by settlers, whether intentionally or by accident. Catalina even has a population of bison, ferried over in 1924 for a film shoot.

(gathering place), it was never a gambling venue but was once a famous ballroom and also contained a movie theater. Lovingly restored, today it hosts the Catalina Film Festival in September and the JazzTrax Festival in October.

___

⑤ Wrigley Memorial & Botanic Gardens

🏠 1400 Avalon Canyon Rd, Avalon ⏰ 8am–5pm daily

This large park honoring William Wrigley, Jr., has an imposing memorial to the founder of the largest manu-facturer of chewing gum in the world, and a collection of plants endemic to Catalina, many of which are very rare.

___

⑥ Two Harbors

A popular spot for anchoring yachts, this village has a diving center and is great for hiking, biking, snorkeling, kayaking, and scuba diving. It hosts the October Buccaneer Days festival, which features street parties where people come dressed as pirates.

the present day. There are also exhibits of archaeological digs, including the largest collections of Tongva and Gabrielino arti-facts in the world.

___

Catalina Casino

🏠 Casino Point, Avalon
📞 (310) 510-0179

Daily tours take place at the Catalina Casino, a 1929 Art Deco Jewel. Taking its name from the Italian *casino*

STAY

Zane Grey Pueblo Hotel

Stunning views across Avalon are the highlight of this 1926 Hopi-style pueblo building *(p254)*, once owned by Western author Zane Grey.

🏠 199 Chimes Tower Rd, Avalon
🌐 zanegreyhotel.com

$⑤$⑤$⑤

___

Mt Ada

The former home of William Wrigley, Jr., the founder of Wrigley chewing gum, offers luxurious accommo-dations in what feels like a private residence. Amenities include golf carts, casino tours, and wine receptions.

🏠 398 Wrigley Rd, Avalon
🌐 catalina chamber.com

$⑤$⑤$⑤

The Nixon Presidential Library and Museum's grand entrance hall

forming a food hall and community space. Here, and in the neighboring 1926 former Packard dealership, there are 50 gourmet vendors, who will satisfy any food critic. Diners can sit out in the picnic gardens or on shaded porches.

EXPERIENCE MORE

Bowers Museum

🅰C7 🏠2002 N Main St, Santa Ana 🚌To Anaheim 🚌45 S ⏰10am-4pm Tue-Sun ⏳Jan 1, Jul 4, Thanksgiving, Dec 25 🌐bowers.org

The Bowers has long been considered Orange County's leading art museum. Its serene Mission-style buildings hold rich permanent

---

Nixon Presidential Library and Museum

🅰C7 🏠18001 Yorba Linda Blvd, Yorba Linda 🚌To Fullerton ⏰10am-5pm daily ⏳Thanksgiving, Dec 25 🌐nixonlibrary.gov

The life and achievements of Richard Nixon, president of the United States from 1969 to 1974, are celebrated in this museum and archive. In the grounds is the simple wooden house where the former president was born in 1913. Nearby are a Reflecting Pool and the graves of Nixon and his wife, Pat, marked by black granite tombstones.

In the museum, a walk-through exhibit provides a chronological account of Nixon's rise and fall. In the World Leaders' Room, statues of famous politicians are surrounded by some of the gifts that Nixon received while in office, such as a 6th-century BC statue of the goddess Isis from Egyptian president Anwar Sadat and a malachite jewelry box from Leonid Brezhnev, leader of the Soviet Union.

Historic items exhibited in other galleries include a lump of rock from the moon, a 12-ft (3.5-m) section of the Berlin Wall, and dresses worn by Pat Nixon when she was First Lady. Visitors are also able to eavesdrop on the infamous "Watergate Tapes," which led to Nixon's resignation.

Anaheim Packing District

🅰C7 🏠440 S Anaheim Blvd, Anaheim 🌐anaheim packingdistrict.com

As the name Orange County suggests, citrus groves used to extend for miles across this region. Farmers would take freshly picked oranges and lemons to packing houses where the process of sorting, labeling, and boxing took place, before loading the fruit onto rail cars that would carry it across the country. The Anaheim Packing District has been repurposed into a shopping area, with the Mission Revival-style Anaheim Packing House at its center,

---

Did You Know?

The "Watergate Tapes" were almost destroyed but Congress passed a new Act to protect them in 1974.

EAT

Georgia's
Try classic southern comfort food at this Anaheim Packing District spot.

🅰C7 🏠440 S Anaheim Blvd no. 209A, Anaheim 🌐georgias-restaurant. com

---

Angelo's Hamburgers
Roller-skating servers deliver burgers and hot dogs right to your car.

🅰C7 🏠511 S State College, Anaheim 🌐angeloshamburgers. net

---

collections and high-profile temporary exhibitions. There is a stylish café and a shop packed with world crafts and art books.

The museum's display of African masks is reason enough for a pilgrimage. Other galleries, with treasures from cultures of Southeast Asia, Oceania, Mexico, and America, reflect the museum's commitment to the art of Indigenous peoples, with examples of their crafts illustrating religious beliefs and daily life. The upstairs galleries, decorated with 1930s murals and plasterwork, cover the mission and rancho periods of California and Orange County. Guided tours run on Saturdays and Sundays.

One block away, a former bank has been converted into the companion **Kidseum**, where kids can enjoy arts-related activities and try on masks and costumes from all over the world.

Kidseum

📍1802 N Main St, Santa Ana
📞(714) 480-1520
🕐10am–3pm Tue–Fri, 11am–3pm Sat & Sun

8

Heritage Museum of Orange County

🅰C7 📍3101 W Harvard St, Santa Ana 🚉To Anaheim 🚌45 S 🕐1–5pm Fri, 10am–2pm Sat, 11am–3pm Sun 🕐Jan 1, Easter Sun, Thanksgiving, Dec 25 🌐heritagemuseumoc.org

Victorian times in Orange County are brought to life in this three-story mansion, built in 1898 by civil engineer Hiram Clay Kellogg. Fascinated by ships, Kellogg incorporated several nautical design features into his residence. The floor in the oval, cabin-like dining room is laid in strips to resemble a ship's deck. Some of the drawers in the built-in wooden cabinets can also be opened from the kitchen, on the other side of the wall.

The mansion now houses a child-friendly museum, where young visitors can dress up in genuine antique clothing and experience life as it was at the turn of the 20th century. Upstairs, rooms are furnished with antique school desks, dolls' houses, and period games. Downstairs, visitors can see a hand-crank telephone and an old-fashioned kitchen.

9

Christ Cathedral

🅰C7 📍13280 Chapman Av, Garden Grove 🚌45 N 🕐10am–3pm Mon–Fri, 9am–4pm Sat 🌐christcathedralcalifornia.org

Constructed from an intricate maze of white steel trusses covered with more than 10,000 panes of silvered glass, the Christ Cathedral (formerly known as the Crystal Cathedral) is a shimmering monument to the television-led evangelism that enthrals millions of Americans. The Crystal Cathedral was the main place of worship for R. Schuller's Reformed Church of America which, after a lengthy evangelical crusade, filed for bankruptcy in 2010. The Roman Catholic Diocese of Orange bought the church in 2012 and reopened it as Christ Cathedral in 2017.

Designed in 1980 by the influential American architect Philip Johnson, the star-shaped cathedral is both a spiritual shrine and an architectural wonder accommodating a congregation of 4,000.

Beside the church, the 236-ft (72-m) steeple, added in 1990, is adorned with polished stainless-steel prisms.

← The mirror-like exterior of Christ Cathedral, and *(inset)* the organ, said to be the biggest in the world

⑩

Huntington Beach

🅰B7 🅸 325 Pacific Coast Hwy; www.surfcityusa.com

A long sandy beach and a consistent wave break have long drawn generations of surfers to Huntington Beach. In summer, the area south of the pier hosts the largest surfing competition in the world: the US Open of Surfing.

The **Huntington Beach International Surfing Museum** displays surfboards, clothing, posters, and even the Bolex camera used to film the seminal 1964 surf documentary *The Endless Summer*. Nearby, on the Surfing Walk of Fame, plaques in the sidewalk honor famous surfers.

Adjacent to Huntington Beach are the salt marshes, lowlands, and mesa that make up the **Bolsa Chica Ecological Preserve**, which shelters 200 species of migratory birds.

Huntington Beach International Surfing Museum

 🅰411 Olive Av 🕒Noon-5pm Tue-Sun 🅆huntington beachsurfingmuseum.org

Bolsa Chica Ecological Preserve

🅰Interpretive Center, 3842 Warner Av 🅆bolsachica.org

SURF CITY, USA

Huntington Beach's nickname Surf City comes from the eponymous 1963 song by Jan and Dean. Other beaches have their own reputation: the Wedge in Newport Beach is famed for its shore breaks, while Lower Trestles near San Clemente has a reef break that gives a long ride. With its own language, style, and music, surfing is the hallmark of the Southern California lifestyle.

⑪

Newport Beach

🅰B7 🅆visitnewport beach.com

The picturesque Newport Beach consists of several neighborhoods spread out along the coast, around a harbor, and into the hills. The Balboa Peninsula is marked by two piers – the Newport Pier and the Balboa Pier – with 3 miles (5 km) of beach between them and a board-walk popular with cyclists and joggers.

A harbor cruise with the **Fun Zone Boat Company** allows visitors to admire expensive homes and yachts from the water. The Balboa Island Ferry links the peninsula to Balboa Island, which is filled with flower-covered cottages on narrow streets named for precious gems. Marine Avenue, its principal shopping street, is lined with enticing boutiques and sunny cafés.

Fun Zone Boat Company

 🅰700 E Edgewater Pl 🕒11am-4pm Thu-Mon 🅆funzoneboats.com

12

Laguna Beach

 E7 ℹ️ 381 Forest Av;
www.visitlaguna
beach.com

When architect and painter
Norman St. Clair discovered
the dramatic landscape and
special light of Laguna Beach
in 1903, other artists soon
followed. Today Laguna's
vibrant art scene and festivals
continue to draw visitors,
and the **Laguna Art Museum**
presents a superb collection
of Californian art.

Just north of Laguna Beach,
Crystal Cove State Park
encompasses coastal hillsides
laced with hiking trails and
beaches with tidal pools.
On the eastern edge of the
park, you learn about how
rescued sea lions and seals
are rehabilitated at the **Pacific
Marine Mammal Center**.

Laguna Art Museum

♿ 🏛️ 307 Cliff Dr 🕐 11am–
5pm Thu–Tue 🌐 lagunaart
museum.org

Crystal Cove State Park

🏛️ 8471 N Coast Hwy
🌐 crystalcovestatepark.org

**Pacific Marine Mammal
Center**

🏛️ 20612 Laguna Canyon Rd
🕐 10am–4pm daily
🌐 pacificmmc.org

13

Dana Point and San Clemente

 E7 ℹ️ 101 W Avenida
Vista Hermosa, Suite 190;
www.sanclemente.com;
www.danapoint.org

Dana Point takes its name
from 19th-century adventure
writer Richard Henry Dana. The
town centers around a busy
harbor filled with pleasure,
fishing, and excursion boats.
At the nearby Ocean Institute,
kids can learn about tall ships
and discover mysteries of the
ocean. Just south of Dana
Point, San Clemente is a beach
town with a long pier popular
among fishermen.

The ocean off this stretch
of coast is home to one of
the richest marine mammal
preserves in the world. Humpback, blue, and California gray
whales are common sightings,
as well as megapods (huge
schools) of dolphins.

EAT

Sugar Shack Café
This local favorite
serves up substantial
plates of omelets,
pancakes, and
breakfast burritos.

 B7 🏛️ 213 Main St,
Huntington Beach
🍽️ Dinner 🌐 hbsugar
shack.com

$ $ $

Rasta Taco
Mexican tacos with
Jamaican spices and
flavorings are the
specialty here.

 E7 🏛️ 170 Beach St,
Laguna Beach
🌐 rastataco.com

$ $ $

Ruby's Diner
A small chain serving
quality hamburgers
and shakes in a fun
1940s atmosphere.
Each venue has its own
theme, such as trains
or vintage cars.

 E7 🏛️ Balboa Pier
Laguna Beach
🌐 rubys.com

$ $ $

STAY

**Crystal Cove State
Park Beach Cottages**
Twenty-one restored
beach cottages dating
from the 1920s to the
1940s offer charming
accommodations.

 B7 🏛️ 5 Crystal Cove,
Newport Coast
🌐 crystalcove.org/
beach-cottages

$ $ $

← Huntington Beach pier,
one of the longest public
piers on the West Coast

SAN DIEGO COUNTY

The area occupied by San Diego County was originally home to the Kumeyaay people. The first European to reach here was Spaniard Juan Rodríguez Cabrillo, who put ashore at Point Loma, 10 miles (13 km) from today's downtown San Diego, in 1542. European settlement, however, didn't begin in earnest until 1769, when Spanish friar Junípero Serra laid down the first link in the chain of 21 missions that underpins the modern state of California. When Serra was canonized by the Catholic Church in 2015 many Native Americans objected, charging him with enslaving and abusing the Indigenous population at the time.

The original settlement, known today as Old Town, remained small long after California was absorbed by the US in 1848. It wasn't until the late 1860s that real estate developer Alonzo Horton began to promote his "New Town" closer to the bay, which ultimately became downtown San Diego. In 1915, the city's national reputation was established by the first of two international expositions in Balboa Park – the Panama-California Exposition, held in 1915–17, and the 1935–36 Pacific International Exposition.

The history of San Diego is intertwined with the US Navy, who arrived here in 1904. During World War II much of San Diego's economy came to be dominated by the military, and the population more than doubled between 1930 and 1950. After the Cold War ended in the 1990s the military sector reduced dramatically, but the city is still the largest military establishment in the world. In recent years, San Diego has also become a biotech industry hub.

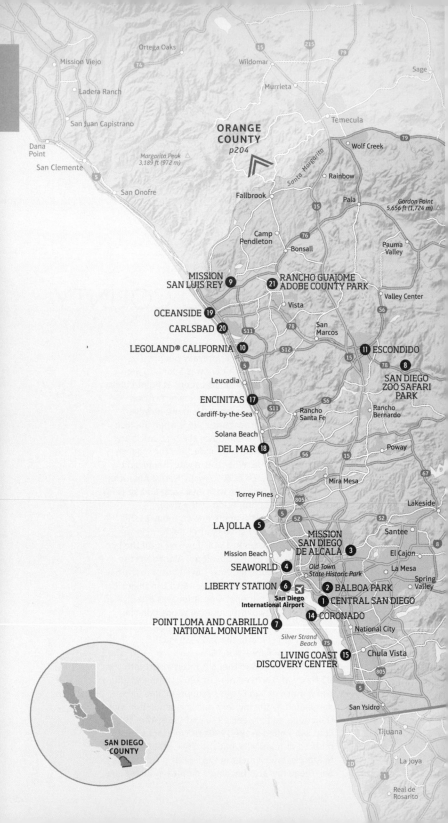

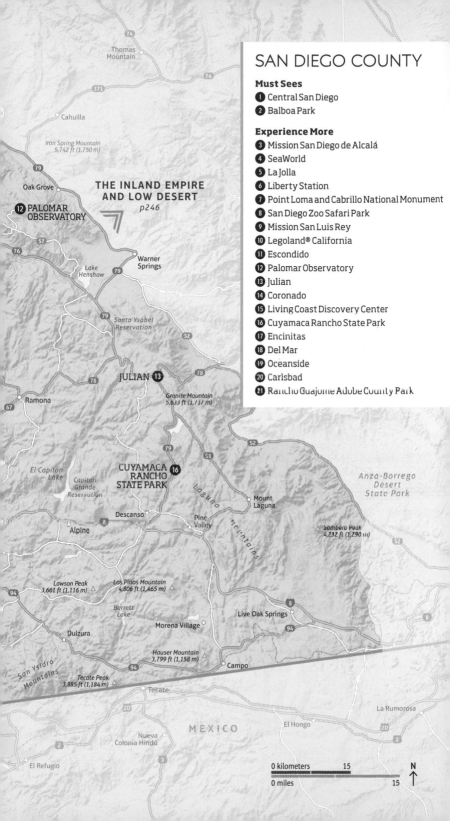

SAN DIEGO COUNTY

Must Sees
① Central San Diego
② Balboa Park

Experience More
③ Mission San Diego de Alcalá
④ SeaWorld
⑤ La Jolla
⑥ Liberty Station
⑦ Point Loma and Cabrillo National Monument
⑧ San Diego Zoo Safari Park
⑨ Mission San Luis Rey
⑩ Legoland® California
⑪ Escondido
⑫ Palomar Observatory
⑬ Julian
⑭ Coronado
⑮ Living Coast Discovery Center
⑯ Cuyamaca Rancho State Park
⑰ Encinitas
⑱ Del Mar
⑲ Oceanside
⑳ Carlsbad
㉑ Rancho Guajome Adobe County Park

THE INLAND EMPIRE
AND LOW DESERT
p246

0 kilometers   15
0 miles   15

N

Soaring skyscrapers
lining the waterfront
of San Diego Bay ↑

1

CENTRAL SAN DIEGO

Ⓐ E7 ✈ **Lindbergh Field Airport** 🚌 **1050 Kettner Blvd**
🚏 **102 W Bdwy** ℹ **1140 N Harbor Dr; www.sandiego.org**

San Diego Bay forms a natural harbor around which
the second-largest city in California has grown. The
military expedition that arrived to secure Alta
California for Spain in 1769 built a presidio near the
San Diego River, an area now known as Old Town State
Historic Park *(p232)*. The growth of modern San Diego
began in the 1870s, when the waterfront was developed,
including the streets of the Gaslamp Quarter *(p230)*,
which form the centerpiece of San Diego's Downtown.

Embarcadero and Seaport Village

🏠 **Corner of N & E Harbor Dr**

The Embarcadero presents an
important part of San Diego's
character – its connection with
the sea. Today's cruise ships
moor alongside historic sailing
ships and an aircraft carrier..

At the south end, Seaport
Village offers over 50 unique
shops, as well as several
waterfront restaurants and
cafés. Close to the village, the

Headquarters, the former
headquarters of the San
Diego Police, now holds high-
end restaurants and shops, as
well as a small museum.

2

Maritime Museum

🏠 **1492 N Harbor Dr** 🕐 **9am-
8pm daily (to 9pm summer)**
🌐 **sdmaritime.com**

The *Star of India*, an 1863
merchant ship, and the San
Francisco Bay passenger ferry,

the *Berkeley* (1898), are
moored here. Alongside them
are the steam yacht *Medea*
(1904) and the HMS *Surprise*,
a replica of an 18th-century
frigate from the 2003 film
Master and Commander.

3

Museum of Contemporary Art

🏠 **1001 Kettner Blvd**
🕐 **11am-5pm Thu-Tue**
🚫 **Jan 1, Dec 25** 🌐 **mcasd.org**

This museum is the Downtown
counterpart of the museum
that shares its name in La Jolla
(p238). The museum comprises
two buildings, directly across
from each other. The four
galleries display changing
exhibitions of new work by
living artists, and selections
from the museum's large
permanent collection.

⑤ 🍴 🖥 🛍
Little Italy

📍 **Between W Laurel St and W A St, Pacific Hwy and Front St** 🌐 **littleitalysd.com**

Little Italy, sometimes known as Middletown, was originally a fishing neighborhood but has now gentrified, although it retains its artistic character. Of note is the iconic Little Italy sign; its nautical theme pays tribute to the Italian immigrants who worked in San Diego's once world-famous tuna and canning industry. At Little Italy's heart is the cobblestoned Piazza della Famiglia, which is lined with shops and cafés, and is the site of cultural events and the Saturday morning farmers' market.

Antique firefighting wagons and other memorabilia are on display at the **San Diego Firehouse Museum**. A key exhibit is a piece of New York's World Trade Center.

San Diego Firehouse Museum

📍 **1572 Columbia St** 🌐 **san diegofirehousemuseum.com**

④
USS Midway Museum

📍 **910 N Harbor Dr** 🕙 **10am–5pm daily** 🚫 **Thanksgiving, Dec 25** 🌐 **midway.org**

Over 60 exhibits, including the engine room and pilots' ready rooms, are on display aboard one of America's longest-serving aircraft carriers.

DRINK

Vin de Syrah
A subterranean bar that serves wines, spirits, and beers, complemented by cheese plates.

📍 **901 5th Av** 🌐 **syrahwineparlor.com**

False Idol
A Tiki-themed speakeasy with drinks that pack a punch.

📍 **675 W Beech St (inside the Craft & Commerce)** 🌐 **falseidoltiki.com**

Pure Project Balboa Park
Great craft beers at an upscale taproom with a large terrace.

📍 **2965 5th Av** 🌐 **purebrewing.org**

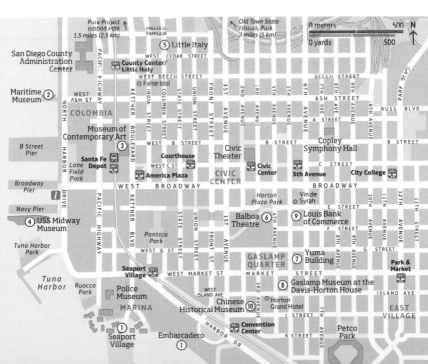

THE GASLAMP QUARTER

Balboa Theatre

📍 868 4th Av
🌐 broadwaysd.com

This landmark 1,500-seat venue, built in Moorish and Spanish Revivial style in 1924, started out as a grand vaudeville movie theater with waterfalls flanking the stage. Notice the beautiful tiled dome on the roof. After World War II

> The Balboa Theatre hosts the annual Mainly Mozart Festival in May and June, and touring Broadway productions.

the Balboa closed as a movie theater. A restoration project converted the building into a performing arts venue in 2008. Today it hosts the annual Mainly Mozart Festival in May and June, and touring Broadway productions.

---

⑦
Yuma Building

📍 631 5th Av

Built in 1882, this was one of the first brick buildings to be constructed during the Gaslamp Quarter's boom years of the 1880s. It was home to a variety of businesses; the most infamous was a brothel that operated here in the early 20th century. By this time, the Gaslamp Quarter was notorious for prostitution, gambling, and drinking and was known as the "Stingaree." In 1912 the police raided the red-light district in an attempt to rid the area of prostitution – the Yuma Building's brothel was the first one to be closed. This beautiful building now houses retail space on street level and a grand, private townhouse on the upper floors.

 INSIDER TIP
ArtsTix in Horton Plaza Park

San Diego supports a vibrant performing arts community. A few paces from the Balboa Theatre, this not-for-profit ticket kiosk in Horton Plaza Park offers tickets for just about any theater, dance, or music performance in the county. Some tickets are sold at full price, but substantially discounted tickets are very often available. They also sell tickets to most of the area's theme parks and attractions, including Legoland, San Diego Zoo & Safari Park, SeaWorld, and the USS Midway Museum.

⑧
Gaslamp Museum at the Davis-Horton House

📍 410 Island Av 🕐 10am-4:30pm Tue-Sat, noon-3:30pm Sun 🌐 gaslamp foundation.org

This museum, home to the Gaslamp Quarter Historical Foundation, is named after William Heath Davis and Alonzo Horton. Davis was a merchant and trader, who

A tram trundling past the Balboa Theatre in the heart of the Gaslamp Quarter

↑ The ornate facade of the historic Louis Bank of Commerce building

tried unsuccessfully to develop San Diego closer to San Diego Bay in 1850. This house was constructed as part of the project. Real estate developer Horton, who many consider to be the founder of San Diego, lived here from 1860 to 1869. It's the oldest wooden structure in the downtown area. Each room is furnished to reflect a period of the house's history, including areas showing it as a pre-Civil War military officers' barracks, a county hospital, and private home.

Louis Bank of Commerce

🚫 To the public

This Victorian Baroque Revival structure is one of the most photographed buildings in the Gaslamp Quarter. Businessman Louis Isadore, in partnership with the Bank of Commerce, erected this building in the 1880s. Home to the bank until 1883, it was converted into an oyster bar in 1893 and became a favorite haunt of Old West lawman and gambler Wyatt Earp. The upper floors of the building later contained a notorious brothel.

→

Entrance to the Chinese Historical Museum, guarded by an imperial guardian lion

STAY

Horton Grand Hotel
Furnished in 1880s period style, this luxurious boutique hotel is housed in two beautiful Victorian Italianate buildings in the heart of the Gaslamp Quarter. Rooms have gas log fireplaces and balconies.

🏠 311 Island Av
Ⓦ hortongrand.com

$$$

After restoration work, the structure was sold to a real estate firm in 2016 and is being redeveloped.

⑩

Chinese Historical Museum

🏠 404 3rd Av Ⓒ 10:30am-4pm Wed-Sun Ⓦ sdchm.org

Founded in 1896, the San Diego Chinese Historical Society was established to uphold Chinese and Chinese American History. The society founded this museum in 1996 to share the heritage of San Diego's Chinese community. Housed in an old mansion, the exhibits show the history of the local Chinese population and its art and culture through fine art, folk art, decorative arts, clothing, historic photographs, miniature models, and archaeological finds. The museum also regularly hosts lectures, educational programs on Chinese history, and special events such as celebrations of Chinese New Year, the Moon Festival, and Veterans Day.

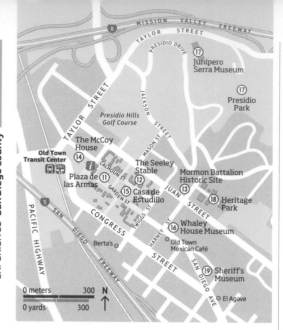

The McCoy House

📍 4002 Wallace St 📞 (619) 220-5422 🕙 10am-4pm Mon-Thu (to 5pm Fri-Sun)

San Diego sheriff and state senator James McCoy built this wood-frame home in 1869 as a wedding present for his wife Winifred. Inside is a small museum with a reproduced Victorian parlor. The museum is a good source of information about the Old Town State Historic Park's history

Casa de Estudillo

📍 4000 Mason St 📞 (619) 220-5422 🕙 10am-5pm daily

Of the original adobe and wooden buildings in Old Town, this is one of the most impressive. It was constructed by the commander of the presidio, José María de Estudillo, in 1829. The house, built around an internal courtyard, is furnished in the Mexican-California style.

OLD TOWN STATE HISTORIC PARK

Plaza de las Armas

Considered the "birthplace" of California, this plaza is lined with some of San Diego's earliest restored and rebuilt 19th-century buildings, and served as the center for public activities such as political and religious gatherings. The Robinson-Rose House, a replica of a house built by lawyer and politician James Robinson in 1853, houses the Old Town's visitor center. A short walk away is the First San Diego Courthouse Museum, with displays on the building's role in the town's civic history.

The Seeley Stable

📍 2648 Calhoun St 📞 (619) 220-5422 🕙 9am-5pm daily

The museum housed in this reconstructed stable displays a collection of horse-drawn carriages and stagecoaches, as well as some interesting Wild West memorabilia.

Mormon Battalion Historic Site

📍 2510 Juan St 📞 (619) 298-3317 🕙 10am-8pm Mon-Sat, 1-8pm Sun (to 9pm in summer)

The Mormon Battalion served in the Mexican-American War. Between 1846 and 1847, 500 men marched from Council Bluffs, Iowa, to San Diego, advancing America's westward expansion.

Docents dressed in character lead visitors through an interactive tour to dramatize the sacrifices of this religious military unit's epic journey.

→

The restored Victorian Sherman-Gilbert House in Heritage Park

Whaley House Museum

🏠 2476 San Diego Av
🕐 Times vary, check website 🌐 whaleyhouse.org

Some years before this house was built in 1857, one of San Diego's most infamous thieves, Yankee Jim, was convicted of larceny and hanged here. Whaley House now enjoys a reputation as one of the most haunted houses in America. Ghost tours are available in the evenings, as well as self-guided day tours.

Presidio Park and Junípero Serra Museum

🏠 2727 Presidio Dr
🕐 10am–4pm Sat & Sun

Overlooking the San Diego River, this park occupies the site of the presidio fort and mission built by the Spanish in 1769. The ruins of the presidio are still being explored by archaeologists, whose finds can be seen in the museum. Exhibits upstairs describe daily life in the presidio and the changing face of San Diego. On a hill within the park, the Junípero Serra Museum is named after the controversial founder of California's mission chain (*p225*).

Heritage Park

🛈 2454 Heritage Park Row
🕐 8am–5pm Mon–Fri
🌐 sandiegocounty.gov

On the east side of Old Town, Heritage Park is a collection of immaculately restored Victorian buildings from all over the city. Of note is the Temple Beth Israel, San Diego's first synagogue and one of the few buildings in Heritage Park where visitors can tour the interior. The 1887 Sherman-Gilbert House was a venue for receptions hosting internationally famous entertainers, such as dancer Anna Pavlova and pianist Artur Rubinstein.

Sheriff's Museum

🏠 2384 San Diego Av
🕐 Noon–5pm Wed–Sun
(to 6pm in summer)
🌐 sheriffsmuseum.org

This museum gives a great insight into the work of law enforcement past and present. A huge variety of firearms is on display, and there's even a replica jail cell where you can have your photo taken. Other rooms feature the history of women in the force and stories of notorious San Diego crimes. Outside, kids can sit in a sheriff's vintage police car and on a real life motorcyle.

EAT

Old Town Mexican Café
This spot is known for generous portions of the best handmade tortillas in San Diego.

🏠 2489 San Diego Ave
🌐 oldtownmexcafe.com

$$$

Berta's
Berta serves all manner of Latin American dishes from Costa Rica to Argentina.

🏠 3928 Twiggs St
🌐 bertasinoldtown.com

$$$

El Agave
Intricate Mexican mole sauces are a specialty at this award-winning restaurant and well-stocked tequileria.

🏠 2304 San Diego Ave
🌐 elagave.com

$$$

→ A gushing fountain in Plaza de Panama by the Balboa Park Visitor Center

BALBOA PARK

 E7 🏛1549 El Prado, San Diego 🚌7 ⏰9:30am–4:30pm daily 🚫Jan 1, Thanksgiving, Dec 25 🌐balboapark.org

Founded in 1868, Balboa Park was the site of the 1915–17 Panama–California Exposition, a world fair celebrating the opening of the Panama Canal. Several of the Spanish Revival-style pavilions survive, forming the basis for a rich collection of museums and venues.

INSIDER TIP
Tickets and Tours

Balboa Park's museums are each independently run with separate admissions. If planning to visit multiple museums, a 1-day or 7-day Balboa Park Explorer Pass is good value for money. These are available online or at the Visitors' Center. Ranger and docent-led tours leave from the House of Hospitality on Tuesday and Sunday. Other tours explore Balboa Park's architectural heritage, the Botanical Building, and the Japanese Friendship Garden.

①
San Diego Museum of Man

🏛1350 El Prado ⏰10am–5pm daily 🚫Thanksgiving, Dec 25, and for some events 🌐museumofman.org

The landmark pavilion of the Panama–California Exposition of 1915–17, also known as the California Building, houses an anthropological museum on the early history of mankind. The building is one of the most recognizable in the park, with an ornate cathedral-like facade and a soaring bell tower that was used by director Orson Welles in *Citizen Kane* (1941). Exhibits cover topics such as the cultures of ancient Egypt and the Mayans, and Native American crafts.

②
San Diego Museum of Art

🏛1450 El Prado ⏰10am–5pm Mon-Tue & Thu-Sat (to 8pm Fri), noon-5pm Sun 🚫Jan 1, Thanksgiving, Dec 25 🌐sdmart.org

This museum's large, varied art collection is boosted by a program of special exhibitions. European and American art from the mid-18th to the 20th centuries is shown in the first-floor galleries, along with exhibits from southern Asia, Japan, and China. The displays on the second floor feature work from 1300 to 1850, including *Coronation of the Virgin* (1508) by Luca Signorelli.

---

③
Timken Museum of Art

🏛1500 El Prado ⏰10am–4:30pm Tue-Sat, noon-4:30pm Sun 🌐timkenmuseum.org

Opened in 1965, the Timken exhibits exquisite works in an inviting space and is the only museum in the park with free admission. Works include those by European masters such as Frans Hals (c. 1581–1666),

 ④

Museum of Photographic Arts

📍1649 El Prado ⏰10am-5pm Tue-Sun (to 8pm Fri in summer) 🚫Some Federal hols 🌐mopa.org

This museum is located on the main floor of the ornate Casa de Balboa. It specializes in high-quality traveling exhibitions that demonstrate the art and power of photography. There is also a good bookstore.

---

⑤

Mingei International Museum

📍1439 El Prado ⏰Times vary, check website 🌐mingei.org

This museum is dedicated to the world of folk art, craft, and design. In the museum's collection are

Did You Know?

Balboa Park is named after Vasco de Balboa, the first European to see the Pacific Ocean, in 1513.

some 26,000 art objects from 141 countries, including pieces by several of Mexico's most famous folk artists, Indonesian and Chinese textiles, and painted carousel horses. A multipurpose theater offers performances, lectures, and concerts, while an educational center has dedicated space for hands-on art and craft for all ages.

François Boucher (1703–70), and Paul Cézanne (1839–1906). The Timken also houses some outstanding pieces by 19th-century American artists, including *The Yosemite Fall* (1864) by Albert Bierstadt, and a collection of Russian icons.

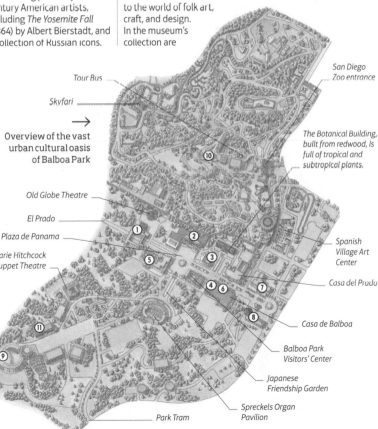

→
Overview of the vast urban cultural oasis of Balboa Park

Tour Bus
Skyfari
San Diego Zoo entrance
The Botanical Building, built from redwood, is full of tropical and subtropical plants.
Old Globe Theatre
El Prado
Plaza de Panama
Marie Hitchcock Puppet Theatre
Spanish Village Art Center
Casa del Prado
Casa de Balboa
Balboa Park Visitors' Center
Japanese Friendship Garden
Spreckels Organ Pavilion
Park Tram

San Diego History Center

⌖1649 El Prado ⏲10am-5pm daily ⊘Thanksgiving, Dec 25 🌐sandiego history.org

Located in the Casa de Balboa, this center showcases the region's unique and colorful history, exhibiting artifacts, costumes, textiles, art, furniture, and photographs. The Research Library has extensive archives of maps, architectural drawings, and one of the largest collections of photographs in the western US.

San Diego Natural History Museum

⌖1788 El Prado ⏲10am-5pm daily ⊘Jan 1, Thanksgiving, Dec 25 🌐sdnhm.org

The Natural History Museum, jovially known as "The Nat," was founded in 1874 and is still an active research institution, dedicated to improving our understanding of the evolution and diversity of the Southern and Baja California regions. There's a giant-screen theater that shows 2-D and 3-D films and a variety of programs for all ages.

Reuben H. Fleet Science Center

⌖1875 El Prado ⏲10am-5pm Mon-Thu, 10am-6pm Fri-Sun; check website for IMAX® show times 🌐rhfleet.org

Named after the man who founded the US airmail service, the Science Center's greatest attraction is the vast dome of the IMAX® cinema in the Space Theater, where films about the world around us are projected onto an enormous tilting screen. Planetarium shows are also staged.

> **The Apollo 9 has Landed exhibit features the only display west of the Rockies of an Apollo Command Module flown in space.**

The complex has a Science Center with over 100 hands-on exhibits that demonstrate the laws of science. There is also a café, and a shop selling books, games, and puzzles.

San Diego Air and Space Museum

⌖2001 Pan American Plaza ⏲10am-4:30pm daily ⊘ Jan 1, Thanksgiving, Dec 25 🌐sandiegoairandspace.org

The Air and Space Museum covers five centuries of aviation history, demonstrating the

← Dinosaur statues facing off in the San Diego Natural History Museum

↑ Magnificent flying machines packed into the Air and Space Museum's main hall

⑪
San Diego Automotive Museum

⌂2080 Pan American Plaza
◷10am–5pm daily ✕Jan 1, Thanksgiving, Dec 25
ⓦsdautomuseum.org

Dream cars and motorcycles from both the United States and Europe shine on in the highly nostalgic San Diego Automotive Museum. Because most of the cars come from private collections, the displays are constantly changing, but gleaming paintwork and whitewall tires are guaranteed. The museum's on-site library has a large collection of vintage perodicals, manuals, and magazines.

remarkable progress of flight from hot-air balloons to space age technology. It has more than 60 air- and spacecraft on display (including originals and full-scale reconstructions). The Apollo 9 has Landed exhibit features the only display west of the Rockies of an Apollo Command Module flown in space. There is also a 3-D and 4-D cinema experience.

⑩
San Diego Zoo

⌂2920 Zoo Dr ◷9am–5pm daily (Jul–Aug: to 9pm)
ⓦzoo.sandiegozoo.org

San Diego Zoo is one of the best-known zoos in the world, famous both for its conservation programs and for housing one of the largest collections of rare and endangered animals in the world. With some 4,000 animals dispersed over 100 acres (40 ha), the best introduction is to take the 35-minute narrated bus tour that covers most of the zoo. The aerial Skyfari ride, which offers a trip across the south of the park in gondola cars 180 ft (55 m) up, is also quite rewarding. After these, visitors can track down their favorites in the animal world by strolling along the paths and moving walkways. There is also a Children's Zoo, and in summer the zoo is open for nocturnal exploration.

A 1940s Oldsmobile station wagon on show at the Auto Museum ↓

EXPERIENCE MORE

 3

Mission San Diego de Alcalá

⒜E7 ⒞10818 San Diego Mission Rd, San Diego 🚌13, 20 🕙9am–4:30pm daily 🚫Jan 1, Thanksgiving, Dec 25 🌐mission sandiego.org

The first mission to be built in the California chain (p47) is today engulfed by freeways and urban development, but its harmonious buildings and gardens retain an atmosphere of peace. A small museum honors the life of the state's first Christian martyr, Padre Luis Jayme, who was killed when a group of 600 Native Americans attacked the newly established mission in 1775.

4

SeaWorld

⒜E7 ⒞500 SeaWorld Dr, San Diego 🚌9 🕙Daily; hours vary, check website 🌐seaworld.com

This large marine life adventure park on Mission Bay offers thrill rides and the chance to get close to many ocean creatures. Since the release of the 2013 documentary *Blackfish*, which questioned the ethics of keeping killer whales in captivity, SeaWorld has come under strong criticism, seeing a considerable drop in visitor numbers. As a result, the park has stopped breeding whales in captivity and has increased its conservation efforts.

5

La Jolla

⒜E7 🚌From San Diego 🛈7590 Fay Av; www.lajollabythesea.com

La Jolla is an upscale coastal resort set amid beautiful cliffs and coves with beaches perfect for swimming, scuba diving, and snorkeling. To appreciate the setting, take the Coast Walk Trail running on the top of the bluffs, with views of elegant homes on one side and the ocean on the other. Spy sea lions basking in the sun at La Jolla Cove or head down the 144 steps of an old smuggler's tunnel into Sunny Jim's sea cave.

TOP 3 **BEACHES**

Mission Beach
⒜E7
Cycle or rollerblade along the boardwalk, play beach volleyball, or ride a roller coaster.

Ocean Beach
⒜E7
Cool coffee houses, surf shops, and dive bars give a chilled-out vibe.

Pacific Beach
⒜E7
Bars and clubs draw a young crowd. Just north of the pier is a wide, family-friendly beach.

La Jolla's streets are lined with designer boutiques, top-name jewelers, and chic restaurants. There are also many galleries and the oceanfront **Museum of Contemporary Art**.

The town is also home to the University of California at San Diego and to the famous **Salk Institute for Biological Studies**, founded in 1960 by Dr.

STAY

Crystal Pier Hotel & Cottages

Wake up to the sound of ocean waves in a 1930s cottage (with a private patio) right on the Pacific Beach pier.

⒜E7 ⒞4500 Ocean Blvd, San Diego 🌐crystalpier.com

$ $ $

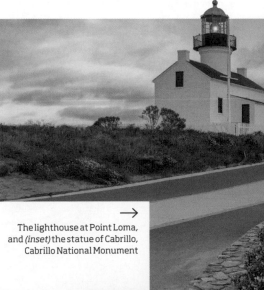

→ The lighthouse at Point Loma, and *(inset)* the statue of Cabrillo, Cabrillo National Monument

Jonas Salk, who famously developed the polio vaccine. Overlooking Scripps Beach is the Scripps Institution of Oceanography, where the **Birch Aquarium at Scripps** provides an insight into the world of oceanography, with exhibits, interactive displays, and feeding shows in the kelp tank. In the aquarium, visitors can observe sea life from the waters of the north Pacific as well as the tropics, including an Alaskan giant octopus.

The **La Jolla Historical Society** organizes interesting exhibitions on local history, art, and culture.

Museum of Contemporary Art
♿ 🏠700 Prospect St ⏰For renovation 🌐mcasd.org

Salk Institute for Biological Studies
♿ 🏠10010 N Torrey Pines Rd ⏰8am-5:30pm Mon-Fri 🔒Federal hols 🌐salk.edu

Birch Aquarium at Scripps
♿ 🏠2300 Expedition Way ⏰9am-5pm daily 🔒Jan 1, Thanksgiving, Dec 25 🌐aquarium.ucsd.edu

La Jolla Historical Society
🏠780 Prospect St ⏰Noon-4pm Wed-Sun 🌐lajollahistory.org

Liberty Station
🅰E7 🏠Historic Decatur Rd, San Diego 🌐liberty station.com

Between Downtown and Point Loma, Liberty Station, a former naval training center, has restaurants, shops, grassy areas, and museums. The **New Americans Museum** explores the experiences of recent immigrants. The **Visions Art Museum** displays quilts.

New Americans Museum
🏠2825 Dewey Rd ⏰11am-5pm Wed-Sun 🌐new americansmuseum.org

Visions Art Museum
 🏠2825 Dewey Rd ⏰10am-2pm Thu-Sat 🌐visionsartmuseum.org

---

❼
Point Loma and Cabrillo National Monument
🅰E7 🏠Tip of Point Loma Peninsula ⏰9am-5pm daily 🌐nps.gov/cabr

The gently rising Cabrillo National Monument park straddles the southern part of the Point Loma Peninsula. The monument was named after Juan Rodríguez Cabrillo, the first European explorer to step ashore in California in 1542. His statue overlooks the ships passing in and out of San Diego Bay.

From late December to late February, the Whale Overlook is a popular place from which to watch gray whales undertaking their annual southward migration. Visitors can also follow the 2-mile (3-km) Bayside Trail around the Point.

The lighthouse operated from 1855 until 1891. Its tower is usually closed to the public, but lower rooms illustrate what the lighthouse keepers' living quarters were like in the 1880s. The excellent visitors' center near the park entrance has a small museum.

← Giraffes in the African Plains area of San Diego Zoo Safari Park

San Diego Zoo Safari Park

⓪F7 ⓪Hwy 78, 15500 San Pasqual Valley Rd ⓪Escondido ⓪9am-5pm daily ⓪sdzsafaripark.org

A rural counterpart to San Diego Zoo (p237), this wildlife park displays a huge variety of birds and mammals in carefully landscaped grounds that sprawl over gently rolling hills. Opened in 1972, the park was conceived as a breeding sanctuary for the world's most endangered species and has remained at the forefront of conservation practice. Among the program's success stories is that of the California condor, a native species of vulture once close to extinction.

A good way to get your bearings is to take the Journey into Africa tour. This 25-minute, 2-mile (3-km) guided tram ride through African habitats visits giraffes, rhinos, and gazelles. It also stops at a waterhole where there are ostriches, herons, and many other birds.

For many, the big animals, including elephants, lions, and rhinos, are the stars. However, the park's various simulated natural environments, such as the Australian Rainforest and the Hidden Jungle, are also engrossing, and the Petting Kraal is popular with children.

Mission San Luis Rey

⓪E7 ⓪Hwy 76 (Mission Av), Rancho del Oro Dr, San Luis Rey ⓪From San Diego ⓪9:30am-5pm Mon-Fri, 10am-5pm Sat-Sun ⓪sanluisrey.org

One of the most prosperous estates in the California mission chain (p47), San Luis Rey de Francia was founded by the Spanish priest Padre Fermín Lasuén in 1798 and named after the canonized 13th-century French king, Louis IX. More than 3,000 Native Americans lived and worked in Mission San Luis Rey, keeping livestock and cultivating grain and fruit.

Visitors are guided first into a **museum** outlining the history of the mission and displaying vestments and other religious artifacts. The church has a cruciform shape like San Juan Capistrano (p216), but it was the only one in the chain with a domed wooden ceiling. The

→ Dramatic sculpture of one of the Stations of the Cross at the Mission San Luis Rey

🔍 HIDDEN GEM
Mission San Antonio de Pala Asistencia

Dating back to 1816, this is California's last Spanish sub-mission (asistencia) still ministering to an Indigenous population living in the Pala Reservation.

wooden pulpit is original, and the painted designs are based on surviving stencils. The mission still functions as a church.

Museum
⓪ ⓪Eastern Cloister ⓪Daily ⓪Jan 1, Thanksgiving, Dec 25

10

Legoland® California

E7 **1** Legoland Drive, Carlsbad **S** Carlsbad **O** Daily; check website for hours **w** legoland.com

This expansive park is aimed primarily at children under 12 years old. It offers over 60 rides, shows, and attractions, including an aquarium with a Lego® Deep Sea Adventure and a water park. For younger visitors, the DUPLO section showcases African wildlife such as giraffes and lions made of bricks.

The main attraction is the display of seven miniature areas of the United States, created using more than 20 million Lego bricks.

 11

Escondido

E7 **i** 235 E Grand Av; www.visitescondido.com

Escondido's Downtown has hundreds of beautifully preserved listed buildings – from Victorian mansions and Craftsman bungalows, to Art Deco homes. Several of these form part of the **Escondido History Center** complex. Here you can step inside an 1887 Santa Fe railroad depot or an authentic Pullman train car. On Tuesdays and Saturdays, the Bandy Blacksmith and Wheelwright Shop comes alive with demonstrations.

Community pride takes center stage at the **California Center for the Arts**, a large hub with a concert hall, a collection of contemporary visual arts, and a theater, while a tiny museum in the **San Diego Archaeological Center** explores how the first San Diegans lived 10,000 years ago.

Niki de Saint Phalle's **Queen Califia's Magical Circle**, a dazzling mosaic sculpture representing the mythology of California's beginnings, can be found in Kit Carson Park.

Escondido History Center
321 N Broadway **1–4pm** Tue–Thu & Sat **w** escondidohistory.org

California Center for the Arts
340 N Escondido Blvd **10am–5pm** Tue–Sat, 1–5pm Sun **w** artcenter.org

San Diego Archaeological Center
16666 San Pasqual Valley Rd **9am–4pm** Mon–Fri, 10am–2pm Sat **w** sandiegoarchaeology.org

Queen Califia's Magical Circle
3333 Bear Valley Pkwy **(760)** 839-4000 **9am– noon** Tue–Thu; also 9am– 2pm 2nd & 4th Sat of month

 12

Palomar Observatory

F7 **35899** Canfield Rd, Palomar Mountain **From** Julian **9am–3pm** daily **Dec 24 & 25** **w** astro.caltech.edu/palomar

Palomar Mountain, in the state park of the same name, is topped by the white dome of the Palomar Observatory, first opened 1948. The large observatory houses a computer-controlled Hale Telescope with a 200-inch (510-cm) mirror, capable of studying areas of the universe that are more than a billion light years away. It is now home to three telescopes that are used for a wide variety of astronomical research. Guided tours cover contemporary and historical scientific research, with an emphasis on the Hale Telescope. An exhibition area and photo gallery explain how the telescope works.

↑ The white dome of the Palomar Observatory, in Palomar Mountain State Park

❸ Julian

🅰 F7   🚌 From San Diego
ℹ 2129 Main St; www.
visitjulian.com

When San Diegans want to go for a pleasant drive or spend a romantic weekend in the "backcountry," they often head for the mountain town of Julian. Gold was discovered here in 1870, and the restored 19th-century wooden buildings that line the main street help to re-create the atmosphere of those pioneer days.

In fall, the "Apple Days" of October attract hundreds of visitors, who come to taste Julian's famous apple pie and buy rustic souvenirs in the quaint gift shops. The family-run **Julian Cider Mill** uses a vintage press for making its cider, and also sells honey and fudge. The delightful **Julian Pioneer Museum** is packed floor-to-ceiling with curiosities and photographs documenting the town's history. Visitors can also explore a gold mine at the **Eagle Mining Company**, which shows the tools and machinery of the early gold-diggers. At the rural **California Wolf Center**, visitors can learn about conservation and see North American and Mexican gray wolves before they are released back into the wild.

> In fall, the "Apple Days" of October attract hundreds of visitors, who come to taste Julian's famous apple pie and buy rustic souvenirs in the quaint gift shops.

Julian Cider Mill

🏠 2103 Main St   🕐 9:30am-5pm daily   🌐 juliancider mill.com

Julian Pioneer Museum

♿ 🏠 2811 Washington St
🕐 Apr–Nov: Fri–Sun; Dec–Mar: Sat & Sun   🌐 julianpioneer museum.org

Eagle Mining Company

♿ 🏠 2320 C St   🕐 Times vary, check website   🕐 Jan 1, Easter Sun, Thanksgiving, Dec 25
🌐 theeaglemining.com

California Wolf Center

♿ 🏠 470 K Q Ranch Rd
🕐 9am–5pm daily
🌐 californiawolfcenter.org

---

❹

Coronado

🅰 E7

The city of Coronado, at the head of a 6.5-sq-mile (17-sq-km) peninsula in the middle of San Diego Bay, is moneyed and self-confident. Businessman Elisha Babcock, Jr. bought the land in 1885 and set out to develop a world-class resort.

Coronado is now the location of San Diego's most exclusive homes, boutiques, hotels, and restaurants. The **Coronado Museum of History and Art** has photographs, early maps, and other artifacts related to the history of the town.

Until the opening of the San Diego–Coronado Bay Bridge in 1969, the **Coronado Ferry** was the area's principal link with the mainland, a service that has since been revived for the enjoyment of tourists and locals alike. The 15-minute trip between the Broadway Pier on the Embarcadero, or the San Diego Convention Center, and the Ferry Landing Marketplace is breathtaking at sunset, when the skyline of Downtown is bathed in a warm glow.

Coronado's stunning white sandy beach is bordered at its southern end by the **Hotel del Coronado**. Opened in 1888 and given National Historic Landmark status in 1977, the affectionately named "Del" is a meticulously preserved grand Victorian seaside hotel. It was built using the skills of architects and laborers from the railroads – a heritage that is most obvious

↑ Hotel del Coronado, a luxury resort dating from 1888, and its adjoining beach

in the domed ceiling of the Crown Room, which is built from sugar pine without using a single nail. The long list of guests who have stayed here is impressive, from presidents Franklin D. Roosevelt and Bill Clinton to film stars Marilyn Monroe and Brad Pitt. The Del has also been the location for several seminal movies, including the 1959 classic *Some Like It Hot*, starring Marilyn Monroe, Jack Lemmon, and Tony Curtis.

Coronado Museum of History and Art

🏛 1100 Orange Av 📞 (619) 435-7242 ⏰ 10am–4pm daily 🌐 coronadohistory.org

Coronado Ferry

🏛 1050 N Harbor Dr ⏰ Daily 🌐 sdhe.com

Hotel del Coronado

🏛 Orange Av ⏰ Daily 🌐 hoteldel.com

Living Coast Discovery Center

📍 E7 🏛 1000 Gunpowder Point Dr, Chula Vista 🚌 C St, Bay Blvd ⏰ 10am–5pm daily ❌ Federal hols 🌐 thelivingcoast.org

This remarkable wildlife park and aquarium beside San Diego Bay allows visitors to observe the stunning animal species of California's coastal wetlands. A free bus takes visitors to the Nature Center from a parking lot located by the I-5, and from the San Diego Trolley Station.

Visitors will learn about the fragile environment of this protected land and children can get up close to a variety of creatures. Birds that can be seen all year round include herons, ospreys, and kestrels.

Cuyamaca Rancho State Park

📍 F7 🏛 12551 Hwy 79 🚌 ⏰ Daily in season; check website for details 🌐 parks.ca.gov

Cuyamaca Rancho State Park is a place to get away from it all. Almost half of its 39-sq-mile (100-sq-km) domain is an officially designated wilderness that is home to skunks, bobcats, coyotes, mule deer, and mountain lions.

As well as horseback riding, camping, and mountain biking facilities, there are 130 miles (210 km) of hiking trails in the park. The Cuyamaca Peak Trail is an arduous but rewarding

↑ A field of wildflowers in bloom at Cuyamaca Rancho State Park

ascent by paved fire road. From the summit, hikers can enjoy unparalleled views of the forested hills of northern San Diego County as far as Palomar Mountain (p241).

At the northern end of the park, Lake Cuyamaca offers boating as well as fishing facilities.

17

Encinitas

E7 **535 Encinitas Blvd, Suite 116; www.encinitas visitorscenter.com**

This laid-back beach city, about 25 miles (40 km) north of San Diego, is famous for its surfing – Swami's Beach has attracted surfers from all over the world ever since the 1960s when it was named in the Beach Boys hit "Surfin' USA."

For a meditative moment, look for the gold domes of the **Self-Realization Fellowship Temple**, founded in 1920 by Paramahansa Yogananda to disseminate the universal teachings of Kriya Yoga, a sacred spiritual science originating millennia ago in India. Here you can explore the lush gardens or spend a few days in meditation at a peaceful retreat.

At the **San Diego Botanic Garden**, paths wind through rare bamboo groves, blooming cacti, and tropical rainforests. The botanic garden strives to conserve rare and endangered plants.

Nature lovers can also visit the beautiful **San Elijo Lagoon Ecological Reserve and Nature Center**, one of San Diego's largest wetlands, where trails lead around a shallow-water estuary that is home to an impressive range of animals and plants.

Self-Realization Fellowship Temple

 939 Second St 9am–5pm Tue-Sat, 11am-5pm Sun encinitastemple.org

San Diego Botanic Garden

230 Quail Gardens Dr 9am–5pm daily sdbgarden.org

San Elijo Lagoon Ecological Reserve and Nature Center

2710 Manchester Av, Cardiff 9am–5pm daily sdparks.org

18

Del Mar

E7 **visitdelmar village.com**

With its rural atmosphere and pristine, family-friendly beach, Del Mar has long been a popular destination. During the Golden Age of Hollywood, celebrities flocked to the **Del Mar Racetrack and Fairgrounds**. Built in 1937 with crooner Bing Crosby supplying much of the financing, the racetrack is now considered one of the most beautiful in the USA. On the same land, the Del Mar Fairgrounds is home to events like the large San Diego County Fair, held every summer, with live music and drama and contests from cooking to flower arranging.

Del Mar Racetrack and Fairgrounds

 2260 Jimmy Durante Blvd delmarfairgrounds.com

Swami's Beach in Encinitas, as seen from the Pacific Coast Highway; *(inset)* two surfers walking toward the waves

the surfboard that champion Bethany Hamilton was on when she was attacked by a tiger shark in Hawaii. The **Oceanside Museum of Art** showcases quilts, sculpture, and glasswork by local artists.

California Surf Museum

 312 Pier View Way 🕙 10am–4pm daily (to 8pm Thu) 🌐 surfmuseum.org

Oceanside Museum of Art

📍 704 Pier View Way 🕙 11am–5pm Tue–Sat (to 8pm Thu & Fri), noon–5pm Sun 🌐 oma-online.org

---

20

Carlsbad

📍 E7 🛈 400 Carlsbad Village Dr; www. visitcarlsbad.com

In the 1880s, the water in this town was believed to have health-giving properties similar to those of the water in Karlsbad, Bohemia (today's Czech Republic). People soon traveled here to benefit from the therapeutic offerings. Mementos of this era can now be explored at the **Carlsbad Alkaline Water**.

The **Leo Carrillo Ranch**, former home of an actor and conservationist, is a leafy, picturesque site complete with a lake, bougainvillea, and period whitewashed adobes.

Carlsbad Alkaline Water

📍 2802 Carlsbad Blvd 🕙 9am–6pm daily 🌐 carlsbadalkalinewater.com

Leo Carrillo Ranch

📍 6200 Flying Leo Carrillo Ln 🕙 9am–5pm daily 🌐 carrillo-ranch.org

---

DRINK

Burgeon Beer Co
This brewery has won numerous awards for its range of IPAs.

📍 E7 📍 6350 Yarrow Dr, Carlsbad 🌐 burgeonbeer.com

Wavelength Brewing Company
The on-tap menu changes regularly at this science-themed brewery. Here, you'll find space memorabilia, telescopes, and weekly science talks.

📍 E7 📍 236 Main St, Vista 🌐 wavelengthbrewco.com

Bagby Beer
Choose from an extensive list of beers and pick a seat on the deck with ocean views.

📍 E7 📍 601 S Coast Hwy, Oceanside 🌐 bagbybeer.com

21

Rancho Guajome Adobe County Park

📍 E7 📍 2210 N Santa Fe Ave, Vista 🕙 9:30am–4pm Wed–Sun 🌐 sdparks.org

The California Rancho period comes to life at this lovingly preserved Mexican American adobe ranch house, a National Historic Landmark since 1970. In 1851 army lieutenant Cave Johnson Couts married Ysidora Bandini, the daughter of a prominent Mexican family. The land was given to them as a wedding present, and Couts built this elegant 22-room house as a social hub for fiestas and rodeos. Everything has been preserved as it was in the mid-19th century.

19

Oceanside

📍 E7 🛈 928 North Coast Hwy; www.visitocean side.org

The down-to-earth city of Oceanside has 3.5 miles (5.5 km) of sandy beach and one of the longest wooden piers on the West Coast (1,942 ft/592 m). Every July, the pier area gives way to the Supergirl Pro, an exciting competition drawing the best female surfers in the world.

Among the items at the **California Surf Museum** is

THE INLAND EMPIRE AND LOW DESERT

The southern deserts of California were once the domain of the Serrano, the Chemehuevi, and the Cahuilla. In fact, the Cahuilla still own much of Palm Springs, as a large area of the city sits within the Agua Caliente Indian Reservation. Anglo-American cattle farmers arrived in the 1850s, along with low-key mining operations, which continued until the 1940s. This and the importation of navel orange trees and Valencia orange trees in the 1870s sparked explosive growth.

Modern Palm Springs was established in the 1880s and gradually attracted "health tourists" with its dry climate and hot springs. The term "Inland Empire" was invented around 1914 to help boost the region by highlighting its unique geography. The Salton Sea was accidently created by flooding in 1905, and its shores became extremely fashionable among wealthy vacationers in the 1950s, before a series of storms in the mid-1970s caused the lake to swallow the shoreline developments.

In the 1940s and 1950s Palm Springs' "Desert Modern" architecture became the model for mass-produced suburban housing in the US, and tourism blossomed. From the 1950s onward, the city also became a haven for the LGBTQ+ community, and in 2018 America's first all-LGBTQ+ city council was elected here. The area was later made famous by the Coachella Festival, which was founded in 1999 and is now one of the largest and most profitable music festivals in the world.

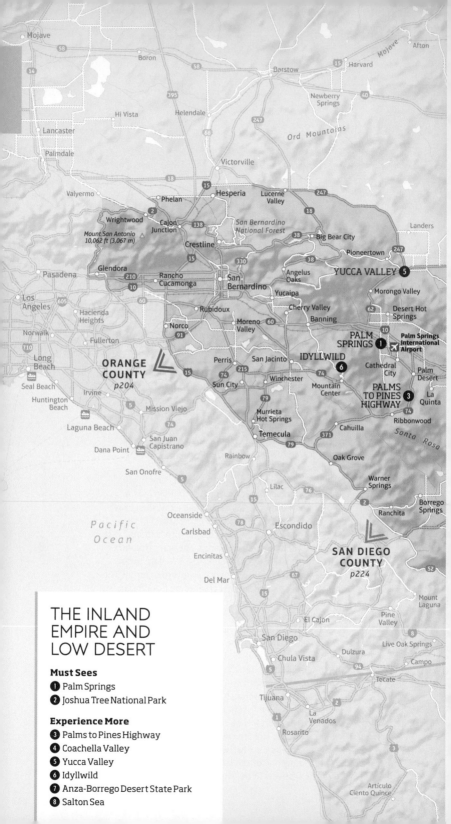

THE INLAND EMPIRE AND LOW DESERT

Must Sees
1. Palm Springs
2. Joshua Tree National Park

Experience More
3. Palms to Pines Highway
4. Coachella Valley
5. Yucca Valley
6. Idyllwild
7. Anza-Borrego Desert State Park
8. Salton Sea

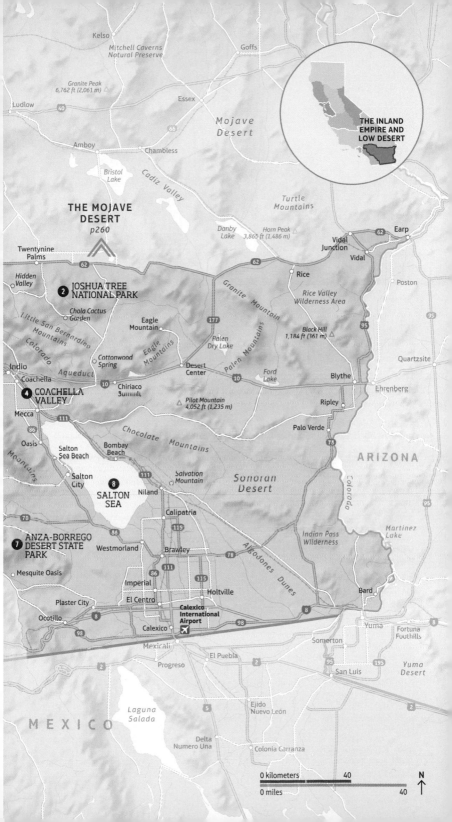

①

PALM SPRINGS

F6 **✈**1 mile (1.5 km) NE of Downtown **🚌**Indio **🚍**3111 N Indian Av **ℹ**70100 Hwy 111, Rancho Mirage; www.visit greaterpalmsprings.com

Located within the Coachella Valley, the area occupied by Palm Springs was first inhabited by the Cahuilla people. From 1853, wealthy European settlers started to arrive here after surveyors came across a mineral pool bubbling up out of the desert – by the start of the 20th century, Palm Springs was a thriving health spa. Today the resort city is also noted for its Modernist architecture.

①

Village Green Heritage Center

🏛221 S Palm Canyon Dr **🕐**Times vary, check website **🚫**Federal hols **w**palmsprings.com

This quiet enclave in the heart of Palm Springs' shopping district contains four historical buildings. Walking tours leave from the McCallum Adobe, which was built in 1884 near the village of Agua Caliente and moved to its present location during the 1950s.

The Cornelia White House (1893) is furnished with antiques dating from Palm Springs' pioneer era.

The heritage of the area's Cahuilla people is related through artifacts and photographs in the Agua Caliente Cultural Museum.

Also in the Village Green Heritage Center is Ruddy's 1930s General Store Museum, an immaculate replica of a Depression-era shop.

Did You Know?

The McCallum Adobe was built by John Guthrie McCallum, Palm Springs' first white resident.

②

Palm Springs Aerial Tramway

🏛1 Tram Way **🕐**Daily **w**pstramway.com

The Aerial Tramway's two revolving Swiss-built cars, each holding 80 passengers, are one of Palm Springs' most popular attractions. The trams depart from Valley Station, 6 miles (10 km) northwest of Palm Springs. The 2.5-mile (4-km) trip over spectacular scenery takes 10 minutes, ascending to the Mountain Station in the Mount San Jacinto State Park and Wilderness Area.

Passengers travel through five distinct ecosystems, and the temperature changes dramatically – the heat of the valley floor can differ wildly from the temperature at the peak, so dress appropriately.

At the top there are 54 miles (85 km) of hiking trails. The Adventure Center is open in the winter, with rentals available for cross-country skiing. There are also campsites and picnic areas.

Observation decks perched on the edge of the 8,500-ft- (2,600-m-) high lookout offer views of the Coachella Valley, Palm Springs, and the San Bernardino Mountains.

← The late afternoon sun hitting the hills along Palm Canyon Drive in Palm Springs

Palm Springs Air Museum

🏠 745 N Gene Autry Trail
🕐 10am–5pm daily 🌐 palm springsairmuseum.org

About 60 beautifully restored vintage aircraft are displayed here in four hangars. On Saturday afternoons from November to May there are flight demonstrations. Volunteer docents, many of them veterans, are on hand to answer questions and tell the stories of those who flew these planes.

Palm Springs Art Museum

🏠 101 Museum Dr 🕐 10am–5pm Tue, Wed & Fri–Sun, noon–8pm Thu 🚫 Federal hols 🌐 psmuseum.org

This museum focuses on painting and sculpture dating from the 19th century to the present day, as well as Native American art, Mesoamerican artifacts, and photography. The museum also houses the extensive William Holden Collection, a gift from the estate of the late actor. The adjoining Annenberg Theater is a 433-seat center for the performing arts.

A 2-mile (3-km) Museum Trail, starting from the museum, enables visitors to explore the flora and fauna of this desert region. The trail climbs 800 ft (244 m) up into the Mount San Jacinto State Park and joins the Lykken Trail at Desert Riders Overlook.

Palm Springs Art Museum Architecture & Design Center

🏠 300 S Palm Canyon Dr
🕐 10am–5pm Fri–Tue, noon–8pm Thu 🌐 psmuseum.org

The former Santa Fe Federal Savings and Loan building has been repurposed as a depository of drawings, photos, and plans of the area's architectural heritage. Designed in 1961 by E. Stewart Williams, architect of many of Palm Springs' iconic mid-century buildings, a number of the bank's features have been retained. The original teller window is still there, as is the vault, which is now a gift shop.

Indian Canyons

🏠 38520 S Palm Canyon Dr
🕐 Mid-Jul–Aug: 8am–5pm Fri–Sun; Sep–mid-Jul: 8am–5pm daily 🌐 indian-canyons.com

Approximately 5 miles (8 km) south of Palm Springs are four spectacular natural palm oases, set in stark, rocky gorges and surrounded by barren hills. Clustered along small streams fed by mountain springs, the canyons are located on the land of the Cahuilla people of Agua Caliente. Rock art and other traces of the area's early inhabitants can still be seen.

The 15-mile- (24-km-) long Palm Canyon is the largest of the gorges. Refreshments and picnic tables are available near the parking lot.

TOP 3 LGBTQ+ VENUES

Toucans Tiki Lounge
🏠 2100 N Palm Canyon Dr
🌐 toucanstikilounge.com
Home to the longest-running drag show in town.

Hunters
🏠 302 E Arenas Rd
🌐 hunterspalmsprings.com
High-energy nightclub where karaoke, cabaret, and leather pride are all part of the fun.

Chill Bar
🏠 217 E Arenas Rd
🌐 chillbarpalmsprings.com
Chill out with a drink or dance with go-go dancers, stripteasers, or drag queens.

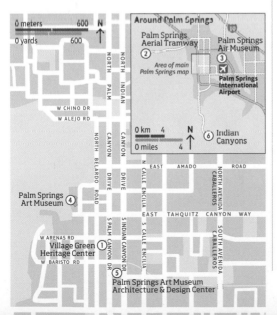

JOSHUA TREE NATIONAL PARK

🅰 F6   🏠 74485 National Park Dr, Twentynine Palms   🚌 Desert Stage Lines from Palm Springs to Twentynine Palms   🕑 Dec 25   🌐 nps.gov

Taking its name from the Joshua trees that thrive here, Joshua Tree National Park is a captivating 1,240 sq miles (3,200 sq km) of wilderness. The formations of pink and gray rocks, abandoned mines, and oases make it a climber's and hiker's paradise.

The Joshua tree was named by early Mormon travelers, who saw the gnarled, upraised arms of the biblical Joshua in its twisted branches. The area was designated a national park in 1944 to preserve the groves of the unusual, spiny-leaved Joshua tree. This large member of the agave family is unique to the area and can grow up to 30 ft (9 m) tall, living for 250 to 300 years. The park covers parts of two deserts – the higher Mojave Desert in the west and the lower Colorado Desert in the east, each with different ecosystems – with the Little San Bernardino Mountains crossing the park's southwest corner. In springtime the park has a wealth of desert flowers. Despite the harshness of the desert environment, a variety of animals thrive here. The kangaroo rat gets its food and water from seeds alone, and the jack rabbit has a coat of muted fur to camouflage it from local predators such as the coyote, bobcat, and eagle.

↑ A desert coyote, typically seen after sunset or early in the morning

ROCK CLIMBING AND BIKING

The park's creviced, rough granite boulders are a celebrated rock-climbing destination, with more than 8,000 routes for climbers of all skill levels, particularly in Hidden Valley's Wonderland of Rocks. Cyclists can ride along the paved Park Boulevard; several backcountry roads are also open for mountain biking.

↑ Distinctive spiky Joshua trees in Joshua Tree National Park and *(inset)* desert flowers

Highlights

Joshua Trees

Large groves of Joshua trees thrive in the higher, wetter, and somewhat cooler desert areas of the park's northwestern half.

Cottonwood Spring

▷ This man-made oasis of palms and cottonwood trees attracts desert birds. There is a visitors' center nearby.

Key's View

The summit of this viewpoint gives sweeping views of the stunning valley, desert, and mountain terrain.

Hidden Valley

◁ The gigantic boulders here formed natural corrals, making this a legendary hideout for cattle rustlers in the days of the Wild West. It's now a popular rock-climbing spot.

Lost Horse Mine

A 2-mile (3-km) trail leads to this historic gold mine, which was found by a cowboy searching for his lost horse. More than $270,000 in gold was extracted during the mine's first year of operation.

Cholla Cactus Garden

▷ A dense concentration of cholla cacti are the focal point of a trail through desert flora and fauna. But beware – the cactus's fluffy-looking fingers are really sharp spines.

Lost Palms Oasis

A 4-mile (6-km) trail leads to the largest group of palms in the park. It is one of the few areas where water occurs naturally near the surface.

Keys Ranch

Join a ranger-guided tour at this ranch to hear the story of William F. Keys and his family, who embodied the hard work it took to settle and prosper here.

Skull Rock

◁ This rock, near Jumbo Rock Campground, on the main park road, was shaped by water erosion.

EXPERIENCE MORE

 3

Palms to Pines Highway

AF7 **W**visitgreater palmsprings.com

One of the most interesting drives in Southern California begins at the junction of Hwy 111 and Hwy 74 in Palm Desert. As you climb Hwy 74, you gradually leave behind the desert ecosystem, with its palms, creosote, and desert ironwood trees, and move into a mountain scenery of pines and juniper. The view from Santa Rosa Summit, just under 5,000 ft (1,500 m) high, is spectacular. Continue northwest on Hwy 74 to reach Mountain Center and the lush meadows of Garner Valley.

DESERT GOLF

With fertile land, stunning scenery, and golf courses designed by renowned architects, Palm Springs is now known as the golf capital of the United States. More than 100 courses can be found across the region, most of which belong to private clubs or hotel complexes. Some, however, are open to the public, including the Desert Dunes course, which is particularly noted for its desert terrain.

 4

Coachella Valley

AF7 **i**70100 Hwy 111, Rancho Mirage; www.visit greaterpalmsprings.com

Stunning mountain views, ritzy resorts, and golf courses define the affluent Coachella Valley. Several attractions are particularly worth seeing here. In 1941 an artist named Cabot Yerxa built a pueblo in the style of the Hopi (a Native American tribe from Arizona). Now known as **Cabot's Pueblo Museum**, the building hosts his impressive collection of Native American art.

The **Palm Springs Art Museum in Palm Desert** has contemporary paintings and

↑ Sunset over the mountains surrounding the Coachella Valley

INSIDER TIP
Coachella Music Festival

If you're heading to this April music festival, it's worth downloading the app. This includes maps and alerts for upcoming acts. You can even sync and share your schedule with friends.

photographs, plus outdoor sculptures, while the **Living Desert Zoo and Botanical Gardens** covers the desert habitats of North America and Africa, with paths leading visitors through 40 different gardens. The wild birds and animals in the zoo include golden eagles and mountain lions.

Finally, a visit to the Palm Springs area is incomplete without a pilgrimage to the grave of one of its most famous residents, Frank Sinatra, at Desert Memorial Park in Cathedral City.

Over 250,000 rock, hip-hop, and indie aficionados gather in Indio every April for the Coachella Valley Music and Arts Festival, the largest of its kind in the world. Tickets usually sell out in hours.

Cabot's Pueblo Museum
Ⓧ 🏠 67616 E Desert View Av, Desert Hot Springs ◷ 9am-4pm Tue-Sun (Jun-Sep: to 1pm) 🅦 cabotsmuseum.org

Palm Springs Art Museum in Palm Desert
Ⓧ 🏠 72567 Hwy 111, Palm Desert ◷ 10am-5pm Tue-Sun 🅦 psmuseum.org/visit/palm-desert

Living Desert Zoo and Botanical Gardens
Ⓧ 🏠 47900 Portola Av, Palm Desert ◷ 8am-5pm daily (Jun-Sep: 7am-1:30pm) 🅦 livingdesert.org

---

⑤

Yucca Valley
🇦F6 🚌 🛈 56711 Twentynine Palms Hwy; www.yuccavalley.org

Yucca Valley is a small town west of the Joshua Tree National Park (p252). On a hillside, the **Desert Christ Park** has

over 40 statues depicting scenes from the life of Jesus. They were sculpted by Antone Martin in the 1950s. The town's **Hi-Desert Nature Museum** has various exhibits on the region's geology, crafts, flora, and fauna.

Pioneertown, 4 miles (6 km) northwest of Yucca Valley, is a hamlet built in 1947 as a Western film set.

Desert Christ Park
🏠 End of Mohawk Trail ◷ Sunrise-sunset daily 🅦 desertchristpark.org

Hi-Desert Nature Museum
🏠 57116 Twentynine Palms Hwy ◷ 10am-5pm Wed-Sat 🅧 Federal hols 🅦 hidesertnaturemuseum.org

→ One of the sculptures in Desert Christ Park, Yucca Valley

⑥
Idyllwild

🅰F6 🛈54325 North Circle; www.idyllwild.com

The alpine village of Idyllwild is located in Mount San Jacinto State Park, where over 50 miles (80 km) of hiking trails twist through pristine wilderness. A scenic 8-mile (13-km) trek leads to the Mountain Station of the Palm Springs Aerial Tramway, and the well-known Pacific Crest Trail also passes through the park. Maps and permits are available at the ranger station.

Among the top destinations for rock climbers in Southern California, Tahquitz Rock and Suicide Rock, in the awesome San Jacinto range, challenge both beginners and pros.

At the family-friendly **Idyllwild Nature Center**, just northwest of Idyllwild, visitors can learn all about Cahuilla Indigenous culture and mountain ecological habitats at a small museum, while docents at the **Idyllwild Area Historical Society Museum** have stories on the village's history, the mountains, and even Elvis Presley, who spent several weeks here in 1961 while filming *Kid Galahad*.

Idyllwild Nature Center
♿ 🏠25225 Highway 243 🕑9am–4pm Wed–Sun 🅦rivcoparks.org/idyllwild-nature-center

Idyllwild Area Historical Society Museum
🏠54470 N Circle Dr 🕑10am–5pm Fri–Sun 🅦idyllwildhistory.org

⑦
Anza-Borrego Desert State Park

🅰F7 🏠200 Palm Canyon Dr 🚌Escondido 🕑Daily 🅦parks.ca.gov

Starting with the Gold Rush of 1848 *(p47)*, the Southern Emigrant Trail, the only all-weather land route into California, brought tens of thousands of miners and early

Flowers in Anza-Borrego Desert, and *(inset)* a sculpture in Galleta Meadows ↓

→
Walking on the sandy shore of Salton Sea, California's largest lake

settlers through the Anza-Borrego Desert. Today, this former overland gateway is a remote and pristine park, offering a rare insight into a unique desert environment.

The desert's well-equipped visitors' center is in Borrego Springs. Here, the Palms at Indian Head is a mid-20th-century hotel that was once a favorite haunt of Hollywood stars like Marilyn Monroe and Clark Gable. Nearby, a colony of enormous metal sculptures by artist and welder Ricardo Breceda, including a dragon emerging from the sand, make Galleta Meadows a surreal and unique visit.

The Box Canyon Historical Monument is 31 miles (50 km) southwest of the visitors' center on County Road S2. Here you can view the old road once used by miners who braved the desert climate in the hope of finding their fortune in the goldfields, which lay 500 miles (800 km) to the north. The Anza-Borrego Desert is

> **Enormous metal sculptures by artist and welder Ricardo Breceda, including a dragon emerging from the sand, make Galleta Meadows a surreal and unique visit.**

inhospitable for most of the year. In spring, however, the burning land bursts into life. Cacti and desert flowers such as brittle-bush, desert poppies, and dune primroses produce a riot of color.

The desert's geology is as fascinating as its ecosystem. Over the millennia, a network of earthquake faultlines lifted and tilted the ground. Winter rains then carved through the shattered landscape, leaving multicolored "layer-cake" bluffs, dramatic ravines, and jagged canyons such as the famous Borrego and Carizzo Badlands.

8
Salton Sea

F7 🚉Mecca 🚉Indio
🕐Daily 🖥desertusa.com/salton-sea/about-salton-sea.html

California's largest lake, the Salton Sea was created by accident in 1905 when the Colorado River flooded and flowed into an irrigation canal leading to the Imperial Valley. It took a team of engineers two years to stem the flow. By then a 35-mile (55-km) inland sea had formed in

the Salton Sink, 230 ft (70 m) below sea level.

There are hiking trails and campsites within the Salton Sea State Recreation Area, as well as boating opportunities.

On the southwest shore of the lake, the Sonny Bono Salton Sea National Wildlife Refuge shelters resident and migratory bird species, such as the burrowing owl and the white-faced ibis.

The Salton Sea has been experiencing rising salinity due to its landlocked nature. It is bogged down with algae in summer, and both fish and birds in adjoining marshlands are disappearing at alarming rates. Governmental agencies have begun restoration plans; however, no firm timetable has yet been announced.

 HIDDEN GEM
Salvation Mountain

Just east of Salton Sea is artist Leonard Knight's man-made mountain. The structure, built from adobe bricks, is painted with images of nature and Bible verses *(www.salvationmountain.us).*

A DRIVING TOUR
RIM OF THE WORLD

Length 115 miles (185 km) **Stopping-off points** There are many hotels, cabins, and restaurants in the resort town of Big Bear Lake, such as The Lodge at Big Bear Lake. The town of Redlands also has a good range of places to stay and restaurants. Picnic areas and campsites are plentiful along the route.

From San Bernardino this invigorating drive winds across the forested San Bernardino Mountains, offering spectacular views of the desert beyond. The altitude provides for distinct seasons, with warm, pine-scented air in the summer, and brisk, cool days in the winter, when the snow-covered mountain trails are perfect for cross-country skiing. The tour passes through the resorts at Big Bear Lake and ends at Lake Arrowhead Village, both favorite destinations for those wanting to escape the heat and smog of LA. In Redlands visitors are offered a sense of the area's heady 19th-century past, and yet another pleasure: the sweet smell of orange groves.

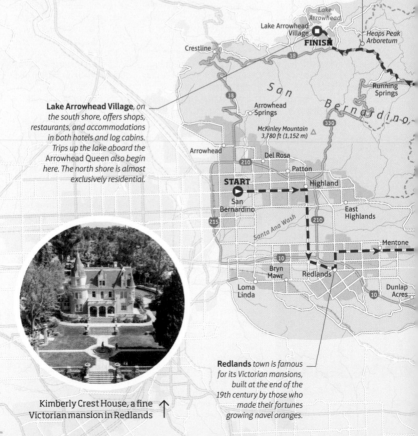

A 1-mile (1.5-km) nature trail winds through the wooded **Heaps Peak Arboretum**, planted with native and other trees. Species include dogwoods, Jeffrey pine, ponderosa pine, black oaks, live oaks, and white fir.

Lake Arrowhead Village, on the south shore, offers shops, restaurants, and accommodations in both hotels and log cabins. Trips up the lake aboard the Arrowhead Queen also begin here. The north shore is almost exclusively residential.

Lake Arrowhead

Lake Arrowhead Village
FINISH

Heaps Peak Arboretum

Crestline

Running Springs

San

Bernardino

Arrowhead Springs

McKinley Mountain 3,780 ft (1,152 m)

Arrowhead

Del Rosa

Patton

START

San Bernardino

Highland

East Highlands

Santa Ana Wash

Mentone

Bryn Mawr

Redlands

Loma Linda

Dunlap Acres

Kimberly Crest House, a fine Victorian mansion in Redlands ↑

Redlands town is famous for its Victorian mansions, built at the end of the 19th century by those who made their fortunes growing navel oranges.

↑ Kayaking on Big Bear Lake, surrounded by the San Bernadino National Forest

Locator Map
For more detail see p248

*Located in the San Bernardino National Forest, **Children's Forest** aims to educate youngsters on forest ecology and involve them in regeneration work.*

*A popular resort area, **Big Bear Lake** offers a range of sports including fishing, sailing, kayaking, swimming, and, in the winter, skiing. Its two commercial centers are Big Bear City, to the east, and Big Bear Village, to the south.*

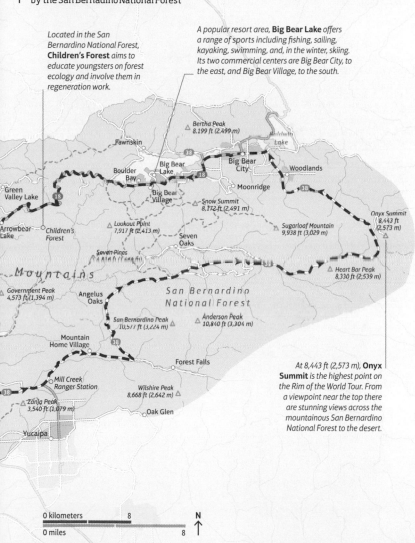

*At 8,443 ft (2,573 m), **Onyx Summit** is the highest point on the Rim of the World Tour. From a viewpoint near the top there are stunning views across the mountainous San Bernardino National Forest to the desert.*

0 kilometers 8
0 miles 8

N ↑

THE MOJAVE DESERT

The Mojave Desert was home to the Timbisha Shoshone, Mojave, Kawaiisu, Koso, and bands of Southern Paiute, including the Chemehuevi, peoples. In 1775, Francisco Garcé, a Spanish missionary, was the first European to meet the Indigenous peoples of the desert. For much of the 19th century, the desert functioned as a gateway to California. Trappers, traders, and early settlers traveled hundreds of miles along the Old Spanish Trail from Santa Fe in New Mexico to Los Angeles. There was frequent conflict between the Indigenous peoples and those crossing through their lands. In the 1860s the US government created reservations into which the Indigenous populations were moved, many by force. Today, Mojave Desert's resident Mojave and Chemehuevi peoples, numbering less than 2,000 in total, live on reservations in California, Nevada, and Arizona.

In the 1870s, gold, silver, borax, and other precious minerals in the region attracted large numbers of miners. Instant cities such as Calico sprang up, but when the mines became exhausted, many of these settlements were abandoned. In 1883 commercial mining became more viable when the Santa Fe Railroad was completed. Towns located along the route, like Barstow, prospered.

Tourism developed relatively late: the Mitchell Caverns were opened in 1932, Death Valley was declared a national monument in 1933, and the Mojave National Preserve was established in 1994.

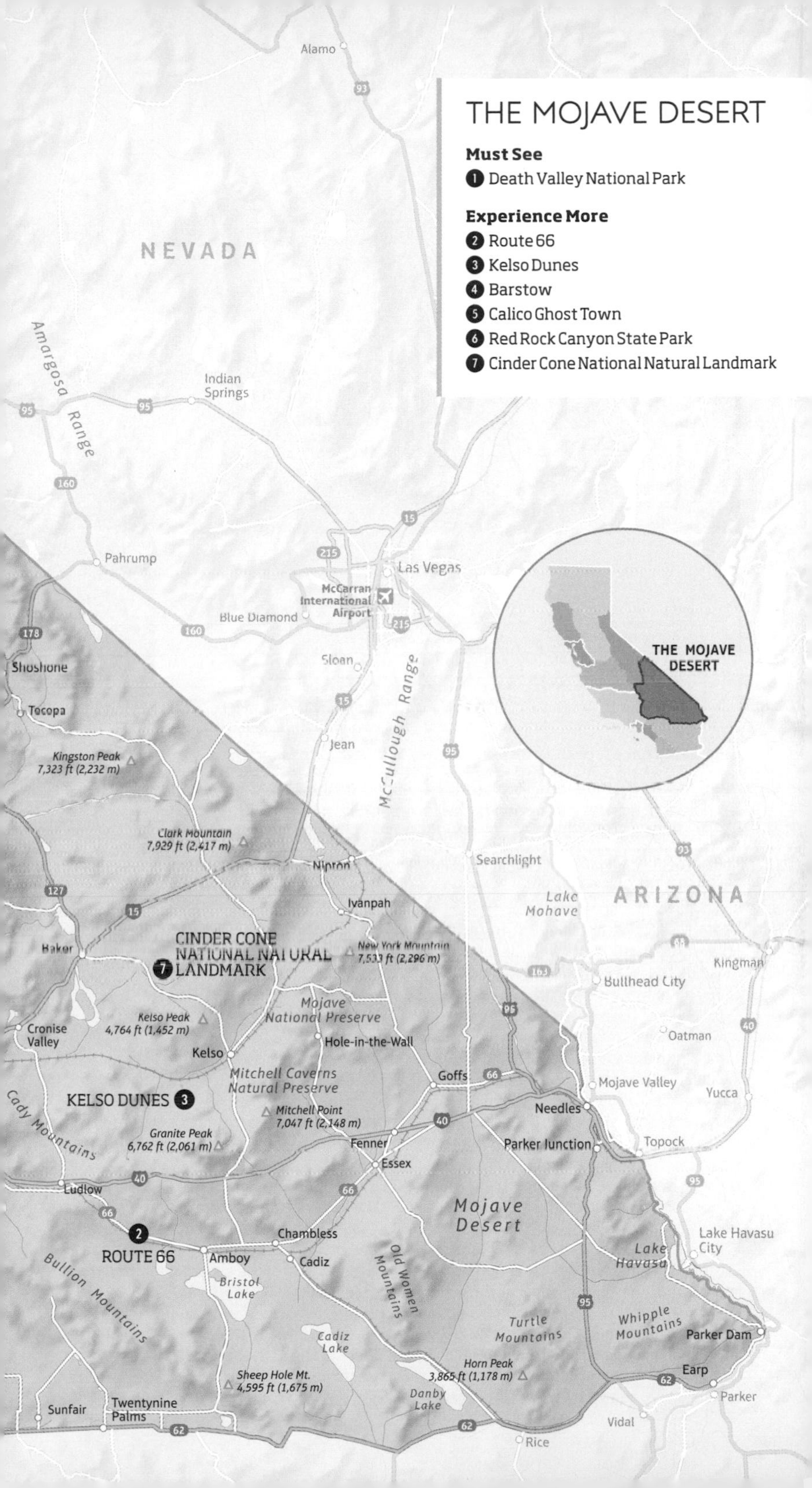

THE MOJAVE DESERT

Must See
1 Death Valley National Park

Experience More
2 Route 66
3 Kelso Dunes
4 Barstow
5 Calico Ghost Town
6 Red Rock Canyon State Park
7 Cinder Cone National Natural Landmark

NEVADA

ARIZONA

THE MOJAVE DESERT

Alamo

Indian Springs

Las Vegas

McCarran International Airport

Pahrump

Blue Diamond

Shoshone

Tecopa

Sloan

Jean

Searchlight

Kingston Peak
7,323 ft (2,232 m)

Clark Mountain
7,929 ft (2,417 m)

Nipton

Lake Mohave

Baker

Ivanpah

CINDER CONE
NATIONAL NATURAL
LANDMARK

New York Mountain
7,533 ft (2,296 m)

Kingman

Bullhead City

Cronise Valley

Kelso Peak
4,764 ft (1,452 m)

Mojave
National Preserve

Oatman

Kelso

Hole-in-the-Wall

KELSO DUNES 3

Mitchell Caverns
Natural Preserve

Mojave Valley

Yucca

Granite Peak
6,762 ft (2,061 m)

Mitchell Point
7,047 ft (2,148 m)

Goffs

Ludlow

Fenner

Needles

Parker Junction

Topock

Essex

ROUTE 66 2

Chambless

Mojave
Desert

Lake
Havasu City

Amboy

Cadiz

Lake
Havasu

Bullion Mountains

Bristol
Lake

Old Women Mountains

Turtle
Mountains

Whipple
Mountains

Parker Dam

Cadiz
Lake

Horn Peak
3,865 ft (1,178 m)

Earp

Sheep Hole Mt.
4,595 ft (1,675 m)

Danby
Lake

Parker

Sunfair

Twentynine
Palms

Rice

Vidal

Did You Know?

Death Valley is the site of the highest recorded temperature in the US: 134° F (57° C) in the shade, in July 1913.

DEATH VALLEY NATIONAL PARK

E4 ☐ **Furnace Creek Visitor Center, Hwy 190; www.nps.gov**

A land of wrenching extremes, Death Valley is a sunken trough in the earth's crust that reaches the lowest point in North America, guarded on both sides by rugged mountains. Polished canyons, burning salt flats, silken sand dunes, and delicate rock formations form this unique expanse.

Death Valley stretches for some 140 miles (225 km) north to south, with the mountain range on the western side soaring 11,000 ft (3,350 m) to form razor-sharp peaks.

Millennia of flash floods have carved a natural gateway into Death Valley. Today, the same abundant springs make Furnace Creek, located in the heart of the valley, a desert oasis. Shaded by date-bearing palms are restaurants and motels. The Borax Museum Furnace Creek displays mining tools and transport machinery used at the 19th-century refinery. Nearby are the ruins of the Harmony Borax Works. A remnant of the valley's former freshwater lake can be seen at Salt Creek.

Just 4 miles (6 km) southeast of Furnace Creek on Hwy 178, Zabriskie Point offers stunning 360-degree views of canyons and gulches. A little south is Devil's Golf Course, an expanse of salt pinnacles. Until about 2,000 years ago, successive lakes covered this area. As surface moisture evaporated from the lakes, ridges and spires of crystallized salt

> With the ground temperature at Badwater 50 percent higher than the air temperature, it is possible to fry an egg on the ground.

formed. The Badwater Basin, 10 miles (6 km) south of here, is the lowest point in North America. The air at Badwater can reach 120° F (49° C). With the ground temperature 50 percent higher than the air temperature, it is possible to fry an egg on the ground.

The northern part of Death Valley includes the large volcanic Ubehebe Crater and Scotty's Castle, a Moorish-style ranch (p266). Sand dunes cover 15 sq miles (39 sq km) on the western side of the park, not far from the second-largest outpost in Death Valley, Stovepipe Wells. A walk along the undulating Mesquite Flat Sand Dunes north of Stovepipe Wells is one of the greatest experiences of Death Valley. Shifting winds blow the sand into the classic crescent dune configuration.

↑ The dramatic mudstone formations of the Death Valley badlands seen from Zabriskie Point

[1] Palm trees fill the Furnace Creek desert oasis.

[2] Borax, used for producing heat-resistant glass, was mined at the Harmony Borax Works in the 1880s. The site consists of ruins today.

[3] Geometric patterns of salt cover nearly 200 sq miles (518 sq km) of the Badwater Basin.

STAY

Inn at Death Valley
In the heart of the national park, this historic hotel that was a favorite with Old Hollywood stars continues to be a glamorous retreat.

🏠 Hwy 190, Death Valley 🌐 oasisat deathvalley.com

$$$

Panamint Springs Resort
With scenic views of sand dunes and mountains, this small, family-owned motel and campground is on the park's western edge.

🏠 40440 Hwy 190, Panamint Springs 🌐 panamint springs.com

$$$

The Ranch at Death Valley
Located near the park's visitor center, this Western-style resort has casual rooms and cabins and a spring-fed pool.

🏠 Hwy 190, Death Valley 🌐 oasisat deathvalley.com

$$$

Stovepipe Wells Vintage Hotel
Surrounded by desert, this retreat, with contemporary rooms set around an inner courtyard, is a perfect base for hiking the dunes.

🏠 51880 Hwy 190, Death Valley 🌐 death valleyhotels.com

$$$

A DRIVING TOUR
DEATH VALLEY

Length 235 miles (380 km) **Stopping-off points** The Inn at Furnace Creek (and the affiliated resort), Stovepipe Wells Village Hotel, and Panamint Springs Resort *(p265)* are the only lodging and eating places in the park. Shoshone, Amargosa, and Tecopa, outside the park, also have motels.

Once an insurmountable barrier to travelers and miners, Death Valley is California desert at its harshest and most awe-inspiring. The Timbisha tribe called the valley Tomesha, referring to the ocher-colored rock in the surrounding hills. The valley and environs were declared a National Park in 1994, making it accessible to visitors, who can discover this stark and unique landscape by car and by taking short walks from the main roads to spectacular viewpoints. The best time to visit is October to April when temperatures average 65° F (18° C). May to September, when the ground temperature can be extremely hot, should be avoided. Check the weather forecast and always carry water, a map, a first-aid and snakebite kit, a cell phone, a jack, and a spare tire.

The Moorish-style **Scotty's Castle** *(also known as Death Valley Ranch) was commissioned by wealthy businessman Albert Johnson in the 1920s. His friend Walter Scott lived in the ranch after Johnson's death.*

Scotty's Castle

Ubehebe Crater

Cottonwood Mountains

One of a dozen volcanic craters in the Mojave area, **Ubehebe Crater** *is at least 2,000 years old. It is more than 900 yds (800 m) wide and 500 ft (150 m) deep.*

△ Hunter Mountain
7,329 ft (2,234 m)

Panamint

Panamint Springs

↑ Telescope Peak and the Badwater Basin seen from Dante's View

Locator Map
For more detail see p262

N ↑

Stovepipe Wells Village, *founded in 1926, was the valley's first tourist resort. According to legend, a lumberjack traveling west struck water here and stayed. An old stovepipe, similar to the ones that were then used to form the walls of wells, marks the site.*

The springs at **Furnace Creek** *are one of the few freshwater sources in the desert. They are thought to have saved the lives of hundreds of gold prospectors crossing the desert on their way to the Sierra foothills. There is a full-service visitors' complex here.*

Made famous by Michelangelo Antonioni's 1960s film of the same name, **Zabriskie Point** *offers views of the multicolored mud hills of Golden Canyon. The spot was named after a former general manager of the borax operations in Death Valley.*

The multicolored hills of cemented gravels known as **Artist's Palette** *were created by mineral deposits and volcanic ash. The colors are at their most intense in the late afternoon sun.*

Amargosa Range

Death

Stovepipe
Wells
**START/
FINISH**

Mosaic
Canyon

Harmony Borax
Works

Furnace Creek

Valley

∧ Aguereberry Point
6,286 ft (1,916 m)

Zabriskie
Point

Artist's
Palette

Death Valley
Junction

Badwater
Basin

△ Telescope Peak
11,053 ft (3,369 m)

Range

Dante's View

The lowest point in North America, **Badwater** *lies 282 ft (85 m) below sea level and is one of the world's hottest places. The water, filled with sodium chloride and sulfates, is not poisonous but is unpalatable.*

At 5,475 ft (1,650 m), **Dante's View** *takes in the entire valley floor and is best seen in the morning. The name of the viewpoint was inspired by writer Dante's famous poem,* Inferno. *In the distance is Telescope Peak in the Panamint Range.*

0 kilometers   20
0 miles   20

Death
Valley

THE MOJAVE
DESERT

EXPERIENCE MORE

Route 66

F6 **W** historic66.com

In 1926, when it received its official designation, Route 66 was one of the few ways to get to California. People drove along it looking for jobs or to see the ocean at the road's end. Tiny towns sprang up on the route to provide gas stations, motels, and cafés. When the Interstate was completed in 1973, these towns declined into near oblivion until a resurgence of enthusiasm brought life back to this mythical road.

Start off with a visit to the **California Route 66 Museum**, where you can pick up kitsch gifts and souvenirs. Home to the landmark Roy's Hotel & Café (open for cold drinks and souvenirs), the ghost town of Amboy is also where you'll find the Amboy Crater National Natural Landmark. During winter months only, a hike to the rim of the volcano rewards you with panoramic views.

California Route 66 Museum

◎ **♠** 16825 South D St, Victorville ◎ 10am–4pm Mon & Thu–Sat, 11am–3pm Sun **W** califrt66museum.org

Kelso Dunes

F6 **ⓡ** Baker **ⓘ** Mojave National Preserve; www.nps.gov/moja

Towering more than 600 ft (160 m) above the desert floor, Kelso Dunes are formed from grains of golden rose quartz that have been blown from the Mojave River basin, 35 miles (56 km) to the west. Known as the "singing" dunes, they emit buzzing and rumbling sounds caused by the upper layers of sand sliding down the face of the dune, producing vibrations that are then amplified by the underlying sand.

Barstow

E6 **ⓡ** **ⓘ** 681 North First Av; www.barstowchamber.com

During the 19th century, this was a small settlement that served farmers as well as immigrants and miners on the Old Spanish Trail (*p261*). From 1937 to the late 1950s, Barstow was an important town along Route 66, the only surfaced road from Chicago to the West

 HIDDEN GEM
Mitchell Caverns

Near Kelso Dunes, in the Providence Mountains State Recreation Area, these caverns feature limestone stalagmites and stalactites. They are accessible only by guided tour (*www.parks.ca.gov*).

Coast. The town is best known today as being the midpoint on I-15 between Los Angeles and Las Vegas. To the 41 million people who make this journey each year, it is a convenient stopping-off point. Many also come here in search of the precious minerals and gemstones that are found in the surrounding desert plains.

The **Desert Discovery Center** has informative indoor displays on the Mojave Desert's flora and fauna, plus maps of the area, and restaurant and hotel information.

Desert Discovery Center

♠ 831 Barstow Rd ◎ 11am–4pm Tue–Sat **ⓧ** Federal hols **W** desertdc.com

---

Calico Ghost Town

F6 **ⓡ** Yermo ◎ 9am–5pm daily **ⓧ** Dec 25 **W** calicoghosttown.net

Calico Ghost Town, 12 miles (19 km) east of Barstow, is a late 19th-century mining town, which is part-authentic and part-reconstruction. Silver was discovered in abundance in the Calico Mountains in 1881, precipitating the arrival of

← Visitors on the streets of Calico Ghost Town, a 19th-century mining community

↑ A Joshua tree in front of red-and-pink cliffs, Red Rock Canyon State Park

hundreds of miners. In 1883 borax was discovered 3 miles (5 km) east of Calico, and the town's prosperity seemed assured. However, after the price of silver fell and the equally valuable borax gave out, the miners left. By 1907, Calico was a ghost town.

Walter Knott, founder of Knott's Berry Farm (p214), began the restoration process in the 1950s. Calico's desert setting reinforces the sense of a rough old mining town. Many of the original buildings remain, and visitors can take a ride in a mine train or explore tunnels in Maggie Mine, one of the most famous silver mines on the West Coast. Theatrical "shoot-outs" are performed on the main street daily.

Red Rock Canyon State Park

🅰 E5 🚌 From Mojave, Ridgecrest 🕐 Daily 🌐 parks.ca.gov

Alternate layers of white clay, red sandstone, pink volcanic rocks, and brown lava are spectacularly combined in Red Rock Canyon, a beautiful state park in the El Paso Mountains, which lie at the southern end of the Sierra Nevada Mountains. Three major desert ecozones overlap here, providing a wealth of plant and animal life, including eagles, hawks, and coyotes.

Cinder Cone National Natural Landmark

🅰 F5 🕐 Daily 🌐 nps.gov/moja

These 32 cinder cones were designated a National Natural Landmark in 1973. The hills of red and black volcanic rocks, and the black basalt lava flows surrounding them, are the result of volcanic activity that occurred here about 7.6 million years ago. Cinder cones are formed when small streams of scorching lava are spewed through the cooler air, making the lava solidify and preserving pockets created by escaping gases. The lightweight cratered rocks formed by the eruption accumulated around the vent to create conical hills that look otherworldly today. The lava that did stream out across the desert ground created lava tubes or tunnels.

The cinder cones left here today form a serene landscape that tourists can either hike to or view from Kelbaker Road.

EAT

Bagdad Café
Named after the cult movie that was filmed here, this café serves burgers, omelets, and sandwiches.

🅰 F6 🏠 46548 National Trails Hwy, Newberry Springs 📞 (760) 257-3101

💲💲💲

Slash X Run
Bikers and off roaders flock to this roadhouse for burgers and beers.

🅰 E6 🏠 28040 Barstow Rd, Barstow 🕐 Mon–Thu 📞 (760) 252-1197

💲💲💲

Emma Jean's Holland Burger Café
Tuck into a big breakfast at this roadside café.

🅰 E6 🏠 17143 N D St, Victorville 🕐 Sun 🌐 hollandburger.com

💲💲💲

SAN FRANCISCO AND THE BAY AREA

Fog rolling under the Golden Gate Bridge into San Francisco Bay

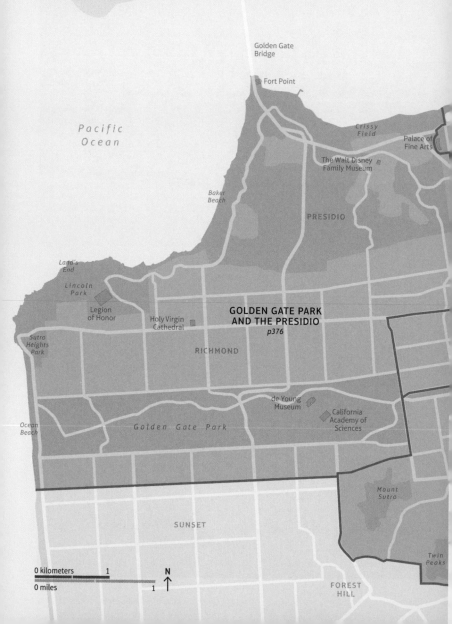

EXPLORE
SAN FRANCISCO

This guide divides San Francisco into seven sightseeing areas, as shown on this map. Find out more about each area on the following pages.

Golden Gate
Bridge

Fort Point

Crissy
Field

Palace of
Fine Arts

The Walt Disney
Family Museum

*Pacific
Ocean*

*Baker
Beach*

PRESIDIO

*Land's
End*

*Lincoln
Park*

Legion
of Honor

Holy Virgin
Cathedral

**GOLDEN GATE PARK
AND THE PRESIDIO**
p376

*Sutro
Heights
Park*

RICHMOND

de Young
Museum

California
Academy of
Sciences

*Ocean
Beach*

Golden Gate Park

*Mount
Sutro*

SUNSET

*Twin
Peaks*

0 kilometers   1
0 miles   1

N

FOREST
HILL

THE BAY AREA
p396

CALIFORNIA

SAN FRANCISCO

Pacific
Ocean

Alcatraz
Island

San Francisco
Bay

USS
Pampanito

PIER
39

Fort
Mason

FISHERMAN'S
WHARF

MARINA

FISHERMAN'S WHARF
AND NORTH BEACH
p324

Coit Tower

Exploratorium

COW
HOLLOW

RUSSIAN
HILL

NORTH
BEACH

Cable Car
Museum

FINANCIAL
DISTRICT

Ferry
Building

PACIFIC HEIGHTS
AND THE CIVIC CENTER
p342

CHINATOWN
AND NOB HILL
p306

Old St Mary's
Cathedral

PACIFIC
HEIGHTS

DOWNTOWN

THEATER
DISTRICT

Japantown

SFMOMA

St. Mary's
Cathedral

CIVIC
CENTER

Yerba Buena
Gardens

DOWNTOWN
AND SOMA
p282

City Hall

Asian Art
Museum

Oracle
Park

HAYES
VALLEY

SOMA

HAIGHT-
ASHBURY

LOWER
HAIGHT

MISSION
BAY

Buena
Vista Park

Mission Dolores

GLBT History
Museum

MISSION

POTRERO

HAIGHT-ASHBURY
AND THE MISSION
p360

NOE
VALLEY

GETTING TO KNOW
SAN FRANCISCO
AND THE BAY AREA

On the northern tip of a peninsula surrounded by ocean on three sides, San Francisco is made up of around 50 hills, after which some of its most famous neighborhoods are named. A global cultural and tech hub, the area overflows with icons and is a pioneer in organic farm-to-table food.

PAGE 282

DOWNTOWN AND SOMA

San Francisco's business and financial center, Downtown has gleaming skyscrapers either side of Market Street, the main drag. Nearby Union Square, encircled by department stores and shopping malls, is the city's fashion hub. To the south, SOMA (South of Market) is a hotspot for museums, galleries, and nightlife – the once-derelict district has been transformed in the 21st century, thanks in part to the Salesforce Transit Center and Yerba Buena Gardens.

Best for
Cable cars, hip restaurants, shopping, modern architecture, and art galleries

Home to
San Francisco Museum of Modern Art, Ferry Building

Experience
Riding the city's iconic cable cars up steep slopes

CHINATOWN AND NOB HILL

PAGE 306

The alleys of San Francisco's historic Chinatown are strung with red lanterns and crammed with restaurants, Buddhist temples, markets, and Chinese-inspired architecture. This is also the best place to see the city's famed cable cars trundling through the streets. They take passengers high above Downtown to the upscale residential district of Nob Hill, famous for its plush hotels, cathedral, and jaw-dropping vistas of the city.

Best for
Chinese food, Chinese temples, and city views

Home to
Cable Car Museum, Grace Cathedral

Experience
Sipping cocktails while enjoying the views from Top of the Mark

PAGE 324

FISHERMAN'S WHARF AND NORTH BEACH

One of the city's most popular destinations, bayside Fisherman's Wharf is loaded with cafés, knick-knack stores, crab shacks, and legendary seafood restaurants. The cultural history of North Beach, also known as "Little Italy," lives on in the Beat Museum and City Lights Bookstore. Nearby are iconic San Francisco sights such as Art Deco Coit Tower, twisting Lombard Street, and the infamous prison on Alcatraz Island.

Best for
Seafood, classic cafés and bars, maritime history

Home to
Alcatraz Island, Exploratorium

Experience
Eating freshly boiled crabs at Fisherman's Wharf

→

PAGE 342

PACIFIC HEIGHTS AND THE CIVIC CENTER

The streets of Pacific Heights, today an exclusive residential neighborhood, are lined with fine Victorian houses. To the north lies the Marina District, where the waterfront features Fort Mason – a top spot for art. To the south, the Civic Center contains City Hall and the greatest Beaux-Arts structures in the city. The beautiful architecture continues on nearby Alamo Square, home to the iconic "Painted Ladies" houses.

Best for
Victorian architecture, Asian art, and Japanese food

Home to
Asian Art Museum, Fort Mason

Experience
Seeing a live jazz performance at SFJazz Center.

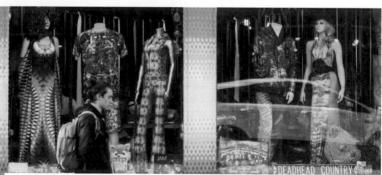

PAGE 360

HAIGHT-ASHBURY AND THE MISSION

Vintage clothing, tattoo parlors, and record stores left over from the hippie-era "Summer of Love" comprise a colorful collage in the Haight-Ashbury neighborhood. To the south, the Mission District remains a multicultural area with a large Latin American community. Home of the legendary Mission burrito, the neighborhood is full of venerable taquerias, as well as a multitude of hipster bars. The Castro district, to the east, has been the center of the city's LGBTQ+ community since the 1960s.

Best for
Mexican food, hippie memorabilia, LGBTQ+ culture, and street art

Home to
Haight-Ashbury, Castro Street

Experience
A guided walking tour of the Mission District murals

GOLDEN GATE PARK AND THE PRESIDIO

The spectacular Golden Gate Park is one of the world's largest urban green spaces. It houses numerous museums, botanical gardens, biking and walking trails, a boating lake, and even a herd of American bison. Land's End, the city's wildest region and home to the art-filled Legion of Honor, lies just to the north. The Presidio, overlooking San Francisco Bay and the Golden Gate Bridge, is now a National Park site, featuring vast woodlands sprinkled with cultural attractions.

Best for
Hiking, museums, parks, and gardens

Home to
California Academy of Sciences, Legion of Honor, Golden Gate Bridge

Experience
Sipping a cup of tea and strolling in the Japanese Tea Garden

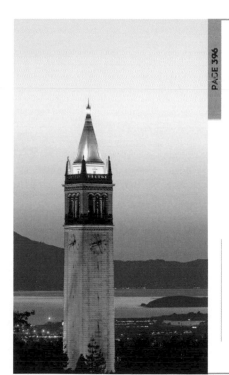

THE BAY AREA

North of San Francisco is Marin County, featuring beautiful parks, dense redwood forests, and small towns such as Tiburon and Sausalito. Oakland's museums and harbor and Berkeley's gardens and famous university take up much of the East Bay area, while farther south are the tech enclaves of Silicon Valley and Stanford. The booming city of San Jose has emerged as the region's newest commercial and cultural center, combining some fine museums with historical architecture.

Best for
Hiking, museums, famous universities, and superb cuisine

Home to
Berkeley, Oakland, San Jose

Experience
A hike in the Marin Headlands to see the Golden Gate Bridge against the San Francisco skyline

7 DAYS

in San Francisco and the Bay Area

Day 1

Start your tour with an organic breakfast at HEYDAY *(555 Mission St)* in San Francisco's Mission District before heading up to the skydeck of the Salesforce Tower *(p298)* for a jaw-dropping overview of the city. Walk off your breakfast en route to SFMOMA *(p286)*, home to leading contemporary art. In the afternoon, wander to Chinatown, where you can pick up snacks from the Golden Gate Fortune Cookie Factory *(p316)* and browse the crafts shops. In the evening, head into North Beach for dinner at Tony's Pizza Napoletana *(www.tonyspizza napoletana.com)* and cocktails at the former Beats hangout, Vesuvio Café *(p339)*.

Day 2

Enjoy an all-American breakfast at the Eagle Café on PIER 39 *(www.eaglecafe.com)* before browsing the pier's many shops. Continue to Fisherman's Wharf, where you can watch the basking sea lions and clamber aboard the historic ships at the Maritime National Historical Park *(p336)*. From here, ferries depart to Alcatraz Island *(p328)* and around the Golden Gate Bay. If you aren't inclined to set sail, hop

on the Powell-Hyde Cable Car for cityscape and ocean views as it rattles up the steep streets to Columbus Avenue and visit Coit Tower *(p338)* to take in 1930s-era frescoes. Then ride a vintage streetcar down Market Street to the Embarcadero and dine on Vietnamese cuisine at the Slanted Door in the Ferry Building *(p290)*.

Day 3

Follow breakfast at the historic Beach Chalet *(p393)* overlooking the Pacific with a stroll along Ocean Beach and onto Golden Gate Park *(p376)*. Wander along the park's shaded pathways, stopping to admire the art at the de Young Museum *(p388)* and the blossoms in the Japanese Tea Garden *(p389)*. If there's enough time, take a taxi north to the wild Land's End promontory, laced with trails and topped by the art-filled Legion of Honor *(p382)*. Park Chalet Coastal Beer Garden *(www.parkchalet.com)* is a lovely gastropub for dinner and drinks.

Day 4

Spend the morning strolling the shops and sights of Haight Street, the main drag of

1 **Vesuvio Café**, which preserves its Beat-era spirit.
2 Basking sea lions on PIER 39.
3 de Young Fine Arts Museum.
4 Stores in Haight-Ashbury.
5 Greek Theatre, Berkeley.

former hippie central Haight-Ashbury (p360). Lunch at Mexican Nopalito (www.nopalitosf.com) in the adjacent Panhandle district. From here it's a short walk to Alamo Square (p354) and the elegant row of "Painted Ladies" Victorian houses. Next, grab a cab to Mission Dolores (p368) – the oldest structure in the city. A stroll through the Mission neighborhood's streets turns up striking murals and the Mission Cultural Center for Latino Arts (p370). End the day with dinner at La Taqueria (2889 Mission St).

Day 5

From Pier 41, take an early ferry to Oakland (p404) for a waterfront breakfast on Jack London Square. Spend a couple of hours in the Oakland Museum of California to learn about the state's art and history, then take the BART railway to Berkeley's Shattuck Avenue, which offers excellent farm-to-table options for lunch. In the afternoon explore Berkeley Art Museum (p403) and the University of California, Berkeley campus (p400) before rounding out the day with live music at the Greek Theatre and drinks on Telegraph Avenue.

Day 6

After heading out of the city to Marin County, have breakfast at the Dipsea Café (www.dipseacafe.com) in Mill Valley. Then get an early start at Muir Woods and Beach (p410), a wonderful hiking and cycling area and a haven for old-growth redwoods. Take a beach stroll or go waterfowl-spotting before heading to Sausalito (p410) for a gourmet dinner and cocktails with views of the bay and Golden Gate Bridge at Cavallo Point lodge (www.cavallopoint.com), a former military base.

Day 7

After breakfast at the Bayside Café in Sausalito (1 Gate 6 Rd), take the short ferry ride from Tiburon to Angel Island (p410) for dazzling Bay Area vistas and a seafood lunch. When you've had your fill of exploring this island state park on its excellent walking and cycling trails, take the ferry back to San Francisco for an evening of gallery viewing at Fort Mason (p348) and dinner at the excellent vegetarian Green's restaurant (www.greensrestaurant.com).

Did You Know?

The original rainbow flag was created by Gilbert Baker for the 1978 San Francisco Pride parade.

SAN FRANCISCO FOR
LGBTQ+
CULTURE

Dubbed "the gay capital of the world," San Francisco has a vibrant LGBTQ+ culture, which started in the 1920s, albeit underground. Castro was the original center of the LGBTQ+ community, but today other areas of the city, such as SOMA, the Mission District, and Haight-Ashbury, have thriving scenes too.

Community History

The city is steeped in LGBTQ+ history. The first Gay Liberation organization in the US emerged here in 1965, and with the first Pride march in 1970, the LGBTQ+ community began to come out and stand proud across the city. Learn about San Francisco's LGBTQ+ history at the GLBT Historical Society Museum *(p368)*. Then head to Castro's main drag, which has rainbow "Walk of Fame" bronze plaques honoring the neighborhood's long history of queer activism. Nearby, Pink Triangle Park is home to the USA's only memorial to the thousands of LGBTQ+ community members who were persecuted in Nazi Germany in World War II.

↑ An exhibit at the Pink Triangle Park Memorial, San Francisco

Iconic Festivals

San Francisco's Pride festival at the end of June is world-famous. While the focus is on fun, the event also aims to commemorate the highs and lows of LGBTQ+ history and to educate. Held to coincide with Pride are Frameline, an LGBTQ+ film festival with screenings at venues all over the city, and Fresh Meat Productions, which hosts live music and dance performances, from opera to pop and voguing to hip hop.

←

Performers in the world-famous San Francisco Pride parade

HARVEY MILK

In 1977, local business-owner Harvey Milk was elected to the San Francisco Board of Supervisors, becoming one of the first gay elected officials in the US. His tenure was cut short in 1978 when he and Mayor George Moscone were shot and killed in City Hall by Dan White, a conservative supervisor. White was found guilty only of manslaughter and given a light sentence, sparking riots and protests. Milk was posthumously awarded the Presidential Medal of Freedom in 2009.

↑ City Hall illuminated in rainbow colors to celebrate San Francisco Pride

The Castro District

The Castro (p366) is San Francisco's most famous LGBTQ+ neighborhood. The welcoming shops, clubs, and cafés are a huge draw for visitors. For a great introduction to the area, join a walking tour (www.sfcityguides.org) to learn about local history and sights. Check out the Castro Street Fair during the first weekend in October when dance parties, performances, crafts stalls, and much more take place.

↑ A rainbow crosswalk heralding gay pride in the Castro district

DOWNTOWN AND SOMA

The original inhabitants of the San Francisco area were the Ohlone people. With the arrival of the Spanish in 1776, the effects of aggressive colonization combined with the spread of European diseases decimated the Ohlone within a few generations. The foundations of modern San Francisco were laid in 1835, when former English sailor William Richardson got permission to settle at what was then known as Yerba Buena Cove. The town developed slowly, its inhabitants trading hides and tallow with visiting ships. In 1849, San Francisco's population exploded thanks to the California Gold Rush, and modern Downtown began to take shape along Montgomery Street, where miners came to weigh their gold dust. By the time the transcontinental railroad was completed in 1869, San Francisco was a rowdy boomtown.

In 1906 a massive earthquake, followed by three days of fire, destroyed three-quarters of the city. Rebuilding began immediately. Today, old-style banking halls from the early 20th century stand in the shadow of glass and steel skyscrapers. Bordering this high-profile hub is SOMA – "South of Market." Once a residential area, the neighborhood is now a contemporary and bustling district of galleries, fine dining, and tech companies.

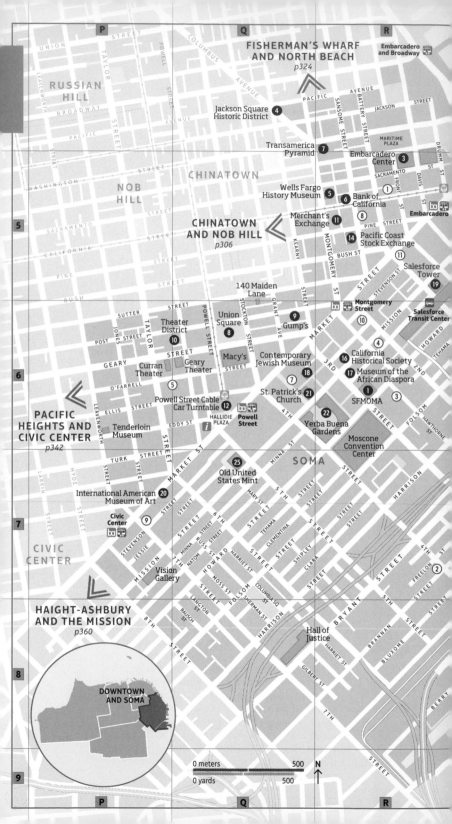

DOWNTOWN AND SOMA

Must Sees
1 SFMOMA
2 Ferry Building

Experience More
3 Embarcadero Center
4 Jackson Square Historic District
5 Wells Fargo History Museum
6 Bank of California
7 Transamerica Pyramid
8 Union Square
9 Gump's
10 Theater District
11 Merchant's Exchange
12 Powell Street Cable Car Turntable
13 Rincon Annex
14 Pacific Coast Stock Exchange
15 Embarcadero Plaza
16 California Historical Society
17 Museum of the African Diaspora
18 Contemporary Jewish Museum
19 Salesforce Tower
20 International American Museum of Art
21 St. Patrick's Church
22 Yerba Buena Gardens
23 Railway Museum
24 Oracle Park
25 Old United States Mint

Eat
① Tadich Grill
② Marlowe
③ Benu
④ The Bird

Drink
⑤ Cityscape Bar & Lounge
⑥ 21st Amendment Brewery
⑦ Press Club

Stay
⑧ Loews Regency San Francisco
⑨ YOTEL San Francisco

Shop
⑩ Alexander Book Company
⑪ Fog City News

❶ 🛝 🎨 🍴 🖥 🛍

SFMOMA

📍R6 🏛151 3rd St 🚌5, 9, 12, 14, 30, 38, 45 🚊J, K, L, M, N, T ⏰10am–5pm Thu–Tue (to 9pm Thu) 🌐sfmoma.org

Standing on the northeast side of the Yerba Buena Gardens art and entertainment complex *(p300)*, the San Francisco Museum of Modern Art (SFMOMA) houses innovative works of modern and contemporary art and is one of the world's largest museums of its kind.

This museum forms the nucleus of San Francisco's reputation as a leading center of modern art. Opened in 1935 at the Veterans Building *(p354)*, it moved into its current quarters in 1995, and in spring 2016 reopened after a major three-year $365 million expansion that doubled its capacity. Designed by the international architecture firm Snøhetta, the 235,000-sq-ft (21,832-sq-m) expansion is seamlessly integrated with Swiss architect Mario Botta's 1995 Modernist building. The museum offers a dynamic schedule of special exhibitions and permanent collection presentations.

Museum Highlights

SFMOMA is both an outstanding repository of modern and contemporary art and a powerhouse of inspiration and encouragement to the local art scene. With more than 30,000 works in the museum's permanent collection, you'll see a wide range of art, including traditional paintings, media arts, architecture, and design. The museum's main strengths lie in US and Latin American Modernism, Fauvism, Surrealism, Abstract Expressionism, Minimalism and post-Minimalism, Pop Art, postwar German art, and the art of California. The 2016 expansion brought a notable addition: the 15,000-sq-ft (1,393-sq-m) Pritzker Center for Photography, the largest space dedicated to this artform in any art museum in the US.

↑ The Howard Street entrance and *(inset)* visitors at a media arts exhibit

Gallery Guide

Level One

Here you'll find the excellent museum store, the Michelin-starred restaurant In Situ, a theater, and large abstract works by Julie Mehretu.

Level Two

The permanent collection, Education Center, and library are housed on the second floor, interspersed with temporary exhibits.

↑ The vibrant *Figures with Sunset* (1978) by Roy Lichtenstein

Level Three

△ The fabulous Pritzker Center for Photography sits on the third floor along with a sculpture terrace, Graphic Design Gallery, and the 30-ft- (9-m-) high Living Wall.

Level Four

△ The Agnes Martin and Kelly Elsworth galleries, event space, and many temporary exhibits are found on Level Four.

Level Five

△ The fifth floor houses a variety of museum highlights including the Oculus Bridge, Andy Warhol gallery, and a sculpture garden.

Level Six

△ The Anselm Kiefer and Gerhard Richter galleries are here.

Level Seven

The top level has media arts displays and the Sculpture Terrace.

LOWER FLOORS

California Arts

On the second floor are galleries dedicated to works by California artists. These painters and sculptors have drawn their inspiration from local materials and scenes to create a body of art unique to the West Coast. Collage and assemblage works by these artists, exhibited on rotation from the museum's collection, make use of every-day materials such as felt-tip pens, junkyard scraps, and old paintings, producing art with a distinctive West Coast flavor.

Photography

Drawing on its enormous permanent collection of over 17,800 photographs, the museum presents wonderful exhibitions of the photographic arts in the Pritzker Center for Photography, located on the third floor.

The collection of Modernist American masters includes Berenice Abbott, Walker Evans, Edward Steichen, and Alfred Stieglitz, with special attention paid to California photographers. Here you will find the finest collection of Japanese photography outside of Japan, as well as extensive collections from Latin America and Europe, including German avant-garde photographers of the 1920s, and European Surrealists of the 1930s.

Did You Know?

SFMOMA includes works from the collection of Doris and Donald Fisher, founders of the Gap.

A display in the Pritzker Center for Photography ↓

Paintings and Sculpture

Included in the museum's permanent holdings are over 8,000 paintings, sculptures, and works on paper. American Abstract Expressionism is well represented at the museum by Philip Guston, Franz Kline, and Jackson Pollock, whose first ever museum exhibition took place here at SFMOMA.

Other prominent North and Latin American artists whose works are displayed in the museum collections include Frida Kahlo, Diego Rivera, and Georgia O'Keeffe. Another exhibition area permanently shows works by Jasper Johns, Robert Rauschenberg, and Andy Warhol, among others. There is a good collection of the European Modernists, including notable paintings by Pablo Picasso from various periods. A large collection of works by Paul Klee are accommodated in an individual gallery; works by the famous French painter of the Fauvist school, Henri Matisse, are found nearby on the second floor.

An actively changing schedule of contemporary art exhibits supplements the museum's historical collection and does much to encourage today's art scene.

↑ Alexander Calder sculptures, and *(inset)* *Frieda and Diego Rivera* (1931), by Frida Kahlo

Leeson, Bill Viola, Doug Hall, and Mary Lucier.

UPPER FLOORS

Architecture and Design

SFMOMA's Department of Architecture and Design was founded in 1983. Its function is to procure and maintain a collection of historical and contemporary architectural drawings, models, and design objects, and to examine and illuminate their influences on modern art. Its current holding of over 6,000 items focuses on architecture, furniture, product design, and graphic design, and is widely considered one of the most significant in the United States. The sixth-floor galleries offer rotating exhibitions.

Among items included in the permanent collection are models, drawings, prints, and prototypes by well-known and emerging designers. These include the architect Bernard Maybeck, who was responsible for some of the most beautiful buildings in the Bay Area, including the Palace of Fine Arts *(p350)*. Other noted Bay Area architects represented are Timothy Pflueger, William Wurster, and Willis Polk, known for his design of the glass-and-steel Hallidie Building (130 Sutter St), as well as the California design team of Charles and Ray Eames. The permanent collection also includes works by Frank Lloyd Wright, Frank Gehry, and Fumihiko Maki.

Media Arts

The seventh-floor galleries deploy state-of-the-art equipment to present film, video, photographic, multi-image and multimedia works, and interactive media artwork.

The museum's growing permanent collection includes pieces by Nam June Paik, Don Graham, Peter Campus, Joan Jonas, Lynn Hershman

Contemporary Art and Special Exhibitions

The fourth floor features special exhibition galleries. An actively changing schedule of contemporary art exhibits supplements the museum's historical collection and does much to encourage today's art scene. The museum also has regular film screenings and public talks in the theater.

EAT

In Situ
Chef Corey Lee's three-star Michelin restaurant.

🅰 Level 1 🆆 insitu. sfoma.org

⑤⑤⑤

Cafe 5
A relaxed restaurant in the sculpture garden.

🅰 Level 5 ☎ (415) 615-0515

⑤⑤⑤

2 🎧 🍴 🍽 👜

FERRY BUILDING

📍S4 🚇Embarcadero at Market St 🚌2, 6, 21, 31, 82 🚊E, F, J, K, L, M, N 🚋California St ⛴SF Bay Ferry 🕐Times vary, check website 🌐ferrybuildingmarketplace.com

This historic entry point into the city is now a chic marketplace and food hall. Everything on offer is made with flair and care by local producers devoted to sustainability and traditional production techniques.

The Ferry Building Marketplace houses many gourmet shops and several restaurants. It has a distinctly northern California feel in the way it celebrates regional produce and local and artisan producers. On Tuesdays, Thursdays, and Saturdays the highly acclaimed Ferry Plaza Farmers' Market sees stalls full of high-quality fresh farm produce and artisan foods. The market provides visitors with an opportunity to learn more about food and local agriculture.

History

The Ferry Building, constructed between 1896 and 1903, survived the great fire of 1906 through the intercession of fireboats pumping water from the bay. The clock tower is 235 ft (71 m) high, and was inspired by the Moorish bell tower of Seville Cathedral. In the early 1930s more than 50 million passengers a year passed through the building. With the opening of the Bay Bridge in 1936, the Ferry Building ceased to be the city's main point of entry, but even today ferries still cross the bay to Larkspur and Sausalito in Marin County and Alameda and Oakland in the East Bay.

The Ferry Building and *(inset)* lavender for sale at the farmers' market ↑

LAVENDER $6 bunch

← The Ferry Building's clock tower, an iconic feature of the downtown skyline

→ Inside the Ferry Building Marketplace, a renowned food market hall

Did You Know?

The arched arcades of the Ferry Building were modeled on the aqueduct in Rome.

EAT

Donut Farm
Vegan-friendly menu with delightful donuts and great breakfast options.

📅 Sat only 🌱 vegan donut.farm

$ $ $

El Porteño Empanadas
Argentinian empanadas created using an old family recipe.

🌐 elportenosf.com

$ $ $

The Slanted Door
A highly acclaimed Vietnamese restaurant overlooking the Bay.

🌐 slanteddoor.com

$ $ $

Gott's Roadside
A 1950s-style restaurant serving burgers, seafood, and sandwiches. Dine inside or out on the pier.

🌐 gotts.com

$ $ $

EXPERIENCE MORE

③ Embarcadero Center

📍R5 🚌1, 32, 41 🚃J, K, L, M, N 🚋California St
🌐embarcaderocenter.com

The Embarcadero Center was completed in 1981, the largest redevelopment project in the city's history. The complex comprises five 35- to 45-story towers rising above landscaped plazas and elevated walkways. Adjacent to the fourth tower is the Hyatt Regency Hotel, whose atrium holds *Eclipse*, a huge sculpted globe by Charles Perry.

④ Jackson Square Historic District

📍Q4 🚌12, 15, 41, 83

This neighborhood contains many brick, cast-iron, and granite facades dating from the Gold Rush era. The best can be seen in Jackson Street, Gold Street, Montgomery Street, and Hotaling Place. From 1850 to 1910 the area was known as the Barbary Coast, notorious for its squalor and the crudeness of its inhabitants. The bawdy relief sculptures in the front of the old Hippodrome theater at No. 555 Pacific Street recall the risqué shows that were performed there. Today the buildings are used as showrooms, law offices, top-notch restaurants, design and fashion boutiques, art galleries, and antiques shops.

---

⑤ Wells Fargo History Museum

📍R5 🏛420 Montgomery St 🚌1, 3, 10, 41
🚇Montgomery St 🕐9am–5pm Mon–Fri 🔒Federal hols 🌐wellsfargo history.com

Founded in 1852, Wells Fargo & Co. became the greatest banking and transportation company in the West and was influential in the development of the American frontier. The company moved people and goods from the East to the West Coast, transported gold from the West Coast to the East, and delivered mail. It also played a major role in the Pony Express mail venture.

The stagecoaches displayed are famous, particularly for the legendary stories of their heroic drivers and the bandits who robbed them. The best-known bandit was Black Bart, who left poems at the scene of his crimes. In one holdup he also mistakenly left a handkerchief with a distinctive

A mail coach on display in the Wells Fargo History Museum

 The *Eclipse* sculpture in the lobby of the Hyatt Regency Hotel, Embarcadero Center

⑦
Transamerica Pyramid

📍 R4 🏠 600 Montgomery St 🚌 1, 10, 12, 30, 41 🕐 8am–5pm Mon–Fri (lobby only) 🚫 Public hols 🌐 thepyramidcenter.com

Designed by William Pereira & Associates and capped with a pointed spire, this 48-story pyramid reaches 853 ft (260 m). The pyramid stands on what is the former site of the Montgomery Block, which was built in 1853 to house many important offices. After the Financial District was extended south in the 1860s, the office workers moved into the new buildings and artists and writers took up residence in the Montgomery Block. By the 1940s the block became rundown and was demolished in 1959. The site was home to a parking lot before the Transamerica Pyramid was built between 1969 and 1972.

laundry mark, revealing him to be a mining engineer named Charles Boles (*p474*). Visitors can experience how it felt to sit for days in a jostling stagecoach, see gold nuggets from the 1848 Gold Rush, and listen to the recorded diary of an immigrant.

⑥
Bank of California

📍 R5 🏠 400 California St 📞 (415) 705-7142 🚌 1, 3, 10, 12, 41 🚋 California St 🕐 Museum: 9am–5pm Mon–Fri 🚫 Federal hols

Businessmen William Ralston and Darius Mills founded this bank in 1864. Ralston invested profitably in the Comstock mines and used the bank and his personal fortune to finance many civic projects in San Francisco, including the city's water company. The present colonnaded building was completed in 1908. The Bank of California Museum, in the basement, displays gold, old banknotes, and diagrams of the Comstock mines.

→ The Transamerica Pyramid, one of San Francisco's most recognizable sights

Union Square

Q6 30, 38, 45
J, K, L, M, N, T Powell-Mason, Powell-Hyde
visitunionsquaresf.com

Union Square was named after the big, pro-Union rallies that were held here during the American Civil War of 1861–65. The rallies were instrumental in galvanizing popular support for the Northern cause, which resulted in California entering into the war on the side of the Union.

The original synagogue, churches, and gentlemen's clubs have long been replaced by shops and offices. The palm-lined square is at the heart of San Francisco's shopping district and marks the edge of the Theater District. On the west side is the luxurious Westin St. Francis Hotel, whose first wings were built in 1904 in the style of Louis Sullivan. In the center, a bronze statue of the Goddess of Victory stands at the top of a 90-ft (27-m) Corinthian column. Sculpted by Robert Aitken in 1903, it commemorates Admiral Dewey's victory at Manila Bay during the Spanish-American War of 1898.

Gump's

Q6 135 Post St
2, 3, 4, 30, 38, 45
J, K, L, M, N Powell-Mason, Powell-Hyde
11am–5pm Mon–Sat
gumps.com

Founded in 1861 by German immigrants who were once mirror and frame merchants, this luxurious San Francisco department store has become a leader in design-savvy retail and a favorite local institution.

Gump's houses one of the largest collections of crystal in the United States, created by prestigious designers such as Baccarat, Steuben, and Lalique.

The store is also known for its oriental treasures, furniture, and rare works of art. Its Asian art offering is particularly fine, especially the jade collection, which enjoys an international reputation. In 1949 Gump's imported a great bronze Buddha and presented it to the Japanese Tea Garden in Golden Gate Park (p389).

Gump's has a very refined atmosphere and is often frequented by the rich and famous. It is renowned for its extravagant window displays.

Theater District

P6 2, 3, 4, 38
J, K, L, M, N, T Powell-Mason, Powell-Hyde

Several theaters are located near Union Square, all within a six-block area. The two largest are on Geary Boulevard: the Curran Theater, designed in 1922 by Alfred Henry D. Jacobs,

> HIDDEN GEM
> ### Tenderloin Museum
>
> This museum tells the story of the Tenderloin area northeast of the Theater District, which was once home to jazz bars and speakeasies. (www.tenderloin museum.org).

↑ Bustling Union Square, centered on a column topped by the Goddess of Victory

which imports hit Broadway shows, and the Geary Theater, with the ornate Edwardian facade. The Geary Theater is now home to the American Conservatory Theater (ACT), which shows classical and contemporary pieces.

San Francisco has a strong reputation for the variety and quality of performances it has on offer, and has historically attracted great actors. Isadora Duncan, the innovative 1920s dancer, was born nearby at No. 501 Taylor Street, which is now marked by a plaque.

A cable car being rotated at the Powell Street Cable Car Turntable ↑

⓫ Merchant's Exchange

🔲 R5 🏠 465 California St
🚌 1, 4, 10, 12, 41
Ⓜ Montgomery St
🕐 Banking Hall: 9am–5pm Mon–Fri 🌐 clintreilly.com/the-merchants-exchange

The exchange, designed by architect Willis Polk in 1903, survived the great fire of 1906 with little damage. The building, which once dominated the skyline, was the focal point of San Francisco's commodities exchange in the early 20th century, when lookouts in the tower relayed news of ships arriving from abroad. Today, the Merchant's Exchange is dwarfed by skyscrapers. The California Bank occupies the main hall, whose walls are covered with William Coulter's stunning seascapes depicting epic maritime scenes from the age of steam and sail. The Julia Morgan Ballroom on the 15th floor is an events space.

Did You Know?

San Francisco's cable cars are the only moving National Historic Landmark.

⓬ Powell Street Cable Car Turntable

🔲 Q6 🏠 Hallidie Plaza, Powell St at Market St
🚌 Many buses 🚈 J, K, M, N
🚋 Powell-Mason, Powell-Hyde 🌐 sfcablecar.com

The Powell–Hyde and the Powell–Mason cable car lines are the most spectacular routes in San Francisco. They start and end their journeys to Nob Hill, Chinatown, and Fisherman's Wharf at the corner of Powell Street and Market Street. Unlike the double-ended cable cars that are found on the California Street line, the Powell Street cable cars were built to move in one direction only – hence the need for a turntable at the end of each line.

After the last passengers have disembarked, the car is pushed onto the turntable and rotated manually by the conductor and gripman. The next passengers for the return journey wait for the half-circle to be completed amid an ever-changing procession of street musicians, local shoppers, and office workers.

The other two turntables in the city are at the corner of Taylor and Bay streets, and at Hyde and Beach streets.

DRINK

Cityscape Bar & Lounge
Craft cocktails and a vast selection of wines are served up with views of the Golden Gate Bridge at this chic rooftop bar.

🔲 P6 🏠 333 O'Farrell St
🌐 cityscapesf.com

21st Amendment Brewery
Sip a flight of refreshing blood-orange India pale ales and spiced ales at this haunt near Oracle Park.

🔲 S7 🏠 563 2nd St
🌐 21st-amendment.com/pub

Press Club
This underground bar is the place to be for happy hour, with generous discounts on local craft brews and wines by the glass.

🔲 Q6 🏠 20 Yerba Buena Lane 🌐 pressclubsf.com

SHOP

Alexander Book Company

This labyrinthine, independent bookstore has stacks of new and used tomes spread over three floors. Comfy chairs dotted between shelves give you a chance to sit down and browse through the wonderful books.

📍R6 📫563 2nd St
🌐21st-amendment.com/pub

Fog City News

Thousands of magazines (including many foreign-language), greetings cards, and a huge array of artisan chocolate bars from all over the world can be found at this legendary, quirky store.

📍R5 📫455 Market St
🌐fogcitynews.com

The portico of the Pacific Coast Stock Exchange building ↓

Rincon Annex

📍S5 🚌14

The Rincon Annex Post Office Building dates from 1940 and is best known for its series of murals by the Russian-born artist Anton Refregier. The panels, in Social-Realist style, decorate the lobby and depict several periods in the history of San Francisco, starting with the Native Americans that first inhabited the area, and then with the arrival of the Spanish conquistadors. The narrative progresses to the establish-ment of the missions, the Gold Rush of 1848, the catastrophic earthquake of 1906, and the construction of the iconic Golden Gate Bridge.

The murals caused much controversy in the politically conservative aftermath of World War II. Detractors questioned the artist's harsh depictions of events and his political leanings.

Pacific Coast Stock Exchange

📍R5 📫301 Pine St 🚌3, 8, 30X, 41 🔒To the public

This was once America's largest stock exchange outside New York City. Founded in 1882, it

occupied these buildings, which were remodeled by Miller and Pflueger in 1930 from the existing US Treasury. The monumental granite statues that flank the Pine Street entrance to the building were made by the renowned San Francisco sculptor, painter, and muralist Ralph Stackpole, also in 1930. No longer a stock exchange, the building now houses a fitness club. Some trading continues at the Mills Building and Tower nearby.

 15

Embarcadero Plaza

📍 S5 🚌 Many buses 🚋 F, J, K, L, M, N 🚃 California St

Popular with lunchtime crowds from the nearby Embarcadero Center (p292), this plaza is best known for its avant-garde Vaillancourt Fountain, created in 1971 by the Canadian artist Armand Vaillancourt. The fountain is modeled from huge concrete blocks, and some people find it ugly, especially when it is allowed to run dry during times of drought. You are allowed to climb through it, and with its splashing pools and columns of falling water, it is an intriguing, if divisive, work of interactive art. The plaza is often rented out to musicians during the lunch hour – the popular rock band U2 performed a lunchtime concert here in 1987, after which they drew criticism for spray-painting the fountain without the city's permission.

> **The Vaillancourt Fountain, with its splashing pools and columns of falling water, is an intriguing, if divisive, work of interactive art.**

 16

California Historical Society

📍 R6 🏛 678 Mission St 🚌 9, 30, 45 🚃 Montgomery St 🕐 Noon–5:30pm Fri–Sun 🌐 californiahistorical society.org

This society is dedicated to preserving and interpreting the history and culture of California. Its Mission Street address offers a reference and research library, museum galleries, and a well-stocked bookstore. The galleries have an impressive photographic collection, more than 900 oil paintings and watercolors by American artists, and a unique costume collection.

↑ The Vaillancourt Fountain in the Embarcadero Plaza

17

Museum of the African Diaspora

📍 R6 🏛 685 Mission St 🚌 5, 6, 9, 14, 30 🚃 J, K, L 🕐 11am–6pm Wed–Sat, noon–5pm Sun 🌐 moadsf.org

One of the few museums in the world focused on the African Diaspora, MoAD aims to raise awareness of the art, history, and culture of this dispersed people. Founded in 2005, the museum explores the varied cultural heritage of Africa and African descendant cultures around the world.

The exhibitions and public events program trace the evolution of the diaspora through the interpretation of visual arts and crafts, music, dance, and much more. Interactive features include iPads and narratives, which cover subjects such as the international slave trade.

18 Contemporary Jewish Museum

📍 Q6 📍 736 Mission St
🚌 8, 14, 30, 45, 81X
🚉 J, K, L, M, N, T ⏰ 11am-5pm Thu-Sat ⏳ Major Jewish holidays
🌐 thecjm.org

This museum partners with national and international cultural institutions to present a variety of art, photography, and installations celebrating and exploring Judaism. The innovative changing displays make use of historical objects, interactive activities, film, music, and more. Past exhibits have explored wide-ranging subjects such as cartoonist Rube Goldberg, the history of Levi Strauss and blue jeans, and the 20th-century tattoo artist Lew Alberts.

The museum is housed in an early 20th-century Pacific Gas & Electric (PG&E) power substation, adapted and redesigned by renowned Polish American architect Daniel Libeskind, and a new geometric steel structure, also by Daniel Libeskind. It has more than 10,000 sq ft (930 sq m) of exhibition space and an impressive education center.

Did You Know?

The foundations of the Salesforce Tower go down a whopping 300 ft (91 m).

19 Salesforce Tower

📍 R5 📍 415 Mission St
🌐 salesforcetower.com

Rising 1,070 ft (326 m) above the East Cut neighborhood, the gleaming Salesforce Tower (formerly the Transbay Tower) has been the tallest building in San Francisco since 2018, when it overtook the 853-ft (260-m) iconic Transamerica Pyramid (p293).

Popular hour-long tours of the 61st floor take place on the last Saturday of every month, allowing visitors to marvel at the city's loftiest view; check tour times on the website and be sure to reserve well in advance as only 50 guests are admitted per month. The 360-degree panorama of the entire city and the Bay Area is truly spectacular, especially on a sun-drenched California day.

20 International American Museum of Art

📍 P7 📍 1023 Market St
⏰ 10am-5pm Tue-Sun
🌐 iamasf.org

A haven of tranquility on this otherwise bustling stretch of Market Street, the International American Museum of Art showcases a fascinating and diverse collection of European and Asian artworks. Among the pieces on display are ink paintings from China, including elegant examples of calligraphy; European and American landscape art from the 17th century to the present day; and contemporary 3D-art. Also on the premises are the Tendergold Gallery, which houses temporary exhibitions of up-and-coming California-based artists, and the Light-space Gallery, which features quarterly rotating displays of installation art, sculpture, and photography.

The gallery runs regular guided tours, some suitable

The Contemporary Jewish Museum, adapted by Libeskind ↓

← The striking Flamboyant Gothic interior of St. Patrick's Church

for children, and there are free walk-throughs of the gallery's highlights every third Sunday of the month.

 21
St. Patrick's Church

📍 Q6 🏠 756 Mission St
🌐 stpatricksf.org

Built in Flamboyant Gothic style, this red-brick Catholic church offers an attractive contrast to the high-rise buildings that surround it. It was built in 1851 and has served successive waves of San Franciscans – first the Irish community, followed by mainly Spanish and Filipino worshippers. The church is named for Ireland's patron saint, and its vibrant Tiffany-style windows depict Irish traditions and the 32 patron saints of each Irish county. Even the interior columns, made from green Connemara and gold-and-white Botticino marble, reflect the colors of the Irish flag. Damaged in the earthquake of 1906, the church was repaired brick by brick in the same distinctive style, becoming a designated landmark in 1968.

🔍 HIDDEN GEM
140 Maiden Lane

Architect Frank Lloyd Wright's only building in San Francisco is the former V. C. Morris Gift Shop at 140 Maiden Lane, a 10-minute walk from St. Patrick's Church. He experimented with the use of ramps in what is considered to be one of his most influential designs.

EAT

Tadich Grill
In business since 1849, this old-school favorite pulls in the after-work crowds with large portions of seafood.

📍 R5 🏠 240 California St
🌙 Sun 🌐 tadichgrillsf.com

$$$

Marlowe
Enjoy bacon cheeseburgers and moreish bar snacks, such as brussels sprout fries, at this gastropub. The cocktails are great too.

📍 R7 🏠 500 Brannan St
🌐 marlowesf.com

$$$

Benu
Seoul-born chef Corey Lee deftly combines Korean, Japanese, and Cantonese flavors at this triple Michelin-starred eatery.

📍 R6 🏠 22 Hawthorne St 🌙 Sun & Mon
🌐 benusf.com

$$$

The Bird
This casual counter-service restaurant is famous for its fried chicken sandwiches.

📍 R6 🏠 115 New Montgomery St
🌐 thebirdsf.com

$$$

Yerba Buena Gardens

📍 R6 🚇 Mission, 3rd, Folsom, and 4th sts 🚌 9, 14, 15, 30, 45, 🚋 J, K, L, M, N ⏰ 6am-10pm daily 🌐 yerbabuenagardens.com

The construction of San Francisco's largest venue for conventions in 1981 - the Moscone Center - was a continuation of ambitious plans to transform a once-industrial area into a green spot for residents and tourists alike. New housing, hotels, museums, galleries, shops, and restaurants have been established to rejuvenate this once-disused area.

There are a number of themed gardens, including the Butterfly Garden, planted with species that attract colorful winged visitors such as monarch butterflies, and the Sister City Gardens, which showcase plants and flowers typical of San Francisco's twinned cities around the world, from Assisi in Italy to Sydney, Australia.

The **Children's Creativity Museum** is located in the Yerba Buena Children's Garden, which is built on top of the Moscone Center. The museum offers an ongoing program of events and provides countless opportunities for youngsters and artists to collaborate in the design and creation of anything from aircraft, robots, and futuristic buildings to mosaics and sculptures. There's also the Making Music Studio, and the Animation Studio, where kids can make their own clay-mation film.

The **Yerba Buena Center for the Arts** is an arts forum with galleries and screenings of contemporary films, and the Lam Research Theater offers performances that reflect the cultural diversity of San Francisco.

Children's Creativity Museum
📷 🏛 🎭 📞 (415) 820-3349 ⏰ 10am-4pm Wed-Sun

Yerba Buena Center for the Arts
📷 🎭 ⏰ Noon-8pm Thu-Sat, noon-6pm Wed & Sun 🚫 Federal hols 🌐 ybca.org

---

SOMA'S LEATHER AND LGBTQ+ CULTURE

In the mid-1960s SOMA emerged as a hub of San Francisco's leather scene. The first leather bar, The Tool Box, opened in 1961 at 339 4th St (today a Whole Foods store). In 1964 *Life* magazine published an article called "Homosexuality in America," profiling The Tool Box, which cemented San Francisco and SOMA as America's capital of LGBTQ+ culture. Several minutes' walk from Yerba Buena Gardens, the Leather and LGBTQ Cultural District *(www. sfleatherdistrict.org)* honors the history of the leather subculture and helps protect the community's businesses.

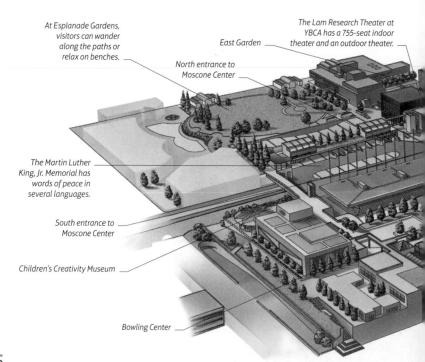

At Esplanade Gardens, visitors can wander along the paths or relax on benches.

The Lam Research Theater at YBCA has a 755-seat indoor theater and an outdoor theater.

East Garden

North entrance to Moscone Center

The Martin Luther King, Jr. Memorial has words of peace in several languages.

South entrance to Moscone Center

Children's Creativity Museum

Bowling Center

Oracle Park, home to the San Francisco Giants baseball team →

23

Railway Museum

♀ S5 ⌂ 77 Steuart St
⏰ 10am–5pm Tue–Sun
🌐 streetcar.org/museum

The unmistakable rattling and chiming of streetcars is still the soundtrack of many San Francisco streets. This small museum illustrates the impact of the street and cable car system on the social fabric of the city. It also induces nostalgia, with its black-and-white photos of a bygone era of city transportation, plus a replica of a 1911 streetcar, where kids can become train conductors. Part of the museum's appeal is the delightful gift shop, featuring transport-themed memorabilia, including replicas of vintage posters from the 1920s and 1930s.

24

Oracle Park

♀ S7 ⌂ 24 Mille Ways Plaza
🚊 N, T 🌐 mlb.com

A short walk south of the San Francisco Visitor Information Center, Oracle Park stadium is home to the San Francisco Giants. Between March and September, a baseball game here, with a spectacular backdrop of the bay, is quintessential San Francisco. The Giants were transplanted from New York City to San Francisco in 1958. In the West Coast's first Major League Baseball match, the Giants defeated the Los Angeles Dodgers and a long-standing rivalry was born. A buddy system connects local Giants fans with tourists; look for the SportsHosts section on the website.

25

Old United States Mint

♀ Q7 ⌂ 5th St and Mission St ☎ (415) 537-1105
🚌 14, 14L, 26, 27 🚊 J, K, L, M, N 🚫 To public

San Francisco's Old Mint produced its final coins in 1937. It was built of granite in the Classical style by A. B. Mullet between 1869 and 1874, hence its nickname, the "Granite Lady." Its windows were fortified by iron shutters and its basement vaults are impregnable. The building was one of the few to survive the great 1906 earthquake. Plans are under way to convert The Mint into a history museum.

> **The Mint was built of granite in the Classical style by A. B. Mullet between 1869 and 1874, hence its nickname, the "Granite Lady."**

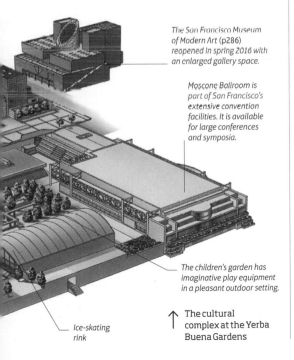

The San Francisco Museum of Modern Art (p286) reopened in spring 2016 with an enlarged gallery space.

Moscone Ballroom is part of San Francisco's extensive convention facilities. It is available for large conferences and symposia.

The children's garden has imaginative play equipment in a pleasant outdoor setting.

Ice-skating rink

↑ The cultural complex at the Yerba Buena Gardens

A SHORT WALK
FINANCIAL DISTRICT

Distance 0.5 miles (1 km) **Time** 15 minutes
Nearest buses 1, 8AX, 8BX, 10, 12, 41

San Francisco's vibrant economic engine is fueled largely by the Financial District, one of the chief commercial centers in the US. It reaches from the imposing modern towers and plazas of the Embarcadero Center to staid Montgomery Street, sometimes known as the "Wall Street of the West." All the principal banks, brokers, exchanges, and law offices are situated within this compact area, along with a few leafy squares for office workers to unwind in. The Jackson Square Historical District, just north of busy Washington Street, was once the heart of the business community.

Embarcadero Center (p292) *houses both commercial outlets and offices. A shopping arcade occupies the first three tiers of the towers.*

Jackson Square Historic District (p292) *recalls the Gold Rush era more than any other.*

Hotaling Place, *a narrow alley leading to the Jackson Square Historic District, has several good antiques shops.*

The Golden Era Building, *built during the Gold Rush, was the home of the* Golden Era *newspaper for which Mark Twain wrote.*

WASHINGTON STREET

BATTERY STREET

CLAY STREET

SANSOME STREET

START

Once the tallest skyscraper in the city, the **Transamerica Pyramid** (p293) *has now been eclipsed by the Salesforce Tower.*

MONTGOMERY STREET

The Wells Fargo History Museum (p292) *has displays on transportation and banking. An original stagecoach, evoking the wilder days of the old West, is one of the many exhibits.*

The grand banking hall in the **Bank of California** (p293) *is guarded by fierce stone lions carved by sculptor Arthur Putnam.*

The former world headquarters of the Bank of America at **555 California** *was the city's tallest skyscraper until 1972.*

Epic paintings line the walls of **Merchant's Exchange** (p295).

0 meters 100
0 yards 100
N

Financial
District

DOWNTOWN
AND SOMA

Locator Map
For more detail see p284

Did You Know?

The California Street Cable Car is double-ended as there is no turnaround at the end of the street.

The **Ferry Building** (p290) *houses gourmet shops and eateries.*

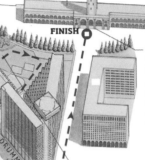

FINISH

The Gandhi Monument *(1988) was designed by K.B. Patel and sculpted by Z. Pounov and S. Lowe. It bears an inscription of Gandhi's words.*

DAVIS STREET

DRUMM STREET

SACRAMENTO STREET

FRONT STREET

CALIFORNIA STREET

Embarcadero Plaza (p297) *is filled with lunchtime crowds on sunny days.*

California Street, *busy with clanging cable cars, sweeps to the top of Nob Hill.*

MARKET STREET

PINE STREET

First Interstate Center, *home of the Mandarin Oriental Hotel*

The **Pacific Coast Stock Exchange** (p296) *was once the focal point of the city's trade.*

→
The iconic Ferry Building, a San Francisco landmark

A LONG WALK
AROUND SOMA

Distance 2.5 miles (3.5 km) **Time** 45 minutes
Terrain Flat streets, busy with pedestrians
and traffic **Nearest BART station** Powell
Street

Once a grubby warehouse district, SOMA (a
contraction of "South of Market") is a model
of urban revitalization. This was once the
"wrong side" of the Market Street cable-
car tracks when Gold Rush-era immigrants
worked in the factories here in the 19th
century. Today, the four-block square area
surrounding the Moscone Convention Center
is packed with major art galleries and history
museums, high-rise hotels, and shops. On
this walk you will encounter vestiges of the
city's lively past among its dazzling 21st-
century architecture.

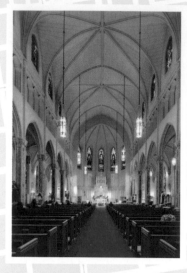

↑ The elegant Flamboyant Gothic
interior of St. Patrick's Church

*Turn left on Howard Street, then take a right
on 5th Street. At the corner of Mission Street,
you will see the facade of the "Granite Lady,"
the Classical-style **Old United States Mint**
(p301), erected in 1869–74 to make coins
from California gold and Nevada silver. Its
last coins were produced in 1937.*

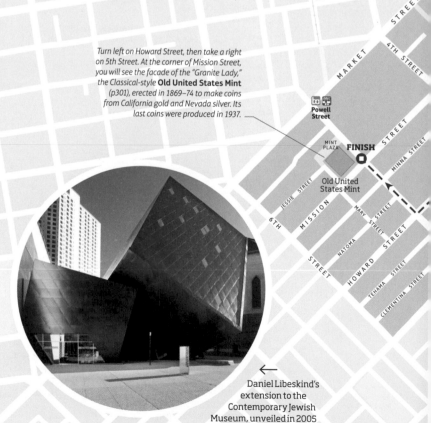

← Daniel Libeskind's
extension to the
Contemporary Jewish
Museum, unveiled in 2005

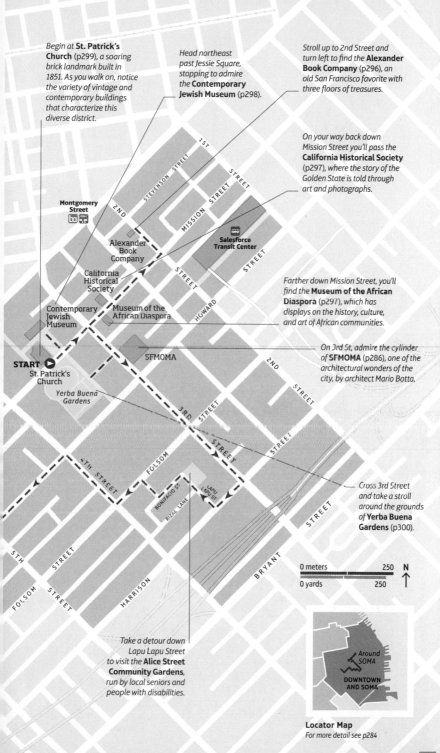

Begin at **St. Patrick's Church** (p299), a soaring brick landmark built in 1851. As you walk on, notice the variety of vintage and contemporary buildings that characterize this diverse district.

Head northeast past Jessie Square, stopping to admire the **Contemporary Jewish Museum** (p298).

Stroll up to 2nd Street and turn left to find the **Alexander Book Company** (p296), an old San Francisco favorite with three floors of treasures.

On your way back down Mission Street you'll pass the **California Historical Society** (p297), where the story of the Golden State is told through art and photographs.

Farther down Mission Street, you'll find the **Museum of the African Diaspora** (p297), which has displays on the history, culture, and art of African communities.

On 3rd St, admire the cylinder of **SFMOMA** (p286), one of the architectural wonders of the city, by architect Mario Botta.

Cross 3rd Street and take a stroll around the grounds of **Yerba Buena Gardens** (p300).

Take a detour down Lapu Lapu Street to visit the **Alice Street Community Gardens**, run by local seniors and people with disabilities.

Montgomery Street

1ST STREET

STEVENSON STREET

MISSION STREET

2ND STREET

Salesforce Transit Center

Alexander Book Company

California Historical Society

Contemporary Jewish Museum

Museum of the African Diaspora

HOWARD STREET

START ▶
St. Patrick's Church

SFMOMA

Yerba Buena Gardens

2ND STREET

3RD STREET

STREET

4TH STREET

FOLSOM

BONIFACIO ST.

RIZAL LANE

LAPU LAPU ST.

STREET

BRYANT STREET

5TH STREET

FOLSOM STREET

HARRISON STREET

| 0 meters | 250 |
| 0 yards | 250 |

N ↑

Locator Map
For more detail see p284

Around SOMA

DOWNTOWN AND SOMA

CHINATOWN AND NOB HILL

Chinese immigrants, keen to benefit from the Gold
Rush and the transcontinental railroad, settled on
Stockton Street in the 1850s, rapidly creating one
of the largest Chinese communities in the world
outside Asia. San Francisco is still known in China
as *Jiùjīnshān* ("Old Gold Mountain"). Nevertheless,
times were often hard; the city became the epicenter
of anti-Chinese racism, with the two-day riot of
1877 destroying swaths of Chinatown. Although
the Chinese Exclusion Act of 1882 effectively
ended Chinese immigration to the US, Chinatown
survived and prospered in the 20th century. Today
its shops and markets recall the atmosphere of a
typical southern Chinese town (albeit with distinctly
American variations on a Cantonese theme),
attracting visitors and locals alike.

Looming above Chinatown, Nob Hill is San
Francisco's most celebrated hilltop, famous for its
cable cars, plush hotels, and breathtaking views.
"Nobs" was a name for the entrepeneurs who
amassed huge fortunes during the development
of the American West. In the late 19th century,
the cable cars made Nob Hill more accessible to
Gold Rush millionaires, and later the "Big Four" –
Central Pacific Railroad barons Leland Stanford,
Collis P. Huntington, Mark Hopkins, and Charles
Crocker – built their mansions here. The earthquake
and fire of 1906 leveled all but one of these houses,
but the area's contemporary hotels still recall the
opulence of Victorian times.

CHINATOWN AND NOB HILL

Must Sees
1. Cable Car Museum
2. Grace Cathedral

Experience More
3. Chinatown Gateway
4. Old St. Mary's Cathedral
5. Golden Gate Fortune Cookie Company
6. Tin How Temple
7. Kong Chow Temple
8. Chinese Historical Society of America
9. Portsmouth Square

10. Pacific Heritage Museum
11. Grant Avenue and Stockton Street

Eat
1. China Live
2. Mister Jiu's
3. Far East Café
4. Mee Mee Bakery

Drink
5. Top of the Mark
6. Tonga Room and Hurricane Bar

RUSSIAN HILL

PACIFIC HEIGHTS AND THE CIVIC CENTER
p342

Lafayette Park

Haas-Lilienthal House

Great American Music Hall

Cathedral of Saint Mary of the Assumption

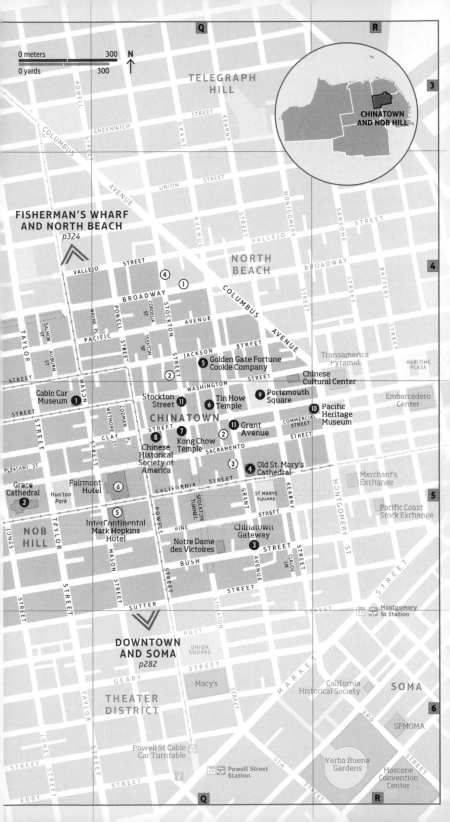

0 meters 300
0 yards 300

N

TELEGRAPH
HILL

CHINATOWN
AND NOB HILL

FISHERMAN'S WHARF
AND NORTH BEACH
p324

GREENWICH STREET

COLUMBUS STREET

UNION STREET

VALLEJO STREET

POWELL STREET

TAYLOR STREET

SALMON ST

AUBURN ST

NORTH
BEACH

BROADWAY

① ④

CORDELIA ST

TRENTON ST

STOCKTON STREET

PACIFIC AVENUE

COLUMBUS AVENUE

BROADWAY

VALLEJO STREET

MONTGOMERY STREET

SANSOME STREET

BATTERY STREET

Transamerica
Pyramid

MARITIME
PLAZA

JACKSON STREET

② ⑤ Golden Gate Fortune
Cookie Company

Chinese
Cultural Center

Cable Car
Museum ❶

MASON STREET

WETMORE ST

CODMAN PL

CLAY STREET

Stockton
Street ⑪

WASHINGTON STREET

CHINATOWN

⑦ ⑧

Chinese
Historical
Society of
America

Kong Chow
Temple

⑥ Tin How
Temple

② ⑪ Grant
Avenue

SACRAMENTO

⑨ Portsmouth
Square

COMMERCIAL STREET

⑩ Pacific
Heritage
Museum

Embarcadero
Center

Merchant's
Exchange

PLEASANT ST

**Grace
Cathedral** ❷

TAYLOR STREET

JONES STREET

**NOB
HILL**

Hun'ton
Park

Fairmont
Hotel ⑥

MASON STREET

POWELL STREET

CALIFORNIA STREET

STOCKTON TUNNEL

PINE STREET

③ ④ Old St. Mary's
Cathedral

ST MARYS
SQUARE

GRANT AVENUE

KEARNY STREET

Pacific Coast
Stock Exchange

MONTGOMERY ST

InterContinental
Mark Hopkins
Hotel ⑤

Notre Dame
des Victoires

BUSH STREET

Chinatown
Gateway ❸

CLAUDE LN

Montgomery
St Station

SUTTER STREET

**DOWNTOWN
AND SOMA**
p282

POST STREET

UNION
SQUARE

Macy's

GEARY STREET

**THEATER
DISTRICT**

California
Historical Society

MARKET STREET

SOMA

SFMOMA

Powell St Cable
Car Turntable

Powell Street
Station

Yerba Buena
Gardens

Moscone
Convention
Center

EDDY STREET

1 ⌂

CABLE CAR MUSEUM

📍P5 🏠1201 Mason St 🚌1, 10, 12 🚋Powell-Mason, Powell-Hyde
🕐10am–6pm daily (Nov–Mar: to 5pm) 🚫Jan 1, Thanksgiving, Dec 25
🌐cablecarmuseum.org

Get up close to the inner workings of the city's famous cable-car system. Here you're right in the middle of the action, feeling the vibrations and hearing the whirring mechanics of public transportation at work.

This is both a museum and the powerhouse of today's cable-car system (p312). Anchored to the first floor are the engines and wheels that wind the cables through the system of channels and pulleys beneath the streets. Observe them from the mezzanine, then descend to below street level in order to view the large underground chamber where the haulage cables are routed out to the street. The museum houses an early cable car and examples of the mechanisms that control the individual cars. The system is the last of its kind in the world, so after you're done getting a close-up look in the car barn don't miss a chance to experience a journey on either the Powell-Mason or Powell-Hyde cable car line right outside.

→

An old cable car stoplight on display at the museum

Timeline

1869
△ Inventor Andrew Hallidie's desire to put a stop to the use of horse-drawn trams allegedly inspires the cable-car system.

1873
△ Construction begins on San Francisco's first cable-car line in May, with regular service starting in September.

1906
△ The San Francisco earthquake destroys most of the system's cars and lines, and electric streetcars replace most of the old cable-car lines when the city is rebuilt.

1947
△ The mayor attempts to have the remaining lines closed, but a committee led by Friedel Klussmann succeeds in preserving the city's cable-car system.

↑ The Cable Car Museum, also housing the city's cable-car system

REBUILDING THE CABLE CARS

San Francisco's cable-car system, introduced in 1873, remained in use even with the advent of more modern public transportation over the years. Despite regular maintenance, the aging system began to deteriorate to the point where drastic measures had to be taken, but as a beloved and iconic feature of the city there was no chance of simply closing the lines. Instead the city initiated the Cable Car System Rehabilitation Program, an immense upgrade that resulted in closing the whole cable-car system from 1982 to 1984. The work involved replacing old tracks across 69 city blocks, tidying up the cars, and carrying out important upgrades at 1201 Mason St - both on the structure of the car barn as well as the mechanisms of the powerhouse. In June 1984 the system reopened and San Franciscans celebrated its return with four days of festivities.

SAN FRANCISCO'S CABLE CARS

In their heyday, cable cars ran on 23 lines throughout the city. While San Franciscans mostly use other public transportation on their commute these days, the cable cars are still a beloved and iconic feature of the city.

The cable car system was launched in 1873, with its inventor Andrew Hallidie riding in the first car. He was purportedly inspired to tackle the problem of transporting people up the city's steep slopes after seeing a horrible accident: a horse-drawn tram slipped down a hill, dragging the horses with it. His system was a great success, and by 1889 cars were running on eight lines. With the advent of the internal combustion engine, cable cars became almost obsolete, and in 1947 attempts were made to replace them with buses. However, after a public outcry – led by Friedel Klussmann's "Citizens' Committee to Save the Cable Cars" – the present three lines, using 17 miles (25 km) of track, were retained.

↑ Two of the 12 California Street cable cars passing by on the streets of San Francisco

Did You Know?

A cable-car bell-ringing contest is held in Union Square every July.

→ Cross-section illustration of a Powell Street car and cable-car tracks

Bell

Grip handle

Sandbox

Emergency brake

Center plate and jaws grip the cable

Wheel brake

HOW CABLE CARS WORK

Engines in the central powerhouse wind a looped cable under the city streets, guided by a system of grooved pulleys. When the gripman in the cable car applies the grip handle, the grip reaches through a slot in the street and grabs the cable. This pulls the car along at a steady speed of 9.5 mph (15.5 km/h). To stop, the gripman releases the grip and applies the brake. Great skill is needed at corners where the cable passes over a pulley. The gripman must release the grip to allow the car to coast over the pulley.

PRESERVING HISTORY

Maintenance and renovations on the cable cars are done with attention to historical detail, because they are designated historic monuments. A cable car celebration was held in 1984 after a two-year renovation of the system. Each car was restored, and all lines were replaced with reinforced tracks, allowing the system to work safely for another 100 years.

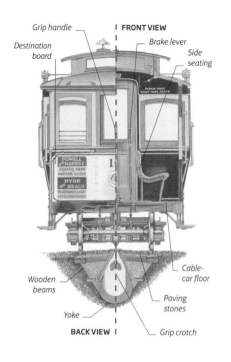

Grip handle

FRONT VIEW

Destination board

Brake lever

Side seating

POWELL MARKET
AQUATIC PARK
MARITIME MUSEUM
HYDE
BEACH

Wooden beams

Cable-car floor

Paving stones

Yoke

BACK VIEW

Grip crotch

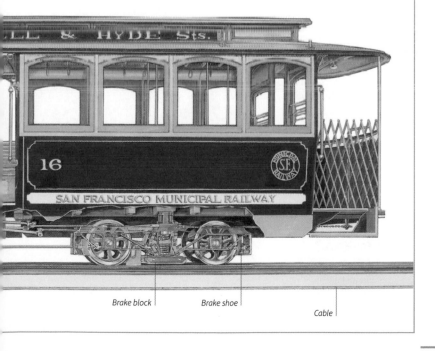

LL & HYDE Sts.

16

S.F.
MUNICIPAL
RAILWAY

SAN FRANCISCO MUNICIPAL RAILWAY

Brake block

Brake shoe

Cable

② Ⓜ️ 🛍️

GRACE CATHEDRAL

📍 P5 🏛️ 1100 California St 🚌 1 🚋 California St
🕐 7am–6pm Mon–Fri, 8am–6pm Sat, 7am–7pm Sun
🌐 gracecathedral.org

Located on Nob Hill, the soaring neo-Gothic Grace Cathedral has many stunning works of medieval-style art. The cathedral is committed to social justice and has a lively, all-inclusive program of services and events.

Designed by architect Lewis P. Hobart, Grace Cathedral is the third-largest Episcopal Cathedral in the United States. Building started in 1928, but it did not near completion until 1964; the interior vaulting remains unfinished. The cavernous building is inspired by Notre Dame in Paris.

The cathedral's entrance doors are cast from Lorenzo Ghiberti's "Doors of Paradise," made for the Baptistry in Florence in the 15th century, considered an early Italian Renaissance masterpiece. The cathedral has a rich collection of stained glass. The 34 leaded medieval-style windows were designed by Charles Connick, using the blue glass of Chartres as his inspiration. The rose window, designed by Lewis P. Hobart, is made of 1-inch- (2.5-cm-) thick faceted glass, which is illuminated from inside the building at night. Other windows were made by Marguerite Gaudin, Henry Willett, and Gabriel Loire. These include the Human Endeavor series, which depicts more than 1,000 figures in science, including Albert Einstein and astronaut John Glenn.

Historical artifacts held within the cathedral include a 13th-century Catalonian crucifix and a 16th-century Brussels tapestry. The AIDS Interfaith Memorial Chapel holds a gold-leaf three-part altarpiece by pop artist Keith Haring, his last work before his own death from AIDS in 1990.

The spire is 117 ft (35 m) tall from the roof to the top

The Chapel of Grace, funded by the Crocker family, has a 15th-century French altarpiece.

Did You Know?

Grace Cathedral may look like it's built of stone, but it is in fact made of concrete.

The New Testament Window, made in 1931 by Charles Connick, is on the south side of the church.

↑ The elegant Grace Cathedral, built in the 20th century

① The facade has replicas of Ghiberti's doors from the Baptistry in Florence.

② A medieval-style labyrinth decorates the floor inside the church.

③ *The Life of Christ* bronze-and-white-gold altarpiece by Keith Haring is one of his few religious pieces.

The Carillon Tower houses 44 bells made in England in 1938.

The Rose Window was made in Chartres in 1964.

Entrance

The Doors of Paradise are decorated with scenes from the Bible and portraits of Ghiberti and contemporaries.

Entrance

> **INSIDER TIP**
> **Events**
>
> Look up the varied events on the cathedral's website. These include spectacular choral Evensongs and gospel, classical, and jazz concerts. There are also regular candlelit meditation services and yoga classes. Every year there are exhibits or performances from the artist in residence, which range from art installations to spoken word to dance.

EXPERIENCE MORE

 3

Chinatown Gateway

Q5 **Grant Av at Bush St** **2, 3, 30, 45**

This ornate south-facing portal, inspired by the ceremonial entrances of traditional Chinese villages, was designed by Chinese American architect Clayton Lee to mark the entrance to Chinatown's main tourist strip, Grant Avenue. The gateway's three arches are capped with green roof tiles and a host of propitiatory animals, all crafted from glazed ceramic. The gate was erected by the Chinatown Cultural Development Committee.

It is guarded by two stone lions that are suckling their cubs through their claws, in accordance with ancient lore. Once through the gate, visitors can find stores selling antiques, embroidered silks, and precious gems, but sometimes at high prices, aimed at tourists.

 4

Old St. Mary's Cathedral

Q5 **660 California St** **2, 3, 8, 8AX, 8BX, 8X, 15, 30, 45** **California St** **oldsaintmarys.org**

San Francisco's first Catholic cathedral, Old St. Mary's, was consecrated on Christmas Day 1854 as the seat of the Roman Catholic bishop of the Pacific Coast. It served a largely Irish congregation until 1891, when the larger St. Mary's Cathedral was built on Van Ness Avenue. The clock tower of the church bears a large inscription, "Son, observe the time and fly from evil," said to have been directed at the brothels that stood across the street. It was one of the few buildings to remain unharmed by the 1906 earthquake and retains its original foundations and walls. The graceful interior, with stained-glass windows, vaulted ceiling, and a balcony, was completed in 1909.

> **CHINATOWN MURALS**
>
> Vivid, handpainted images, from the Buddha and Bruce Lee to joyful dancing and fierce golden dragons, adorn facades in San Francisco's Chinatown. A symbol of power, strength, and wisdom in Chinese culture, dragons are believed to bring good luck.

 5

Golden Gate Fortune Cookie Company

Q4 **56 Ross Alley** **1, 8, 8AX, 8BX, 30, 45** **California St, Powell-Hyde, Powell-Mason** **9am–6:30pm Mon–Fri, 9am–7pm Sat & Sun** **goldengatecookies.com**

A San Francisco institution, the Golden Gate Fortune Cookie Company has been

↑ The grand, green-tiled Chinatown Gateway, at the entrance to Grant Avenue

↑ Colorful murals of Chinese dancing dragons in Chinatown

in business since 1962. The cookie-making machine nearly fills the tiny bakery, where dough is poured onto griddles and baked on a conveyor belt. An attendant inserts the "fortunes" (slips of paper bearing mostly positive predictions) before the cookies are folded. Almost 10,000 fortune cookies are made every day. As well as the traditional vanilla variety, the cookies are also made in multiple flavors, including chocolate, strawberry, and green tea.

Ironically, despite its associations with Chinese culture, the fortune cookie is unknown in China. It was actually invented in 1909 in San Francisco's Japanese Tea Garden by then Chief Gardener, Magota Hagiwara.

Did You Know?

Fortune-telling sticks at Kong Chow Temple said that Harry Truman would become president in 1948.

6

Tin How Temple

◉ Q5 ⬚ Top floor, 125 Waverly Pl ☎ (415) 986-2520 🚍 1, 10, 12, 30, 41, 45 🚋 Powell-Hyde, Powell-Mason ⏱ 9am–4pm daily

This unusual temple dedicated to Tin How, the divine Queen of Heaven and protector of seafarers and visitors, is the oldest running Chinese temple in the United States. It was originally founded in 1852 by Day Ju, one of three Chinese immigrants who were the first to land in San Francisco. The temple, at the top of three steep, wooden flights of stairs, which are considered to place it closer to heaven, is filled with the smoke from both incense and burned paper offerings, and is decorated with hundreds of gold and red lanterns. Gifts of fruit lie on the carved altar in front of the wooden statue of the temple's namesake deity.

7

Kong Chow Temple

◉ Q3 ⬚ 4th floor, 855 Stockton St ☎ (415) 788-1339 🚍 30, 45 ⏱ 9am–4pm daily

From the top floor above the district's post office, the Kong Chow Temple looks out over Chinatown and the Financial District. The building itself dates from 1977, but the Taoist temple was founded in 1857 and the altar and statuary are thought to form the oldest Chinese religious shrine in the country. The main shrine is presided over by a carved wooden statue of the deity Guan Di dating from the 19th century. Guan Di is frequently seen in the city's Chinatown district: his face looks down from Taoist shrines in many of the area's restaurants. He is typically depicted holding a large sword in one hand and a book in the other.

EAT

China Live

Wash down beef noodle soup, pork dumplings, and Peking-style duck with cocktails made with ingredients such as lemongrass syrup and yuzu lemonade.

◉ Q4 ⬚ 644 Broadway 🌐 chinalivesf.com

$$$

Mister Jiu's

This smart restaurant in a historic building serves thoughtfully sourced and beautifully presented food, including crunchy pork buns and seafood *cheong fun* (flat rice noodle rolls).

◉ Q4 ⬚ 28 Waverly Pl ⏱ Sun, Mon 🌐 misterjius.com

$$$

Far East Café

The mostly Cantonese and American Chinese menu at this restaurant has changed little since the 1920s; the egg *foo young* (omelet) is a favorite.

◉ Q5 ⬚ 631 Grant Av ⏱ Mon 🌐 fareastcafe sf.com

$$$

Mee Mee Bakery

Open since 1950, Mee Mee is best known for mooncakes, traditional pies stuffed with honeydew and red beans. Locals also line up for almond cookies and salty-sweet "cow ears."

◉ Q4 ⬚ 1328 Stockton St 🌐 meemeebakery.com

$$$

↑ Re-created quarters in the Chinese Historical Society of America

8

Chinese Historical Society of America

📍 Q5 🏠 965 Clay St
🚌 1, 30, 45 🚋 Powell St
🕐 11am–4pm Wed–Sun
🚫 Federal hols 🌐 chsa.org

Founded in 1963, this is the oldest organization in the US dedicated to the interpretation, promotion, and preservation of the history and contributions of Chinese people in America. Exhibits include a multimedia display chronicling the complex history of the Chinese in America, replicas of the Angel Island barracks and interrogation room, and paintings by Chinese American artists such as Jake Lee and Stella Wong, including a mural by James Leong.

The Chinese contribution to California's development was extensive despite the poor treatment that they faced. Wealthy merchants used them for cheap labor in the gold mines. Chinese workers also helped build the western half of the first transcontinental railroad, constructed dikes throughout the Sacramento River delta, were pioneers in the fishing industry, and planted the first vines in many of California's early vineyards. The society sponsors oral history projects, an "In Search of Roots" program, and a monthly speakers' forum.

Did You Know?

A memorial in Portsmouth Square honors Scottish writer Robert Louis Stevenson.

9

Portsmouth Square

📍 Q5 🚌 1, 41

San Francisco's original town square was laid out in 1839. It was once the social center for the village of Yerba Buena. On July 9, 1846, just after US rebels in Sonoma declared California's independence from Mexico (*p47*), US Marines raised the American flag above the plaza, officially seizing the port as part of the United States. In the 1850s the area was the hub of this new dynamic city, but in the 1860s the city's business district shifted to flatlands reclaimed from the bay and the plaza lost much of its civic importance.

Today Portsmouth Square is the social center of Chinatown. Children play, people practice *t'ai chi* or gather in the evening to play cards.

10

Pacific Heritage Museum

📍 R5 🏠 608 Commercial St
☎ (415) 399-1124 🚌 1, 8, 8AX, 8BX, 30X, 41
🕐 10am–4pm Tue–Sat

As elegant as the frequently changing collections of Asian arts displayed within it, this is actually a synthesis of two distinct buildings. The US Sub-Treasury was built here in 1875–77 by William Appleton Potter, on the site of the city's original mint. You can look into the expansive old coin vaults through a cutaway section on the first floor, or descend in the elevator

AUTUMN MOON FESTIVAL

San Francisco Chinatown's annual Autumn Moon Festival, held every year in early or mid-September, follows the tradition of the Autumn Moon festivals that take place in China to celebrate seasonal change and give thanks to a bountiful summer harvest. A parade, arts and crafts bazaars, and martial arts performances are held in the heart of Chinatown. Bakeries sell traditional mooncakes (pastries filled with sweet bean paste and egg) and people light paper lanterns.

for closer inspection. In 1984, architects Skidmore, Owings, and Merrill designed the 17-story headquarters of the Bank of Canton (now East West Bank) above the existing building, incorporating the original street-level facade and basement.

Grant Avenue and Stockton Street

📍 Q5 🚌 10, 12, 30, 45
🚋 California St 🌐 sanfranciscochinatown.com

Grant Avenue, the main artery that runs through Chinatown, is historically important for being the first street of Yerba Buena, the village that preceded San Francisco. A plaque at No. 823 Grant Avenue marks the block where William A. Richardson and his wife, Maria Antonia Martinez, erected Yerba Buena's first edifice, a canvas tent, on June 25, 1835. By October, they had replaced this with a wooden house, and

the following year with a yet more permanent adobe (sun-dried brick) home, called Casa Grande. The street in which the Richardsons' house stood was named Calle de la Fundación, the "Street of the Founding." An estimated 25,000 Chinese settled in this area during the Gold Rush era.

In 1885 the street was renamed Grant Avenue in memory of Ulysses S. Grant, the US president and Civil War general who died that year.

Most of the buildings on Grant Avenue were built after the 1906 earthquake. Today, Grant Avenue is lined with a huge array of touristy shops and is Chinatown's busiest street. Distinctive red lantern lights, installed in the 1930s, overhang the street. Many of the more authentic shops and markets have moved from Grant Avenue to neighboring Stockton Street, which provides a more authentic shopping experience.

In between Grant Avenue and the parallel-running Stockton Street are some of the most characterful streets in Chinatown – the Chinatown Alleys – containing many old buildings, temples, and

traditional shops, such as Chinese herbalists. The largest alley is Waverley Place, known as the "Street of Painted Balconies" for reasons apparent to any passerby. Throughout the alleys, small restaurants, both above and below street level, serve cheap, delicious, home-cooked food.

Chinese street lamps and lanterns on Grant Avenue and *(inset)* ingredients on sale in a food market

A SHORT WALK
CHINATOWN

Distance 1 mile (1.5 km) **Time** 20 minutes
Nearest buses 8, 30, 45, 91

Grant Avenue is the tourist Chinatown of dragon lampposts, upturned rooflines, and stores packed to the rafters with everything from kites to cooking utensils. Locals shop on Stockton Street, where the freshest produce and fish spill over in boxes onto crowded sidewalks. In the alleys in between, look for traditional temples, shops, and family-run restaurants.

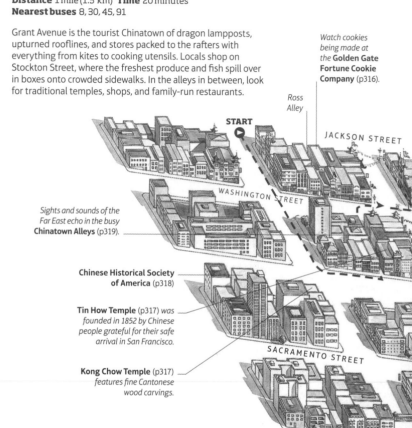

Watch cookies being made at the **Golden Gate Fortune Cookie Company** (p316).

Ross Alley

START

JACKSON STREET

WASHINGTON STREET

Sights and sounds of the Far East echo in the busy **Chinatown Alleys** (p319).

Chinese Historical Society of America (p318)

Tin How Temple (p317) *was founded in 1852 by Chinese people grateful for their safe arrival in San Francisco.*

Kong Chow Temple (p317) *features fine Cantonese wood carvings.*

SACRAMENTO STREET

Cable cars (p312) *run down California Street and are an key part of the area's atmosphere. Any of the three lines will take you there.*

CALIFORNIA STREET

0 meters   80   N
0 yards   80   ↑

BUSH

← Grant Avenue, Chinatown's main commercial thoroughfare

← A cable car passing through Chinatown

Locator Map
For more detail see p308

Portsmouth Square (p318) *was the social center for the village of Yerba Buena, the original settlement that became San Francisco. Today people gather here to play cards and mahjong.*

Did You Know?

San Francisco's historic Chinatown is the oldest one in the US.

The **Chinese Cultural Center** *contains an art gallery and a small crafts shop. It sponsors a lively series of lectures and seminars.*

Housed in an elegant building, the small **Pacific Heritage Museum** (p318) *has fine exhibitions of Asian art.*

In the mid 19th century, **Grant Avenue** (p319) *was the main thoroughfare of Yerba Buena. It is now the busy commercial center of Chinatown.*

The clock tower of **Old St. Mary's Cathedral** (p316), *built while the city was still in its infancy, bears an arresting inscription.*

St. Mary's Square *is a quiet haven in which to take a rest.*

Also known as the "Dragons' Gate," **Chinatown Gateway** (p316) *marks Chinatown's southern entrance.*

KEARNY STREET

CLAY STREET

GRANT AVENUE

STOCKTON STREET

PINE STREET

STREET

FINISH

A SHORT WALK
NOB HILL

Distance 0.5 miles (1 km) **Time** 15 minutes
Nearest buses 1, 27

Nob Hill is the highest summit of the city center, rising 338 ft (103 m) above the bay, and affording splendid views of the city. Its steep slopes were treacherous for carriages and kept prominent citizens away until the opening of the California Street cable car line in 1878. After that, the wealthy "nobs" soon built new homes on the peak of the hill. Though many of the grandiose mansions were burned down in the great fire of 1906, Nob Hill still attracts the affluent to its many splendid hotels. A stroll through this well-heeled neighborhood will lead you past some of the most expensive real estate in the US.

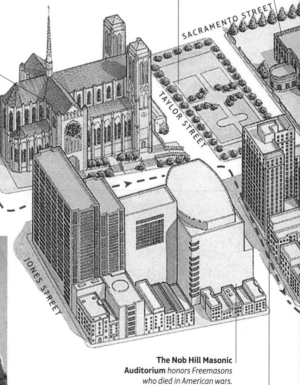

The **Pacific-Union Club**, now an exclusive men's club, was once the mansion of Comstock millionaire James Flood.

Huntington Park is on the site of Collis P. Huntington's mansion.

Grace Cathedral (p314) is a replica of Notre Dame in Paris.

SACRAMENTO STREET

TAYLOR STREET

JONES STREET

START

The **Nob Hill Masonic Auditorium** honors Freemasons who died in American wars.

Huntington Hotel, with its Big Four Bar and Restaurant, exudes the opulent urbane atmosphere of the 19th century on Nob Hill.

← The interior of Grace Cathedral, with beautiful stained-glass windows

← The lobby of the Fairmont Hotel, one of the grandest hotels on Nob Hill

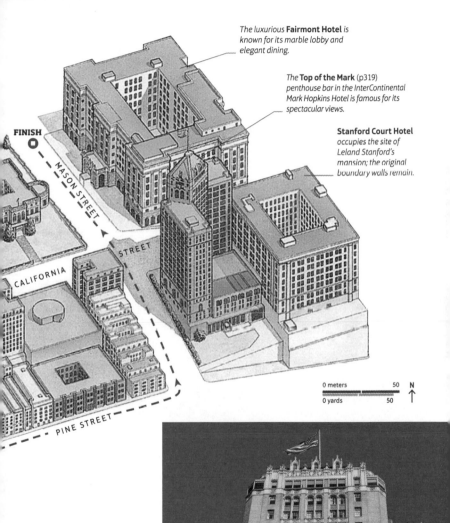

The luxurious **Fairmont Hotel** is known for its marble lobby and elegant dining.

The **Top of the Mark** (p319) penthouse bar in the InterContinental Mark Hopkins Hotel is famous for its spectacular views.

Stanford Court Hotel occupies the site of Leland Stanford's mansion; the original boundary walls remain.

FINISH

MASON STREET

STREET

CALIFORNIA

PINE STREET

0 meters 50
0 yards 50

N

→ The grand exterior of the 1920s InterContinental Mark Hopkins Hotel

FISHERMAN'S WHARF AND NORTH BEACH

Chinese and Italian immigrants made a living catching fish at San Francisco's northern waterfront during the days of the Gold Rush in the mid-19th century, thus founding the San Franciscan fishing industry. In 1893, Genoese chocolatier Domenico Ghirardelli located the headquarters of his chocolate company here (commemorated at today's Ghirardelli Square). Fishing has slowly given way to tourism since the 1950s – San Francisco Maritime National Historical Park got its start in 1951 and PIER 39 was developed in 1978 – but brightly painted boats still set out from the harbor on fishing trips early each morning.

To the south of Fisherman's Wharf lies North Beach, also known as "Little Italy." Italian immigration to the city was ignited by the Gold Rush, but it gained momentum after the 1906 earthquake, when focaccia bakeries, salami grocers, and Italian cafés sprung up on empty lots. Italian American baseball hero Joe DiMaggio grew up in the area in the 1920s and the late Lawrence Ferlinghetti, another famous Italian American resident, opened the City Lights Bookstore on Columbus Avenue in 1953. This still-operating store was a leading light in the Beat Movement and North Beach was home to beatniks Allen Ginsberg and Gregory Corso. Today, the neighborhood still attracts hipsters and young professionals, but few Italian Americans live here.

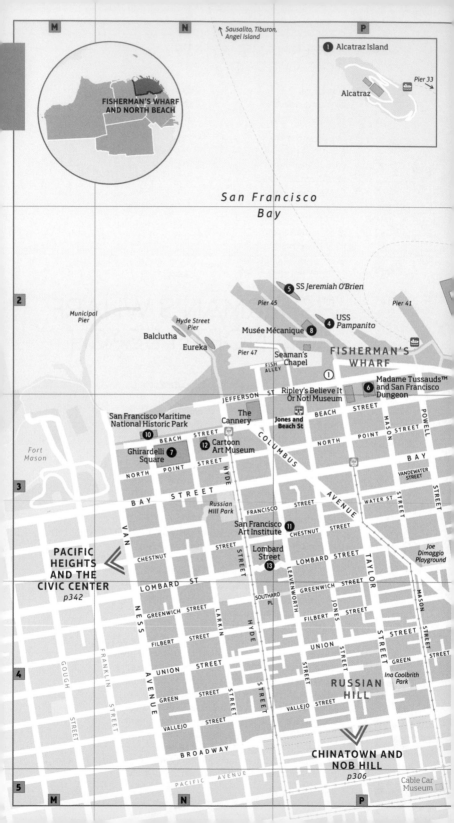

FISHERMAN'S WHARF AND NORTH BEACH

① Alcatraz Island

Alcatraz

Pier 33

↑ Sausalito, Tiburon, Angel Island

San Francisco Bay

⑤ SS Jeremiah O'Brien

Pier 45

Pier 41

Municipal Pier

Hyde Street Pier

Musée Mécanique ⑧

④ USS Pampanito

Balclutha

Eureka

Pier 47

FISH ALLEY

Seaman's Chapel

FISHERMAN'S WHARF

①

JEFFERSON ST

Ripley's Believe It Or Not! Museum

⑥ Madame Tussauds™ and San Francisco Dungeon

San Francisco Maritime National Historic Park

⑩

The Cannery

BEACH STREET

Jones and Beach St

NORTH POINT STREET

MASON STREET

POWELL STREET

BEACH STREET

Ghirardelli Square ⑦

⑫ Cartoon Art Museum

BAY

VANDEWATER STREET

STREET

Fort Mason

NORTH POINT STREET

COLUMBUS

WATER ST

BAY STREET

AVENUE

STREET

Russian Hill Park

FRANCISCO STREET

STREET

San Francisco Art Institute ⑪

CHESTNUT STREET

Joe Dimaggio Playground

PACIFIC HEIGHTS AND THE CIVIC CENTER
p342

CHESTNUT STREET

STREET

Lombard Street ⑬

LOMBARD STREET

TAYLOR STREET

VAN NESS

LOMBARD ST

SOUTHARD PL

LEAVENWORTH

GREENWICH STREET

MASON STREET

GREENWICH STREET

FILBERT STREET

JONES STREET

RUSSIAN HILL

Ina Coolbrith Park

FRANKLIN STREET

FILBERT STREET

LARKIN STREET

HYDE STREET

UNION STREET

UNION STREET

STREET

GREEN STREET

GOUGH STREET

AVENUE

GREEN STREET

STREET

VALLEJO STREET

VALLEJO STREET

CHINATOWN AND NOB HILL
p306

BROADWAY

PACIFIC AVENUE

Cable Car Museum

FISHERMAN'S WHARF AND NORTH BEACH

Must Sees
1. Alcatraz Island
2. Exploratorium

Experience More
3. PIER 39
4. USS *Pampanito*
5. SS *Jeremiah O'Brien*
6. Madame Tussauds™ and San Francisco Dungeon
7. Ghirardelli Square
8. Musée Mécanique
9. The Beat Museum
10. San Francisco Maritime National Historical Park
11. San Francisco Art Institute
12. Cartoon Art Museum
13. Lombard Street
14. Coit Tower
15. Saints Peter and Paul Church
16. Levi's Plaza
17. Washington Square

Eat
1. Crab Shacks
2. Liguria Bakery
3. Mario's Bohemian Cigar Store Café
4. Caffè Trieste

Drink
5. Vesuvio Café
6. Tony Nik's

Shop
7. City Lights Bookstore

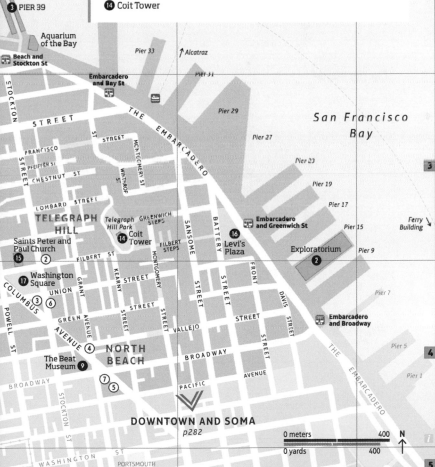

1 🗺️ Ⓜ️ 🛍️

ALCATRAZ ISLAND

📍P1 ⛴️Pier 33 🕐Times vary, check website
🌐nps.gov/alcatraz; www.alcatrazcruises.com

Visible from the crowded shores of San Francisco, this compelling rocky island and abandoned prison is the city's most notorious attraction.

Alcatraz means "pelican" in Spanish, a reference to the first inhabitants of this rocky, steep-sided island. Lying 3 miles (5 km) east of the Golden Gate Bridge (p384), its location is both strategic and exposed to harsh ocean winds that elicit a chilling atmosphere. In 1859, the US military established a fort here that guarded San Francisco Bay until 1907, when the fort became a military prison. From 1934 to 1963, it served as a maximum-security Federal Penitentiary. Abandoned until 1969, the island was occupied by Indians of All Tribes, who claimed the island as their land. The group was expelled in 1971, and Alcatraz is now part of the Golden Gate National Recreation Area.

The former prison and its lighthouse standing atop Alcatraz Island ↑

Did You Know?

There were 14 escape attempts during the 29 years Alcatraz Federal Penitentiary was in operation.

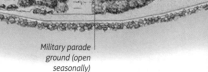

Lighthouse

Warden's house

The officers' apartments stood here.

Agave Trail (open seasonally)

Military parade ground (open seasonally)

1854
▼ First Pacific Coast lighthouse activated on Alcatraz.

1775
△ Spanish explorer Juan Manuel de Ayala names Alcatraz after the "strange birds" that inhabit it.

1848
△ Governor of California, John Frémont, buys Alcatraz from Francis Temple.

1850
Alcatraz is declared a military reservation by President Fillmore.

1859
△ Fort Alcatraz completed; equipped with 100 cannon and 300 troops.

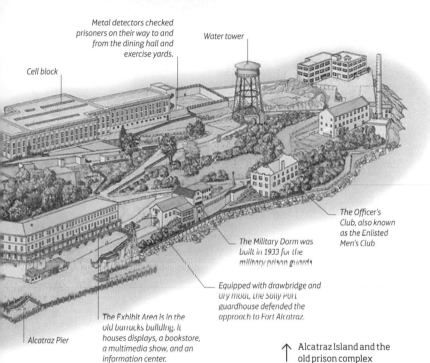

Metal detectors checked prisoners on their way to and from the dining hall and exercise yards.

Water tower

Cell block

The Officer's Club, also known as the Enlisted Men's Club

The Military Dorm was built in 1933 for the military prison guards

Equipped with drawbridge and dry moat, the Sally Port guardhouse defended the approach to Fort Alcatraz.

The Exhibit Area is in the old barracks building. It houses displays, a bookstore, a multimedia show, and an information center.

Alcatraz Pier

↑ Alcatraz Island and the old prison complex

1909

▽ Army prisoners begin construction on the cell house.

1934

△ Federal Bureau of Prisons turns Alcatraz into a civilian prison.

1962

▽ Famed criminal Frank Morris escapes (p331).

1963

Prison closed.

1972

△ Alcatraz becomes a national park.

Inside Alcatraz

The maximum-security prison on Alcatraz, dubbed "The Rock" by the US Army, housed an average of 264 of the country's most incorrigible criminals, who were transferred here for disobedience while serving time in prisons elsewhere in the US. The strict discipline at Alcatraz was enforced by the threat of a stint in the isolation cells and by loss of privileges, including special jobs, time for recreation, use of the prison library, and visitation rights.

 INSIDER TIP
Plan Ahead

Tickets for Alcatraz go on sale 90 days in advance, and sell out particularly fast in summer months. Make sure you bring a jacket or sweater, as the weather can be far wilder and colder out here than it is in the city.

↑ The corridor that separates C and B blocks, nicknamed Broadway by the prisoners

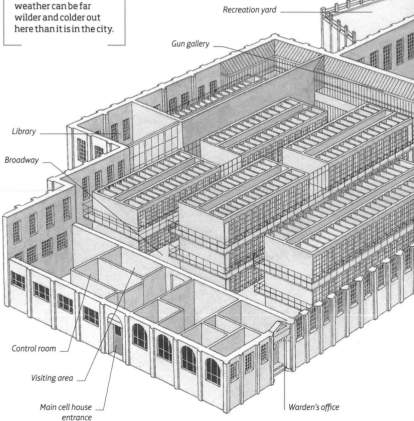

Recreation yard

Gun gallery

Library

Broadway

Control room

Visiting area

Main cell house entrance

Warden's office

↑ Cross-section of the interior of Alcatraz Federal Penitentiary

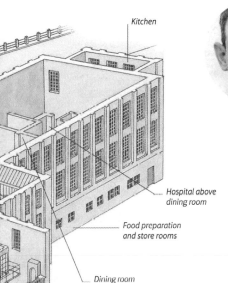

Kitchen

Hospital above
dining room

Food preparation
and store rooms

Dining room

↑ The prison kitchen, off the dining room where inmates were well fed to help quell rebellion

Al Capone

▶ The notorious Prohibition-era gangster "Scarface" Capone was convicted, in 1934, for income tax evasion. He spent much of his 10-year sentence in a hospital isolation cell, and finally left Alcatraz with a mental illness after contracting syphilis years before his conviction.

Robert Stroud

◀ Convicted murderer Stroud spent all of his 17 years on The Rock in solitary confinement. Despite assertions to the contrary in the film *The Birdman of Alcatraz* (1962), Stroud was in fact prohibited from keeping birds in his prison cell.

Carnes, Thompson, and Shockley

In May 1946, a group of prisoners led by Clarence Carnes, Marion Thompson, and Sam Shockley overpowered guards and captured their guns. The prisoners failed to break out of the cell house, but three inmates and two officers were killed in the "Battle of Alcatraz." Carnes received an additional life sentence, and Shockley and Thompson were executed at San Quentin prison, for their part as ringleaders of the insurrection.

Anglin Brothers

▶ John and Clarence Anglin, along with Frank Morris, chipped through the back walls of their cells, hiding the holes with cardboard grates. They left dummy heads in their beds and made a raft to enable their escape. They were never caught. Their story was dramatized in the film *Escape from Alcatraz* (1979).

George Kelly

▶ "Machine Gun Kelly" served 17 years on The Rock for kidnapping and extortion. He was then sent to a Kansas jail, where he later died.

15595

2 🛝 🍴 🖥 🛍

EXPLORATORIUM

📍R3 🅰Pier 15 🚌1, 2, 6, 10, 12, 14, 21, 31, 38, 41 🚊E, F 🚇Embarcadero
🕐10am–5pm Wed–Sat, noon–5pm Sun 🌐exploratorium.edu/visit

One of the world's first hands-on science museums, the popular Exploratorium is an interactive playground of exhibits that ignite the senses. Covering everything from vast topics like the science of human behavior right down to local geography, there's a subject to inspire everyone's curiosity – from kids to adults alike.

Since 1969 this renowned museum and global learning center has been influencing people of all ages with its creative and interactive exhibits. The museum uses unique hands-on displays that promote playful learning, and with so many topics to explore there's endless fun to be had. Learn how reflections work, understand how certain genes are passed on from parent to child, and examine local microorganisms and their Bay Area habitats. The top draw is the Tactile Dome, a pitch-dark network of chambers and mazes that you find your way out of using only the sense of touch. When you need a break from all the excitement, the all-glass Fisher Bay Observatory Gallery and Terrace offers excellent views of the Bay.

There are also a variety of events to look out for on the museum's calendar, including a guided walk during the highest tide of the year (known as the "King Tide"), and Community Days when patrons can pay whatever they wish (though admission is first-come-first-served and can't be guaranteed). After Dark Thursdays also give adults a chance to explore the exhibits in their own time (18+ only: 6–10pm Thursdays).

→

Colored light bathing visitors in the Central Gallery and *(inset)* a child blowing bubbles

MUSEUM GUIDE

The long building is laid out into five galleries. The Bernard and Barbro Osher Gallery 1 contains the Human Phenomena exhibit on topics such as emotions and human behavior. Gallery 2's tinkering exhibits and the Bechtel Gallery 3 on seeing and listening take up a large part of the museum, followed by Gallery 4 on living systems. Covering both the natural sciences and local history and geography are the outdoor Gallery 5 and the Fisher Bay Observatory Gallery on the upper level of the museum.

↑ The skyline of downtown San Francisco seen from the Exploratorium

EXPERIENCE MORE

3

PIER 39

Q2 **25** **10am-9pm daily (but hours can vary)** **pier39.com**

Refurbished in 1978 to resemble a quaint wooden fishing village, this 1905 cargo pier now houses souvenir and specialty stores on two levels.

The pier's street performers and amusements are popular and appeal particularly to families with children. You can ride on the two-level carousel, or visit the 7D Experience, which offers a couple of high-tech, exhilarating attractions.

The Aquarium of the Bay houses 20,000 sea creatures including sharks, bat rays, and skates. You can take a closer look at the pier's most famous residents at the Sea Lion Center; exhibits include a sea lion skeleton and interactive videos. Step outside afterward to view the sea lions at close range.

4

USS Pampanito

P2 **Pier 45** **8X, 47** **F** **10am-6pm daily (stays open late some days; check website)** **maritime.org**

This World War II submarine fought in, and survived, a number of bloody battles in the Pacific, sinking six enemy ships and severely damaging others. Tragically for the Allies, two of its fatal targets were carrying British and Australian prisoners of war. The *Pampanito* managed to rescue 73 men, however, and carry them to safety in the US. A self-guided tour of the ship takes visitors from stern to bow and includes visits to the torpedo room, the claustrophobic galley, and officers' quarters. In the days when the USS *Pampanito* was in service, it had a crew of 10 officers and 70 enlisted seamen.

EAT

Crab Shacks

If you're visiting Fisherman's Wharf during crab season (November–June), head to the pop-up shacks along Taylor Street for fresh seafood.

P2 **Taylor St (north end)**

$ $ $

5

SS Jeremiah O'Brien

P2 **Pier 45** **10am–5pm Fri–Sun** **ssjeremiahobrien.org**

Moored by Pier 45 is the last unaltered Liberty warship, one of 2,710 American-built vessels launched in World War II. Taking her name from the

→

Ghirardelli Square shopping center, site of the original famous chocolate factory

first American to succeed in capturing a British navy ship during the Revolutionary War, the SS *Jeremiah O'Brien* crossed the globe seven times before retiring north of San Francisco. Abandoned for 33 years, the ship was eventually restored and now offers an evocative snapshot of navy life. Visit on the third Saturday and Sunday of the month, when her boilers are lit. Alternatively, book a cruise; on the 4th of July the ship offers unrivaled views of the spectacular fireworks.

Madame Tussauds™ and San Francisco Dungeon

♥ P2 **⌂** 145 Jefferson St **🚌** 32 **🚋** F **🕐** 10am–7pm Mon–Thu, 10am–8pm Fri–Sun **🌐** madametussauds.com/sanfrancisco

After 50 years at Fisherman's Wharf, the Fong family finally closed-up their famous Wax Museum, handing the keys to the world-renowned Madame Tussauds™, which opened a fully revamped waxworks in 2014. The family-friendly attraction is a fun, interactive, star-studded experience with numerous wax figures of celebrities including sports stars, music legends, TV icons, film characters, and local A-list celebrities.

The building is also home to the San Francisco Dungeon – a thrill-filled journey through the darkest sections of the city's history – and the Rainforest Café, with its own indoor waterfall.

←

The huge crab sculpture standing at the entrance to PIER 39

Ghirardelli Square

♥ N3 **⌂** 900 North Point St **🚌** 19, 30, 47, 49 **🚋** F **🚋** Powell-Hyde **🕐** Times vary, check website **🌐** ghirardellisq.com

This former chocolate factory and woolen mill is the most attractive of the city's many refurbished sites, with shops and restaurants lining its pleasant square. The Original Ghirardelli Ice Cream & Chocolate Shop is a café with old chocolate-making tools and an ice-cream fountain, while the massive Ghirardelli Chocolate Marketplace sells

> ### GHIRARDELLI CHOCOLATE
>
> Ghirardelli chocolate is one of San Francisco's best-loved brands. Its originator, Domingo Ghirardelli, sailed to the US from Italy in 1849. Through a combination of confectionery expertise and smart suggestions from his employees, the "Broma process" was born. This chocolate-refining technique squeezes out cocoa butter to produce smooth, intensely flavorful chocolate.

the confection, which is now made in San Leandro, across the bay. The shopping center retains the famous Ghirardelli trademark clock tower and the original electric roof sign. Andrea's Fountain, the square's centerpiece, is a popular gathering point for shoppers.

Musée Mécanique

♥ P2 **⌂** Pier 45, at the end of Taylor St **🚌** 1 **🚋** E, F **🕐** 10am–8pm daily **🌐** museemecaniquesf.com

Kids and adults alike will love the experience of combing through and playing at this museum of penny-arcade games from the early 20th century. The collection consists of more than 300 items, including automatons, early examples of pinball machines, laughing fortune tellers, coin-operated pianos, and antique slot machines. This was an insiders-only spot for many years, and it is still popular with young San Franciscans looking for a fun evening out. Located close to Fisherman's Wharf, Musée Mécanique can be part of a nostalgic, fun-filled day. Admission is free, but the cost to play games ranges from a penny (true to their name!) up to a dollar.

9
The Beat Museum

📍 Q4 🏠 540 Broadway
🚌 30, 41, 45 🕐 10am-7pm
Thu-Mon 🌐 kerouac.com

Celebrating the famous Beat movement of 1950s San Francisco, this compact museum showcases artifacts linked to nearly everyone and everything ever linked to the phenomenon. With references galore to Allen Ginsberg's *Howl* poem, including a warning of an emergency exit that will "howl" if opened, the museum's collection features letters, photos, newspaper clippings, books, and album covers.

10
San Francisco Maritime National Historical Park

📍 N3 🏠 900 Beach St at Polk St 🚌 10, 19, 30, 47
🚃 Powell-Hyde 🕐 9:30am-5pm daily 🌐 nps.gov/safr

Resembling a beached ocean liner, the 1939 Aquatic Park Bathhouse building reopened as the Maritime Museum in 1951. On display is a collection

Balclutha, at the San Francisco Maritime National Historical Park ↓

🔍 HIDDEN GEM
Beat Generation

Although prominent Beat figure Jack Kerouac never really lived in San Francisco, his life and work are intrinsically linked to the city. An alley to the south of the City Lights Bookstore was named for him in 2007, and it contains plaques dedicated to the Beat Generation.

of ship models, old nautical instruments, paintings, and photographs illustrating local nautical history. In the lobby, visitors can also see colorful, historical murals depicting the underwater world.

Moored at the nearby Hyde Street Pier is the USA's largest collection of National Historic Landmark ships. The star here is the *Balclutha*. Launched in 1886, she sailed between Britain and California twice a year, trading wheat. Other ships include the *CA Thayer*, a three-masted schooner built in 1895 and retired in 1950. It carried lumber along the Northern California coast, and later was used in Alaskan fishing. Also at the pier is the 2,320-ton side-wheel ferryboat, *Eureka*, built in 1890 to ferry trains between Hyde Street Pier and

the counties north of San Francisco Bay. It carried 2,300 passengers and 120 cars and was the largest passenger ferry of its day.

11

San Francisco Art Institute

📍 P3 🏠 800 Chestnut St
🚌 30, 45, 91 🌐 sfai.edu

San Francisco's Art Institute dates from 1871 and once occupied an imposing Gothic-style wooden mansion built by railroad tycoon Mark Hopkins on Nob Hill *(p307)*, which was destroyed in the fire of 1906 *(p48)*. Today the Institute is housed in a Spanish Revival-style building from 1926, complete with cloisters, a courtyard fountain, and bell tower. A modern extension was added at the rear of the building in 1969. The **Diego Rivera Gallery**, named for the famous Mexican muralist and containing a significant example of his work, sits to the left of the main entrance.

The Institute holds temporary shows, exploring topics from contemporary photography to design and technology.

Diego Rivera Gallery
🕐 9am-5pm daily
🚫 Federal hols

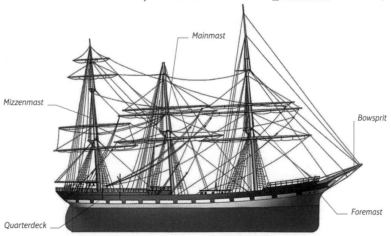

Mainmast
Mizzenmast
Bowsprit
Quarterdeck
Foremast

Cars driving down the
dramatically winding
Lombard Street ↑

⑫

Cartoon Art Museum

📍 N3 🏠 781 Beach St
🕐 11am–5pm Thu–Tue
🌐 cartoonart.org

The power of cartoons is
colorfully explored at the
Cartoon Art Museum, housed
in a 1912 building overlooking
the bay. Among the 7,000
items on display are political
caricatures, anime, graphic
novels, and iconic cartoons
from Warner Bros and Walt
Disney. Visitors are offered a
nostalgic look at the stories of
Snoopy and Donald Duck.

Occasional workshops
encourage guests of all ages
to try their hand at visual
storytelling. The museum is
small but offers a broad over–
view of this appealing medium.
On Tuesdays, the admission
fee is flexible and visitors can
decide what to pay.

⑬

Lombard Street

📍 N3 🚌 45 🚋 Powell–Hyde

Banked at a natural incline
of 27 degrees, this hill proved
too steep for vehicles to climb.
In the 1920s the section of
Lombard Street close to the
summit of Russian Hill was
revamped, and the severity
of its gradient was lessened
by the addition of eight
hairpin bends.

Today this beautifully
landscaped one-way street
is known as "the crookedest
street in the world." Cars
can travel downhill only at
a speed of 5 miles per hour
(8 km/h), while pedestrians
can take the steps up, as well
as down from the Powell-
Hyde cable car stop. There are
spectacular views of San
Francisco from the summit of
the street.

SHOP

City Lights
Bookstore

A favorite of the Beat
poets, this independent
bookstore was founded
in 1953 by the poet
Lawrence Ferlinghetti
and sociology professor
Peter D. Martin.
Browsing the shelves
and exploring the
unique titles, it's easy to
be transported back to
the 1960s. The upstairs
aisles focus on poetry
and offer plenty of cozy
nooks to settle down
into with a new book.

📍 Q4 🏠 261 Columbus
Av 🌐 citylights.com

 14

Coit Tower

Q3 Telegraph Hill Blvd
39 10am–6pm daily
(Nov–Apr: to 5pm)
sfrecpark.org

The 210-ft (64-m) reinforced concrete Coit Tower was built in 1933 at the top of 284-ft- (87-m-) high Telegraph Hill, with funds left to the city by Lillie Hitchcock Coit, an eccentric San Franciscan pioneer and philanthropist. The view of the North Bay area from the observation platform (reached by an elevator) is quite spectacular.

In the lobby of the tower are absorbing murals (p372). These were sponsored in 1934 by a government-funded program designed to keep artists in employment during the Great Depression.

Twenty-five artists worked together on the vivid portrait of life in modern California, painting in Social Realist style and addressing themes such as racial inequality. Many of the faces in the paintings belong to the artists and to local figures such as Colonel William Brady, the caretaker of Coit Tower. The work's political subject matter caused some controversy and delayed its official unveiling.

Descending from Telegraph Hill Boulevard, Filbert Steps is a picturesque stairway made of wood, brick, and concrete, where fuchsia, rhododendron, and bougainvillea thrive; it offers great panoramic views. Roughly parallel to Filbert Steps, the steps of Greenwich Street, with luxuriant foliage from adjoining gardens over-flowing onto them, also have splendid vistas. Going up one set of steps and down the other makes a delightful walk around the eastern side of Telegraph Hill.

15

Saints Peter and Paul Church

Q3 666 Filbert St
8X, 30, 39, 45 Powell-
Mason 7:30am–4pm
daily salesiansspp.org

Still known by many as the Italian Cathedral, this large church is situated at the heart of North Beach. The building, designed by architect Charles Fantoni, has an Italianesque facade, with a complex interior notable for its many columns and ornate altar. The concrete and steel structure of the church, with its twin spires rising over the surrounding rooftops, was completed in 1924.

← Coit Tower, and (inset) the fascinating 1930s murals in the lobby, depicting everyday California life

Cecil B. DeMille filmed the workers laying the church's foundations and used the scene to show the building of the Temple of Jerusalem in his film *The Ten Commandments*, made in 1923.

↑ Saints Peter and Paul Church, also known as the Italian Cathedral

⑯
Levi's Plaza

📍 R3 🚌 10, 12, 39, 42, F

This square is where the headquarters of Levi Strauss & Co., manufacturers of the famous blue jeans brand, can be found. Landscaped by Lawrence Halprin in 1982,

the plaza is studded with granite rocks and cut by flowing water, symbolizing the Sierra Nevada canyon scenery in which the miners who first wore the jeans worked. Generations of jeans are on show in the lobby of the Levi's Plaza Store, while The Vault, the adjoining one-room museum, traces the evolution of blue jeans from 1873 to the present day.

LEVI STRAUSS AND HIS JEANS

Denim jeans have only grown in popularity since they first burst onto the market in the days of the Gold Rush (*p47*). In the 1860s, Levi Strauss pioneered the use of a durable, brown, canvaslike material to make work trousers, sold directly to miners. Soon his company began to use metal rivets to reinforce the stress points in the garments, and demand increased. Levi's jeans are now a cultural institution, sold and worn all over the world.

⑰
Washington Square

📍 Q4 🚌 8BX, 8X, 30, 39, 41, 45, 91 🚋 Powell-Mason

This simple expanse of lawn – surrounded by benches and trees, and set against the twin towers of Saints Peter and Paul Church – has an almost Mediterranean atmosphere, appropriate for the "town square" of Little Italy. Near the center of the square stands a statue of Benjamin Franklin. A time capsule was buried under the statue in 1979 and is scheduled to be reopened in 2079. It is said to contain some Levi's jeans, a bottle of wine, and a poem written by Lawrence Ferlinghetti, one of San Francisco's famous Beat poets.

EAT

Liguria Bakery
Focaccia comes studded with black olives, or laced with rosemary and garlic, at this long-standing Italian bakery.

📍 Q3 📍 1700 Stockton St 🕐 Sun

⑤⑤⑤

Mario's Bohemian Cigar Store Café
Wholesome home cooking attracts a loyal clientele to this no-frills Italian spot.

📍 Q4 📍 566 Columbus Av

⑤⑤⑤

Caffè Trieste
Francis Ford Coppola wrote parts of *The Godfather* screenplay here; grab an espresso and cannoli to fuel your own masterpiece.

📍 Q4 📍 601 Vallejo St 🌐 caffetrieste.com

⑤⑤⑤

DRINK

Vesuvio Café
Jack Kerouac and Allen Ginsberg were regulars at this pub with a bohemian ambience.

📍 Q4 📍 255 Columbus Av 🌐 vesuvio.com

Tony Nik's
This bar, a speakeasy during the Prohibition years, features a lost-in-time ambience and classic cocktails.

📍 Q4 📍 1534 Stockton St 🌐 tonyniks.com

A SHORT WALK
FISHERMAN'S WHARF

Distance 1 mile (1.5 km) **Time** 20 minutes **Nearest streetcars** E, F

World-class dining, shopping, and lively entertainment are the focus of this vibrant neighborhood. The center of San Francisco's fishing industry, Fisherman's Wharf is the perfect place to try the city's celebrated Dungeness crab (served from November to June) at one of the countless seafood restaurants, see the fishing boats along Jefferson Street, and watch fishermen at work on Fish Alley. The Wharf is also the launching point for bay cruises. Tickets for Alcatraz can be purchased from Pier 33.

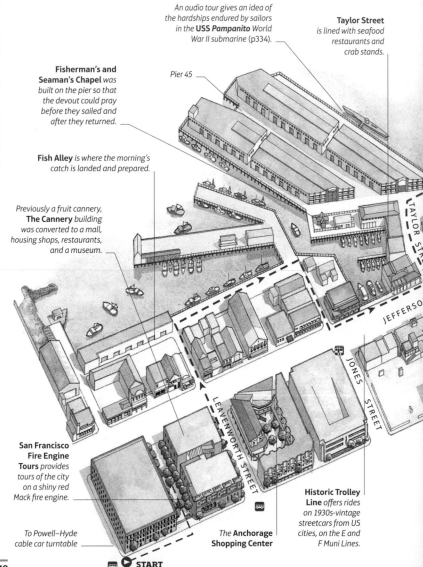

An audio tour gives an idea of the hardships endured by sailors in the **USS Pampanito** World War II submarine (p334).

Taylor Street is lined with seafood restaurants and crab stands.

Fisherman's and Seaman's Chapel was built on the pier so that the devout could pray before they sailed and after they returned.

Pier 45

Fish Alley is where the morning's catch is landed and prepared.

Previously a fruit cannery, **The Cannery** building was converted to a mall, housing shops, restaurants, and a museum.

TAYLOR STREET

JEFFERSON

JONES STREET

San Francisco Fire Engine Tours provides tours of the city on a shiny red Mack fire engine.

LEAVENWORTH STREET

To Powell–Hyde cable car turntable

The **Anchorage Shopping Center**

Historic Trolley Line offers rides on 1930s-vintage streetcars from US cities, on the E and F Muni Lines.

▶ START

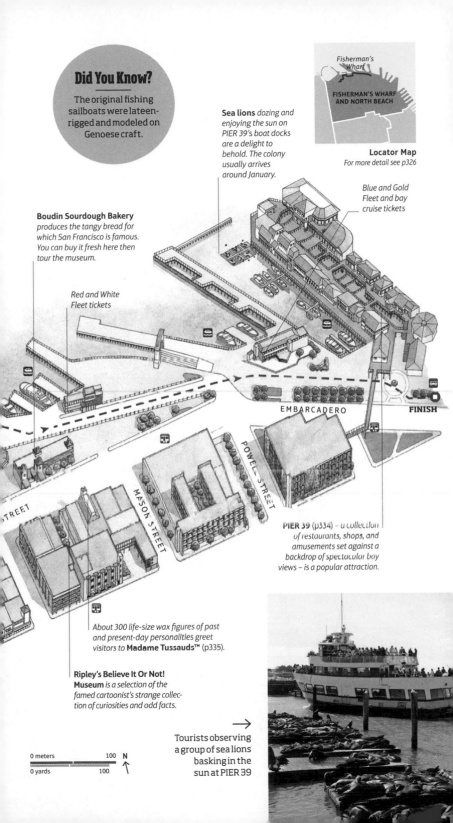

Did You Know?

The original fishing sailboats were lateen-rigged and modeled on Genoese craft.

Sea lions *dozing and enjoying the sun on PIER 39's boat docks are a delight to behold. The colony usually arrives around January.*

Fisherman's Wharf

FISHERMAN'S WHARF AND NORTH BEACH

Locator Map
For more detail see p326

Blue and Gold Fleet and bay cruise tickets

Boudin Sourdough Bakery *produces the tangy bread for which San Francisco is famous. You can buy it fresh here then tour the museum.*

Red and White Fleet tickets

EMBARCADERO

FINISH

POWELL STREET

MASON STREET

STREET

PIER 39 (p334) – *a collection of restaurants, shops, and amusements set against a backdrop of spectacular bay views – is a popular attraction.*

About 300 life-size wax figures of past and present-day personalities greet visitors to **Madame Tussauds™** (p335).

Ripley's Believe It Or Not! Museum *is a selection of the famed cartoonist's strange collection of curiosities and odd facts.*

0 meters   100   N
0 yards   100   ↑

→
Tourists observing a group of sea lions basking in the sun at PIER 39

PACIFIC HEIGHTS AND THE CIVIC CENTER

Pacific Heights was developed in the 1880s after cable cars linked it with the city center. With its magnificent views, it quickly became a desirable place to live, and elegant Victorian houses line its tree shaded streets. To the north of Broadway, the once marshy site descending all the way to San Francisco Bay was cleared and drained for the 1915 Panama-Pacific Exposition, of which the Palace of Fine Arts is the sole survivor. Anchored by the boutiques and restaurants on Fillmore Street, today Pacific Heights is one of the most expensive neighborhoods in the US.

After the earthquake of 1906, the Civic Center was built to the south of Pacific Heights to a masterplan by local architects led by John Galen Howard. It contains many of the city's important cultural and government institutions. The 50 United Nations Plaza Federal Office Building, completed in 1934, was where the UN Charter was signed in 1945, as was the 1951 Treaty of San Francisco in 1951, which officially ended the Pacific War. Today the Civic Center remains the home of the Supreme Court of California, and the seat of government for the City and County of San Francisco.

PACIFIC HEIGHTS AND THE CIVIC CENTER

Must Sees
1 Asian Art Museum
2 Fort Mason

Experience More
3 Palace of Fine Arts
4 Spreckels Mansion
5 Haas-Lilienthal House
6 Wave Organ
7 Fillmore District
8 Japantown
9 Cow Hollow
10 African American Art and Culture Complex
11 Octagon House
12 Bill Graham Civic Auditorium
13 San Francisco War Memorial and Performing Arts Center
14 Cathedral of St. Mary of the Assumption
15 Alamo Square
16 City Hall
17 Hayes Valley

Eat
1 Jane on Fillmore
2 Café Boho
3 Nopa
4 State Bird Provisions

Drink
5 The Snug
6 The Tipsy Pig

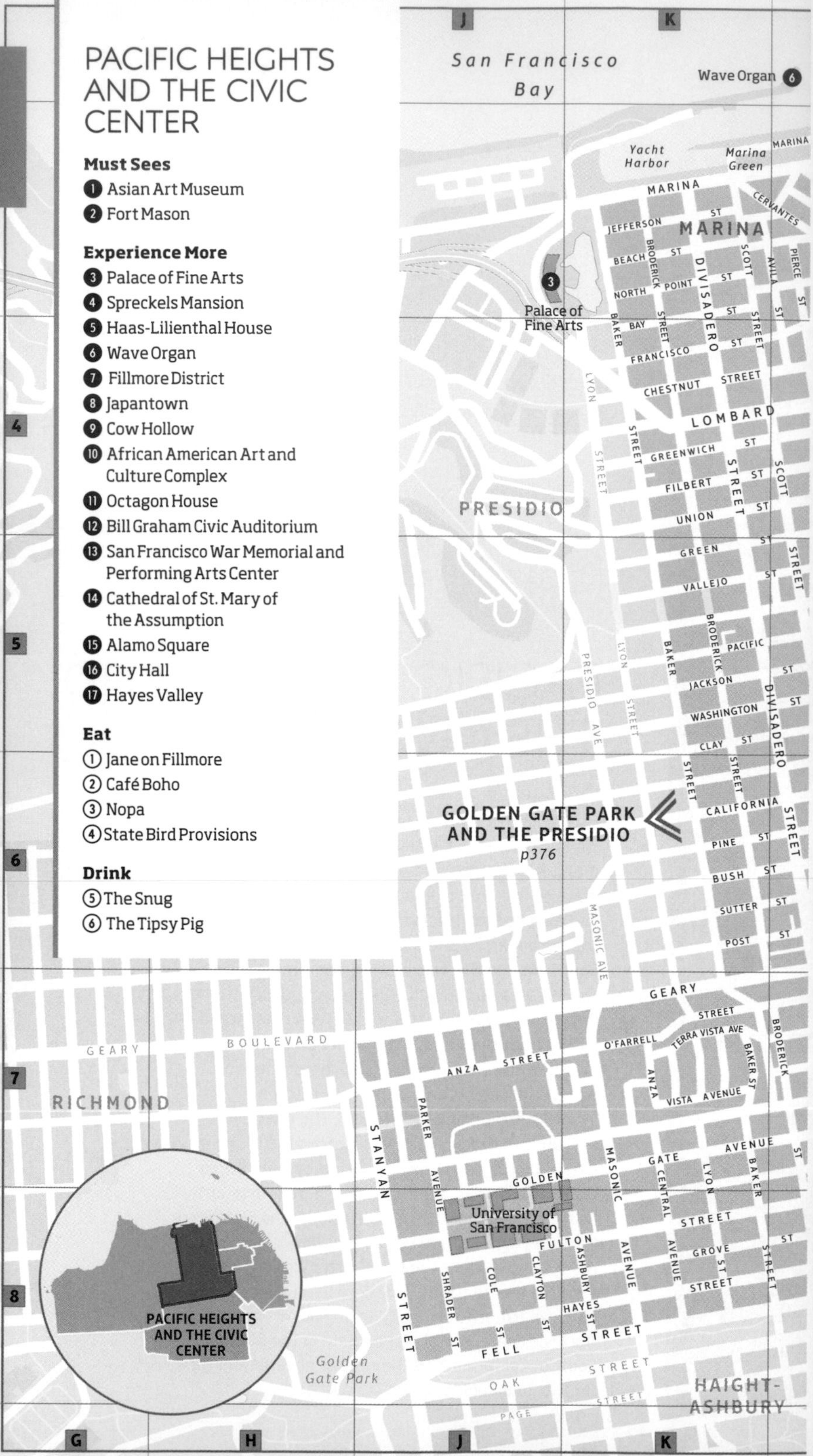

San Francisco Bay

Wave Organ 6

Yacht Harbor
Marina Green
MARINA

MARINA ST
JEFFERSON ST
BEACH ST
NORTH POINT ST
BAY ST
FRANCISCO ST
CHESTNUT STREET
LOMBARD
GREENWICH ST
FILBERT STREET
UNION ST
GREEN ST
VALLEJO ST
PACIFIC
JACKSON ST
WASHINGTON
CLAY ST
CALIFORNIA
PINE ST
BUSH ST
SUTTER ST
POST ST

CERVANTES
DIVISADERO ST
SCOTT ST
AVILA ST
PIERCE ST
BRODERICK ST
LYON STREET
BAKER STREET
BRODERICK STREET
SCOTT STREET
DIVISADERO

Palace of Fine Arts 3

PRESIDIO
PRESIDIO AVE
LYON STREET
MASONIC AVE

GOLDEN GATE PARK AND THE PRESIDIO
p376

GEARY STREET
O'FARRELL
ANZA STREET
VISTA AVENUE
GOLDEN GATE AVENUE
FULTON STREET
GROVE STREET
HAYES STREET
FELL STREET
OAK STREET
PAGE

TERRA VISTA AVE
BAKER ST
BRODERICK
ANZA
LYON
BAKER ST
CENTRAL AVENUE
MASONIC AVENUE
ASHBURY AVENUE

GEARY BOULEVARD

RICHMOND

STANYAN STREET
PARKER AVENUE
SHRADER ST
COLE ST
CLAYTON ST

University of San Francisco

Golden Gate Park

HAIGHT-ASHBURY

PACIFIC HEIGHTS AND THE CIVIC CENTER

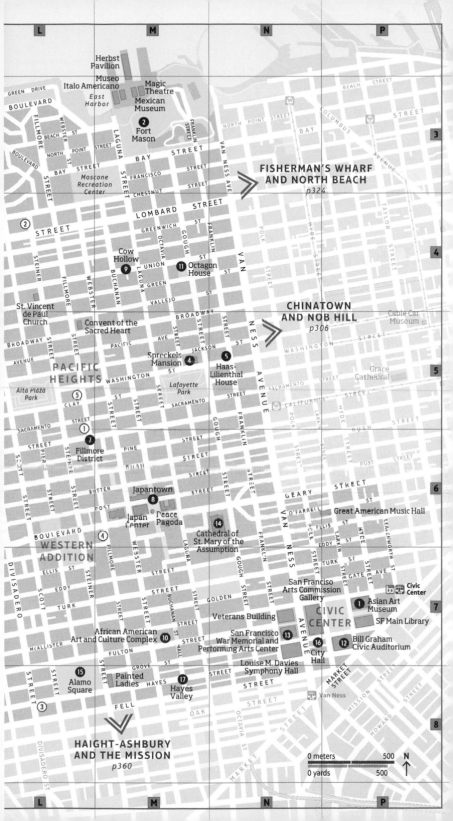

① ⊘ ⊗ ▢ ⊕

ASIAN ART MUSEUM

📍 P7 📍 200 Larkin St 🚌 5, 7X, 9, 19, 21, 31, 47, 49 🚋 F, J, K, L, M, N, T
Ⓜ Civic Center 🕐 10am–5pm Mon & Fri–Sun, 1–8pm Thu 🌐 asianart.org

Head up the grand staircase of the Asian Art Museum to embark on a historical and cultural tour of the world's largest continent. The 2,000 works on display celebrate both tradition and history as well as the contemporary cultures of many Asian nations.

Housed in the former San Francisco city library building, the Asian Art Museum contains one of the USA's largest collections of paintings, sculptures, ceramics, and textiles from Asia. Galleries are arranged by region and time period, beginning with ancient South Asia (India, Pakistan, Bangladesh, and Sri Lanka) on the third floor. Much of this level is taken up with religious statuary, though there are also displays of Javanese puppets and precious gold jewelry from Indonesia (room 11). The Chinese collection begins with a fabulous room full of intricate jade objects (room 13) and ancient ritual bronze vessels from the Shang dynasty (room 14). Room 16 contains the oldest known Chinese Buddha, a gilded bronze statue dating to 338 AD. The Chinese collection continues on the second floor with porcelain and scroll paintings from the later Qing dynasty and the Lingnan School. This floor also houses the Korean and Japanese collections. The latter begins with ancient Jōmon pottery (room 25). Other Japanese highlights include miniature sculptures and samurai armor (room 27) and screen paintings (room 28). The first floor is usually given over to temporary exhibitions.

↑ Facade of the Asian Art Museum, a Beaux-Arts building dating back to 1917

↑ Children painting copies of artworks from the museum's collection

Highlights

1000 BC

The museum's pair of sculptures of Shiva and Parvati are from the inner sanctuary of a Hindu temple in Cambodia.

c. 1500

◀ From China's Ming Dynasty, this complex Buddha sculpture is made of many small pieces that were fitted together before firing.

1870

△ This watercolor portrait of Maharaja Mahinder Singh of Patiala was copied from a photograph, which was a common practice.

2014

△ Painted in vibrant colors, artist Hung Yi's *Dragon Fortune* is a joyful enameled-steel sculpture that stands outside the museum.

A visitor admiring some
of the museum's more
modern artworks

2 🍴 💻 🏛

FORT MASON

📍 M3 🏠 2 Marina Blvd 🚌 22, 28, 30, 30X, 43, 49 🕐 9am–5pm Mon–Fri
Ⓦ fortmason.org

Once a military base, Fort Mason is now a vibrant arts and culture center, and a hot spot for foodies. Some of the city's finest views across the bay can be enjoyed from here.

Part of the National Register of Historic Places, Fort Mason reflects the military history of San Francisco. The original buildings were private houses, erected in the late 1850s, which were confiscated by the US Government when the site was taken over by the US army during the American Civil War (1861–65). The fort remained an army command post until the 1890s, and later housed refugees left homeless by the 1906 earthquake. During World War II, Fort Mason Army Base was the point of embarkation for around 1.6 million soldiers.

↑ Guests at a fine art exhibition in the Fort Mason Center for Arts and Culture

It was converted to peaceful use in 1972. The original barracks and the old hospital – which serves as a Visitor Center and the headquarters of the Golden Gate National Recreation Area (GGNRA) – are both open to the public.

Fort Mason Center for Arts and Culture

Part of the fort is now occupied by one of San Francisco's prime art complexes. Fort Mason Center for Arts and Culture is home to over 25 cultural organizations, art galleries, museums, and theaters. Particular highlights include the SFMOMA Artists Gallery, which offers artworks from Northern Californian artists for sale or rent, and the Museo Italo Americano, with works by Italian and Italian American artists. The Mexican Museum has a unique collection of over 12,000 objects representing thousands of years of Mexican history. Among the many places to eat at Fort Mason Center is Greens, one of the city's best vegetarian restaurants. Times vary for each venue, so check the website. Fort Mason Center also hosts thousands of events every year.

↑ The buildings of the Fort Mason complex on the piers in the Marina District

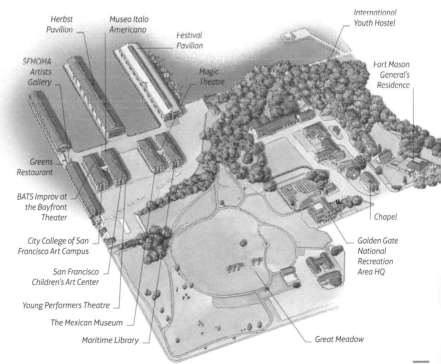

Herbst Pavilion

Museo Italo Americano

Festival Pavilion

SFMOMA Artists Gallery

Magic Theatre

International Youth Hostel

Fort Mason General's Residence

Greens Restaurant

BATS Improv at the Bayfront Theater

City College of San Francisco Art Campus

San Francisco Children's Art Center

Young Performers Theatre

The Mexican Museum

Maritime Library

Chapel

Golden Gate National Recreation Area HQ

Great Meadow

EXPERIENCE MORE

3
Palace of Fine Arts

📍 J3 🏛 3601 Lyon St 🚌 22, 28, 29, 30, 43, 45, 47, 49 🌐 palaceoffinearts.org

This Neo-Classical folly is the sole survivor of the many grandiose monuments built as part of the 1915 Panama-California Exposition, a world fair celebrating San Francisco's recovery from the earthquake of 1906. Today it is a space for theater, music, and dance performances. Its spacious auditorium has a capacity for 1,000 spectators.

The designer, Bernard R. Maybeck, took inspiration from the drawings of the Italian architect Piranesi and from the painting *L'Isle des Morts* by Swiss symbolist painter Arnold Böcklin. Originally built of wood and plaster, the Palace eventually began to crumble, until one concerned citizen raised funds for its reconstruction in 1959. It was restored to its original splendor between 1962 and 1968 using reinforced concrete.

The central feature is the rotunda, perched on the edge of a landscaped, swan-filled lagoon. Its dome is decorated with allegorical paintings, all of which depict the defense of art against materialism.

PANAMA-CALIFORNIA EXPOSITION

In 1915 San Francisco celebrated its successful recovery from the 1906 earthquake and fire with a monumental fair that was officially intended to mark the opening of the Panama Canal. The halls and pavilions of the fair were donated by all the states, plus 25 foreign countries, and they lined a concourse 1 mile (1.5 km) long. The brilliant Tower of Jewels, at the center of the concourse, was encrusted with glass beads and lit by spotlights, while to the west the beautiful Palace of Fine Arts could be reached by gondola across a landscaped lagoon.

4
Spreckels Mansion

📍 M5 🏛 2080 Washington St 🚌 1, 47, 49 🕐 To the public

Dominating the north side of Lafayette Park, this imposing Beaux-Arts mansion is sometimes known as the "Parthenon of the West." It was built in 1912 for the flamboyant socialite Alma de Bretteville Spreckels and her husband, Adolph, heir to the sugar fortune of Claus Spreckels. The house contains 26 bathrooms, and a large swimming pool in which Alma Spreckels swam daily until the age of 80. Her love of French architecture inspired the design. The architect of Spreckels mansion was George Applegarth, who in 1916 also designed the California Palace of the Legion of Honor in Lincoln Park *(p382)*. The mansion was donated to the city by Alma and Adolph Spreckels in 1924.

Today Spreckels Mansion is owned by the bestselling novelist Danielle Steel.

---

5 🖾 🏛
Haas-Lilienthal House

📍 N5 🏛 2007 Franklin St 🚌 1, 12, 19, 27, 47, 49, 76X, 83, 90 🕐 Noon–3pm Wed & Sat, 11am–4pm Sun (times may vary, check website) 🌐 haas-lilienthal house.org

This attractive Queen Anne-style mansion *(p357)* was built in 1886 for the rich merchant William Haas. Alice

The grandiose Palace of Fine Arts, now an events and performance space

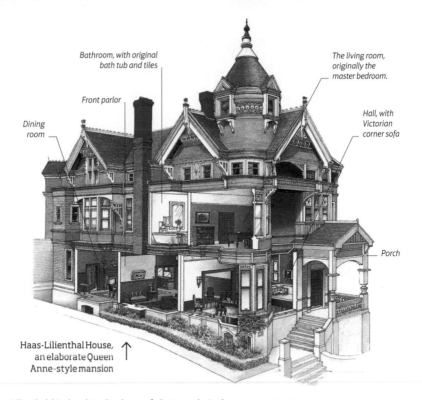

Bathroom, with original bath tub and tiles

The living room, originally the master bedroom.

Front parlor

Dining room

Hall, with Victorian corner sofa

Porch

↑ Haas-Lilienthal House, an elaborate Queen Anne-style mansion

Lilienthal, his daughter, lived here until 1972, when it was given to the Foundation for San Francisco's Architectural Heritage. It is the only intact private home of the period in San Francisco open as a museum, complete with authentic furniture.

A fine example of an upper-middle-class Victorian home, the house has elaborate wooden gables and luxurious ornamentation. A display of photographs in the basement describes the history of the building and reveals that this grandiose abode was modest in comparison with some of the mansions destroyed in the great fire of 1906 (p48).

 6

Wave Organ

📍 L2 🏠 1 Yacht Rd 🚌 30
🌐 exploratorium.edu

Sitting at the tip of the breakwater that protects the Marina is the world's most peculiar musical instrument. Built by scientists from the Exploratorium (p332), the Wave Organ consists of 25 underwater pipes that echo and hum with the changing tides. Listening tubes are imbedded in a sculptural mini-amphitheater that has views of Pacific Heights and the Presidio. The sounds created by the organ can be relaxing and ambient.

EAT

Jane on Fillmore
The scent of freshly brewed coffee and home-baked sourdough bread wafts from the door of this café, a popular lunch spot.

📍 L6 🏠 2123 Fillmore St
🌐 itsjane.com

$$$

Café Boho
Fresh, local seafood takes center stage here, particularly with the signature "seacuterie board": a sharing platter with tuna pastrami and octopus dip.

📍 L4 🏠 3321 Steiner St
🌐 cafebohosf.com

$$$

The pagoda at the center of the Peace Pagoda Garden, Japantown

Fillmore District

L6 **1, 2, 3, 22, 24**

Fillmore District managed to survive the 1906 earthquake and fire virtually intact, so for several years afterward this area served as the civic heart of the ruined city. Government departments, as well as several independent businesses, were housed in local shops, homes, and even churches. Today the main commercial district linking Pacific Heights and the Civic Center is located here, from Jackson Street to the outskirts of Japantown around Bush Street. This area is filled with fine bookstores, fashionable restaurants, and exclusive boutiques, plus the Fillmore Heritage Center, a historic venue for live music.

HISTORY OF FILLMORE JAZZ

In the 1940s and 1950s the Fillmore District had the largest jazz community on the West Coast of the United States and attracted many jazz stars such as Louis Armstrong, Ella Fitzgerald, and Billie Holliday to its night-clubs. During the late 1960s and 1970s, the district underwent a large-scale redevelopment, which led to a decline of the jazz scene. Today jazz finds a spotlight at the SFJAZZ Center *(www.sfjazz.org)* in the nearby Hayes Valley district *(p355)*.

Japantown

M6 **2, 3, 38**
sfjapantown.org

In the early 1900s, this neighborhood was the heart of the local Japanese American community, and had the look and feel of downtown Tokyo. That changed when those of Japanese birth and descent were forcibly interned during World War II. In the 1960s, when the **Japan Center** shopping complex was built as part of a scheme to revitalize the Fillmore District, the area regained some of its historic character. At the heart

> **In the early 1900s, this area was the heart of the local Japanese American community, and had the look and feel of downtown Tokyo.**

of the three shopping malls in the complex, and centered upon a five-tiered pagoda, is the Peace Pagoda Garden. Taiko drummers and other artists perform here at the Northern Cherry Blossom Festival in April. Each side of the pagoda is a mall with shops, sushi bars, bathhouses, and *Shiatsu* massage centers, modeled on Tokyo's Ginza district. One of the city's best movie theaters, the Sundance Kabuki Cinema, is also here.

More Japanese shops line the open-air mall across Post Street, flanked by sculptures by Ruth Awawa. On nearby Buchanan Street is Benkyodo, a cult bakery, which sells *manju* sweets and mochi rice cakes.

Japan Center

Geary, Post, Fillmore & Laguna sts
7am–midnight daily

Cow Hollow

📍 M4 🚌 22, 41, 45

Cow Hollow is a shopping district along Union Street. It is so called because it was used as grazing land for the city's dairy cows up until the 1860s. It was then taken over for development and turned into a residential neighborhood. In the 1950s the area became fashionable, and chic boutiques, antique shops, and art galleries took over the old neighborhood stores. Many of these are in restored 19th-century buildings, lending an old-fashioned air to the district, in stark contrast to the sophistication of the merchandise on display.

Union Street itself has more than 300 boutiques, and open-air arts, crafts, and food fairs are held regularly in the area.

African American Art and Culture Complex

📍 M7 🏠 762 Fulton St 🕐 9am–8pm Mon–Fri, 9am–5pm Sat; Gallery: noon–5pm Tue–Sat 🌐 aaacc.org

An epicenter of African art, music, and debate in San Francisco, the African American Art and Culture Complex is made up of several on-site spaces. It runs a broad-ranging events calendar that includes activist conferences, special exhibitions, and seasonal festivities. Performances are staged at the 206-seat Buriel Clay Theater and Hall of Culture, and dance studios

and other events venues are available to the local community. The gallery spaces are dedicated to exhibition work from and about the African diaspora.

Octagon House

📍 M4 🏠 2645 Gough St 🚌 10, 41, 42, 45, 47, 49, 70, 80, 90 🕐 Feb–Dec: noon–3pm on 2nd Sun and 2nd & 4th Thu of the month 🌐 nscda-ca.org/octagon-house

Built by William C. McElroy in 1861, the Octagon House, with its eight-sided cupola, is a well-preserved example of a house style that was once popular throughout the United States. Now run by the Colonial Dames of America, the first floor has been opened up into one large room, and this and the second floor house a small but engaging collection of decorative arts as well as historic documents dating from the 17th, 18th, and 19th centuries. Among the exhibits are furniture, paintings, porcelain, silver, pewter, samplers, playing cards from the American Revolutionary era, and signatures of 54 of the 56 signatories to the Declaration of Independence.

DRINK

The Snug

Classic cocktails are given a fresh update in this bright, stylish spot founded by four friends with a passion for great drinks. The hip clientele lounge on comfy leather sofas to sip raspberry negronis or bourbon sours with Chinese plum.

📍 L5 🏠 2301 Fillmore St 🌐 thesnugsf.com

💲💲💲

The Tipsy Pig

Low lighting and polished wood surfaces give this bar a warm, old-fashioned feel, but the craft cocktails – shaken and muddled with fresh fruit, herbs, and house-made syrups – are thoroughly modern. There's also an outdoor terrace.

📍 L4 🏠 2231 Chestnut St 🌐 thetipsypigsf.com

💲💲💲

→
The Victorian Octagon House, now housing a collection of decorative arts

12

Bill Graham Civic Auditorium

📍P7 🏠99 Grove St
🚌5, 19, 21, 47, 49, 71 🚃J, K, L, M, N 🚇Civic Center
🌐billgrahamcivic.com

Built during the architectural renaissance that followed the great earthquake and fire of 1906, the city's Civic Auditorium was designed in Beaux-Arts style by architect John Galen Howard. It was inaugurated by the French pianist and composer Camille Saint-Saëns in 1915, and it has since become one of the city's major performance venues, seating 7,000 people. In 1964 its name was changed in honor of Bill Graham, the local rock music impresario.

San Francisco War Memorial and Performing Arts Center

📍N7 🏠401 Van Ness Av
🌐sfwarmemorial.org

This stately complex in the Fillmore District is a nexus of local history and performing arts. The War Memorial Opera House is the home of the San Francisco Opera and Ballet, and the Veterans Building also houses lavish performance spaces: the ornate, Beaux-Arts Herbst Theater and the Green Room, featuring gilt detailing and towering columns. In 1980, the 2,739-seat Louise M. Davies Symphony Hall joined the ensemble and became home to the San Francisco Symphony.

You can join guided tours of the impressive interiors (10am to 2pm Mon), or stop for a light lunch and quality coffee at Café Valor, in the War Memorial Veterans Building lobby (open Mon to Fri).

14

Cathedral of St. Mary of the Assumption

📍N6 🏠1111 Gough St
🚌2, 3, 31, 38 🕐8:30am-5pm Mon-Fri, 9am-5:30pm Sat, 9am-5pm Sun
🌐stmarycathedralsf.org

Situated at the summit of Cathedral Hill, St. Mary's is one of San Francisco's most prominent architectural landmarks. Created by Modernist architects Pietro Belluschi and Pier Luigi Nervi, it was completed in 1971. The four-part arching paraboloid roof stands out like a white-sailed ship. The 200-ft- (60-m-) high concrete structure, which seems to hover effortlessly above the nave, supports the cross-shaped stained-glass ceiling. A canopy of aluminum rods sparkles above the altar.

HIDDEN GEM
Great American Music Hall

Cutting-edge sounds meet old-world glamour at this venue near the Cathedral of St. Mary of the Assumption. (www.slimspresents.com/great-american-music-hall).

15

Alamo Square

📍L8 🚌21, 22

The city's most photographed row of Queen Ann-style houses lines the eastern side of this sloping green square, offering great views of City Hall and Downtown. Alamo Square was laid out at the same time as the beautiful squares in Pacific Heights, but it developed later, with speculators building nearly identical houses.

So many grand old Victorian houses line the streets around Alamo Square that the area has been declared a historic district.

→ The eye-catching "Painted Ladies" Victorian houses, facing onto Alamo Square

16

City Hall

📍 N7 🏠 400 Van Ness Av
🚌 5, 8, 19, 21, 26, 47, 49, 71
🚈 J, K, L, M, N 🕐 8am-5pm
Mon-Fri 🌐 sfgov.org/
cityhall

City Hall, completed in 1915, was designed by the architect Arthur Brown at the height of his career. Its grand Baroque dome was modeled after St. Peter's Basilica in Rome and is higher than that of the United States Capitol in Washington, DC. The upper levels of the dome are open to the public.

The Beaux-Arts building stands at the heart of the Civic Center complex. Allegorical figures evoking the city's Gold Rush past fill the pediment above the Polk Street entrance, which leads into the elegant rotunda. Tour guides share stories from the building's past, such as the assassinations of Mayor George Moscone and Supervisor Harvey Milk in 1978.

17 🍴 🖥 🛍

Hayes Valley

📍 M8 🚌 21, 22

Situated west of City Hall, these few blocks of Hayes Street have become one of San Francisco's trendier shopping districts. After US Highway 101 was damaged in the 1989 Loma Prieta earthquake, the road was entirely demolished. The former highway had previously divided Hayes Valley from the wealthy power-brokers and theatergoers who frequented the rest of the Civic Center. A small number of up-and-coming cafés and restaurants, such as Ivy's and Mad Magda's Russian Tea Room, had already established themselves alongside Hayes Street's second-hand furniture and reject shops. Today an influx of art galleries, interior design shops, trendy cafés, and independent clothing and jewelry boutiques has made the area a more stylish destination.

EAT

Nopa
This convivial and chic restaurant offers a seasonal, organic menu. The pork chop with sauerkraut is a dinnertime standout.

📍 L8 🏠 560 Divisadero St 🌐 nopasf.com

💲💲💲

State Bird Provisions
Chefs Nicole Krasinki and Stuart Brioza create tapas-style dishes from seasonal ingredients. Highlights include the buttermilk-fried quail and baked duck eggs.

📍 M6 🏠 1529 Fillmore St 🌐 statebirdsf.com

💲💲💲

VICTORIAN HOUSES IN SAN FRANCISCO

Despite earthquakes, fires, and the inroads of modern life, thousands of ornate, late 19th-century houses still line the streets of San Francisco. In fact, in many neighborhoods they are by far the most common type of housing. Victorian houses are broadly similar, in that they all have wooden frames, elaborately decorated with mass-produced ornament. Most were constructed on narrow plots to a similar floor plan, but they differ in the features of the facade. Four main styles prevail in the city, although in practice many houses, especially those built in the 1880s and 1890s, combine aspects of two or more styles.

Balustrades on the porch betray the origins of the style in the Deep South.

Wide porches can be reached by a central staircase.

Tall cornices, often with decorative brackets, conceal a pitched roof.

A gabled roof with decorated vergeboards is the clearest mark of Gothic Revival.

The pitched roof over the main facade often runs lengthwise, allowing the use of dormer windows.

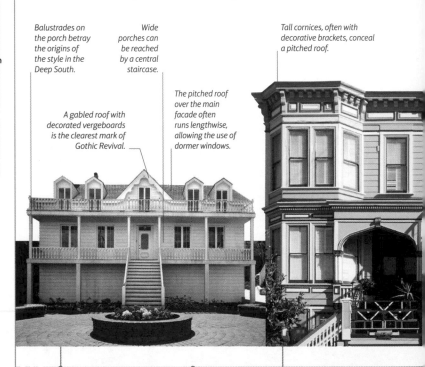

Architectural Styles

Gothic Revival (1850–80)

These houses are the easiest to identify, since they always have pointed arches over the windows, and sometimes over the doors. Other features are pitched gabled roofs, decorated vergeboards, and porches that run the width of the building. The smaller, simpler houses of this type are usually painted white, rather than the vibrant colors often associated with later styles.

Italianate (1850–85)

The Italianate style was more popular here than elsewhere in the US, perhaps because the compact form was suited to San Francisco's high building density. The most distinctive feature of the Italianate style is the tall cornice, usually with a decorative bracket, which adds a palatial air even to modest homes. Elaborate decoration around doors and windows is another typical feature.

↑ Neo-Classical doorways on an Italianate house

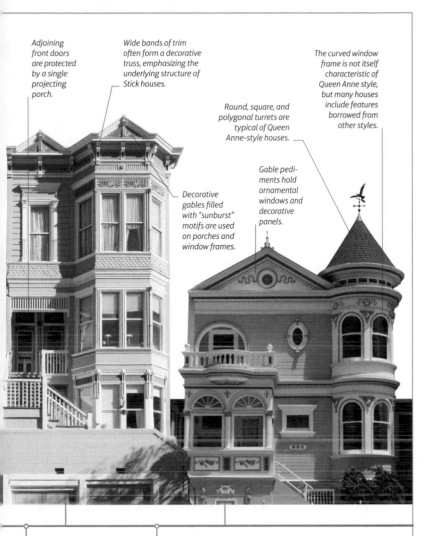

Adjoining front doors are protected by a single projecting porch.

Wide bands of trim often form a decorative truss, emphasizing the underlying structure of Stick houses.

Round, square, and polygonal turrets are typical of Queen Anne-style houses.

The curved window frame is not itself characteristic of Queen Anne style, but many houses include features borrowed from other styles.

Decorative gables filled with "sunburst" motifs are used on porches and window frames.

Gable pediments hold ornamental windows and decorative panels.

Stick
(1860–90)

This style is perhaps the most prevalent among Victorian houses in the city. Sometimes also called "Stick-Eastlake" after London furniture designer Charles Eastlake, the style was intended to be architecturally "honest." Vertical lines are emphasized, both in the wood-frame structure and in ornamentation. Bay windows, false gabled cornices and square corners are key identifiers.

Queen Anne
(1875–1905)

The name "Queen Anne" does not refer to a historical period; it was coined by the English architect Richard Shaw. Queen Anne houses freely combine elements from many decorative traditions, but are marked by their turrets and towers and large, often decorative, panels on wall surfaces. Most houses also display intricate spindle-work on balustrades, porches, and roof trusses.

WHERE TO FIND THEM

Haas-Lilienthal House *(p350)*

Octagon House *(p353)*

Pacific Heights *(p358)*

Painted Ladies *(p354)*

Clarke's Folly *(250 Douglass St)*

A SHORT WALK
PACIFIC HEIGHTS

Distance 1 mile (0.5 km) **Time** 20 minutes
Nearest buses 3, 10, 24

The blocks between Alta Plaza and Lafayette Park are at the heart of Pacific Heights. The streets in this upscale neighborhood are quiet and tidy, lined with smart apartment blocks and palatial houses. Some date from the late 19th century, while others were built after the earthquake and fire of 1906 *(p283)*. To the north of the area, the streets drop steeply toward the Marina District, affording outstanding views of the bay. Wander through the large Alta Plaza and Lafayette parks and past the luxuriant gardens of the mansions in between, then visit lively Fillmore Street, with its numerous fashionable bars, cafés, restaurants, and shops.

↑ Colorful Victorian houses on Washington Street

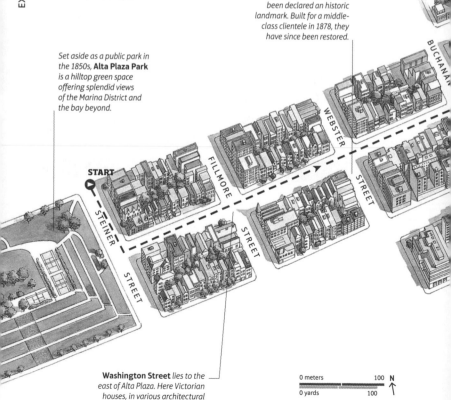

*Row houses (terraced houses) on **Webster Street** have been declared an historic landmark. Built for a middle-class clientele in 1878, they have since been restored.*

*Set aside as a public park in the 1850s, **Alta Plaza Park** is a hilltop green space offering splendid views of the Marina District and the bay beyond.*

START

Washington Street lies to the east of Alta Plaza. Here Victorian houses, in various architectural styles, fill an entire block.

BUCHANAN

WEBSTER STREET

FILLMORE STREET

STEINER STREET

0 meters   100   N
0 yards   100

Locator Map
For more detail see p344

The Victorian **Haas-Lilienthal House** (p350) is the headquarters of the Foundation for San Francisco' Architectural Heritage Foundation.

The impressive limestone **Spreckels Mansion** (p350) is constructed on the lines of a Beaux-Arts palace.

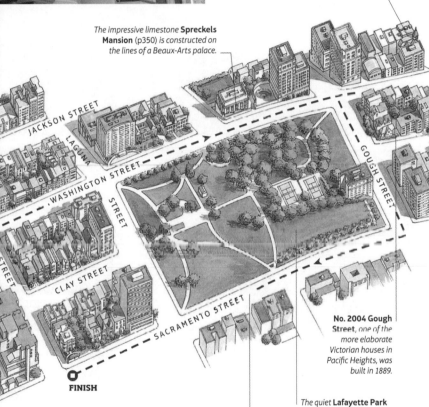

No. 2004 Gough Street, one of the more elaborate Victorian houses in Pacific Heights, was built in 1889.

The quiet **Lafayette Park** offers good views of the Victorian houses that surround it.

No. 2151 Sacramento Street is an ornate French-style mansion. A plaque commemorates a visit by the author Sir Arthur Conan Doyle in 1923.

FINISH

Did You Know?

A little north of this map, 2640 Steiner Street is the house where *Mrs Doubtfire* was filmed.

HAIGHT-ASHBURY AND THE MISSION

With its rows of beautiful late Victorian houses, Haight-Ashbury was once a typical San Franciscan neighborhood, developed after the cable car connected the area with Downtown in the 1880s. After World War II, its wealthy upper-middle classes fled to the suburbs, resulting in low rents, which made the area a haven for hippies in the 1960s. This was the epicenter of the "Summer of Love" In 1967, home to the Grateful Dead, Janis Joplin, the Hell's Angels, and a host of counterculture icons. Though that rebellious past is long over, Haight-Ashbury has kept its alternative subculture vibe.

The Castro District, to the east, is the nexus of San Francisco's LGBTQ+ community and has the largest number of gay bars in the city. Well known for its wild hedonism in the 1970s, the area is quieter these days, but its cafés and bars are still lively. The Mission District, farther east still, takes its name from the Mission San Francisco de Asis, founded by Spanish Franciscans in 1776. From the 1940s to 1960s, Central and South American immigrants moved into the neighborhood. Latin American artistic and cultural institutions, including vibrant street murals, still flourish here, despite gentrification in the 1990s.

HAIGHT-ASHBURY
AND THE MISSION

Must Sees
1. Haight-Ashbury
2. Castro Street

Experience More
3. Randall Museum
4. Golden Gate Park Panhandle
5. GLBT Historical Society Museum
6. Mission Dolores
7. Mission Cultural Center for Latino Arts
8. Carnaval Mural
9. Buena Vista Park
10. Twin Peaks
11. Vulcan Street Steps
12. Lower Haight Neighborhood

Eat
1. Bi-Rite Creamery
2. Craftsman & Wolves
3. Foreign Cinema

Drink
4. Ritual Coffee Roasters
5. Woods Cervecería

Shop
6. Amoeba Music
7. Booksmith
8. 826 Valencia Pirate Supply Store

GOLDEN GATE PARK AND THE PRESIDIO
p376

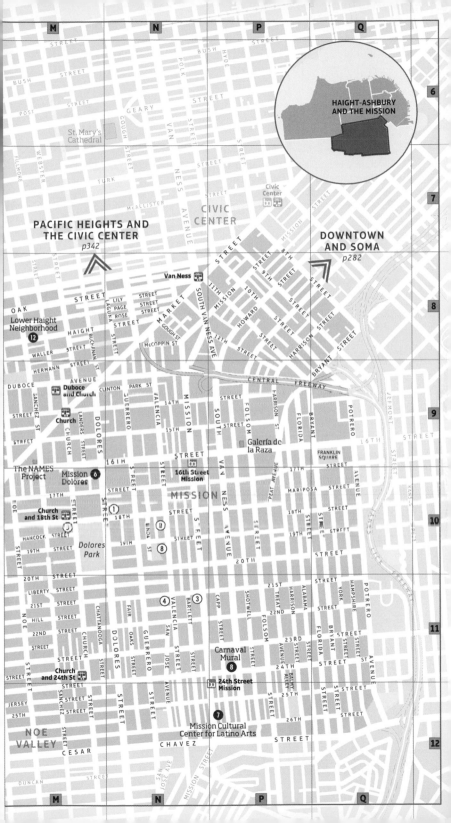

1 🍴 🖼 🛍

HAIGHT-ASHBURY

🚇 K9 🚌 5, 6, 7, 24, 31, 33, 37, 43 🚋 N

The birthplace of hippie counterculture in the 1960s, the Haight retains its antiestablishment atmosphere, and an aura of the past can still be found in its congenial cafés and vintage clothing shops.

Taking its name from the junction of two main streets – named after the San Francisco pioneers Henry Haight and Munroe Ashbury – this district contains independent bookstores, large Victorian houses, cafés, and hip clothing boutiques. The neighborhood's origins date back to the 1890s, when the area was rapidly built up following the reclamation of Golden Gate Park (p394) and the opening of a large amusement park called The Chutes. The district became a middle-class suburb – hence the dozens of elaborate Queen Anne-style houses (p357) lining its streets.

The Hippie Haight

After the streetcar tunnel under Buena Vista Park was completed in 1928, the middle classes began their exodus to the suburbs. After World War II the area reached its lowest ebb, and the big Victorian houses were divided into apartments offering low rents. While North Beach became the place for the beatniks in the 1950s, many creatives and freethinkers began to venture to Haight-Ashbury, as it was the cheaper place to live. By the 1960s the Haight had become host to a rebellious community that was a hotbed of anarchy.

A component of this "hippie scene" was rock music, but the area stayed low-key until 1967. Then the media-fueled "Summer of Love" brought some 75,000 young people in search of free love, music, and drugs, and the area became the focus of a major worldwide youth culture.

← Street-side seating at Cafe Cole in the Haight

← A row of elaborate Victorian houses in Haight-Ashbury

> While North Beach became the place for the beatniks in the 1950s, many creatives and free-thinkers began to venture to Haight Ashbury, as it was the cheaper place to live.

← Vintage secondhand clothing at the Decades of Fashion store

THE SOUNDS OF THE 1960S

Famous musicians who lived and performed in Haight-Ashbury include Big Brother and the Holding Company and their lead singer Janis Joplin *(right)*, who moved to her apartment at 635 Ashbury Street with her lover Peggy Caserta in 1967. Band members of The Grateful Dead lived at 710 Ashbury Street from 1965 to 1968. Graham Nash, the singer-songwriter, also lived in The Haight in the 60s and 70s, opposite Buena Vista Park.

CASTRO STREET

L11 **24, 33, 35, 37** **F, K, L, M, T**

The hilly neighborhood around Castro Street between Twin Peaks and the Mission District is the heart of San Francisco's high-profile LGBTQ+ community. It's a lively district of entertainment venues and nightlife with a side of beautiful architecture and proud history.

Focused on the intersection of Castro Street and 18th Street, the self-proclaimed "Gayest Four Corners of the World" emerged as an LGBTQ+ nexus during the 1970s. The LGBTQ+ Flower Power generation moved into this predominantly working-class district and opened gay bars such as Mary Ellen Cunha and Peggy Forster's Twin Peaks Tavern on the corner of Castro Street and 17th Street. With large windows, the Twin Peaks Tavern was the city's first gay bar where passersby could see inside. Though the many shops and restaurants attract all kinds of visitors, the Castro's openly queer identity has made it a place of pilgrimage for members of the LGBTQ+ community. Castro's most famous resident, Harvey Milk, the first openly gay man elected to public office in California, is remembered with a plaza outside the Muni stop on Market Street. The Human Rights Campaign Store (575 Castro Street), on the site of Milk's former home, sells all manner of LGBTQ+ apparel.

> **The Castro's openly queer identity has made it a place of pilgrimage for LGBTQ+ people.**

A rainbow-colored street crossing and *(inset)* the famous Twin Peaks Tavern

CASTRO THEATRE

Completed in 1922, this brightly lit neon marquee is a Castro Street landmark. It is the most sumptuous and best preserved of San Francisco's neighborhood film palaces, with a lavish interior inspired by *Arabian Nights* and a glorious Wurlitzer organ that rises from the floor between screenings. The venue hosts the San Francisco International LGBTQ+ Film Festival, held each June.

Rainbow Honor Walk

Bronze plaques on the Castro Street sidewalk commemorate important figures in the international LGBTQ+ community. While the honorees come from various backgrounds, they all shared in the battle for equality and are held up as inspirational figures in this walk of fame. Names range from famous artists like Freddie Mercury to local heroes like Major League Baseball's Glenn Burke, who is credited with inventing the high five.

EXPERIENCE MORE

3

Randall Museum

⚐ L9 ⌂ 199 Museum Way 🚍 24, 37 🕙 10am–5pm Tue–Sat 🌐 randallmuseum.org

Clinging to the side of Corona Heights Park, this unusual museum for children has a menagerie of more than 100 animals, including a raccoon, owls, snakes, and tortoises. There are also exhibitions on earthquakes, ocean life, and the Native American tradition of basket-making, as well as hands-on experiences with woodworking, ceramics, theater, and much more.

Corona Heights' bare red-rock peak offers great views over the city and East Bay.

4

Golden Gate Park Panhandle

⚐ K8 🚍 3, 5, 6, 21, 43, 66, 71

Dotted with old eucalyptus trees, this one-block-wide and eight-block-long stretch of parkland forms the narrow "Panhandle" to the giant pan that is Golden Gate Park (p394).

Its winding carriage roads and bridle paths were first laid out in the 1870s, and the upper classes came here to walk and ride. Today the old roads and paths are frequented by large crowds of joggers and cyclists.

During the "Flower Power" heyday of the 1960s, young hippies flocked to the park to listen to impromptu concerts by the new psychedelic bands from Haight-Ashbury. It is still a popular spot for street musicians and hippie guitarists.

5

GLBT Historical Society Museum

⚐ L10 ⌂ 4127 18th St 🚍 24, 33, 35, 37 🚋 F, K, L, M, S, T 🕙 11am–6pm Wed–Mon, noon–5pm Sun 🚫 Tue in fall and winter months 🌐 glbthistory.org

This is the first full-scale, stand-alone museum devoted to the history of the liberation of the gay, lesbian, bisexual, and transgender community in the United States. Though fairly small, the museum packs a punch, celebrating San Francisco's queer past through dynamic exhibits.

Treasures from the archives of the GLBT Historical Society reflect the fascinating stories of this vibrant community.

6

Mission Dolores

⚐ M10 ⌂ 16th St & Dolores St 🚍 22, 33 🚋 J 🕙 9am–4:30pm (to 4pm in winter) 🚫 Thanksgiving, Dec 25 🌐 missiondolores.org

Dating from 1776, Mission Dolores is the oldest building in the city and an embodiment of San Francisco's religious Spanish roots (p47). The mission was founded by Father Junípero Serra and is formally known as the Mission of San Francisco de Asis. The

> 🏔 GREAT VIEW
> **Dolores Park**
>
> A short walk from Mission Dolores, this park sits high on a hill with great views. To the south and west above the park, the streets rise so steeply that many turn into pedestrian-only stairways.

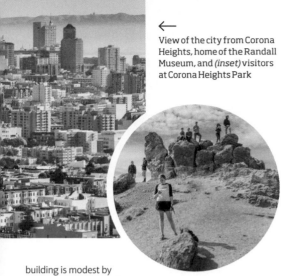

← View of the city from Corona Heights, home of the Randall Museum, and *(inset)* visitors at Corona Heights Park

building is modest by mission standards, but its thick walls have survived the years without serious decay and Native American paintings adorn the ceiling.

There is a fine Baroque altar and reredos, and a display of historical documents in

Mission Dolores, preserved since 1791 ↓

the small museum. The cemetery contains graves of San Franciscan pioneers. A statue marking the mass grave of 5,000 Native Americans, most of whom died in measles epidemics in 1804 and 1826, was later stolen. All that now remains is a pedestal, reading "In Prayerful Memory of our Faithful Indians."

SHOP

Amoeba Music
Leaf through a large selection of vinyl and CDs at this cult store in a former bowling alley.
📍 J9 🏠 1855 Haight St
🌐 amoeba.com

Booksmith
You'll find helpful staff and a wide collection of titles, as well as author events, at this independent bookstore.
📍 J9 🏠 1727 Haight St
🌐 booksmith.com

826 Valencia Pirate Supply Store
Yes, there are pirate-themed T-shirts, eye patches, and hooks, but also homewares, toys, and quirky gifts.
📍 N10 🏠 826 Valencia St
🌐 shop.826valencia.org

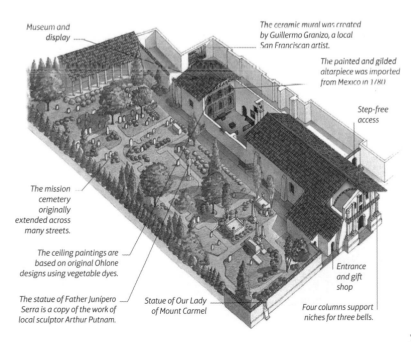

Museum and display

The ceramic mural was created by Guillermo Granizo, a local San Franciscan artist.

The painted and gilded altarpiece was imported from Mexico in 1780.

Step-free access

The mission cemetery originally extended across many streets.

The ceiling paintings are based on original Ohlone designs using vegetable dyes.

The statue of Father Junipero Serra is a copy of the work of local sculptor Arthur Putnam.

Statue of Our Lady of Mount Carmel

Entrance and gift shop

Four columns support niches for three bells.

7

Mission Cultural Center for Latino Arts

📍 P12 🏛 2868 Mission St
🚌 14, 22, 27, 48, 49 🚊 J
🚇 24th Street Mission
🕐 10am-6:30pm Tue-Sat
(to 5pm Sat) 🌐 mission
culturalcenter.org

This dynamic arts center, partly funded by the city, offers music and dance classes, concerts, theater, two art galleries, and a silk-screen print shop for the local Latin American community. It also hosts the district's Day of the Dead (p45) celebration.

8

Carnaval Mural

📍 P11 🏛 3195 24th St and
South Van Ness Av 🚌 12,
14, 48, 49, 67 🚊 J 🚇 24th
Street Mission 🌐 sfmural
arts.com

The *Carnaval Mural*, one of many murals in the Mission District, was created in 1983 by muralist Daniel Galvez and a group of local artists. It celebrates the diverse people who come together for the Carnaval festival, an annual spring event that is the highlight of the year. Guided tours of the other murals,

some with political themes, are given by civic organizations like the **Precita Eyes Muralists Association**.

There is also an outdoor gallery with murals in Balmy Alley (p373), near Treat and Harrison streets. Many of these murals are protests against government injustice.

Precita Eyes Muralists Association
🌐 precitaeyes.org

9

Buena Vista Park

📍 K9 🚌 6, 7, 37, 43, 66, 71
🌐 sfrecpark.org

Buena Vista Park rises steeply above the geographical center of San Francisco, with views

---

CALLE 24 LATIN AMERICAN CULTURAL DISTRICT

Calle 24 (*www.calle24sf.org*) is an organization that aims to preserve the Latin American character of the Mission District. Its successes are visible along the stretch of 24th Street between Mission Street and Potrero Avenue, and include Galería de La Raza (*www.galeriadelaraza.org*), an artist collective that runs exhibitions, workshops, and poetry readings, Balmy Alley's murals (*www.balmy alley.com*), and Mini Park's mosaic snake, a kids' favorite.

over the Bay Area. First landscaped in 1894, it is a pocket of land left to nature. Numerous overgrown and eroded paths wind up from Haight Street to the crest, but there is a paved route from Buena Vista Avenue.

10

Twin Peaks

📍 K12 🚌 33, 36, 37

These two hills lie at the heart of San Francisco and reach a height of 900 ft (274 m) above sea level. Twin Peaks Boulevard circles both hills

The colorful *Carnaval Mural*, celebrating the
↓ popular spring event

↑ Far-reaching views from the observation deck at the top of the Twin Peaks

near their summits; there is a parking lot and viewing point that overlooks the city. Those who are prepared to climb up the steep path to the very top on foot can leave the crowds behind and get a breathtaking 360-degree view.

⑪
Vulcan Street Steps

📍K10 🏠Vulcan St 🚌37

There is no link between the cult TV program *Star Trek* and this block of houses climbing between Ord and Levant streets. However, the Vulcan Steps do feel light years away from the busy Castro District below. The pretty gardens of the houses spill out and soften the edges of the steps, and a canopy of pines muffles the city sounds. There are great views of the Mission District and the southern waterfront.

⑫
Lower Haight Neighborhood

📍M8 🚌6, 7, 22, 66, 71 🚋K, L, M, N, T

Located halfway between City Hall and Haight-Ashbury,

and marking the southern border of the predominantly African American Fillmore District, the Lower Haight is Haight-Ashbury's grungier cousin. Unusual art galleries and boutiques, including the Used Rubber USA shop, which sells clothes and accessories made entirely of recycled rubber, began to open here in the mid-1980s. These joined the inexpensive small cafés, bars, and restaurants serving an arty clientele already in business in the area. This combination has created one of the most lively districts in San Francisco.

As in nearby Alamo Square *(p354)*, the Lower Haight has dozens of houses known as "Victorians" *(p356)*, built between the 1850s and the early 1900s, including picturesque, Queen Anne-style Nightingale House at No. 201 Buchanan Street, which dates to the 1880s. The 1950s public housing blocks have discouraged wholesale gentrification here. Commonsense safety precautions, such as not walking alone, should be taken if visiting the area at night.

EAT

Bi-Rite Creamery
Caramel and fresh fruit are among the top flavors at this ice-cream joint. There are dairy-free options too.

📍N10 🏠3692 18th St 🌐biritemarket.com

⑤⑤⑤

Craftsman & Wolves
The specialty here is The Rebel Within, a soft-cooked egg baked into a muffin of Italian cheese, spring onions, and sausage.

📍N10 🏠746 Valencia St 🌐craftsman-wolves.com

⑤⑤⑤

Foreign Cinema
New California cuisine is on the menu at this movie-loving venue.

📍N11 🏠2534 Mission St 🌐foreigncinema.com

⑤⑤⑤

DRINK

Ritual Coffee Roasters
This Bay Area coffee chain is worth a visit for its blended espresso drinks and trendy decor.

📍N11 🏠1026 Valencia St 🌐ritualroasters.com

Woods Cervecería
Small-batch beers here include the MateVeza, which is inspired by the South American tea drink *maté*.

📍M10 🏠3801 18th St 🌐woodsbeer.com

SAN FRANCISCO'S MURALS

The elaborate murals that decorate San Francisco's walls and fences, mainly in the Mission District, are testament to its pride in its reputation as a culturally rich and cosmopolitan city. Some murals were painted in the 1930s, with many more created since the 1970s.

PAST MASTERS

Some of the best examples of San Francisco's historical mural art can be found inside Coit Tower (p338), where a series of panels, funded during the Great Depression of the 1930s by President Roosevelt's New Deal program, is typical of the period. Many local artists participated in creating the work, inspired by Mexican mural artist Diego Rivera. Between 1941 and 1948, Russian-born artist Anton Refregier created the 27 History of California murals inside the Rincon Annex (p296) in a similar Social Realist style.

INTO THE PRESENT

In the 1970s the Mission District became a hotbed for mural art, much of it painted or sponsored by the Precita Eyes Muralists

↑ *City Life* fresco (1934) by Victor Arnotauff in Coit Tower

MaestraPeace on the ↑
Women's Building, one of
the city's largest murals

Association, founded by Susan Cervantes and Luis Cervantes (p370). Las Mujeres Muralistas, an all-female Chicana artist collective, began to decorate Balmy Alley in the early 1970s and a further 27 murals by various artists were added in 1985. The alley remains the city's most concentrated collection of murals.

Clarion Alley has been similarly adorned with street art since 1992, with works created by well-known artists such as Maya Hayuk, Rigo 23, and Megan Wilson. Anchored by tree-lined 24th Street, the Calle 24 Latin American Cultural District (p370) brings much of the area's cultural and artistic heritage together (it's the home of Precita Eyes and Balmy Alley), with notable murals at the 24th Mini Park, and on stores' rolldown gates, lit at night.

Today Precita Eyes runs lively mural tours around the Mission and operates two arts centers (in the Mission and adjacent Bernal Heights). It also continues to sponsor new murals by established artists; Strength of Community was completed in 2020 at 1296 Shotwell Street in the Mission, while the huge Baobab Rising debuted in 2018 at 350 Ellis Street.

↑ *After the Storm* by Tina Wolfe in Balmy Alley

↑ *Swan* by Daniel Doherty In Clarion Alley

ᵀᴼᴾ5 MURALS

Carnaval Mural
A huge mural depicting the energy and spirit of the city's Carnaval festival (p370).

No Ceiling
⌖ Jessie and Mission St, SOMA
A 1971 feminist image by BiP (Believe in People).

Fantasy for Children
⌖ 24th St Mini Park, Mission
Painted in 1975 by Las Mujeres Muralistas.

MaestraPeace
⌖ 3543 18th St, Mission
Mural by seven female artists made in 1994.

Women of the Resistance
⌖ Balmy Alley, Mission
Global female heroines painted by Lucia Ippolito in 2018.

A SHORT WALK
HAIGHT-ASHBURY

Distance 1 mile (1.5 km) **Time** 20 minutes
Nearest buses 7, 33

Stretching from the hilly Buena Vista Park to the flat expanses of Golden Gate Park, Haight-Ashbury was a place to escape to from the city center in the 1880s. It developed into a residential area, but between the 1930s and 1960s it changed dramatically to become the center of the "Flower Power" world. It is now one of the liveliest and most liberal and artsy places in San Francisco, with an eclectic mix of people, excellent book and record stores, and good cafés. This route takes you past some of the area's main highlights.

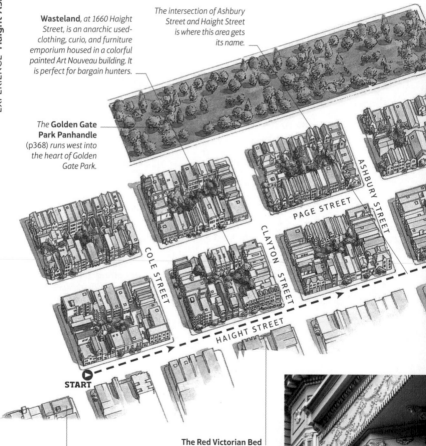

Wasteland, at 1660 Haight Street, is an anarchic used-clothing, curio, and furniture emporium housed in a colorful painted Art Nouveau building. It is perfect for bargain hunters.

The intersection of Ashbury Street and Haight Street is where this area gets its name.

The **Golden Gate Park Panhandle** (p368) runs west into the heart of Golden Gate Park.

ASHBURY STREET

PAGE STREET

CLAYTON STREET

COLE STREET

HAIGHT STREET

START

Cha Cha Cha (1801 Haight St) is one of the liveliest places to eat in San Francisco, serving Latin American food in a variety of small dishes.

The Red Victorian Bed and Breakfast (1665 Haight St) is a relic of the hippie 1960s. It caters to a New Age clientele with rooms with transcendental themes.

↑ Downtown San Francisco skyline seen from Buena Vista Park

Locator Map
For more detail see p362

OAK STREET

CENTRAL STREET

LYON STREET

MASONIC STREET

0 meters 100 N
0 yards 100 ↑

Through its mass of twisting trees, the dramatic **Buena Vista Park** *(p370) offers magnificent views over the city.*

BUENA VISTA WEST

No. 1220 Masonic Avenue *is one of many ornate Victorian mansions built on a steep hill to the south of Haight Street.*

FINISH

← Kooky artwork in the window of the Piedmont Boutique on Haight Street

GOLDEN GATE PARK AND THE PRESIDIO

The Presidio, a large park, was home to an 18th-century Spanish fort, which fell under Mexican rule when the nation became independent from Spain in 1821. It was taken over again by the US military during the Mexican-American War (1846–48), and continued to play a role in American military endeavors in the Pacific until 1994. Since then, it has been developed by the National Park Service and is now a mix of parkland (with 24 miles/ 39 km of trails), homes, museums, and private businesses, such as Lucasfilm.

Lying to the south is the spectacular Golden Gate Park. Once a sandy wasteland, it was designed in 1871 by Park Commissioner William Hall in the style of Frederick Law Olmsted (the creator of New York City's Central Park), but completed in the 1890s by Scottish horticulturalist John McLaren. Little grows here, and trees have been planted where they will best deflect the prevailing winds. Some of the park's buildings date from the 1894 California Midwinter Exposition, the first World's Fair held in California. More parklands lie to the north and west, where rugged Land's End meets the sea.

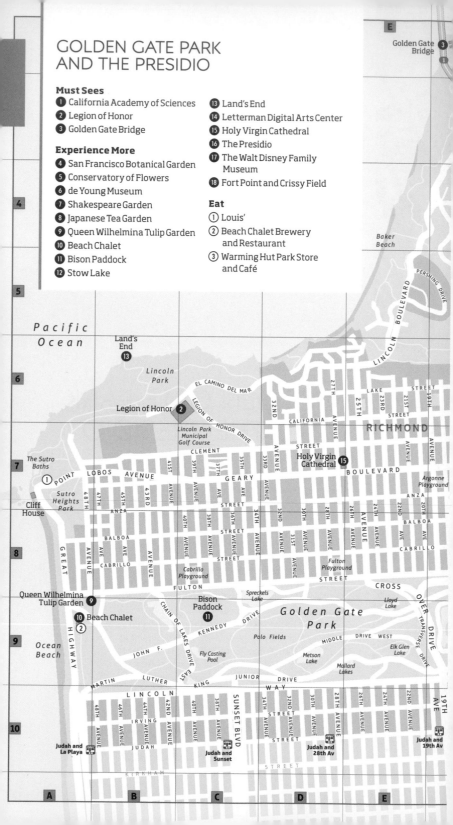

GOLDEN GATE PARK AND THE PRESIDIO

Must Sees
1. California Academy of Sciences
2. Legion of Honor
3. Golden Gate Bridge

Experience More
4. San Francisco Botanical Garden
5. Conservatory of Flowers
6. de Young Museum
7. Shakespeare Garden
8. Japanese Tea Garden
9. Queen Wilhelmina Tulip Garden
10. Beach Chalet
11. Bison Paddock
12. Stow Lake
13. Land's End
14. Letterman Digital Arts Center
15. Holy Virgin Cathedral
16. The Presidio
17. The Walt Disney Family Museum
18. Fort Point and Crissy Field

Eat
1. Louis'
2. Beach Chalet Brewery and Restaurant
3. Warming Hut Park Store and Café

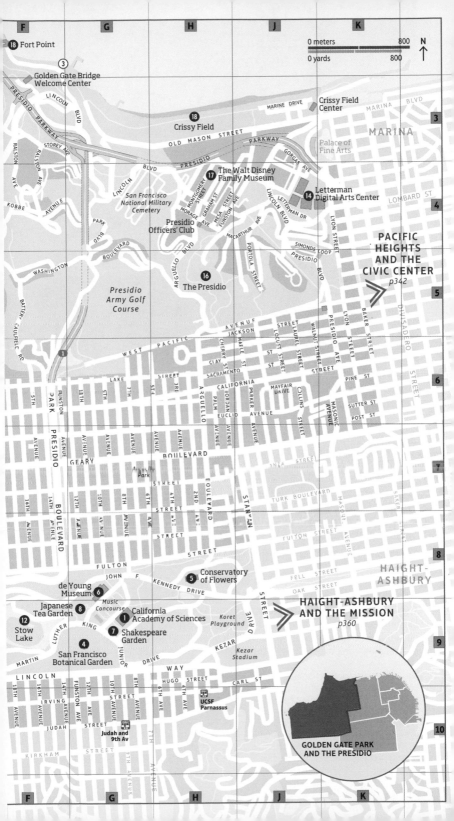

① ⊘ ⊛ Ⓨ ⊡ 🛍

CALIFORNIA ACADEMY OF SCIENCES

📍 G9 🏠 55 Music Concourse Dr 🚌 5, 44 🚇 N
🕘 9:30am–5pm Mon–Sat, 11am–5pm Sun 🌐 calacademy.org

The California Academy of Sciences lets curious minds get close to nature with exciting exhibits such as an indoor rainforest, a vast aquarium, and a natural history museum. An environmentally friendly structure with a roof covered in local plant life, the building itself blends in with the natural surroundings of Golden Gate Park.

The California Academy of Sciences has been located in Golden Gate Park since 1916, settling into a new building in late 2008. It houses the Steinhart Aquarium, Morrison Planetarium, and the Kimball Natural History Museum, and combines innovative green architecture with flexible exhibition spaces. A lovely piazza is at the heart of the building. The 2.5-acre (1-ha) living roof, which can be seen from the rooftop deck, is filled with native plant species, creating a beautiful oasis for birds, insects, and other creatures. Explore the museum's fascinating exhibits at your own pace or flit between the many workshops and talks held throughout the day. The museum's calendar is also full of lectures, weekly late-night events for adults 21 years and over, and sleepovers for kids aged 5 to 17.

Must See

Morrison Planetarium

Visitors leave planet Earth behind as stunning films send them flying through space and time.

Living Roof

▽ An observation deck offers views of the park and allows visitors to see the green roof up close.

↑ Visitors in the Osher Rainforest exhibit, a four-story indoor rainforest

Osher Rainforest

Inside a large glass dome, this neo-tropical rainforest has more than 1,600 live plants and animals.

T. Rex

▷ Part of the Kimball Natural History Museum, the skeleton of a *Tyrannosaurus rex* sits at the museum entrance. This gigantic predator was the most powerful carnivore ever to walk the Earth.

Steinhart Aquarium

◁ The amazing aquarium exhibit on the lower floor includes the world's largest indoor reef.

MUSEUM GUIDE

Steinhart Aquarium displays are spread throughout the museum, but most of the tanks are on the lower level beneath the piazza. The main floor is the gateway to all the other key exhibits, including the Kimball Natural History Museum, Morrison Planetarium, and Osher Rainforest, with some exhibits extending up several floors. An auditorium above the café hosts traveling exhibits as well as special performances and programs. The third floor houses the geology collection and Naturalist Center, and on the roof there is an observation deck.

Tusher African Hall

▷ Preserved animals from Africa are displayed here in lifelike dioramas. This area is also home to a colony of endangered African penguins.

② LEGION OF HONOR

⊙C6 🏛Lincoln Park, 100 34th Av (at Clement St) 🚌1, 18, 38 ⏰9:30am-5:15pm Tue-Sun 🌐legionofhonor.famsf.org

Set in the gorgeous natural landscape of Land's End and housed in a replica of the Palais de la Légion d'Honneur in Paris, this museum features medieval to 20th-century European art, and is famous for hosting superb temporary exhibits.

Alma de Bretteville Spreckels (heiress to the Spreckels sugar fortune) commissioned the Legion of Honor in the 1920s to promote French art in California and to commemorate the state's casualties in World War I. It contains mostly European art from the last eight centuries, with paintings by famous figures including Monet, Rubens, and Rembrandt, as well as over 70 sculptures by Rodin. The gallery also houses collections of photography and ancient art covering 6,000 years of world history and cultures. The Achenbach Foundation, a famous collection of around 90,000 graphic works, is displayed in rotating exhibits.

WAL

GALLERY GUIDE

The museum's permanent collection is displayed in 19 galleries on the first floor. Beginning at the left of the entrance, works are arranged chronologically from the medieval period to the 20th century.

Gallery Highlights

c. 1880

▽ This oval-leaf molded plate was designed by the famous Wedgwood Factory.

c. 1904

▽ The bronze cast of Rodin's *The Thinker* was made by Rodin's assistant, Henri Lebossé.

1642

△ *The Raising of Lazarus*, one of several hundred Rembrandt works in the Achenbach Foundation collection.

1889

△ Konstantin Makovsky's *The Russian Bride's Attire* depicts a Russian woman preparing for her wedding day.

PHYLLIS SHORENSTEIN COURT

↑ A gallery of European sculptures and the museum facade (*inset*), inspired by a historic palace in Paris

1924

▽ The Skinner pipe organ was built by the Ernest M. Skinner Organ Company, and is used in organ concerts here throughout the year.

c. 1914

△ This version of *Water Lilies* is just one of around 250 paintings Monet created of the water lilies in his garden.

→ A copy of Rodin's *The Thinker* (c. 1904), outside the gallery

→

The Golden Gate Bridge against the San Francisco skyline

Jan 5, 1933

Construction officially begins.

Dec 1933

▽ Repairs begin after the same trestle is damaged in a storm.

Timeline

Aug 11, 1930

△ After decades of debate and deliberation a construction permit is finally issued for a suspension bridge over the Golden Gate strait.

Feb 26, 1933

△ The official ground-breaking ceremony takes place – a festive event with over 100,000 attendees eager to celebrate the long-awaited bridge project.

Aug 14, 1933

△ Part of the access trestle is destroyed by a ship.

③

GOLDEN GATE BRIDGE

⑨ F2 🚌 2, 28, 76 Ⓦ goldengate.org

You may expect such a famous city landmark to feel familiar, but visitors to the Golden Gate Bridge are sure to find themselves in awe when they see it in person. Whether you journey across or just view it from the shore, this iconic bridge is sure to capture your imagination and get you itching for a stunning photo of your own.

Named for the entrance to the Strait of San Francisco Bay called "Golden Gate" by John Fremont in 1846, the bridge opened in 1937, connecting San Francisco with Marin County. Measuring 4,200 ft (1,280 m) in length, it was the world's longest suspension bridge at the time it was built. Breathtaking views are offered from this world-famous landmark, which has six lanes for vehicles, plus a pedestrian and bicycle path.

Cars driving southbound from the Marin County side toward San Francisco must pay a toll, and pedestrians and cyclists are only permitted on the eastern sidewalk.

> INSIDER TIP
> **Welcome Center**
>
> The Welcome Center (open 9am–6pm daily) offers practical information, has exhibits on the history of the bridge, and sells merchandise.

The Opening of the Bridge

The bridge that most people said could never be built was completed on time and under budget in the midst of the Great Depression, under chief engineer Joseph Strauss. On May 27, 1937, Golden Gate Bridge opened only for pedestrians, and an estimated 200,000 people came to be the first to walk across. The roadway opened the next day, and an official convoy of Cadillacs and Packards were the first vehicles to cross the bridge.

→ The first pedestrians on the Golden Gate Bridge, May 27, 1937

THE BRIDGE IN FIGURES

Crossing the Bridge
Every year approximately 41 million vehicles cross the bridge (about 112,000 a day).

Incredible Cables
The two great 7,650-ft (2,332-m) main cables are more than 3 ft (1 m) thick, and contain 80,000 miles (128,744 km) of steel wire, enough to encircle the Earth at the equator three times.

The Concrete
The volume of concrete poured into the piers and anchorages during the bridge's construction would be enough to lay a 5-ft- (1.5-m-) wide sidewalk stretching from New York to San Francisco.

Built to Last
The bridge was designed to withstand 100 mph (160 km/h) winds. Each pier has to withstand a tidal flow of more than 60 mph (97 km/h), while supporting a 22,000-ton steel tower.

Timeline

Jun 1935
The south tower (closest to San Francisco) is completed.

Jun 1934
△ The north tower (near the Marin County end of the Bridge) is completed, although some records claim it was finished in November.

Must See

TOP 3 VIEWS OF THE BRIDGE

Baker Beach
This large, popular beach may not be ideal for swimming, but it makes up for it with stunning views.

Fort Point
The northernmost point of San Francisco offers angles that highlight the incredible scale of the bridge (p393).

Vista Point
Head to this popular spot on the Marin County side to get a photo of Golden Gate Bridge with a stunning San Francisco backdrop.

↑ Photographers setting up to capture the Golden Gate Bridge from Baker Beach

Jun 1936
△ Work begins on the roadway that will connect San Francisco and Marin County.

Feb 17, 1937
Ten workers are killed when a safety net fails.

Apr 27, 1937
▽ The last gold rivet is driven into the bridge during a ceremony marking its completion.

May 27, 1937
△ Opening day. Every siren and church bell in San Francisco and Marin sounds in unison as part of a huge celebration. The following day, President Roosevelt holds a dedication ceremony via telegraph.

Palm trees and flower beds around a glasshouse at San Francisco Botanical Garden ↑

EXPERIENCE MORE

4

San Francisco Botanical Garden

📍G9 🏠9th Ave at Lincoln Way, Golden Gate Park 🚌44, 71 🕐7:30am-6pm daily (Nov-Mar: to 5pm) 🌐sfbotanicalgarden.org

On display here are more than 8,000 species of plants, trees, and shrubs from around the world. There are Mexican, South American, African, and Australian gardens, and one that is devoted entirely to native California plants. The enchanting Moon-Viewing Garden exhibits Far Eastern plants in a naturalistic setting, while in the Garden of Fragrance, designed for blind plant-lovers, the emphasis is on the senses of taste, touch, and smell, and all the plants are identified in Braille. Another area re-creates the flora of a northern Californian coastal forest. There is also a New World Cloud Forest, with flora from the mountains of Central America.

The garden has a shop, selling seeds and books, and also houses the Helen Crocker Horticultural Library, which is open to the public. Free tours run daily at 1:30pm. A flower show is held every spring.

5

Conservatory of Flowers

📍H8 🏠100 John F. Kennedy Drive, Golden Gate Park 🚌5, 33, 44 🕐10am-4:30pm Tue-Sun 🌐conservatoryof flowers.org

This ornate greenhouse, inspired by the one in London's Kew Gardens, is the oldest building in the park. A property developer, James Lick, imported the frame from Ireland, but died before its erection in 1879. Ferns, palms, and orchids thrived for over a century until a hurricane in 1995 largely destroyed the conservatory. San Franciscans campaigned for its repair, and it reopened in 2003.

6

de Young Museum

📍G8 🏠50 Tea Garden Drive, Golden Gate Park 🚌5, 21, 44 🕐9:30am-5:15pm Tue-Sun (Apr-Nov: to 8:45pm Fri) 🌐de young.famsf.org

The de Young is a fine arts museum founded in 1895. In 1989 the original building was too damaged by an

earthquake to be saved. The collection is now housed in a state-of-the-art facility with a copper exterior designed by Herzog & de Meuron. The museum contains a broad range of American art from the 17th to the 21st centuries. With pieces by Native Americans, early immigrants, and enslaved Africans, the collection offers a look at the diversity of American experiences and cultures. Alongside displays of American origin are exhibits from the Department of Africa, Oceania, and the Americas, which owes its collection mainly to donations. These have developed into a broad and fascinating selection of exhibits from cultures around the world, and one of the most impressive textile and costume collections in the US.

← Sculpture of Diana at the de Young Museum

❼ Shakespeare Garden

📍 G9 🎵 Music Concourse, Golden Gate Park 🚌 44

Gardeners here have tried to cultivate all 200 flowers and plants mentioned in Shakespeare's works. The quotations are inscribed on plaques set in the wall at the back of the garden.

❽ Japanese Tea Garden

📍 G9 🎵 Music Concourse, Golden Gate Park 🚌 5, 38, 44 🕐 Mar–Oct: 9am–5:30pm daily; Nov–Feb: 9am–4:45pm daily 🌐 japanese teagardensf.com

Established by George Turner Marsh for the 1894 California Midwinter Fair, this garden was later tended by Japanese gardener Makota Hagiwara. He and his family maintained and expanded the garden until World War II, when, like many other Japanese Americans, they were interned. A plaque by Ruth Asawa now commemorates their work.

The best time to visit is when the cherry trees blossom in April. Don't miss the delicious matcha tea and fortune cookies that are served in the Teahouse.

⑨ Queen Wilhelmina Tulip Garden

📍A9 🚌5, 18 📮1690 John F. Kennedy Dr, Golden Gate Park

This garden was named after the Dutch Queen Wilhelmina, and hundreds of tulip bulbs are donated each year by the Dutch Bulb Growers' Association. In the spring, the area is carpeted with the flowers in full bloom. The Dutch Windmill, near the northwest corner of Golden Gate Park, was built in 1903. Its purpose, along with its companion, the Murphy Windmill, erected in the park's southwest corner in 1905, was to pump water from a source underground, in order to irrigate the park. The increasing volume of water required – about 5 million gallons, or 230 million liters per day – soon made the windmills obsolete, and they are no longer in use.

> Recognizable by their short horns and humped backs, buffaloes are the symbol of the American plains, and are more properly known as the American bison.

⑩ The Beach Chalet

📍A9 📮1000 Great Hwy, Golden Gate Park 🚌5, 5R, 31, 31AX, 38 🕐Times vary, check website 🌐beachchalet.com

Where Golden Gate Park meets the ocean, you'll find this charming historic building, which is home to a brewery, restaurants, and dining terrace. Architect Willis Polk designed the chalet in 1925, while other artisans have added their own touches over the years, creating a distinctly "only-in-San Francisco" establishment. Elaborate murals by artist Lucien Labaudt, commissioned by the Works Progress Administration in 1936, depict famous places and people in San Francisco. Intricate wood carvings by Michael von Meyer show seaside imagery such as mermaids, octopuses, and old ships, underscoring the sweeping views of the Pacific Ocean right outside the Beach Chalet windows.

⑪ Bison Paddock

📍C9 📮John F. Kennedy Dr, Golden Gate Park 🚌5, 29

The shaggy buffalo grazing in this paddock are the largest of all North American land animals. Recognizable by their short horns and humped backs, buffaloes are the symbol of the American plains, and are more properly known as the American bison. This paddock was opened in 1892, with the aim of protecting the species, then on the verge of extinction. The first herd, brought in from Wyoming, sadly all died of a tuberculosis epidemic and had to be replaced. Today there are some 100 or so bison.

⑫ Stow Lake

📍F9 📮Stow Lake Dr, Golden Gate Park 🚌28, 29, 44

This artificial lake was created around Strawberry Hill, whose summit now forms an island linked to the mainland by two stone-clad bridges. It is a popular spot for boating, picnicking, and birding. Stow Lake's circular stream makes an ideal course for rowing laps from the boathouse, although

↑ Glorious flower beds and the Dutch Windmill in the Queen Wilhelmina Tulip Garden

↑ Rowboats on tree-lined Stow Lake, one of Golden Gate Park's main attractions

the tranquil atmosphere makes leisurely drifting seem more appropriate. Bird-watchers can enjoy spotting great blue herons and buffleheads. A red-and-green Chinese pavilion, beautifully decorated with carvings, sits on the lake's northwestern shore.

In 1894, the railroad baron Collis Porter Huntington donated the money to create the waterfall that cascades into Stow Lake. Known as Huntington Falls, this is now one of the park's most attractive features.

⑬
Land's End

📍B6 🚌1, 1AX, 18, 38

A rugged seascape of rock, cliff, and matted cypress woods, Land's End is reached on foot via the Coastal Trail, which can be accessed by stairs from the Legion of Honor, or from a parking area at Point Lobos. The trail ends at a spectacular viewing point overlooking the Golden Gate Bridge (p384). It is inadvisable to leave the Coastal Trail, as there is a risk of being stranded by incoming

 HIDDEN GEM
Sutro Baths

Developed in Lands End in 1890 by former mayor Adolph Sutro, the baths housed the largest indoor pools in the US. Today all that remains of the Sutro Baths are atmospheric ruins in a wild and rocky setting

tides; call the National Park Service for tide information (415 561-4700).

⑭
Letterman Digital Arts Center

📍J4 🏠Chestnut St and Lyon St 🚌28, 43 🕘9am–5pm Mon–Fri 🌐presidio.gov/places/letterman-digital-arts-center

A pilgrimage spot for *Star Wars* fans, the Letterman Digital Arts Center was

founded by filmmaker George Lucas and the Presidio Trust in 2005 to house Industrial Light and Magic, Lucasfilm Ltd., and other visual effects companies. The sprawling campus includes four buildings, beautiful grounds created by landscape designer Lawrence Halpin, a natural lagoon, and photo-worthy views of the Golden Gate Bridge and the Palace of Fine Arts. Another draw is the life-size statue of Yoda, the popular *Star Wars* character. Take a peek in the lobby to see more life-size figures of Darth Vader and Boba Fett, as well as other movie memorabilia such as props and costumes.

→ The statue of Yoda, in the grounds of the Letterman Digital Arts Center

↑ The spectacular interior and *(inset)* golden domes of the Holy Virgin Cathedral

15

Holy Virgin Cathedral

📍 D7 🏠 6210 Geary Blvd 🚌 2, 29, 38 🕐 9:30–11:30am Tue & Wed 🌐 sfsobor.com

Gold onion-shaped domes crown the Russian Orthodox Holy Virgin Cathedral of the Russian Church in Exile in the suburban Richmond District. Built in the early 1960s, it is generally only open to the public during services.

The cathedral and the many Russian-owned businesses surrounding it, such as the lively Russian Renaissance restaurant, are situated at the heart of San Francisco's extensive Russian community. This reached its highest population when immigrants arrived after the Russian Revolution of 1917.

16

The Presidio

📍 H5 ℹ️ 210 Lincoln Blvd, on the Main Post; www. presidio.gov 🕐 10am–5pm daily

A national park and former military fort, the Presidio has been occupied longer than any other part of the city. Remnants of its military past, including barracks, are all around. There are also 24 miles (39 km) of hiking trails, cycle paths, and beaches, as well as three installations by British artist Andy Goldsworthy. The free PresidiGo bus stops at over 40 destinations in the park. Get your bearings at the William Penn Mott, Jr. Presidio Visitor Center, where you can also find out about ranger walks, live music, and family activities.

The Presidio Officers' Club (50 Moraga Ave) overlooks the parade grounds and the 19th-century barracks. Built in Spanish Mission style in the 1930s, it incorporates the adobe remains of the original 18th-century Spanish fort and hosts events and exhibits on California history.

A HISTORY OF THE PRESIDIO

In 1776 José Joaquín Moraga, one of the first Spanish settlers, founded a military camp of adobe buildings on the edge of San Francisco Bay to defend the Mission Dolores *(p368)*. Following Mexican independence from Spain, the site remained the northernmost fort of the short-lived republic until the United States took it over in 1847. The Presidio was used for military purposes until 1994.

From the 1850s to the 1930s, the adobe buildings were replaced, first with wooden barracks, then with concrete Mission- and Georgian-style cottages for the officers and their families. These buildings remain.

about the man himself. This museum, founded by his daughter Diane Disney Miller, explores the remarkable life and times of Walt Disney through photographs, documents, animation art, and fun interactive exhibits. The museum also hosts regular art and animation workshops, daily classic Disney film screenings, talks, and other events.

 18

Fort Point and Crissy Field

📍F2 & H3 🏠Marine Dr
🕐10am-5pm Thu-Tue
(winter: Fri-Sun only)
🌐nps.gov/fopo

Completed by the US Army in 1861, this fort was built partly to protect San Francisco Bay from any attack and partly to defend ships carrying gold from the Californian mines. The most prominent of the many fortifications on the coast, it is a classic example of a pre-Civil War brick fortress. The building soon became obsolete, as its 10-ft- (3-m-) thick brick walls would not stand up to powerful modern weaponry. It was closed in 1900, never having come under attack.

The brickwork vaulting is unusual for San Francisco, and may have saved the fort in the 1906 earthquake. It was nearly demolished in the 1930s to make way for the Golden Gate Bridge, but it survived and is now a good place from which to view the bridge. National Park Service rangers in Civil War costume conduct guided tours.

A tidal marsh once covered the area known as Crissy Field. After two centuries of military use, the Field was transformed into a waterfront park. At the Military Service Historic Learning Center (open on weekends), visitors can learn about the US Army's secret program of recruiting

 17

The Walt Disney Family Museum

📍H4 🏠104 Montgomery St 🚌28L, 43 🕐10am-6pm Wed-Mon 🚫Jan 1, Thanksgiving, Dec 25
🌐waltdisney.org

Walt Disney (1901–66) is most famous for entertaining the world with the characters he created, from Mickey Mouse to Goofy, but less is known

↑ Looking at Mickey Mouse memorabilia at The Walt Disney Family Museum

EAT

Louis'
Louis' offers stellar views of the wild coastline as you dine on classic American fare. It doesn't take reservations, but it's worth trying your luck as a walk-in.

📍F7 🏠902 Point Lobos Av 🌐louissf.com

💲💲💲

Beach Chalet Brewery and Restaurant
Crab cake Benedict, seafood, and steaks are served at this spot at the western edge of Golden Gate Park.

📍A9 🏠1000 Great Hwy 🌐beachchalet.com

💲💲💲

Warming Hut Park Store and Café
Fuel long walks in the Presidio with filled ciabattas and cinnamon rolls.

📍F2 🏠983 Marine Dr 🌐parksconservancy. org/services/warming hut-park-store-cafe

💲💲💲

Japanese American soldiers and training them in Japanese military language.

Just west of Crissy Field, the beachfront Greater Farallones National Marine Sanctuary Visitor Center (open Wed–Sun) has a small aquarium and information on local ecosystems. A few minutes' walk east, the Crissy Field Center offers a rich array of programs, including many geared toward kids, such as wildlife treks and kite-flying.

A SHORT WALK
GOLDEN GATE PARK

Distance 0.5 mile (1 km) **Time** 10 minutes
Nearest buses 5, 44

Golden Gate Park is one of the largest urban parks in the world. It stretches from the Pacific Ocean to the center of San Francisco, forming an oasis of greenery and calm where locals go to escape from the bustle of city life. There are a range of enticing activities, both sporting and cultural, available in the park. The lush landscaped area around the Music Concourse, with its ornate fountains, plane trees, and benches, is the most popular and developed section. Here you can enjoy free Sunday concerts at the Spreckels Temple of Music. Two museums stand on either side of the Concourse, and the beautiful Japanese and Shakespeare gardens are easily within walking distance.

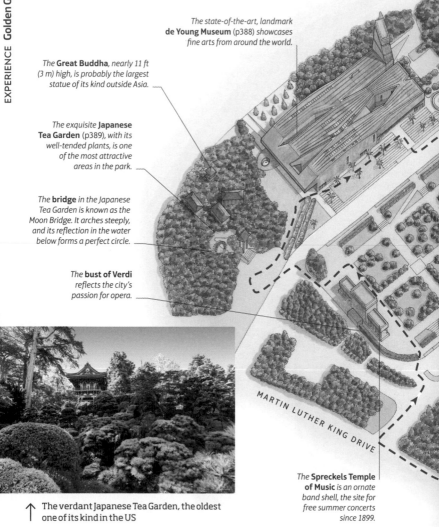

The state-of-the-art, landmark **de Young Museum** (p388) *showcases fine arts from around the world.*

The **Great Buddha**, *nearly 11 ft (3 m) high, is probably the largest statue of its kind outside Asia.*

The exquisite **Japanese Tea Garden** (p389), *with its well-tended plants, is one of the most attractive areas in the park.*

The **bridge** *in the Japanese Tea Garden is known as the Moon Bridge. It arches steeply, and its reflection in the water below forms a perfect circle.*

The **bust of Verdi** *reflects the city's passion for opera.*

MARTIN LUTHER KING DRIVE

The **Spreckels Temple of Music** *is an ornate band shell, the site for free summer concerts since 1899.*

↑ The verdant Japanese Tea Garden, the oldest one of its kind in the US

← The stunning Spreckels Temple of Music band shell

GOLDEN GATE PARK AND THE PRESIDIO

Golden Gate Park

Locator Map
For more detail see p378

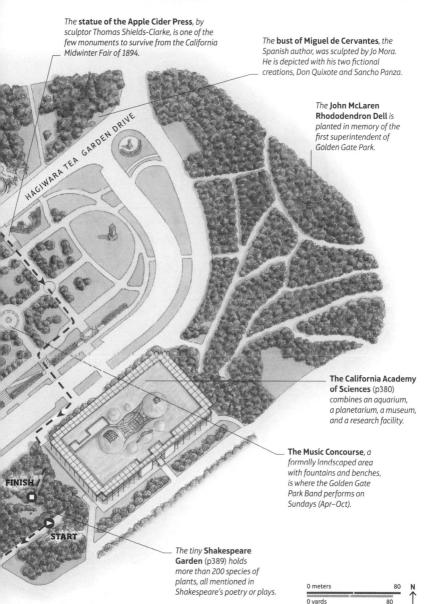

The **statue of the Apple Cider Press**, by sculptor Thomas Shields-Clarke, is one of the few monuments to survive from the California Midwinter Fair of 1894.

The **bust of Miguel de Cervantes**, the Spanish author, was sculpted by Jo Mora. He is depicted with his two fictional creations, Don Quixote and Sancho Panza.

The **John McLaren Rhododendron Dell** is planted in memory of the first superintendent of Golden Gate Park.

HAGIWARA TEA GARDEN DRIVE

The **California Academy of Sciences** (p380) combines an aquarium, a planetarium, a museum, and a research facility.

The **Music Concourse**, a formally landscaped area with fountains and benches, is where the Golden Gate Park Band performs on Sundays (Apr–Oct).

FINISH

START

The tiny **Shakespeare Garden** (p389) holds more than 200 species of plants, all mentioned in Shakespeare's poetry or plays.

| 0 meters | 80 |
| 0 yards | 80 |

N ↑

THE BAY AREA

San Francisco is the smallest of the nine counties that encircle San Francisco Bay. To the north of Golden Gate Bridge, the wild, windswept coastline and redwood forests of Marin County were once home to the Miwok people. Oakland, meanwhile, in the East Bay, is highly developed. Constructed in 1868, Oakland Long Wharf became the genesis of today's massive Port of Oakland, and the city flourished as a major shipping and transportation hub. Manufacturing also boomed from the 1920s, attracting thousands of African Americans from the South. Huey Newton and Bobby Seale founded the Black Panther Party here in 1966, but Oakland went into decline in the 1970s. Since then the city has seen much regeneration, though gentrification remains a controversial issue. Neighboring Berkeley is most associated with its iconic University of California campus, established here in 1868.

The Peninsula area to the south of San Francisco is home to Silicon Valley, which began with Hewlett and Packard's efforts in 1938 around Stanford University. Everything from Intel's silicon transistors in the 1960s to 21st-century internet giants Google and Facebook has started here. Farther south, San Jose was founded by the Spanish in 1777. The city was a largely agricultural hub until World War II, but it has since seen phenomenal growth, and its population surpassed San Francisco's in the 1990s.

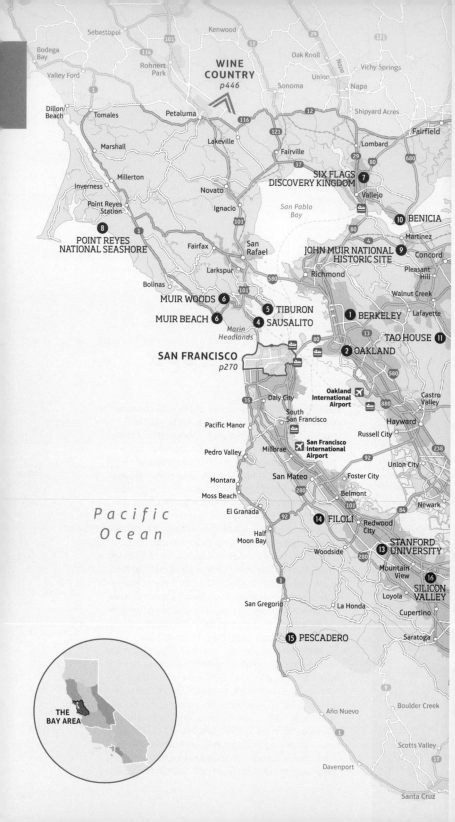

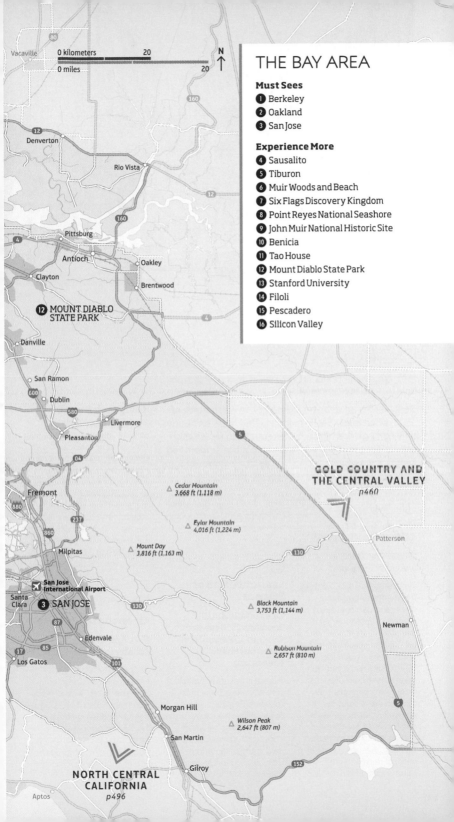

THE BAY AREA

Must Sees
1 Berkeley
2 Oakland
3 San Jose

Experience More
4 Sausalito
5 Tiburon
6 Muir Woods and Beach
7 Six Flags Discovery Kingdom
8 Point Reyes National Seashore
9 John Muir National Historic Site
10 Benicia
11 Tao House
12 Mount Diablo State Park
13 Stanford University
14 Filoli
15 Pescadero
16 Silicon Valley

Shops and cafés on
Telegraph Avenue,
popular with students

❶

BERKELEY

🅰F1 **✈Oakland, 12 miles (19 km) SW of Berkeley** **🚌2160
Shattuck Av** **ℹ2015 Center St; www.visitberkeley.com**

Berkeley began to boom following the earthquake of
1906, when many San Franciscans fled here. Its famous
university gained a worldwide reputation for political
activism in the 1960s with the birth of the student-led
Free Speech Movement. Today the city is famous for its
arts venues, bookstores, and liberal politics.

①

University of
California, Berkeley

**🏛2227 Piedmont Av;
www.berkeley.edu**

The reputation of UC Berkeley
for countercultural move-
ments sometimes eclipses its
academic reputation, yet it is
one of the largest and most
prestigious universities in the
world. Since its founding in
1868, Berkeley has numbered
at least ten Nobel laureates
among its professors. The
campus was laid out by the
pioneering landscape architect Frederick Law Olmsted.
The university has more than
30,000 students and a wide
range of museums and
cultural amenities. The Koret

Visitor Center has information
and maps and organizes free
walking tours.

②

Lawrence Hall of
Science

**🏛Centennial Dr, UC
Berkeley** **🕐10am–5pm
Tue–Sun** **🚫Federal hols
🌐lawrencehallof
science.org**

Science is fun at this public
center, located in the hills
above UC Berkeley. Hands-
on exhibits encourage visitors
to manipulate a hologram,
track earthquakes, or plot
stars in the planetarium.
There is also a program of
changing exhibitions. At night,

the view of the lights around
the northern Bay Area from
the hall's large plaza is an
extraordinary sight.

③

Telegraph Avenue

Berkeley's most fascinating
street is Telegraph Avenue,
especially the blocks between
Dwight Way and the university.
It has a plethora of coffee
houses and low-cost eateries,
as well as clothing boutiques.
The district was the center of
student protests against the
Vietnam War in the 1960s. It
still swarms with students
from dawn to dark, along with
street vendors and musicians.

④

Claremont Club & Spa

**🏛41 Tunnel Rd
🌐claremontresort.com**

The Berkeley hills form a backdrop to this half-timbered
fairy-tale castle. The enormous
Claremont Hotel construction
began in 1906 and ended in
1915. In the early years the
hotel failed to prosper, partly
due to a law that forbade the
sale of alcohol within a 1-mile
(1.5-km) radius of the UC

Berkeley campus. In 1937 an enterprising student actually measured the distance and discovered that the radius line passed through the *center* of the building. The Terrace Bar was opened beyond the line, in the same corner of the hotel that it occupies today.

⑤
University of California Botanical Garden

🏛 200 Centennial Dr, Berkeley Hills ⏰ 9am-5pm daily 🚫 Federal hols 🌐 botanicalgarden.berkeley.edu

More than 12,000 species from all over the world thrive in the Mediterranean-style climate of Berkeley's Strawberry Canyon. Although primarily used for research, the collections can be visited by the public and are arranged in thematic gardens linked by paths. Of particular note are the Asian,

African, South American, European, and California sections. The Chinese medicinal herb garden, the orchid houses, the cactus garden, and the carnivorous plants are also well worth a visit.

---

⑥
Magnes Collection of Jewish Art and Life

🏛 2121 Aliston Way ⏰ Mid-Sep-mid-Dec & Feb-May: 11am-4pm Tue-Fri 🚫 Jewish and Federal hols 🌐 magnes.berkeley.edu

Located in a sleek terra-cotta-colored building, the Magnes Collection has been safeguarding the evidence of Jewish lives around the world since 1962. Comprised of nearly 15,000 items dating back to 440 BC, the collection is a testimony to the contributions made by Jewish communities to world cultures. Ritual objects, ethnographic materials, fine art, and historical documents

Must See

SHOP

Moe's Books
Founded in 1959 by creative bookseller Moe Moskowitz, Moe's has rare books on fine arts, photography, and architecture.

🏛 2476 Telegraph Av 🌐 moesbooks.com

Pegasus Books
Books are beautifully displayed at this large independent bookseller.

🏛 1855 Solano Av 🌐 pegasusbook store.com

serve as powerful witnesses that connect generations to a shared history and sense of peoplehood. Exhibitions change regularly.

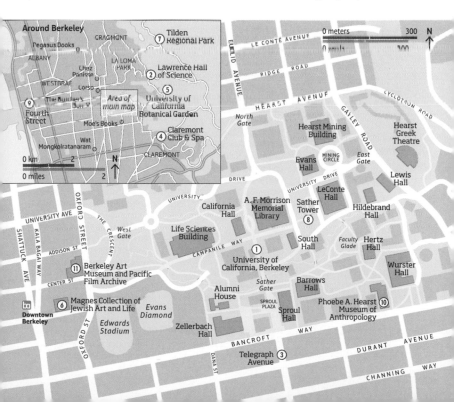

EAT

Wat Mongkolratanaram

The monks prepare brunch at this working temple. Swap cash for plastic coins (monks don't handle money) then grab some delicious green curry, pad thai, or coconut griddle cakes.

 1911 Russell St
 Sun only

$$$

The Butcher's Son

All-vegan American comfort food is served here. Tofu forms the basis of the "steak and eggs." Fried mozzarella burgers are made from plant-based ingredients, as are the cannoli and cheesecake.

1954 University Ave
thebutchers veganson.com

$$$

Chez Panisse

Founded in 1971, Chez Panisse is an epicenter of locally sourced, sustainable California cuisine where the menu moves with the seasons.

1517 Shattuck Av
chezpanisse.com

$$$

Corso

Craft cocktails and an entirely Italian wine list complement the Tuscan dishes prepared at Corso. Ingredients are authentically Italian.

1788 Shattuck Av
corsoberkeley.com

$$$

Sather Tower soaring above the fall foliage on the Berkeley campus ↑

 ⑦

Tilden Regional Park

Wildcat Canyon Rd & Grizzly Peak Blvd
ebparks.org/parks/tilden

Though preserved for the most part in a natural wild condition, Tilden Park offers a variety of attractions. It is noted for the enchanting **Botanical Garden**, specializing in native plants, including some rare and endangered species. Visitors can stroll from alpine meadows to desert cactus gardens by way of a redwood glen, or join a guided nature walk. Kids will enjoy the antique **Herschell–Spillman Merry-Go-Round** and the **Redwood Valley Railway**, which offers a peaceful ride on a model steam train.

Botanical Garden

8:30am–5pm daily

Herschell-Spillman Merry-Go-Round

11am–5pm Fri–Sun (daily in summer)

Redwood Valley Railway

11am–5pm Sat & Sun (daily in summer)

 ⑧

Sather Tower

Carillon Rd ⏱ 10am–3:45pm Mon–Fri, 10am–4:45pm Sat, 10am–1:30pm & 3–4:45pm Sun ⊕ visit.berkeley.edu

Rising 307 ft (94 m) above the UC Berkeley campus, and visible from miles around, the Beaux-Arts Sather Tower is the world's third-tallest university bell-and-clock tower after Moscow State University, Russia, and the University of Birmingham, UK. Surrounded by London plane trees, the "Campanile" (as locals call it) is UC Berkeley's most postcard-perfect sight, drawing worthy comparisons to Venice's own Campanile di San Marco ever since it opened to the public in 1916. The tower is named after philanthropist Jane K. Sather (1824–1911), one of the university's most influential benefactors. An elevator will whisk you up to the tower's observation deck, where you can enjoy panoramic views of the Bay Area. Listen out for the carillon of 61 bells, which rings out three times daily during spring and fall.

Fourth Street

📍 1834 4th St; www.fourthstreet.com

This gentrified enclave north of University Avenue is lined with fine art galleries and design stores. Here you can pick up sleek contemporary furniture, sustainable fashion, plant-based skincare products, and designer garden tools. The street comes alive on weekends, when families, hipsters, and bargain-hunters come looking to find that special something. There are also plenty of cafés and restaurants with outdoor seating.

Did You Know?

The California concept of cooking with fresh, local foods was born in Berkeley.

Phoebe A. Hearst Museum of Anthropology

🏛 102 Kroeber Hall
🕐 11am–5pm Wed, Fri & Sun, 11am–8pm Thu, 10am–6pm Sat 🌐 hearstmuseum.berkeley.edu

More than 3.8 million objects from across continents and historical periods are amassed at this trove in UC Berkeley. The largest collection is North American, including 8,000 California Native American baskets. There are also rare sculptures and metalwork from the African continent plus thousands of ancient Egyptian artifacts spanning four millennia of history. The original collections of the museum, which was founded in 1901, were assembled by philanthropist and suffragist Phoebe Elizabeth Apperson Hearst; the museum was renamed after her in 1991.

Berkeley Art Museum and Pacific Film Archive (BAMPFA)

🏛 2155 Center St
🕐 11am–7pm Wed–Sun
🌐 bampfa.org

Some 23,000 pieces of art and 17,500 films and videos comprise the dizzying, multicultural collections at this leading visual arts center. More than 20 exhibitions are held each year, including eclectic sculpture, photography, and graphic art, along with hundreds of film screenings. The museum is housed in a shimmering steel structure whose north-facing galleries are flooded in natural light during the day.

The glistening steel exterior of the Berkeley Art Museum and Pacific Film Archive ↑

②
OAKLAND

🅰 F1 ✈ 5 miles (8 km) SW of Oakland 🚉 1245 Broadway St
ℹ 475 14th St; visitoakland.org

Once a small, working-class suburb, Oakland grew when it became the West Coast terminus of the transcontinental railroad. Many of the African American railroad workers settled here, followed by a Hispanic population, giving the city a multicultural atmosphere. Oakland's literary associations, including Jack London and Gertrude Stein, have made it a cultural center.

①
Lake Merritt

Lake Merritt and its surrounding park form an oasis of rich blue and green in the urban heart of Oakland. Boats can be rented from the west and north shores, and joggers and cyclists can circle the lake on a 3-mile (5-km) path. The north shore has flower gardens, an aviary, and kids' puppet shows.

Jack London Square

Author Jack London (1876–1916) grew up in Oakland in the 1880s and was a frequent visitor to the Oakland waterfront. Today the area is a bright promenade of shops, hotels, restaurants, and boats. London's footsteps can be traced to the First and Last Chance Saloon and the Yukon cabin, occupied by him in 1898.

African American Museum and Library

🏛 659 14th St 🕐 Noon–5:30pm Tue-Sat 🌐 oakland library.org

The history and culture of African Americans in Northern California and the Bay Area

THE BLACK PANTHER PARTY

Founded in Oakland in 1966 by students Huey P. Newton and Bobby Seale, the Black Panther Party was a left-wing revolutionary political organization that fought for social and economic equality for Black Americans and for their protection against police brutality. Their influence soon spread to other major cities in the US and the rest of the world. The group declined after internal schisms and it disbanded in 1982.

are thoughtfully conserved at this museum and library. Changing exhibitions are hosted in the second-floor museum. The huge reference library, a significant resource on African American experiences, has an invaluable collection of more than 12,000 volumes by or about African Americans, including Martin Luther King, Jr., Malcolm X, the Black Panther Party, religion, and California history.

Lake Merritt overlooked by the skyscrapers of downtown Oakland ↑

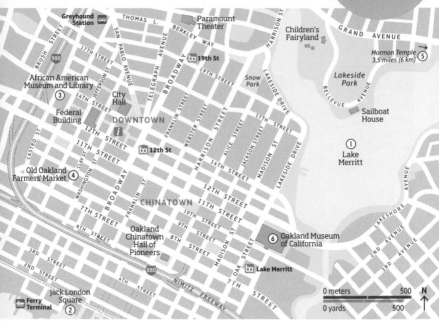

④
Old Oakland Farmers' Market

🅐 Clay St & 9th St **🕓 8am–2pm Fri** **🅦 uvfm.org/old-oakland-fridays**

The Old Oakland Farmers' Market is located in what is known as Victorian Row – two blocks built between the 1860s and 1880s and renovated in the 1980s. Stalls sell super-fresh produce, including fruit and vegetables, eggs, cheeses, baked goods, locally caught fish, and flowers, as well as tasty street foods. There are also local handicrafts.

⑤
Mormon Temple

🅐 4770 Lincoln Av **🚇 Fruitvale, then AC Transit 46 bus** **🅦 churchofjesuschrist.org**

Designed in 1963 and built on a hilltop, the Oakland Temple of the Church of Jesus Christ of Latter Day Saints is Northern California's only Mormon temple. Floodlit at night, it is sometimes referred to as "the beacon on the hill" as it can be seen from all over Oakland and from San Francisco. The central ziggurat is surrounded by four towers, clad with white granite and capped by golden pyramids.

From the temple there are magnificent views over the entire Bay Area.

⑥
Oakland Museum of California

🅐 Oak & 10th sts **🕓 11am–5pm Wed & Thu, 11am–9pm Fri, 11am–5pm Sat & Sun** **🅦 museumca.org**

This interdisciplinary museum, dedicated to documenting California's art, history, and natural sciences, first opened in 1960 and has since undergone several massive renovations and expansions.

The art collection consists of more than 70,000 pieces by local artists and designers, the history section includes an impressive array of Native California crafts, and the Natural Sciences exhibits emphasize the state's huge biodiversity. Visitors can also enjoy interactive and digital features depicting the many people and stories of California.

↑ Contemporary art on show at the Oakland Museum of California

3

SAN JOSE

G3 150 W San Carlos St; sanjose.org San Jose International Airport, 2 miles (3 km) NW of San Jose 65 Cahill St 70 Almeden St

San Jose was founded in 1777 and has grown to become the state's third-largest city. Now the commercial and cultural center of the South Bay and civic heart of the Silicon Valley region (p415), San Jose is a bustling and modern city that has preserved its historic buildings.

1

Mission Santa Clara de Asis

500 El Camino Real
Daily scu.edu

On the campus of the Jesuit University of Santa Clara, 5 miles (8 km) northwest

INSIDER TIP
Cosplay Days

Over Memorial Day weekend, visitors to downtown San Jose will likely find the streets filled with robots and superheroes, thanks to FanimeCon, one of the country's largest anime and comics conventions.

of downtown San Jose, this grand mission is a modern replica of the adobe original, first built in 1777. Relics include bells donated by the Spanish monarchy. There are carefully tended gardens adjacent to the church.

2

De Saisset Museum at Santa Clara University

500 El Camino Real
11am–4pm Tue–Sun
scu.edu/desaisset

Next to the Santa Clara Mission, this museum exhibits artifacts from the 18th-century mission and other eras of California history, along with a collection of paintings and photographs.

3

Rosicrucian Egyptian Museum and Planetarium

Naglee Av & Park Av
9am–5pm Wed–Fri, 10am–6pm Sat & Sun
Jan 1, Easter Sun, Thanksgiving, Dec 25
egyptianmuseum.org

This large museum displays the most extensive collection of ancient Egyptian artifacts west of the Mississippi. Housed in a complex of Egyptian- and Moorish-style buildings, each gallery represents a different aspect of Egyptian culture.

4

Peralta Adobe

175 W St. John St (408) 287-2290 8am–5pm Mon–Fri Federal hols

One block to the west of Market Street is San Jose's oldest surviving building, the Peralta Adobe. Built in 1797, by Apache Manuel González, it is the sole remnant of the Spanish pueblo. Inside, the rooms have been furnished to show how they might have looked in González's time.

←

Downtown San Jose, encircled by mountains of the Santa Clara county

(5)

San Jose Museum of Art

📍110 S Market St ⏰11am–5pm Tue–Sun 🚫Jan 1, Thanksgiving, Dec 25 🌐sjmusart.org

This small but daring modern and contemporary art museum is known for some of the Bay Area's most interesting and popular exhibits of West Coast art.

(6)

The Tech Interactive

📍201 S Market St ⏰10am–5pm daily 🌐thetech.org

Located in the heart of San Jose, this fascinating science and technology center has its eyes set on the future. Hands-on exhibits and activities for all age groups encourage visitors to discover how various technologies work. The on-site IMAX Dome Theater shows educational and mainstream movies.

(7)

History San Jose

📍1650 Senter Rd ⏰Noon–5pm Tue–Sun 🚫Jan 1, Jul 4, Thanksgiving, Dec 25 🌐historysanjose.org

A number of historic structures have been reassembled to form this indoor/outdoor museum that relates the history of San Jose. The 19th-century Pasetta House has a permanent collection of paintings by Santa Clara Valley artists, and the 1880 Pacific Hotel hosts changing art exhibitions on subjects like Fifty Years of Queer Resistance and Resilience in Silicon Valley. Other key buildings include a doctor's office and print shop from the late 1800s and a 1920s gas station.

(8)

California's Great America

📍4701 Great America Pkwy ⏰Seasonal, check website 🌐cagreatamerica.com

The best amusement park in Northern California packs in a wide variety of attractions. The park is divided into several areas,

EAT

Original Joe's

This is a bastion in San Jose's rapidly changing downtown, defined by its gracious welcomes and Italian home cooking.

📍301 S 1st St 🌐sanjose originaljoes.com

$$⑤

Paper Plane

Truly original cocktails accompany the food at this chic, brick-walled bar-restaurant.

📍72 S 1st St 🌐paperplanesj.com

$$$

each designed to evoke various regions of the United States. These include Orleans Place, Yankee Harbor, and the Yukon Territory. Along with high-speed roller coasters, many rides incorporate themes from films and TV shows, such as *Top Gun* and *Star Trek*.

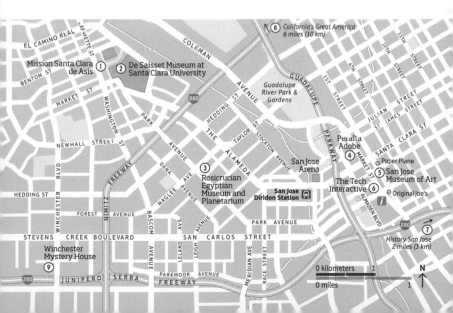

⑨ 🗡 🎿 🖥 🎒

WINCHESTER MYSTERY HOUSE

🏠 525 S Winchester Blvd 🚌 25, 60, 85 🕐 9am–5pm daily (end Apr–mid-Jun: 9am–5pm Sun–Thu, 9am–7pm Fri & Sat) 🚫 Dec 25
🌐 winchestermysteryhouse.com

With no blueprints and seemingly no plan, Sarah Winchester's new San Jose home steadily grew from an unfinished eight-room farmhouse into a sprawling architectural wonder that continues to baffle and amaze – a secret attic was discovered as recently as 2016.

Winchester Mystery House is a mansion with a remarkable history. Sarah Winchester, heiress of the Winchester Rifle fortune, moved from Connecticut to San Jose in 1884 and bought a small farmhouse. Convinced by a medium that its expansion would exorcise the spirits of those killed by the rifle that made her rich, she kept builders laboring on the house 24 hours a day,

7 days a week, for 38 years, until her death in 1922. The result is a bizarre complex of 160 rooms, with stairs that lead nowhere, doors that open onto walls, and windows set into floors. The house has been refurbished with authentic 19th-century furniture, while the immaculate Victorian gardens include several fine statues and fountains.

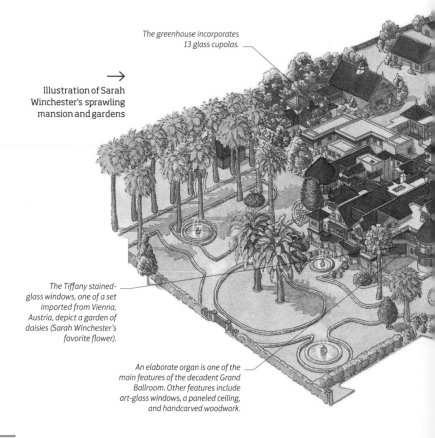

The greenhouse incorporates 13 glass cupolas.

→ Illustration of Sarah Winchester's sprawling mansion and gardens

The Tiffany stained-glass windows, one of a set imported from Vienna, Austria, depict a garden of daisies (Sarah Winchester's favorite flower).

An elaborate organ is one of the main features of the decadent Grand Ballroom. Other features include art-glass windows, a paneled ceiling, and handcarved woodwork.

↑ Cupid's fountain in the Victorian gardens
of the Winchester mansion

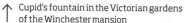

Each of the 44 steps on the Switchback Staircase is only 1.5 inches (3.8 cm) high, and the staircase rises only 9 ft (2.7 m). It is thought they were built in this way to ease Sarah Winchester's arthritis.

Tour entrance

The Winchester Firearms Museum features an extensive display including the Henry Repeating Rifle and the Model 1873, which came to be known as "The Gun that Won the West."

A stairway leading directly up into the ceiling is just one of the many inexplicable oddities within the house.

The Winchester Antique Products Museum contains items such as roller skates, electric irons, and lawn mowers.

This plush room was Sarah Winchester's bedroom. At night she would play the harmonium that is today situated opposite the ornately carved bed.

10,000

The estimated number of windowpanes in the Winchester estate.

A yacht sailing past the colorful houses and leafy hills of Sausalito →

EXPERIENCE MORE

④ Sausalito

 F1 🚌🚈 **ℹ 780 Bridgeway Ave; www.sausalito.org**

In this small town that was once a fishing community, Victorian bungalows cling to steep hills rising from San Francisco Bay. Parallel to the waterfront, Bridgeway Avenue serves as a promenade for the weekend crowds.

The **US Army Corps of Engineers Bay Model Visitor Center** is well worth a look to see a working hydraulic scale model that simulates the movement of the tides and currents in San Francisco Bay, and in the bay-delta system.

US Army Corps of Engineers Model Visitor Center

📍 2100 Bridgeway Av
🕐 9am–4pm Tue–Sat (Jun–Aug: 10am–5pm Sat) 🚫 Federal hols
🌐 spn.usace.army.mil

⑤ Tiburon

F1 🚌🚈 **ℹ 96B Main St; www.townoftiburon.org**

The main street of this elegant waterfront town is lined with fashionable shops and restaurants, some housed in "arks." These unique buildings are in fact houseboats from the early 20th century that have been pulled ashore and refurbished. They now stand in what is called "Ark Row." Less hectic than Sausalito, Tiburon is a good town for

> 💬 **INSIDER TIP**
> ### Angel Island
> Reached by ferry from Tiburon and San Francisco, wooded Angel Island rises to 776 ft (237 m) above sea level. No motor vehicles are allowed, so it's a great place for walking or cycling.

walking. Parks are situated along the waterfront, from which you can contemplate the bay, and are a popular spot for hikers and cyclists.

⑥ Muir Woods and Beach

E1 🏠 **1 Muir Woods Rd** 🚌 **Mill Valley ℹ Hwy 1, Mill Valley; www.nps.gov/muwo**

Nestling at the foot of Mount Tamalpais is Muir Woods National Monument, one of the few remaining stands of old-growth coastal redwoods. These tall trees (the oldest dates back at least 1,000 years) once covered the coastal area of California. The woods were named after John Muir, the 19th-century naturalist responsible for turning Yosemite into a national park (p412).

Redwood Creek bubbles out of Muir Woods and makes its way down to the ocean at

Muir Beach, a wide expanse of sand popular with beach combers and picnickers.

Muir Beach is often crowded with families and sunseekers on weekends, especially during the hot summer months, but visitors who are prepared to walk for 15 minutes or more along the sand are rewarded with peace and quiet.

Walking amid the giant redwoods in Muir Woods National Monument

---

7

Six Flags Discovery Kingdom

🅰F1 🅰1001 Fairgrounds Dr 🚌🚍 🕐Times vary, check website 🅦sixflags.com/discoverykingdom

A unique wildlife park, theme park, and oceanarium, Six Flags Discovery Kingdom attracts 1.6 million visitors every year. The park aims to educate and entertain. In the Shark Experience, visitors pass through a transparent tunnel surrounded by a tank filled with sharks and tropical fish. Similar to SeaWorld in San Diego (*p238*), Six Flags has come under criticism from animal rights groups, although it was thanked by PETA for ending elephant rides in the facility.

8

Point Reyes National Seashore

🅰B3 🅰Hwy 1 to Olema; then follow signs for Point Reyes National Seashore 🚌Golden Gate Transit buses 70 & 101 to San Rafael Center, then West Marin Stage 60 🅦nps.gov/pore

Wild and windswept, Point Reyes peninsula is a haven for wildlife, including a herd of tule elk. The peninsula is due west of the San Andreas Fault, which caused the devastating 1906 earthquake (*p283*). A displaced fence on the Earthquake Trail near Bear Valley Visitor Center shows how the Fault caused the peninsula to move a full 20 ft (6 m) north of the mainland.

At the peninsula's tip, Point Reyes Lighthouse, built in the late 19th century, may be the

---

EAT

Curled around the edge of Richardson Bay, Sausalito has plenty of options for dining with a waterfront view.

The Spinnaker
Classic seafood in a room with floor-to-ceiling glass walls.
🅰F1 🅰100 Spinnaker Dr 🅦spinnakersausalito.us

$$$⑤

The Trident
Known for its psychedelic 1960s murals and as the birthplace of the Tequila Sunrise cocktail.
🅰F1 🅰558 Bridgeway 🅦thetrident.net

$$$

Barrel House Tavern
New California cuisine in a sleek interior.
🅰660 Bridgeway 🅰F1 🅦barrelhousetavern.com

$$$

Fish.
Fresh, sustainably sourced seafood.
🅰F1 🅰350 Harbor Drive 🅦331fish.com
$$⑤

---

windiest and foggiest place on the Pacific Coast. The lighthouse is reached via a 307-step staircase from the clifftop **Lighthouse Visitor Center** – a great place to spot migrating whales.

Lighthouse Visitor Center
🅰27000 Sir Francis Drake Blvd 🕐10am–4:30pm Fri-Mon 🅦nps.gov/pore/planyourvisit/lighthouse.htm

9
John Muir National Historic Site

⚠F1 🏛4202 Alhambra Av, Martinez ⏱10am–5pm daily 🚫Jan 1, Thanksgiving, Dec 25 🌐nps.gov/jomu

Set amid the suburban neighborhood of Martinez, the John Muir National Historic Site preserves the home where the naturalist and writer lived from 1890 until his death in 1914. The 17-room Italianate house is typical of a late 19th-century, upper-middle-class dwelling, conveying little of Muir's simple tastes. Only the library, which Muir called his "scribble den," gives a real sense of who he was. The house was once surrounded by 4 sq miles (10 sq km) of orchards, in which Muir grew fruit and nuts. Only a fraction of the orchards survive today, but rangers aim to preserve the many varieties grown by Muir. In season, fruit is picked for visitors to sample.

The visitor center, in keeping with Muir's own conservation ethics, features eco-conscious design elements, such as bamboo wood flooring and a recycled-redwood front desk. The center includes exhibits on Muir that educate the public about his life and achievements in conservation. Kids can learn about the duties of a park ranger by filling in a Junior Park Ranger activity booklet, which earns them a Junior Ranger badge.

Nearby are a handful of hiking trails, which pass through fruit orchards and wildflower fields. Full moon walks are also available.

THE LIFE OF JOHN MUIR

John Muir (1838–1914) dedicated his life to preserving the USA's wild landscapes. Muir's efforts led to the formation of the National Parks Service (NPS), the government agency charged with conserving and managing historic and natural treasures. However, his legacy has been called into question by Native Americans, who looked after their ancestral lands long before white settlers took them over. Muir largely excluded the Native Americans in the transformation of their land for recreational use.

10
Benicia

⚠F1 🚌🚇 ℹBenicia Chamber of Commerce, 601 1st St; www.visitbenicia.com

Set on the north side of the Carquinez Straits, the narrow waterway through which the Sacramento and the San Joaquin rivers flow from the Sierra Nevada to San Francisco Bay, Benicia is one of California's most interesting historic towns. From February 1853 until February 1854, Benicia served as an early state capital. The Greek Revival building that once housed the government has been preserved as part of the **Benicia Capitol State Historic Park**, complete with many original fixtures and furnishings. Next door to the former capitol, the Fisher-Hanlon House, a former Gold Rush hotel, has also been restored to its original condition.

At the other end of Main Street from the capitol complex is the Benicia waterfront, where ferries shuttled to Port Costa during the 1850s. The former Benicia Arsenal, which stored army weapons from the 1850s to the 1950s, has been converted into live-work studio spaces and **Arts Benicia**, an artists' hub with exhibition space, family events, and art classes.

Benicia Capitol State Historic Park
♿ 🏛115 West G St
⏱10am–5pm Sat & Sun
🌐parks.ca.gov

Arts Benicia
🏛991 Tyler St, Suite 114
⏱Noon–5pm Wed–Sun
🌐artsbenicia.org

←
A room in the house at the John Muir National Historic Site

A serene lakeside setting, with Mount Diablo in the distance ↑

Tao House

🏛️ F1 📍Danville ⏰For tours only, 10am & 12:30pm Wed–Sun; reservation required (except on Sat) 🌐eugeneoneill.org/about-tao-house

When the American playwright Eugene O'Neill (1888–1953) won the Nobel Prize for Literature in 1936, he used the stipend to build a home for himself and his wife in the then-rural San Ramon Valley at the foot of Mount Diablo. Tao House, a hybrid of Spanish and Chinese architecture, was completed in 1937. Over the next six years O'Neill worked in this house on what is now considered to be his best work, the semi-autobiographical series of tragic plays, including *The Iceman Cometh*, *A Moon for the Misbegotten*, and *Long Day's Journey Into Night*. In 1944 O'Neill was diagnosed with Parkinson's disease and his condition steadily deteriorated. The remote location of Tao House, and the lack of local nursing staff due to World War II, forced O'Neill to leave his home. He died in a Boston hotel in 1953, leaving behind a considerable literary legacy.

The surrounding valleys have now been developed into suburbs, but Tao House and its beautiful landscaped grounds have been turned into a national historic site, operated by the National Park Service. Both have been preserved in the condition the playwright left them in.

Mount Diablo State Park

🏛️ G1 🚉🚌Walnut Creek ℹ️Walnut Creek Visitor Center; Summit Rd; www.parks.ca.gov

Rising over the inland suburbs, the 3,849-ft- (1,173-m-) high Mount Diablo dominates the East Bay region. From its summit, on a clear day, it is possible to see for more than 200 miles (320 km), from Mount Lassen (p441) and the Cascade Mountains in the north to Mount Hamilton in the south, and from the Sierra Nevada in the east to the Farallon Islands to the west. Much of the land around the summit has now been set aside as a state park, and there is a wide range of hiking trails, as well as biking and horseback riding. A twisting road takes vehicles

within 50 ft (15 m) of the mountain's summit. Once there, the Visitors' Center offers helpful information on the mountain's cultural history and its fauna and flora, including the wildflowers that cover the mountainside in spring.

DRINK

The Rellik Tavern
This downtown bar has craft beers, fine wines, and live music most nights. Comfy couches add to the relaxed, friendly vibe.

🏛️ F1 📍726 1st St, Benicia 🌐therellik tavern.com

Auburn Lounge & Wine Bar
Located in the heart of Danville, this laid-back, speakeasy-style bar offers craft cocktails and specialty wines. There's live music on weekends.

🏛️ F1 📍321 Hartz Av, Danville 🌐auburn lounge.com

13 Stanford University

⚐F2 ⏷Junípero Serra St ⏰8:30am–5pm Mon–Fri, 10am–5pm Sat & Sun ⏷University hols ℹ215 Galvez St; www.stanford.edu

Founded by the railroad tycoon Leland Stanford (*p473*) in honor of his son who died in 1885 at the age of 16, Stanford University opened in 1891. The campus occupies the former Stanford family farm, covering 13 sq miles (33 sq km) – larger than the entire downtown district of San Francisco. It was designed in a mixture of Romanesque and Mission styles by the architect Frederick Law

↑ The Romanesque-style arches of the Memorial Church, Stanford University

Olmsted, and its sandstone buildings and numerous arcades are capped by red-tiled roofs. At the heart of the university campus is the Main Quadrangle, where the Memorial Church is decorated with a gold-leaf and tile mosaic. Also on the campus, the Cantor Art Center holds a large collection of sculptures by Auguste Rodin, including the impressive *Gates of Hell*, while the Anderson Collection displays contemporary and modern American art.

STAY

Stanford Park Hotel
This hotel at the heart of California's innovation hub oozes grandeur, from the antiques in the lobby to the elegant large grounds.

⚐F1 ⏷100 El Camino Real, Menlo Park ⓦstanfordparkhotel.com

$$$

Pescadero Creak Inn
In a quiet and charming country setting, this inn in an old farmhouse is an ideal retreat for those looking to escape the busy cities of the Bay Area and head back to nature. White-sand beaches and redwood forests are nearby.

⚐F3 ⏷393 Stage Rd, Pescadero ⓦpescaderocreekinn.com

$$$

14 Filoli

⚐F2 ⏷86 Cañada Rd ⏰10am–5pm daily ⏷Federal hols ⓦfiloli.org

The Filoli estate was the home of energy companies entrepreneur William Bourn. Designed in Palladian style by Willis Polk in 1916, it encloses more than 36,000 sq ft (3,345 sq m) of living space on two fully furnished floors, with a red-brick exterior that resembles a Georgian terrace. The house is surrounded by formal gardens that provide colorful blooms all year. The estate's name, Filoli, is an acronym for the motto "Fight for a just cause, Love your fellow man, Live a good life."

---

15 Pescadero

⚐F3 ℹ235 Main St, Half Moon Bay; www.visit halfmoonbay.org

Only an hour's drive from San Francisco to the north, the town of Pescadero is a pleasant escape from the fast-paced world around it. Although it contains little more than a whitewashed

→

Pigeon Point Lighthouse, overlooking the rocky coastline near Pescadero church (the oldest in the county), a general store, a post office, and the popular Duarte's Tavern along its two main streets, the town has the charming appearance of an old movie set. The tradition of whitewashing the town's buildings dates back to the 19th century, when a cargo of white paint was rescued from a nearby shipwreck and used on the buildings.

Eight miles (12 km) south is **Pigeon Point Light Station State Historic Park**, where visitors can enjoy unspoiled scenery and expansive views. Tours of the area are at 1pm Thursday to Monday (call 650 879-2120 to reserve a place).

About 7 miles (11 km) south, families can enjoy Swanton Berry Farm's **Coastways Ranch U-Pick** for an afternoon of fruit-picking.

Pigeon Point Light Station State Historic Park
🕙🏛 🏠 210 Pigeon Point Rd
🕐 8am-sunset daily
🌐 parks.ca.gov

Coastways Ranch U-Pick
🏛 🏠 640 Hwy 1 🕐 May-Oct: 8am-5pm daily 🌐 swanton berryfarm.com

Silicon Valley
🅰 F2

In the southern part of the Bay Area, this innovation hub ballooned into a technological juggernaut from the 1970s thanks to universities and the development of silicon transistor technology. San Jose (p406), Silicon Valley's largest city, is the headquarters of Hewlett Packard, while Palo Alto is the HQ of Tesla, Inc. Most company HQs aren't open to visitors. However, you can pose by the colorful Google Android Lawn Statues illustrating versions of the Android operating system, just next to the Googleplex (Google Campus) in Mountain View, or by the thumbs-up sign at the main campus of Facebook's Menlo Park HQ.

The **Computer History Museum** offers the most comprehensive overview of tech development, from truck-sized computer processors through to state-of-the-art, self-driving cars. Nearby is **NASA Ames Research Center**, where visitors can browse

space-themed souvenirs at the excellent gift shop. In Santa Clara, you can catch a glimpse of a silicon chip factory at the **Intel Museum**.

Computer History Museum
♿ 🏠 1401 N Shoreline Blvd, Mountain View 🕐 10am-6pm daily (to 5pm Sat & Sun) 🌐 computerhistory.org

NASA Ames Research Center
🏛 🏠 Mountain View 🕐 10am-6pm Mon-Sat 🌐 nasa.gov/ames

Intel Museum
🏠 2200 Mission College Blvd, Santa Clara 📞 (408) 765-5050 🕐 9am-6pm Mon-Fri, 10am-5pm Sat (call ahead to ensure they are open)

A LONG WALK
THE MARIN HEADLANDS

Distance 2 miles (3 km) **Time** 45 minutes
Terrain Hilly; some paved roads; the Coastal
Trail is a woodland track **Nearest transport-
ation** Bus 76X to Bunker Rd & Field Rd

At its northern end, the Golden Gate Bridge is
anchored in the rolling green hills of the Marin
Headlands. This is an unspoiled wild area of
windswept ridges, sheltered valleys, and
deserted beaches, once used as a military
defense post and now part of the vast Golden
Gate National Recreation Area. This walking
route passes several vantage points that offer
spectacular views of San Francisco and the sea
and, in the fall, you might see migrating eagles
and ospreys gliding past Hawk Hill.

Barracks *house various
offices, among them the
Headlands District Office,
the Golden Gate Raptor
Observatory, and an energy
and resources center.*

Barracks

MITCHELL   ROAD

*Wooden
footbridge*

Rodeo
Beach

COASTAL

Locator Map
For more detail see map on p398

The Marin
Headlands

SAN
FRANCISCO

*From the beach, turn inland
again as you approach the
tip of the lagoon, crossing a
wooden footbridge.*

*A 15-minute walk from the
visitor center parking area
will bring you to the sandy
Rodeo Beach. Fishing boats
may be seen bobbing out
at sea, but the beach is
mostly empty of people.*

South
Rodeo
Beach

*From Rodeo Beach
there is a fine view
of **Bird Island** lying
to the south.*

Bird
Island

0 meters   300   N
0 yards   300   ↑

←
Rodeo Lagoon
at dusk, bordered by
windswept hillsides

The **Marine Mammal Center** is run by volunteers who rescue and care for sick or injured sea lions and seals. After being examined and treated they are put back in the sea.

After crossing the bridge, take the path down to the right into the dense shrubbery and then continue up the hill again, via steps that will return you to the path at the visitor center parking area.

Just before the paved road that runs past the lagoon crosses a bridge, stop to watch the water birds. There are plenty to be seen in the tall grasses.

Before starting the walk, pause at the **Marin Headlands Visitor Center**, a museum with a natural history bookstore. Here you can learn about the history of the Marin Headlands.

The Marine Mammal Center

BUNKER ROAD

BUNKER ROAD

Rodeo Lake

BUNKER ROAD

FINISH

START

Marin Headlands Visitor Center

Rodeo Lagoon

COASTAL TRAIL

TRAIL

FIELD ROAD

CONZELMAN ROAD

SIMMONDS RD

ROSENSTOCK RD

Marin Headlands Hostel

Battery Smith-Guthrie

Battery Alexander

FIELD ROAD

Walk back up Rosenstock Road until you reach the **Coastal Trail**. Take the path to the sea, but beware of the poison oak bushes.

After the visitor center, head down to the three-story wooden **Marin Headlands Hostel**, which is listed on the National Historic Registry. It previously served as officers' headquarters, a hospital, and a missile command center.

Battery Mendell

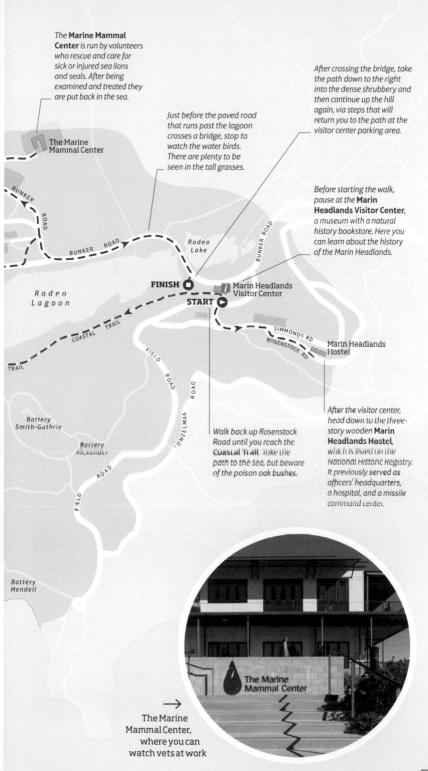

→ The Marine Mammal Center, where you can watch vets at work

A DRIVING TOUR
BAY AREA COASTLINE

Length 120 miles (195 km) **Stopping-off points** Saltwater Oyster Depot (www.salt wateroysterdepot.com), a seafood restaurant in Inverness, is convenient for Point Reyes. Pacifica, Pillar Point Harbor, and Half Moon Bay have many ocean-side restaurants and cafés.

The Pacific coastline north and south of San Francisco varies a great deal, its rugged cliffs alternating with sandy surf beaches to make a blissfully wild contrast to the western fringes of the city. As you drive on Hwy 1, which is known as the Shoreline Highway north of the Golden Gate, and Cabrillo Highway to the south, you'll pass a series of beautiful state and federal parks, beginning with Point Reyes National Seashore and ending at Pigeon Point. You'll also get to cross the Golden Gate Bridge halfway along.

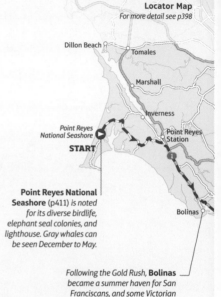

Locator Map
For more detail see p398

Dillon Beach · Tomales
Marshall
Inverness
Point Reyes National Seashore · **START** · Point Reyes Station
Bolinas

Point Reyes National Seashore (p411) *is noted for its diverse birdlife, elephant seal colonies, and lighthouse. Gray whales can be seen December to May.*

Following the Gold Rush, **Bolinas** *became a summer haven for San Franciscans, and some Victorian buildings still survive. The town is also a winter home to monarch butterflies.*

0 kilometers 20
0 miles 20

N ↑

↑ Chimney Rock Point, at the easternmost end of Point Reyes National Seashore

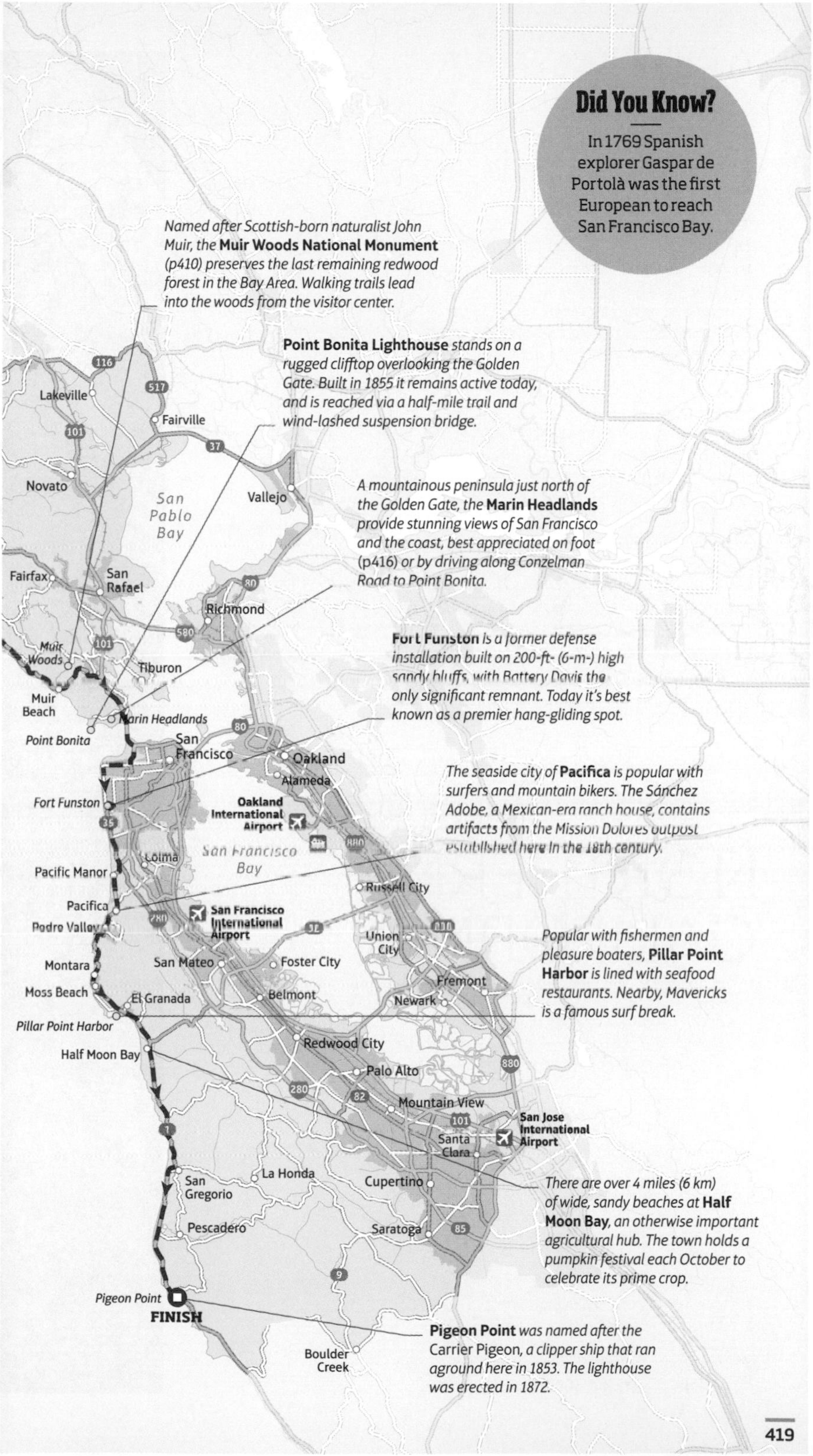

Named after Scottish-born naturalist John Muir, the **Muir Woods National Monument** (p410) preserves the last remaining redwood forest in the Bay Area. Walking trails lead into the woods from the visitor center.

Point Bonita Lighthouse stands on a rugged clifftop overlooking the Golden Gate. Built in 1855 it remains active today, and is reached via a half-mile trail and wind-lashed suspension bridge.

A mountainous peninsula just north of the Golden Gate, the **Marin Headlands** provide stunning views of San Francisco and the coast, best appreciated on foot (p416) or by driving along Conzelman Road to Point Bonita.

Fort Funston is a former defense installation built on 200-ft- (6-m-) high sandy bluffs, with Battery Davis the only significant remnant. Today it's best known as a premier hang-gliding spot.

The seaside city of **Pacifica** is popular with surfers and mountain bikers. The Sánchez Adobe, a Mexican-era ranch house, contains artifacts from the Mission Dolores outpost established here in the 18th century.

Popular with fishermen and pleasure boaters, **Pillar Point Harbor** is lined with seafood restaurants. Nearby, Mavericks is a famous surf break.

There are over 4 miles (6 km) of wide, sandy beaches at **Half Moon Bay**, an otherwise important agricultural hub. The town holds a pumpkin festival each October to celebrate its prime crop.

Pigeon Point was named after the Carrier Pigeon, a clipper ship that ran aground here in 1853. The lighthouse was erected in 1872.

FINISH

419

NORTHERN CALIFORNIA

Walking in Redwood National Park among giant sequoia trees

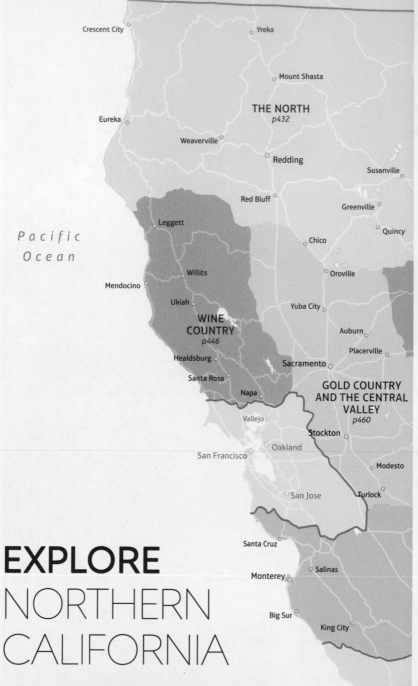

Pacific
Ocean

OREGON

Crescent City

Yreka

Mount Shasta

THE NORTH
p432

Eureka

Weaverville

Redding

Susanville

Red Bluff

Greenville

Leggett

Chico

Quincy

Oroville

Willits

Mendocino

Ukiah

Yuba City

WINE
COUNTRY
p446

Auburn

Healdsburg

Placerville

Santa Rosa

Sacramento

Napa

GOLD COUNTRY
AND THE CENTRAL
VALLEY
p460

Vallejo

Stockton

San Francisco

Oakland

Modesto

San Jose

Turlock

Santa Cruz

EXPLORE
NORTHERN
CALIFORNIA

Monterey

Salinas

Big Sur

King City

Atascadero

San Luis Obispo

This section divides Northern California into five color-coded sightseeing areas, as shown on this map. Find out more about each area on the following pages.

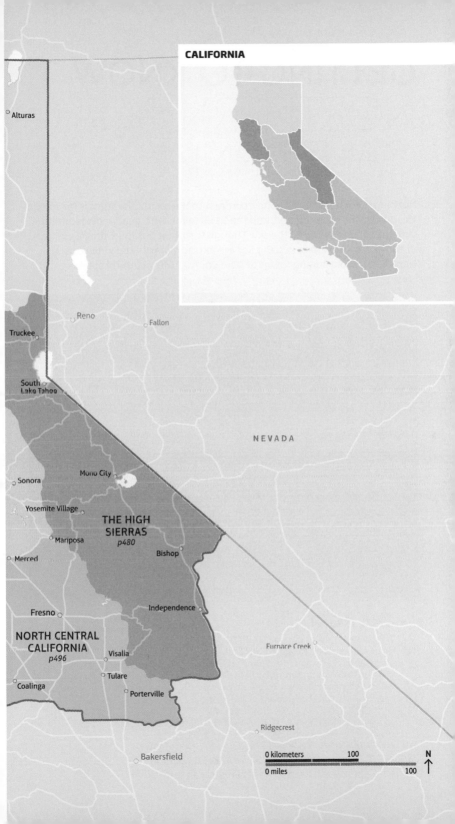

GETTING TO KNOW
NORTHERN CALIFORNIA

Northern California makes quite a contrast to the south; the coast is far wilder, the mountains snow-topped, and the trees taller, with giant redwoods and sequoia soaring high into the sky. Though the great outdoors provides much of the allure – Yosemite and Big Sur are extraordinary – the vineyards of Napa and the old mining towns of Gold Country offer cultural appeal.

THE NORTH

PAGE 432

From deserted beaches strewn with driftwood to dense forests of pine, fir, and redwood at the foot of alpine peaks, the far north of California is the state at its most wild and rugged. Along the coast, Eureka makes a good base for exploring the often deserted beaches and coastal redwood groves. Inland, the Sacramento Valley provides access to the beautiful snowcapped Mount Shasta, the volcanic spectacles of Lassen Volcanic National Park, and the Lava Beds National Monument.

Best for
Skiing, redwood forests, mountains, and volcanoes

Home to
Redwood National and State Parks, Lava Beds National Monument, Lassen Volcanic National Park

Experience
Climbing Mount Shasta

WINE COUNTRY

PAGE 446

Famous throughout the world for its superlative vintages, the Wine Country of Napa and Sonoma has a temperate climate, huge stretches of vine-covered rolling hills, and spectacular winery architecture, from the Mission-style Robert Mondavi to French chateau Inglenook. The small town of Calistoga is famed for its restorative mud baths, enormous geysers, and hot mineral-water tubs. To the west lie the dramatic, rocky landscapes of the Sonoma and Mendocino coastlines. A wide choice of excellent food and, of course, premium wine, is available throughout.

Best for
Wine and vineyards, historic sites, and gourmet restaurants

Home to
Napa Valley Wine Country, Sonoma

Experience
A guided tour of the Napa Valley wineries

→

PAGE 460

GOLD COUNTRY AND THE CENTRAL VALLEY

Named after the Gold Rush boom that transformed the state, Gold Country is today anchored by Sacramento, the state capital, which has the highest concentration of sights. The highlight of this area is in driving its many scenic routes, passing through historic mining communities such as Sutter Creek and Nevada City. The adjacent Sacramento Valley lies at the heart of the state's thriving agricultural industry, and is dotted with small historic towns.

Best for
Restaurants, gold-mining towns and museums, and Victorian architecture

Home to
Sacramento

Experience
A boat trip along the Sacramento River

PAGE 480

THE HIGH SIERRAS

The densely forested High Sierras rise to over 14,000 ft (4,270 m), sprinkled with crystalline lakes, towering trees, waterfalls, and ski trails, preserved in a series of stunning national parks. Yosemite – one of the absolute must-sees in California – is accompanied by Sequoia and Kings Canyon National Parks, home to the last few stands of giant sequoia trees. To the north, Lake Tahoe is one of the bluest bodies of water in the US, and is a skier's paradise in winter.

Best for
Mountains and rock climbing, waterfalls, giant redwoods and sequoias, alpine lakes, and skiing

Home to
Yosemite National Park, Sequoia and King's Canyon National Parks, Lake Tahoe

Experience
Hiking up Half Dome

PAGE 496

NORTH CENTRAL CALIFORNIA

From the sweeping sandy expanses of Santa Cruz to the jaw-dropping cliffs of Big Sur, it's the coastline that makes North Central California so enticing. The landscape holds an embarrassment of riches, with golden beaches, splendid wilderness, and the pancake-flat San Joaquin Valley inland, one of the world's most productive agricultural regions. Monterey retains a unique Spanish flavor, with its many historic buildings. On a rugged peninsula nearby stand the wealthy resorts of Pacific Grove, with its grand Victorian houses, and artsy Carmel, full of quaint cottages.

Best for
Beaches, hiking, and Spanish Colonial architecture and history

Home to
Santa Cruz, Monterey, Big Sur

Experience
Bathing at Esalen Hot Springs

←

1 Napa Valley vineyards.

2 Old Faithful Geyser, Calistoga.

3 Wine tasting at the Sterling Vineyards near Calistoga.

4 Lunch plate at The Girl and the Fig, Sonoma.

3 DAYS
in Wine Country

Day 1

Morning Start this tour of California's most celebrated wine regions with breakfast at Jax White Mule Diner *(www.jaxwhitemulediner.com)* in historic downtown Napa. Hire a driver and spend the day touring the vineyards and wine tasting between here and tiny St. Helena, 18 miles (29 km) north on Hwy 29 – aim to visit a maximum of four wineries for a full experience. Begin with a pop at Domaine Chandon *(p451)*, the sparkling wine specialist in Yountville, set in beautifully landscaped grounds. From here it's a short drive through the heart of the bright, sunlit Napa Valley to the Spanish Mission-style Robert Mondavi Winery *(p451)*, where you can have lunch after a tour.

Afternoon Your next stop is the Inglenook Estate winery *(www.inglenook.com)*, owned by movie director Francis Ford Coppola, which features a grand European-style chateau. Follow this with a visit to the vast Charles Krug Winery *(p450)*, Napa's oldest and home to the original 19th-century Redwood Cellar.

Evening End the day strolling along St Helena's Main Street, lined with galleries, charming shops, and wine-tasting rooms. The Goose & Gander gastropub *(www.goosegander.com)* is a great dinner spot. Stay overnight at the Wydown Hotel *(www.wydownhotel.com)*.

Day 2

Morning Rent a car in St. Helena and head 8 miles (12 km) north to Calistoga *(p459)* to admire the Old Faithful Geyser as it spouts boiling water. Then continue 3 miles (5 km) east to Clos Pegase winery *(www.clospegase.com)* to view its superb modern art collection and sample the wines. You can have a picnic lunch here.

Afternoon Walk ten minutes south and you will reach an aerial tram to take you to the Mediterranean-style Sterling Vineyards *(www.sterlingvineyards.com)*. Tour the winery and enjoy magnificent views of the Napa Valley from its hilltop perch.

Evening End the day by soaking in a mineral mud bath in Calistoga, followed by classic American cuisine at Café Sarafornia *(www.cafesarafornia.com)* and an overnight stay at Craftsman Inn *(www.lodginginnapavalley.com)*.

Day 3

Morning Drive 17 miles (27 km) southwest to Santa Rosa *(p458)* to admire the cartoons of artist Charles M. Schulz at Snoopy's Gallery and Gift Shop. Then tour the rose garden at Luther Burbank Home and Gardens before heading into Sonoma Valley *(p452)* and making for the charming town of Sonoma. Check into the downtown Sonoma Hotel, dating to 1879, where you can lunch at the on-site The Girl and the Fig restaurant *(www.sonomahotel.com)*.

Afternoon Explore the atmospheric 19th-century Spanish-Mexican buildings around Sonoma Plaza. Then, if you are feeling energetic, head on to Jack London State Historic Park *(p459)* for an invigorating hike.

Evening End your tour with fine wine, cheese, and charcuterie at the chic Pangloss Cellars *(www.panglosscellars.com)* in downtown Sonoma.

→

1 The emerald-sapphire waters of Lake Tahoe.

2 California State Railroad Museum, Sacramento.

3 Panning for gold in Columbia State Historic Park.

4 Yosemite Falls, one of the world's tallest waterfalls, Yosemite National Park.

5 DAYS

Touring the Gold Country and Sierra Nevada

Day 1

Start in Sacramento (p464), California's capital city, born during the 1848 Gold Rush. Visit the fascinating California State Railroad Museum before paying homage to California's Chinese heritage with lunch at the original Frank Fat's (p467), an institution since 1939. In the afternoon take a guided tour of the Neo-Classical California State Capitol (p466). End the day with dinner and cocktails at 1920s-style Shady Lady Saloon (www.shadyladybar.com) and a show at the Sacramento Theatre (www. sactheatre.org). Stay overnight aboard the atmospheric Delta King Riverboat (p465).

Day 2

After picking up a rental car, drive through the Sierra foothills to Nevada City (p468). Visit the Empire Mine State Historic Park (p469) for a tour of a restored 19th-century gold mine before having lunch in the Crazy Horse Saloon and Grill (www.crazyhorsenc. com). In the afternoon drive through pine forests to the Wild West town of Truckee (p492) and continue via Highway 267 to Lake Tahoe (p490). Book yourself into the Franciscan Lakeside Lodge (www.franciscan lodge.com) and dine at Gar Woods Grill & Pier (www.garwoods.com), with lake views.

Day 3

Circle the western shore of Lake Tahoe, stopping to photograph vistas of the Emerald Bay State Park and Vikingsholm.

Then follow the scenic Lincoln Highway (Route 50) to Placerville (p471) and visit the El Dorado County Historical Museum before continuing south to Sutter Creek (p473), a Gold Rush town full of antiques shops. Dine and stay overnight at Hotel Sutter (p472) in the center of town.

Day 4

Drive uphill from Sutter Creek to the quaint hamlet of Volcano and visit Indian Grinding Rock State Historic Park (p472), one of the best-preserved Native American sites in the US. Continue south 46 miles (74 km) to Columbia State Historic Park (p476) for an afternoon panning for gold in this perfectly preserved Gold Rush-era town. End your day in Sonora (p477); try the famed burgers at the Diamondback Grill (www. diamondbackgrillsonora.com) before turning in for the night at the Gunn House Hotel (www.gunnhousehotel.com).

Day 5

Today head into the High Sierras and Yosemite National Park (p484). Begin by exploring Yosemite Valley, with its spectacular monoliths and plunging waterfalls. Then drive to Glacier Point (p485) for jaw-dropping views of Yosemite Valley and Half Dome. Continue south to Mariposa Grove to hike among giant sequoias before ending your trip at Wawona Hotel (8308 Wawona Rd).

THE NORTH

The Wiyot, Yurok, Karuk, Chilula, and Whilkut have lived in Northern California since at least 10,000 BC, painting pictographs on cave walls. When the Europeans arrived in the area in the 19th century, the Native American population declined rapidly due to exposure to diseases. The first European settlers were fur trappers, in search of beavers, sea otters, and other pelts. Soon afterwards, gold seekers arrived, hoping for similar riches to those found in the Sierra Nevada. Some gold was found, but the real wealth was made when lumber companies began to harvest the forests of coastal redwoods. Eureka and Mendocino, founded in 1850, became "timber capitals." The rapid deforestation inspired the foundation of the Save the Redwoods League in 1918, which eventually led to the creation of the Redwood National and State Parks.

Inland, the completion of the Central Pacific Railroad in 1887 kick-started tourism in the Mount Shasta region. The region's popularity was cemented by the designation of the Lassen Volcanic National Park in 1907 and the Lava Beds National Monument in 1925. The latter was the site of the notorious Modoc War (1872–73) during which a band of Modocs led by chief Kintpuash (also known as Captain Jack) was defeated by the US Army. Today this wild quarter of Northern California remains a popular vacation spot.

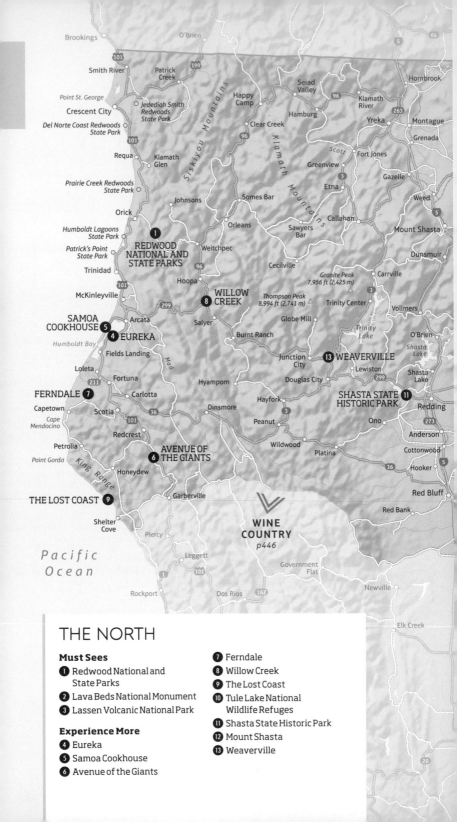

THE NORTH

Must Sees

1 Redwood National and State Parks

2 Lava Beds National Monument

3 Lassen Volcanic National Park

Experience More

4 Eureka

5 Samoa Cookhouse

6 Avenue of the Giants

7 Ferndale

8 Willow Creek

9 The Lost Coast

10 Tule Lake National Wildlife Refuges

11 Shasta State Historic Park

12 Mount Shasta

13 Weaverville

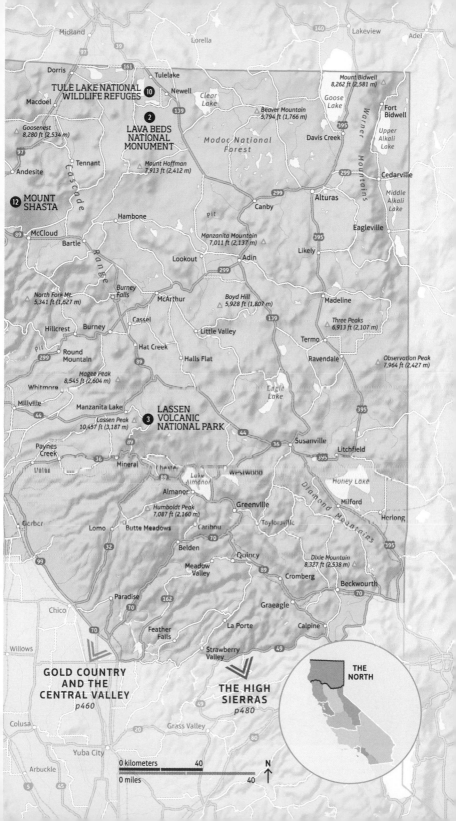

❶

REDWOOD NATIONAL AND STATE PARKS

🅰A1 🆙332 1st St, Eureka; www.visitredwoods.com; www.nps.gov

Stretching along 40 miles (60 km) of rugged Northern California coastline, Redwood National and State Parks are home to some of the largest original redwood forests in the world and many of the tallest and oldest trees on Earth.

Three state parks – Prairie Creek Redwoods, Del Norte Coast Redwoods, and Jedediah Smith Redwoods – together with Redwood National Park comprise the Redwood National and State Parks. Established in 1968, this large World Heritage Site and International Biosphere Reserve encompasses redwood forests, prairies, riverways, oak woods, and beaches. The adjacent Humboldt Lagoons and Patrick's Point state parks also protect lagoons, wetlands, wildflower meadows, and shoreline. Many Native American groups, such as the Yurok and Chilula, have historical ties to the region.

> 💬 INSIDER TIP
> **Visiting the Parks**
>
> September and October are ideal months to visit. Though spring and summer can be foggy, many flowering plants are on view during this time. Winter is often rainy but is best for whale-watching. Crescent City, Arcata, and Eureka are the nearest cities and have a range of restaurants, motels, and other facilities.

↑ Stone Lagoon in Humboldt Lagoons State Park surrounded by wildflowers in spring

↑ Standing next to a giant redwood tree in Redwood National Park

○ *Humboldt Lagoons State Park*

Big Lagoon, a freshwater lake stretching for 3 miles (5 km), and two other estuaries form Humboldt Lagoon State Park.

Trees of Mystery

◁ Located near the coastal town of Klamath, this attraction features giant fiberglass statues of the fictional lumberjack Paul Bunyan and his ox Babe. The two characters were popularized in early 20th-century folklore stories about their journey from Maine to California.

○ *Gold Bluffs Beach*

This 11-mile (18-km) beach is rated by many as one of the most beautiful in California.

○ *Patrick's Point State Park*

In winter, the headlands are a good place to watch for migrating gray whales. Rock pools abound with smaller marine life.

○ *Del Norte Coast Redwoods State Park*

▷ This park became the first protected area in 1926. Part of the old Redwood Highway has been maintained as a hiking trail. In spring, wildflowers cover the hillsides.

○ *Jedediah Smith Redwoods State Park*

Some of the most awe-inspiring coastal redwoods are found here. The park was named after the fur-trapper Jedediah Smith, the first white man to walk across the US. He explored this region in 1828.

○ *Prairie Creek Redwoods State Park*

▷ One of the world's tallest trees, a 378-ft (115-m) giant, stands in the aptly named Tall Trees Grove at the southern end of Prairie Creek Redwoods State Park. The park also provides a habitat for one of the last remaining herds of Roosevelt elk on Earth.

2 🧭 🌋 🛍️

LAVA BEDS NATIONAL MONUMENT

🅰️ C1 🏠 1 Indian Well HQ, Tulelake 🌐 nps.gov/labe

A striking landscape sculpted by molten earth, Lava Beds National Monument contains volcanic tablelands and more than 700 caves. These surreal elements were formed 10,500–65,000 years ago when the outer edges of flowing lava began to cool, forming tubes.

Despite its seemingly desolate topography, the volcanic fields have a rich diversity of plant and animal life. Amid the scraggly expanses of sagebrush and juniper are wildflowers, while a variety of ferns, lichens, and mosses grow in the cave entrances. Mule deer, pronghorn antelope, bobcat, coyote, a variety of birds, and several species of bats thrive in the semi-arid environment.

←

Modoc pictograph at Symbol Bridge cave in Lava Beds National Monument

Until white settlers arrived in the 19th century, this region was home to the Modoc peoples. Ancient pictographs can be seen on cave walls and Petroglyph Point contains one of the largest panels of Native American rock art in the US.

The area has the largest concentration of lava tubes in North America. The cylindrical tunnels were created when the top of a lava flow cooled and hardened, while the hot lava flowed underneath. Inside are fascinating lavacicles, dripstone, and other speleothems. The greatest concentration of caves lies along Cave Loop Road, 2 miles (3 km) south of the visitor center. Caves are rated for difficulty from least to most challenging. Check first with the visitor center, as some caves are periodically closed to protect hibernating bats.

Much of the national monument is designated wilderness, and 13 hiking trails wind through this extraordinary landscape.

↑ The volcanic landscape of the Lava Beds National Monument, covered in grasslands, sagebrush, and juniper

Ancient pictographs can be seen on cave walls and Petroglyph Point contains one of the largest panels of Native American rock art in the US.

Most are short out-and-back trails of under a mile each way, with longer trails leading into the backcountry. Popular routes include the Petroglyph Point Trail, Captain Jack's Stronghold Trail, and the Big Nasty loop trail with its beautiful sunset views.

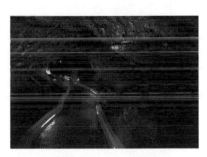

↑ The interior of Mushpot Cave, the only cave with lights and a paved floor

THE MODOC WAR

The Modoc War of 1872–73, the only major war between the US and the Indigenous peoples in California, took place within the volcanic fields. After being forced into a reservation in Oregon by the US government, a group of Modoc returned under the command of Chief Kintpuash, or "Captain Jack" *(left)*. For six months they evaded the US Cavalry in the lava beds and caves, but Captain Jack was eventually captured and hanged, and others were moved to a reservation in Oklahoma. Captain Jack's Stronghold is along the area's north border.

Did You Know?

With a volume of 0.6 cubic miles (2.5 cubic km), Lassen Peak is the largest lava dome on Earth.

GREAT VIEW
Cinder Cone

The challenging 4-mile (6-km) Cinder Cone Trail from Butte Lake winds through stark, rugged lava beds to the top of Cinder Cone – an extinct volcano. Enjoy views of Lassen Peak, the Painted Dunes, and more, before descending into the yawning crater.

Snowcapped Lassen Peak, looming over the lunar landscape of the park ↑

3

LASSEN VOLCANIC NATIONAL PARK

🅰️ C2 🏠 38050 Hwy 36 East, Mineral 🚌 Chester, Red Bluff
🌐 nps.gov/lavo

There's a stunning volcanic world to explore in this remote and beautiful national park. Tread an intrepid boardwalk trail through steaming, sulfurous pools of boiling water, and hike or bike beneath snowcapped peaks to wildflower meadows and clear mountain lakes.

It may look peaceful today, but a century ago this area was a dangerous place to be. Lassen Peak erupted nearly 300 times between 1914 and 1917, laying waste to 100,000 acres (40,500 ha) of the surrounding land. At 10,457 ft (3,187 m), this still-active volcano looms over what became one of the country's oldest national parks – an unspoiled wilderness that has fascinating volcanic features and pristine mountain landscapes.

The winding Lassen Volcanic Scenic Byway runs for 30 miles (48 km) through the park, and takes you to most of its main sights, with viewpoints to stop and soak up the magnificent vistas along the way. The road is open only in summer, as this high-altitude park gets over 30 ft (9 m) of snow between October and June. But the park offers a wealth of recreational activities year-round, from sledding, snowshoeing, and cross-country skiing in winter to traffic-free biking in spring.

A perennial park activity is hiking the more than 150 miles (240 km) of trails that lace the park. As well as tackling the ashen gray summit of Lassen Peak, popular routes take in Summit Lake, boiling mudpots and hissing fumaroles from boardwalk trails at Sulphur Works and Bumpass Hell, and the bleak landscape of rough volcanic mudflows at the Devastated Area. Here, in the northwest corner of the park, the Loomis Museum has a photographic record of Lassen Peak's many eruptions.

↑ A hiker surveying the view of Lassen Peak from the shore of Lake Helen

> **The park offers a wealth of recreational activities year-round, from sledding, snowshoeing, and cross-country skiing in winter to traffic-free biking in spring.**

Bumpass Hell, named after a guide who lost his leg in one of the mudpots in 1865 ↓

EXPERIENCE MORE

EXPERIENCE The North

4

Eureka

A1 ✈ Arcata/Eureka Airport, 15 miles (25 km) N of Eureka 🚌 ℹ 240 E St; www.visiteureka.com

Founded in 1850 on a natural harbor by gold miners, and named for the state's ancient Greek motto meaning "I have found it," Eureka has since expanded into the northern coast's largest industrial center, although its fishing operations now far outstrip the dwindling logging industry. The Old Town behind the waterfront is full of restored 19th-century buildings, many with cast-iron facades, which have been converted into cafés, bars, and restaurants. The absorbing **Clarke Historical Museum** explores the region's history and houses the visitor center. Nearby, the extravagant Gothic-style Carson Mansion (M & 2nd sts), built for millionaire lumber baron William Carson in 1885, is

deceptively painted to resemble stone. Further afield are the **Morris Graves Museum of Art**, with its sculpture garden, the amusing **Kinetic Museum Eureka**, which showcases vehicles from the quirky annual Kinetic Sculpture Race, and **Fort Humboldt State Historic Park**.

Clarke Historical Museum

♿🕐 🏛 240 E St ⏰ 10am–4pm Wed–Sun 🌐 clarke museum.org

Morris Graves Museum of Art

♿🕐🚻🏛 636 F St ⏰ Noon–5pm Wed–Sun 🌐 humboldtarts.org

Kinetic Museum Eureka

🏛 518 A St ⏰ 2:13–6:32pm Fri–Sun 🌐 kineticgrand championship.com

Fort Humboldt State Historic Park

🕐 🏛 3431 Fort Av 📞 (707) 445-6547 ⏰ 8am–5pm daily 🌐 parks.ca.gov

5

Samoa Cookhouse

A1 🏛 908 Vance Av, Samoa ⏰ 9am–8pm Sun–Thu (till 9pm Fri & Sat) 🚫 Thanksgiving, Dec 25 🌐 samoacookhouse.net

The Samoa Cookhouse was built in 1890 as a dining room for workers at the adjacent Louisiana Pacific pulp mill, one of many lumber mills on the narrow Samoa Peninsula. It was opened to the public in the 1960s, when automation in the mills had reduced the size of the workforce and the need for on-site dining facilities. The restaurant has retained its rustic decor and its giant-sized portions of traditional American dishes. Antique logging equipment adds to the unique ambience.

6

Avenue of the Giants

B2 🚌 Garberville ℹ Weott; www.avenue ofthegiants.net

The world's tallest redwood trees and the most extensive primeval redwood groves

Hikers in Humboldt Redwoods State Park, which is crossed by the Avenue of the Giants ↑

stand along the banks of the Eel River in the impressive 80-sq-mile (200-sq-km) Humboldt Redwoods State Park. The 33-mile (53-km) Avenue of the Giants, a two-lane highway running parallel to US 101 through the park, offers a good overall sense of these trees. For the best experience, however, leave your car in one of the many parking areas and walk around the groves, taking in the full immensity of the trees.

The visitors' center, halfway along the Avenue of the Giants on US 101, has displays on the natural history of these forests. It also supplies maps and information on the hiking, biking, camping, picnicking, and swimming facilities available within the park.

❼ Ferndale

🅰A2 ✈ Arcata/Eureka Airport, 40 miles (65 km) N of Ferndale 🌐 visit ferndale.com

A pastoral respite from the wilderness of California's northern coast, Ferndale was founded in 1852 by Danish, Swiss-Italian, and Portuguese immigrants who together established a lucrative dairy industry here. Exhibits of the town's history can be seen in the **Ferndale Museum**.

During the annual Kinetic Sculpture Race, contestants ride self-made vehicles from Arcata to Ferndale's Main Street.

Ferndale Museum

🏛 Shaw Av & 3rd St 🕐 11am–4pm Wed–Sat, 1–4pm Sun 🚫 Jan 🌐 ferndale-museum.org

❽ Willow Creek

🅰B1 ✈ Arcata/Eureka Airport, 45 miles (70 km) E of Willow Creek 🚌 🌐 willow creekchamber.com

The tiny town of Willow Creek is perhaps best known for the **Willow Creek – China Flat Museum** , featuring the world's largest assortment of curios related to the legendary Bigfoot. The term "Bigfoot" was coined in 1958 after giant footprints and sightings of the fabled man-beast were reported by locals. Kids can pour over the unique collection of Bigfoot pictures, footprint casts, and maps. The annual Bigfoot Days festival takes place each Labor Day weekend.

Willow Creek - China Flat Museum

🏛 38949 CA-299 Willow Creek 🕐 May–Sep: 10am–4pm Wed–Sun; Oct: noon–4pm Fri–Sun 🌐 bigfoot country.net

DRINK

Lost Coast Brewery & Café

Here you can sample a wide range of ales, especially hoppy IPAs, and ciders. Brewery tours are also available.

🅰A1 🏛 617 Fourth St, Eureka 🌐 lostcoast.com

Dunsmuir Brewery Works

This intimate microbrewery provides an eclectic selection of ales served by friendly staff.

🅰B1 🏛 5701 Dunsmuir Av, Dunsmuir 🌐 dunsmuir breweryworks.com

Etna Brewing Company

Tucked in a remote corner of the wide-open north, this homey microbrewery makes exquisite ales, such as the XX Imperial IPA, which you can sup with a tasty bite.

🅰B1 🏛 131 Callahan St, Etna 🌐 etna brewing.com

STAY

Lost Whale Inn

Located on a wooded bluff above a secluded beach where seals often play, this romantic and luxurious B&B offers ocean- and garden-view rooms. It is also conveniently placed for visiting Redwood National Park.

🅰A1 🏛 3452 Patrick's Point Dr, Trinidad 🌐 lostwhaleinn.com

⑤⑤⑤

EAT

Black Bear Diner
Pancakes, eggy breakfasts, and classic American diner meals.

🅰B1 🏠401 W Lake St, Mt Shasta 🌐black beardiner.com

Ⓢ Ⓢ Ⓢ

Café Maddalena
Cuisine inspired by Mediterranean flavors.

🅰B1 🏠5801 Sacramento Av, Dunsmuir 🌐cafe maddalena.com

Ⓢ Ⓢ Ⓢ

VI: 400
Both diner classics and upscale California fare.

🅰A2 🏠400 Ocean Av, Ferndale 🌐virestaurant.com

Ⓢ Ⓢ Ⓢ

⑨
The Lost Coast

🅰A2 🚌Garberville 🚹782 Redwood Dr; www.garber ville.org

Covering a small section of coastline so craggy and wild that no road could reasonably be built along it, the so-called Lost Coast stretches for more than 40 miles (64 km) and is the largest remaining stretch of undeveloped shoreline in California.

The salmon-fishing port of Shelter Cove, tucked away within a tiny bay, is at the center of the Lost Coast. Its remote location has kept the village small, but it remains a good base for hikers and wildlife enthusiasts. Sixteen miles (25 km) of hiking trails, inhabited only by fauna such as black bears, deer, mink, and bald eagles, run along the clifftops, interspersed with free campsites. Shelter Cove is accessible only via a winding but well-maintained road.

A good feel for the Lost Coast can be had by taking Hwy 211 west of US 101 and then following the scenic road between Humboldt Redwoods State Park and Ferndale (p443). This beautiful 50-mile (80-km) road runs to the edge of the Pacific Ocean around Cape Mendocino, the westernmost point on the coast of California.

⑩
Tule Lake National Wildlife Refuges

🅰C1 🚌Klamath Falls 🚹4009 Hill Rd; www.fws. gov/refuge/Tule_Lake

Six refuges on both sides of the California–Oregon border form one of the most popular bird-watching spots in the western US. Centering upon Tule Lake and the Lower Klamath River, much of the region has been set aside as wildlife refuges. In the fall the refuges attract hundreds of thousands of wildfowl as they migrate south, from Canada to the Central Valley and beyond. Tule Lake is also the winter home to as many as 1,000 bald eagles. You can also see a variety of mammals, reptiles, and amphibians.

← Stormy clouds on the wild, rugged landscape of the Lost Coast

⑪ Shasta State Historic Park

B2 🚉Redding
ⓦparks.ca.gov

In the 1850s, Shasta was one of the largest gold-mining camps in the state and the base of operations for prospectors working along the Trinity, Sacramento, McCloud, and Pit Rivers. As the Gold Rush faded, the town faded too and became a ghost town.

In the early 1920s the state of California, realizing Shasta's historical importance, began to restore it. Numerous old brick buildings are preserved in a state of arrested decay, but the **Shasta Courthouse** has been restored to its original condition and now houses the **visitors' center**. Here, there are exhibits tracing the town's history.

One mile (1.5 km) west of Shasta town, the land around Lake Whiskeytown forms the smallest parcel of the three-part Shasta-Whiskeytown-Trinity National Recreation Area, a forest preserve surrounding the three reservoirs.

 HIDDEN GEM
Burney Falls

President Theodore Roosevelt named this waterfall, located 70 miles (113 km) north-east of Shasta State Historic Park, "the eighth wonder of the world." The 129-ft (40-m) falls can be seen year-round.

Lake Shasta is the largest, and all three lakes are popular with fishermen, waterskiers, houseboat owners, and other recreational users.

Shasta Courthouse and Visitors' Center

🅰Main St 📞(530) 243-8194
🕐10am–5pm Thu–Sun

---

⑫ Mount Shasta

B1 🚆Dunsmuir
🚌Siskiyou, Shasta
🚶300 Pine St, Mt Shasta;
www.mtshastaca.gov

Mount Shasta rises abruptly to a height of 14,162 ft (4,316 m) and is the second highest of the Cascade Mountains after Mount Rainier in Washington State. Usually covered with snow, the summit of this volcano (which last erupted in 1786) is popular with experienced mountaineers. The lower slopes offer skiing at **Mount Shasta Ski Park** in winter and easy walking trails through wildflower-filled meadows and cool forests in summer.

Shasta-Trinity National Forest has many lakes and recreational facilities.

Mount Shasta Ski Park

😊🎿🅰4500 Ski Park Hwy, McCloud
ⓦskipark.com

Shasta-Trinity National Forest

🚶😊🅰fs.usda.gov/stnf

---

⑬ Weaverville

 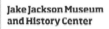

B2 ✈Redding Municipal Airport, 40 miles (65 km) E of Weaverville 🛈509 Main St; www.weavervilleca.org

This small rural town has changed little since it was founded by gold prospectors in the 19th century. At the heart of the small commercial district is the **Jake Jackson Museum and History Center**, where displays trace the history of the town and its surrounding gold-mining and lumber region. Adjacent to the museum, the Joss House State Historic Site is the oldest and best-preserved Chinese Temple in the country. Built in 1874, it serves as a reminder of the Chinese immigrants who arrived in the US to mine gold and stayed in the state, helping to build the California railroads.

To the north, the Trinity Alps, part of the Salmon Mountain Range, attract hikers in the summer and cross-country skiers in the winter months.

Jake Jackson Museum and History Center

🅰780 Main St
🕐11am–4pm Thu & Sat (daily in summer)
ⓦtrinity museum.org

→ Carving of a miner in the small town of Weaverville

WINE COUNTRY

For 10,000 years the Wappo, Pomo, and Miwok peoples lived in this region, one of California's longest inhabited areas. They established villages and an agricultural way of life. This changed dramatically with the arrival of the Russians at Fort Ross in 1812 and the Spanish, who established their most northerly mission at Sonoma in 1823. A large number of the native population died from smallpox, introduced by the settlers, and many of those who survived were forced off their lands to make way for the planting of grape vines by the Franciscan fathers to produce sacramental wines for the missions. This was the start of California's wine industry.

In 1857, the Hungarian Count Agoston Haraszthy brought modern winemaking to California. Using imported European grape varieties, he planted the state's first major vineyard at Sonoma's revered Buena Vista Winery. Haraszthy made a name not only for himself (he is known as the "father of California wine") but also for this previously unrecognized wine-producing region.

Over the years, many wine producers have followed in his footsteps, most of them favoring the rich, fertile soil of the Napa Valley. Russian-born winemaker André Tchelistcheff is credited with re-establishing the industry after Prohibition in the 1930s, and Robert Mondavi founded his celebrated Mission-style vineyard in 1965. Hundreds of wineries now stand side by side along the length of the valley floor, most of them offering tours of their facilities and wine tastings.

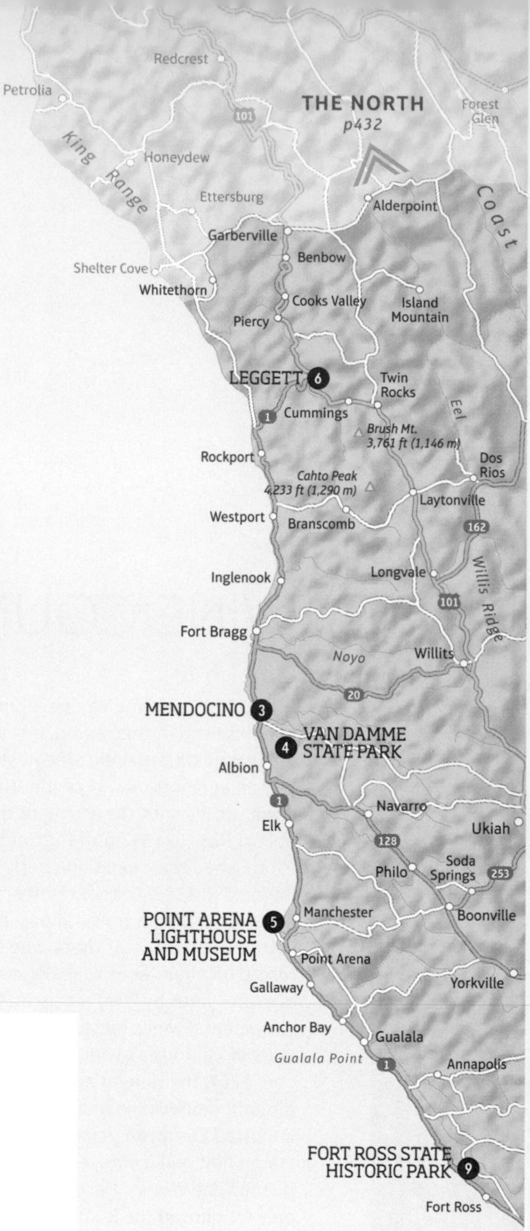

Pacific
Ocean

THE NORTH
p432

Redcrest
Petrolia
Forest Glen
Honeydew
Ettersburg
Alderpoint
Garberville
Benbow
Shelter Cove
Whitethorn
Cooks Valley
Island Mountain
Piercy

LEGGETT 6
Twin Rocks
Cummings
Brush Mt. 3,761 ft (1,146 m)
Rockport
Cahto Peak 4,233 ft (1,290 m)
Dos Rios
Laytonville
Westport
Branscomb
Inglenook
Longvale
Fort Bragg
Noyo
Willits
MENDOCINO 3
VAN DAMME STATE PARK 4
Albion
Navarro
Ukiah
Elk
Philo
Soda Springs
Boonville
POINT ARENA LIGHTHOUSE AND MUSEUM 5
Manchester
Point Arena
Yorkville
Gallaway
Anchor Bay
Gualala
Gualala Point
Annapolis
FORT ROSS STATE HISTORIC PARK 9
Fort Ross

King Range
Coast
Eel
Willits Ridge

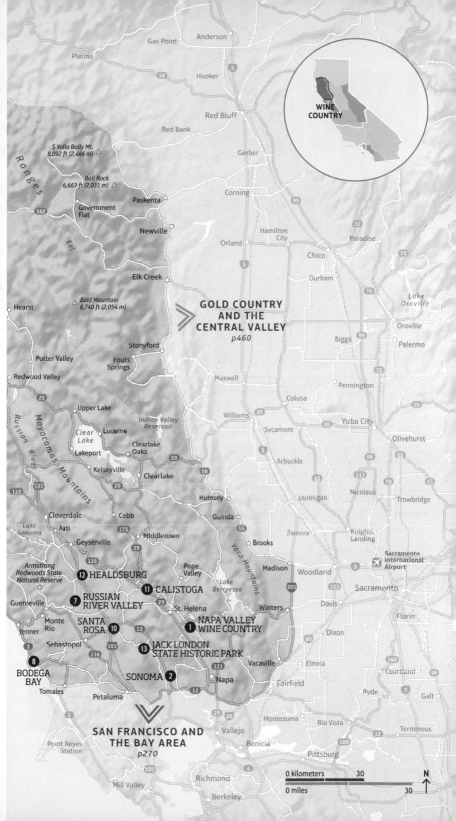

❶

NAPA VALLEY WINE COUNTRY

🅰B3 📧 ℹ️ 1331 1st St, Napa; www.visitnapavalley.com

Since the legendary Judgment of Paris in 1976 – when the Napa Valley wines beat Burgundy to top honors in both the red and white categories – this region has been a hotspot for wine-lovers. Aside from purchasing award-winning wine, people also come here for the experience: to tour grand chateaux, dine at renowned restaurants, and sip small-batch wines in boutique tasting rooms.

Charles Krug Winery

🄰2800 Main St, St. Helena ⏱10:30am–5pm daily 🅆charleskrug.com

Many firsts can be attributed to Napa Valley's oldest winery. Charles Krug, who founded the estate in 1861, was a pioneer of varietal labeling. He was also the first to import French oak barrels for wine aging. The tasting room, yet another first in California when it opened to the public in 1882, is the crowning glory, with a soft peach, Tuscan-style exterior leading to a sleek space with daily tastings of limited-release wines.

V. Sattui

🄰1111 White Lane, St. Helena ⏱9am–6pm daily (winter: to 5pm) 🅆vsattui.com

With tasting room staff pouring everything from estate Cabernet to champagne-method bubbles, you can't really go wrong at V. Sattui. Even those who aren't wine-lovers can delight in exploring the vast grounds, with vine-combed slopes and shaded picnic areas. Reserve in advance to take a tour through the cellars and listen to the fascinating history of this family-run winery, which was started in San Francisco in the 19th century, destroyed by Prohibition and, finally, resurrected here in 1976.

Robert Mondavi Winery

🄰7801 St. Helena Hwy, Oakville 📧10 ⏱10am–4pm daily 🅆robert mondaviwinery.com

The flagship estate of one of Napa's pioneering vineyard owners is styled to resemble

↑ A glass of Twin Oaks wine being served at Robert Mondavi winery

↑ The rolling hills and stunning golden vineyards of Napa Valley

California's Spanish missions, with graceful arches and a vast, elegant courtyard. A passionate ambassador for Napa Valley wines until his death in 2008, Robert Mondavi is credited with helping to elevate the area to one of the world's most recognized wine regions. Still family-run, the winery continues to pour its renowned Cabernets and signature Fumé Blanc.

EAT

The French Laundry
This cozy French restaurant, run by Thomas Keller, is a Napa Valley favorite. It features an imaginative nine-course menu and also boasts three Michelin stars.

🏠 6640 Washington St, Yountville ◯ Dinner daily, reservations only ⓦ thomaskeller.com

$ $ $

---

fermented with Sauvignon Blanc grapes. Visitors can join wine tasting sessions, cellar tastings with reserve wines, and barrel room tours.

---

④ Ⓜ 🏛

Opus One Winery

🏠 7900 St. Helena Hwy, Oakville 🚌 10 ◯ By appointment only
ⓦ opusonewinery.com

Opus One was founded in 1979 as an unprecedented joint venture between two wine legends – Napa Valley's Robert Mondavi and Baron Philippe de Rothschild, founder of Château Mouton Rothschild in Bordeaux, France. Their plan was to create a single, world-class Bordeaux blend based on California Cabernet, and their legacy is a wine that is consistently considered one of Napa's best.

The striking stone building of the winery, tucked low against the hillside, hosts intimate, appointment-only tastings of the current

---

vintage, or you can reserve a tour to explore the vast grounds and production areas.

---

⑤ Ⓜ 🍴 🏛

Domaine Chandon

🏠 1 California Dr, Yountville 🚌 29 ◯ Shop: 10am–4pm daily; tastings: 10am–4pm Thu–Mon by reservation
ⓦ chandon.com

From classic brut to blushing rosé, it's all about the bubbles at this lavish estate founded by Moët & Chandon in 1973. While it exudes a French elegance, there's nothing formal about the atmosphere. As befits a spot specializing in fizz, a visit here is all about having a good time.

Experiences range from tasting flights, including the estate's still varieties, to weekend mixology classes, when participants can make and sip cocktails using the signature sparkling wine.

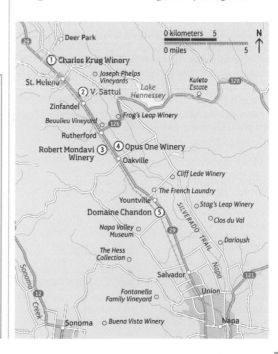

↑ A lush vineyard covering the rolling hills of the Sonoma Valley

②

SONOMA

🅐 B3 ℹ️ Historic Plaza: 453 1st St E; www.sonoma.com
✖️ Sonoma County Airport, 6 miles (10 km) N of Santa Rosa
🚌 90 Broadway & W Napa St, Sonoma Plaza

Nestling in the narrow Sonoma Valley, cradled by the Mayacama mountains to the east and by the Sonoma mountains to the west, is a seemingly endless expanse of land covered in vineyards. At the foot of the valley lies the tiny town of Sonoma, whose main attractions are its internationally renowned wineries and the Spanish-style Sonoma Plaza, lined with dozens of meticulously preserved historical sights. Many of the adobe buildings around the square house wine shops, charming boutiques, and chic restaurants serving excellent California and Wine Country cuisine.

①

General Joseph Hooker House

🏠 414 1st St East, El Paseo 🕐 11am–3:30pm Wed–Sat by appointment 🌐 bedrock wineco.com

This 1855 gabled house once belonged to Civil War veteran "Fighting Joe" Hooker, who later sold it to settlers Pedro and Catherine Vasquez. The house now serves as a tasting room for the Bedrock Wine Company and includes a display of mid-19th century photographs that trace Sonoma's history.

②

Toscano Hotel

🏠 20 E Spain St 📞 (707) 938-5889 🕐 10am–5pm daily

Located on the north side of Sonoma Plaza, the restored Toscano Hotel is now a historic monument. The two-story wood-frame building dates from the 1850s, when it was used as a general store and library. It was converted into a hotel for gold miners in 1886 and now belongs to the state. The Toscano is furnished in 1850–1950 style and is open for tours.

③

Lachryma Montis

🏠 3rd St W 🕐 10am–5pm daily 🌐 parks.ca.gov

Visitors can glimpse the lavish lifestyle of Mexican General Mariano Vallejo by exploring Lachryma Montis, his former home. This Gothic Revival house was built of redwood in 1852. It features an eclectic array of Vallejo memorabilia, ranging from the general's silver epaulettes and a cattle brand to a collection of his favorite books. The name of the house is Latin for "mountain tear," a reference to the Native American name for the area, Chiucuyem

→ The spartan accommodations of Sonoma Barracks

("Crying Mountain"), given for the free-flowing mineral spring on the property.

 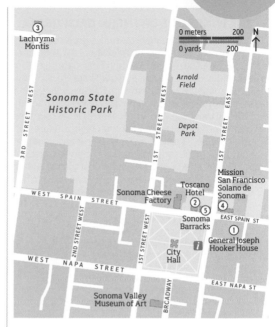

Mission San Francisco Solano de Sonoma

🏠 114 E Spain St
🕙 10am–5pm daily
🌐 sonomaparks.org

Named after a Peruvian saint, this beautifully restored old mission (commonly called the Sonoma Mission) was the last of the historic chain of 21 Franciscan missions built in California. Father José Altimira of Spain founded the mission in 1823 at a time when California was under Mexican rule. Today all that survives of the original building is the corridor of Father Altimira's quarters. An adobe chapel was built by General Vallejo in 1840 to be used by the town's families and soldiers (who were stationed at the barracks just across the street). This was severely damaged by the 1906 earthquake, but was carefully restored by the newly formed California Historic Landmarks League.

Sonoma Barracks

🏠 20 E Spain St 🕙 10am–5pm daily 🌐 sonomaparks.org

Native American labor was used to build this two-story

adobe structure between 1836 and 1840, when it served as the headquarters for Mexican General Vallejo and his troops. After the 1846 Bear Flag Revolt – when a small group of American settlers, seeking to establish their own California Republic, rebelled against the ruling Mexican government – it became an outpost for the United States Army for about a decade.

In the late 1950s it was purchased by the state and the building was carefully restored. It is now a California Historical Landmark.

SONOMA VALLEY WINERIES

The Sonoma Valley has the perfect combination of soil, sun, and rain for growing superior wine grapes. The climate varies slightly in each region, creating different environments suitable for particular grape varieties, including Cabernet Sauvignon and Chardonnay. In 1824, Fr. José Altimira planted Sonoma's first grapevines, in order to produce sacramental wine for the masses held at the Mission San Francisco Solano de Sonoma. Today the valley is home to more than 300 wineries. Some of the best are Sebastiani Vineyards, Gundlach-Bundschu Winery, and Château St. Jean. Most of the wineries offer picnic areas, though many charge for tastings.

THE WINES OF NORTHERN CALIFORNIA

California is the most important wine-growing area in the United States, producing roughly 90 percent of the nation's wine. More than 635,000 acres (216,140 ha) of the state's land is used for viticulture. Half of the grapes grown here are harvested from the fertile soil of the interior region, particularly the stretch of land bordered by the Sacramento Valley to the north and the San Joaquin Valley to the south. The north coast region accounts for less than a quarter of California's total wine-growing acreage, but many of the country's best Chardonnay, Sauvignon Blanc, Cabernet Sauvignon, and Merlot grapes are grown here. The north coast is also home to most of the state's 3,300 wineries. Chardonnay and Pinot Noir grapes are the mainstays of the central coast region, which extends from the San Francisco Bay Area to Santa Barbara.

LOCATION AND CLIMATE

California's latitude, proximity to the ocean, and sheltered valleys create a mild climate. Winters tend to be short and mild, while the growing season is long and hot but cooled by summer fogs. Combined with fertile soil, these factors mean that large areas have ideal grape-growing conditions.

GRAPE VARIETIES

California's most widely planted grape is Chardonnay, used to make a dry wine with a balance of fruit, acidity, and texture. Other popular whites include Sauvignon Blanc (also known as Fumé Blanc), Chenin Blanc, Pinot Blanc, Gewürztraminer, and Johannisberg Riesling. Red wines are dry with some tannic astringency and include the full-bodied Cabernet Sauvignon, Merlot, Syrah, Pinot Noir, and Zinfandel.

↑ Vineyard in the Alexander Valley, Sonoma County

Lake County

▽ Located north of Napa Valley, Lake County's vineyards are planted at a high elevation. The pure air helps to produce excellent Cabernet Sauvignan, Sauvignan Blanc, and other varietals.

Mendocino County

△ California's largest and most climatically diverse wine-growing region is one of the state's leading areas for organic viticulture.

Anderson Valley

△ World-class Pinot Noir, Chardonnay, Riesling, Gewürztraminer, Pinot Blanc, and Pinot Gris are produced in this valley 110 miles (180 km) north-west of San Francisco.

PRODUCERS

There are at least 800 wineries in northern California. Producers range from boutique wineries making a few hundred cases a year to vast industrial operations such as Ernest and Julio Gallo, and Kendall-Jackson.

Many wineries are increasing the number of acres farmed using organic, biodynamic, and sustainable farming techniques. Fetzer in Mendocino was a pioneer of organic viticulture in California and the winery still produces organic wines under its Bonterra label. The white wines are lean and fresh; the red packed with fruit and flavor. Navarro in Anderson Valley produces some of California's finest Rieslings, backed with vivid acidity. The wineries of Napa and the Sonoma valley *(p450, p453)* are some of the most famous.

↑ Visitors on a vineyard and winery tour in Napa Valley

THE STORY OF ZINFANDEL

This versatile grape is thought to have been brought to America from Croatia's Dalmatian coast. Zinfandel arrived in California in the 1850s, and is now the third-leading grape variety in the state. The Zinfandel reds, particularly those from the Dry Creek and Russian River valleys, are in great demand. Some have oaky flavors, while others have strong, fruity flavors. The rosé White Zinfandel was created by winemakers to use up their surplus red grapes.

Redwood Valley

▽ Best known for its red wines, such as Merlot, Cabernet Sauvignon, Pinot Noir, and Zinfandel, Redwood Valley has a red soil that gives a distinct character to its grapes.

Napa Valley

▽ Several hundred vineyards make up one of the world's leading wine regions. The Mediterranean climate produces superb Cabernet Sauvignon, Merlot, Cabernet Franc, Pinot Noir, and Zinfandel, among others.

Sonoma Valley

△ In the 1950s this region became the birthplace of the California wine industry. Today it is home to more than 300 wineries and tasting rooms and among the top grapes are Zinfandel, Merlot, Cabernet Sauvignon, and Chardonnay.

EXPERIENCE MORE

3

Mendocino

A3 **45035 Main St; www.mendoparks.org/ visitor-centers**

The settlers of this fishing village came to California from New England in 1852. They built their new homes to resemble as closely as possible those they had left behind on the East Coast, with pointed gables and decorative wooden trims. As a result, the Mendocino coastline is often referred to as "California's New England Coast." Perched on a rocky promontory high above the Pacific Ocean, Mendocino has retained the picturesque charm of its days

as a major fishing and logging center. The small, distinctive Temple of Kwan Tai, at 45160 Albion Street, dates from the mid- to late 1800s.

Although tourism is now Mendocino's main industry, the town is also a thriving arts center, with a large number of bookshops and galleries.

THE SKUNK TRAIN

Since 1885, the Skunk Train *(www.skunktrain.com)* has been running from Fort Bragg, a coastal logging town north of Mendocino, into the heart of the redwood groves. Thanks to the odoriferous mix of diesel and gasoline once used to fuel the locomotive, waiting passengers could always smell the train before they could see it, hence its name. Today locomotive lovers can ride on one of the steam, diesel, or electric trains for a half- or full-day tour through the forests.

HIDDEN GEM
Glass Beach

A ten-minute walk north of Fort Bragg, on Mendocino's coast, Glass Beach is made up of tiny pieces of glass and crockery smoothed by the sea, a legacy of the garbage that was dumped here in the past.

4

Van Damme State Park

B3 **Comptche Ukiah Rd** **From Point Arena** **Times vary, check website** **parks.ca.gov**

This beautiful 2,200-acre (890-ha) preserve has some of California's most scenic forest

trails, shaded by immense redwoods and giant ferns, and accompanied by meandering creeks. The coastal areas of the park are popular with abalone divers. For visitors who want to enjoy a hike or jog through gorgeous countryside, the lush Fern Canyon Trail is one of the best in the park. There are also several cycle trails.

A particular attraction in Van Damme State Park is the peculiar Pygmy Forest, an eerie grove of 100-year-old, stunted trees. Due to a combination of poor soil and bad drainage, these trees grow no taller than about 4 ft (1.2 m). Situated in the southeast corner of the park, the Pygmy Forest Trail is accessible for wheelchair users.

New England-style houses overlooking a beach in Mendocino ↑

Point Arena Lighthouse and Museum

🅰A3 🔲45500 Lighthouse Rd 🚌 🕐10am–3:30pm daily 🌐pointarena lighthouse.com

One mile (1.5 km) north of the Point Arena fishing village stands this impressive 115-ft (35-m) lighthouse. Erected in 1870, the original brick building was destroyed in the earthquake of 1906. The present reinforced concrete structure was inaugurated in 1908.

A climb up the 145 steps to the top of the lighthouse provides a stunning view of the coast. Tours of the lighthouse offer a chance to see its huge original Fresnel lens close-up. Built in France, it measures over 6 ft (1.8 m) in diameter, weighs more than 2 tons, and floats in a large pool of mercury.

The adjacent fog signal building, which dates from 1869, now houses a museum. Exhibits include compressed-air foghorns and displays on the history of the lighthouse.

6

Leggett

🅱B2 🚌 ℹ70400 Hwy 101; www.visitmendocino.com

This lush, green valley, separated from the Pacific Ocean by the King Mountain Range, is famous for its majestic giant redwoods. In the 1930s a hole was cut in the trunk of one enormous redwood to allow motorists to drive through the tree.

Hikers come to this area to enjoy the atmospheric redwood forest trails (part of the forest here was used to film scenes for George Lucas's science-fiction epic, *Star Wars*). The local wildlife population includes raccoons and deer, and golden eagles can often

↑ Rows of grapevines on a verdant hillside in the Russian River Valley

be seen soaring above the trees, searching the forest floor for unsuspecting prey.

South Fork Eel River, which is rich in salmon and steelhead trout, attracts many birds, including herons. The river is also popular with anglers and, in summer, swimmers.

7

Russian River Valley

🅰B3 🚌From Healdsburg ℹ16209 First St, Guerneville; www. russianriver.com

Bisected by the Russian River and its tributaries, the area known as the Russian River Valley is so vast that it contains several smaller valleys, some dominated by hillsides planted with grapevines and apple

> In the 1930s a hole was cut in the trunk of one enormous redwood in Leggett to allow motorists to drive through the tree.

orchards, others by redwood groves, family farms, and sandy river beaches. About 60 wineries, many of which are open for wine tastings, are scattered throughout the valley.

The tiny, friendly town of Guerneville is a summertime haven for San Francisco Bay Area residents, particularly popular with the LGBTQ+ community. Every year in September, the town plays host to the Russian River Jazz Festival at Johnson's Beach. Johnson's is also a good place from which to take a canoe or rafting trip down the gentle Russian River, where turtles, river otters, and great blue herons are often sighted. Hikers and equestrians flock to Guerneville to visit the 805-acre (330-ha) **Armstrong Redwoods State Natural Reserve**, the site of one of the few remaining old-growth redwood forests in California. Among the mighty redwoods in the park is a 308-ft (94-m) giant – a 1,400-year-old tree named Colonel Armstrong.

Armstrong Redwoods State Natural Reserve
🔲17020 Armstrong Woods Rd, Guerneville 🕐Daily 🌐parks.ca.gov

↑ Waves breaking against the cliffs near Bodega Bay, and *(inset)* a seal at Goat Rock Beach

8
Bodega Bay

🅰 B3 🚌 ⓘ 913 Hwy 1;
www.bodegabay.com

The coastal town of Bodega Bay is known as the setting for Alfred Hitchcock's classic 1963 film *The Birds*.

Bodega Head, the small peninsula sheltering Bodega Bay, is one of California's best whale-watching points. The northern end of Bodega Bay marks the start of the Sonoma Coast State Beach, a 10-mile (16-km) stretch of ten beaches, separated by rocky bluffs. At the northernmost tip of this chain of beaches sits the little town of Jenner. Here, the wide Russian River spills into the Pacific Ocean, and hundreds of gray harbor seals bask in the sun and breed on Goat Rock Beach. The best time to watch the seals is during their "pupping season" (Mar–late Jun).

9
Fort Ross State Historic Park

🅰 B3 🏛 1900 Coast Hwy 1, Jenner 🚌 From Point Arena ⏰ Sunrise-sunset daily ❌ Thanksgiving, Dec 25 🌐 parks.ca.gov

On a windswept headland, 12 miles (19 km) north of Jenner, stands the grand Fort Ross State Historic Park. A Russian trading outpost founded in 1812, the fort was occupied until 1841 (the name "Ross" is a derivative of the Russian word "Rossyia," meaning Russia). Built in 1836, the original house of the fort's last manager, Alexander Rotchev, is still intact today, and several other buildings have been painstakingly reconstructed within the wooden palisade. The most impressive structure in Fort Ross is the Russian Orthodox chapel, which was constructed from local redwood in 1824.

Every year, on the last Saturday of July, more than 200 costumed participants re-create life at the outpost in the 1800s.

10
Santa Rosa

🅰 B3 ✈ Sonoma County Airport, 6 miles (10 km) N of Santa Rosa 🚌 ⓘ 9 4th St; www.visitsantarosa.com

Santa Rosa is best known as the home of the horticulturist Luther Burbank (1849–1926) and Charles Schulz (1922–2000), creator of the *Peanuts* series. Burbank became world famous for developing 800 new plant varieties. Self-guided tours explore the one-acre (0.5-ha) site of the **Luther Burbank Home and Gardens**. The garden features plants often found in domestic gardens in the 1880s.

In a restored 1909 post office, the **Sonoma County Museum** explores the history of Sonoma County through rare historical photographs, documents, and artifacts.

Fans of Charles Schulz's cartoon characters can visit **Snoopy's Gallery and Gift Shop**, which stocks the world's widest range of Charlie Brown and *Peanuts* products.

Luther Burbank Home and Gardens

⏱ 🏛 204 Santa Rosa Av ⏰ Home: 1-4pm Tue-Sun; Gardens: 8am-dusk Sat-Mon & Wed, 1pm-dusk Tue, Thu & Fri 🌐 lutherburbank.org

Sonoma County Museum
🏛425 7th St 🕐11am–5pm Tue–Sun 🌐museumsc.org

Snoopy's Gallery and Gift Shop
 🏛1665 West Steele Lane 🕐10am–6pm daily 🚫Federal hols 🌐snoopygift.com

---

⑪
Calistoga

🅰B3 🚍 🛈1133 Washington St; www.calistogavisitors.com

Visitors have had mineral or mud baths in this little spa town since it was founded in the mid-1800s by the state's first millionaire, Sam Brannan (1819–89). Specialized spa treatments still draw crowds here, along with good Wine Country cuisine.

Two miles (3 km) north of the town, the **Old Faithful Geyser** spouts jets of boiling mineral water 60 ft (18 m) into the sky about once every 40 minutes. To the west lies the **Petrified Forest**. Here hikers can see huge redwoods turned to stone by a volcanic eruption over three million years ago.

Old Faithful Geyser
⊘ 🏛1299 Tubbs Lane 🕐Daily 🌐oldfaithfulgeyser.com

Petrified Forest
⊘ 🏛4100 Petrified Forest Rd 🕐9am–6pm daily 🚫Dec 25 🌐petrifiedforest.org

---

⑫
Healdsburg

🅰B3 🛈217 Healdsburg Av; www.healdsburg.com

Nestled in the Alexander Valley and surrounded by the nation's top wine regions, Healdsburg is a beautiful town with a small-village feel. Its tree-shaded streets are lined with Victorian mansions that house boutiques, restaurants, and wine-tasting rooms. At its heart is a classic 19th-century Spanish plaza, shaded by coast redwoods and surrounded by antiques stores. The Russian River runs through town, and visitors can enjoy canoeing and kayaking along its length. On one bend of the river, in the south side of town, Veterans Memorial Beach offers quiet swimming in summer.

---

⑬
Jack London State Historic Park

🅰B3 🏛2400 London Ranch Rd, Glen Ellen 🕐Park: 9am–5pm daily; Museum: 10am–5pm daily 🚫Dec 25 🌐jacklondonpark.com

In the early 1900s, the world-famous author of *The Call of the Wild (p404)* abandoned his hectic lifestyle to live in this tranquil expanse of oaks, madrones, California buckeyes, and redwoods. London (1876–1916) aptly named this territory the Beauty Ranch, and it still contains his stables, vineyards, and the cottage where he lived and died. After London's death, his widow, Charmian Kittredge, built a magnificent home on the ranch, called the House of Happy Walls. The house is now a museum displaying London memorabilia, such as his writing desk and early copies of his work. The park is ideal for a quiet picnic and a hike.

 The cottage where author Jack London spent the last years of his life, now part of Jack London State Historic Park

GOLD COUNTRY AND THE CENTRAL VALLEY

The Nisenan, Patwin, Miwok, and Yokuts peoples lived in villages in this region for centuries. They were unaffected by the influence of the early Spanish settlers in the early 1800s and their meeting with the Spanish was peaceful. The California Gold Rush, which began in 1848 at Sutter's Mill, changed everything. Thousands of prospectors poured into the region, bringing with them diseases that decimated the Indigenous population. Though most of the gold was gone within 15 years, former mining camps, such as Placerville, Murphys, Nevada City, and Sonora, survived, albeit seeing very little action as the decades passed. Sacramento flourished from its inception in 1848 and, by 1854, had become the de facto capital of California. Today it's home to the California Legislature and the Governor of California.

In the 1860s, the Geological Survey of California described the San Joaquin Valley south of Sacramento as "bone dry, parched, and baked and crisped." Over the ensuing decades a vast system of levees, aqueducts, and reservoirs transformed the valley into farming country, and the abundance of low-paying agricultural jobs has encouraged immigration from Central America and Mexico.

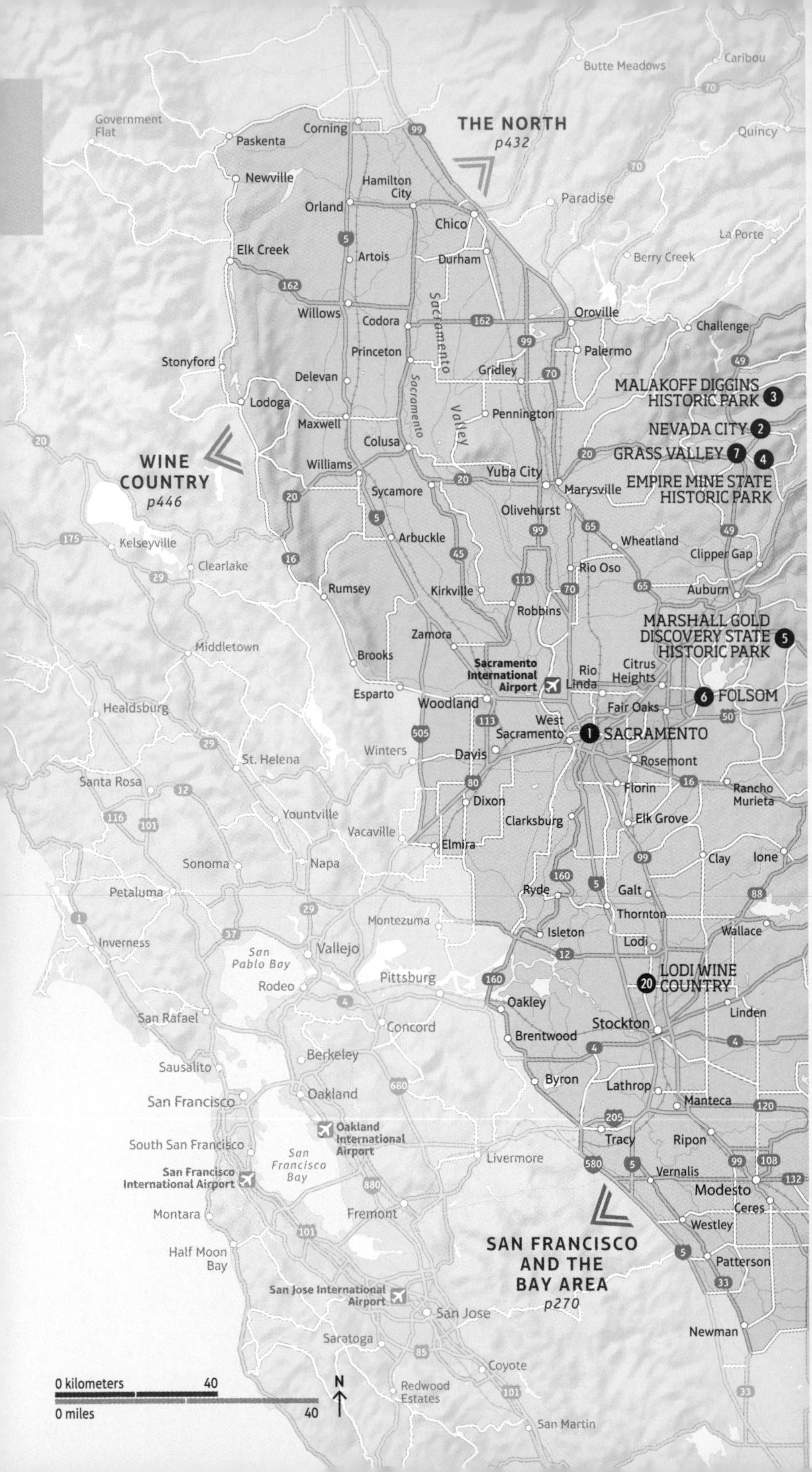

Butte Meadows
Caribou
THE NORTH
p432
Government Flat
Corning
Paskenta
Quincy
Newville
Hamilton City
Orland
Paradise
Chico
La Porte
Elk Creek
Artois
Durham
Berry Creek
Willows
Codora
Sacramento
Oroville
Challenge
Princeton
Palermo
Stonyford
Delevan
Gridley
MALAKOFF DIGGINS HISTORIC PARK 3
Lodoga
Pennington
Maxwell
Sacramento
Valley
NEVADA CITY 2
Colusa
GRASS VALLEY 7 4
WINE COUNTRY
p446
Williams
Yuba City
EMPIRE MINE STATE HISTORIC PARK
Sycamore
Marysville
Olivehurst
Arbuckle
Wheatland
Kelseyville
Clipper Gap
Clearlake
Rio Oso
Rumsey
Kirkville
Auburn
Robbins
MARSHALL GOLD DISCOVERY STATE HISTORIC PARK 5
Zamora
Middletown
Brooks
Sacramento International Airport
Rio Linda
Citrus Heights
Esparto
Woodland
6 FOLSOM
Fair Oaks
Healdsburg
West Sacramento
1 SACRAMENTO
Winters
Davis
St. Helena
Rosemont
Santa Rosa
Florin
Rancho Murieta
Dixon
Yountville
Clarksburg
Elk Grove
Vacaville
Elmira
Napa
Sonoma
Clay
Ione
Petaluma
Ryde
Galt
Thornton
Montezuma
Inverness
Isleton
Wallace
Lodi
San Pablo Bay
Vallejo
Pittsburg
Rodeo
LODI WINE COUNTRY 20
Oakley
San Rafael
Concord
Linden
Stockton
Brentwood
Berkeley
Sausalito
Byron
Lathrop
Oakland
San Francisco
Manteca
Oakland International Airport
South San Francisco
San Francisco Bay
Tracy
Ripon
Livermore
San Francisco International Airport
Vernalis
Modesto
Ceres
Montara
Fremont
Westley
SAN FRANCISCO AND THE BAY AREA
p270
Half Moon Bay
Patterson
San Jose International Airport
San Jose
Newman
Saratoga
Coyote
0 kilometers 40
0 miles 40
N
Redwood Estates
San Martin

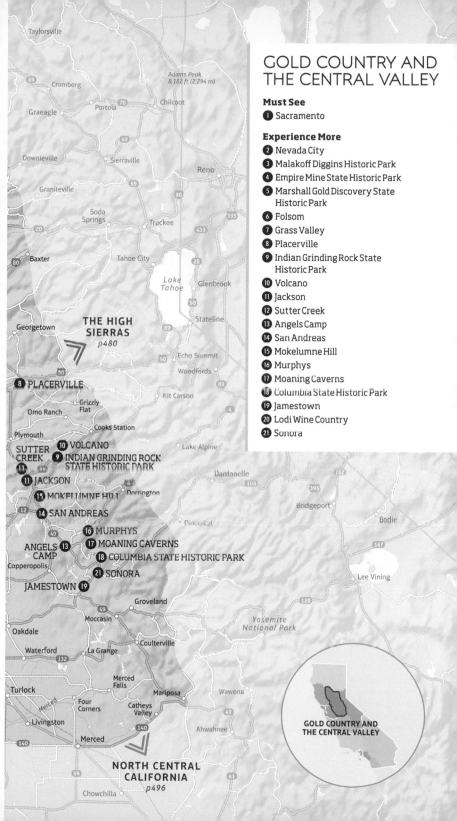

GOLD COUNTRY AND THE CENTRAL VALLEY

Must See

1. Sacramento

Experience More

2. Nevada City
3. Malakoff Diggins Historic Park
4. Empire Mine State Historic Park
5. Marshall Gold Discovery State Historic Park
6. Folsom
7. Grass Valley
8. Placerville
9. Indian Grinding Rock State Historic Park
10. Volcano
11. Jackson
12. Sutter Creek
13. Angels Camp
14. San Andreas
15. Mokelumne Hill
16. Murphys
17. Moaning Caverns
18. Columbia State Historic Park
19. Jamestown
20. Lodi Wine Country
21. Sonora

THE HIGH SIERRAS
p480

8 PLACERVILLE

SUTTER CREEK
10 VOLCANO
9 INDIAN GRINDING ROCK STATE HISTORIC PARK
11 JACKSON
15 MOKELUMNE HILL
12
14 SAN ANDREAS
16 MURPHYS
ANGELS CAMP 13
17 MOANING CAVERNS
18 COLUMBIA STATE HISTORIC PARK
21 SONORA
JAMESTOWN 19

NORTH CENTRAL CALIFORNIA
p496

GOLD COUNTRY AND THE CENTRAL VALLEY

↑ The skyline of downtown Sacramento seen from across the river

1

SACRAMENTO

🅰C3 🚻1002 2nd St; www.visitsacramento.com

The capital of California is one of the oldest incorporated cities in the state. Old Sacramento preserves many old buildings, mostly dating from the 1860s and 1870s. A handful of museums trace the area's historic importance. The Old Sacramento Waterfront district is ideal for walking and cycling.

the Sacramento History Museum contains exhibits on the Gold Rush and mining, the Nisenan and Maidu peoples, agriculture, and the cultural heritage of the city.

In the 1860s Sacramento raised its streets to avoid severe floods. Tours of Old Sacramento Underground, organized by the museum, show the remains of the original streets.

1

California State Railroad Museum

🏛111 I St ⏰10am–5pm daily ⏰Jan 1, Thanksgiving, Dec 25 🌐california railroad.museum

Immaculately restored locomotives and train cars, some dating to 1862, are part of this collection that explores the history of the California railroad. Exhibits show how the railroads changed daily life for Americans. Between April and October, the museum operates the Sacramento Southern Railroad, which takes passengers on a 45-minute round-trip along a portion of the former Southern Pacific Railroad on an old locomotive.

2

The Sacramento History Museum

🏛101 I St ⏰10am–5pm daily ⏰Jan 1, Thanksgiving, Dec 24 & 25 🌐sachistorymuseum.org

Housed in a reproduction of the 1854 City Hall and Waterworks brick building,

Did You Know?

Sacramento was home to the original Pony Express mail delivery service that ran all the way to Missouri.

3

Leland Stanford Mansion State Historic Park

🏛800 North St 📞(916) 324-0575 ⏰10am–5pm daily

This imposing pastel-shaded mansion is an excellent example of Californian Victorian architecture. Originally built in 1856 by Gold Rush merchant Sheldon Fogus, it was twice redesigned by railroad baron Leland Stanford, who also acted as California governor from 1862 to 1863. Now open as a museum, the grand edifice features gilded mirrors, historic paintings, and original period furnishings. You can also walk in the lush 19th-century-style gardens.

STAY

Delta King Riverboat
This restored 1927 moored paddle-wheel steamer has been converted into an atmospheric hotel and restaurant.

 1000 Front St
w deltaking.com

$$$

---

④ Ⓜ 🛍
Cathedral of the Blessed Sacrament

 1019 11th St ⏰ 10am-4pm daily w cathedral sacramento.org

Dedicated on June 30, 1889, the Roman Catholic Cathedral of the Blessed Sacrament was largely the vision of Sacramento's first bishop, Patrick Manogue, who had studied in a Parisian seminary and took inspiration for the building's Italian-Renaissance exterior design from the Eglise de la Sainte-Trinité in Paris. It is one of the largest churches west of the Mississippi River. The characteristic clock was added to the central tower in 1902 and the cathedral's bells were another later addition. The cavernous Victorian-style interior is decorated with numerous colorful ceiling frescoes and stained-glass windows, while the 115-ft- (35-m-) high dome centers upon a dramatic image in the oculus depicting the dove that represents the Holy Spirit.

---

⑤
Old Schoolhouse Museum

 1200 Front St
📞 (916) 483-8818
⏰ Mon–Sat

This one-room building run by volunteers is a replica of an 1800s California schoolhouse, with a pot-bellied stove, vintage student desks, and other furnishings typical of the period. Interpreters dressed as teachers in period costume are available to give insight into school life in 19th-century California. It's a fun place for kids, who can engage in role play with the "teachers."

↑ The 1800s-style Old Schoolhouse Museum in the historic center

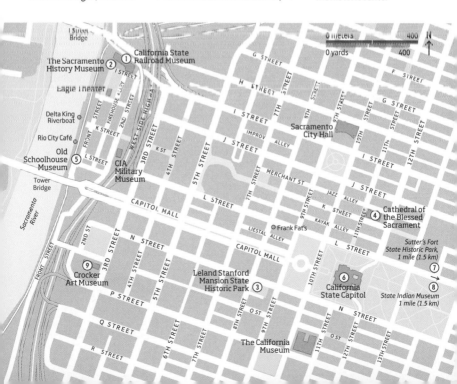

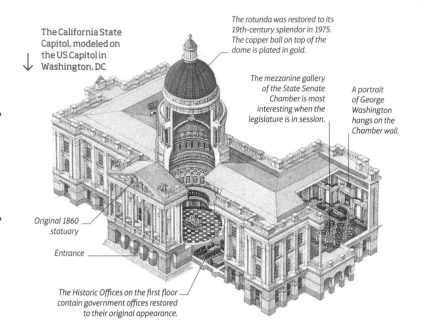

The California State Capitol, modeled on the US Capitol in Washington, DC

The rotunda was restored to its 19th-century splendor in 1975. The copper ball on top of the dome is plated in gold.

The mezzanine gallery of the State Senate Chamber is most interesting when the legislature is in session.

A portrait of George Washington hangs on the Chamber wall.

Original 1860 statuary

Entrance

The Historic Offices on the first floor contain government offices restored to their original appearance.

California State Capitol

🏛10th St & L St, Capitol Mall, Capitol Park 🕐7:30am-6pm Mon-Fri, 9am-5pm Sat & Sun 🚫Jan 1, Thanksgiving, Dec 25 🖥capitolmuseum. ca.gov

Standing at the center of a vast, landscaped park, the California State Capitol is Sacramento's primary landmark and one of the state's handsomest buildings. It was designed in 1860 in grand Greek Revival style, with Corinthian porticos and a tall central dome. The building was completed in 1874 after almost 15 years of construction, and expanded during the 1920s and 1950s. The Governor of California operates from his Capitol office, but the building also stands as a shining example of the Golden State's proud past. Along with the chambers of the state legislature, which are open to visitors even when they are in session, the Capitol serves as a museum of the state's political and cultural history.

Sutter's Fort State Historic Park

🏛2701 L St 🕐10am-5pm daily 🚫Jan 1, Thanksgiving, Dec 25 🖥suttersfort.org

Now somewhat marooned amid the suburban streets of the modern state capital, Sutter's Fort in its heyday was one of the most important and populous sites in early California history. Established by John Sutter in 1839, the fort became the cultural and economic center of northern California in the years leading up to the Gold Rush. Apart from the 21 Spanish missions along the coast, it was then the only European settlement in California. Throughout the 1840s, new immigrants following the overland trails from the eastern states stopped here for the fort's blacksmith shop, grain mill,

JOHN SUTTER

The story of the early California entrepreneur John Sutter is a classic real-life rags-to-riches-to-rags adventure. Following bankruptcy in his native Switzerland, Sutter emigrated to California in 1839. After becoming a citizen he founded a colony called New Hevetia. His land and recovered wealth made him virtual lord and master over most of northern California. However, after the discovery of gold flakes at his mill in 1848 (p470), thousands of miners swarmed to the region and took over his land. Sutter died almost penniless in 1880.

> **Sutter's Fort in its heyday was one of the most important and populous sites in early California history.**

and many other facilities. The three-story central building is all that survives of the original fort. The rest of the complex has been reconstructed to give a picture of frontier life. A walled courtyard houses historical exhibits along a self-guided audio tour, including a prison, a bakery, and a black-smith's. This is one of the few official sites in California where the Mexican flag still flies.

8

State Indian Museum

📍2618 K St 🕐10am–5pm daily 🚫Jan 1, Thanks-giving, Dec 25 🌐parks.ca.gov

This area of California was once occupied by the Maidu people. Set in a park adjacent to Sutter's Fort, this small but fascinating museum explores the different Native American cultures that existed in the state before the arrival of the first Europeans in the 16th century. Displays of handicrafts focus on the beautiful reed baskets that held both a practical and spiritual value to the Maidu, and a series of dioramas re-create the look and feel of Native American reservations. Slide shows, tape recordings, and films document other aspects of indigenous culture, from language to agricultural skills.

Special programs, generally held on weekends, celebrate the survival of ancient Native American traditions into the present day.

---

9 〰️ 〰️

Crocker Art Museum

📍216 O St 🕐10am–5pm Thu–Sun 🚫Jan 1, Thanksgiving, Dec 25 🌐crockerart.org

Founded in 1873, this is the oldest public art museum west of the Mississippi. The collection includes 19th century painting and sculpture from Asia, Europe, and the US, but its real strength is the Native American ceramics, California art and photography, and the touring shows.

The Italianate building, designed by the architect Seth Babson, is an attraction in itself. The gallery includes polychrome tiled floors, intricately carved woodwork, and a graceful central staircase. It also houses the large Teel Family Pavilion – a contemporary building added in 2010 that complements the historic structures. The museum is free to visit on public holidays.

EAT

Rio City Café
This superb restaurant with river views offers California cuisine made with local ingredients.

📍1110 Front St
🌐riocitycafe.com

💲💲💲

Frank Fat's
Running since 1939, this renowned, family-owned restaurant serves superb modern Chinese cuisine.

📍806 L St
🌐frankfats.com

💲💲💲

↑ A gallery displaying world-class works of art in the Crocker Art Museum

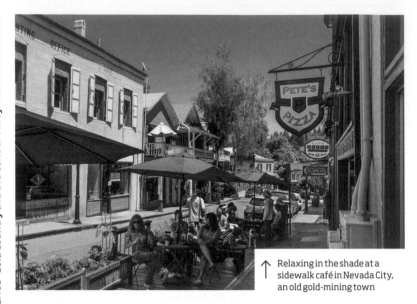

↑ Relaxing in the shade at a sidewalk café in Nevada City, an old gold-mining town

EXPERIENCE MORE

 2

Nevada City

🅐C3 🚌 ℹ️ 132 Main St; www.nevadacity chamber.com

With Victorian houses and commercial buildings lining its steep streets, picturesque Nevada City deserves its reputation as "Queen of the Northern Mines." Located at the northern end of the Mother Lode goldfields, Nevada City thrived until gold mining peaked in the 1860s, then it faded into oblivion. Nearly a century later, the city was resurrected as a tourist destination, with galleries, restaurants, and inns re-creating the Gold Rush era.

Hwy 49 takes visitors arriving in Nevada City to the foot of Broad Street. Looking up the street, the large building on the left is the National Hotel. One of California's oldest hotels, it first opened in the mid-1850s.

A block east of the hotel is **Firehouse Number 1 Museum**, one of the region's most photographed facades. Dainty balconies and a white cupola decorate the exterior, and inside, a small museum displays artifacts made by the local Maidu people, pioneer relics, including some relating to the tragic Donner Party (p492), and the altar from a Gold Rush Chinese temple. Antique mining devices are displayed in the park opposite, and several plaques on the city's walls commemorate events from its past.

Back on Broad Street, the arcaded brick facade marks the historic **Nevada Theatre**, which has been in use as a performance venue since 1865. A block to the south is the Miner's Foundry, an old metalworks where the innovative Pelton wheel was first developed and produced. A block to the north is the Art Deco facade of the city's County Courthouse, one of the city's few 20th-century works of architecture.

Firehouse Number 1 Museum

🅐214 Main St
🕐Times vary, check website
🌐nevadacountyhistory.org

Nevada Theatre

🅐401 Broad St
🌐nevadatheatre.com

 3

Malakoff Diggins Historic Park

🅐C3 🚌From Nevada City
🕐Park: sunrise-sunset; Museum: noon-4pm Thu, 10am-4pm Fri-Sun
🔒Buildings: Oct-Apr
🌐sierragoldparks foundation.org

As the original gold-mining techniques became less rewarding in the late 1850s, miners turned to increasingly powerful and destructive ways of extracting the ore. When the more easily recoverable surface deposits disappeared, the miners began to strip away the soil with powerful jets of pressurized water. Spraying more than 200,000 gallons (115,000 liters) of water per hour, the jets washed away entire mountainsides in search of gold, a process known as hydraulic mining. In 1884 the California legislature forbade the dumping of gravel into streams, but huge swaths of land had already been ruined and the rivers had been clogged up with debris. The largest of these hydraulic mining operations was at Malakoff Diggins in the mountains above Nevada City. The eroded hillsides created a canyon that now forms an eerily beautiful historic park, with several preserved buildings from the 1870s abandoned mining town of North Bloomfield.

Empire Mine State Historic Park

C3 10791 Empire St, Grass Valley From Nevada City 10am–5pm daily (winter: to 4pm) Jan 1, Thanksgiving, Dec 25 parks.ca.gov

One of the longest surviving and most lucrative gold-mining operations in the state, the Empire Mine was in business until 1956. It has now been preserved by the state as a historic park. Starting with surface workings in the 1850s, the Empire Mine grew to include 365 miles (585 km) of underground tunnels, from which pure gold estimated at 5.8 million ounces (16.5 million grams) was recovered. Head frames, which held the mine's elevator shafts and other mining equipment, are scattered over the park's 785 acres (318 ha).

To get a real sense of how much money was made here, visit the Empire Cottage. Designed by San Franciscan architect Willis Polk in 1897 for the mine's owner, William Bourn and his wife Agnes, the granite and red-brick exterior resembles an English manor house, while the redwood interior gives an air of casual affluence. The lovely gardens next door to the cottage contain nearly 1,000 rose bushes, a large greenhouse, and a tennis court.

More exhibits on the history of the Empire Mine and on hard-rock gold mining are displayed in the visitors' center, along with samples of the precious metal.

EAT

Friar Tuck's
This popular spot hosts live music nightly and serves fondue dinners and pasta.

C3 111 N Pine St, Nevada City friartucks.com

$$$

Three Forks
Wash down sandwiches and wood-fired pizzas with craft ale brewed on the premises.

C3 211 Commercial St, Nevada City threeforksnc.com

$$$

Kaldo
Top-notch sushi, sashimi, and tempura are the mainstays of this sleek restaurant.

C3 207 W Main St, Grass Valley kaidosushi.com

$$$

← Mining equipment on display in the grounds of the Empire Mine State Historic Park

5

Marshall Gold Discovery State Historic Park

🅐C3 🏠310 Back St, Coloma 🚌From Placerville ⏰8am-6pm daily 🚫Jan 1, Thanksgiving, Dec 25 🌐parks.ca.gov

Covering some 250 acres (101 ha) along the banks of the American River, this peaceful state park protects and interprets the site where gold was first discovered in January 1848. It was James Marshall who spotted shiny flakes in the water channel of a sawmill he and his fellow workmen were building for John Sutter (466), and the rest is history.

Within a year, some 10,000 miners had turned Coloma into a thriving city, but with news of even richer deposits elsewhere the boom went bust as quickly as it began. Today little remains from this momentous era.

A reproduction of Sutter's Mill stands on the original site, and a statue of James Marshall, decorated with the classic prospector's tools, including a gold pan and a pickaxe, sits on a nearby hill to mark the spot where he is buried. The park's visitors' center includes the small **Gold Discovery Museum**, which displays Native American artifacts, films, and other exhibits on the discovery of gold, as well as fascinating items relating to James Marshall.

Did You Know?

James Marshall died penniless after the gold mine he became a partner of yielded nothing.

Gold Discovery Museum

 🏠310 Back St, Coloma ⏰10am-5pm daily (Nov-Feb: 9am-4pm) 🚫Thanksgiving, Dec 25 🌐parks.ca.gov

6

Folsom

🅐C3 🚌 ℹ️200 Wool St; www.folsomchamber.com

Folsom is now a pleasant Sacramento suburb, despite being the site of the state penitentiary made famous by Johnny Cash's 1970s song "Folsom Prison Blues."

It played an important role as the last station on the Pony Express and transcontinental railroad. Folsom is now one of the few remaining transcontinental railroad sites, as documented in the local **Folsom History Museum**. Antique shops line the Wild West-style Sutter Street, set amid boxcars and other railroad memorabilia.

At the foot of Riley Street, behind Folsom Dam, there is a large lake, which is a popular summer vacation spot for boating and fishing. Another body of water, the Folsom Lake can be reached via the Johnny Cash Trail, a bike and pedestrian path that goes through the historic district. Future plans for the trail include the addition of eight large art installations related to Johnny Cash.

→

Old buildings in Placerville, once a thriving supply center for local miners

Folsom History Museum

🏠823 Sutter St ⏰11am-4pm Tue-Sun 🚫Federal hols 🌐folsomhistoricalsociety.org

7

Grass Valley

🅐C3 🚌 ℹ️128 E Main St; www.grassvalleychamber.com

Long the largest and busiest town in the northern Gold Country, Grass Valley served the Empire Mine and other nearby hard-rock gold mines.

In the 1870s and 1880s Grass Valley welcomed workers from the tin mines of Cornwall, England, who were known as "Cousin Jacks." Their expertise enabled the local mines to recover underground ore deposits and so remain in business after the rest of the area had fallen quiet. Grass Valley also has one of California's best mining museums. The **North Star**

←

Statue of James Marshall in Marshall Gold Discovery State Historic Park

MARSHALL

Mining Museum and Pelton Wheel Exhibit is situated in the powerhouse of the former North Star Mine. Surrounding the entrance are the giant Pelton wheels that increased production in the region's underground mines. Displays include a stamp mill (a giant pulverizer used to crush ore), a Cornish pump (used to filter out underground water), and artifacts relating to the local miners' Cornish background.

North Star Mining Museum and Pelton Wheel Exhibit
🏠 Mill St at Allison Ranch Rd
🕐 May–Oct: noon–4pm Wed–Sun 🌐 nevadacounty history.org

 8

Placerville
🅰 C3 🚌 ℹ 542 Main St; www.visit-eldorado.com

During the Gold Rush, Placerville was a busy supply center for the surrounding mining camps. Still located on one of the main routes to Sacramento, Placerville has retained its importance as a transportation center, although the stagecoaches have long since given way to cars and trucks along US 50.

The downtown business district preserves a handful of historic structures and sites, but the best sense of Placerville's past comes from the Placerville History Museum on Main Street and the **El Dorado County Historical Museum**. The displays here range from old mining equipment and a replica of a 19th-century general store to artifacts from the Chinese settlement and other local historical exhibits.

A little way out of town, **Gold Bug Park** is a former gold mine offering a number of family-friendly activities, from self-guided tours of the mine and museum, to looking for gems in a panning trough.

El Dorado County Historical Museum
🏠 104 Placerville Dr
🕐 10am–4pm Wed–Sat, noon–4pm Sun 🚫 Federal hols 🌐 museum.edcgov.us

Gold Bug Park
🏠 2635 Goldbug Lane
🕐 10am–5pm daily
🌐 goldbugpark.org

STAY

Cary House Hotel
In the heart of Placerville, this quiet boutique hotel is full of elegant period furnishings dating to the mid-1800s.
🅰 C3 🏠 300 Main St, Placerville
🌐 caryhousehotel.com

💲💲💲

EAT

The Sutter Restaurant

The elegant dining room of the Victorian Hotel Sutter offers quality California cuisine and a tempting wine list.

🅰C3 🏠53 Main St, Sutter Creek
🌐hotelsutter.com

$⑤⑤$

Taste

The stylish menu here includes dishes such as Alaskan halibut with black quinoa.

🅰C3 🏠9402 Main St, Plymouth
🌐restauranttaste.com

$⑤⑤$

Mel & Faye's Diner

This classic roadside diner is a fine stop to fill up on huge breakfasts, lunchtime sandwiches, or a succulent steak.

🅰C3 🏠31 Hwy 88, Jackson 🌐melandfayes.homestead.com

⑤$⑤

Union Inn & Pub

A former Wild West saloon, this is now a pub serving comfort food.

🅰C3 🏠21375 Consolation St, Volcano
🌐volcanounion.com

$⑤⑤

Grounds

Classic American breakfast, lunch, and dinner are served here.

🅰C3 🏠402 Main St, Murphys 🌐groundsrestaurant.com

$⑤⑤

↑ Holes made for grinding acorns at Indian Grinding Rock State Historic Park

9

Indian Grinding Rock State Historic Park

🅰C3 🏠14881 Pine Grove, Volcano Rd, Pine Grove 🚍From Sacramento 🚌From Sacramento or Jackson 🕐Park: sunrise–sunset; Museum: 10am–4pm daily 🌐parks.ca.gov

Tucked away amid the oak trees in the hills above Jackson, this 136-acre (55-ha) park protects one of the largest and most complete Native American sites in the country. The area was once home to the Miwok people and the park is dedicated to their past and future. The aim of this comprehensive museum is to increase understanding of Native American life, centering on the Californian foothill peoples. Exhibits include an array of basketry, dance regalia, and ancient tools.

Hundreds of mortar holes form the main focus of the park. These limestone pockets were formed by generations of Miwok grinding meal from acorns. There are also many rock carvings and replica Miwok dwellings.

10

Volcano

🅰C3 🚌 ℹ71A Main St, Sutter Creek; www.amadorcountychamber.com

For a taste of the Gold Rush without the tourist trappings, visit Volcano, a picturesque ghost of a mining town with a wealth of historic sights.

During the Gold Rush, the town had an unusual reputation for sophistication and culture, creating the state's first library and its first astronomical observatory. The old jail, stagecoach office, brewery, and a cannon dating from the Civil War are among the preserved buildings and artifacts on display around

→

Nineteenth-century wooden buildings lining Main Street in Sutter Creek

the four-block town. The most attractive Victorian building is the historic St. George Hotel (16104 Main St) covered in Virginia creeper.

Springtime visitors to the region should also follow the signs to Daffodil Hill, 3 miles (5 km) north of Volcano, when more than 300,000 naturalized daffodil bulbs come into full bloom on the hillside.

⑪ Jackson

C3 🚌 🛈115 Main St; www.amadorcounty chamber.com

Located at the crossroads of two main Gold Rush trails, Jackson was once a bustling gold-mining community and has continued to thrive as a commercial center and lumber mill town since 1850.

The town center features a number of old Gold Rush buildings, but the most interesting stop is the **Amador County Museum**, on a hill above the town. Here you can view working models of stamp mills and a variety of other old mining equipment.

North of the town, in a small park off Hwy 49, are the massive tailing wheels from the Kennedy Mine, one of the deepest in the US. Reaching 58 ft (18 m) in diameter, these wheels were used to dispose of leftover rocks after the gold had been extracted. St. Sava's Serbian Orthodox Church, built in 1894 with a delicate white steeple, is also in the park. It is a testament to one of many cultures that contributed to the history of the Gold Country.

Amador County Museum
📍225 Church St 🕐11am– 3pm Fri–Sun 🚫Federal hols 🌐amadorgov.org

⑫ Sutter Creek

C3 🚌 🛈71-A Main St; www.suttercreek.org

Named after John Sutter (p466), Sutter Creek is one of the prettiest Gold Country towns, full of antiques shops and whitewashed country inns. It grew up around 1860 to service the Old Eureka Mine, which was owned by Hetty Green, reputedly the "Richest Woman in the World." Industrialist and politician Leland Stanford put $5,000 into the town's Lincoln Mine, which produced millions of dollars worth of gold. Along

 INSIDER TIP
Scott Harvey Wines Tasting Room

To sample fine Amador County wines come to this tasting room in Sutter Creek or take a tour of the winery in Shenandoah (www. scottharveywines.com).

with partners Charles Crocker, Collis Huntington and Mark Hopkins, he invested the money in railroads, becoming governor of the Central Pacific Railroad in 1861, and then the eighth governor of California.

In the heart of Sutter Creek is **Knight Foundry**, established in 1873 to provide equipment to gold mines. The last surviving water-powered cast-iron foundry in the US, it displays impressive machinery.

An attractive drive in the region is along Sutter Creek Road via Indian Grinding Rock State Historic Park to Volcano, past remains of former mining equipment.

Knight Foundry
🚶🚲🅿 📍81 Eureka St 🕐10am–4pm daily 🌐knightfoundry. com

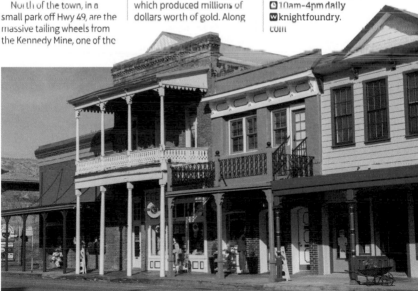

13
Angels Camp

C3 **753 S Main St; www.gocalaveras.com**

Angels Camp is a former gold-mining town that was best known as the real-life location of Mark Twain's classic short story "The Celebrated Jumping Frog of Calaveras County". Today the town has grown into a commercial center for the surrounding area.

A few historic structures, including the Angels Hotel where Twain heard the story of the jumping frog, still line the steep streets of the compact downtown area, which usually comes alive every May for a popular reenactment of the frog-jumping competition (with strict rules regulating the frogs' welfare).

Two huge 19th-century locomotives stand on Hwy 49 in front of the **Angels Camp Museum**, which contains an array of old mining equipment. There is also a large collection of Native American artifacts and exhibits on Mark Twain and the jumping frog.

Angels Camp Museum
⊘ **753 S Main St**
🕙 10am–4pm daily
🚫 Thanksgiving, Dec 25
🌐 angelscamp.gov

14
San Andreas

C3 **753 S Main St, Angels Camp; www.gocalaveras.com**

Home to the Calaveras County government, San Andreas is a small, bustling city. During the Gold Rush era, however, it was a gritty mining camp, originally built in 1848 by Mexicans who were later forcibly removed by white Americans after rich deposits of gold were found. In 1883 the legendary outlaw Black Bart was captured here.

Very little now remains from the Gold Rush days, although there are a handful of historic buildings on Main Street, such as the Odd Fellows Hall (1856) and the Calaveras County Archives. Dating from 1855, the latter is the oldest building in town. San Andreas also houses one of the Gold Country's best museums, the **Calaveras County Historical Museum**, in the old courthouse just north of Hwy 49. Along with exhibits tracing gold-mining history from 1848 to the 1930s, the collection includes Miwok artifacts and the courtroom where Black Bart, the "Gentleman Bandit," was tried and convicted. His prison cell during the trial, situated behind the museum, is now surrounded by a pleasant, if somewhat incongruous, garden of indigenous plants.

BLACK BART

Famous for his habit of leaving poetry at the scene of his crimes, the outlaw known as Black Bart is one of the state's best-loved legends.

After holding up stagecoaches between 1877 and 1883, he was caught when the laundry mark on his handkerchief was traced to San Francisco. Black Bart turned out to be Charles Boles, a mining engineer. Tried and convicted in San Andreas, he spent five years in San Quentin prison.

Calaveras County Historical Museum
⊘ **30 N Main St**
🕙 10am–4pm daily
🚫 Jan 1, Thanksgiving, Dec 25 🌐 calaverasco historical.com

15
Mokelumne Hill

C3 **753 S Main St, Angels Camp; www.gocalaveras.com**

Bypassed by Hwy 49, Mokelumne Hill is one of the most intriguing old Gold Country towns. A handful of historic buildings, including the Hotel Leger, with its

 ←

Ol' Beth, a 19th-century locomotive on display at Angels Camp Museum

→ Grapevine-covered hillside at the scenic Ironstone Vineyards, near Murphys

wraparound balconies, and the old Wells Fargo stagecoach station, form a charming one-block business district. However, the sleepy, old-world ambience of "Moke Hill," as it is commonly known, belies the town's unsavory and violent history.

Although much of the town has fallen into picturesque decay, during the Gold Rush era the hotels and saloons were packed with belligerent miners, whose drunken fights resulted in an average of one killing per week. Many of the victims ended up in the hilltop Protestant Cemetery – a short walk to the west of town. Here the multilingual headstones are now all that remain of the international population who came to the town in search of gold.

> **Although much of Moke Hill has fallen into picturesque decay, during the Gold Rush era the hotels and saloons were packed with belligerent miners.**

 16

Murphys

▲ C3   🛈 753 S Main St, Angels Camp; www.gocalaveras.com

With mature sycamores, elms, and locust trees lining its quiet streets, Murphys is among the prettiest towns in the southern Gold Country. It offers a quiet, pleasant break from the frantic tourism of many of the other Mother Lode towns and sights in the area.

Having played host to such luminaries as Ulysses S Grant, Mark Twain, and Will Rogers, the restored Murphys Hotel, built in 1855 at the intersection of Main and Algiers streets, is now the town landmark. Across the street, the **Old-Timers' Museum** houses a quirky collection of Gold Rush memorabilia. The outside wall displays a series of humorous plaques detailing the town's history.

A short drive north of Murphys takes you to the **Mercer Caverns**, with their fascinating rock formations ranging from stalagmites to calcite flowstones.

Old-Timers' Museum

⊗ 🏠 470 Main St ⏰ Noon–4pm Fri–Sun 🗓 Jan 1, Thanksgiving, Dec 25 🖥 murphysoldtimersmuseum.com

Mercer Caverns

⊗⊗⊗ 🏠 1665 Sheep Ranch Rd ⏰ 9am–5pm daily (winter: 10am–4:30pm) 🗓 Thanksgiving, Dec 25 🖥 mercercaverns.net

TOP 3 **MURPHYS WINE-TASTING TOURS**

Ironstone Vineyards
▲ C3 🏠 1894 Six Mile Rd
🖥 ironstonevineyards.com
Join a tasting tour at this scenic winery.

Aloria Vineyards
▲ C3 🏠 448 Main St
🖥 aloriavineyard.com
Try superb, handcrafted wines on a tour.

Hovey Winery
▲ C3 🏠 350 Main St
🖥 hoveywine.com
Tour the tasting room, which has 13 wine varietals.

17

Moaning Caverns

C3 5350 Moaning Cave Rd, Vallecito Times vary, check website moaningcaverns.com

This large limestone cavern took its name from the groaning sound emitted by the wind flowing out of the entrance. Unfortunately the sound was destroyed when the cavern was enlarged to improve public access. Two types of tours (Spiral Tour and Expedition Tour) explore the cave.

18

Columbia State Historic Park

C3 Hwy 49 22708 Broadway St; www.parks.ca.gov

At the height of the Gold Rush, Columbia was one of the largest and most important towns in the Gold Country. Most of California's mining camps were abandoned; they quickly disintegrated and disappeared after the gold ran out in the late 1850s. Unusually, Columbia remained active. It was proudly kept intact by its remaining residents until 1945, when California's government turned the entire town into a state historic park. Many buildings have been preserved in their original Gold Rush-era state. The state historic park gives a good example of what life was like during one of America's most colorful periods of history.

19

Jamestown

C4 193 S Washington St, Sonora; www.visittuolumne.com/jamestown

Jamestown was home to the largest gold mine in operation until 1993. Some of the historic town was destroyed by fire in 1966, but Main Street still has many picturesque buildings, such as the Jamestown Hotel.

Railtown 1897 State Historic Park, north of downtown, preserves the steam locomotives and historic carriages of the Sierra Railroad. Rides are offered on weekends (April to October).

Railtown 1897 State Historic Park

 5th Av & Reservoir Rd Apr–Oct: 9:30am–4:30pm daily; Nov–Mar: 10am–3pm daily Jan 1, Thanksgiving, Dec 25 railtown1897.org

20

Lodi Wine Country

C3 Stockton, 15 miles (25 km) S of Lodi 2545 W Turner Rd; www.lodiwine.com

Lodi Wine Country centers on the large town of Stockton. The **Haggin Museum** reveals the town's history and includes Native American crafts and 19th-century storefronts.

Just north of Stockton, the fertile valley around Lodi enjoys a Mediterranean-type climate and has become one of California's most respected wine destinations. Vines were first planted here in 1850 and, after Prohibition halted the industry's initial

Tree-lined Main Street in Columbia State Historic Park, and *(inset)* inside the farriery

expansion, there was a boom in dessert wines from the 1940s. In the late 1960s the emphasis changed to premium varietals from Europe, and Lodi was granted its own appellation in 1986. Hundreds of wines are now produced by more than 80 wineries, many adopting sustainable farming practices.

Haggin Museum

 ⌂1201 N Pershing Ave ⏱1:30–5pm Wed–Fri, noon–5pm Sat & Sun 🗓Jan 1, Dec 23–25, 30, 31 🖥hagginmuseum.org

---

㉑

Sonora

🅐C4 🚌 🛈193 S Washington St; www. visittuolumne.com

Known as the "Queen of the Southern Mines," Sonora was established in 1848 by miners who emigrated from the state of Sonora in Mexico. As with many other communities in the area, gold mining was at the heart of the town's early development. Sonora outstripped Columbia for the seat of county government during the Gold Rush. As mining declined in the late 1800s, the lumber industry took over with the arrival of the Sierra Railroad in 1899.

Today Sonora is the Tuolumne County seat and a busy commercial center, which thrives mainly on tourism. Many old narrow streets and historic buildings have been perfectly preserved, including the St. James Episcopal Church and the Sonora Opera Hall on Washington Street, as well as a number of Victorian houses. Sonora's old jail was built in 1857 and renovated after being destroyed in a fire in 1866. It is now home to the **Tuolumne County Museum and History Center**. The museum houses Gold Rush artifacts, including gold nuggets and a number of 19th-century photographs.

Tuolumne County Museum and History Center

⌂158 W Bradford Ave ⏱10am–4pm Sun–Fri, 10am–3:30pm Sat 🗓Jan 1, Dec 25 🖥tchistory.org

↑ St. James Episcopal Church, built in Sonora in the mid-19th century

DRINK

Zane Iron Horse Lounge
This dive bar serves good spirit measures and offers a friendly welcome, as well as a retro jukebox.

🅐C4 ⌂97 S Washington St, Sonora ☎(209) 532-4482

Sonora Tap Room
Sample some of the 20 craft beers on tap or sip great wines in the diminutive interior of this lively bar-restaurant. There is regular live music in the evenings.

🅐C4 ⌂1 Linoberg St, Sonora ☎(209) 288-2423

A SHORT WALK
COLUMBIA STATE HISTORIC PARK

Distance 1 mile (1.5 km) **Time** 20 minutes
Nearest bus Route 4, Columbia State Historic Park

Once a busy Gold Rush town, Columbia (p476) was also one of the largest cities in California by the mid-19th century. Gold from Columbia was used to finance the United States government and the Union Army during the Civil War. Though the town's population dwindled after the decline of the mining boom in the 1860s, Columbia never became deserted. In the 1920s and 1930s local groups worked to preserve its historic buildings. Today visitors can enjoy a stroll through this inhabited open-air museum. Shops, stagecoach rides, and regular tours are run by individuals in period costumes.

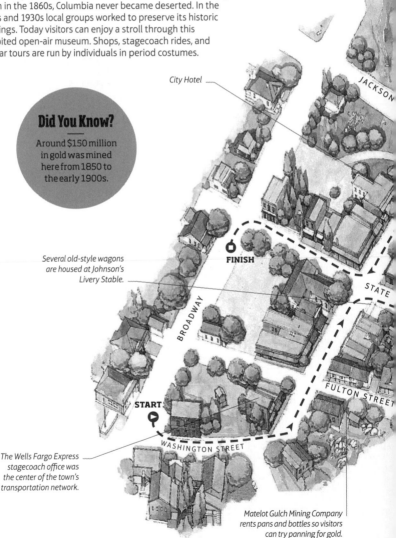

Did You Know?

Around $150 million in gold was mined here from 1850 to the early 1900s.

City Hotel

FINISH

JACKSON

STATE

Several old-style wagons are housed at Johnson's Livery Stable.

BROADWAY

FULTON STREET

START

The Wells Fargo Express stagecoach office was the center of the town's transportation network.

WASHINGTON STREET

Matelot Gulch Mining Company rents pans and bottles so visitors can try panning for gold.

← Historic buildings lining a road in Columbia State Historic Park

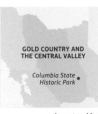
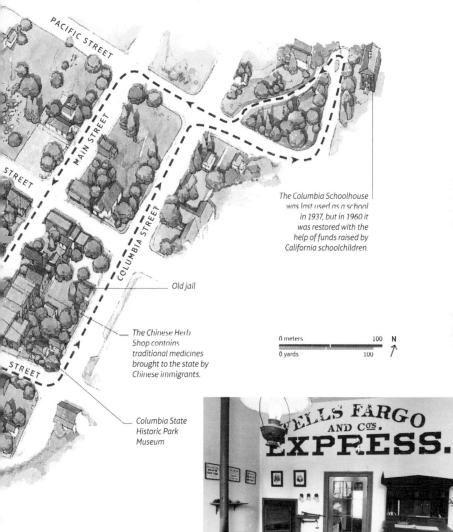

PACIFIC STREET

MAIN STREET

COLUMBIA STREET

STREET

STREET

The Columbia Schoolhouse was last used as a school in 1937, but in 1960 it was restored with the help of funds raised by California schoolchildren.

Old jail

The Chinese Herb Shop contains traditional medicines brought to the state by Chinese immigrants.

Columbia State Historic Park Museum

0 meters 100 N
0 yards 100

→ The perfectly preserved Wells Fargo Express stagecoach office

THE HIGH SIERRAS

The High Sierras of California were once the realm of the Paiute, Mono, Panamint, and Miwok peoples, and, due to the challenging mountainous terrain, completely escaped gold fever. In 1851, Major James Savage led the Mariposa Battalion against the Awahneechee – a Miwok people – trailing them beyond the foothills and becoming the first white men to set foot in Yosemite Valley in the process. His troops forced the Awahneechee off their land to the Fresno River Reservation to make way for white settler farmers. The valley has been protected since 1864, and in 1890, Yosemite became the third US national park, due in part to Scottish naturalist John Muir. A few Ahwahneechee were allowed to stay on their land but only if they agreed to act as guides and weave baskets for visiting tourists.

The land now encompassed by the Sequoia and Kings Canyon National Parks was also widely ignored by Europeans until 1858, when the local Yokuts people led Hale Tharp, a cattleman from Three Rivers, up to the sequoias around Moro Rock. Hale Tharp was the first white man to reach this region. Over the next 40 years, settlers and the California State Militia waged war on the Yokuts people and their population was all but annihilated by the end of the 19th century. In 1890, Sequoia became the country's second national park.

To the north, Lake Tahoe also became a recreational haven in the late 19th century. Tahoe City was founded as a resort community in 1864, and the lake has been a tourist magnet ever since.

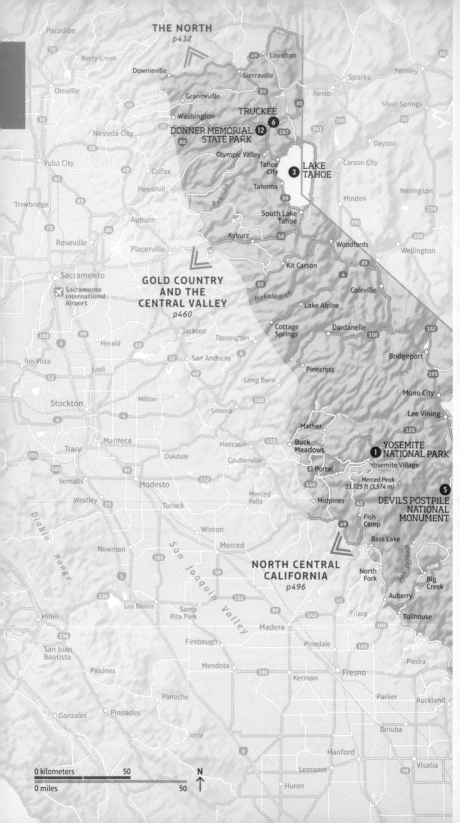

THE HIGH SIERRAS

Must Sees

1 Yosemite National Park
2 Sequoia and Kings Canyon National Parks
3 Lake Tahoe

Experience More

4 Mono Lake
5 Devils Postpile National Monument
6 Truckee
7 Bodie State Historic Park
8 Mammoth Lakes
9 White Mountains
10 Owens Valley
11 Mount Whitney
12 Donner Memorial State Park

YOSEMITE NATIONAL PARK

D4 **To Yosemite Valley** **To Merced, then YARTS shuttle to Yosemite Valley** **nps.gov/yose**

Soaring cliffs, plunging waterfalls, and rugged canyons – some of the world's most beautiful terrain lies within Yosemite National Park. Millions of years of glacial activity have formed these natural beauties.

Standing nearly 1 mile (1.5 km) above the valley floor, the silhouette of the Half Dome cliff has become the symbol of Yosemite. This landmark is in fact a granite ridge, polished by glaciers to create the illusion that it is a round, rock dome cut in half. A formidable trail using steel cable handholds leads to the summit, offering panoramic views of the valley. But you'd be mistaken in thinking that Half Dome is Yosemite's only attraction. Rock-climbers can spend days scaling El Capitan, at the valley's western entrance, while those who prefer a more sedate pace of life can step back in time at the Yosemite Museum or Yosemite Chapel, soak up the views from Glacier Point, or take a gentle hike. Each season offers something different, from the swelling waterfalls of spring to the rustic colors of fall. Numerous roads, bus tours, bike paths, and hiking trails link the spectacular views.

The vista from Tunnel View lookout, with El Capitan on the left and Bridalveil Falls on the right ↑

[1] A popular half-day hike is the Mist Trail, which takes in the 317-ft (97-m) Vernal Falls and 594-ft (180-m) Nevada Falls.

[2] Mariposa Grove, at the southern end of the park, features over 500 giant sequoia trees, some more than 3,000 years old and 250 ft (75 m) tall.

[3] The great Yosemite panorama can be experienced from Glacier Point, which rests on a rocky ledge 3,215 ft (980 m) above the valley, and is only accessible in summer when the road is clear.

Did You Know?

The valley's Native American name was *Ahwahnee*, meaning "gaping, mouth-like place".

EXPLORING YOSEMITE NATIONAL PARK

Over 4 million people visit the 1,170 sq miles (3,030 sq km) of Yosemite National Park each year. The summer months are the most crowded. Parking fills up quickly, so arrive early and use the free shuttle system, well-maintained cycle paths, and hiking trails to get around the park. There are over 750 miles (1,207 km) of hiking trails in Yosemite, ranging from easy walks in popular beauty spots to challenging, multi-day wilderness treks, and 12 miles (19 km) of paved bike paths in Yosemite Valley alone.

The spectacular Yosemite Valley is a good base from which to explore the park. It is easily reached by car and there are 200 miles (320 km) of paved roads from here, providing access to more remote areas. However, during the snowbound winter months several roads are inaccessible. Yosemite Village has the main visitor center, a museum, and plenty of restaurants. It's the perfect place to relax after a day spent trekking, swimming, kayaking, or skiing.

Yosemite Creek drops 2,425 ft (740 m), to form **Lower Yosemite Falls** – the highest waterfall in the US.

Upper Yosemite Falls

Valley Visitors' Center

The history of the Miwok and Paiute people is displayed in the **Yosemite Museum**.

The tiny **Yosemite Chapel** (1879) is all that is left of Yosemite's 19th-century Old Village.

Yosemite Creek

Yosemite Village

Yosemite Lodge

Sunnyside

NORTHSIDE DRIVE

SOUTHSIDE DRIVE

Lower River

Sentinel Creek

FOUR-MILE TRAIL

YOSEMITE FALLS TRAIL

0 kilometers 1
0 miles 1

N

Sentinel Rock 7,038 ft (2,145 m)

Sentinel Falls

Sentinel Dome can be reached via the trail from Glacier Point.

← Yosemite Chapel, nestled in the forest below the hulking silhouette of Half Dome

↑ Mirror Lake, the last remnant of a large glacial lake that once filled Yosemite Valley

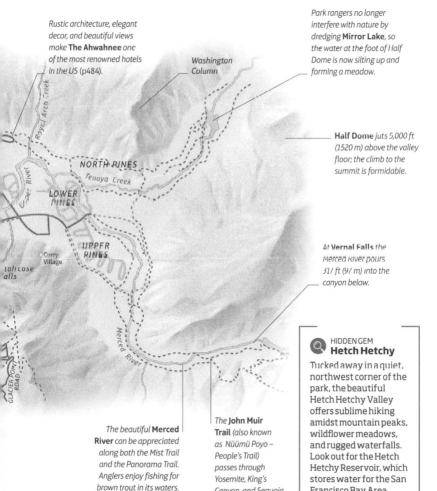

Rustic architecture, elegant decor, and beautiful views make **The Ahwahnee** *one of the most renowned hotels in the US (p484).*

Washington Column

Park rangers no longer interfere with nature by dredging **Mirror Lake***, so the water at the foot of Half Dome is now silting up and forming a meadow.*

Half Dome *juts 5,000 ft (1520 m) above the valley floor; the climb to the summit is formidable.*

Royal Arch Creek

NORTH PINES

Tenaya Creek

LOWER PINES

UPPER PINES

Curry Village

Staircase Falls

At **Vernal Falls** *the Merced River pours 317 ft (97 m) into the canyon below.*

Merced River

GLACIER POINT ROAD

The beautiful **Merced River** *can be appreciated along both the Mist Trail and the Panorama Trail. Anglers enjoy fishing for brown trout in its waters.*

The **John Muir Trail** *(also known as Nüümü Poyo – People's Trail) passes through Yosemite, King's Canyon, and Sequoia national parks.*

> **HIDDEN GEM**
> ### Hetch Hetchy
> Tucked away in a quiet, northwest corner of the park, the beautiful Hetch Hetchy Valley offers sublime hiking amidst mountain peaks, wildflower meadows, and rugged waterfalls. Look out for the Hetch Hetchy Reservoir, which stores water for the San Francisco Bay Area.

SEQUOIA AND KINGS CANYON NATIONAL PARKS

🅰D4 **ℹ** **Kings Canyon Visitor Center: 83918 Hwy 180; www.nps.gov/seki**

Walk among the Earth's largest living trees in these twin national parks. Together they preserve lush forests, rugged granite peaks, and glacier-carved canyons rich in wildlife.

The Sequoia and Kings Canyon National Parks protect 40 groves of giant sequoia, the largest tree species in the world. America's deepest canyon, the south fork of the Kings River, cuts a depth of 8,200 ft (2,500 m) through Kings Canyon. Along the eastern boundary of Sequoia is Mount Whitney (p494), the highest summit on the US mainland, while deep underground is a network of subterranean tunnels and caves with surreal rock formations. Wild and scenic rivers and thousands of lakes and ponds nurture bears, cougars, and many other wild creatures.

Roads serve the western side of the parks; the rest is wilderness, accessible only to serious hikers or with rented pack-trains of horses or mules. Winter visitors can ski cross-country over both marked and unmarked trails.

GREAT VIEW
Moro Rock

A staircase carved into the rock takes you to the top of this granite monolith. The climb of over 350 steps is worth it, giving 360-degree views across the High Sierras and California's Central Valley.

The High Sierras seen from near the top of Moro Rock, and *(inset)* a brown bear and its cub ↑

↑ People standing under the General Sherman Tree, the largest tree on Earth

Mineral King

△ Steep, narrow Mineral King Road winds 25 miles (40 km) up to this beautiful and remote subalpine valley. Hike short loop trails or backpack on wilderness tracks beneath soaring, rugged peaks.

Tunnel Log

▷ Over 2,000 years old, Tunnel Log fell naturally across Crescent Meadow Road in 1937. Smaller vehicles can drive underneath.

Giant Forest

Hiking trails take you through one of the largest groves of sequoias in the world. Learn all about them at the Giant Forest Museum. An array of sequoias border Crescent Meadow, a colorful grassy wetland full of wildlife, which naturalist John Muir called the "gem of the Sierra."

General Sherman Tree

The world's largest living single-stem tree has a trunk measuring 36 ft (11 m) around its base. The tree still grows 0.4 inches (1 cm) every ten years.

Crystal Cave

Chiseled out by an ancient river, this marble cavern is filled with glistening stalagmites and stalactites, and is one of the few caves open to visitors. Sign up well in advance for the mandatory guided tours.

General Grant Tree

The centerpiece of Grant Grove, the General Grant Tree is the world's second-largest sequoia. It is also known as the Nation's Christmas Tree; a ceremony is held here every Christmas.

Cedar Grove

◁ Kings Canyon Scenic Byway leads to this lesser-visited, gorgeous, glaciated valley, a good place to see the mighty Kings River. Follow trails to Roaring River Falls, Mist Falls, and Zumwalt Meadow, beneath towering rock formations like Grand Sentinel and North Dome.

Did You Know?

"Tahoe" is a mispronunciation of the Washoe name for the area – *Da ow a ga*, or "edge of the lake."

3 🍴 🖥 🛍

LAKE TAHOE

🅐 D3 🚗 I-89 and US 50 🚆 Truckee 🚌 South Lake Tahoe
🌐 visitinglaketahoe.com

Surrounded by stunning snowcapped peaks and lush forests that frame its clear, cobalt blue waters, Lake Tahoe is both beautiful and a high-altitude haven for enjoying the great outdoors.

↑ The Heavenly Mountain Gondola, which grants fabulous lake views

Sitting majestically in the Sierra Nevada mountains at 6,225 ft (1,897 m) above sea level, Lake Tahoe is the largest alpine lake in North America. Scenic roads run all the way around its 71-mile (114-km) shoreline, which is dotted with beaches, harbors, and state parks. The area began to develop as a resort after the construction of the first road here in 1915 made it more accessible. Its reputation for recreation was cemented when the first waterside casinos opened on the Nevada side of the lake in the 1930s.

Apart from gambling, the lake is a haven for outdoor enthusiasts, with outstanding hiking and biking trails. The south shore is known for its long stretch of sandy beaches, and offers everything from boating and watersports to snowshoeing and cross-country skiing. Meanwhile, the northern shore of the lake is more laid-back, with smaller towns and beaches, good fishing and river rafting, and winter activities.

Must See

↑ Looking over Lake Tahoe from the inlet of Emerald Bay, on the lake's west shore

[1] The challenging Tahoe Rim Trail climbs to 10,338 ft (3,151 m), and passes through stunning mountain wilderness, as it skirts the lake.

[2] The peaks surrounding Lake Tahoe, particularly on the California side, are famous for their ski resorts.

[3] With a short sweep of golden sand, and beautiful mountain views, Baldwin Beach, on the southern shore, is a great spot for swimming and picnicking. Kayak rentals are also available.

EXPERIENCE MORE

4

Mono Lake

🗺D4 🚉Merced
ℹHwy 395 & 3rd St;
www.monolake.org

The 70 sq miles (180 sq km) of this ancient lake are among the most visually striking anywhere in the United States. The Sierra Nevada is reflected in the clear waters of the lake, which formed between two volcanic islands. Evaporation and water diversion to Los Angeles have resulted in a shrunken, incredibly brackish lake – some three times saltier than seawater. Twisting natural limestone sculptures (called "tufa spires") poke out of the lake, making for some truly otherworldly scenery. The lake and its striking formations are protected by local bylaws.

Did You Know?

In the 1860s, writer Mark Twain called Mono Lake "the Dead Sea of California."

Visitors can find out the best ways to explore the area at the **Mono Lake Committee Information Center & Bookstore** and the **Mono Basin National Forest Scenic Area Visitor Center**.

Mono Lake Committee Information Center & Bookstore

🗺Hwy 395 & 3rd St, Lee Vining 🌐monolake.org/visit/infocenterbookstore

Mono Basin National Forest Scenic Area Visitor Center

🗺1 Visitor Center Dr, Lee Vining 🌐fs.usda.gov

5

Devils Postpile National Monument

🗺D4 🚌Shuttle from Mammoth Mountain Inn 🕐Mid-Jun–Oct: daily 🌐nps.gov/depo

On the west of the Sierra Nevada crest, but most easily accessible from the eastern resort town of Mammoth Lakes, Devils Postpile National Monument protects one of the most impressive geological formations in the state.

Basalt columns, in varying geometrical shapes, cover a 545-sq-yard (652-sq-m) area and are more than 60 ft (18 m) tall. The columns, which look like a tiled floor from above, were formed around 100,000 years ago, when molten lava cooled and fractured. The monument is only accessible in summer via shuttle bus.

Rainbow Falls, 2 miles (3 km) from the Postpile, are named after the refraction of sunlight in their spray.

6

Truckee

🗺D3 🚉🚌 ℹ10065 Donner Pass Rd; www.truckee.com

One of the highest and coldest towns in California, Truckee is thought to have gained its name when the Paiute people greeted the first white settlers with *Trokay*, meaning "peace." A popular base for winter skiers and

→ A visitor admiring the striking tufa formations dotting Mono Lake

↑ An abandoned, rusting car in front of deserted buildings in Bodie State Historic Park

summer hikers, Truckee sits along the main highway (I-80) and rail route across the Sierra Nevada Mountains. Its history as a transportation center goes back to 1863, when it was founded as a changeover point for crews along the transcontinental railroad. Much of the town's Wild West character and history as a lumber center survives, especially along Commercial Row in the heart of town, where a line of old brick and wooden buildings now house atmospheric shops, restaurants, and cafés.

Another evocative survivor of the town's past is the **Old Truckee Jail**, built in 1875. It is a small museum depicting the wilder side of frontier life.

Old Truckee Jail
⊘ 🅳 Jibboom & Spring sts
🕒 Times vary, check website 🅲 Federal hols
🅆 truckeehistory.org

❼
Bodie State Historic Park

🅰 D3 🚍 From Bridgeport
🕒 Mar–Oct: 9am–6pm daily;
Nov–Feb: 9am–4pm daily
🅸 End of Hwy 270; www.
parks.ca.gov

High up in the foothills of the eastern Sierra Nevada, Bodie is the largest ghost town in California. Now protected as a state historic park, Bodie was, during the second half of the 19th century, a bustling gold-mining town, with a population that topped 8,000 in 1880. Named after the gold prospector Waterman S. Bodey, who first discovered placer deposits (surface gold) here in 1859, Bodie boomed with the discovery of hard-rock ore in the mid-1870s. Soon many different mines had been established in the area, but it all came to an end when the gold ran out in 1882. Later, a series of fires destroyed much of the town. Only the Standard Mine remained in business, but it closed in 1942 because of a wartime ban on mining.

The state acquired the entire town in 1962, and has maintained the 170 buildings in a condition of "arrested decay." The result is an evocative experience of empty streets lined by deserted wooden buildings. The Miners' Union Hall has been converted into a visitors' center and museum.

Mammoth Lakes

D4 **2510 Main St;**
www.visitmammoth.com

The Mammoth Lakes area is a year-round adventure destination. In winter, visitors flock to the resorts around Mammoth, Old Mammoth, June Lake, and Snowcreek, and take to the slopes of Mammoth Mountain to ski and snow-board. In spring and summer, activities center around hiking, mountain biking, and fishing.

⑨ White Mountains

E4 **798 Main St,**
Bishop; (760) 873-2500

Rising along the eastern side of Owens Valley, the White Mountains soar to around 12,000 ft (3,660 m). Little vegetation grows here, but a species that survives is the ancient bristlecone pine (*Pinus aristata*). These contorted, gnarled trees that grow on the lower slopes look pre-historic and can live for around 4,000 years. Equally ancient, the Palisade Glacier is the southernmost glacier in the western hemisphere.

⑩ Owens Valley

E4 **Lone Pine** **120 S**
Main St, Lone Pine; www.
lonepinechamber.org

Sparsely populated but ruggedly beautiful, Owens Valley has more in common with Nevada than with the rest of California. The land here was bought secretly in 1905 by the City of Los Angeles. LA needed a water supply, and the aque-ducts still drain the valley.

In 1942 a detention camp was established at Manzanar for 10,000 Japanese American men, women, and children, deemed a threat to national security after the attack on Pearl Harbor. The former camp has been preserved and can be visited at the **Manzanar National Historic Site**. Exhibits on this chapter of Japanese-American history and other aspects of Owens Valley can be seen at the **Eastern**

Climbing Mount Whitney, ↑ a popular activity in the summer months

California Museum, in the town of Independence.

Manzanar National Historic Site
🏠5001 Hwy 395, Independence
🕐9am–4:30pm daily
🌐nps.gov/manz

Eastern California Museum
🏠155 N Grant St, Independence 🕐10am–5pm daily 🌐inyocounty.us

⑪ Mount Whitney

E4 **640 S Main St, Lone**
Pine; www.fs.usda.gov

The highest peak in the lower 48 states of the US, Mount Whitney rises to a height of 14,496 ft (4,420 m), forming a sheer wall above the town of Lone Pine. A steep 11-mile (18-km) trail leads to the summit and panoramic views over the High Sierras. A permit is required to hike the trail.

←

Fishing at Lake George, in the Mammoth Lakes area, with views of the mountains

12
Donner Memorial State Park

🅰D3 🚉🚌Truckee ⏱Sunrise-sunset daily 🌐parks.ca.gov

This tranquil park marks the site of one of the most tragic episodes of the volatile US frontier era. In the winter of 1846–7, the Donner Party, a group of 89 emigrants from Missouri, were traveling to California along the Oregon

Monument remembering the tragic story of the ↓ Donner Party

Trail. Halfway into their journey, they decided to leave the established trail and try a shortcut. This turned out, however, to be a far more difficult route, and added three weeks to their journey. The party finally arrived at the eastern foot of the Sierra Nevada Mountains in October 1846, having lost most of their cattle.

After resting for a week they were caught by an early winter storm. A few members struggled on foot across the mountains to seek help from Sutter's Fort (p466), but the rest of the party, trapped by the snow and with insufficient supplies, had to resort to cannibalism in order to survive. When rescuers reached them in mid-February 1847, 42 of the pioneers had already died.

A statue of a family from this group, atop a 22-ft (6.7-m) pedestal indicating the depth of the snow they encountered, marks the site. The **Visitor Center** documents this story. Other exhibits feature the Chinese construction of the railroad and early road trips over Donner Pass.

Visitor Center
🏠12593 Donner Pass Rd 📞(530) 582-7892 ⏱10am–5pm daily

EAT

Mt. Whitney Restaurant
This wood-paneled diner serves a range of American classics.

🅰E4 🏠227 S Main St, Lone Pine 📞(760) 876-5751 ⏱Sun

$⑤$⑤$⑤

Still Life Café
If you're after French cuisine - snails, beef Bourguignon, onion soup - this is the place.

🅰E4 🏠135 S Edwards St, Independence 📞(760) 878-2555

$⑤$⑤$⑤

Erick Schat's Bakkery
Sample a Basque loaf known as Sheepherder Bread at this jauntily decorated café.

🅰E4 🏠763 N Main St, Bishop 🌐schatsbakery.com

$⑤$⑤$⑤

Mahogany Smoked Meats
Smoked meats fill stuffed sandwiches and come as jerky or cured selections.

🅰E4 🏠2345 N Sierra Hwy, Bishop 🌐smokedmeats.com

$⑤$⑤$⑤

Whiskey Creek
The elevated menu here includes herb-crusted calamari and smoked duck pasta.

🅰E4 🏠524 N Main St, Bishop 🌐whiskeycrk.com

$⑤$⑤$⑤

NORTH CENTRAL CALIFORNIA

The Salinan, Esselen, Rumsen, Mutsen, Awaswas, and Yokuts peoples lived along the coast and inthe inland valleys of North Central California for over 6,000 years. These peoples were moved from their lands into the missions built by Spanish colonizers, who first settled the area at Monterey on June 3, 1770. The aim of the missionaries was to convert the Indigenous peoples to Catholicism, resulting in all but destroying their cultural practices. After the Spanish missions fell into disuse in the 1920s following the Mexican Revolution, the surviving Indigenous peoples were released to fend for themselves, their lands having been confiscated by European settlers. They remained landless for centuries until 2020 when the remaining small population of Esselen peoples of Monterey County finally managed to purchase their old lands in the hills of Big Sur with the help of Western Rivers Conservancy. Their mission is to preserve their ancestral sacred sites and revive their cultural history and native languages.

Monterey remained the capital of Upper California until the United States took formal control in 1848. Thereafter, the city became something of a backwater, barely affected by the waves of immigration that soon flowed into California. By the 1950s, even the local fishery had collapsed and tourism is now Monterey's main livelihood.

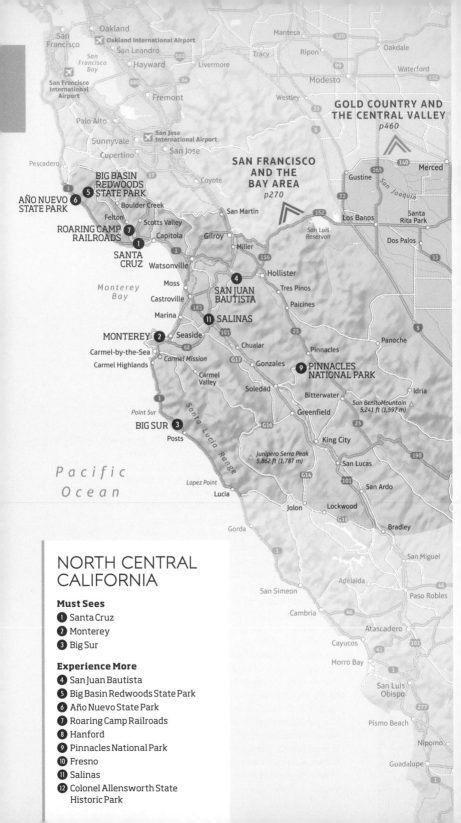

NORTH CENTRAL CALIFORNIA

Must Sees

1. Santa Cruz
2. Monterey
3. Big Sur

Experience More

4. San Juan Bautista
5. Big Basin Redwoods State Park
6. Año Nuevo State Park
7. Roaring Camp Railroads
8. Hanford
9. Pinnacles National Park
10. Fresno
11. Salinas
12. Colonel Allensworth State Historic Park

GOLD COUNTRY AND THE CENTRAL VALLEY
p460

SAN FRANCISCO AND THE BAY AREA
p270

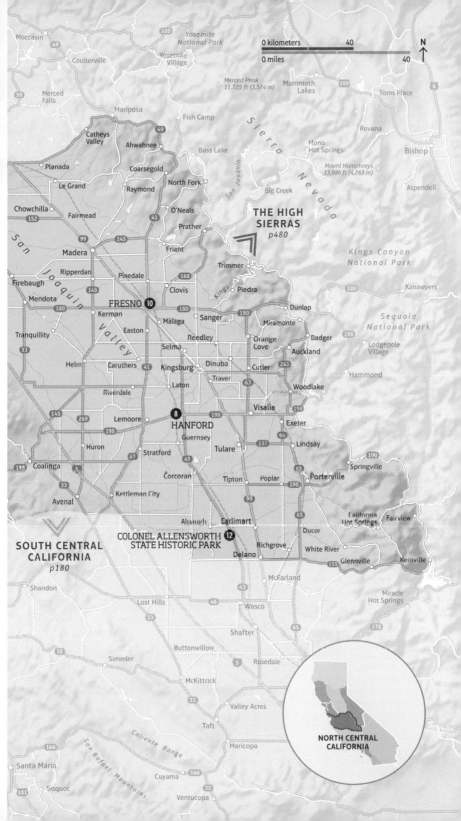

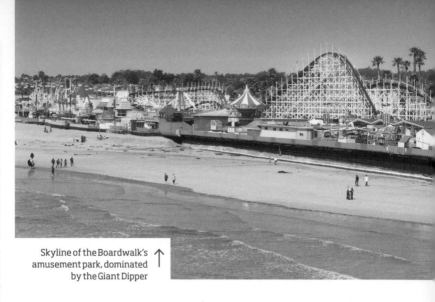

Skyline of the Boardwalk's amusement park, dominated by the Giant Dipper ↑

SANTA CRUZ

AB4 **✈**San Jose International Airport, Monterey Peninsula Airport **🚌**920 Pacific Ave **ℹ**303 Water St, No. 100; www.santacruz.org

Perched at the northern tip of Monterey Bay, Santa Cruz is a composite of small-town agricultural California. The mountains that rise to the east separate Santa Cruz from the more urban Silicon Valley and, along with the scenic coastline, provide residents and visitors with easy access to nature.

Santa Cruz Beach Boardwalk

🏠400 Beach St **🕐**Times vary, check website **🌐**beachboardwalk.com

The last surviving old-style amusement park on the West Coast, the Santa Cruz Beach Boardwalk offers a variety of attractions and games lined up along the beachfront. The main attraction is the Giant Dipper roller coaster, built in 1924 by Arthur Looff and now a National Historic Landmark. The carousel nearby features horses and chariots hand-carved by Looff's father, craftsman Charles Looff, in 1911. The ride is accompanied by an antique pipe organ. The park also has 27 more modern rides and an Art Deco dance hall.

Santa Cruz Mission

🏠126 High St **🕐**10am–4pm Thu–Mon **🌐**parks.ca.gov

On top of a hill overlooking the town, Santa Cruz Mission was founded in 1791 by Father Lasuén, as the 12th Franciscan mission in California. The buildings were completed three years later. The mission was never a great success, however, due to frequent earthquakes, poor weather, and its isolated location, all of which have eliminated any remains of the original structure. A park outlines the site, and a 1931 replica of the mission houses a small museum.

Museum of Art and History at the McPherson Center

🏠705 Front St **🕐**Noon–6pm Thu–Sun **🚫**Jan 1, Thanksgiving, Dec 25 **🌐**santacruzmah.org

This huge cultural center opened in 1993 to house the local art and history galleries. It has over 7,000 items. The Art Gallery shows works primarily by north central artists depicting the local landscape. The History Gallery includes a series of displays tracing the development of

Did You Know?

The Museum of Art and History was built on the site of the former county jail.

④
Natural Bridges State Beach

📍 **2531 W Cliff Dr** ⏰ **8am-sunset daily** 🌐 **parks.ca.gov**

This beach takes its name from the picturesque archways carved into the cliffs by the ocean. Two of the three original arches collapsed but one still remains, through which waves roll into a small sandy cove. The park also has a eucalyptus grove, a monarch butterfly preserve, and a nature trail.

⑤
Santa Cruz Surfing Museum

📍 **Lighthouse Point, 701 W Cliff Dr** 📞 **(831) 420-6289** ⏰ **Noon-4pm Fri-Sun** 🚫 **Federal hols**

In a lighthouse overlooking the region's main surfing area, this museum represents every era of Santa Cruz surfing. The sport was brought here from Hawaii, making Santa Cruz the birthplace of surfing on the US mainland. Surfboards range from 1930s redwood planks to today's high-tech laminates.

Santa Cruz County, from the time of the Ohlone peoples through to the era of the missions through to the present day. It also documents the region's agricultural and industrial heritage, with photographs of late 19th-century and early 20th-century farms and logging operations.

The museum incorporates the adjacent red-brick octaganol Octagon Gallery that was completed in 1882 as the County Hall of Records.

💬 INSIDER TIP
Abbott Square Market

Head to this space near the Museum of Art and History for a real community buzz. There is an indoor food hall and an outdoor space for live music and theater. Murals and public art adorn the plaza.

⑥
Mystery Spot

📍 **465 Mystery Spot Rd** ⏰ **10am-4pm Mon-Fri, 10am-5pm Sat & Sun** 🌐 **mysteryspot.com**

Two miles (3 km) east of Santa Cruz, this redwood grove has been drawing visitors since its discovery in 1940 due to various strange events. Balls roll uphill, parallel lines converge, and the laws of physics and gravity appear to be suspended. Part tourist trap, part genuine oddity, it's a fun outdoor adventure.

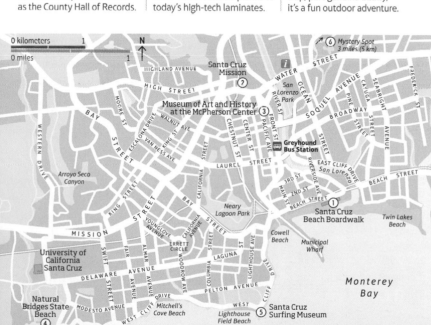

2

MONTEREY

 B4 Tyler, Pearl & Munras sts 🛈 401 Camino El Estero; www.seemonterey.com

After serving as the capital of Mexican Alta California from 1776 to 1848, Monterey lost its status to San Francisco following the Gold Rush, and settled into the role of a hardworking fishing port, market town, and military base. Today visitors come here to tour the town's many historic sites, attend the annual jazz festival in September, and explore the spectacular coastline of the Monterey Peninsula.

① 🏠

Custom House

🏠 20 Custom House Plaza
🕐 10am–4pm Tue–Sun
ⓦ parks.ca.gov

Under Mexican rule the port of Monterey was a major trading center, attracting traders from many parts of the world. The Mexican government built the adobe Custom House in the 1820s to collect taxes on imported goods, including sugar, coffee, rice, and tools. The Custom House remained a busy place under United States rule through the 1840s. It is the oldest government building in California and the first government building on the west coast. Preserved as it was in the 1830s and 1840s, today it is a museum, open to the public for visits and tours.

> You can enjoy panoramic views of the Bay from Old Fisherman's Wharf - spot pelicans and sea otters, as well as seals sunbathing on the rocks and buoys.

②

Larkin House

🏠 464 Calle Principal
🕐 By appointment only
ⓦ parks.ca.gov

Thomas Larkin, a New England merchant, built this house in 1832. The architecture, with its two stories of adobe brick and a wooden portico, became representative of Monterey style. The home is filled with early 19th-century antiques. Tours of the house can be arranged by appointment.

③

Old Fisherman's Wharf

ⓦ montereywharf.com

Once the center of the fishing and whaling industries, Old Fisherman's Wharf is now known for its plentiful seafood restaurants, shops, and markets. Be sure to taste the clam chowder, a local specialty. You can enjoy panoramic views of the Bay from the wharf – spot pelicans and sea otters, as well as seals sunbathing on the rocks and buoys. Whale-watching expeditions and Monterey Bay cruises depart from here. This is also the departure point for kayaking and yachting trips.

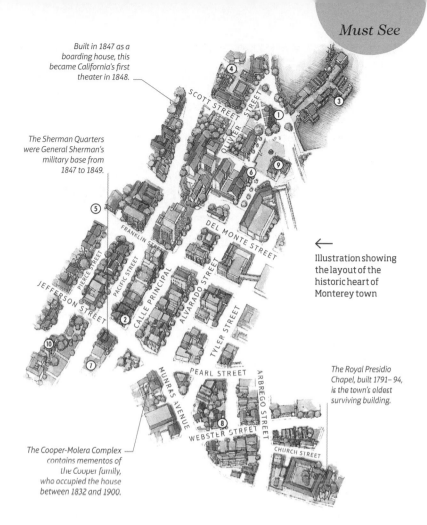

Built in 1847 as a boarding house, this became California's first theater in 1848.

The Sherman Quarters were General Sherman's military base from 1847 to 1849.

Illustration showing the layout of the historic heart of Monterey town

The Royal Presidio Chapel, built 1791– 94, is the town's oldest surviving building.

The Cooper-Molera Complex contains mementos of the Cooper family, who occupied the house between 1832 and 1900.

 Old Whaling Station

🏠 391 Decatur St
☎ (831) 375-5356
🕙 10am-2pm Tue-Fri
(garden open daily)

Built in 1847 by Scottish adventurer David Wight as a family home, this adobe became the headquarters of the Old Monterey Whaling Company in 1855. The pavement outside the building was

← Seafood restaurants and shops lining Old Fisherman's Wharf

made using whale bones. Inside, mementos of the local whaling industry are on display. The house and gardens are open to the public for self-guided tours.

 Presidio of Monterey Museum

🏠 76th Artillery St & Corporal Ewing Rd ☎ (831) 646-3456 🕙 10am-1pm Mon, 10am-4pm Thu-Sat, 1-4pm Sun

Due to its strategic location, Monterey has a long military history. On the site of the

Presidio dating to 1770, this museum's exhibition halls trace the story of the changing face of this site and Monterey's military operations, starting with Indigenous peoples through the Spanish and Mexican rule to the present day. A mural of a Native American woman greets visitors at the museum's entrance as a mark of the Indigenous peoples for whom the historic Presidio site was home for more than 6,000 years, long before it became a military base. Much of the museum is dedicated to the story of the development of the site as a military training center.

↑ Historical artifacts in the Pacific House Museum, and *(inset)* the adobe building in which it is housed

⑥ Ⓐ Ⓜ Ⓐ
Pacific House Museum

🏠 10 Custom House Plaza
🕐 10am–4pm Tue–Sun
🌐 parks.ca.gov

This two-story adobe house, formerly a government building dating back to 1847, houses an informative museum of California's history. As the former capital of Mexican California, Monterey has a fascinating past. Interactive exhibits and self-guided tours give an overview of events from the time of the Ohlone peoples to the present day. The second story houses the superb Monterey Museum of the American Indian, with showcases of Indigenous pottery and other crafts and a wealth of historic artifacts. At the back, the tranquil Memory Garden has a fountain and a well-tended collection of plants. The museum store is a great resource for local history books.

⑦ Ⓐ
Monterey Museum of Art

🏠 559 Pacific St 🕐 11am–5pm Thu–Sat 🌐 monterey art.org

Founded in 1959, the main site of the Monterey Museum of Art has eight galleries with a focus on American and early California painting (1875–1945), photography, and contemporary art. Among its 14,000 objects are works by Evelyn McCormick, Armin Hansen, William Ritschel, Nathan Oliveira, and Ansel Adams. Many exhibits concentrate on the artistic heritage of the Monterey region. The museum also has an impressive collection of Asian art, including historic woodblock prints, jade and lacquer objects, and ceramics.

The other branch of the museum, La Mirada, is located in a stone Mexican adobe at 720 Via Marida, surrounded by magnificent gardens. Its four galleries are used for special exhibitions. La Mirada also hosts events such as lectures and workshops.

⑧ Ⓐ
Robert Louis Stevenson House

🏠 530 Houston St 🕐 Times vary, call ahead 📞 (831) 649-7118

The writer Robert Louis Stevenson stayed at this former boarding house, then known as the French Hotel, for a few months in the fall of 1879 in his youth. It was here that Stevenson penned the *Old Pacific Capital,* an account of his stay in Monterey. Many

→ Colton Hall, the birthplace of the California State Constitution in 1849

believe that his walks along the Monterey Peninsula were the inspiration for the setting of *Treasure Island*. Today the Stevenson House has been restored and is a museum with several rooms devoted to Stevenson memorabilia.

(9)

MHAA Salvador Dalí Museum

🏠 5 Custom House Plaza
🕐 11am–8pm daily
🌐 mhaadali.com

In 2016 private collector Dimitri Piterman offered his huge Salvador Dalí collection to the Monterey History and Art Association (MHAA) and their Custom House site. One of the largest collections of the works of Dalí in the US, it encompasses some 580 pieces by the renowned Surrealist artist. As well as the paintings that Dalí is more famous for, the museum houses some of his etchings, tapestries, and rare sculptures. Other exhibits recount local links to Dalí, who spent the 1940s wartime in Pebble Beach.

(10)

Colton Hall Museum

🏠 570 Pacific St
📞 (831) 646-3933
🕐 10am–4pm daily

Colton Hall was built by the Reverend Walter Colton, who served as the first *alcalde* (mayor) of Monterey from 1846 to 1849. The former schoolhouse and town hall now houses a museum containing a re-creation of the meeting room where the California State Constitution was first signed in 1849. Other exhibits document early Monterey history. The Old Monterey Jail, built in 1854, stands adjacent to the museum.

EAT

Old Monterey Cafe
Located in Monterey's historic center, this homey café with a long narrow dining room takes pride in its made-to-order breakfasts.

🏠 489 Alvaro St
📞 (831) 646-1021
🕐 Breakfast & lunch only

$ $ $

Alvarado Street Brewery & Grill
More than 20 draft beers are brewed on site, from sours to IPAs, complemented by a comprehensive menu that blends small bar-style plates with steaks, burgers, and pizzas.

🏠 426 Alvarado St
🌐 asb.beer.com

$ $ $

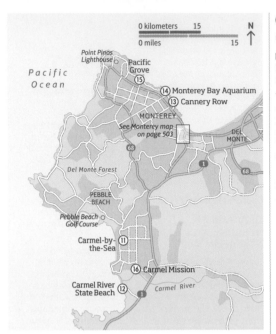

See Monterey map on page 503

Point Pinos Lighthouse
Pacific Grove
⑮
⑭ Monterey Bay Aquarium
⑬ Cannery Row
MONTEREY
DEL MONTE
Pacific Ocean
⑥⑧
Del Monte Forest
PEBBLE BEACH
Pebble Beach Golf Course
Carmel-by-the-Sea ⑪
⑯ Carmel Mission
Carmel River State Beach ⑫
Carmel River
①

EXPLORING THE MONTEREY PENINSULA

⑬
Cannery Row

◭ 800 Cannery Row, Monterey ⓦ cannery row.com

This six-block harborfront street, celebrated by John Steinbeck in his novels *Cannery Row* and *Sweet Thursday (p517)*, was once the site of more than 20 fish-packing plants that processed sardines from Monterey Bay. The canneries thrived from the early 20th century, reaching their greatest volume of production in the early 1940s. By 1945 the sardines had disappeared, perhaps as a result of overfishing, and most of the canneries were abandoned, later to be demolished. The buildings that remain today house an eclectic collection of shops and restaurants. No. 800 is the old laboratory of "Doc" Ricketts, marine biologist and friend of Steinbeck. It is now a private club.

⑪
Carmel-by-the-Sea

ⓘ Carmel Plaza, 2nd floor, Ocean Av; www.carmel california.com

Known for its rich artistic, musical, and literary heritage, the picturesque town of Carmel is full of art galleries and hosts regular exhibitions, an annual playwriting contest, and a Bach Festival. The varied houses border the steep hillsides down to the ocean. City ordinances restrict streetlights, mail deliveries, and sidewalks, giving the town its quaint atmosphere.

> **💬 INSIDER TIP**
> **Pebble Beach Golf Course**
>
> Located on a stretch of spectacular coastline a little north of Carmel-by-the-Sea, Pebble Beach is the site of one of the best golf courses in the US *(www.pebble beach.com)*.

⑫
Carmel River State Beach

◭ Carmelo & Scenic rds ⓦ parks.ca.gov

This 109-acre (270-ha) state park straddles the mouth of the Carmel River. It contains a lagoon and wetland nature preserve for a bountiful population of native and migratory birds. The beach is a favorite picnic spot among locals. It is also popular with scuba divers and kayakers, and fishing is permitted. However, swimming is discouraged because of dangerous currents and cold temperatures.

↑ Visitor watching a blue groper fish, Monterey Bay Aquarium

Monterey Bay Aquarium

🏠 886 Cannery Row, Monterey ⏱ 10am–5pm Thu–Mon 🌐 montereybay aquarium.org

Monterey Bay Aquarium is one of the largest aquariums in the US, with more than 500 species and tens of thousands of specimens from the Monterey Bay area. Among the exhibits are an enclosed kelp forest, a rock pool, and a live jellyfish display. A pool connected to the open bay attracts sea otters. The Outer Bay Wing has a huge tank in which the conditions of the ocean are re-created. It contains yellow-fin tuna, ocean sunfish, green sea turtles, and barracuda.

The Research Institute offers educational programs where visitors can watch the marine scientists at work and learn more about ocean conservation.

---

⑮ Pacific Grove

📍 584 Central Av; www.pacificgrove.org

This town was founded in 1875 as a religious retreat, where alcohol, dancing, and even newspapers were banned. Today it is best known for its Victorian wooden houses, many now converted into bed-and-breakfasts, Its beautiful coastal parks, and the monarch butterflies that arrive between October and April. The annual return of the insects, which are protected by city ordinance, occasions a parade and bazaar on the first Saturday of every October.

Nearby, the Point Pinos Lighthouse, built in 1852, is now the oldest continuously operating lighthouse on the US West Coast.

THE 17-MILE DRIVE

One of the best ways to tour the Monterey Peninsula is the circular 17-Mile Drive toll road. While there is a fee to drive along it, cycling and walking are free. The route affords spectacular views of what the area has to offer, including crashing surf, coastal flora, and the Del Monte Forest. The extra-ordinary beauty of the region has drawn the rich to build beautiful mansions here. Most celebrated of all the area's attractions are the championship golf courses.

A unique oak tree in
↓ the historic heart of Pacific Grove

(16) ⟨⟩ 🛍

CARMEL MISSION

🏠 3080 Rio Rd, Carmel 🕐 10am–4pm Wed–Thu, 10am–5pm Fri & Sat,
12:30–5pm Sun 🔒 Easter, Thanksgiving, Dec 24–26 🌐 carmelmission.org

One of the most authentically restored Catholic churches in California, Carmel Mission, built of adobe brick by Native American laborers, was founded in 1770 by Father Junípero Serra. Its courtyard and lush gardens are peaceful places to linger.

Carmel Mission served as the administrative center for all the 21 Northern California missions. Father Serra *(p225)*, one of the leaders of the Franciscans when they traveled north from Mexico in the 18th century, resided here until his death in 1784 and is now buried at the foot of the altar. The mission was secularized and abandoned in 1834, quickly falling into disrepair. Restoration work began in 1924, carefully following the plans of the original mission, and replanting the gardens. The reconstructed living quarters detail 18th-century mission life. The mission still functions as a Catholic church.

Bell tower

The sarcophagus depicts Father Serra recumbent in death, surrounded by three mourning padres. It is among the finest of its type in the US.

The restored kitchen shows it as it was in missionary days, including the oven brought from Mexico. A section of the original adobe wall can be seen.

Dining room

→
The restored buildings of Carmel Mission

Father Serra's simple way of life is evident in this sparse cell. The wooden bed, chair, desk, and candlestick were the only pieces of furniture he possessed.

←
Statue of Father Junípero Serra, founder of the Carmel Mission

Set within the beautiful front courtyard, a statue of Father Serra faces the mission church he founded.

Did You Know?

Father Serra originally estabished the Mission in Monterey but relocated it to Carmel a year later.

The Gothic arch of Carmel's main altar, with its ornate decoration, is the only one of its kind among all of the 21 Franciscan missions in California.

Father Serra's burial place under the altar is marked with a plaque.

Munras Museum ↗

The chapel window is the only place where the original paintwork can still be seen.

The cemetery contains the graves of 18th-century missionaries.

The museum, in the old living quarters, contains several relics belonging to Father Serra.

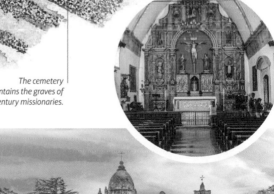

→
The Spanish-Moorish facade of Carmel Mission, and *(inset)* the interior with its elaborate altar

③

BIG SUR

🅐C5 🚌Nepenthe Park 🌐bigsurcalifornia.org

The novelist Robert Louis Stevenson called Big Sur "the greatest meeting of land and sea in the world," and the breathtaking mountains, cliffs, and coves still leave visitors grasping for adjectives. There are no large towns and very few signs of civilization. Most of the shoreline is protected in a series of state parks, with dense forests, broad rivers, and crashing surf, all easily accessible.

①

Andrew Molera State Park

🏠 20 miles (30 km) S of Carmel, off Hwy 1
🌐 parks.ca.gov

Opened in 1972, this park is still relatively undeveloped and includes 10 miles (16 km) of hiking trails through lush meadows, high ridges, forests of redwood and sycamore trees, and a quiet, sandy beach. The park is also home to the year-round Highbridge Falls.

The Ventana Wildlife Society has a **Discovery Center** in the park with displays on local wildlife, including the Bringing the Condors Home exhibit dedicated to California condors and the efforts to recover the birds to the wild. The center runs Condor-spotting tours.

Discovery Center
 🏠 Andrew Molera State Park 🕙 10am–4pm Sat & Sun

②

Sand Dollar Beach

🏠 60 miles (95 km) S of Carmel, off Hwy 1
🌐 californiabeaches.com

Located halfway between Cambria and Big Sur Station, this beach is especially popular among surfers, given that it's one of the few surf-friendly spots in this region. The name is slightly misleading given the clear absence of sand dollars (a type of invertebrate related to sea urchins) here. Wide and sandy, the spacious beach is great for families. A fun activity is to look for the polished jade stones that wash up in and around Jade Cove. You can stay overnight at Plaskett Creek Campground.

③

Point Lobos State Reserve

🏠 3 miles (5 km) S of Carmel, off Hwy 1 🕗 8am–sunset daily 🌐 pointlobos.org

Named after the offshore rocks at Punta de los Lobos Marinos, ("Point of the Sea Wolves"), where the sound of the resident sea lions carries all the way inland, this spectacular reserve contains headlands, coves, and rolling meadows. The offshore area forms one of the richest underwater habitats in the world, popular with certified divers. You can

→

The graceful Bixby Creek Bridge stretching across the rocky Big Sur coastline

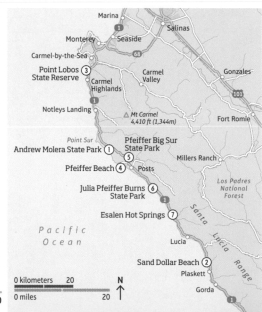

spot seals, sea lions, sea otters, and migrating gray whales (usually December through May). The Reserve is also home to thousands of seabirds and is the habitat of the Monterey cypress, the only tree to survive the region's mixture of fog and salt spray. Its branches are shaped by the sea winds.

Hiking trails along the shoreline lead to hidden coves. The area used to be the home of an early 20th-century whaling and abalone industry. A small cabin built by Chinese fishermen from that time at Whalers Cove houses a cultural history museum displaying documents and artifacts of the peoples who lived and worked in the region, from the Rumsen people to Chinese, Japanese, Portuguese, and Americans.

Pfeiffer Beach

📍 **30 miles (50 km) S of Carmel, off Hwy 1**
🌐 **californiabeaches.com**

One of the best-kept secrets among locals, this beach has a couple of notable features – the craggy and dramatic sea stacks that rise out of the water and the distinctive purple sand, caused by the natural drainage of minerals from the surrounding hills. Note the extreme north end of the beach has a

clothing-optional policy, and there is no beach access from Pfeiffer Big Sur State Park (approach the beach from Sycamore Canyon around mile marker 45.64). Just 4 miles (6 km) east along the highway is Nepenthe (p513), a Big Sur dining institution, with some of the most enviable views anywhere on the coast.

 HIDDEN GEM
Henry Miller Memorial Library

About 4 miles (6 km) east of Pfeiffer Beach, this nonprofit arts center, bookstore, and performance venue is dedicated to the late writer, artist, and Big Sur resident Henry Miller. It contains a large number of books, manuscripts, and letters by Miller, and hosts regular music, lectures, signings, and community events (www.henry miller.org).

↑ A group of sea lions sunbathing on rocks in Point Lobos State Reserve

Following a trail through a redwood forest in Pfeiffer Big Sur State Park

Big Sur Lodge
 47225 Hwy 1
🌐 bigsurlodge.com

Pfeiffer Big Sur State Park Campground
Pfeiffer Big Sur Rd, near mile marker 47.2 on Hwy 1
🌐 reservecalifornia.com

Julia Pfeiffer Burns State Park

Marker 35.8 on Hwy 1, 35 miles (60 km) S of Carmel; 12 miles (20 km) S of Pfeiffer Big Sur SP on Hwy 1 ⏰ 8am–sunset daily 🌐 parks.ca.gov

This park, smaller but even more beautiful than Pfeiffer Big Sur State Park, is named after pioneer Julia Pfeiffer Burns, who was a lifelong resident and rancher in Big Sur and led expeditions to the beach here. The park stretches from the coastline into nearby high ridges and features redwood, tan oak, madrone, and chaparral trees. Starting from the parking lot, the Overlook Trail ducks under Hwy 1, leading to the 100-ft- (30-m-) high bluff from which the McWay Falls spill onto a pristine beach in an enchanting cove by the ocean. Visitors are not allowed onto the beach itself, which maintains its unspoiled quality. Just north of McWay Falls, the slightly more vigorous Partington Cove Trail leads through a tunnel carved into the rock to an isolated cove. An alternative route leads to a small beach graced by giant boulders. A panoramic view of the Pacific and miles of rugged coastline can be enjoyed from the loftier points along the trails east of the highway.

⑤ Pfeiffer Big Sur State Park

Pfeiffer Big Sur Rd, 25 miles (40 km) S of Carmel 🌐 parks.ca.gov

This scenic park has developed around the fertile banks of the Big Sur River. There's a spectacular abundance of nature here, from the redwood and conifer trees to the wide open meadows. There are miles of hiking trails, where visitors can look out for wildlife, which includes bobcats, black-tail deer, skunks, and kingfishers.

The park is a favorite with families for camping, biking, swimming, picnicking, and fishing. The **Big Sur Lodge** offers everything from basic family rooms to fully equipped cottages with wood-burning fireplaces and furnished decks. The hugely popular **Pfeiffer Big Sur State Park Campground** has excellent facilities, with 189 RV and tent sites, hot showers, Wi-Fi, and several self-guided nature trails. The campground can get booked up months in advance, even in winter, so reserve online in advance.

Note that, despite the name, there is no access to Pfeiffer Beach from this park.

7

Esalen Hot Springs

📍 40 miles (65 km) S of Carmel, off Hwy 1
🌐 esalen.org

Outside of the world-class scenery, Big Sur also has several large resorts based around natural hot springs. This is the most well known, followed by the Sykes and Tassajara hot springs. The Esalen Institute was founded on this site in 1962 and became the birthplace of the countercultural Human Potential Movement – a quasi-spiritual rebellion against mainstream psychology and organized religion. In the years to come, Esalen would become an influential personal development retreat and wellness center, offering a host of activities and workshops on anything from meditation, massage, and yoga to theater, visual arts, and creative writing.

Esalen offers 24-hour access to the hot springs for guests, but they are open to the public between the hours of 1am and 3am (although reservations are required), so be prepared to stay up late if you're not staying at the retreat itself. The resort has a range of accommodations available, but be aware that even the most basic – a sleeping bag in a shared room – will set you back several hundred dollars, and there is no camping on site. However, prices include meals, workshops, and other facilities, including indoor and outdoor hot tubs.

EAT

Deetjen's Big Sur Inn
This cabin retreat and high-end restaurant is on the National Register of Historic Places.

📍 48865 Hwy 1
🌐 deetjens.com

$$(S)$$($)$

Nepenthe / Café Kevah
Nepenthe serves hearty modern American cuisine, while Kevah has more casual dishes, such as paninis.

📍 48510 Hwy 1
🌐 nepenthe.com

$$(S)$$($)$

Fernwood Resort Bar & Grill
The homespun ambience and no-nonsense menu attract many loyal customers.

📍 47200 Hwy 1
🌐 fernwoodbigsur.com

$$(S)$$($)$

Big Sur Bakery & Restaurant
This intimate ranch house often sees a line out the door for their pastries and wood-fired pizzas.

📍 47540 Hwy 1
🌐 bigsurbakery.com

$$(S)$$($)$

Big Sur Roadhouse
Seasonal, organic, and fresh are the watchwords at this modern-rustic restaurant.

📍 47080 Hwy 1
🌐 glenoaksbigsur.com

$$(S)$$($)$

↑ McWay Falls flowing onto a secluded beach in Julia Pfeiffer Burns State Park

EXPERIENCE MORE

4

San Juan Bautista

 C4 🚍 From Hollister
ℹ️ 319 Third St; www.
sanjuanbautistaca.com

The small town of San Juan Bautista has retained its rural character, despite being a mere 30 miles (50 km) from the heart of the high-tech Silicon Valley *(p415)*.

The town's main attraction, Mission San Juan Bautista, stands to the west of the central plaza. The largest of the Spanish missions built during 1834 to 1839, it is the only one to have aisles along the nave. Alfred Hitchcock used the mission's facade for the final scenes of his film *Vertigo* (1958). The adjacent monastery now houses a museum with mission artifacts and photographs of the town at various stages of development. On the north side of the church there is a cemetery, next to which a faint trail marks the historic El Camino Real. This 650-mile (1,050-km) path linked the 21 California missions, all within a day's journey of their nearest mission. By complete coincidence, the El Camino Real trail also follows the San Andreas Fault, the underlying source of all California's earthquakes. A seismograph on the edge of the town's plaza monitors tectonic activity.

The east and south sides of the plaza are lined by three historic buildings, all of which have been preserved as part of San Juan Bautista State Historic Park. The Plaza Hotel incorporates part of the original barracks built in 1813. The town's stables now house antique carriages and stagecoaches. The Castro-Breen Adobe facing the plaza was owned by Patrick Breen and his family, famous survivors of the ill-fated Donner Party *(p495)*.

↑ The Spanish Colonial Mission San Juan Bautista, and *(inset)* its aisled interior

> Alfred Hitchcock used the mission's facade for the final scenes of his film *Vertigo* (1958).

5

Big Basin Redwoods State Park

 B4 🚃 Santa Cruz, Boulder Creek ℹ️ 21600 Big Basin Way, Boulder Creek; www. parks.ca.gov

In the year 1900 a group of environmentalists formed the Sempervirens Club with the aim of preventing the logging of redwoods. This resulted in Big Basin Redwoods State Park, California's first state park, being established in 1902. It covers 16,000 acres (6,475 ha) and protects the southernmost groves of the coastal redwood tree *(p436)* and forests of Douglas fir and other conifers. It is also home to wildlife such as black-tailed deer and the mountain lion.

Trails lead through redwood groves to the park's many waterfalls, including the popular Berry Creek Falls. There are also more than 100 miles (160 km) of other routes, such as the Skyline-to-Sea Trail, which drops down to the Pacific Ocean at Waddell Creek.

Año Nuevo State Park

🅰B4 🚌Santa Cruz, Waddell Creek 📍1 New Years Creek Rd, Pescadero; daily; www.parks.ca.gov

The Año Nuevo State Park, 60 miles (95 km) north of Monterey, has as its main point of interest the breeding grounds of the northern elephant seal. A short stretch of sandy beach and a small offshore island are populated each winter by hundreds of these giant mammals, which arrive here from all over the Pacific Ocean to mate and give birth.

The seals are named after the dangling proboscis of the male, which resembles an elephant's trunk. Each December, the male seals arrive here and begin the battle for dominance, engaging in violent fights. Only a handful of the most powerful males are able to mate, but one male can father pups with as many as 50 different females in one season. After spending most of the year at sea, the females arrive in January to give birth to young conceived the previous winter. Mating follows soon after, although conception is delayed for up to four months while the female recovers from giving birth. The name Año Nuevo

("New Year") was given to the island by explorer Sebastián Vizcaíno, who sailed past the area on January 1, 1603. The park is open all year, but during the winter when the elephant seals are present, visitors are allowed only on guided tours. Tickets are available through the California State Parks reservation service.

Roaring Camp Railroads

🅰B4 🚉5401 Graham Hill Rd, Felton 🚌Santa Cruz 🕐Times vary, check website 🚫Federal hols 🌐roaringcamp.com

High up in the Santa Cruz Mountains, a pair of historic logging railroads have been kept in operation as the focus of a family-orientated theme park devoted to the late 19th-century and early 20th-century logging town, complete with general store, schoolhouse, and opera house. A narrow-gauge train with open-top cars, usually pulled by a steam engine, departs on a 6-mile (10-km) round-trip through the adjacent forests of Henry Cowell Redwoods State Park. From April through early fall, the standard-gauge Big Trees, Santa Cruz, and Pacific Railroad sets off from Roaring

Camp on an hour-long trip through the mountains and down to Santa Cruz. There is a two-hour stopover, during which passengers can enjoy the beach and Boardwalk Amusement Park (p500) before the return journey. The trip can also be taken as a round-trip from Santa Cruz.

A steam engine driving through a forest on the Roaring Camp Railroads

8 Hanford

D5 **113 Court St; www.hanford chamber.com**

The farming community of Hanford has a multicultural heritage. The China Alley neighborhood was once inhabited by one of California's largest Chinese communities, many of whom worked on the construction of the transcontinental railroad. East of the town center is the historic **Taoist Temple**, built in 1893. The temple operated as a hostel for Chinese immigrants and a Chinese school, as well as a religious shrine.

Nearby, the **Children's Storybook Garden and Museum**, with its themed gardens based on art and children's literary classics, is a delight for adults as well as kids.

Taoist Temple

12 China Alley **By appt only** **chinaalley.com**

Children's Storybook Garden and Museum

175 E Tenth St **9am–noon Mon, Sat & Sun, 6–9pm Tue–Thu** **childrensstory bookgarden.org**

9 Pinnacles National Park

C5 **500 Hwy 146, Paicines** **King City & Soledad** **Times vary, check website** **nps. gov/pinn**

High in the hills above the Salinas Valley, the Pinnacles National Park preserves 16,000 acres (6,500 ha) of volcanic landscape. A solid ridge of former lava flows runs through the center of the park, in places forming cliffs more than 500 ft (150 m) tall. There are no roads in the park, but there are many well-maintained hiking trails.

The Balconies formation can be reached by a 1.5-mile (2.5-km) leisurely trail. Here red-gold cliffs rise high above the ground, attracting rock-climbers, photographers, and bird-watchers.

The park is best visited in spring, when the wildflowers are in bloom.

10 Fresno

D4 **Fresno Air Terminal** **1180 E Shaw Av Suite 201; www. visitfresnocounty.org**

The city of Fresno is often referred to as the "Raisin Capital of the World" because of its abundant production of the dried fruit. Worth a visit are

---

EAT

La Elegante Taqueria

This tiny Chinatown taco spot has a reputation beyond its size thanks to its outstanding Adobada tacos.

D4 **1423 Kern St, Fresno** **(559) 497-5844** **Dinner Mon**

$$$

Roger Rocka's Dinner Theater

Sit back and enjoy a theatrical presentation as you tuck into a modern American dinner menu.

D4 **1226 N Wishon Av, Fresno** **rogerrockas.com**

$$$

← The spire-like volcanic rock formations at Pinnacles National Park

the **Forestiere Underground Gardens**, a network of tunnels and grottoes that were excavated in 1906. Nearby, the 1890 Victorian Gothic **Meux Home Museum** has period furniture.

In Kearney Park, 7 miles (11 km) west of Fresno, is the French Renaissance-style **Kearney Mansion**, built in 1903 by Theodore Kearney, an agriculturalist who helped found California's raisin industry. The house is now a period museum.

Forestiere Underground Gardens

⊛⊛ 🏠5021 W Shaw Ave ⊙Mid-Mar–mid-Dec: 9am– 3pm daily 🔳underground gardens.com

Meux Home Museum

⊛⊛ 🏠1007 R St ⊙Noon–3pm Fri–Sun 🔳meuxhome museum.org

Kearney Mansion

⊛⊛ 🏠7160 W Kearney Blvd, Hwy 99 ☎(559) 441-0862 ⊙Times vary, call ahead

⓫ Salinas

🅰C4 🚊🚌 🛈119 E Alisal St; www.salinaschamber.com

At the north end of the Salinas Valley, which stretches between San Francisco and San Luis Obispo, Salinas is the region's primary agricultural center. Vegetable-packing plants and canneries line the major highways and railroad tracks. The town is perhaps best known as the birthplace of the author John Steinbeck (1902–68), who set many of his naturalistic stories here and in the surrounding area. A selection of books, manuscripts, photographs, and personal memorabilia relating to the author is on display at the **National Steinbeck Center Museum**, while Steinbeck House *(132 Central Av)*, where the novelist was

↑ Displays on author John Steinbeck at Salinas' National Steinbeck Center Museum

born, is now a restaurant. The Steinbeck Festival is held in Salinas every August.

National Steinbeck Center Museum

⊛⊛⊛ 🏠1 Main St ⊙10am–5pm Wed–Sun 🔒Federal hols 🔳steinbeck.org

⓬ ⊛ Colonel Allensworth State Historic Park

🅰D5 🏠4011 Grant Dr, off Hwy 99 on County Rd J22, Earlimart ⊙9am–sunset daily 🔳parks.ca.gov

In 1908, Colonel Allen Allensworth and a group of African American families established a unique farming community in this remote spot in the San Joaquin Valley. Through dedication and hard work, they aimed to escape discrimination and improve life for African Americans. For a number of years the town flourished, with public buildings, a church, schoolhouse, and even a glee club. Although tough farming conditions and other setbacks made it impossible to maintain their vision long-term, a few families stayed on until the early 1960s and it became known as "the town that refused to die." Memorabilia of this independent community are now on display in the old farmhouses and restored buildings at this State Historic Park south of Hanford.

COLONEL ALLEN ALLENSWORTH

Allen Allensworth was born in into slavery in 1842, but escaped and fought in the Civil War for the Union Army. He became the first African American to reach the rank of lieutenant colonel and was then appointed an army chaplain. He believed his fellow African Americans could combat racism by building their own future, and founded his namesake town in 1908. He died in 1914, in a motorcycle accident in Monrovia, where a monument now stands.

A DRIVING TOUR
NORTH CENTRAL COASTLINE

Length 80 miles (130 km) **Stopping-off points** Monterey, Capitola, and Santa Cruz have many waterside restaurants and cafés.

The coast of North Central California encompasses long, thin stretches of beaches pounded by Pacific surf and handsome seaside towns with Spanish roots, including Monterey, and Santa Cruz, and Carmel-by-the-Sea. This driving tour begins at Año Nuevo State Reserve, a pristine preserve of wild beaches and giant dunes, and home to northern elephant seals and flocks of pelicans. The route then follows Hwy 1 (Cabrillo Hwy), which hugs the coast for most of this drive. Between the towns, the area is surprisingly undeveloped and rich in marine life, from seal colonies and sea otters to shore birds and tidepool-dwellers. The route ends at upscale Carmel-by-the-Sea, which combines a popular art gallery and restaurant scene with a white sandy beach and an opulent Spanish mission.

*Part of the Big Basin Redwoods State Park (p514), the golden-sanded **Waddell Creek Beach** is a favorite spot for picnickers, anglers, and windsurfers.*

START
Año Nuevo State Reserve

Big Basin

Boulder Creek

Waddell Creek Beach

Ben Lomond

Felton

Bonny Doon

Davenport

Wilder Ranch State Park

Majors

__Wilder Ranch State Park__ was originally a coastal dairy farm, complete with ranch house and outbuildings dating from the 1890s. Today you can see farm animals or hike the coastal bluffs.

↑ The Pacific Ocean coast during high tide, Wilder Ranch State Park

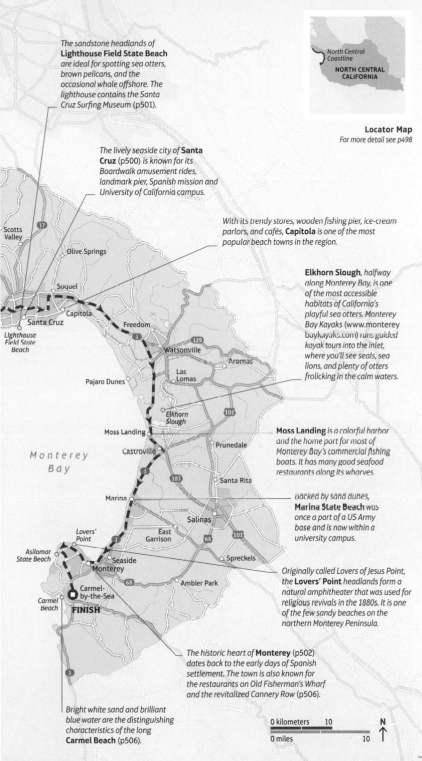

The sandstone headlands of **Lighthouse Field State Beach** are ideal for spotting sea otters, brown pelicans, and the occasional whale offshore. The lighthouse contains the Santa Cruz Surfing Museum (p501).

The lively seaside city of **Santa Cruz** (p500) is known for its Boardwalk amusement rides, landmark pier, Spanish mission and University of California campus.

With its trendy stores, wooden fishing pier, ice-cream parlors, and cafés, **Capitola** is one of the most popular beach towns in the region.

Elkhorn Slough, halfway along Monterey Bay, is one of the most accessible habitats of California's playful sea otters. Monterey Bay Kayaks (www.monterey baykayaks.com) runs guided kayak tours into the inlet, where you'll see seals, sea lions, and plenty of otters frolicking in the calm waters.

Moss Landing is a colorful harbor and the home port for most of Monterey Bay's commercial fishing boats. It has many good seafood restaurants along its wharves.

Backed by sand dunes, **Marina State Beach** was once a part of a US Army base and is now within a university campus.

Originally called Lovers of Jesus Point, the **Lovers' Point** headlands form a natural amphitheater that was used for religious revivals in the 1880s. It is one of the few sandy beaches on the northern Monterey Peninsula.

The historic heart of **Monterey** (p502) dates back to the early days of Spanish settlement. The town is also known for the restaurants on Old Fisherman's Wharf and the revitalized Cannery Row (p506).

Bright white sand and brilliant blue water are the distinguishing characteristics of the long **Carmel Beach** (p506).

North Central Coastline

NORTH CENTRAL CALIFORNIA

Locator Map
For more detail see p498

Scotts Valley

Olive Springs

Soquel

Capitola

Santa Cruz

Lighthouse Field State Beach

Freedom

Watsonville

Aromas

Pajaro Dunes

Las Lomas

Elkhorn Slough

Moss Landing

Prunedale

Castroville

Santa Rita

Monterey Bay

Marina

Salinas

East Garrison

Lovers' Point

Asilomar State Beach

Seaside

Monterey

Spreckels

Ambler Park

Carmel Beach

Carmel-by-the-Sea

FINISH

0 kilometers 10

0 miles 10

N

NEED TO KNOW

Bixby Creek Bridge on the Big Sur coast

BEFORE
YOU GO

Things change, so plan ahead to make the most of your trip. Be prepared for all eventualities by considering the following points before you travel.

AT A GLANCE

CURRENCY
US Dollar (USD)

AVERAGE DAILY SPEND

SAVE	SPEND	SPLURGE
$100	$250	$500+

BOTTLED WATER	COFFEE	BEER	DINNER FOR TWO
$2	$2–3	$8	$80+

CLIMATE

 It is sunny for an average of 75 percent of daylight hours through the year.

 Much of California has warm, dry summers and mild, wet winters.

 Coastal ranges and the Sierras have the most rain in winter; at the highest elevations there is snow.

ELECTRICITY SUPPLY

Standard voltage is 110 volts. Power sockets are type A and B, fitting two- or three-pronged plugs.

Passports and Visas

For entry requirements, including visas, consult your nearest US embassy or check the **US Department of State** website. Canadian visitors require a valid passport to enter the US. Citizens of Australia, New Zealand, the UK, and the EU do not need a visa, but must apply in advance for the Electronic System for Travel Authorization (**ESTA**) and have a valid passport to enter. All other visitors will need a passport and tourist visa to enter the US.
ESTA
W esta.cbp.dhs.gov
US Department of State
W state.gov

Government Advice

Now more than ever, it is important to consult both your and the US government's advice before traveling. The **UK Foreign and Commonwealth Office**, the **Australian Department of Foreign Affairs and Trade**, and the US Department of State *(see above)* offer the latest information on security, health, and local regulations.
Australian Department of Foreign Affairs and Trade
W smartraveller.gov.au
UK Foreign and Commonwealth Office
W gov.uk/foreign-travel-advice

Customs Information

You can find information on the laws relating to goods and currency taken in or out of the US on the **US Customs and Border Protection Agency** website.
US Customs and Border Protection Agency
W cbp.gov

Insurance

We recommend that you take out a comprehensive insurance policy, covering theft, loss of belongings, medical care, cancellations, and delays, and read the small print carefully. There is no universal health care in the US for citizens or visitors and health care is very expensive so it is particularly important to take out comprehensive medical insurance.

Vaccinations

No specific inoculations are required to visit the US. For information regarding COVID-19 vaccination requirements, consult government advice.

Booking Accommodations

If visiting in summer (June to September), book accommodations well in advance as they are snapped up fast. Beware that prices are often inflated during this high season. Sales taxes, when added to the resort fees that are imposed by some larger hotels, sometimes raise the actual hotel rate by up to 25 percent. These taxes are usually paid on top of the advertised rates.

Money

Major credit and debit cards, including American Express, are widely accepted, as are prepaid currency cards and most device contactless payment methods. Many cafes and some restaurants have become cashless.

Tipping is customary. In restaurants it is normal to tip 15–20 percent of the total bill. Allow for a tip of 15 percent for taxi drivers and bar staff. Hotel porters and housekeeping expect $1–$2 per bag or day.

Travelers with Specific Requirements

Nearly all Federal and public buildings, including museums, hotels, and restaurants, provide wheelchair facilities with ramps and wide doors. However, some lodgings in historic buildings may not have these so always check in advance.

Trains, buses, and taxis are designed to accommodate wheelchairs. Amtrak trains offer a 10 percent discount to adult passengers with a disability. Car rental agencies offer hand-controlled vehicles and vans with wheelchair lifts.

A Wheelchair Rider's Guide to the California Coast gives information on the accessibility of beaches, parks, and trails. **Accessible Features in State Parks** has a useful map showing

accessible trails and facilites. For accessible accommodations, tours, and transportation in the northern part of the state, consult **Access Northern California**.
A Wheelchair Rider's Guide to the California Coast
 wheelingcalscoast.org
Access Northern California
 accessnca.org
Accessible Features in State Parks
 access.parks.ca.gov/home.asp

Language

English is the main language spoken in California, with Spanish as a close second. You will hear multiple other languages too, especially Chinese, Vietnamese, and Korean.

Opening Hours

> **COVID-19** Increased rates of infection may result in temporary opening hours and/or closures. Always check ahead before visiting museums, attractions, and hospitality venues.

Mondays Some museums and tourist attractions are closed for the day.
Sundays Most shops and businesses are open for limited hours; banks are closed.
Federal holidays Many museums and attractions and all banks are closed.

FEDERAL HOLIDAYS	
Jan 1	New Year's Day
3rd Mon Jan	Martin Luther King Jr. Day
3rd Mon Feb	President's Day (Washington's Birthday)
Last Mon May	Memorial Day
Jun 19	Juneteenth Independence Day
Jul 4	Independence Day
1st Mon Sep	Labor Day
2nd Mon Oct	Columbus Day
Nov 11	Veterans Day
4th Thu Nov	Thanksgiving Day
Dec 25	Christmas Day

GETTING
AROUND

Whether you are planning on city-hopping or retreating to the national parks, discover how best to reach your destination and travel like a pro.

PUBLIC TRANSPORT COSTS

LONG BEACH

$1.25

Single bus journey

LOS ANGELES

$1.75

Single bus and subway/metro journey

PALM SPRINGS

$1

Single bus journey

TOP TIP
Avoid on-the-spot fines – be sure to stamp your ticket to validate your journey.

SPEED LIMITS

FREEWAYS

65 mph (105 km/h)

TWO-LANE UNDIVIDED HIGHWAYS

55 mph (89 km/h)

URBAN AREAS

35 mph (55 km/h)

NEIGHBORHOOD SLOW ZONE

25 mph (40 km/h)

Arriving by Air

California's largest international airports are at Los Angeles (LAX), San Francisco (SFO), and San Diego (SAN). Greater Los Angeles is also served by John Wayne Airport Orange County (SNA), Ontario International Airport (ONT) in San Bernardino County, Bob Hope Airport in Burbank (BUR), and Long Beach Airport (LGB). Other airports serving the Bay area are Oakland International Airport (OAK) and San Jose International Airport (SJC).

All of California's international airports are well served by bus and taxi services, and rented cars. Smaller airports depend more on taxis to surrounding areas. The table opposite lists popular transport options to and from California's main international airports.

Train Travel

Passenger trains in California are dwindling, though Los Angeles to San Diego services remain fast and frequent and California High-Speed Rail is projected to connect LA with San Francisco within the next 10 years.

For now, all long-distance passenger train routes are operated by **Amtrak**, the national rail operator. In general, Amtrak tickets should be booked well in advance (tickets are more expensive closer to departure).

Those visiting San Francisco by train will arrive at the Amtrak station in Emeryville, to the north of Oakland. From here, take a free 45-minute shuttle to the city center. Alternatively, you can arrive by Amtrak to San Jose, then transfer via the **CalTrain** commuter rail to San Francisco. **Metrolink** provides commuter train services in southern California.

The California Rail Pass, available to buy on the Amtrak website, allows for up to seven days of travel in California over a 21-day period for $159.

Amtrak
w amtrak.com
CalTrain
w caltrain.com
Metrolink
w metrolinktrains.com

GETTING TO AND FROM THE AIRPORT

Airport	Distance to city	Taxi fare	Public transport	Journey time
Los Angeles (LAX)	15 miles (24 km)	$50-65	Bus/light rail	60-90 mins
San Diego (SAN)	3 miles (5 km)	$15-22	Bus	15-30 mins
San Francisco (SFO)	14 miles (22 km)	$60-70	Light rail (BART)	20-40 mins
Oakland (OAK)	19 miles (30 km)	$40-50	Light rail (BART)	60 mins

CAR JOURNEY PLANNER

This map is a handy reference for traveling between California's main cities and sights by car. The times given reflect the fastest and most direct routes available, in non-rush hour traffic and with no breaks.

Downtown LA to Death Valley National Park	3 hrs 40 mins
Downtown LA to Joshua Tree National Park	2 hrs 30 mins
Downtown LA to Palm Springs	2 hrs
Downtown LA to San Diego	3 hrs
Downtown LA to San Francisco	7 hrs
Downtown LA to Santa Barbara	2 hrs
Downtown LA to Sequoia and Kings Canyon National Parks	3 hrs 45 mins
San Francisco to Big Sur	2 hrs 45 mins
San Francisco to Lake Tahoe	4 hrs
San Francisco to Monterey	2 hrs
San Francisco to Napa	1 hr 20 mins
San Francisco to Redwood National Park	6 hrs 30 mins
San Francisco to Sacramento	2 hrs
San Francisco to Yosemite National Park	4 hrs

Redwood National Park

Lake Tahoe

Sacramento

Napa

San Francisco

Yosemite National Park

Sequoia and Kings Canyon National Parks

Death Valley National Park

Monterey

Big Sur

··· Direct train routes

Joshua Tree National Park

Santa Barbara

Los Angeles

Palm Springs

San Diego

Long-Distance Bus Travel

Buses are typically the most economical way to get around California. **Greyhound** takes passengers from Los Angeles to San Francisco in around nine hours. It also runs to Bakersfield, Barstow, Eureka, El Portal (Yosemite), Fresno, Monterey, Palm Springs, Redding, Sacramento, San Diego, San Jose, San Luis Obispo, Santa Barbara, and Santa Cruz.

Budget operator **Megabus** serves LA, San Francisco, and the Bay Area, offering very low rates. Most buses offer free Wi-Fi.

If you want a more leisurely journey, the **Green Tortoise** bus company offers a friendly way to see California, with passengers enjoying meals together along the way, and also often stopping at tourist sights.

Green Tortoise
🅦 greentortoise.com
Greyhound
🅦 greyhound.com
Megabus
🅦 us.megabus.com

Public Transportation

California's cities are well served by buses, subways, ferries, or light rail systems, which are often a more efficient and eco-friendly way of getting around than driving. Some transport systems offer multi-day passes – check their websites before visiting. Safety and hygiene measures, timetables, ticket information, transport maps, and more can be obtained from kiosks, customer service offices, or the websites of the transport authorities.

LA Metro runs buses, subways, and light rail in Los Angeles. Greater Los Angeles and surrounding counties are served by **Metrolink** commuter trains. The **San Francisco Municipal Railway (MUNI)** runs the city's bus, cable car, and streetcar systems, while the Bay area is served by the **Bay Area Rapid Transit (BART)** rail and subway system. San Diego's buses, light rail, and streetcars are run by the **San Diego Metropolitan Transit System**.

Commuter boat services provide a scenic way to travel between some cities. **Catalina Express** boat services run a fast link from LA to Catalina Island. In San Francisco you can sail across the bay to Marin County with the **San Francisco Bay Ferry** and **Golden Gate Ferry**. The **Coronado Ferry** runs regular services between San Diego and Coronado.

Bay Area Rapid Transit (BART)
🅦 bart.gov
Catalina Express
🅦 catalinaexpress.com
Coronado Ferry
🅦 flagshipsd.com

Golden Gate Ferry
🅦 goldengate.org
LA Metro
🅦 metro.net
Metrolink
🅦 metrolinktrains.com
San Diego Metropolitan Transit System
🅦 sdmts.com
San Francisco Bay Ferry
🅦 sanfranciscobayferry.com
San Francisco Municipal Railway (MUNI)
🅦 sfmta.com/muni

Driving

Exploring California by car is one of the most convenient ways to travel around the state, especially when visiting a remote rural area or national park. California's highway network is excellent and generally well maintained. However, city-center traffic congestion and expensive parking fees mean that visitors to LA and San Francisco may find that public transportation is quicker and cheaper than driving.

Car Rental

Foreign drivers' licenses are valid in the US, but if your license is not in English, you must get an International Driver's License. Drivers must have held their licenses for at least one year, and visitors under 25 years of age may encounter restrictions when renting, usually having to pay an extra $20–30 a day (check in advance). If you're under 21, you will likely not be able to rent a car (there are some exemptions, but usually only for US license holders, and then with a hefty surcharge). Unlike most US states, in California all additional drivers are free (you must still list the additional driver on the contract, though).

Many car rental companies have offices at city airports and towns across the US, and rentals are easily arranged before arriving in California. When picking up your rental car, you may be asked to show your passport and return airline ticket – you will also need a credit card. Most rental companies offer GPS (SatNav) for an additional daily fee, and child seats with advance notice. Free unlimited mileage is usually included, but leaving the car in a different city than the one in which you rent it may incur a substantial drop-off fee. Standard rental cars in the US have automatic transmissions.

Car Insurance

When you rent a car in California you will be asked to add on a bewildering array of insurance extras. California requires you to have at least some type of liability insurance. Note that the rental company is not required to enforce this and may assume you are covered by your own policy. Complying with California's law on rental car insurance is the responsibility of the renter. In brief, loss-damage waiver (LDW) or collision damage waiver (CDW) allows you to avoid paying for any damage to the rental vehicle or theft of the car. However, there are sometimes "minimums" as opposed to "full" coverage, which can mean you are liable for the first $1,000 of damage, for example. Punctured tires and windshield (windscreen) damage are often not covered. Supplemental liability protection (SLP) will pay for damage you cause to other drivers' vehicles or property – again, check how much this actually covers. Personal accident insurance covers medical costs if the car is involved in an accident. In general it's a good idea to take at least LDW plus SLP – even a minor accident can result in astronomical costs. Check to see if your own car insurance will cover rentals (this is most likely if you own a car in the US or Canada).

Rules of the Road
Everywhere in California (and throughout the US) driving is on the right-hand side of the road, and all distances are measured in miles. Seat belts are compulsory. Right turns on a red traffic light (unless otherwise indicated) are allowed after coming to a complete stop. All vehicles must give way to emergency service vehicles, and traffic in both directions must stop for a school bus until it moves away again.

California prohibits the use of cell phones while driving, with the exception of a "hands-free" system. Speeding will usually result in a fine which you should pay in person if possible – if you are renting the car, the rental company will otherwise charge hefty additional administration fees. Driving under the influence of alcohol is a very serious offence, likely leading to arrest. It is illegal for any person aged 21 or over to drive a car if their BAC (blood alcohol content) level is 0.08 percent or higher (0.01 percent for those under 21).

Toll Roads
There are a number of toll roads in California (mostly in and around LA and San Francisco). These tolls are collected electronically – there are no toll booths at which to stop and pay. If you drive on a toll road without an electronic pass, you face a hefty fine and administraton fees from your rental company. Your car may be fitted with an electronic pass, but using this may incur a daily fee from the rental company (plus tolls incurred), regardless of usage – make sure you understand the billing structure before you drive off. If you expect to be driving on toll roads a lot, it may be worth buying a transponder (an electronic toll collector) from **FasTrak**.
FasTrak
w fastrak.org

Parking
Most cities and towns have paid on- and off-street parking with parking meters and designated parking lots (car parks). Parking in the downtown core of major cities is usually very expensive. Hotels in major cities charge $25–60 per day for on-site parking. Even the cheapest parking lots in downtown San Francisco, for example, charge $16 per day, and parking meters range from $2 to $6 per hour.

Cycling
Cycling is a great way to get around the more rural parts of the state and its popularity is on the rise. Most urban centers have dedicated bike lanes stretching hundreds of miles, and almost all cities allow bikes to be taken on public transportation. The **California Bicycle Coalition** has more information.
California Bicycle Coalition
w calbike.org

Bicycle Rental
All major cities have shops that rent bikes. Specialty bike shops also rent electric and mountain bikes. **Metro Bike Share** in LA, **Breeze** in Santa Monica, **Bay Wheels** in San Francisco, and **HOPR** in Santa Barbara are bike-share programs with docking stations that allow cyclists to make one-way bike trips for a nominal fee. **Jump** is a GPS-powered dockless system that offers e-bikes and scooters in many cities including Los Angeles, Sacramento, San Diego, San Francisco, Santa Cruz, and Santa Monica.
Bay Wheels
w lyft.com/bikes/bay-wheels
Breeze
w santamonicabikeshare.com
HOPR
w gohopr.com/ucsb
Jump
w jump.com
Metro Bike Share
w bikeshare.metro.net

Walking
A well-maintained network of trails crosses the state's many parks and protected wilderness areas. You may need a special permit for some wilderness trails; the most popular need to be reserved weeks to months in advance as there are daily quotas.

The downtown areas and historic centers of many towns and cities, such as San Francisco and San Diego, are easily explored on foot, and even though Los Angeles is very spread out, some districts, such as Downtown, Old Pasadena, and the Golden Triangle in Beverly Hills, are pedestrian-friendly.

PRACTICAL
INFORMATION

A little local know-how goes a long way in California. Here you will find all the essential advice and information you will need during your stay.

AT A GLANCE

EMERGENCY NUMBERS

ALL EMERGENCIES

911

TIME ZONE

California falls within Pacific Standard Time (PST). DST (Daylight Savings Time) is observed from the second Sunday in March to the first Sunday in November.

TAP WATER

Unless stated otherwise, tap water in California is safe to drink.

WEBSITES AND APPS

Incident Information System
Website with instant updates on wildfires, incidents, and emergencies (*www.inciweb.nwcg.gov*).

National Park Service
Practical information about all US national parks (*www. nps.gov*).

Visit California
California's official tourist board website (*www.visitcalifornia.com*).

Gas Buddy
Website and app showing the locations of nearby gas stations and prices (*www. gasbuddy.co*).

Personal Security

California is generally a safe place and, by exercising commonsense, visits are nearly always trouble free. Car break-ins are not uncommon in San Francisco; be sure not to leave valuables in your vehicle.

The state is experiencing a homelessness crisis, and thousands of people are living in encampments in Los Angeles *(p70)*, San Francisco, San Diego, and many other cities. Tackling this issue is a priority for local government but it may take some years before things visibly improve.

It is important to be well prepared before hiking in the wilderness. Notify someone of your plans before setting off. Check the **California State Parks** website for hiking tips, facilities, and current weather conditions. The **Department of Forestry and Fire Protection** website has maps showing the locations of any wildfires. The worst of these have occurred in the High Sierras north of Sacramento and in Wine Country from spring through fall in recent years. Be careful in the desert. At lower levels, it is very hot and dry; at high elevations temperatures often drop to below freezing at night. Always carry extra gas and water in your car.

As a rule, Californians are very accepting of all people, regardless of their race, gender or sexuality. The state has one of the most multi-cultural and diverse populatons in the US and has a long history of celebrating LGBTQ+ rights. Homosexuality was legalized in 1976, followed by same-sex marriages in 2013. California's large LGBTQ+ community is mainly focused in the major cities, particularly in the Castro District of San Francisco, Hillcrest in San Diego, the West Hollywood area of LA, and in Palm Springs.
California State Parks
W parks.ca.gov
Department of Forestry and Fire Protection
W fire.ca.gov

Health

The US has a private health care system, and though excellent, it is very expensive. It

is therefore very important to arrange comprehensive medical insurance before traveling. The cost of basic care can rise incredibly quickly. Keep all medical receipts for reimbursement later.

Pharmacies are an excellent source of advice. They can diagnose minor ailments and suggest appropriate treatment. The main pharmacy chains in California are **Walgreens** and **CVS**; some are open 24 hours.

CVS
W cvs.com
Walgreens
W walgreens.com

Smoking, Alcohol, and Drugs

You must be at least 21 years of age to drink or purchase alcohol or buy cigarettes and any other tobacco products throughout the US; expect to show photo ID even if you look much older. In California smoking is banned in all indoor public places, including restaurants, bars, and hotels and in many outdoor public spaces, such as all parks, beaches, and pedestrian plazas.

US Federal law prohibits cannabis use, but California has legalized limited amounts of 1 ounce (8 g) for recreational use for anyone over the age of 21, including visitors. However, it is illegal to smoke cannabis in public places. Taking any amount of cannabis across state lines or international borders is illegal, and being caught doing this or being in possession of any other drug will likely result in a jail sentence.

ID

There is no requirement for visitors to carry ID, but due to occasional checks (especially at Federal sites) you may be asked to show a passport or other picture ID.

Responsible Travel

The Visit California tourism website has tips for how to travel around the state responsibly. In particular, when visiting national and state parks, respect the lands and native communities. Use marked paths, respect signage, and don't climb on any sites except where it is officially allowed to do so. Always deposit trash in the available receptacles, or take it with you.

Cell Phones and Wi-Fi

Free Wi-Fi spots are available in most towns and cities, at major airports, libraries, and most hotels. Cafés and restaurants generally permit the use of their Wi-Fi on the condition that you make a purchase. Local SIM cards from US providers can be used in compatible phones. Canadian residents can usually upgrade their domestic cell phone plan to extend to the USA.

Post

US Postal Service (USPS) runs the postal system in the US. Post offices are generally open Monday to Friday from 9am to 5pm (though some open earlier), and Saturday from 9am to noon or later.
US Postal Service (USPS)
W usps.com

Taxes and Refunds

The state-wide sales tax is 7.25 percent, though supplementary local sales taxes may be added by cities and counties. Most cities in Los Angeles County charge at least 9.5 percent and San Francisco charges 8.5 percent. Because none of these taxes are levied at a national level, tourists cannot claim sales tax refunds.

Discount Cards

The US National Park Service's **America the Beautiful Pass** covers entrance fees for a driver and all passengers in a personal vehicle at US national parks. The pass costs $80 for one year; seniors pay $20 a year or $80 for life. California state parks *(p528)* have separate multi-use passes.

Most cities operate some form of discount card: **Go City** offers up to 50 percent off many sights in LA, San Diego, and San Francisco. **CityPASS** offers discounts on theme parks in Southern California and top attractions in San Francisco and San Diego.
America the Beautiful Pass
W store.usgs.gov/pass
CityPASS
W citypass.com
Go City
W gocity.com/en-us

INDEX

ACKNOWLEDGMENTS

DK would like to thank the following for their contribution to the previous edition: Sally Davies, Mary–Ann Gallagher, Ben Ffrancon Davies, John Ardagh, David Baird, Vicky Hayward, Adam Hopkins, Lindsay Hunt,Nick Inman, Paul Richardson, Martin Symington, Nigel Tisdall, Roger Williams

The publisher would like to thank the following for their kind permission to reproduce their photographs:

Key: a–above; b–below/bottom; c–centre; f–far; l–left; r–right; t–top

123RF.com: Jon Bilous 153br; coralimages 346bl; Brian Kinney 88–89b; Nick Kontostavlakis 384–85t; Chon Kit Leong 234–35t; Wasin Pummarin 328–29t.

4Corners: Pietro Canali 174c; 180–81; Susanne Kremer 176cb; 246–47.

Alamy Stock Photo: agefotostock / Douglas A. Holck 512–13b, / Herbert Hopfensperger 310crb, / Lucid Images 50–51t, / Tono Balaguer 358–59t, 364–65t; Agencja Fotograficzna Caro / Kaiser 458cla; All Canada Photos / Chris Cheadle 253crb; andreamful / Stockimo 231br; Arcaid Images / Michael Halberstadt 298–99b; Kevin Archive 50bl; Archwhite 410–11t; Art Directors / Spencer Grant 372cra; Artokoloro 81cra; Gonzalo Azumendi 365clb; Sergio Torres Baus 338bl; Debra Behr 23b; 71b; Nancy Hoyt Belcher 459br; Judy Bellah 16bl; Benoneimages 479br; Bildagentur–online / Schickert 169tl; 315tr; Jon Bilous 368–69t; Russ Bishop 37tr; blickwinkel / AGAMI / M. Verdoes 253tl; Phillip Bond 31b; 417br; Kanwarjit Singh Boparai 380–81t; Richard Broadwell 38br; Allen Brown 139tl; Larry Brownstein 99tl; 102–03b; Evan Burnett 13cr; David L. Moore – CA 72t; 72cr; California Collective 504t; Ed Callaert 437crb; 444–45t; 454clb; 489bc; Cannon Photography LLC / BrownWCannonIII 178crb; 428crb; Cavan Images 28–29t; , Cavan Images / Aurora Open / Josh Miller Photography 469b; / CI2 29br; 455cb; / Kevin Steele / Aurora Photos 33t; cfc photography 218br; Lorne Chapman 18cra; Felix Choo 281br; 356–57c; 372–73b; Chronicle 386crb; Ronnie Chua 295tr; Chuck Place 196tl; Citizen of the Planet / Peter Bennett 151bl; 163tr; 200bl; 237br; Classic Collection A17 47br; Classic Image 310cb; 328cb; 439bl; Robert Clay 50cb; 301tr; Corbin17 266bl; Core Imagery 73br; Dennis Cox 23cl; Gary Crabbe 489cra; 491br; Gary Crabbe / Enlightened Images 475t; John Crowe 18tl; 198tl; 241br; Richard Cummins 465cra; Curved Light USA 319clb; Ian Dagnall 51tr; 62bl; 91tl; 430br; 453bl; 468t; 472tr; 476–77b; Ian G Dagnall 21tr; 119tl; 221bl; 400t; 489tl; Rachid Dahnoun 454cr; Danita Delimont / Jon Alves 454crb, / Peter Bennett 16cl, 144bl, / Stuart Westmorland 190b, / Walter Bibikow 20cra, / Chuck Haney 310–11t, / Jaynes Gallery / Christopher Talbot Frank 243tr; © David Zanzinger 254bl; David R. Frazier Photolibrary; Inc. 109br; Oden's Dawn 132crb; Design Pics Inc / Brand B / Debra Brash 252cr, 253bc; Directphoto Collection 338crb; Terry Donnelly 20–21tc; California Dreamin 148br, 335tr, 458t; Randy Duchaine 236–37t, 287cb (Oculus), 310ca; DumbTube 455cl; Eagle Visions Photography / Craig Lovell 44clb, 253tr; ekunau / Stockimo 31tr; Enlightened Images / Gary Crabbe 201tr; 436bl, 455bl; EuroStyle Graphics 40–41b; Everett Collection Historical 46t; Everett Collection Inc 387crb; Everett Collection Inc / CSU Archives 69tr; Eye Ubiquitous / Nick Bonetti 74bl, 162–63b; eye35 stock 357cr; eye35.pix 493t; EyeEm / Hosni Marharvie 100–01b; Michele Falzone 322bl; Ryan Fidrick 152bl; Stephen Finn 375tl; Tim Fleming 370b; Neil Fraser 304bl; Dennis Frates 269t, 455br; Robert Fried 455tr; Gado Images / Smith Collection 353br; Tom Gardner 476clb; Larry Geddis 252–53b; David George 101tr, 106–07b;

Benjamin Ginsberg 222tc; GL Archive 329bc, 331ca, 331br; Paul Christian Gordon 389bl; GoUSA 221crb; Jeremy Graham 114–115t, 139cla, 258bl; Granger Historical Picture Archive; NYC 49tr, 191br, 310cb (cable–car); Brian Green 240br; Michele and Tom Grimm 60tl, 110–11; Have Camera Will Travel | North America 341br; Yuval Helfman 390bl, 416bl; Hemis.fr / Marc Dozier 68t, / Støphane Lemaire 101cra, / Walter Bibikow 102cra; Heritage Image Partnership Ltd / Curt Teich Postcard Archives 48–49t; The Jon B. Lovelace Collection of California Photographs in 's America Project; ; Prints and Photographs Division.; Gift; The Capital Group Companies Charitable Foundation in memory of Jon B. Lovelace; 2012; (DLC/PP–2012:063).; Forms part of: Jon B. Lovelace Collection of California Photographs in 's America Project in the Archive.; 2012 445br; Historic Images 26tl, 287br; History and Art Collection 346cb, 474cr; The History Collection 310clb; Radek Hofman 222–23b; Peter Horree 268bl, 321tl; Ken Howard 99br; Della Huff 290–91t; imageBROKER / Moritz Wolf 394bl; Images–USA 39tr, 189cra, 316b; incamerastock / ICP 167tc; INTERFOTO / Personalities 331tr; INTERFOTO / Travel 239crb; Anton Ivanov 381crb; J.H.Miller 101tl; Jamie Pham Photography 141cra, 142–43t; Brian Jannsen 270–71; jejim120 356br; Inge Johnsson 191tl; Dee Jolie 391br; Jon Arnold Images Ltd 274c, 282–83, 427, 496–97; Jim Kidd 485tr; Paul Kim 178t; Victor Korchenko 159cl; Art Kowalsky 381cb; Ken L Howard 178cr; Robert Landau 24–25t, 25cla, 62cr; 62crb, 114bl, 123tr, 125cra; Chon Kit Leong 146tr; 152t, 208cra; LHB Photo 45cla; Michael Lingberg 367cra; David Litschel 265bl; lucky–photographer 414–15b; m–images 392cl; Stefano Politi Markovina 315cra; Benny Marty 115bl; mauritius images GmbH / Axel Schmies 323br; Buddy Mays 36b; Chad McDermott 211tr; Brian McGuire 328bc; Jon McLean 39cla; Michael DeFreitas North America 209br; Mike Kipling Photography 387bc; Diane Modafferi 99tr; David L. Moore 27clb; Geoffrey Morgan 348–49t; Robert Mullan 279tl; Naeblys 296b; Jonathan Nguyen 21cla; Ron Niebrugge 45crb; Nikreates 293br, 304tr; 346cra; NiKreative 338–39t; North Wind Picture Archives 466br; Oldtime 328clb; Jonathan ORourke 103br; Efrain Padro 236bl, 311br; David Parker 329crb; parkerphotography 278tl; Sean Pavone 148–49tr; Susan Pease 315tl, 322–23t; PersimmonPictures.com 452t; Jamie Pham 142br; 175, 204–05; Pictorial Press Ltd 189tc, 365br, 412cra; The Picture Art Collection 103tr; Eric Plante 511bl; Prisma by Dukas Presseagentur GmbH / Heeb Christian 87tl, / Raga Jose Fuste 504cla; RAIMUND KOCH–VIEW 59bl, 92–93, 109cla; RGB Ventures / SuperStock / Fred Hirschmann 47tl; Ed Rhodes 371tl; Robertharding / Alan Copson 502b, / Frank Fell 16t, / Michael Defreitas 259tl, / Miles Ertman 456b, / Richard Cummins 61, 131bl, 154–55, / Roy Rainford 486bl, / Toms Auzins 485cra; Rohan Van Twest Creative 369ca; RooM the Agency / shutterjack 8cla; RooM the Agency / tristan 13t; scott sady / tahoelight.com 12t, 37cla; Nandakumar Sankaran / Crooked Trunk 412bl, 514cra; Maurice Savage 240t; R Scapinello 374–75bc; Peter Schickert 250t; Duncan Selby 18cla, 192–93t; Macjules Sevilla 317tl; Hayk Shalunts 122br; Ian Shaw 290crb, 507tl; SiliconValleyStock 140tl, 332–33b, 409t, 504–05b; Shangara Singh 146–47b; Witold Skrypczak 474bl, 477tr; Smith Collection / Gado Images 333tr; Inga Spence 436–37; Spring Images 438bl; Rosemarie Stennull 168bl; Stephen Saks Photography 437ca, 470bl; StockimoNews / Lisa Werner 44cra; Rebecca Stunell 500–01t; SuperStock 491bl; tahoelight.com / scott sady 437br, 491crb; Jeff Tangen 454bc; Leta Taylor 70tl; The Reading Room 517br; Terry Thomas 18–19tc; Bryan Toro 489tr; Tribune Content Agency LLC / McClatchy 430cb; Scott Tucker 158–59b; Rohan Van Twest 367tl, 391t; UPI / Jim Ruymen 44cla; UrbanTexture 292br, 403b; Michael Urmann 395tl; Yoshiki Usami 210crb; Martin Valigursky 414tr; Greg Vaughn 194br, 253c, 517tr; Michael Ventura 430t; Jurgen Vogt 118b; Ike Waits 265cb; David Wall 320bl; Anthony Wallbank 473b; WaterFrame_jdo 10clb; Nik Wheeler 495bl; Philip Willcocks 232–33b; Scott

Photography 33cl; Kohls / imageBROKER 330–31t; Hans Kwiotek 333br; Rafael Ramirez Lee 277bl, 396–97; Kit Leong 11t, 115crb, 138–39b, 139ca; Let Go Media 35cra; LnP images 62t; melissamn 428cr; meunierd 242–43b; Moviestore 42cla; Harun Ozmen 230bl; pablopicasso 10ca; Paramount / Kobal 42b; UA / Lions Gate / Kobal 43cl; Umomos 37bl.

Sarah Snelling: 34cla.

TopFoto.co.uk: AP 329clb; The Image Works 386bl, 387clb.

Universal Studios Hollywood: 130–31t, 131tr, 132cl, 132clb, 133cb, 133bl.

Unsplash: Jack Finnigan / @jackofallstreets 52–53; Gerson Repreza / @gersonrepreza 54–55.

Volakis Gallery: 27t.

Wolfgang Puck Fine Dining Group: 34bl.

Cover images:
Front & Spine: Three Brothers rock formation reflected in the Merced River, Yosemite National Park – **4Corners:** Jordan Banks; *Back:* **4Corners:** Jordan Banks b; **Getty Images:** Moment / Claude LeTien c; **iStockphoto.com:** LUNAMARINA cla; **Shutterstock.com:** Bertl123 tr; Front Flap: **4Corners:** Susanne Kremer cb; **Alamy Stock Photo:** Michele and Tom Grimm bl; Robertharding / Frank Fell br; **AWL Images:** Matteo Colombo cra; **Getty Images:** Rich Fury t; **iStockphoto.com:** mbbirdy cla.

All other images © Dorling Kindersley

Main Contributors Stephen Keeling, Christopher Baker, Pamela Barrus, Anita Isalska, Nick Edwards, Paul Oswell, Jamie Jensen, Barry Parr, Ellen Payne, J Kingston Pierce, Rebecca Poole Forée, Nigel Tisdall, John Wilcock, Stanley Young

Senior Editor Alison McGill

Senior Designers Sarah Snelling, Tania Da Silva Gomes, Stuti Tiwari

Project Art Editors Bharti Karakoti, Van Anh Le, Ben Hinks

Project Editor Rada Radojicic

Editors Sophie Adam, Parnika Bagla, Rebecca Flynn, Matthew Grundy Haigh, Arushi Mathur, Zoë Rutland, Mark Silas, Sands Publishing Solutions, Lucy Sara-Kelly, Danielle Watt

Updaters Pamela Barrus, Anita Isalska, Matt Charnock

Proofreader Kathryn Glendenning

Indexer Hilary Bird

Picture Researcher Åsa Westerlund

Illustrators Arcana Studios, Joanna Cameron, Stephen Conlin, Dean Entwhistle, Nick Lipscombe, Lee Peters, Robbie Polley, Kevin Robinson, John Woodcock

Assistant Picture Research Administrator Vagisha Pushp

Jacket Coordinator Bella Talbot

Jacket Designer Jordan Lambley

Senior Cartographic Editor Casper Morris

Cartographic Editor Ashif, Subhashree Bharati

Cartography Manager Suresh Kumar

Senior DTP Designer Tanveer Zaidi

Senior Production Editor Jason Little

Production Controller Kariss Ainsworth

Deputy Managing Editor Beverly Smart

Managing Editors Hollie Teague, Shikha Kulkarni

Managing Art Editor Bess Daly

Senior Managing Art Editor Priyanka Thakur

Art Director Maxine Pedliham

Publishing Director Georgina Dee

First edition 1997

Published in Great Britain by Dorling Kindersley Limited, DK, One Embassy Gardens, 8 Viaduct Gardens, London SW11 7BW

The authorised representative in the EEA is Dorling Kindersley Verlag GmbH. Arnulfstr. 124, 80636 Munich, Germany

Published in the United States by DK Publishing, 1450 Broadway, Suite 801, New York, NY 10018

Copyright © 1997, 2022 Dorling Kindersley Limited
A Penguin Random House Company

21 22 23 24 10 9 8 7 6 5 4 3 2 1

A CIP catalog record for this book is available from the British Library.

A catalog record for this book is available from the Library of Congress.

ISSN: 1542 1554
ISBN: 9780241418413

Printed and bound in China.

www.dk.com

A NOTE FROM DK EYEWITNESS

The rapid rate at which the world is changing is constantly keeping the DK Eyewitness team on our toes. While we've worked hard to ensure that this edition of California is accurate and up-to-date, we know that opening hours alter, standards shift, prices fluctuate, places close and new ones pop up in their stead. So, if you notice we've got something wrong or left something out, we want to hear about it. Please get in touch at travelguides@dk.com